fluency4

WITH INFORMATION TECHNOLOGY

skills, concepts, & capabilities

lawrence snyder
UNIVERSITY OF WASHINGTON

Addison-Wesley

Boston Columbus Indianapolis New York San Francisco Upper Saddle River
Amsterdam Cape Town Dubai London Madrid Milan Munich Paris Montreal Toronto
Delhi Mexico City Sao Paulo Sydney Hong Kong Seoul Singapore Taipei Tokyo

Editor-in-Chief: Michael Hirsch
Acquisitions Editor: Matt Goldstein
Editorial Assistant: Chelsea Bell
Managing Editor: Jeffrey Holcomb
Senior Production Project Manager: Marilyn Lloyd
Marketing Manager: Erin Davis
Marketing Coordinator: Kathryn Ferranti
Media Producer: Katelyn Boller
Senior Manufacturing Buyer: Carol Melville
Senior Media Buyer: Ginny Michaud
Production Services, Illustrations, and Text Design: Gillian Hall/The Aardvark Group
Copyeditor: Rebecca Greenberg
Proofreader: Holly McLean-Aldis
Indexer: Jack Lewis
Art Director, Exterior: Linda Knowles
Cover Designer: Joyce Cosentino Wells/JWells Design
Cover Image: © 2009 Josh Bernard/iStockphoto

Credits and acknowledgments borrowed from other sources and reproduced, with permission, in this textbook appear on appropriate page within text (or on pages 795–796).

Library of Congress Cataloging-in-Publication Data

Snyder, Lawrence.
Fluency with information technology : skills, concepts & capabilities / Lawrence Snyder.— 4th ed.
p. cm.
ISBN 978-0-13-609182-0
1. Information technology. 2. Computer literacy. I. Title.
T58.5.S645 2010
004--dc22

2009052461

Addison-Wesley
is an imprint of

www.pearsonhighered.com

ISBN-13: 9780136091820
ISBN-10: 0136091822
2 3 4 5 6 7 8 9 10—CRK—13 12 11

Preface

WELCOME to the Fourth Edition of *Fluency with Information Technology: Skills, Concepts, & Capabilities*. This book moves beyond the click-here-click-there form of technology instruction to one firmly founded on ideas. Today the majority of college and post-secondary students are already familiar with computers, the Internet, and the World Wide Web, and do not need rudimentary instruction in double-clicking and resizing windows. Rather, they need to be taught to be confident, in-control users of IT. They need to know how to navigate independently in the ever-changing worlds of information and technology, to solve their problems on their own, and to be capable of fully applying the power of IT tools in the service of their personal and career goals. They must be more than literate; they must be fluent with IT.

What's New in This Edition?

This revision has been enhanced to keep it fully current with both the level of preexisting student knowledge and the advancement of technology. For example, the Web-based code is now fully compliant with the XHTML standard. All programs validate, and a new section explains to students how they can validate their programs. Also, the text is now fully compliant with the Cascading Style Sheet standard, and a new section has been added giving a comprehensive overview of CSS. Two new sections have been added on Lab Practice; the goals are to make students more productive while working on projects and to reduce the number of errors introduced in their code.

Chapter 12, Social Implications of IT, and Chapter 13, Privacy and Digital Security, have been completely redeveloped. The security sections teach security principles, but they are also formulated to give students practical tools for keeping their computers both safe and secure. Certain topics—firewalls and social engineering—that have been treated in passing in earlier editions are now covered more thoroughly and in context.

Substantial content improvements are included; many are to be found in Part 1, Becoming Skilled at Computing (Chapters 1–6). In past years it has been necessary to teach certain very basic information. In the current edition, however, understanding that students come to class knowing much more, the text adopts a strategy of explaining to students *why* what they know is the way it is, and how to extend it further. Chapter 5 contains an entirely new treatment of Web searching, including a deeper description of how PageRank works. It explains, for example, why the search terms might not be in the text of the pages that hit. Not only is effective searching taught, but so too are critical algorithmic issues. Chapter 6 fully revises Web research to conform to the students' level of familiarity with Google Search and progress in Web content.

In every chapter, additional in-line Try It exercises have been added. These enable students to test their knowledge as they progress through a chapter. In addition, several new exercises have been added to most chapters.

What Is Fluency with Information Technology?

This book is inspired by a report from the National Research Council (NRC), *Being Fluent with Information Technology*. In that study, commissioned by the National Science Foundation, the committee asserted that traditional computer literacy does not have the "staying power" students need to keep pace with the rapid changes in IT. The study concluded that the educational "bar needs to be raised" if students' knowledge is to evolve and adapt to that change. The recommended alternative, dubbed *fluency with information technology*, or *FIT*, was a package of skills, concepts, and capabilities wrapped in a project-oriented learning approach that ensures that the content is fully integrated. The goal is to help people become effective users immediately, and to prepare them for lifelong learning.

The Vision

This textbook largely implements the vision of the NRC committee. To summarize the main components, recall that they proposed a three-part content and recommended integrating that content using projects.

Three-Part Content

To make students immediately effective and launch them on the path of lifelong learning, they need to be taught three types of knowledge: Skills, Concepts, and Capabilities.

- **Skills** refers to proficiency with contemporary computer applications such as email, word processing, Web searching, etc. Skills make the technology immediately useful to students and give them practical experience on which to base other learning. The Skills component approximates traditional computer literacy content; that is, Fluency *includes* literacy.
- **Concepts** refers to the fundamental knowledge underpinning IT, such as how a computer works, digital representation of information, assessing information authenticity, etc. Concepts provide the principles on which students will build new understanding as IT evolves.
- **Capabilities** refers to higher-level thinking processes such as problem solving, reasoning, complexity management, and troubleshooting. Capabilities embody modes of thinking that are essential to

exploiting IT, but they apply broadly. Reasoning, problem solving, and so forth are standard components of education; their heavy use in IT makes them topics of emphasis in the Fluency approach.

For each component, the NRC report lists ten recommended items. These are shown in the accompanying table.

The NRC's List of Top Ten Skills, Concepts, and Capabilities

Fluency with Information Technology
Skills
1. Set up a personal computer
2. Use basic operating system facilities
3. Use a word processor to create a document
4. Use a graphics or artwork package to manipulate an image
5. Connect a computer to the Internet
6. Use the Internet to locate information
7. Use a computer to communicate with others
8. Use a spreadsheet to model a simple process
9. Use a database to access information
10. Use online help and instructional materials
Concepts
1. Fundamentals of computers
2. Organization of information systems
3. Fundamentals of networks
4. Digital representation of information
5. Structuring information
6. Modeling and abstraction
7. Algorithmic thinking and programming
8. Universality
9. Limitations of information technology
10. Social impact of computers and technology
Capabilities
1. Engage in sustained reasoning
2. Manage complexity
3. Test a solution
4. Find problems in a faulty use of IT
5. Navigate a collection and assess quality of the information
6. Collaborate using IT
7. Communicate using IT about IT
8. Expect the unexpected
9. Anticipate technological change
10. Think abstractly about information technology

Projects

The Skills, Concepts, and Capabilities represent different kinds of knowledge that are co-equal in their contribution to IT Fluency. They span separate dimensions of understanding. The overall strategy is to focus on the Skills instruction in the lab, the Concepts instruction in lecture/reading material, and the Capabilities instruction in lecture/lab demonstrations. The projects are the opportunity to use the three kinds of knowledge for a specific purpose. They illustrate IT as it is often applied in practice—to solve information processing tasks of a substantial nature.

A project is a multiweek assignment to achieve a specific IT goal. An example of a project might be to create a database to track medical patients in a walk-in clinic, and to give a presentation to convince an audience that patient privacy has been preserved. Students apply a variety of Skills such as using database design software, Web searching, and presentation facilities. They rely on their understanding of Concepts such as database keys, table structure, and the `Join` query operator. And they use Capabilities such as reasoning, debugging, complexity management, testing, and others. The components are applied together to produce the final result, leading students to an integrated understanding of IT and preparing them for significant "real life" applications of IT. The labs can be found on the book's Web site.

Audience

This book is designed for freshmen "non-techies," students who will not be majoring in science, engineering, or math. ("Techies" benefit, too, but because "hot shots" can intimidate others, they should be discouraged from taking the class, or better, encouraged to join an accelerated track or honors section.) Except for one short paragraph about encryption, which can be skipped, no mathematical skills are required beyond arithmetic. There are no prerequisites.

Most students who take Fluency will have used email, surfed the Web, and word processed, and this is more than enough preparation to be successful. Students with no experience are advised to spend a few hours acquiring some exposure to IT prior to starting Fluency.

Chapter Dependencies

I have written *Fluency with Information Technology* so it can be taught in a variety of ways. In addition to the preliminary material in Chapters 1 and 2, social issues in Chapters 12 and 13, and the wrap-up in Chapter 24, the overall structure of the book includes standalone chapters with few dependencies, as well as small chapter sequences devoted to a sustained topic. The sequences are:

- 3, 4, and 5—networking, XHTML, and information
- 8, 9, 10, and 11—data representations, computers, and algorithms
- 14, 15, 16, and 17—spreadsheets and database principles
- 18, 19, 20, and 21—programming in JavaScript

One effective way to use this design is to present one of the chapter sequences as the basis for a project assignment. Then, while the students are working on the project—projects may span two or more weeks—material from standalone chapters is covered.

Though there are many sequences, three stand out to me as especially good ways to present the material:

- **Networking cycle.** The linear sequence of chapters is designed to begin with information and networking and progressively advance through computation and databases to JavaScript, where it returns to the networking theme. This is the basic Chapter 1 to 24 sequence, adjusted by local reordering to accommodate the timing of projects as needed.
- **Internet forward.** I teach Fluency in the 1–10, 18–22, 11–17, 23–24 order. This approach begins with information and XHTML, progresses through to algorithms, then jumps to JavaScript to continue the Web page building theme, and finally wraps up with databases. The strategy is dictated largely by the logistics of teaching the class in a quarter (10 weeks), and is recommended for that situation.
- **Traditional.** In this approach, the material is taught to parallel the time sequence of its creation. So, information representation and computers come well before networking. In this case, the order is 1–2, (23), 8–15, 3–7, 16–24. Chapter 23, which contains more philosophical content like the Turing test and Kasparov/Deep Blue chess tournament, might optionally be presented early for its foundational content.

Each of these strategies has a compelling pedagogical justification. Which is chosen depends more on the instructor's taste and class logistics than on any need to present material in a specific order.

Pedagogical Features

- **Learning Objectives:** Each chapter opens with a list of the key concepts that readers should master after reading the chapter.

There are several boxed features that appear throughout the text to aid in students' understanding of the material:

- fluencyTIP Practical hints and suggestions for everyday computer use.
- fluencyBIT **and** fluencyBYTE Interesting facts and statistics.
- fluencyALERT Warnings and explanations of common mistakes.
- TRY IT Short, in-chapter exercises with solutions provided.
- ✓checkLIST A useful list of steps for completing a specific task.

Throughout the text, we also distinguish notable material by the following features:

- fluency FLASHBACK A historical look at some of the major people and milestones in computing.

- **Glossary:** Important words and phrases appear in boldface type throughout the text, and a glossary of terms is included at the end of the book. Terms in the glossary also appear in bold in the book's index.
- **Answers:** Solutions are provided to the odd-numbered exercises for the multiple-choice and short-answer questions.
- **Appendix A:** XHTML reference including a chart of Web-safe colors.
- **Appendix B:** The XML database and the XSL template style information for iDiary in Chapter 17.
- **Appendix C:** JavaScript programming rules.
- **Appendix D:** Bean Counter Program: A complete JavaScript and XHTML example.
- **Appendix E:** Memory Bank Code: A complete JavaScript and XHTML example.
- **Appendix F:** Smooth Motion Program: A complete JavaScript and XHTML example.

Supplements

The Companion Website for *Fluency with Information Technology* is located at www.aw.com/snyder/ and is where you can find the various HTML sources, database designs, and JavaScript programs used in the textbook examples. Students are encouraged to retrieve these files to explore along with the text.

The following supplements are available to all users of this book:

- **Fluency Lab materials.** Learning Fluency is a hands-on activity, and so 14 complete laboratory exercises (contained in the Computer Skills Workbook) are available at the Web site.
- **VideoNotes.** VideoNotes are short tutorial videos, available online, that enhance concepts presented in the textbook. Many present an example solution to an end-of-chapter exercise.
- **JavaScript reference card.**
- **Glossary flashcards.**
- **A downloadable workbook (in PDF format) on Alice and the Alice development environment.** This workbook can be used as a substitute for the JavaScript programming chapters in the text.

The following instructor supplements are available to qualified instructors only. Please contact your local Addison-Wesley sales representative, or send email to computing@aw.com for information about how to access them.

- **PowerPoint slides.** A convenient resource for teaching Fluency is the collection of PowerPoint slides available online.
- **Instructor's manual with solutions.**
- **Test bank.**
- **Test generator.**

- **Excel labs with solutions.** Since understanding how to solve problems with Excel is an important skill, a series of problem-oriented labs using Excel are available.

In addition to the Companion Website, the course content is available in CourseCompass™, Blackboard™, and WebCT. CourseCompass is a nationally hosted, dynamic, interactive online course management system powered by Blackboard, leaders in the development of Internet-based learning tools. This easy-to-use and customizable program enables professors to tailor content and functionality to meet individual course needs. Visit www.coursecompass.com to see a demo. Please contact your local Addison-Wesley sales representative for more information on obtaining course content in these various formats.

Pearson Custom Textbooks

Pearson Custom allows you to create your own customized version of the fourth edition of Fluency. Insert material from the accompanying Computer Skills Workbook by Scollard or add chapters from popular textbooks on Alice programming logic, ethics, Dreamweaver®, and more. You can also change the chapter sequence, remove chapters you don't use, and even insert your own material. The Pearson Custom Database creates a unique pagination, table of contents, and index for your customized book. For a full listing of available titles, pricing, ordering information, or to create your own book, please visit www.pearsoncustom.com (keyword search: computer science).

Note to Students

Fluency is a somewhat unusual topic, making this a somewhat unusual book. There are two things that I think you should know about using this book.

- **Learn Skills in the lab.** Of the three kinds of knowledge that define Fluency—Skills, Concepts, and Capabilities—very little of the Skills material is included in this book. The Skills content, which is mostly about how to use contemporary computer applications, changes very rapidly, making it difficult to keep up to date. But the main reason few skills are included is that they are best learned in the lab, seated in front of a computer. The lab exercises, which are online and are up to date, provide an excellent introduction to contemporary applications. They provide great coverage of the Skills.
- **Study Fluency steadily.** If this book is successful, it will change the way you think, making you a better problem solver, better at reasoning, better at debugging, and so forth. These Capabilities are useful in IT and elsewhere in life, so they make learning Fluency really worthwhile. But changing how you think won't happen just by putting the book under your pillow. It'll take some studying. To learn Fluency you must apply good study habits: read the book, do the end-of-chapter exercises (answers to odd-number exercises are printed at the back of the book), start on your assignments early, ask questions, and so on. I think it's best if you spend some time in the

> lab studying Fluency (not reading email) every day, because it takes some time for the ideas to sink in. Students with good study habits tend to do well in Fluency class, and because it improves their problem-solving abilities, and more, they become even better students! It takes some discipline but it pays.

Finally, reading this book is enhanced by having a computer handy so you can try out examples. All files used here are available at www.aw.com/snyder/. Good luck! Writing this book has truly been a pleasure. I hope reading it is equally enjoyable.

Acknowledgments

Many people have contributed to this work. First to be thanked are my collaborators in the creation of the Fluency concept, the NRC Committee on Computer Literacy—Al Aho, Marcia Linn, Arnie Packer, Allen Tucker, Jeff Ullman, and Andy van Dam. Special thanks go to Herb Lin of the NRC staff who assisted throughout the Fluency effort, tirelessly and in his usual great good humor. Two enthusiastic supporters of Fluency—Bill Wulf of the National Academy of Engineering and John Cherniavski of the National Science Foundation—have continually supported this effort in more ways than I am aware. It has been a pleasure to know and work with this team.

As the material was developed for this book, many have contributed: Ken Yasuhara and Brian Bannon, teaching assistants on the first offering of CSE100, contributed in innumerable ways and injected a needed dose of practicality into my ideas. Grace Whiteaker, Alan Borning, and Batya Friedman have been generous with their ideas regarding Fluency. Martin Dickey of CSE and Mark Donovan of UWired have been constant sources of support. The original offerings of CSE100 benefited greatly from contributions by Nana Lowell, Anne Zald, Mike Eisenberg, and Fred Videon. Colleagues who have contributed include Frank Tompa, Martin Tompa, Carl Ebeling, Brian Kerninghan, Dotty Smith, Calvin Lin, and David Mizell.

I am particularly grateful for the keen insights and valuable feedback from the reviewers of this book. For this edition, my thanks go to: Syed Ahmed (North Georgia College and State University), Brooke Bourassa (Southern New Hampshire University), Jim Bowring (College of Charleston), Kyungsub Choi (Manhattan College), Toni Farley (Arizona State University), Michael Gelotte (Bellevue Community College), Joseph Kolb (Ocean County College), Ronald Mummaw (Antelope Valley College), Laurie J. Patterson (UNC Wilmington), R. Perkoski (University of Pittsburgh), C. Robert Putnam (California State University – Northridge), Jay Shaffstall (Muskingum College), Trevor Smith (University of Arizona), and Mehmet Ulema (Manhattan College).

Also, the following, who have provided helpful reviews for previous editions: Nazih Abdallah (University of Central Florida), Robert M. Aiken (Temple University), Diane M. Cassidy (University of North Carolina at Charlotte), Anne Condon (University of British Columbia), Lee D. Cornell (Minnesota

State University, Mankato), Nicholas Cravotta (University of California, Berkeley), Gordon Davies (Open University), Peter J. Denning (George Mason University), Rory J. DeSimone (University of Florida), Richard C. Detmer (Middle Tennessee State University), David L. Doss (Illinois State University), John P. Dougherty (Haverford College), Philip East (University of Northern Iowa), Michael B. Eisenberg (University of Washington), Robert S. Fenchel (University of Wisconsin, Madison), Michael Gildersleeve (University of New Hampshire), Jennifer Golbeck, Michael H. Goldner, Esther Grassian (UCLA College Library), Raymond Greenlaw (Armstrong Atlantic State University), Steve Hodges (Cabrillo College), A. J. Hurst (Monash University, Australia), Malcolm G. Lane (James Madison University), Doris K. Lidtke (Towson University), Wen Liu (ITT Technical Institute), Daniela Marghitu (Auburn University), C. Dianne Martin (George Washington University), Peter B. Miller (University of Virginia), Namdar Mogharreban (Southern Illinois University, Carbondale), Paul M. Mullins (Slippery Rock University), David R. Musicant (Carleton College), Alexander Nakhimovsky (Colgate University), Brenda C. Parker (Middle Tennessee State University), Dee Parks (Appalachian State University), Thomas Parks (Colgate University), Laurie J. Patterson (University of North Carolina, Wilmington), Roger Priebe (University of Texas at Austin), Paul Quan (Albuquerque Technical Vocational Institute), Glenn Ray (University of Pittsburgh), John Rosenberg (Monash University, Australia), Robert T. Ross (California Polytechnic State University), Carol Schwartz (Rutgers University), Zhizhang Shen (Plymouth State College), Robert J. Shive, Jr. (Millsaps College), Patrick Tantalo (University of California, Santa Cruz), and Mark Urban-Lurain (Michigan State University).

Thank you to Jim McKeown and Tim Gottleber for contributing to the end-of-chapter exercises.

The Fluency material has been a topic of discussion with many international colleagues. Discussions with Hans Hinterberger, John Rosenberg, and John Hirsch have been especially valuable in critiquing the material from an overseas perspective. Other helpful international commentary came from Anne Condon, Hannes Jonsson, Jerg Nievergelt, Clark Thomberson, Barbara Thomberson, Ewan Tempero, and Kazuo Iwama.

Among the many thoughtful computer users who have either generously described their misunderstandings about IT or patiently listened to my explanations about IT, I wish to thank Esther Snyder, Helene Fowler, Judy Watson, Brendan Healy, Victory Grund, Shelley Burr, Ken Burr, and Noelle Lamb.

As this textbook evolves to keep pace with technological advances, more and more generous people contribute, for which I am deeply appreciative. In the third edition, Noelle Lamb enabled the revisions of the database chapters; Rich LeBlanc, Ben Lerner, and Bern Martens caught errors that I am delighted to have fixed. In the fourth edition, I am grateful to Susan Marx for catching another error. Rebecca Greenberg's editing has improved the content and presentation significantly; as always it is a great pleasure to work with Gillian Hall. And, once again it is my pleasure to thank Matt Goldstein and the whole Addison-Wesley team of Michael Hirsch, Marilyn Lloyd, Jeff Holcomb and Chelsea Bell.

Finally, my wife, Julie, and sons, Dan and Dave, have been patient, encouraging, and, most important, a continual source of good humor throughout this effort. It is with my deepest appreciation that I thank them for everything.

—Larry Snyder, December 2009

For Julie Ann, Dan, and Dave

Contents

part 1 Becoming Skilled at Computing

The Master said: "To learn something and then put it into practice at the right time. Is this not a joy?"

—THE ANALECTS OF CONFUCIUS

1 PART

Becoming Skilled at Computing

chapter

1

PART

Introduction

OUR STUDY of computing begins with an introduction to information, technology, and information technology. If your contact with computers has been limited, an introduction is essential. If you are like most readers, you've used computers enough to be familiar with MP3 music, Googling, email, Web surfing, Facebook, and perhaps office applications like word processing; but, you think, there must be many other cool and interesting ways to use computers. You're right! And establishing a firm foundation is the fastest way to move forward.

Part 1 focuses on becoming skilled at using an Internet-connected personal computer. You will learn new applications—in fact, you will *learn how to learn* new applications—and you will discover new ways to use the Internet and World Wide Web. By the end of Part 1 you will be able to apply information technology to your studies, work, and recreation.

The goal of this book is to help you become a confident and knowledgeable computer user. You can achieve this goal by combining the information in Part 1 with daily computer and Internet use. Part 1 presents practical, useful information that requires practice and use, making Fluency a subject in which you can immediately apply what you learn.

Defining Information Technology

1 chapter

Terms of Endearment

learning objectives

- Explain why it's important to know the right word
- Define basic hardware and software terms
- Describe how the mouse clicks a button
- Define and give examples of "idea" terms
- Develop the ability to think more analytically
  - Compare speed records
  - Express an improvement in speed as a factor
- Explain the benefits of analytical thinking

It would appear that we have [as a society] reached the limits of what it is possible to achieve with computer technology, although one should be careful with such statements as they tend to sound pretty silly in 5 years.

—JOHN VON NEUMANN, COMPUTER PIONEER 1947

TO BECOME FLUENT, we need to learn the language of computing and information technology (IT). The people who create the technology are notorious for using acronyms, jargon, and everyday words in unusual ways. Acronyms like WYSIWYG (WHIZ·zee·wig), "what you see is what you get," are often meaningless even after you learn what the letters stand for. (We'll come back to the WYSIWYG story later.) Jargon like "clicking around," for navigating through an application or a series of Web pages, is meaningful only after you have actually done it. And an everyday term like **window**, which was originally chosen to suggest the idea of a portal to the computer, may no longer be an appropriate metaphor for that sophisticated computer concept. It is not surprising that coming across computing terms for the first time is confusing. But is such techno-speak any weirder than, say, medical or musical terms? (For example, *bilirubin* and *hemidemisemiquaver* may sound like odd words unless you're a doctor or a musician.) Technology, like medicine and music, makes more sense when we are familiar with the vocabulary.

Our first goal is to understand why learning the right term is essential to any new endeavor. Next, we ask some simple questions about computers (like "Where's the **Start** button?") to review terms you may already know. But, for almost every familiar term, there is a new word or idea to learn. We also introduce some new words for the physical and computational parts of the computer. These are mostly terms you have probably heard before, but learning exactly what they mean will help you make them part of your everyday vocabulary. Along the way, we explain basic ideas like how buttons are created and how they are clicked. This starts to demystify the computer's virtual world and introduces the ideas of process and algorithm. Then we introduce the "idea" terms of computing, words like *abstraction* and *generalization*. These terms refer to deep concepts, and devoting a few minutes to understanding them will pay off throughout the rest of your Fluency study. Finally, we close with interesting stories about how people and computers have advanced, as we become more analytical in our thinking.

Why Know Just the Right Word

Computing adopts many strange terms because it is filled with new ideas, concepts, and devices that never before existed. The inventors name them so they can describe and explain their ideas to others. Acronyms are common, because as engineers and scientists develop ideas, they often abbreviate them with the letters of the concept's description. The abbreviation sticks, and if the concept is important, its use extends beyond the laboratory. For example, when engineers invented the "small computer system interface," they abbreviated it SCSI. People began to pronounce it "skuzzy" rather than saying S-C-S-I. Naming-by-abbreviation creates a terminology full of acronyms. Critics call it "alphabet soup." But we can understand the terms once we understand what all the letters stand for. For example, ROM is short for "read-only memory." Even without knowing much about computers, you can guess that ROM is a special type of memory that can be read but not written to.

Using the right word at the right time is one characteristic of an educated person. Perhaps the best term to learn to use well is the French (now also English) term *le mot juste* (luh·MO·joost), which means the right word or exact phrasing.

There are two important reasons for knowing and using *le mot juste*. First, understanding the terminology is basic to learning any new subject. When we learn what new words mean, we learn the ideas and concepts that they stand for. Our brains seem to be organized so that when we name a thing or idea, we remember it. For example, in ice hockey, *icing* is the term for hitting the puck across the blue lines and the opponent's goal line. We might not even notice this amid all the passing and slap shots. By knowing this new definition for the familiar word *icing*, we start watching for it, increasing our understanding and enjoyment of the game. Precision in using the term means precision in understanding the idea. Eventually the word stops sounding weird and becomes a part of our vocabulary. At that point, we use the right word without even thinking about it.

The second reason for knowing and using the right word is to communicate with others. If we use terms properly, people understand us. We are able to ask questions and receive help—something everyone starting out in a field needs to do. When seeking help in computing, using the right word is especially important because we often must rely on email, the telephone, or an online help facility. We have to be precise and articulate because no one is by our side to help us describe what we need. A goal of Fluency is to be able to get help from such resources. The ability to use *le mot juste* allows us to communicate, get help, and ultimately, be self-reliant.

You can learn vocabulary by reading a computer dictionary, of course, but that's *waaay* too boring. Instead, we introduce the basic terminology by asking some simple IT questions that have unexpected answers.

Where's the Start Button?

Most computers are on all the time, which is why screen savers were invented. Screen savers—animations such as a kitten prancing around the screen or a changing geometric design—are programs that sleep when the computer is in use and wake up when the computer is idle. These moving images "save the screen." Without them, a single, unchanging image can "burn" into the screen of older monitors, permanently changing the phosphorous surface and creating a "ghost" of the image, which interferes with viewing. Burn-in is less of a problem on newer monitors and many computers simply turn off the screen when the system is idle. You can reactivate the computer by moving or clicking the mouse, or by pressing any key.

If computers are usually on, why bother to learn where the **Start** button is? Because sometimes they are off, and as we will see later, we might need to **cycle power**—turn the computer off and then back on. To know where to look for the power button, we need to know how a computer is organized.

Two Basic Organizations: Monolithic or Component

Some computers are sold as *components* with a separate monitor, computer and hard drive, speakers, and other devices. (We'll discuss the individual devices later.) Many desktop PCs are organized this way. The **monolithic** package, like a Mac or a laptop, has all the devices bundled together, as shown in Figure 1.1(a). The component approach lets you mix and match parts to fit your needs, as shown in Figure 1.1(b). The all-in-one monolithic design is simpler because manufacturers decide for you which components will form a balanced, effective system. Laptops are monolithic, of course, because it is inconvenient to carry around multiple parts.

In a monolithic design, the **power switch** (⏻) is on the front of the chassis or, often with Macs, on the keyboard. For component systems, the power switch is usually on a separate box near the display containing the CD/DVD drive. Most component monitors also have their own power switches, but they control power only for the screen, not the whole computer.

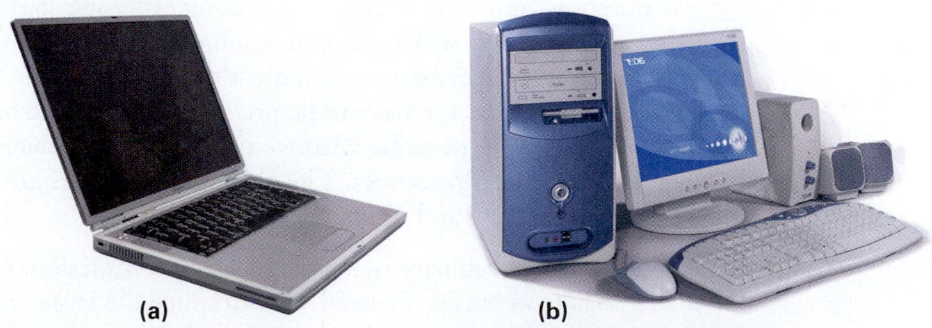

Figure 1.1 Examples of the (a) monolithic and (b) component systems.

The Monitor

The **monitor** is a video screen like a TV, but there are many differences. Unlike passive TVs, computers are interactive, so the monitor becomes more like a blackboard showing the information created by both the computer and the user as they communicate. Modern monitors are **bit-mapped**, meaning that they display information stored in (the bits of) the computer's memory, as illustrated in Figure 1.2. TVs generally display images live or from recorded tape, captured with a camera. The big, bulky monitors are **cathode ray tubes** (CRTs), whereas the slim, flat displays are **liquid crystal displays** (LCDs).

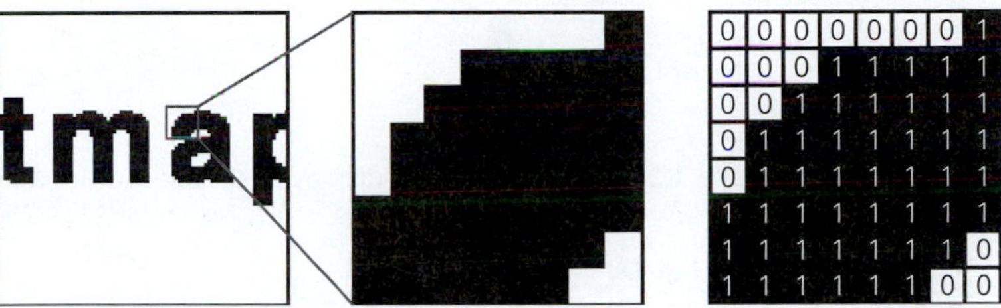

Figure 1.2 An enlargement of a monitor's display of the word *bitmap* and the corresponding bits for each pixel.

To emphasize the contrast between TVs and computers, notice that television can only show "reality"—the images *recorded* through a camera's lens. A computer creates the images it displays in its memory; the images don't have to exist in physical reality. The world that a computer creates is called **virtual reality**.

Cables

The components and the computer must be connected to each other and they must be connected to an electrical power source. For power-hungry devices like monitors, separate **power cables** are usually used, which is why there is a separate power switch. For simple devices like the keyboard or mouse, the **signal** and power wires are combined into one cable. To help us plug in the cables correctly, the computer's sockets and the cable's plugs are usually labeled with icons, as shown in Figure 1.3. So, we simply match up the icons.

Computer component plugs fit into their sockets in only one way. After you figure out which way the plug goes in, insert it into the socket gently to make sure that the pins (the stiff wires making the connections) align and do not bend. Once the plug is inserted, push it in firmly.

fluency ALERT

Damage Control. When connecting computer components (or other electronic devices), plug in the external power connection last. When disconnecting, remove the power connection first. Remember PILPOF—plug in last, pull out first.

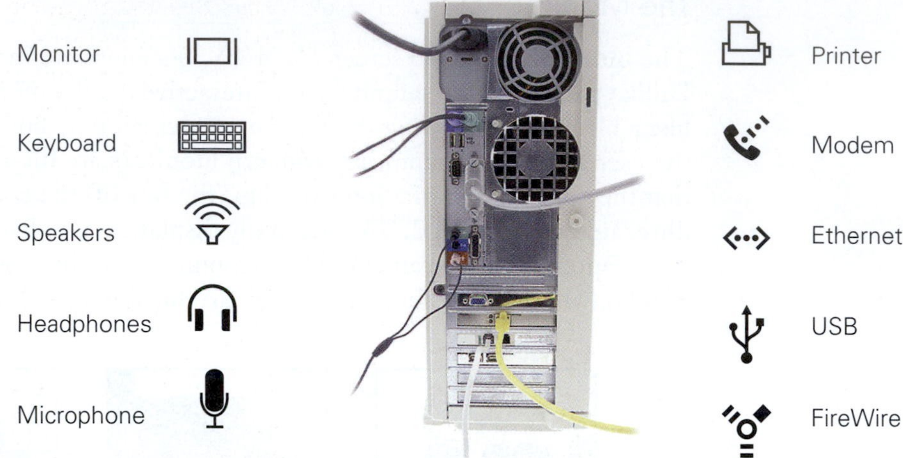

Figure 1.3 Icons commonly displayed on computer cables and sockets.

Colors: RGB

Combining different amounts of three colors of light—red, green, and blue (RGB)—produces the colors you see on your computer monitor, as shown in Figure 1.4. The computer tells the monitor the right proportions of light to display with signals sent through the RGB cable. Any color can be created with some combination of intensities of these three colors. In computer applications, when we select a color from a "palette"—to change the color of text, for example—we are really telling the computer how much of these three colors of light to use.

It may seem odd that red and green combine to produce yellow, as shown in Figure 1.4. As children we learned the primary colors as yellow, red, and blue, and when mixing paints, we discovered that yellow and blue make green. The difference is that monitors mix light and in painting we mix pigment. Stage lighting is another case where we mix colored light, and as we mix more colors (red, green, and blue are enough), we get closer to white. When we mix

Figure 1.4 Mixing of red, green, and blue light.

pigments, we get closer to black. Why? Because pigments absorb and reflect light. Figure 1.4 shows the color mixing of the reflected light. When white light shines on yellow pigment, it absorbs blue and reflects red and green, making yellow as you can see in Figure 1.4. Cyan pigment, a light blue, absorbs red and reflects blue and green (see Figure 1.4). Mix those two pigments together and they absorb the red and blue, reflecting only the green as we learned in kindergarten.

Pixels

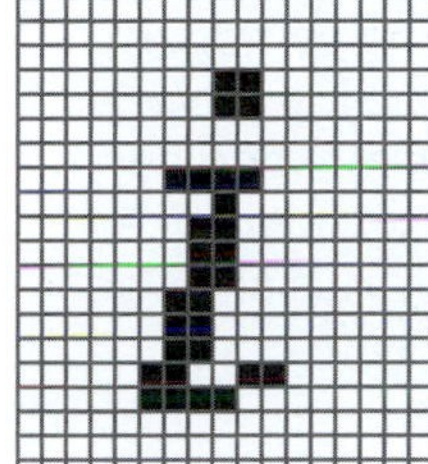

The monitor's screen is divided into a grid of small units called **picture elements** or **pixels**. The size of a pixel is under your control, but it is substantially less than the size of the dot on an *i*. (Check this out on your monitor with a magnifying glass.) The computer displays information on the screen by drawing each pixel in the color designated for the figure or image. For example, in text, the pixels forming the words are colored black and the surrounding pixels are colored white. The size of the grid in pixels—1024 × 768 is typical for a laptop—is important because the more pixels in each row and column, the higher the resolution of the screen image, and the smoother and crisper the result.

The computer must first create in its memory everything displayed on the screen, pixel by pixel. For computer-animated movies like *WALL•E*, creating images of an engaging robot is extremely complex. But the appearance of reality that we see on a computer screen is much easier to generate, as we demonstrate in the following *fluencyBYTE*.

Image Change. The size of the pixel grid displayed on the screen can be increased or decreased using the Display Control Panel for Windows or the Display System Preferences for Mac.

A Virtual Button. It is simple to color the screen's pixels to make a figure that looks like a believable button. On a medium-gray background, the designer colors the top and left sides of a rectangle white and the bottom and right sides black (look at the bottom image in Figure 1.5). This makes the interior of the rectangle appear to project out from the surface, because the white part is highlighted and the dark part looks like a shadow from a light source at the upper left. (If the figure doesn't look much like a button, look at it from a distance.) There is nothing special about the medium-gray/white/black combination except that it gives the lighted/shadowed effect. Other colors work, too. And, by using colors with less contrast, it is possible to give the button a different "feel"; for example, less metallic, as shown in the top image in Figure 1.5.

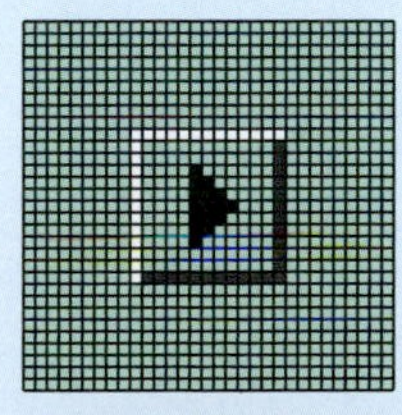

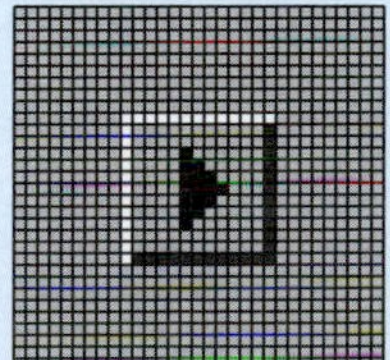

Figure 1.5 Two virtual buttons using different color combinations.

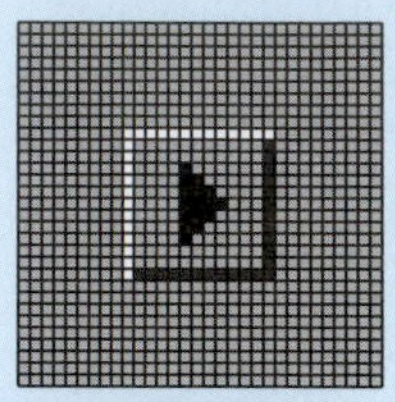

Figure 1.6 Pushing a button.

The Illusion of Button Motion

To show that the button has been pressed, the designer reverses the black and white colors and translates the icon one position down and to the right (see Figure 1.6). To **translate** a figure means to move it, unchanged, to a new position. Because our brains assume that the light source's position stays the same, the reversal of the colors changes the highlights and shadows to make the inside of the rectangle appear to be pushed in. The translation of the icon creates motion that our eyes notice, completing the illusion that the button is pressed. Notice however, that the translation of the icon down and to the right is not really a correct motion for a button "pushed into the screen," but accuracy is less important than the perception of motion.

There is no real button anywhere inside the computer. The bits of the computer's memory have been set so that when they are displayed on the screen, the pixels appear to be a picture of a button. The computer can change the bits when necessary so that the next time they are displayed, the button looks as if it has been pushed in. The designer can add a "click" sound that makes the illusion even more real. But there is still no button.

Pressing a Virtual Button

If there is only a picture of a button, how can we "click" it with the mouse? That's a good question, which we can answer without becoming too technical.

We begin with the mouse pointer. The mouse pointer is a white arrow point with a black border and, like the button, must be created by the computer. When we move the mouse, the computer determines which direction it is moving and redraws the pointer translated a short distance in that direction. By repeatedly redrawing the pointer in new positions that are redisplayed rapidly, the computer produces the illusion that the pointer moves smoothly across the screen. It's the same idea as cartoon flipbooks or motion pictures: A series of still pictures, progressively different and rapidly displayed, creates the illusion of motion. The frequency of display changes is called the **refresh rate** and, like motion-picture frames, is typically 30 times per second. At that rate, the human eye sees the sequence of still frames as smooth motion.

As the mouse pointer moves across the screen, the computer keeps track of which pixel is at the point of the arrow. In Figure 1.7, the computer records the position by the column and row coordinates because the pixel grid is like graph paper. So (1003, 141) in Figure 1.7(a) means that the pixel pointed out is in the 1003rd pixel column from the left side of the screen and at the 141st pixel row from the top of the screen. With each new position, the coordinates are updated. When the mouse is clicked, as shown in Figure 1.7(d), the computer determines which button the mouse pointer is hovering over and then redraws the button to look pushed in.

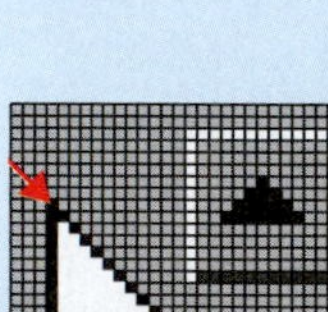

(a) column 1003, row 141

(b) column 1011, row 140

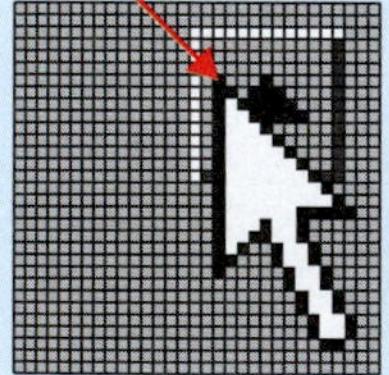

(c) column 1017, row 139

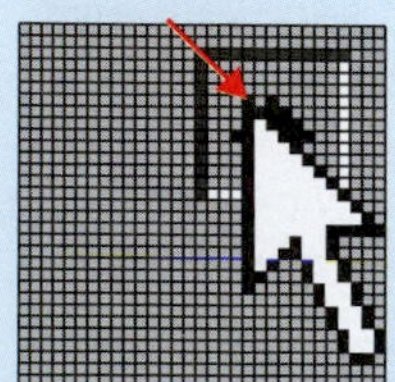

(d) Click

Figure 1.7 Mouse pointer moving toward (a, b), pointing to (c), and then clicking (d) a button; the coordinates of the point of the pointer are given by their column and row positions.

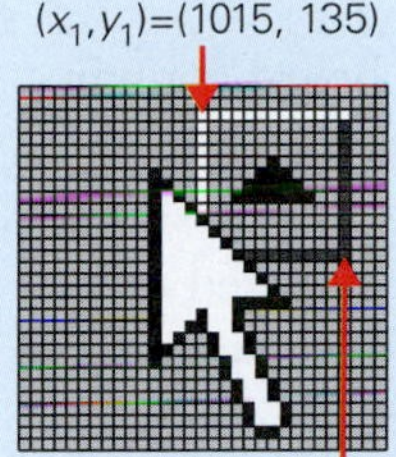

Figure 1.8
A button's location is completely determined by the positions of its upper-left and lower-right corners.

Coordinating the Button and the Mouse

How does the computer know which button the mouse pointer is hovering over? It keeps a list of every button drawn on the screen, recording the coordinates of the button's upper-left and lower-right corners. In Figure 1.8, the button has its upper-left corner at pixel (1015, 135) and its lower-right corner at pixel (1027, 147). The two corners, call them (x_1, y_1) and (x_2, y_2), determine the position of the rectangle that defines the button: the top row of white pixels is in row y_1, the left-side column of white pixels is in column x_1, the bottom row of black pixels is in row y_2, and the right-side column of black pixels is in column x_2.

Now, if the mouse pointer's point has a row coordinate between y_1 and y_2, the pointer is somewhere between the top and bottom of the button, although it may be to the left or right of the button rather than on top of it. But if the pointer's point also has a column coordinate between x_1 and x_2, the pointer is between the left and right sides of the button; that is, it is somewhere on the button. So, for each button with coordinates (x_1, y_1) and (x_2, y_2), the computer tests whether

x_1 < column coordinate of mouse pointer point < x_2

and

y_1 < row coordinate of mouse pointer point < y_2

are *both* true. If so, the mouse pointer's point is over that button and the button is redrawn in the "clicked configuration." This tells the user that the command has been received and the program performs the appropriate action.

Creating a button and keeping track of the positions of the button and the mouse pointer may seem like a lot of work, but it makes using a computer easier (and more fun) for us. The metaphor of pressing a button to cause an action is so natural that software developers believe it's worth the trouble to make buttons.

Where Is the Computer?

This may seem like an odd question, but it's not. In casual conversation, most of us call the monitor "the computer." Technically speaking, we're usually wrong. If we are referring to a laptop or iMac, the part that actually does the computing *is* inside the same unit as the monitor, so in those cases we're right. But for component systems, the computer is not in the monitor unit, but rather in a separate box on the floor or somewhere else nearby. Calling the monitor the computer is not so much a mistake as an acknowledgment that the monitor is our interface to the computer, wherever it is.

In the component approach, the computer and most of its parts (for example, hard disk, and CD/DVD drive) are packaged together in a box called the **processor box**, though it often has a fancy marketing name (for example, minitower) that has no technical meaning. In the monolithic approach, the associated disks and drives are in the same package as the monitor; it's as if the monitor were attached to the processor box. The information in this section applies to both component and monolithic systems.

Motherboard

Inside the processor box is the **motherboard**, a printed circuit board containing most of the circuitry of a personal computer system, as shown in Figure 1.9. The name comes from the fact that smaller printed circuit boards, sometimes called **daughter boards** but more often called **cards**, are plugged into the motherboard for added capacity or functionality. A motherboard is impressive to look at with all of its fine wire patterns, colorful resistors, economy of space, and so forth. (Ask your computer dealer to show you one—it's safer than looking at the one in your computer and risking harm to it.) The motherboard is a **printed circuit** or PC board. (This use of "PC" predates "PC" meaning "personal computer" by decades.) Of the many parts on this PC board, only the microprocessor chip and the memory interest us at the moment.

Microprocessor

The **microprocessor**, found on the motherboard, is the part of a personal computer system that computes. The microprocessor is involved in every

Figure 1.9 A computer motherboard.

activity of the system, from making the mouse pointer appear to move around the screen to locating information stored on the hard disk. The microprocessor is the "smart" part of the system, so engineers often describe the other parts of a computer as "dumb." It is surprisingly easy for a computer to be "smart," as we will see. Eventually, we will even ask, "Can a computer think?"

The "micro" part of microprocessor is archaic and no longer accurate. The term "microprocessor" was adopted around 1980 when all of the circuitry for a computer first fit onto a single silicon chip. These were technically computer processors, but they were small and primitive compared to the mainframes and the "minicomputers" of the day, so they were called *micro*processors. But improvements came so quickly that in a few years microprocessors were more powerful than the largest computers of 1980. Today's microprocessors are fast, highly optimized, loaded with features, and very sophisticated. In fact, today's microprocessor chips come with *multiple* processors known as **processor cores**. Because there is nothing "micro" about today's microprocessors, we will simply use the term **processor** for the rest of this book.

Memory

The **memory** of a computer is where a program and its data are located while the program is running. For example, when you are using a word processor, the word processing program and the document being edited are stored in the computer's memory. (When they're not in memory, programs and data are stored on the hard disk; see the next section.) Computer memory is often called **RAM**, short for **random access memory**; unlike the ROM, the read-only memory mentioned earlier, RAM can be electronically read and written, making it more versatile. The basic unit of memory is a **byte**, which is described in Chapter 8. Today's personal computers have millions or billions of bytes of RAM memory, that is, **megabytes** (from the Greek prefix **mega-** meaning million) or **gigabytes**. See Figure 9.11 in Chapter 9 for a list of prefixes.

There are two basic ways to locate and retrieve, or *access*, information: sequential and random. Information stored sequentially is arranged in a line, so that when you want to find a specific item, you have to skip everything else stored before it, as shown in Figure 1.10. Cassette tapes, VCR tapes, and so on are examples of **sequential access**. **Random access** means that any item can be retrieved directly. Finding dictionary entries, library books, and phone numbers are examples of random access. Random access is faster than sequential access, as anyone trying to locate the last scene of a TV show on a VCR tape knows.

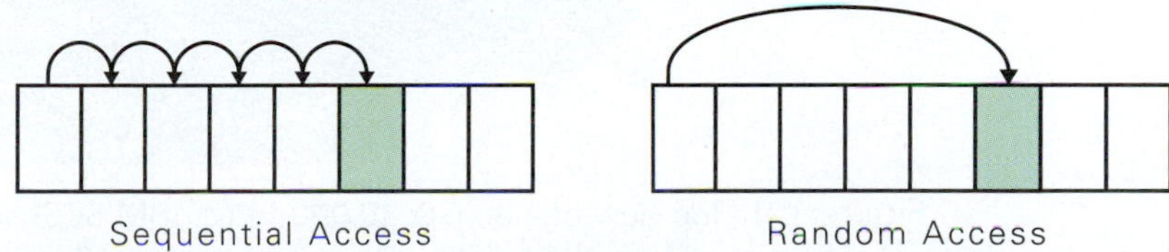

Figure 1.10 Sequential versus random access.

Hard Disk

The **hard disk** is not really part of the computer—technically it is a high-capacity, persistent storage peripheral device. But it is so fundamental to personal computer systems that it's helpful to think of it as a basic part. The hard disk is also referred to as the **hard drive**, or simply the **disk**. The disk stores programs and data when they are not in immediate use by a computer. Disks are made from an iron compound that can be magnetized. Because the magnetism remains even when the power is off, the encoded information is still there when the power comes back on. So a disk is said to be *permanent* or *persistent* storage. A hard disk is usually located in the same box as the processor, because without access to permanent storage, the effectiveness of a processor is limited.

The hard disk looks like a small stack of metal washers with an arm that can sweep across and between them, as shown in Figure 1.11. The "popping" or "clicking" sound we sometimes hear coming from the computer is the arm moving back and forth as it accesses information on various tracks of the disk.

Saving from RAM to Hard Disk. Successful computer users save their work regularly. For example, when writing a term paper using a word processor, run the *Save* command every half hour or perhaps after completing a few pages or a section. Saving copies the information, that is, your term paper, from the RAM memory to the hard disk memory. This action is important because of the differences between the two types of memory.

Figure 1.11 Top view of a 36 GB, 10,000 RPM, IBM SCSI server hard disk, with its top cover removed. Note the height of the drive and the 10 stacked platters. (The IBM Ultrastar 36ZX.)

Recall that hard disk memory is made from a magnetic material that "remembers," even when the power is off. Today's RAM memory, however, is made from **integrated circuit (IC)** technology, informally called microchips. One property of IC memory is that it is volatile, meaning that the information is lost when the power is turned off. That is, when IC memory loses power, it "forgets." This difference wouldn't matter if computers didn't fail. But they do.

When a computer crashes—that is, when it no longer works correctly or it stops running entirely—it must be restarted, a process called **rebooting**. If the computer is not working correctly, the *Restart* command will run. The first step in restarting is to erase the memory, causing the information stored in the RAM to be lost. If it's not working at all, then the power must be cycled—turned off, and then after a few seconds turned on again—also causing the information stored in the RAM to be lost, because IC memory is volatile. Either way, anything that was in the RAM, such as the latest version of your term paper, will be lost. Only the copy that is on the hard disk, which is the copy from the last time it was saved, is available when the computer "comes up." All the work since the last save is lost.

Crashes are not common, but they happen. Frequently saving your file limits the amount of work you will have to redo if your computer crashes.

How Soft Is Software?

The term hardware predates computers by centuries. Originally it meant metal items used in construction, like hinges and nails. The word software did not exist until computers were invented.

Software

Software is a collective term for computer programs. The name contrasts with hardware, of course, but what does it mean for software to be "soft"? When a computer function is implemented in software, the computer performs the operation by following instructions. A program that figures out your income taxes is an example of software. If a computer function is implemented in **hardware**, the computer performs the operations directly with wires and transistors. (We say it is **hard-wired**.) The multiplication operation is an example of hardware-implemented functions.

The difference between "hard" and "soft" is like the difference between an innate ability, such as coughing, and a learned ability, such as reading. Innate abilities are "built in" biologically, and they're impossible to change, like hardware. Learned abilities are easily changed and expanded, like software. Typically, only the most primitive operations like multiplication are implemented in hardware; everything else is software. (Computers don't *learn* to perform soft operations, of course, the way we learn to read. Rather, they are simply given the instructions and told to follow them.)

The Hard Reality. The difference between hardware and software was dramatically illustrated in 1994 when a bug was discovered in the hard-wired divide operation of Intel's Pentium processor, an approximately $200 chip. Though the wrong answers were rare and tiny, the error had to be fixed. If divide had been implemented in software, as had been the usual approach in computing's early years, Intel could have sent everyone a simple patch for $1 or $2. But hardware cannot be modified, so the Pentium chips had to be recalled at a total cost estimated at about $500 million.

Algorithms and Programs

An **algorithm** is a precise and systematic method for solving a problem. Another term for a systematic method is a **process**. Some familiar algorithms are arithmetic operations like addition, subtraction, multiplication, and division; the process for sending a greeting card; and searching for a phone number. The method used for determining when a mouse pointer hovers over a button is an algorithm. Because an algorithm's instructions are written down for some other agent (a person or a computer) to follow, precision is important.

We learn some algorithms, like arithmetic. Sometimes we figure out algorithms on our own, like finding phone numbers. In Chapter 10, we introduce **algorithmic thinking**, the act of thinking up algorithms. Writing out the steps of an algorithm is called **programming**. **Programs** are simply algorithms written in a specific programming language for a specific set of conditions.

1.1 Algorithmic Steps. Suppose you want to send a birthday card to your grandmother. Assume the first two steps are: (1) Buy an appropriate card for your grandmother, and (2) Buy an appropriate stamp for the card. Give the remaining steps to complete the task. There isn't one correct answer, but a typical solution will identify five or six more steps.

When we ask a computer to do something for us, we ask it to **run** a program. This is literally what we ask when we click on the icon for an application like Internet Explorer. We are saying, "Run the program from the Microsoft company to browse the Internet." *Run* is a term that has been used since the invention of computers, but *execute* is a slightly better term because it emphasizes an important property of computing.

Execute

A computer **executes** a program when it *performs* instructions. The word *execute* means to follow a set of orders exactly as they are written. Computer pioneers used the word *orders* for what we now call instructions. Orders tell the computer to act in a specific way. When orders are given, the faithful agent is *not* supposed to think. "Following instructions literally" is what computers do when they run programs; it is that aspect that makes "execute" a slightly better term than "run."

In addition to run and execute, **interpret** is also a correct term for following a program's instructions, as explained in Chapter 9.

Boot

Finally, the term **booting** means to start a computer and **rebooting** means to restart it. Because booting most often happens after a catastrophic error or a crash, you might guess that the term is motivated by frustration—we want to kick the computer like a football. Actually, the term *booting* comes from *bootstrap*. Computers were originally started by an operator who entered a few instructions into the computer's empty memory using console push buttons. Those instructions told the computer to read in a few more instructions—a very simple operating system—from punch cards. This operating system could then read in the instructions of the real operating system from magnetic tape, similar to a VCR tape. Finally, the computer was able to start doing useful work. This incremental process was called *bootstrapping*, from the phrase "pulling yourself up by your bootstraps," because the computer basically started itself. Today the instructions to start a computer are stored on a microchip called the boot ROM.

The Words for Ideas

Although understanding the physical parts of IT—monitors, motherboards, and memory—seems very important, we are not too concerned with them here. Instead, we will focus on *concept* words, such as those discussed in this section.

"Abstract"

One of the most important "idea" words used in this book is the verb *abstract*. It has several meanings. In British mysteries, *to abstract* means *to remove*, as in *to steal*: "The thief abstracted the pearl necklace while the jeweler looked at the diamond ring." In computing, *to abstract* also means to remove, but the thing being removed is not physical. The thing being removed is an idea or a process, and it is extracted from some form of information.

To **abstract** is to remove the basic concept, idea, or process from a situation. The removed concept is usually expressed in another, more succinct and usually more general form, called an **abstraction**.

We are familiar with abstraction in this sense. Parables and fables, which teach lessons in the form of stories, require us to abstract the essential point of the story. When we are told about a fox that can't reach a bunch of grapes and so calls them sour, we abstract the idea from the story: When people fail to get what they want, they often decide that they didn't want to have it after all.

Notice two key points here. First, many but not all of the details of the story are irrelevant to the concept. When abstracting, we must decide which details of the story are relevant and which are irrelevant. The "grapes" and the "fox" are unimportant, but "failure" is important. Being able to tell the difference between important and unimportant details is essential to understanding the point of a story, and to abstraction in general. Second, the idea—the abstraction—has meaning beyond the story. The point of repeating the parable, of course, is to convey an idea that applies to many situations.

"Generalize"

A process similar to abstraction is to recognize the common idea in two or more situations. Recognizing how different situations have something basic in common is why we create parables, rules, and so on.

To **generalize** is to express an idea, concept, or process that applies to many situations. The statement summing up that idea is called a **generalization**.

For example, most of us notice that twisting a faucet handle left turns water on and twisting it right turns it off. Not always—some water taps have only a single "joy stick" handle, and others have horizontal bars that pull forward. But since it's true most of the time, we generalize that "on" is to the left and "off" is to the right. Perhaps we also notice that twisting lids, caps, screws, and nuts to the left usually loosens them, and turning them to the right usually tightens them. Again, we generalize that left means loosen and right means tighten. We probably also generalize that both situations are examples of the same thing! A generalization of generalizations.

Noticing patterns and generalizing about them is a very valuable habit. Although generalizations do not always apply, recognizing them gives us a way to begin in a new, but similar, situation.

"Operationally Attuned"

Another term related to extracting concepts and processes refers to being aware of how a gadget works. To be **operationally attuned** is to apply what we know about how a device or system works to simplify its use.

For example, we previously generalized that with few exceptions, all caps, lids, screws, and nuts tighten by turning right and loosen by turning left. We might know this intuitively, but knowing it *explicitly* makes us operationally attuned. Knowing this fact as a rule means that when a lid or nut is stuck, we can twist it very hard, certain that we are forcing it to loosen rather than tighten. Being operationally attuned makes us more effective.

The term operationally attuned is introduced here to emphasize that thinking about how IT works makes it simpler to use. We don't expect to be experts on all of the technology—few are. But by asking ourselves, "How does this work?" and using what we learn by thinking about the answer, we will be more successful at applying IT. Our Fluency study focuses on learning enough to answer many of the "How does this work?" questions well enough to succeed.

fluencyBYTE

Tuning In. In our daily lives, we use hundreds of devices, systems, and processes. For some, like a car ignition, we quickly learn which way to turn the key because it only turns in one direction. We don't think about how it works. Using it becomes a habit. Other gadgets, however, have more leeway, and for them it helps to be attuned to their operation. One example is a deadbolt lock, which moves a metal bar from the door to the doorframe to lock the door. Thinking about how the lock works tells us whether the door is locked or not. Referring to Figure 1.12(a), notice which way the knob is turned. By visualizing the internal works of the lock, we can imagine that the top of the knob is attached to the bar. When the knob is pointing left, the bar must be pulled back—that is, unlocked. When the knob is pointing right, the bar is extended, so the door is locked. We may not know how the lock really works, but explaining its operation in our own terms means that we can see at a distance whether the door is locked or unlocked. It might save us from getting up from the sofa to check if the door is locked.

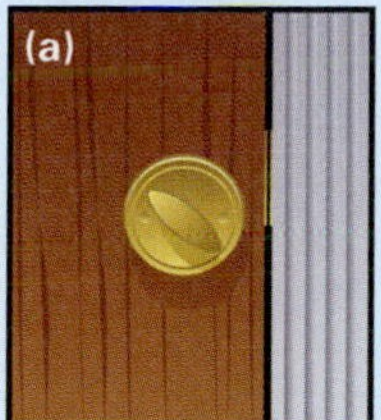

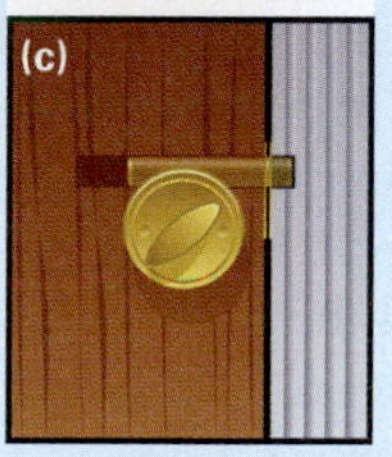

Figure 1.12 Deadbolt lock. (a) The external view. (b) Internal components, unlocked. (c) Internal components, locked. Thinking about how the deadbolt works allows us to see at a glance whether the door is locked or not.

"Mnemonic"

Mnemonic is a rather unusual term that we use in IT and in other fields as well. The silent *m* implies that it's a word with an unusual past.

A mnemonic (ni MÄ·nik) is an aid for remembering something. The reminder can take many forms, such as pronounceable words or phrases. We remember the five Great Lakes between the U.S. and Canada with the acronym HOMES—Huron, Ontario, Michigan, Erie, and Superior. Earlier in this chapter, we mentioned PILPOF—plug in last, pull out first. And when Pluto was downgraded from planetary status, we had to change our mnemonic for the planets: My very educated mother just served us nachos.

There are many IT details that we need to know only occasionally, like when to connect power. They're not worth memorizing, but they're inconvenient to look up. So, if we can think of a mnemonic that helps us remember the details when we need them, using technology is simpler.

Analytical Thinking

Using the right terms makes learning IT simpler. Becoming more analytical is an equally valuable habit to acquire. When we say that the world record in the mile run has improved or that computer performance has improved, we are making very weak statements. They simply assert that things have changed over time for the better. But has the change been infinitesimally small or gigantic? How does the change compare to other changes? Since we can easily find information on the Internet, we can compare an earlier measure of performance with a recent one. Thinking analytically is essential to becoming Fluent in IT, but it is also useful in our other studies, our careers, and our lives.

Mile Runs

When Moroccan runner Hicham El Guerrouj broke the world record on July 7, 1999, the news reports trumpeted that he "smashed," "eclipsed," and "shattered" the world record set six years earlier by Noureddine Morceli of Algeria (see Figure 1.13). El Guerrouj had run a mile in an astonishing 3 minutes, 43.13 seconds, an impressive 1.26 seconds faster than Morceli. The descriptions were not hyperbole. People around the world truly marveled at El Guerrouj's accomplishment, even though 1.26 seconds seems like an insignificant difference.

To put El Guerrouj's run into perspective, notice that 45 years had passed since Englishman Roger Bannister attracted world attention as the first man in recorded history to run a mile in less than 4 minutes (see Figure 1.13). His time was 3:59.4. In 45 years, the world's best runners improved the time for the mile by an astonishing 16.27 seconds. (Notice that El Guerrouj's 1.26 seconds was a significant part of that.) As a rate, 16.27 seconds represents an improvement from 15.038 miles per hour to 16.134 miles per hour, or just over 7 percent. Given that Bannister's time was a world-class starting point, an improvement in human performance of that size is truly something to admire.

Comparing to 20-Year-Olds

How do these world champions compare to average people? Most healthy people in their early 20s—the age group of the world record setters—can run a mile in 7.5 minutes. This number was chosen because it covers the ability of a majority of the people in the age range, and is approximately twice the time El Guerrouj needed. To say El Guerrouj is twice as fast as an average person

Figure 1.13 The runners Hicham El Guerrouj (left) and Roger Bannister (right).

is to say he is faster by a factor of 2. (The factor relating two numbers is found by dividing one by the other; for example 7.5/3.75 = 2.)

This factor-of-2 difference is a rough rule for the performance gap between an average person and a world champion for most physical strength activities such as running, swimming, jumping, and pole vaulting. The factor-of-2 rule tells us that no matter how hard most people try at physical activities, their performance can improve by roughly twice. Of course, most of us can only dream of achieving even part of that factor-of-2 potential. Nevertheless, the factor-of-2 rule is an important benchmark.

Factor of Improvement

When we compared world champions, we said there was a 7 percent improvement and that El Guerrouj's speed was about a factor-of-2 times faster than the speed of an average person. There is a difference between expressing improvement as a *percentage* and expressing improvement as a *factor*. We find a **factor of improvement** by dividing the new rate by the old rate. So, to find El Guerrouj's improvement over Bannister's, we divide their rates (16.134/15.038) to get 1.07. Percentages are a closely related computation found by dividing the *amount of change* by the old rate (16.134 – 15.038)/15.038 = 0.07 and multiplying the result by 100. The added complexity of percentage is potentially confusing, so we use the simpler factor-of-improvement method. El Guerrouj was a factor-of-1.07 times faster than Bannister and about a factor-of-2 times faster than an average person.

Super Computers

As another example of analytical thinking, let's compare computer speeds. The UNIVAC I, the first commercial computer, unveiled in 1951 (and current when Bannister set his record), operated at a rate of nearly 100,000 addition operations (adds) per second. By comparison, a typical PC today—say, the portable IBM ThinkPad—can perform a billion additions per second or so. This factor-of-10,000 improvement over UNIVAC I (1,000,000,000/100,000) is truly remarkable. But, consider this—the ThinkPad is no record setter. It's the sort of computer a college student can afford to buy. Engineering workstations can easily do several billion adds per second, boosting the factor even higher. And an Intel computer called ASCI Red, built for Sandia National Laboratory, held the world record for computer speed in 1999, when El Guerrouj set his record. ASCI Red ran at an astonishing 2.1 trillion floating-point adds per second. (Floating-point adds are decimal arithmetic operations that are more complex than the additions used to measure the speed of the UNIVAC I.) Compared to the UNIVAC I, ASCI Red is a factor of 21 million times faster!

Faster Still. ASCI Red was the fastest of its day, but its day has passed. Several computers have eclipsed its performance, and better designs continue to be developed. For the latest speed tests, see www.top500.org.

Perhaps nothing else in human experience has improved so dramatically. In roughly the same time period that human performance improved by a factor of 1.07 as measured by the mile run, computer performance improved by a factor of 21,000,000. Can we comprehend such a huge factor of improvement, or even the raw speed of ASCI Red?

1.2 Computing the Factor of Improvement. Flyer 1, the aircraft Orville and Wilbur Wright flew at Kitty Hawk, North Carolina, traveled so slowly (10 mph) that the brother who wasn't piloting could run alongside as it flew just off the ground. The SR-71 Blackbird, probably the world's fastest plane, flies at 2,200 mph, three times the speed of sound.

What is the factor of improvement between Blackbird and Flyer 1?

fluencyBIT

Think About It. Most of us can appreciate the 7 percent improvement of El Guerrouj's run over Bannister's, and probably the factor-of-2 improvement in average versus world champion performance. Those we can imagine. But factors of improvement in the thousands or millions are beyond our comprehension. Notice that if El Guerrouj had improved on Bannister by a factor of 21,000,000, he'd have run the mile in 11.4 microseconds. That's 11.4 millionths of a second. What does that mean?

- Human visual perception is so slow that El Guerrouj could run 3,000 miles at that rate before anyone would even notice he had moved.
- The sound would still be "inside" the starting gun 11.4 microseconds after the trigger was pulled.
- Light travels only twice as fast.

Both the raw power of today's computers and their improvement over the last sixty years are almost beyond our comprehension.

Benefits of Analytical Thinking

To summarize, we have made our understanding of recent speed improvements crisper by applying simple analysis: Rather than accepting the statement that the mile run and computers have improved, we learned the facts given as two measurements of performance. But once we had the data, we did not leave it as two separate observations: 100,000 additions in 1951 versus 2.1 trillion additions in 1999. Instead, we analyzed their relationship by figuring the factor of improvement: 2,100,000,000,000/100,000. ASCI Red is faster by a factor of 21 million.

This analysis let us compare the improvement to other advancements, and to put them all into perspective. The mile run, improved by an apparently small factor of 1.07 times in 45 years, is still very impressive when we recall that champions are only about a factor-of-2 better than average people. Computer performance has improved by unimaginable amounts. Although our original statement, "the mile run and computers have improved," is correct, our analysis helps us to be much more expressive and precise. Analytical thinking helps us understand more clearly the world of computing and the physical world in which we live.

Defining WYSIWYG

Our only remaining task is to define the first acronym mentioned in the chapter: **WYSIWYG**. Remember that it stands for "what you see is what you get." To understand the term, recall that the computer creates the virtual world we see on our monitors. The representation the computer uses to keep track of the things on the screen is very different from the picture it shows us. For example, the text you are reading was stored in the computer as one very long line of letters, numbers, punctuation, and special characters, but it is displayed to me as a nicely formatted page like the one you are reading. The computer processes this representation—the long sequence of letters—to create the nicely formatted page. Original text editing software couldn't do that, so users had to work with the long sequence. If you wanted to make a change to the document, you had to imagine what it would look like when printed.

Eventually, text editing systems were programmed to show the user the page as it would appear when printed. Changing the text became much easier. This property was described as "what you see (when editing) is what you get (when it's printed)" or WYSIWYG. Text editors with the WYSIWYG property became known as **word processors**.

Summary

In this chapter we focused on learning IT terms in context. We learned to:

- Know and use the right word because as we learn words, we learn ideas; knowing the right words helps us to communicate.
- Ask questions to review basic and familiar terms, such as monitor, screen saver, RAM, and software.
- Understand a few new terms, such as sequential access, volatile, and motherboard.
- Consider a brief list of "idea" words, such as abstract and generalize.
- Save our work regularly.
- Think analytically by looking at improvements in the mile run and computer speed.

We're not done, however. All of the chapters introduce new terms when new ideas are discussed. Learning and remembering these key terms will help you learn and remember the ideas. Key terms appear in the glossary at the end of the book. Check the glossary when the meaning of a term slips your mind. In addition to the glossary in this book, there are several good online glossaries. It's a good idea to find one with your Web browser and bookmark it—that is, save its URL. We will discuss URLs in Chapter 3. Meanwhile, check the glossary to learn what the acronym URL stands for.

Try It Solutions

1.1 The additional steps could include: (3) Add a personal note to the card and sign it; (4) Place the card in the envelope; (5) Affix the stamp; (6) Address the envelope; (7) Seal the envelope; and (8) Mail the envelope.

1.2 Speed of Blackbird = 2,200 mph
Speed of Flyer 1 = 10 mph
Factor of improvement = 2,200/10 = 220

The Blackbird is a factor-of-220 faster than Flyer 1.

Review Questions

Multiple Choice

1. Computer monitors are different from TVs because
a. monitors are bit-mapped whereas TVs are not
b. TVs are interactive whereas monitors are not
c. monitors are CRTs whereas TVs are not
d. more than one of the above

2. How is the process for clicking a check box similar to clicking a button?
a. The tip of the arrow must be inside the *x*, *y* coordinates that make up the check box.
b. The user must click the mouse button.
c. The configuration of the check box must change from unchecked to checked or vice versa.
d. all of the above

3. The display for a laptop is most likely a
a. TV
b. RGB display
c. LCD
d. CRT display

4. Mice and keyboards do not have power cords because
a. they are not electrical
b. the power and the signal wires are in one cable
c. they run on batteries
d. none of the above

5. The last cable you plug in should be the
a. monitor cable
b. keyboard cable
c. printer cable
d. power cable

6. RGB stands for
   a. red, green, black
   b. red, gray, blue
   c. rust, black, brown
   d. red, green, blue
7. A combination of red light and green light produces
   a. blue
   b. purple
   c. yellow
   d. brown
8. A typical monitor
   a. has over a million pixels
   b. has exactly a million pixels
   c. displays pixels in only one color
   d. none of the above
9. How many pixels make up the button in Figure 1.8 (page 11)?
   a. 19×19
   b. 304
   c. 1024×768
   d. none of the above

Short Answer

1. The _______ is involved in every activity of the computer system.
2. Knowing _______ is important to understanding technology and being understood when talking about it.
3. A(n) _______ saves a CRT monitor from "burn in" when it is not in use.
4. The last cable you should plug in should be the _______.
5. There are _______ pixels on a typical laptop?
6. The number of times a second that images on the screen are redrawn is called the _______.
7. The _______ is the active point of the mouse pointer.
8. A specified result sought through the use of a precise and systematic method is a(n) _______.
9. _______ is the proper term used when a computer performs the instructions in a program.
10. The process of starting a computer is called _______.
11. Recognizing the central idea or concept from a situation is called _______.
12. A device that helps you remember a fact or concept is a(n) _______.

13. A WYSIWYG text editor is called a(n) ______.
14. On the computer, programs and information are stored on the ______.
15. The formulation of an idea, concept, or process that can be applied in many situations is called a(n) ______.

Exercises

1. Here are some of the acronyms found in this chapter. Next to each, write its name and its meaning.
   SCSI ____________________
   IT ____________________
   CRT ____________________
   LCD ____________________
   RGB ____________________
   RAM ____________________
   ROM ____________________
   PC ____________________
   IC ____________________
2. Create a list of mnemonics that you know and their meanings.
3. Answer the following questions about your computer. You may need to use your system's software to answer some of these.
   a. How much memory does your computer have?
   b. How big is your hard drive?
   c. What operating system are you running?
   d. What version of the operating system are you running?
4. It took Magellan's expedition three years to circumnavigate the globe. The space shuttle makes an orbit in about 90 minutes. Calculate the factor of improvement.
5. Ellery Clark of the United States won the long jump in the 1896 Olympiad in Athens, Greece, with a jump of 20 feet 9 3/4 inches. The current men's world record is held by Mike Powell of the United States, who jumped a distance of 8.95 meters. What is the factor of improvement? Be sure to convert between feet and meters.
6. Ray Harroun won the first Indianapolis 500 in 1911 with a speed of 74.59 miles per hour. The 2009 race was won by Hélio Castroneves with a speed of 150.318 mph. What is the factor of improvement?
7. In 2009, Yelena Isinbayeva set the women's world pole vault record at 5.06 meters. William Hoyt had set the men's record in 1896 with a vault of 3.30 meters. What is the factor of improvement that she made over the men's record of 1896? What is the percentage increase?

8. If a button that is the size and kind illustrated in Figure 1.7 (page 10) is located with its upper-left corner at position 100, 100 on the screen, give the positions of its other three corners. Remember that the pixel positions increase to the right and down.

9. Using online research, find an online glossary of computing terms. Look up the following terms in at least two sources, and state in your own words what they mean.
   a. USB memory
   b. TFT display
   c. window

   Include with your answers the name (and link) of the glossary you found most helpful.

2

chapter

Exploring the Human-Computer Interface

What the Digerati Know

learning objectives

- Explain key ideas familiar to experienced users (the digerati):
  - The advantages of having consistent features in information technology
  - The benefits of using feedback from "clicking around" and from "blazing away" when exploring new applications
  - The basic principle of computation: form follows function
- Explain how a basic search is done
- Use common methods to search and edit text:
  - Find (words, characters, spaces)
  - Shift-select
  - The placeholder technique
  - Search-and-replace (substitution)

Exploration is really the essence of the human spirit.

—FRANK BORMAN, US ASTRONAUT

Text processing has made it possible to right-justify any idea, even one which cannot be justified on any other grounds.

—J FINNEGAN, USC

PERHAPS THE MOST uncomfortable part of being a "noncomputer person" is the suspicion that everyone but you knows how to use technology. Everyone seems to know automatically what to do in any situation.

Of course, experienced users don't really have a technology gene. Through experience, however, they have learned a certain kind of knowledge that lets them figure out what to do in most situations. Most people don't "know" this information explicitly—it's not usually taught in class. They learn it through experience. But you can avoid long hours of stumbling around gaining experience. This chapter reveals some secrets of the digerati so that you, too, can "join the club." (Digerati, analogous to the word *literati*, means people who understand digital technology.)

Our major goal in this chapter is to show you how to think abstractly about technology. We do this by asking how people learn technical skills and by considering what technology developers expect from us as users. This chapter will also help you understand that:

- Computer systems use consistent interfaces, standard metaphors, and common operations.
- Computer systems always give feedback while they are working.
- Making mistakes does not break the computer.
- The best way to learn to use new computer software is to experiment with it.
- Asking questions of other computer users is not evidence of being a dummy, but proof of an inquiring mind.

These ideas can help you learn new software quickly. A key abstract idea about software is that it obeys fundamental laws. This fact can help you in your everyday software use, as we illustrate when we explain the principle "form follows function." We show how this principle applies to basic text searching by teaching the subject without using any specific software. Such knowledge applies to every system and makes us versatile users. You too, can become one of the digerati.

fluencyBIT

Desktop. Many creative people have contributed to the invention of personal computing, beginning in the late 1960s with Douglas Englebart and his team at SRI who created devices such as the mouse. In the 1970s, researchers at Xerox's Palo Alto Research Center (PARC) applied the ideas to office automation by creating the Alto, the first personal computer with the features we've come to expect: bit-mapped display, mouse, windows, desktop metaphor, and so on. Although it was never marketed, the Alto motivated Apple to create the Macintosh, launched in 1984. Eventually, Microsoft upgraded its DOS (disk operating system) to have these features, making them effectively universal.

Learning the Technology

Human beings are born knowing how to chew, cough, stand, blink, smile, and so forth. We are not born knowing how to ride a bicycle, drive a car, use a food processor, or start a lawnmower. For any tool more complicated than a stick, we need some explanation about how it works and possibly some training in how it's used. Parents teach their children how to ride bicycles and most products come with an owner's manual.

Some tools, such as music players, are so intuitive that most people living in our technological society find their use "obvious." We don't need to refer to the owner's manual. We can guess what the controls do because we know what operations are needed to play music. (Without this knowledge, the icons would probably be meaningless.) And we can usually recover if we make mistakes.

But the fact that we live in a technological society and can figure out how music players work doesn't mean that we are born with any technological abilities. Instead, it emphasizes two facts about technology that are key to our success:

- Our experience using (related) devices, including software, guides us in what to expect.
- Designers who create these devices, including software, know we have that experience and design products to match what we already know.

New Software

Suppose in December of 2008 you heard all of the hype surrounding the official release of Chrome, a browser written by Google. You're thinking of trying it despite being uncertain what makes it better than your current browser. But will you know how to use it? Of course you will. You've browsed before—that's the first bullet point above—and the designers, wanting you to use Chrome effortlessly, will exploit your knowledge in their new software, which is the second bullet. Let's take a look at Chrome from that perspective to see how you use this sort of knowledge. After downloading and installing the software, your first look is shown in Figure 2.1.

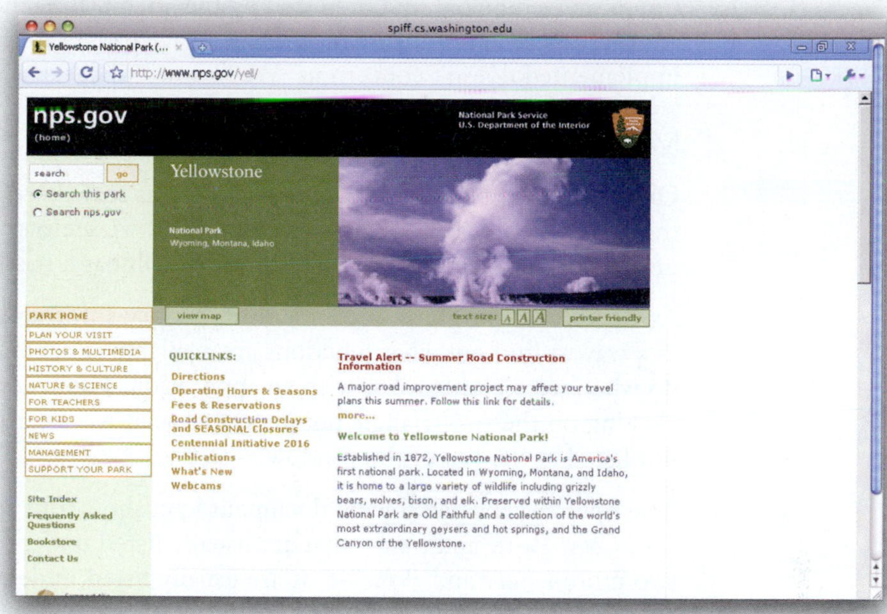

Figure 2.1 Page displayed using the Chrome browser.

Poking Around

Looking at Figure 2.1 we see the Chrome browser, but technically, it is the **Graphical User Interface** (**GUI,** pronounced GOO-ee) to the browser. Most of our interactions with computers use GUIs, and we give them little thought. But they are highly structured and extremely consistent. That's one reason why they are so familiar when we see one we've never seen before. What do we notice?

Unsurprisingly, it looks like a browser: There is an empty window, which you guess is the location window, because displaying Web sites is what browsers do, and they need to be told the URL. That must be what the window is for. You enter a URL and get your page. Immediately, the left pointing arrow is highlighted, and so you guess that that is the Back operation. The other operations around the Location window—Forward, Refresh, Go—are probably self-evident. But if they are not, we know that hovering the cursor over an unknown icon will give us "balloon help."

So, if the star is not suggestive of a familiar operation, hovering over it tells us that it is for bookmarking.

We know all of this because GUIs tend to use a small set of standard icons and metaphors. Of course, an **icon** is a graphic that describes a thing or action pictorially—as in [close icon] for close and [refresh icon] for refresh. In software, a **metaphor** is an object or idea used as an analogy for computation. So, the idea of addition, which is technically a mathematical operation on numbers, is used as a metaphor for creating another window, technically the "new instance" operation discussed below, and indicated by the + icon. But, the idea of "adding" another tab is so intuitive that it doesn't have to be explained, and how it is implemented doesn't concern us. We "know" what it means and what to do.

Menus

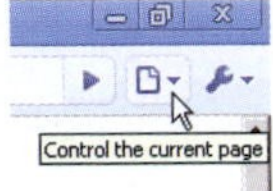

One thing that is curious about this browser is that there are no menus across the top of the GUI. Looking closer, however, we see two icons at the right end of the Location window, and significantly, each has a triangle pointer next to it.

As we know, **triangle pointers** indicate hidden information. Clicking on them as a way to find out what functions are available is generally a good thing to do when we are unfamiliar with an application. Figure 2.2 shows the result of clicking on the two triangle pointers, and what we see are menus. They're just not listed at the top of the window as words.

The operations listed for the document icon show four standard functions—*Cut*, *Copy*, *Paste*, and *Find*—that are usually listed under an *Edit* menu, and two more—*Save* and *Print*—that are usually listed under the *File* menu. Plus, other browser-specific functions are listed. The tools icon bears even less resemblance to standard functionality: The *New* and *Exit* commands are standard operations usually listed under the *File* menu, but the remainder are either gathered from their own menu lists (*Help*) or are browser specific (*Bookmark manager*). The point is that it was easy enough to find these operations, and whether they are old standards or new to you, you can probably guess what they do and how to use them based on your experience. The designers used your familiarity with browsing to give you a design you had never seen, but one that was built with familiar components.

The operations of the last paragraph were classified as "standard." What does that mean? Because software processes information, most applications provide two standard sets of operations in two menus labeled *File* and *Edit*, which you're familiar with. Generally, the operations under the *File* menu apply to

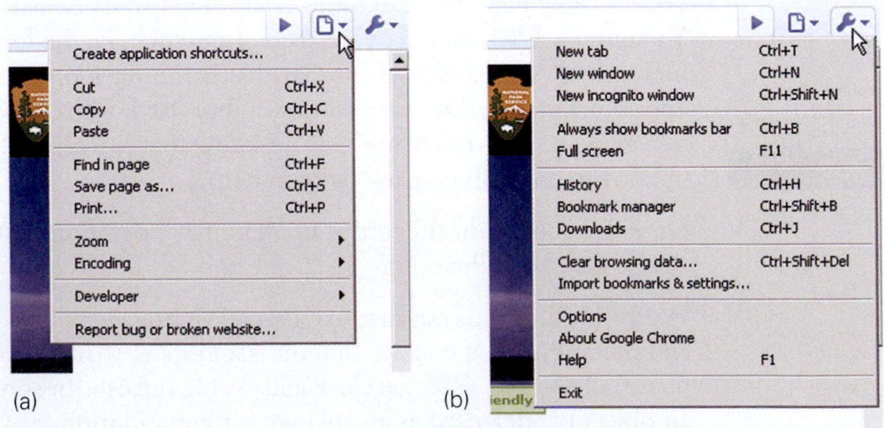

Figure 2.2 Clicking on the triangle pointers for the (a) document and (b) tools icons.

whole instances of the information being processed by an application. An **instance** is one of whatever kind of information the application processes. For example, for word processors, an instance is a document; for MP3 players, an instance is a song; for photo editors, an instance is a picture.

Everyday Menu Items

The *File* menu items treat a whole instance. The operations you can expect under the *File* menu are:

- **New** Create a "blank" instance of the information.
- **Open** Locate a file on the disk containing an instance of the information and read it in.
- **Close** Stop processing the current instance of the information, close the window, but keep the program available to process other instances.
- **Save** Write the current instance to the hard disk or other storage device with the previous name and location.
- **Save As** Write the current instance to the hard disk or other peripheral storage with a new name or location.
- **Page Setup** Specify how the printed document should appear on paper; changes to the setup are rare.
- **Print** Print a copy of the current instance of the information.
- **Print Preview** Show the information as it will appear when printed.
- **Exit** or **Quit** End the entire application.

Other operations unique to the application are usually included.

The *Edit* operations let you make changes within an instance. They often involve selection and cursor placement.

The operations under the *Edit* menu are:

- **Undo** Cancel the most recent editing change, returning the instance to its previous form.
- **Repeat** Apply the most recent editing change again.
- **Cut** Remove the selected information and save it in temporary storage, ready for pasting.
- **Copy** Store a copy of the selected information in temporary storage, ready for pasting.
- **Paste** Insert into the instance the information saved in the temporary storage by *Cut* or *Copy;* the information is placed either at the cursor position or at a standard position, depending on the application.
- **Clear** Remove the selected information.
- **Select All** Make the selection be the entire instance.

Again, other application-specific editing operations are usually included.

Because these operations are standard—available for most applications and consistent across operating systems—it is a good idea to learn their shortcuts, as shown in Table 2.1. A **shortcut** is a combination of two keyboard characters—the operating system's special escape character and a letter—that have the same effect as choosing the menu operation. (See the list on the right side of Figure 2.2(a).) As you know the special character for the Mac is Command ⌘, sometimes referred to as a clover, and for the Windows operating system it is Control Ctrl. To use the shortcut, simply hold down the special key—Command ⌘ or Control Ctrl depending on which operating system you are using—and type the letter. Even though the letter is shown as a capital, it is not correct to hold down the Shift key while performing these shortcuts. (To prevent accidents, *Clear* often does not have a shortcut.) In addition, "double-click"—two (rapid) clicks with the (left) mouse button— is a shortcut meaning *Open*.

Page Two

Clicking on the plus sign (+) by the tab at the top of the Chrome browser's GUI, another window opens under a new tab as shown in Figure 2.3. This may be an unfamiliar part of the browser, as it gives a thumbnail display of your most visited sites, which of course doesn't yet apply because you have only visited one site with this browser. The browsers you are familiar with might not do that. But the concept is explained and it makes sense. Again, exploring the software is a way to quickly familiarize yourself with it.

Summary: Designer's Intent

Everyone who invents a new tool, including software designers, has to teach users how to operate their inventions. Software products are often accompanied by manuals or have online *Help* that explain the software's slick features, but it's much faster and easier if users can figure out the software without studying the documentation. So software designers try to pick easy-to-understand user inter-

Table 2.1 Standard Shortcuts. These common shortcut letters for standard software operations combine with "Control" Ctrl for Windows or "Command" ⌘ for Mac OS X and is indicated by ^.

File Functions		Edit Functions	
New	^N	Cut	^X
Open	^O	Copy	^C
Save	^S	Paste	^V
Print	^P	Select All	^A
Quit, Exit	^Q	Undo	^Z
		Redo	^Y
		Find	^F

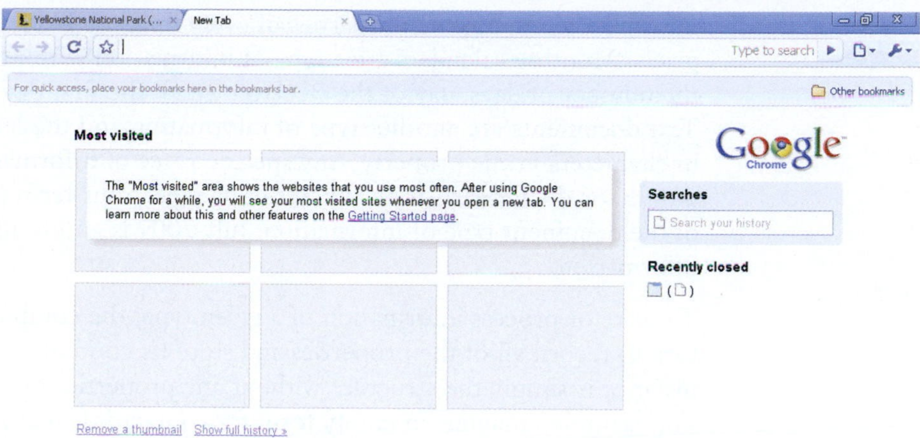

Figure 2.3 The New Tab page when first using the Chrome browser.

faces. We saw that with Chrome, but grab any new application that interests you and see the same thing. Instead of creating a GUI that requires explanation, the designers guessed that using familiar metaphors would be intuitive. And they guessed right. By analogy, the basic features of the software are obvious. Because software designers want to make the GUI intuitive, we should expect that we can "brain out" how it works. We use this idea every time we use new software.

A Win for Users. The Microsoft Windows operating system includes most of the GUI metaphors developed for the Apple Macintosh, so in 1988 Apple sued Microsoft for patent infringement. Apple claimed Microsoft illegally used the "look and feel" of its Mac. The legal issues were complex, but the judge ruled that Microsoft could freely use the metaphors Apple had developed. This might not seem fair to Apple, but it was a great win for users, because it meant that GUIs could work pretty much the same on the Mac and the PC.

Two Concepts of Computing

There are two intuitive aspects of everyday computer usage that should be explained, because understanding them better will help in using a computer better: Instances and Feedback.

New Instance

Notice that *New* under the *File* menu creates a "blank" instance. What is "blank information"?

To understand this fundamental idea, notice that all information is grouped into **types**, based on its properties. Photographs (digital images) are a type of information; among the properties of every image is its height and width in pixels. Monthly calendars are a type of information with properties such as the number of days, day of the week on which the first day falls, and year. Text documents are another type of information and the length of a document in characters is one property. Any specific piece of information—an image, month, or document—is an *instance* of its type. Your term paper is an instance of the document type of information; July 2009 is an instance of calendar type information.

To store or process information of a given type, the computer sets up a structure to record all of the properties and store its content. A "new" or "blank" instance is simply the structure without any properties or content filled in. For example, imagine an empty form for contact information in an electronic address book, as shown in Figure 2.4. That's a new instance, ready to receive its content.

Command and Control. Sometimes it is necessary to refer to an operation like *Copy* by its shortcut without being specific about which operating system is used. In such cases we write ^C to indicate that the operation takes either Command (⌘) or Control (Ctrl), depending on the operating system.

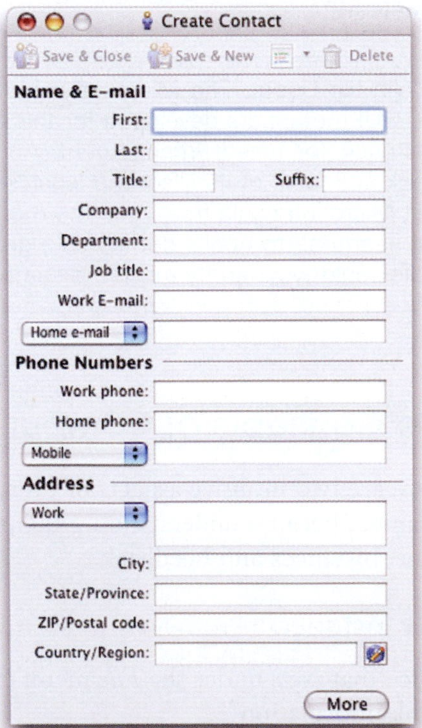

Figure 2.4 A new contact (i.e., a "blank" instance) in an electronic address book.

Expecting Feedback

A computer is our assistant, ready to do whatever we tell it to do. It is natural that when any assistant performs an operation, he, she, or it must report back to the person who made the request, describing the progress. This is especially true when the assistant is a computer, because the user needs to know that the task was done and when to give the next command. So a user interface will always give the user feedback about "what's happenin'."

In a GUI, **feedback** is any indication that the computer is still working, or has completed the request. Feedback takes many forms, depending on what operation a user has commanded. If the operation can be performed instantaneously—that is, so fast that a user does not have to wait for it to complete—the GUI simply indicates that the operation is complete. When the operation is an editing change, for example, the proof that it is done is that the revision is visible. When the effect of the command is not discernable—say, when one clicks a button—then there is some other indication provided; for example, highlighting, shading, graying, underlining, changing color, or an audible click.

The most common form of feedback is the indication that the computer is continuing to perform a time-consuming operation. As the operation is carried out, the cursor is replaced with an icon such as an hourglass ⌛ (on Windows systems) or a rainbow spinner (on Macintosh systems). Applications can also give the user custom feedback. A common indicator is the busy spinner a revolving circle of a dozen radial bars. When the completion time can be predicted, applications show a meter that "fills" as the operation progresses. Often these displays give a time estimate for 100 percent completion, sometimes called a *progress bar*. Finally, when an operation is processing a series of inputs, the "completion count" gives the tally of the completed instances, or equivalently, the number remaining.

Always expect feedback.

Be Selective. Occasionally we can get confused when an operation we want to use is not available (that is, it is "grayed out"). This often happens because the operation needs us to select something and nothing is selected. For example, the computer cannot perform *Copy* until you have selected what you want to copy.

"Clicking Around"

When the digerati encounter new software, they expect a consistent interface. They expect to see the basic metaphors, find standard operations, and receive feedback while the application is working. Digerati automatically look for these interface features and begin to explore. We did it when we first looked at the Chrome browser. The purpose of their exploration is to learn what the software can do.

We call the act of exploring a user interface **clicking around**. It involves noting the basic features presented by the GUI and checking each menu to see what operations are available. "Clicking around" can help us figure out what operations are available without having to be taught or to read the manual. Software manuals and *Help* pages are notoriously dull reading and hard to use. But "clicking around" does not make them obsolete. Manuals—now mostly taking the form of online *Help* resources—are still necessary and useful. "Clicking around" works because, as noted, (a) we come to the new software with technological experience, and (b) software designers try to build on what we know by using metaphors and consistent interfaces. When new software works like the last software did, we already "know" how to use it. The manual is usually needed only to understand advanced features or subtleties of operation. Ironically, then, manuals are most useful for experienced users, not beginners.

A Fast Start. When you're using software for the first time, practice "clicking around":

- Take a minute to study the GUI graphics and icons.
- Open each menu and triangle pointer to see what operations are available.
- Determine the purpose of icons and controls.
- Hover the cursor over unknown buttons or GUI features for a short explanation of their purpose.

"Clicking around" is exploration and may not reveal all of the software's features. We may need to experiment, test repeatedly, and try again. But this "clicking around" technique usually gives useful information quickly. If it doesn't, the software design has undoubtedly failed to some extent.

Following Protocol. Our normal interactive use of computers alternates between our commanding the computer to do something and the computer doing it. If the computer can't finish immediately, it gives feedback showing the operation is in progress. If the computer is finished, we can see the effects of the command. Be attuned to this alternating protocol. If nothing seems to be happening, the computer is waiting for you to give a command.

"Blazing Away"

After getting to know a software application by "clicking around," the next step is to try it. We will call this **blazing away**. The term suggests a user's trying an application assertively—exploring features even without a clear idea of what they will do. "Blazing away" is sometimes intimidating for beginning users because they're afraid they'll break something if they make a mistake. A basic rule of information processing is: *Nothing will break!* If you make a mistake, the software is not going to screech and grind to a halt, and plop on the floor with a clunk. When you make a mistake, the software may "crash" or "hang," but nothing actually breaks. Most of the time nothing happens. The software catches the mistake before doing something wrong and displays an error message. By paying attention to these messages, you can quickly learn what's legal and what isn't. Therefore, "blazing away" is an effective way to learn about the application even if you make mistakes.

Of course, saying that nothing will break is not the same as saying that it's impossible to get into a terrible mess by "blazing away." Creating a mess is often very easy. Beginners and experts do it all the time. The difference between the two is that the experts know another basic rule of information technology: *When stuck, start over.* That may mean exiting the program. It may mean rebooting the computer. It may simply mean "undoing" a series of edits and repeating them. The simple point is that the mess has no value. It does not have to be straightened out or fixed, because it didn't cost anything but your time to create in the first place. Because your time is chalked up to "experience" or "user training," there's no harm in throwing the mess out and starting over. Therefore, an experienced user who is "blazing away" on a new software system will probably exit the software and restart the application over and over, without saving anything.

Usually, we are working with new software because we have something specific we want to do, so it pays to focus on getting that task done. This means that we should "blaze away" on those operations that will contribute to completing the task; we don't have to become experts. It's common for Fluent users to know only the most basic functions of the software systems they use infrequently. And, because they are not regular users of these programs, they usually forget how the applications work and have to "click around" and "blaze away" each time.

fluencyBIT

Getting Out and Getting Back In. Starting over is so common for computer users—it's called *getting out and getting back in*—that it has become the subject of some geek humor. A mechanical engineer, an electrical engineer, and a computer engineer are camped at Mt. Rainier. In the morning, they pack up to leave and get into their car, but it doesn't start. The ME says, "The starter motor is broken, but I can fix it," and he gets out of the car. The EE says, "No way. It's the battery, but I know what to do," and she gets out of the car. The CE says while getting out of the car, "Now, let's get back in."

Obviously, if you are "blazing away" and starting over when you get into trouble, you shouldn't spend too much time creating complicated inputs. For example, if the software asks for text input and gives you space for several paragraphs, just enter `Test text` and continue to explore. Once you understand how to do the task, you can focus on using the software productively.

Watching Others

"Clicking around" and "blazing away" are the first steps when learning new software because you are likely to succeed using your own observation and reasoning skills. And, if you need to know something very specific about the software, you can always read the manual or online *Help*. However, these two extremes may not cover all of the possibilities. Complicated software systems usually have some features that are not obvious, too advanced, or too specialized to learn on our own. They include GUI features that most of us do not think to look for and they provide capabilities that we may not even know we need.

The Shift-Select Operation

An example of a not-so-obvious feature is using the Shift key in selection operations. Suppose we want to select only the red and green circles of the stoplight in Figure 2.5(a). Clicking on the red circle selects it (Figure 2.5(b)), as shown by the small boxes around the circle. Clicking on the green circle selects it and deselects the red circle (Figure 2.5(c)). Dragging the cursor vertically from the red circle to the green circle selects all the circles (Figure 2.5(d)). So how do we select just red and green without the yellow? The problem is that when we select something (e.g., the green circle), anything that is already selected (e.g., the red circle) becomes deselected automatically. We need some way to bypass that automatic protocol.

The solution is to select the first item (e.g., click on the red circle) and then hold down the Shift key while selecting the second item (e.g., clicking on the green circle). Using the Shift key during a selection means to "continue selecting everything that is already selected." Because the red circle is already selected when the green circle is shift-selected, both become selected, completing the task.

Learning from Others

The **shift-select** operation, meaning "continue to select the item(s) already selected," is a common feature in commercial software. Without knowing about shift-select, however, we probably wouldn't discover it by "clicking around" or "blazing away." We would not think to try it. We might not even know that we need the feature in the first place. So how do we learn about this kind of feature?

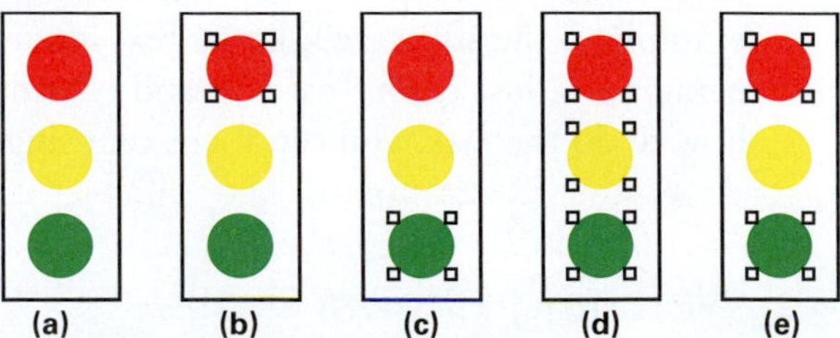

Figure 2.5 Examples of selection.

We can take a class on the specific software or read the user's manual, but an alternative is to observe others as they use a program we are familiar with. As we watch, we should be able to follow what they are doing, though it might seem very fast. If we see an operation that we do not understand, we ask about it. Most people are eager to share their expertise. Many an obscure feature, trick, or shortcut is learned while looking over the shoulder of an experienced user, so it pays to watch others. Equally useful is having an experienced user looking over our shoulder; even if it is somewhat intimidating, it is a terrific way to learn tricks.

Toggling Shift-Select. Generally when you use shift-select, one or more additional items are selected, because you usually click on an unselected item. But what happens when you use shift-select on an item that is already selected? It deselects that item only, leaving all other items selected. This property of changing to the opposite state—selecting if not selected, deselecting if selected—is called **toggling**. It's a handy feature in many situations.

Principle: Form Follows Function

A theme of this chapter is that computer systems are very similar because software designers want us to figure out how to use them based on our previous experience with other software. So, they use consistent interfaces and metaphors. When features of a new system work like the same features in a familiar system, we already know how to use parts of the new system. But there is a much deeper principle at work to explain the similarity among software systems. We state this principle as "form follows function."

The *form follows function* principle states that the fundamental operations of a software system and the way they work are determined by the task being solved. This doesn't mean that two software systems for the same task look alike; it means that they will have the same basic operations and those operations will work similarly. Think of your usual browser and the Chrome browser shown earlier. Of course, their GUIs can be very different with fancier icons and glitzier buttons, but those differences are superficial. At the core, the task defines the operations and how they work. Both browsers need a Location window; both browsers display video. Performing the task requires that the information is processed in a specific way.

Similar Applications Have Similar Features

As another illustration of this principle, text processing applications such as Word, WordPerfect, BBEdit, SimpleText, AppleWorks, Notepad, and a dozen others use a cursor to mark your place in text. They all have operations for typing text, deleting text, selecting text, copying text, searching text, replacing text, and other common actions. The software vendors did not invent these operations; they are fundamental in text processing. Furthermore, the operations work in much the same way in every system. For example, the Backspace (or Delete) key removes the character to the left of the cursor's present position. The applications use the natural and sensible meanings of the operations in the context of text, which is why they share many features.

If vendors cannot make better software by changing the fundamental operations, how can they compete? Easy, they add other nonfundamental features that make their systems more convenient, friendlier, faster, less error prone, and so on. For example, in some, but not all, text processing systems, it's possible to select text and drag it to a new position. This is not a fundamental text processing operation, since it can be achieved with a select, cut, reposition-the-cursor, and paste sequence of operations. But text dragging is convenient, and so it has been added to many systems. Software vendors also try to attract new customers by making their software more appealing by adding cool icons or animated "helpers."

Take Advantage of Similarities

Form follows function in browser software, spreadsheet software, drawing software, photo-editing software, and so on. Because it's a general principle, when we learn an application from one software maker, we learn the core operations for that task as well as the handy features and annoying quirks of that vendor's product. Then when we use software from a different vendor, we should look for and expect to recognize the *basic* operations. The features and quirks may or may not be present. The basic operations may have a different look and feel, but they will still be there and work roughly the same way.

The form follows function principle is important to our everyday use of computers for three reasons:

- When a new version of familiar software is released, we should expect to learn it very quickly because it shares the core functions and many of the features and quirks of the earlier version.
- When we must perform a familiar task using unfamiliar software, we should expect to use its basic features immediately because we're already familiar and experienced with them.
- When we are frustrated with one vendor's software, we should try another's. Because of our experience with the first system, we will learn the new system quickly. (And "voting" by purchasing better software helps to improve overall software quality.)

In summary, because the function determines how a system must work, different software implementations for a task must share basic characteristics. You don't need to feel tied to a particular software system that you learned years ago. You should experiment with new systems because you already know the basic functional behavior of the program.

Mixed Messages. Software is notorious for confusing error messages. It's a difficult problem to fix: Finding errors is easy, but diagnosing the cause is difficult. And programmers explain errors in programming jargon. The result is often an incomprehensible error message. But, don't ignore it entirely; a hint of the cause may be buried in the message. For example, this error message

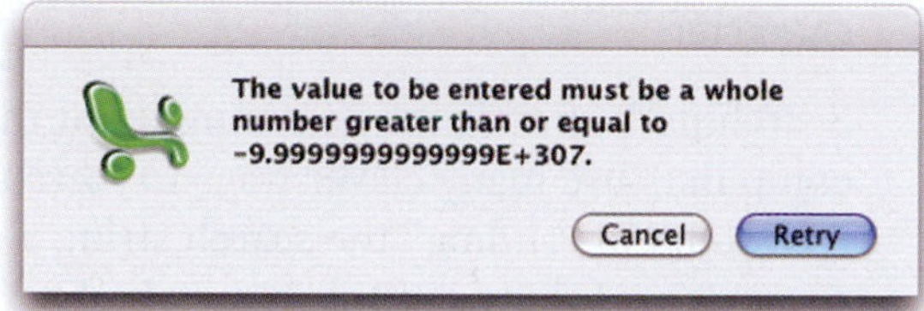

resulted from typing a letter rather than a number. Why doesn't it say, "Enter a number!"? In fact, it does, but in a very complicated way. The conclusion: Spend a moment trying to understand the error message; a useful hint may be hidden there.

Searching Text Using Find

The principle that form follows function has another advantage: It lets us learn how certain computer operations work without referring to any specific software system. Of course, we must focus only on the basic processing behavior rather than on the "bells and whistles" of the GUI, but learning in this way lets us apply our knowledge to any vendor's software. We illustrate this idea with text searching.

Many applications let us search text. Text searching, often called *Find*, is used by word processors, browsers (to look through the text of the current page), email readers, operating systems, and so on. *Find* is typically available under the *Edit* menu, because locating text is the first step in editing it. In cases where editing doesn't make sense—for example, when looking through a file structure in an operating system—*Find* may be listed under the *File* menu or as a "top-level" application. The shortcut for *Find*—Ctrl-F for Windows and ⌘-F for Mac OS X—is standard in most applications.

Things to be searched are called **tokens**. Most often, tokens are simply the letters, numbers, and special symbols like @ and & from the keyboard, which are also called **characters**. However, sometimes we search for composite items, such as dates that we want to treat as a whole. In such cases, the date is the token, not its letters and digits. For the purposes of searching, tokens form a sequence, called the **search text**, and the tokens to be found are called the **search string**. One property of the search string is that it can contain any tokens that may be in the text. In other words, if the text contains unprintable characters like tabs, the search string is allowed to contain those characters. Even though you have used search before, let's take a closer look.

How to Search

To illustrate searching, suppose the search string is content and the text is a sentence from Martin Luther King's "I Have a Dream" speech:

I have a dream that my four little children will one day live in a nation where they will not be judged by the color of their skin, but by the content of their character.

Searching begins at the beginning or at the current cursor position. Although computers use many clever ways to search text, the easiest one to understand is to think of "sliding" the search string along the text. At each position, compare to see if there is a token match. This simply means looking at corresponding token pairs to see if they are the same:

```
I have a dream ...

content
```

(Notice that spaces are characters too.) If there is a match, then the process stops and you see the found instance. But if there is no match, slide the search string along and repeat:

```
... by the content of ...

... ccccccccontent
```

If the search string is not found when the end of the text is reached, the search stops and is unsuccessful. (Search facilities typically give you the option to continue searching from the beginning of the text if the search did not start there.) The search ends where it began when the search string is not found.

Search Complications

Character searching is easy, but to be completely successful, you should be operationally attuned, as explained in Chapter 1. There are four things to keep in mind when you are searching: case sensitivity, hidden text, substrings, and multiword strings.

Case Sensitivity. One complication is that the characters stored in a computer are case sensitive, meaning that the uppercase letters, such as R, and lowercase letters, such as r, are considered different. So a match occurs only when the letters *and* the case are identical. A case-sensitive search for unalienable rights fails on Jefferson's most famous sentence from the *Declaration of Independence:*

We hold these truths to be self-evident, that all men are created equal, that they are endowed by their Creator with certain unalienable Rights, that among these are Life, Liberty and the pursuit of Happiness.

To find unalienable rights in a text that uses the original capitalization, we would have to ignore the case. Search tools are case sensitive if case is important to the application. For example, word processors are sensitive to case, but operating systems are not. If the search has case-sensitive capabilities, the user has the option to ignore them.

Hidden Text. Characters are stored in the computer as one continuous sequence. There are two types of characters: keyboard characters that we type and formatting information added by the software application using tags. Because every system uses a different method for the formatting information and because it is usually not important to the search anyhow, we will show the formatting information using our own invented tags.

Tags are abbreviations in paired angle brackets, such as <Ital>, that describe additional information about the characters (in this case that they should be in italics). Tags generally come in pairs so that they can enclose text like parentheses. The second of the pair is the same as the first, except with a slash (/) or backslash (\) in it. (Tags are used often in our Fluency study, so backslash (\) is used here for the invented tags of this chapter to distinguish them from later uses in HTML, the OED digitization, and XML, which all use slash.) For instance, to show that the word "Enter" should appear in italics, a software application might represent it as <Ital>Enter<\Ital>. These formatting tags are invisible to the reader.

For example, the balcony scene from *Romeo and Juliet* appears in a book of Shakespeare's plays as:

> SCENE II. *Capulet's orchard.*
>
> *Enter* Romeo.
>
> *Romeo.* He jests at scars that never felt a wound.
>
> [*Juliet appears above at a window.*
>
> But, soft ! what light through yonder window breaks?
> It is the east, and Juliet is the sun.

But, this text might be stored in the computer as follows:

```
SCENE·II.·→<Ital>Capulet's·orchard.<\Ital>↵↵<Center><Ital>Ent
er<\Ital>Romeo.<\Center>↵↵<Ital>Romeo.<\Ital>→He·jests·at·sca
rs·that·never·felt·a·wound.↵<Right>[<Ital>Juliet·appears·above·
at·a·window.<\Ital><\Right>↵But,··soft·!·what·light·through·yon
der·window·breaks?·↵It·is·the·east,·and·Juliet·is·the·sun.↵
```

The word processor's tags surround the italic text (<Ital>, <\Ital>), the text to be centered, (<Center>, <\Center>), and right-justified (<Right>, <\Right>). The user typed the other characters and they are the ones we are interested in now. These characters include the text we see as well as formatting characters we can't see: spaces (·), **tabs** (→), and **new lines** (↵). Because these characters control formatting and have no printable form, there is no standard for how they are displayed; for example, the new line character is the **paragraph symbol** (¶) in some systems. Users can ask that all the characters they type be displayed:

```
SCENE·II.·→    Capulet's·orchard.↵
↵
                    Enter·Romeo.↵
↵
Romeo.→        He·jests·at·scars·that·never·felt·a·wound.↵
                              [Juliet·appears·above·at·a·window.
↵
But,··soft·!·what·light·through·yonder·window·breaks?↵
It·is·the·east,·and·Juliet·is·the·sun.↵
```

Because the effects of the formatting are shown, it is easy to see where the nonprinted formatting characters are. During a search, the software's formatting tags are generally ignored, but all of the characters typed by the user are considered. Some systems allow tags to be searched by giving you a way to search for formatted text such as italic.

Substrings. Finding gets more complicated when we think of search strings as having a meaning more complex than tokens. For example, we often look for words, although the tokens are characters. The problem is that the software may be searching for token sequences, not the more complicated objects that we may have in mind. So searches for the search string you in President John Kennedy's inaugural address turn up five hits:

And so, my fellow Americans: ask not what your country can do for you—ask what you can do for your country.
My fellow citizens of the world: ask not what America will do for you, but what together we can do for the freedom of man.

Of the five hits, only three are the actual word we're looking for; the other two hits *contain* the search string. To avoid finding your, we can search for ·you·, because words in text are usually surrounded by spaces. However, that search discovers no hits in this quote because you doesn't appear with spaces on both sides. The five hits for you are followed by r, a dash, a new line, an r, and a comma, respectively. The you at the end of the second line probably should have had a space between it and the new line, but the typist left it out.

Because looking only for the word you and avoiding your means checking for all of the possible starting and ending punctuation characters and blanks, it's probably better to give up on finding the exact word matches and simply ignore the cases where the search string is part of another word. If the search is part of a system such as a word processor, where words are a basic element, the ability to search for words is typically available. Such cases amount to changing the tokens from characters to words.

Multiword Strings. A similar problem occurs with multiword search strings. The words of a multiword string are separated by spaces, but if the number of spaces in the search string is different from the number in the text being searched, no match is found. For example, the search string

That's · one · small · step · for · man

Neil Armstrong's words on first stepping on the moon, will not be found in the quote

That's · one · small · step · for · · man, · one · giant · leap · for · mankind.

because there are two spaces between for and man in the text.

One Small Step. It is a good idea to look for single words in your search instead of longer phrases. For example, looking for *leap* or *mankind* might work because they are probably not used again in the moon walk transcript.

In summary, searching is the process of locating a sequence of tokens, the search string, in a longer sequence of tokens, the text. Character searches are usually limited to the characters typed, even though other characters may be present. Typed characters can include nonprinting formatting characters such as new line characters. Searches look for token sequences, and the tokens (for example, characters) are often more basic than what we can build from them (for example, words). To be successful, we must create search strings so that we find all the matches we're interested in.

Editing Text Using Substitution

Find-and-*Replace*, also known as **substitution**, is a combination of searching and editing documents to make corrections. The string that replaces the search string is called the **replacement string**. Although substitution can apply to a single occurrence of the search string in the text if necessary, there is little advantage to using a search-and-replace facility over simply searching and editing the single occurrence directly. The real power of substitution comes from applying it to all occurrences of the search string. For example, if you typed "west coast" in your term paper but then realized that regions are usually capitalized, it is simple to search for all occurrences of west coast and replace them with West Coast.

Because *Find* and *Replace* is a powerful tool that we want to study closely, we will express it in this book using a left-pointing arrow (←) between the search string and the replacement string. The capitalization example is shown as

west coast ← West Coast

Such an expression can be read "west coast *is replaced by* West Coast" or "West Coast *substitutes for* west coast." Another example is

Norma Jeane Mortenson ← Marilyn Monroe

describing her 1946 name change when she signed her first movie contract.

We emphasize that the arrow is only a *notation* that helps us discuss substitutions in this book; it doesn't appear within the application. When using an application, a GUI is used to specify the replacement (see Figure 2.6). For example, the two text fields of the GUI correspond to the information on each side of the arrow. *Find* is the left side of the arrow and *Replace* is the right side. We don't type the arrow in applications. It is only for our use here.

2.1 Marking Trademarks. Suppose your report contains several uses of trademarked names, but because the text came from the World Wide Web, the trademark symbol was written (R). Use the arrow notation to describe how to convert these characters into ®.

Unwanted Spaces

In the last section, we noted that multiple spaces separating words in a text string complicates searching for multiword strings. Substitution can fix the "multiple spaces in a document" problem: Simply collapse double spaces to single spaces. That is, if the search string is ·· and the replacement string is ·, a find-and-replace of the whole document results in all double spaces becoming single spaces. Expressed using the arrow notation, the "two spaces are replaced by one space" substitution is

·· ← ·

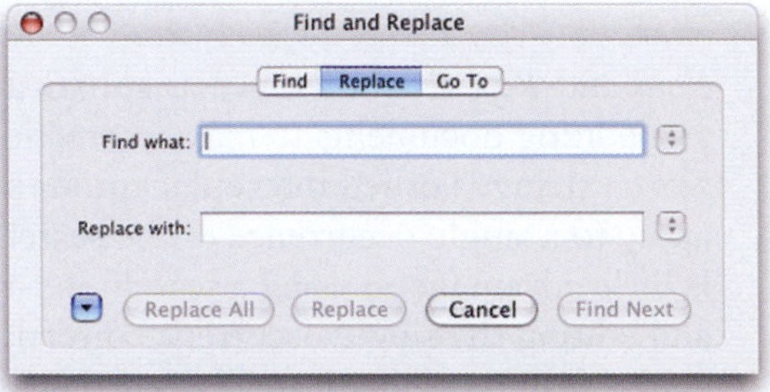

Figure 2.6 A *Find and Replace* GUI.

Changing from curly quotes, often called *smart quotes*, to straight quotes is easy enough by writing

“ ← "

” ← "

Can we change simple quotes to smart quotes? We can’t write

" ← “

because that changes all of the simple quotes to opening smart quotes, including the closing quotes. But we can use the context around the quotes: Opening quotes are preceded by a space, and after changing them, we replace the remaining quotes with close quotes. So we write

·" ← ·“

" ← ”

solving the problem.

Notice that most software for *Find* and *Replace All* reports how many instances of the search string it found and replaced.

2.2 Missing References. In your report you have used [ ] to indicate a place where you need a reference but don’t have the details yet. Your report is finished, but now you wonder how many references are missing. You could go through the text and count them or you could use substitution. How?

Formatting Text

One situation where substitution is particularly handy is when text is imported into a document from another source and the formatting becomes messed up. For example, suppose you find the Articles from the UN’s Universal Declaration of Human Rights on the Web:

Article 1 All human beings are born free and equal in dignity and rights. They are endowed with reason and conscience and should act towards one another in a spirit of brotherhood.

Article 2 Everyone is entitled to all the rights and freedoms set forth in this Declaration, without distinction of any kind, such as race, color, sex, language, religion, political, or other opinion, national or social origin, property, birth or other status.

Furthermore, no distinction shall be made on the basis of political, jurisdictional or international status of the country or territory to which a person belongs, whether it be independent, trust, non-self-governing, or under any other limitation of sovereignty.

Article 3 Everyone has the right to life, liberty and security of person.

But when you copy the first three articles and paste them into your document, they come out looking like this:

```
        Article 1 All human beings are born free and equal in dignity and
rights. They are endowed with reason and
        conscience and should act towards one another in a spirit
of brotherhood.

        Article 2  Everyone is entitled to all the rights and freedoms set forth
 in this Declaration, without distinction of any
        kind, such as race, color, sex, language, religion, political
or other opinion, national or social origin,
        property, birth or other status.

        Furthermore, no distinction shall be made on the basis of
political, jurisdictional or international status of
        the country or territory to which a person belongs, whether
it be independent, trust, non-self-governing,
        or under any other limitation of sovereignty.

        Article 3  Everyone has the right to life, liberty and security of person.
```

The formatting is a mess. Displaying the text with the formatting characters reveals why:

```
········Article·1··All·human·beings·are·born·free·and·equal·in·dignity·and·↵
rights.·They·are·endowed·with·reason·and·↵
········conscience·and·should·act·towards·one·another·in·a·spirit·↵
of·brotherhood.·↵
↵
········Article·2··Everyone·is·entitled·to·all·the·rights·and·freedoms·set·forth↵
·in·this·Declaration,·without·distinction·of·any↵
········kind,·such·as·race,·color,·sex,·language,·religion,·political·↵
or·other·opinion,·national·or·social·origin,·↵
········property,·birth·or·other·status.··↵
↵
········Furthermore,·no·distinction·shall·be·made·on·the·basis·of·↵
political,·jurisdictional·or·international·status·of·↵
········the·country·or·territory·to·which·a·person·belongs,·whether·↵
it·be·independent,·trust,·non-self-governing,·↵
········or·under·any·other·limitation·of·sovereignty.·↵
↵
········Article·3··Everyone·has·the·right·to·life,·liberty·and·security·of·person.·↵
```

We see that extra leading spaces and new lines have been inserted when we imported the text into the document.

Clearly, removing the groups of eight spaces at the beginning of lines is simple: we replace them with nothing. When writing the substitution expression, we express "nothing" with the Greek letter epsilon, which is called the empty string; that is, the string with no letters. (Notice that epsilon is used only for writing out substitution expressions for ourselves. In the Find-and-Replace GUI of an application, we simply leave the replacement string empty.)

········· ← ε

Removing these leading spaces is easy because we want all sequences of eight spaces removed. Correcting the new line characters is more difficult.

We want to get rid of the new line characters that have been inserted within a paragraph but we want to keep the double new lines that separate the paragraphs. But getting rid of the single new line

↵ ← ε

will get rid of *all* the new lines! How can we keep the double new lines but remove the singles?

The Placeholder Technique

An easy strategy, called the **placeholder technique**, solves our problem. It begins by substituting a placeholder character for the strings we want to keep; that is, the new line pairs in the example. We pick # as the placeholder because it doesn't appear anywhere else in the document, but any unused character or character string will work. The substitution expression is

↵↵ ← #

Our text without the leading blanks and double new lines now looks like this:

```
Article·1··All·human·beings·are·born·free·and·equal·in·dignity·and·↵
rights.·They·are·endowed·with·reason·and·↵
conscience·and·should·act·towards·one·another·in·a·spirit·↵
of·brotherhood.#Article·2··Everyone·is·entitled·to·all·the·rights·and·freedoms·set·forth·↵
in·this·Declaration,·without·distinction·of·any↵
kind,·such·as·race,·color,·sex,·language,·religion,·political·↵
or·other·opinion,·national·or·social·origin,·↵
property,·birth·or·other·status.#Furthermore,·no·distinction·shall·be·made·on·the·basis·of·↵
political,·jurisdictional·or·international·status·of·↵
the·country·or·territory·to·which·a·person·belongs,·whether·↵
it·be·independent,·trust,·non-self-governing,·↵
or·under·any·other·limitation·of·sovereignty.#Article·3··Everyone·has·the·right·to·life,·liberty·and·security·of·person.
```

The new lines that remain are the ones to be removed, so we need to replace them with nothing

↵ ← ε

The resulting text has no new line characters left:

```
Article·1··All·human·beings·are·born·free·and·equal·in·dignity·and·rights.·They·are·endowed·
with·reason·and·conscience·and·should·act·towards·one·another·in·a·spirit·of·brotherhood.#
Article·2··Everyone·is·entitled·to·all·the·rights·and·freedoms·set·forth·in·this·Declaration,·
without·distinction·of·any·kind,·such·as·race,·color,·sex,·language,·religion,·political·or·
other·opinion,·national·or·social·origin,·property,·birth·or·other·status.#Furthermore,·no·
distinction·shall·be·made·on·the·basis·of·political,·jurisdictional·or·international·status·of·the·
country·or·territory·to·which·a·person·belongs,·whether·it·be·independent,·trust,·non-self-
governing,·or·under·any·other·limitation·of·sovereignty.#Article·3··Everyone·has·the·right·to·
life,·liberty·and·security·of·person.
```

Finally, replace the placeholder with the desired character string

← ↵↵

which gives us

> Article·1··All·human·beings·are·born·free·and·equal·in·dignity·and·rights.·They·are·endowed·with·reason·and·conscience·and·should·act·towards·one·another·in·a·spirit·of·brotherhood.
>
> Article·2··Everyone·is·entitled·to·all·the·rights·and·freedoms·set·forth·in·this·Declaration,·without·distinction·of·any·kind,·such·as·race,·color,·sex,·language,·religion,·political·or·other·opinion,·national·or·social·origin,·property,·birth·or·other·status.
>
> Furthermore,·no·distinction·shall·be·made·on·the·basis·of·political,·jurisdictional·or·international·status·of·the·country·or·territory·to·which·a·person·belongs,·whether·it·be·independent,·trust,·non-self-governing,·or·under·any·other·limitation·of·sovereignty.
>
> Article·3··Everyone·has·the·right·to·life,·liberty·and·security·of·person.

Except for the bold font for the Article titles and numbers, the resulting file looks like the original document showing the double new lines as appropriate. The final replacements:

Article 1 ←**Article 1**

Article 2 ←**Article 2**

Article 3 ←**Article 3**

complete the task. You may also change the titles to bold directly by editing.

To summarize, the placeholder technique is used to remove short search strings that are part of longer strings that we want to keep. If we were to remove the short strings directly, we would trash the longer strings. The idea is to convert the longer strings into the placeholder temporarily, which "hides" them. Of course, a single placeholder character can replace the long strings because all we're keeping track of is the position of the longer string. With the longer strings replaced by the placeholder, it is safe to remove the short strings. Once they are gone, the longer string can replace the placeholder. The following substitution expressions summarize the idea:

LongStringsContainingInstance(s)OfAShortString ← *Placeholder*

ShortString ← ε

Placeholder ← *LongStringsContainingInstance(s)OfAShortString*

Technology: Take It Personally

We have revealed some secrets known to expert computer users. Now, it's not miraculous that the digerati appear to know how to use software they have never seen before. They expect consistent interfaces and intuitive icons that allow them to apply their previously learned knowledge. Now we can exploit that strategy, too.

The important thing about our discussion of learning to use technology is how we figured it all out. We thought about technology as it relates to us. We thought, "We need to learn how to use this technology," so we asked, "How did the inventors of this technology expect us to learn it?" We thought about tool inventors who want people to use their inventions. Inventors can write manuals and we can read them, but they will have more users and users will have more success if the inventions are intuitive, allowing people to "brain out" how to use them. We concluded that we should expect intuitive interfaces. This approach of thinking about technology as it relates to us personally and analyzing the situation in that context is essential for any technology use.

✓checkLIST

There is a series of similar questions that we should ask ourselves when we need to use new technology, especially software:

- *What do I have to learn about this software to do my task?*
- *What does the designer of this software expect me to know?*
- *What does the designer expect me to do?*
- *What metaphor is the software showing me?*
- *What additional information does the software need to do its task?*
- *Have I seen these operations in other software?*

When we think about information technology in terms of our personal or workplace needs, we may also ask questions such as:

- *Is there information technology that I am not now using that could help me with my task?*
- *Am I more or less productive using this technological solution for my task?*
- *Can I customize the technology I'm using to make myself more productive?*
- *Have I assessed my uses of information technology recently?*

These and similar questions can help you use technology more effectively. Information technology, as a means rather than an end, should be continually assessed to ensure that it is fulfilling your needs as the technology changes and evolves.

2.3 Clearing Italics. Suppose in your term paper you used *italics* really often to *emphasize* your meaning, but now you find that your grumpy professor hates this use of italics. Describe how to remove all italics in the term paper.

Summary

This chapter began by exploring how we learn to use technology. We concluded that:

- People are either taught technology or they figure it out on their own.
- We can figure out software because designers use consistent interfaces, suggestive metaphors, and standard functionality.
- We apply our previous experience to learn new applications.
- In computer software, if we make a mistake, nothing breaks.
- We should explore a new application by "clicking around" and "blazing away."
- We should watch other users and ask questions.
- Form follows function.
- Searching and substituting, which are available with many applications, work consistently, demonstrating the idea behind form follows function.
- We should think personally about technology and apply general principles and ideas to become more expert users.

Try It Solutions

2.1 The arrow notation is (R) ← ®.

2.2 In a two-step process, search for [ ] and *Replace All* of them with some character you haven't used, say #. Notice how many changes were made; that's the number of missing references. Now replace # with [ ] to return the text to its original form. In the arrow notation you do:

[ ] ← #

\# ← [ ]

2.3 Although your word processor might allow you to search for italicized words, changing each occurrence is too slow. Instead, use the idea of toggling: Select all of the text in your term paper before the references, which should have italics, make it all italic, and then make it all italic again—that is, toggle it. When you change the text to italics, the positions of all of the previous italics are lost; when it is italicized again—that is, changed back—all of the italics will be removed.

Review Questions

Multiple Choice

1. Experienced computer users are known as
   a. digerati
   b. literati
   c. maserati
   d. culturati
2. What is a GUI?
   a. graphical update identification
   b. general user identification
   c. graphical user interface
   d. general update interface
3. Software designers use analogies to help a user understand software because doing so
   a. makes it easier for the user to learn and use the software
   b. makes the software more popular
   c. is required by law
   d. more than one of the above
4. An example of a metaphor is
   a. The player played with the heart of a lion.
   b. The silence was deafening.
   c. The computer played chess as well as the best humans.
   d. all of the above
5. Which of the following is not a common computer metaphor?
   a. buttons
   b. door handles
   c. menus
   d. sliders
6. In Windows, closing a subwindow
   a. is not allowed
   b. leaves the application running
   c. quits the application
   d. automatically saves your file
7. Menu options that are unavailable
   a. have a check mark by them
   b. are gray
   c. have a line through them
   d. are hidden

8. Which of the following is not an instance?
   a. an image
   b. a song file
   c. a word processing document
   d. a menu
9. The Greek letter epsilon ε can be used to represent "nothing." In a find and replace, you would have to use
   a. —
   b. null
   c. nothing (empty)
   d. ←

Short Answer

1. _______ is the word used to describe people who understand digital technology.
2. GUI stands for _______.
3. Software designers help users understand their software through the use of _______.
4. A(n) _______ is a figure of speech where one object is compared to another.
5. _______ are used to indicate there is information available that is usually hidden.
6. *Open*, *New*, *Close*, and *Save* can usually be found in the _______ menu.
7. To avoid cluttering the screen with commands, software designers put most of their commands in _______.
8. *Undo*, *Cut*, *Copy*, and *Paste* can usually be found in the _______ menu.
9. The online manual can usually be found in the _______ menu.
10. When the computer needs more information from the user before it completes an action, it gets the information via a _______.
11. Menu choices that are unavailable are generally colored _______.
12. The clover-shaped shortcut key on a Macintosh is called the _______ key.

Exercises

1. Explain the desktop metaphor.
2. Discuss the advantages of a consistent interface. Look at it from the consumer's view and from the developer's view.
3. List the technology tools you can typically use without reading the owner's manual.
4. What are the two keys to success with information technology?

5. What happens when we apply the ** ← * replacement to *****? Try this out with your text editor. How many times did it find and replace? How many were left? Explain how this process worked.

6. Using Lincoln's Gettysburg Address, what appears more often, "that" or "here"?

7. How many times does the word "the" appear in Lincoln's Gettysburg Address? How many times do the letters t-h-e appear together in it?

8. Open your word processor, create a new document, then do the following:
   a. Type each of these items on its own line: your name, street address or dorm and room number, city, state, postal code, your school name, your favorite color, and your favorite type of music. (You should have 8 lines.)
   b. Delete the last 3 lines. (You should have 5 lines now.)
   c. Undo the delete. (You should have 8 lines now.)
   d. Cut the last three lines and paste them after the first line. (You should have 11 lines now.)
   e. Cut the lines with your favorite color in them. (You should have 9 lines now.)
   f. Insert a line between your name and your school name that says, "Using a computer is great fun!"
   g. Save the file as an RTF file to your USB drive. Name it using the form: *Your initials* (in capital letters) followed by *C2N8.rtf.* (For example, if your name is Robyn Banks, the file name would be RBC2N8.rtf.)

9. The chapter describes the process of using the placeholder technique to protect some characters from replacement while editing a document. Perform the steps of the process as described in the text, but with a different character as the placeholder.
   a. First try it using a period as the placeholder. Did that work? Why or why not? Save the file with the name placeholder1.
   b. Now try it using a character other than #. Save the file with the name placeholder2. Submit both documents to your instructor.
   c. Explain the necessary characteristics of a good placeholder.

10. Reopen the document you saved in Exercise 8. Make all the proper names-names of people and places-bold. Using the method described in Try It 2.3, change all bold text to normal.

3

chapter

The Basics of Networking

Making the Connection

learning objectives

- Tell whether a communication technology (Internet, radio, LAN, etc.) is synchronous or asynchronous; broadcast or point-to-point
- Explain the roles of Internet addresses, domain names, and DNS servers in networking
- Distinguish between types of protocols (TCP/IP and Ethernet)
- Describe how computers are interconnected by an ISP and by a LAN
- Distinguish between the Internet and the World Wide Web

The open society, the unrestricted access to knowledge, the unplanned and uninhibited association of men for its furtherance—these are what make a vast, complex, ever growing, ever changing, ever more specialized and expert technological world nevertheless a world of human community.

—J ROBERT OPPENHEIMER, 1953

The presence of humans in a system containing high-speed electronic computers and high-speed accurate communications is quite inhibiting [to the system].

—STUART LUMAN SEATON, 1958

COMPUTERS ALONE ARE USEFUL. Computers connected together are even more useful. Dramatic proof of this occurred in the mid-1990s when the Internet, long available to researchers, became generally available to the public. The Internet is the totality of all wires, fibers, switches, routers, satellite links, and other hardware for transporting information between addressed computers, as shown in Figure 3.1. For the first time, people could conveniently and inexpensively connect their computers to the Internet and thereby connect to all other computers attached to the Internet. They could send email and surf the Web from home. This convenient access to volumes of information, eCommerce, blogs, and other capabilities greatly expanded the benefits people derived from computers.

We begin this chapter by defining fundamental communication terms. These will help you compare the Internet with other forms of communication. Some topics are designed to give you a sense of how the Internet works without the technical details: naming computers, packets, the TCP/IP and Ethernet protocols, and connecting your computer to the Internet. Finally, the World Wide Web and file structures are explained in preparation for our discussion of HTML in Chapter 4.

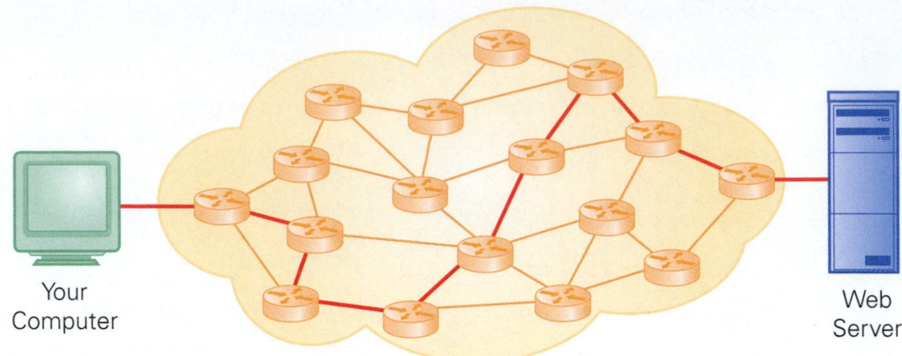

Figure 3.1 A schematic diagram of the Internet.

Comparing Communication Types

To understand the Internet, it's necessary to explain some basic communication vocabulary.

General Communication

Communication between two entities, whether they are people or computers, can be separated into two broad classes: synchronous and asynchronous. **Synchronous communication** requires that both the sender and the receiver are active at the same time. A telephone conversation is an example of synchronous communication because both people in the conversation must perform one of the two parts of the communication—sending (talking) or receiving (listening)—simultaneously. In **asynchronous communication**, the sending and receiving occur at different times. A postcard and text messages are examples of asynchronous communication because they are written at one time and read later. Answering machines and voice mail make synchronous telephones asynchronous because the caller leaves a message that the receiver listens to later. Email is asynchronous; applications like Skype and iChat are synchronous computer communication.

Another property of communication concerns the number of receivers. **Broadcast communication** involves a single sender and many receivers. Radio and television are examples of broadcast communication. The term **multicast** is used when there are many receivers, but the intended recipients are not the whole population. Magazines, often covering specialized topics, are an example of multicast communication. The opposite of broadcasting and multicasting is **point-to-point communication**. Telephone communication is point-to-point. The property of broadcast *versus* point-to-point communication is separate from the property of synchronous *versus* asynchronous communication.

The Internet's Communication Properties

The Internet supports point-to-point asynchronous communication. A fundamental feature of the Internet is that it provides a general communication "fabric" linking all computers connected to it (see Figure 3.1). That is, the computers and the network become a single medium that can be applied in many ways to produce alternatives to established forms of communication. For example, the Internet can act like the postal system, but at electronic speed. In fact, the Internet is fast enough to mimic synchronous communication, enabling chatting: Two or more people can have a conversation by the rapid exchange of asynchronous messages, allowing the Internet to be used like a phone. Also, multicasting is possible, enabling small- to modest-size groups to communicate via blogs or chat rooms. Finally, because it is possible to post a Web page or YouTube video that can be accessed by anyone, the Internet offers a form of broadcasting that compares with radio or television. The Internet is truly a universal communications medium.

The Internet also becomes more effective with each additional computer added to it. That is, if *x* computers are already attached to the Internet, adding one more computer results in *x* potential new connections—that computer with each of the original machines.

fluencyBIT

Internet. The present-day Internet is the commercial descendant of the ARPANET, developed for the U.S. Department of Defense Advanced Research Projects Agency (DARPA). The ARPANET sent its first messages in 1969.

The Client/Server Structure

Most interactions over the Internet use a protocol known as **client/server interaction**. This simple idea is illustrated by following what happens when you browse the Web.

A brief encounter. When you click on a Web link, your computer begins the process of accessing the page for you. At that moment, your computer enters into a client/server interaction. Yours is the client computer and the computer on which the Web page is stored is the server computer, which is why it's called a **Web server** (see Figure 3.2). The term "client" refers to any situation where one computer, the *client*, gets services from another computer, the *server*. As a result of your client request, the server sends the page back over the Internet, fulfilling the request. That completes the operation started with your click on the link, and it ends that client/server relationship.

fluencyBIT

Moving in the Right Direction. When we get files like Web pages from a server, we are **downloading** them; when we put the files on a server, we are **uploading** them. Think of the client as "below" the server.

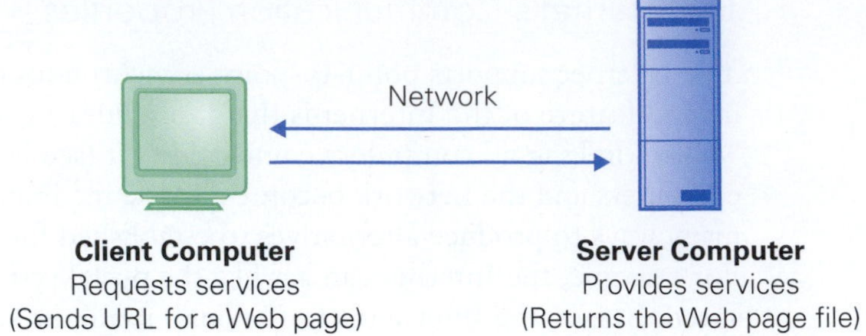

Figure 3.2 The basic client/server interaction, as illustrated by the browser (client) requesting Web pages provided by the Web server.

The client/server structure is fundamental to Internet interactions. A key aspect of the idea is that, as shown in Figure 3.2, only a single service request and response are involved. It is a very brief relationship, lasting from the moment the request is sent to the moment the service is received. Unlike a telephone call, in which a connection is made and *held* for as long as the call lasts, and during which there are many alternating exchanges, the client/server relationship is very short. It only entails the client's single request for a service and the server's reply in response.

Many brief relationships. An important advantage of this approach is that the server can handle many clients at a time. Typically between two consecutive client requests from your browser—between getting a Web page and asking for the next Web page from the same site—that server could have serviced hundreds or perhaps thousands of other clients. This is a very efficient system, because the server is busy with you only for as long as it takes to perform your request. Once it's fulfilled, the relationship is over from the server's viewpoint. But the relationship is over from your viewpoint, too. Your next click could be on a link for a different server. Between that click and the next time you visit the site, if ever, you and your browser could be clients to hundreds or perhaps thousands of other Web servers. Figure 3.3 shows the client/server relationship over an interval of time.

fluencyBIT

> **Staying Connected.** With conventional telephones, callers stay connected even if no one is talking. In a client/server interaction, there is no connection. There is a client-to-server transmission for requests and a server-to-client transmission for replies. But doesn't your computer stay connected to the Internet? Yes, but only to your ISP—that is, to the Internet—not to a Web server.

The Medium of the Message

How does the Internet transmit information such as Web pages and email messages? Complex and sophisticated technologies are used to make today's Internet work, but the basic idea is extremely simple.

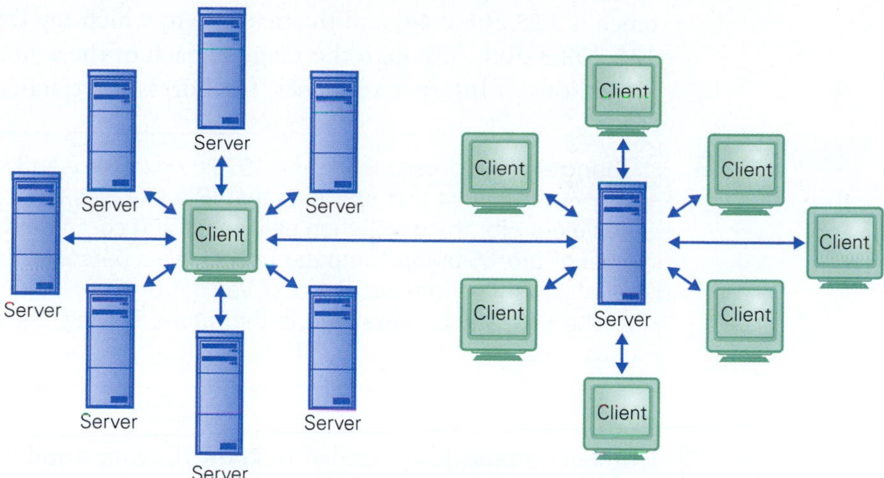

Figure 3.3 Client/server relationships as they might evolve over time.

The Name Game of Computer Addresses

To begin, remember that the Internet uses point-to-point communication. When anything is sent point-to-point—a phone conversation, a letter, or furniture—the destination address is required.

IP addresses. Each computer connected to the Internet is given a unique address called its **IP address**, short for **Internet Protocol address**. An IP address is a series of four numbers separated by dots, as shown in Figure 3.4. For example, the IP address of the computer on which I am typing this sen-

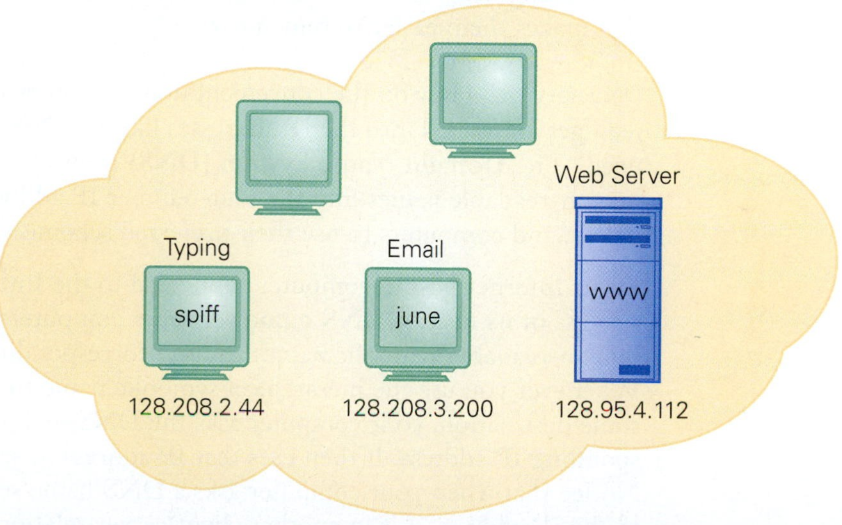

Figure 3.4 Computers connected to the Internet are given IP addresses.

tence is 128.208.2.44, and the machine to which my email is usually sent is 128.208.3.200. Although the range of each of these numbers (0–255) allows for billions of Internet addresses, IP addresses are actually in short supply.

fluencyBIT

Change of Address. Since the 1970s we have used Internet Protocol Version 4 (IPv4). It is IPv4 that specifies that IP addresses are four numbers long. Four was plenty for the days when only about 200 computers were networked. Now most of the 1.5 billion computer users have a personal computer, motivating the development of Internet Protocol Version 6 (IPv6). IPv6 specifies IP addresses will be sixteen numbers long in the future, solving the IP address problem for good.

Domain names. If we needed to know the four numbers of the IP addresses of our friends' computers to send them email, the process would be very annoying and uncivilized. Instead, the Internet uses human-readable symbolic names for computers that are based on a hierarchy of *domains*. A **domain** is a related group of networked computers. For example, the name of my computer is spiff.cs.washington.edu, which reveals its domain membership by its structure. Pulling apart the name, my computer (spiff) is a member of the Computer Science and Engineering Department domain (cs), which is part of the University of Washington domain (washington), which is part of the educational domain (edu), as shown in Figure 3.5(a) and (b). This is a hierarchy of domains because each is a member of the next larger domain. Another of my computers, tracer.cs.washington.edu, has a name with a similar structure, so it is apparently a member of the same domain. Other departments at the University of Washington, such as Astronomy (astro.washington.edu), have names that are peers of cs (on the same level) within the washington domain, and other schools (for example, princeton.edu) have names that are peers with washington within the edu domain. These names are symbolic and meaningful, making them easier to read than numbers, and arranged in a hierarchy that makes them easier to remember.

DNS servers. How do the convenient domain names like spiff.cs.washington.edu get converted into the IP addresses like 128.208.2.44 that computers need? The **Domain Name System (DNS)** translates the hierarchical, human-readable names into the four-number IP addresses. This allows both people and computers to use their preferred scheme.

Every Internet host (a computer connected to the Internet) knows the IP address of its nearest **DNS name server**, a computer that keeps a list of the human-readable symbolic names and the corresponding IP addresses. Whenever you use the hierarchical symbolic name to send information to some destination, your computer asks the DNS server to look up the corresponding IP address. It then uses that IP address to send the information. Notice that when your computer asks a DNS name server to translate a name to the IP address, it is in another client/server relationship.

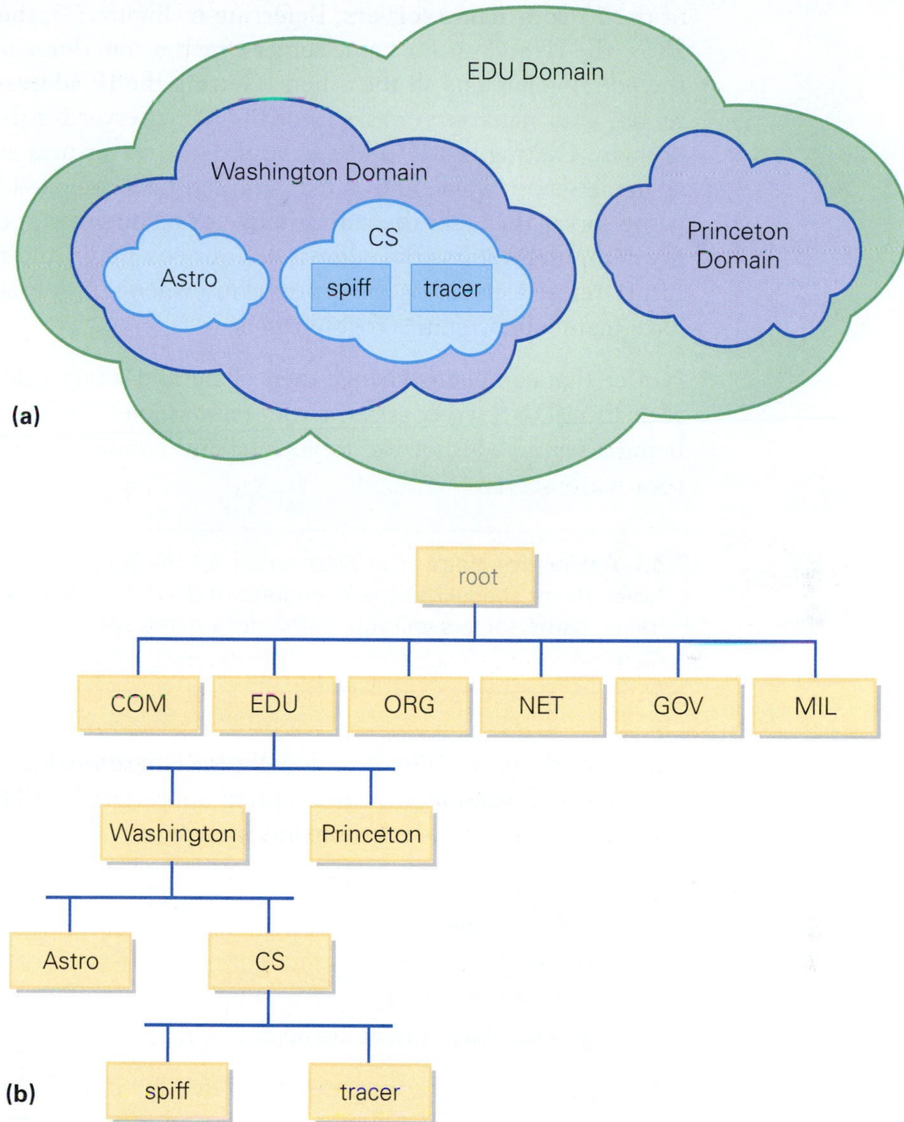

Figure 3.5 Two ways to think of the Internet domain hierarchy.

Usually the DNS server knows the translation for the symbolic name to the IP address because it has processed the IP address before, and so replies immediately. But if it doesn't know, it goes looking for the IP address by asking an **authoritative name server**. *Authoritative* means the name server keeps *the* complete list of the IP addresses and corresponding domain names for all authoritative name servers and computers in its domain. It's the "go to" name server.

If your name server is looking for my IP address, for example, because you have used spiff.cs.washington.edu, the search begins—in principle—with one of the 13 **root name servers**. Referring to Figure 3.5, the root name servers know the IP address for name servers for the com domain, name servers for the edu domain, and all the others. Getting the IP address of the edu name server, your name server asks it for the name server for the washington domain. Getting that IP address, your name server next asks the authoritative cs name server, which knows that spiff has been assigned 128.208.2.44. Your name server then asks the authoritative cs name server, gets the IP address for my computer, returns the address to your computer, and remembers it for future reference. This is the process "in principle," but name servers usually have many opportunities for shortcuts.

Notice that computers change their client and server roles all the time. When your local DNS server asks the root name server for help, it changes from being a server, which it was to your (client) computer, to being a client of the root name server.

3.1 Asking for Help. The Web server for the National Air and Space Museum (www.nasm.si.edu) has the IP address 160.111.252.58. In principle, what authoritative name servers will your computer's name server ask to find this IP address for you?

Top-level domains. The .edu domain for educational institutions is one of several **top-level domain** names, often abbreviated **TLDs**. In addition to .edu, the original top-level domains include:

.com for commercial enterprises
.org for organizations
.net for networks
.mil for the military
.gov for government agencies

The top-level domains were expanded in 2000 to include .biz, .info, .name, .travel, and others; the full list can be found at www.icann.org. The original domains all apply to organizations in the United States. There is also a set of mnemonic two-letter country designators, such as .ca (Canada), .uk (United Kingdom), .fr (France), .de (Germany, as in Deutschland), .es (Spain, as in España), .us (United States), and so on. (See Table 3.1 on the next page for a complete list.) These allow domain names to be grouped by their country of origin. More top-level domain names will be coming because ICANN is expanding to user-defined top-level domain names.

Root Name Servers. If the 13 root name servers are scattered around the world, where are they? Because they are *mirrored*, that is, copies of the same information is stored in multiple sites, they are everywhere. See the map at www.root-servers.org for the root name server nearest you.

Table 3.1 Top-level country domain abbreviations

Country	Code
Afghanistan	af
Albania	al
Algeria	dz
American Samoa	as
Andorra	ad
Angola	ao
Anguilla	ai
Antarctica	aq
Antigua and Barbuda	ag
Argentina	ar
Armenia	am
Aruba	aw
Ascension Island	ac
Australia	au
Austria	at
Azerbaijan	az
Bahrain	bh
Bangladesh	bd
Barbados	bb
Belarus	by
Belgium	be
Belize	bz
Benin	bj
Bermuda	bm
Bhutan	bt
Bolivia	bo
Bosnia and Herzegowina	ba
Botswana	bw
Brazil	br
Brunei	bn
Bulgaria	bg
Burkina Faso	bf
Burundi	bi
Cambodia	kh
Cameroon	cm
Canada	ca
Cape Verde	cv
Central African Republic	cf
Chad	td
Chile	cl
China	cn
Christmas Island	cx
Cocos (Keeling) Islands	cc
Colombia	co
Comoros	km
Congo	cg
Congo, DRC	cd
Cook Islands	ck
Costa Rica	cr
Cote d'Ivoire	ci
Croatia	hr
Cuba	cu
Cyprus	cy
Czech Republic	cz
Denmark	dk
Djibouti	dj
Dominica	dm
Dominican Republic	do
East Timor	tp
Ecuador	ec
Egypt	eg
El Salvador	sv
Equatorial Guinea	gq
Eritrea	er
Estonia	ee
Ethiopia	et
Falkland Islands	fk
Faroe Islands	fo
Fiji	fj
Finland	fi
France	fr
French Guiana	gf
French Polynesia	pf
Gabon	ga
Gambia	gm
Georgia	ge
Germany	de
Ghana	gh
Gibraltar	gi
Greece	gr
Greenland	gl
Grenada	gd
Guadeloupe	gp
Guam	gu
Guatemala	gt
Guinea	gn
Guinea-Bissau	gw
Guyana	gy
Haiti	ht
Honduras	hn
Hong Kong	hk
Hungary	hu
Iceland	is
India	in
Indonesia	id
Iran	ir
Iraq	iq
Ireland	ie
Isle of Man	im
Israel	il
Italy	it
Jamaica	jm
Japan	jp
Jordan	jo
Kazakhstan	kz
Kenya	ke
Kiribati	ki
Korea, DPRK	kp
Korea, Republic of	kr
Kuwait	kw
Kyrgyzstan	kg
Laos	la
Latvia	lv
Lebanon	lb
Lesotho	ls
Liberia	lr
Libya	ly
Liechtenstein	li
Lithuania	lt
Luxembourg	lu
Macao	mo
Macedonia	mk
Madagascar	mg
Malawi	mw
Malaysia	my
Maldives	mv
Mali	ml
Malta	mt
Marshall Islands	mh
Martinique	mq
Mauritania	mr
Mauritius	mu
Mexico	mx
Micronesia	fm
Moldova	md
Monaco	mc
Mongolia	mn
Montserrat	ms
Morocco	ma
Mozambique	mz
Myanmar	mm
Namibia	na
Nauru	nr
Nepal	np
Netherlands	nl
Netherlands Antilles	an
New Caledonia	nc
New Zealand	nz
Nicaragua	ni
Niger	ne
Nigeria	ng
Niue	nu
N. Mariana Islands	mp
Norway	no
Oman	om
Pakistan	pk
Palau	pw
Panama	pa
Papua New Guinea	pg
Paraguay	py
Peru	pe
Philippines	ph
Pitcairn	pn
Poland	pl
Portugal	pt
Puerto Rico	pr
Qatar	qa
Reunion	re
Romania	ro
Russia	ru
Rwanda	rw
Saint Kitts and Nevis	kn
Saint Lucia	lc
St Vincent, Grenadines	vc
Samoa	ws
San Marino	sm
Sao Tome and Principe	st
Saudi Arabia	sa
Senegal	sn
Seychelles	sc
Sierra Leone	sl
Singapore	sg
Slovakia	sk
Slovenia	si
Solomon Islands	sb
Somalia	so
South Africa	za
S Georgia, S Sandwich Islands	gs
Spain	es
Sri Lanka	lk
St. Helena	sh
Sudan	sd
Suriname	sr
Swaziland	sz
Sweden	se
Switzerland	ch
Syria	sy
Taiwan	tw
Tajikistan	tj
Tanzania	tz
Thailand	th
The Bahamas	bs
The Cayman Islands	ky
Togo	tg
Tokelau	tk
Tonga	to
Trinidad and Tobago	tt
Tunisia	tn
Turkey	tr
Turkmenistan	tm
Tuvalu	tv
Uganda	ug
Ukraine	ua
United Arab Emirates	ae
United Kingdom	uk
United States	us
Uruguay	uy
Uzbekistan	uz
Vanuatu	vu
Vatican City State	va
Venezuela	ve
Vietnam	vn
Virgin Islands (British)	vg
Virgin Islands (US)	vi
Western Sahara	eh
Yemen	ye
Yugoslavia	yu
Zambia	zm
Zimbabwe	zw

Following Protocol

Having figured out how a computer addresses other computers to send them information, we still need to describe how the information is actually sent. The sending process uses **Transmission Control Protocol/Internet Protocol (TCP/IP).** It sounds technical—and is—but the concept is easy to understand.

TCP/IP postcard analogy. To explain how TCP/IP works, we repeat an analogy used by Vinton Cerf, one of the pioneers of IP: Sending information over the Internet is like sending your novel from your home in Tahiti to your publisher in New York City using only postcards. How could you do that? You would begin by breaking up the novel into small units, only a few sentences long, so that each unit fits on a postcard. Then number each postcard to indicate where in the sequence of your novel the sentences belong, and write the publisher's address on each. As you complete the postcards, drop them into a mailbox. The postal service in Tahiti sends them to the publisher (eventually), but the cards are not kept together, nor do they all take the same route. Some postcards may go west, via Hong Kong; others may go east, via Los Angeles. From Hong Kong and Los Angeles, there are multiple routes to New York City. Eventually the postcards arrive at the publisher, who uses the numbers to put the postcards in order and reconstruct the novel, as shown in Figure 3.6.

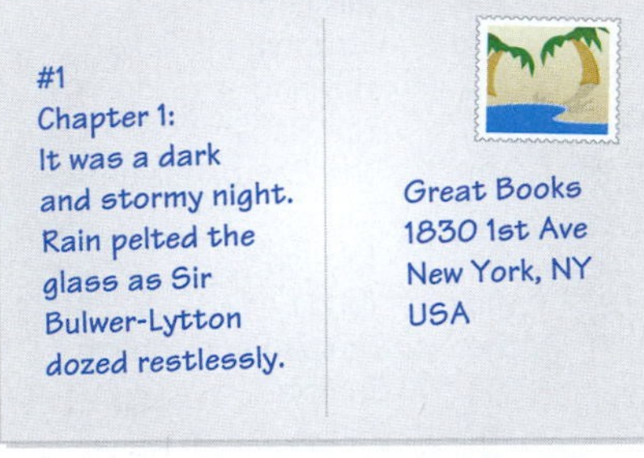

Cerf's postcard analogy makes the concept of TCP/IP clear. Sending any amount of information, including a whole novel, is possible by breaking it into a sequence of small fixed-size units. An **IP packet**, like the postcard, has space for the unit, a destination IP address, and a sequence number. IP packets are filled in order and assigned sequence numbers. The packets are sent over the Internet one at a time using whatever route is available, as shown in Figure 3.7. At the destination, they are reordered by sequence number to assemble the information.

Packets are independent. Consider the advantages of TCP/IP. For example, it is natural to assume that IP packets would take a single path to their destinations, like conventional telephone calls, but they do not. Because each packet can take a different route, congestion and service interruptions do not delay

Figure 3.6 The TCP/IP postcard analogy.

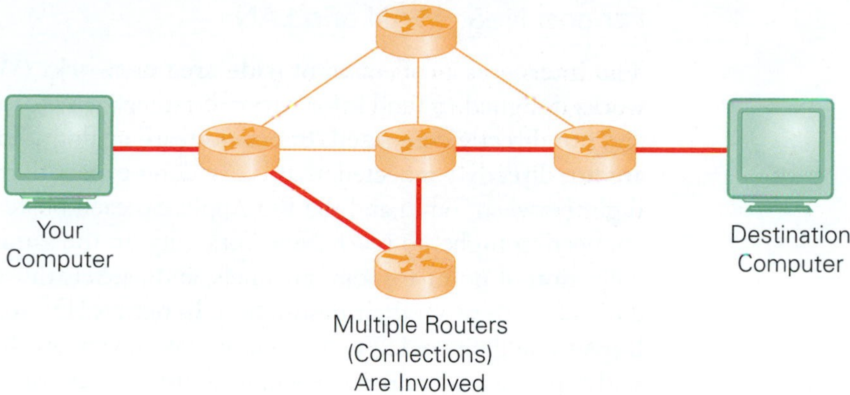

Figure 3.7 The Internet makes use of whatever routes are available to deliver packets.

transmissions. If sending the first postcard via Hong Kong meant that all following postcards had to be sent via Hong Kong, then a typhoon preventing aircraft from flying between Tahiti and Hong Kong would delay the novel's transmission. But if the postcards can take any available route, the transmission can continue via Los Angeles. As a result, all of the novel might be delivered via LA before airline service is restored between Tahiti and Hong Kong. This concept motivated engineers to decide to make TCP/IP packets independent.

Moving packets: wires and more. Although Cerf's analogy uses postcards and airplanes, the Internet uses electrical, electronic, and optical communication means. The original ARPANET used long-distance telephone lines, and the Internet continues to rely on telephone carriers for long-distance connections. However, as the Internet has grown and as new technologies such as fiber optics have matured, the Internet now uses separate dedicated lines as well. Because the TCP/IP protocol describes exactly how IP packets are structured and handled, the technology used to move the packets only concerns the carrier. The computers at each end of the communication do not know or care what medium is used because they simply send and receive IP packets. Indeed, transmissions often rely on multiple technologies as the packets move across the Internet.

Ironically, with the growth of Internet capacity, telephone companies are also sending telephone conversations over the Internet. Speech is digitized, stuffed into IP packets at the speaker's end, sent over the Internet, unpacked at the listener's end, and converted to the analog form acceptable to a phone set. This Voice over IP (VoIP) application suggests that the Internet is fast becoming the universal information carrier.

fluencyBIT

Netting a Prize. Vint Cerf and Bob Kahn received the 2004 Turing Award from the Association of Computing Machinery, computing's Nobel Prize, for the development of TCP/IP.

Far and Near: WAN and LAN

The Internet is a collection of **wide area networks (WAN)**, meaning networks designed to send information between two locations widely separated and not directly connected. In our postcard analogy, Tahiti and New York City are not directly connected; that is, we don't expect there to be a single airline flight between Tahiti and the Big Apple. So each postcard takes a sequence of connecting flights to reach New York City. In the same way, the Internet is a collection of point-to-point channels, and packets must visit a sequence of computers to reach their destination. In networking terms, packets take several **hops** to be delivered. The trace in Figure 3.8 shows that a ping—a "please reply" message—from my machine `spiff` to `eth.ch`, the Swiss Federal Technical University, takes 18 hops on its route from Seattle to Zürich.

When computers are close enough to be linked by a single cable or pair of wires, the interconnection is referred to as a **local area network (LAN)**. Ethernet is the main technology for local area networks, and is appropriate for connecting all the computers in a lab or building. An Ethernet network uses a radically different approach than the Internet, but it's equally easy to understand.

Ethernet party analogy. Depending on the technology, the physical setup for an Ethernet network is a wire, wire pair, or optical fiber, called the **channel**, that winds past a set of computers. (Robert Metcalfe, the inventor of the Ethernet design, described the channel as the "The Ether," giving the technology its name; see Figure 3.9.) Engineers "tap" the channel to connect a computer, allowing it to send a signal (that is, drive an electronic pulse or light flash onto the channel). All computers connected to the channel can detect the signal, including the sender. Thus the channel supports broadcast communication.

Trace My Computer to http:// eth.ch port 80

Table: Traceroute to eth.ch

Hop	IP Address	Node Name	Location	Network
0	128.208.2.44	spiff.cseresearch.cs.washington.edu	Seattle, WA, USA	University of Washington
1	128.208.2.102	acar-atg-02-vlan75.cac.washington.edu	Seattle, WA, USA	University of Washington
2	205.175.108.21	vl3805.uwcr-ads-01.infra.washington.edu	Seattle, WA, USA	University of Washington
3	205.175.101.157	uwcr-ads-01-vlan1839.cac.washington.edu	Seattle, WA, USA	University of Washington
4	205.175.101.2	vl1800.uwbr-chb-01.infra.washington.edu	Seattle, WA, USA	University of Washington
5	209.124.191.134	ge-2-0-0--4013.iccr-sttlwa01-03.infra.pnw-gig	Seattle, WA, USA	Pacific Northwest Gigapop
6	209.124.179.45	iccr-sttlwa01-02-ge-0-2-0--0.infra.pnw-gigapc	Seattle, WA, USA	Pacific Northwest Gigapop
7	209.124.179.46	nlr-packetnet.trans.pnw-gigapop.net	Seattle, WA, USA	Pacific Northwest Gigapop
8	216.24.186.6	denv-seat-58.layer3.nlr.net	Cypress, usa	National LambdaRail
9	216.24.186.4	chic-denv-36.layer3.nlr.net	Cypress, usa	National LambdaRail
10	216.24.186.33	newy-chic-100.layer3.nlr.net	Cypress, usa	National LambdaRail
11	216.24.184.86	-	Cypress, usa	National LambdaRail
12	62.40.112.57	so-6-2-0.rt1.fra.de.geant2.net	Frankfurt, Germany	IP allocation for GEANT network
13	62.40.112.21	so-6-2-0.rt1.gen.ch.geant2.net	Geneva, Switzerland	IP allocation for GEANT network
14	62.40.124.22	swiCE2-10GE-1-1.switch.ch	Chur, Switzerland	DANTE Ltd.
15	130.59.37.2	swiLS2-10GE-1-3.switch.ch	*(Switzerland)?*	SWITCH, The Swiss Education and
16	130.59.36.206	swiEZ2-10GE-1-1.switch.ch	Wetzikon, Switzerland	SWITCH, The Swiss Education and
17	192.33.92.1	rou-rz-gw-giga-to-switch.ethz.ch	Zurich, Switzerland	ETHZ, Swiss Federal Institute of Tec
18	192.33.92.169	rou-fw-rz-rz-gw.ethz.ch	Zurich, Switzerland	ETHZ, Swiss Federal Institute of Tec
?	...	-		-
?	**129.132.97.15**	eth.ch	*(Switzerland)?*	ETH/UNIZH Camp Net

Figure 3.8 A ping from the author's machine to **eth.ch**.

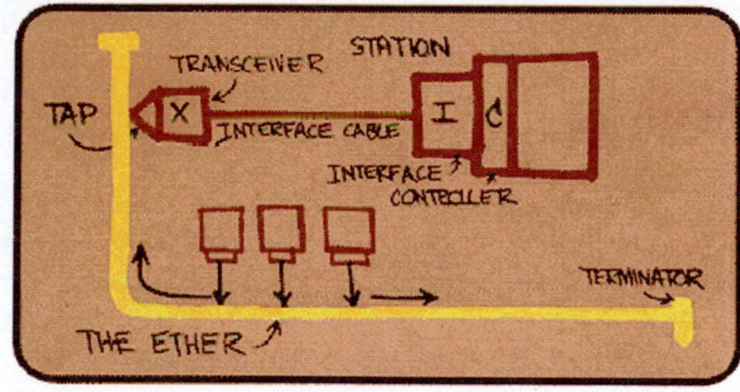

Figure 3.9 Robert Metcalfe's original drawing of the Ethernet design; the unlabeled boxes (computers), "tap" onto the wire that Metcalfe labeled "The Ether."

fluencyBIT

Getting Ether. Robert Metcalfe described the Ethernet (in 1973) as a "multipoint data communication channel with collision detection." His first implementation connected the 100-node *Alto Aloha Network* at Xerox's Palo Alto Research Center.

To understand how an Ethernet network works, consider another analogy. A group of friends is standing around at a party telling stories. While someone is telling a story, everyone is listening. The speaker is broadcasting to the group. When the story is over, how do the friends decide who tells the next story? There may be a momentary pause while the friends wait for someone to speak. Since there is no plan or agreement as to who should speak next, someone typically just begins talking. If no one else begins talking, that speaker continues telling the story to completion. At the end of the story, the same situation arises. There is a pause, and then someone else starts talking. If two or more people begin talking after the pause, they will notice that someone else is speaking and immediately stop. There is a pause while everyone waits for someone to go ahead. Assuming speakers tend to wait a random length of time, someone will begin talking. It's possible that two or more speakers will again start at the same time, notice the situation, stop, and wait a random length of time. Eventually one person will begin telling another story.

In this analogy we have assumed all the friends are equal; that is, there is no difference in status, nor does anyone have an especially loud or soft voice. Even so, the system isn't fair, because it favors the person who waits the shortest length of time at the end of a story. Of course, we all know such people!

Ethernet communication works like the party protocol. When the channel is in use, as when someone is telling a story, all of the computers listen to it. (Unlike storytelling, however, only one computer typically keeps the transmitted information; that is, this broadcast medium is being used for point-to-point communication.) A pause indicates the end of the transmission when no computer is sending signals and the channel is quiet. A computer wanting to transmit starts sending signals and, at the same time, starts listening to the channel to detect what is being transmitted. If it is exactly the information the computer sent, the computer knows it's the only one sending, and it completes its transmission. If the computer's signals are mixed in with signals from one or more other computers, it notices the garbled message and stops transmitting immediately. The other computer(s) stop too. Each machine pauses for a random length of time. The computer that waits the shortest length of time begins sending, and if there are no conflicting computers, it continues. If not, the colliders repeat the process.

fluencyBIT

Many Versus One. There is an important difference between the way the Internet works and the way an Ethernet works. The Internet uses a point-to-point network to implement point-to-point communication. An Ethernet uses a broadcast network for point-to-point communication. The difference is that with the Internet multiple communications can take place at once over different wires, but with the Ethernet only one communication can take place at a time. This limitation is usually not a problem, because Ethernets usually carry much less traffic.

Notice that the Ethernet scheme is completely decentralized and requires no schedule or plan. Each computer listens to the channel, and if it's quiet, it's free. The computer transmits unless some other computer starts at the same moment. When that happens, both computers back off for a brief (random) amount of time and then try again.

Connecting a Computer to the Internet

How are computers actually connected to the Internet? Today there are two basic methods:

- By an Internet service provider (ISP)
- By a campus or enterprise network

Most of us use both kinds of connections daily, depending on where we study or work. Let's look at each approach.

Connections by ISP. As the name implies, Internet service providers sell connections to the Internet. Examples of ISPs are Comcast.com and Earthlink.net, but there are thousands of providers. Most home users connect to the Internet by ISPs. Here's how an ISP connection usually works.

Users plug their computer into the telephone system just as they would connect an extension telephone. (The plug, called an RJ-11, is universal in North America, but an adapter may be needed elsewhere.) Then the computer's modem, which is generally built into modern personal computers, can dial up the ISP and establish a connection. This operation is similar to a fax machine dialing another fax machine. A preferred alternative to dial-up, because it is much faster, is a dedicated connection to the ISP, such as a **digital subscriber line (DSL)**. DSL, which is provided by a phone company or through an equivalent service provided by cable companies, connects "continuously" to the ISP. Either way, the modems—one at each end of the connection—enable the home computer to talk to the ISP's computer so that they can send and receive information. The ISP's computer is connected to the Internet, so it relays information for its customers. For example, when you surf the Web and click on a remote link (that is, a page stored on a distant computer), the request for the page is sent from your computer to the ISP's computer, across the Internet to the remote computer, which then sends the Web page back across the Internet to the computer at the ISP. From there, the page is sent over the ISP's connection to your computer and displayed on your screen.

Enterprise network connections (LAN). The other way to connect to the Internet is as a user of a larger networked organization such as a school, business, or governmental unit. In this case, the organization's system administrators connect the computers and form a local area network (LAN). The Ethernet technology mentioned earlier is an example of a local area network. These local networks, known as **intranets**, support communication within the organization, but they also connect to the Internet by a gateway. Information from a distant Web computer is sent across the Internet, through the gateway to the organization's intranet, and across the LAN to the user's computer.

With either method, ISP or LAN, you usually send and receive information across the Internet transparently—that is, without knowing or caring which method is used.

Wireless networks. The two preceding examples cover the usual cases for fixed location computers, that is, those tethered by the phone or network cables (and power cables, too). Laptops, notebooks, hand-helds, and other mobile computers may be connected to network cables, but they are most convenient when they use wireless communication. **Wireless networking** is a variation on the LAN connection and is often referred to by its protocol name **802.11**, pronounced *eight-oh-two-eleven*; see Figure 3.10. A **router** is physically connected to the Internet and is capable of broadcasting and receiving signals, usually radio frequency (rf) signals, which the mobile computers can also send and receive. The router and any computers within signal range (with their wireless communication turned on) participate in a network based on the Ethernet principles described earlier. The router relays Internet requests for the participating computers.

fluencyBIT

Should I Know My Computer's IP Address? No. If you are dialing into the Internet via an ISP, your computer is assigned a temporary IP address when you log in and you use it until you log out. If you access the Internet via an intranet, one of two cases applies. Your network administrator may have assigned your computer an IP address when it was set up. Alternatively, no permanent address was assigned, and through the Dynamic Host Configuration Protocol (**DHCP**), your computer is assigned an address each time you turn it on. Wireless uses DCHP, too. In any case, the IP address is nothing you have to worry about.

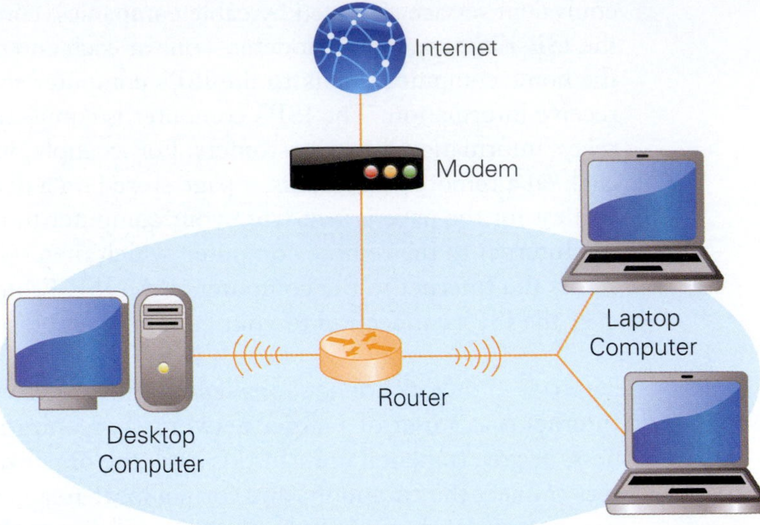

Figure 3.10 Standard Wi-Fi network configuration. A wireless router is connected via the modem to the ISP's Internet modem; laptops and other wireless-enabled devices connect by radio signals to the router.

The World Wide Web

Some of the computers connected to the Internet are **Web servers**. That is, they are computers programmed to send files to browsers running on other computers connected to the Internet. Together these Web servers and their files comprise the **World Wide Web (WWW)**. The files are Web pages, but Web servers store and send many other kinds of files, too. These files are often used to create the Web page (for example, images or animations) or to help with other Web services (for example, software used to play audio or video).

When described in these terms, the Web doesn't seem like much. And technically, it's not. What makes the World Wide Web significant is the information contained in the files and the ability of the client and server computers to process it.

No Confusion. The World Wide Web and the Internet are different. The Internet is all of the wires and routers connecting named computers, that is, the hardware. The World Wide Web is a subset of those computers (Web servers) and their files.

Requesting a Web Page

As noted earlier, Web requests are processed in a client/server interaction. When you request a Web page, such as my university Web page (http://www.cs.washington.edu/homes/snyder/index.html), your browser is a client asking for a file from a Web server computer. The **URL (Universal Resource Locator)**, has three main parts:

- **Protocol.** The http://part, which stands for **Hypertext Transfer Protocol**, tells the computers how to handle the file. There are other ways to send files, such as ftp, File Transfer Protocol.
- **Server computer's name.** The name is the server's IP address given by the domain hierarchy, www.cs.washington.edu. Your computer uses the name to send a request to the server computer for the page.
- **Page's pathname.** The pathname is the sequence following the IP address: /homes/snyder/index.html. The pathname tells the server which file (page) is requested and where to find it.

All URLs have this structure, although you may not think so, because in some cases you can leave parts out and the software fills in the missing part. (This is further explained in the next section.) It is never a mistake to use the full form.

Summarizing, Web browsers and Web servers both "speak" HTTP. When you specify a URL in your browser's location window, you say where the information is to be found (server's name), what information you want (pathname), and what protocol the two computers will use to exchange the information (HTTP).

3.2 **Take It to the Bank.** Classify each part of this URL according to the three parts just described: **https://accts.lastbank.com/newdeposits/welcome/toaster.html**.

Describing a Web Page

As you know, servers do not store Web pages in the form seen on our screens. Instead, the pages are stored as a *description* of how they should appear on the screen. When the Web browser receives the description file (**source** file), it creates the Web page image that it displays. There are two advantages to storing and sending the source rather than the image itself:

- A description file usually requires less information.
- The browser can adapt the source image to your computer more easily than a literal pixel-by-pixel description.

For example, it's easier to shrink or expand the page from its description than to use the image itself. Though browsers show the image, they always give you the option of seeing the description, too. Next time you are online, look under the *View* menu and choose the *Source* or *Page Source* option in your browser. Figure 3.11 shows a simple Web page and its source.

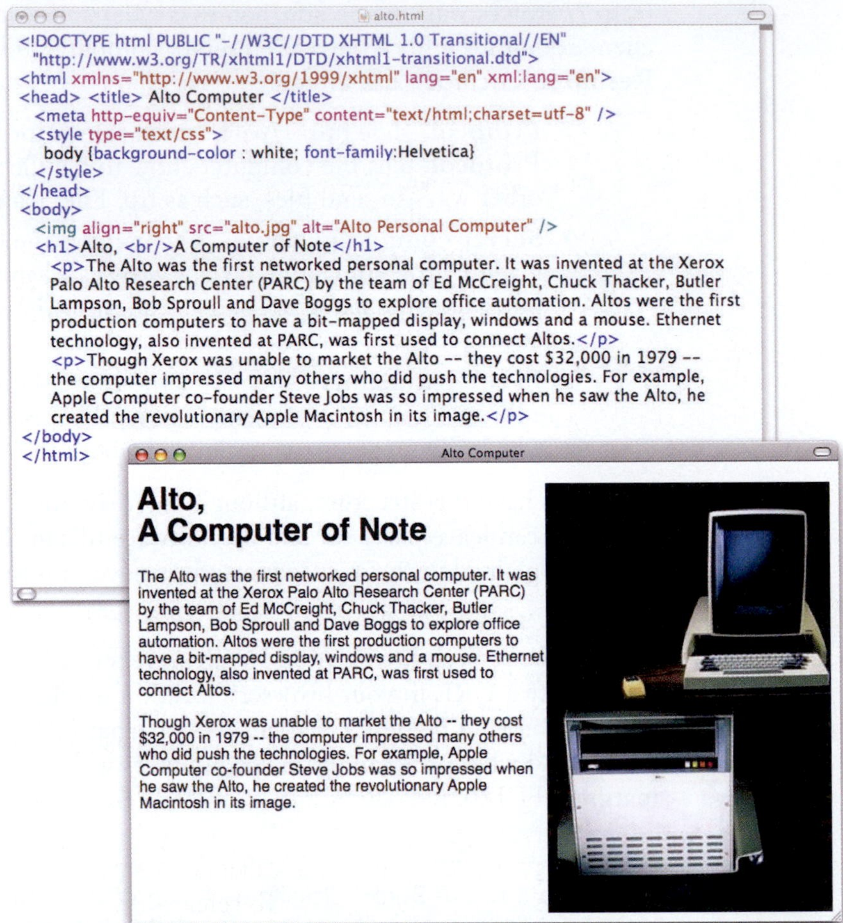

Figure 3.11 A Web page and the HTML source that produced it. Notice that an additional image file, **alto.jpg**, is also required to display the page.

fluencyBIT

Stated Briefly. Tiny URLs, popular with SMS, Twitter, and other users, are not actually URLs at all, but simply short names for the true URL. For example, **TinyURL.com** gave me **d5r9kr** for this book's student resources Web page: **wps.aw.com/aw_snyder_fluency_3/79/20307/5198635.cw/index.html**. Sites supporting tiny URLs are simply Web applications that keep a list of the short names and corresponding URLs; when we use the short name (e.g., **http://tinyurl.com/d5r9kr**), they look it up in their list and open the page.

Hypertext

To describe how a Web page should look, many pages use **Hypertext Markup Language (HTML).** Markup languages, traditionally used in publishing and graphic design, describe the layout of a document, including margin width, font, text style, image placement, and such. Hypertext began as an experiment to break away from the straight sequence of normal text: first paragraph, second paragraph, third paragraph, and so on. With hypertext, it's possible to jump from one point in the text to somewhere else in the text or to some other document and then return. This familiar feature, which breaks a document's linear sequence, gives it a more complex structure. The (usually blue) highlighted words—the **hyperlinks**—provide the point from which we can (optionally) jump and return. The term *hypertext* was coined in the late 1960s by Theodore Nelson, although in his *Literary Machines* he credits the original idea to computer pioneer Vannevar Bush. Combining the two ideas—markup languages and hypertext—was the contribution of Tim Berners-Lee. It lets us build nonlinear documents, which are ideal for the dynamic and highly interconnected Internet. The World Wide Web was born.

In Chapter 4 we study HTML to learn how Web pages are created and processed. In Chapters 5 and 6, we explore the content of the WWW.

The Internet and the Web

Some Web servers have www as part of their domain name, some don't. Some Web servers, like www.cs.washington.edu, seem to add on the www if you leave it out, and some, like New York City's Museum of Modern Art (MoMA), work either way; both www.moma.org and moma.org display the same Web site. When is the www required and when is it optional?

First, remember that names like www.cs.washington.edu are simply names. That is, like spiff, www is the name of a computer, the Web server, in the cs.washington.edu domain. And, like all computers connected to the Internet, Web servers have IP addresses. To refer to a Web server, you *must* give its name exactly, because your computer will ask the DNS server for the Web server's IP address using that name. If the name is wrong, either you will access the wrong IP address or, more typically, the DNS lookup will fail. Your browser will give you an error message (e.g., "404 Not Found") advising you to check the address. So, there is no option: You must give the name exactly.

No organization taking the trouble to put a Web server on the Internet wants visitors to fail to reach them, so their Web administrators try to save users from mistakes. For example, if you try to access my Web page but forget to include the www, your request http://cs.washington.edu/... will reach the wrong computer. However, that computer has been programmed to notice http://requests and to return to your computer, "You probably meant www.cs.washington.edu." Your computer tries it automatically. This is called a **redirection**.

fluencyBIT

Punctuating the Internet. URLs use many slashes (/); that's the correct term. Backslashes (\) are also used in computing; that's also the correct term. The term "forward slash" is not correct, except perhaps with light sabers.

Browsers are designed to try again with the recommended address. So, when you type http://cs.washington.edu/homes/snyder, your location window quickly changes to http://www.cs.washington.edu/homes/snyder, making it seem that the www has been added. What you see is your browser trying the redirection address. The redirection could have been http://www.aw.com/snyder/, the URL for this book. In that case, the redirection looks like a replacement, which is what it really is in both cases. Redirection is used extensively at Web sites to avoid telling users that they made a mistake and to get them to where they want to be.

Rather than using redirection, some organizations, like the Museum of Modern Art, simply make several names work. That is, MoMA has registered both moma.org and www.moma.org to the IP address 12.172.4.131, saving us from making a mistake no matter which choice we make and avoiding redirection. Both names produce the same result because they refer to the same computer.

Web servers don't have to be named www. It's just what people usually name their Web servers. Web servers are named www because as the Web got started, many domains added a separate computer as their Web server. The server needed a name that people could remember, because redirection was not yet widely used. Because the first groups named their servers www, later groups did, too. Now it seems like a requirement, but it is only a tradition.

fluencyBIT

Universal Language. Most people are amazed at the Web's ability to provide access to information around the world. Few have observed, however, that it is the universal HTTP language that makes this communication possible. Every computer—regardless of who manufactured it, how it's configured, its operating system type and version, the applications it runs, the (native) language of its user, and so on—can communicate because the computers "know" this common language. Imagine the benefits if every person on the planet spoke a common language!

File Structure

To use networks well, we need to understand file structures, although the topic is not technically part of networking. Recall from your experience using a personal computer that a **folder**—also known as a **directory**—is a named collection of files or other folders or both.

Directory Hierarchy

Because folders can contain folders, which can contain files and other folders, and on and on, the whole scheme—called the **file structure** of the computer—forms the **directory hierarchy**. Think of any hierarchy as a tree; in the case of file structures, folders are the branch points and files are the leaves. Hierarchy trees are often drawn in odd ways, such as sideways or upside down, but in all cases two terms are standard:

- *Down* or *lower* in the hierarchy means into subfolders; that is, toward the leaves.

› *Up* or *higher* in the hierarchy means into enclosing folders; that is, toward the root.

To illustrate these terms, Figure 3.12 shows part of the hierarchy of this book formed from its parts, chapters, and sections; the "tree" of Figure 3.12 is drawn on its side with the root, Fluency, to the left. The path from the root (the whole book) to the leaf (this section) is highlighted. We move *up* or *higher* in the hierarchy when we move, say, from Chapter 3 to Part 1, since it is more inclusive. We move *down* or *lower* in the hierarchy when we move, say, from Chapter 3 to this Directory Hierarchy section, since it is more specific.

Learning the "directionality" of hierarchical references makes navigating the Web simpler.

Pulling Rank. An easy way to remember the directions of "higher" and "lower" in a hierarchy is to think of the military hierarchy: general, colonel, major, captain, lieutenant, sergeant, corporal, private. Moving up or down in the hierarchy corresponds to moving up or down the chain of command, or to higher or lower rank.

Part of the directory hierarchy is shown in the pathnames of URLs. For example, the URL http://www.nasm.si.edu/exhibitions/gal100/pioneer.html is a National Air and Space Museum's site describing Pioneer 10, the first man-made object to leave the solar system. The page is specified by a path-

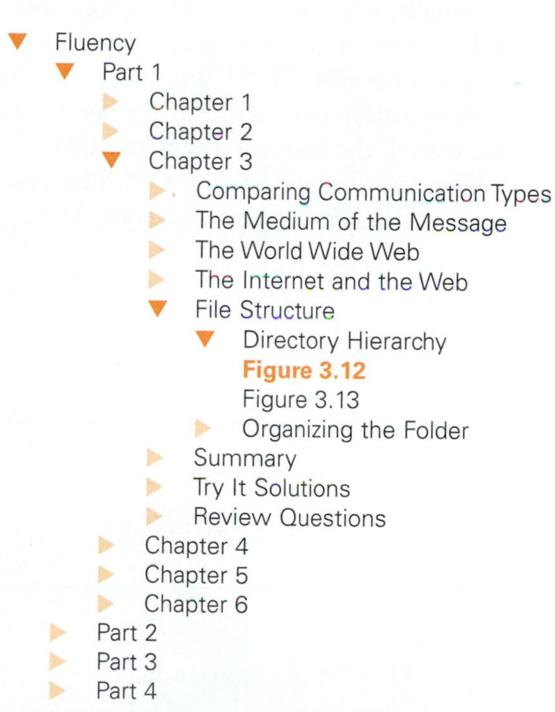

Figure 3.12 The hierarchy of this book highlighting the path to this figure; down-pointing triangles are expanded; right-pointing triangles are not.

name, /exhibitions/gal100/pioneer.html, that tells the computer how to navigate through the Air and Space Museum's directory hierarchy to the file, as shown in Figure 3.13. Each time we pass a slash (/), reading the pathname from left to right, we move into a subfolder or to the file. That is, we go down in the hierarchy. We start at a top-level folder called exhibitions. Within the exhibitions folder, there is a subfolder called gal100, which we might assume refers to Gallery 100, the room containing famous "firsts" in air and space exploration. And in the gal100 folder, there is a file called pioneer.html, the Web page we want.

In general, the path in a URL tells the server computer how to navigate to the requested file in the server's file structure. The server computer follows down the hierarchical structure just as we did in the NASM example.

Case in Point. Remember that case sensitivity means computers treat uppercase and lowercase letters as different characters. In URLs, domain names are not case sensitive, because they are standardized for DNS lookup. Pathnames can be case sensitive, because they tell how to navigate through the Web server's file structure, which may be case sensitive. Be careful when typing pathnames, and when in doubt, try lowercase first.

Organizing the Folder

Normally, when we give a URL, we expect the last item in the sequence to be a file name, such as homepage.html, but it is not always necessary. Other technologies besides HTML are used to produce Web pages. Also, when a URL ends in a slash (which means the last item on the path is a folder rather than a file name), the browser automatically looks for a file called index.html in that folder. So, a request for the URL http://www.cs.washington.edu/homes/snyder/index.html to my university Web page is the same as http://www.cs

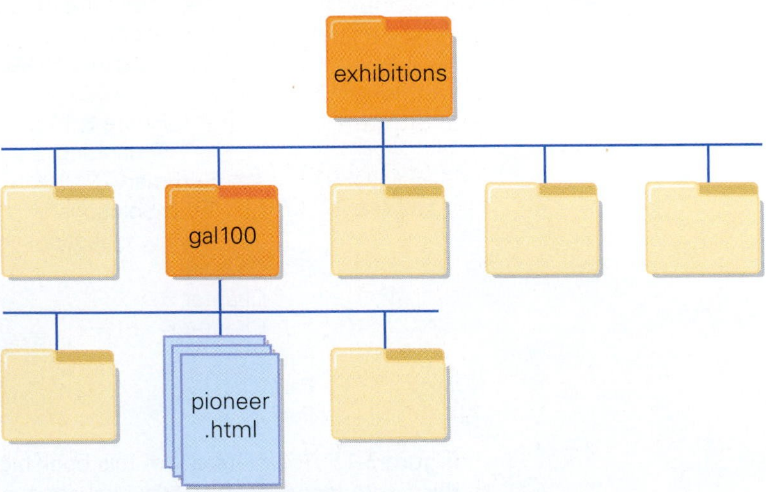

Figure 3.13 The pathname hierarchy ending in pioneer.html.

.washington.edu/homes/snyder/ because a browser that finds the folder named snyder will automatically look for a file called index.html in it. Of course, the index.html file will exist only if the person who set up the Web pages and built the file hierarchy decided to organize it that way and provide the index pages. Some people do and some people don't, but the browser will look for index.html when necessary.

Why build a hierarchy at all? Why not dump all the files into one huge folder and save typing? Most people build hierarchies to organize their own thinking and work. Because directories cost nothing, there is no reason not to use them, and it is highly recommended. (In this book, when we create a Web page, for example, we will always use a subfolder for organizing the pictures on the page.)

fluencyALERT

Look Before You Delete. The "blazing away" discussion in Chapter 2 claiming "nothing can break" applied to the computer on the desk or lap in front of you. When you are using Web services such as Gmail or Yahoo email accessed via a browser, you are using some other computer that may be less forgiving; certain operations may be irreversible. For example, mail downloaded to your computer and then deleted usually ends up in a Trash folder on your computer, from which you can usually retrieve it, but deleting email stored on a server usually deletes it for good. There is no *Undo* command. These systems *always* check to make sure you really want to delete something; when you answer "delete," it's gone.

Summary

In this chapter we have discussed:

- Basic types of communication: point-to-point, multicast, broadcast, synchronous, and asynchronous.
- Networking that included: IP addresses, domains, IP packets, IP protocol, WANS and LANS, Ethernet protocol, ISPs, enterprise networks, and wireless networks.
- The difference between the Internet and the World Wide Web.
- The history of HTML, and we reviewed file hierarchies in preparation for our further study of HTML.

Try It Solutions

3.1 The authoritative name servers ask the A-name server for .edu, then .si, and then (possibly) .nasm.

3.2 The parts of the URL are its protocol, https://, server computer's name, accts.lastbank.com, and page's pathname, /newdeposits/welcome/toaster.html.

Review Questions

Multiple Choice

1. What is the potential number of IPv4 addresses available?
   a. 65,536
   b. 16,777,216
   c. 4,294,967,296
   d. limitless
2. The part of an email address to the right of the @ is most like a
   a. mailbox
   b. post office
   c. letter
   d. return address
3. DNS stands for
   a. Determined Name of Sender
   b. Determined Not Spam
   c. Domain Name System
   d. Domain Number Sequence
4. If the Internet consisted of four computers, there would be six possible connections. If it consisted of five computers, there would be ten possible connections. How many connections are possible with ten computers?
   a. 10
   b. 30
   c. 45
   d. infinite
5. As an aspiring TV exec, the ideal country to locate the top-level domain for your new quiz show "What's My IP?" would be
   a. Papua New Guinea
   b. Cocos Islands
   c. Tuvalu
   d. Nauru
6. Between client requests from a specific IP address, a Web server
   a. cannot handle requests from another client
   b. can handle requests up to the number of clients specified by the administrator
   c. can handle up to 255 other requests
   d. might handle hundreds or even thousands of requests
7. Root name servers
   a. maintain a list of all computer users
   b. manage all emails sent
   c. maintain the relationship between IP addresses and symbolic computer names
   d. maintain a list of all Web pages

8. To connect to the Internet with a wireless connection you'd need to communicate through a device that is physically connected to a network. This device is called a
   a. port
   b. Ethernet
   c. switch
   d. router

Short Answer

1. eCommerce is the shortened term for ________.
2. All IP addresses of authoritative name servers for TLDs are maintained and managed by 13 _______ servers scattered around the world.
3. A communication that goes out to many people within a specific target audience is called a(n) ________.
4. A hierarchy of related computers on a network is called a(n) ________.
5. Computers on the same level of a domain are known as ________.
6. A "please reply" message sent over the Internet is called a(n) ________.
7. Computers on an Ethernet network "tap" into a cable called a(n) ________.
8. A company that supplies connections to the Internet is called a(n) ________.
9. Intranets connect to the Internet via ________.
10. Local networks that support communications wholly within an organization are called ________.
11. Special computers that send files to Web browsers elsewhere on the Internet are known as ________.
12. The `http://` in a Web address is the ________.
13. Files are often sent over the Internet via a process known by the acronym ________.
14. The source file for a Web page contains the _______ of the page, not the actual image of the page.
15. HTML stands for ________.
16. In the client/server structure, the customer's computer is the _______ and the business' computer is the _______.
17. A personal log posted on the Web for public viewing is called a ________.

Exercises

1. There's an adage: "Guns don't kill people. People kill people." How does this relate to human nature and the Internet?

2. Label the following with either an S to indicate synchronous communication or an A to indicate asynchronous communication.

_____ movie	_____ book
_____ chat session	_____ concert
_____ email	_____ text messaging
_____ video conference	_____ Web board
_____ Web page	_____ blog

3. Go to http://www.internettrafficreport.com/namerica.htm and check out the Internet traffic for North America. How does the time of the day affect the traffic? How would the time of the day affect overseas Internet traffic?
4. Try the Web address above without the file name. What do you get?
5. Describe how the Internet is like a bus route, a subway route, UPS, or Federal Express. How is it different from these? Go to http://www.mta.nyc.ny.us/nyct/maps/submap.htm to see a map of the NYC subway system. How does it compare? Compare the Internet to the Prague subway map by going to http://www.myczechrepublic.com/prague/prague_metro.html.
6. What industries have prospered and which ones might have suffered because of the growth of the Internet? Why?
7. Are there more client computers or more server computers on the Internet? Explain.
8. Identify each part of the following URL: http://www.cs.washington.edu/homes/snyder/index.html.
   a. Protocol
   b. Domain
   c. Top-level domain
   d. Pathname
   e. Web page
9. State what the following acronyms stand for, and briefly describe what they are.

a. TCP/IP	e. WWW
b. LAN	f. URL
c. WAN	g. HTML
d. DSL	h. ISP

10. Using Table 3.1, try to find a top-level country code matching your initials. Record the country and the country code. If your initials are not there, pretend you are Kelly Young.
11. Visit Yahoo.com. Using the *Page Source* view, identify at least five different pairs of markup tags. For each pair, give the start tag, the content between the tags, and the end tag.

A Hypertext Markup Language Primer

4
chapter

Marking Up with HTML

learning objectives

- Know the meaning of and use hypertext terms
- Use XHTML tags to structure a document
- Use the basics of XHTML tag attributes
- Use XHTML tags to link to other files
- Explain the differences between absolute and relative pathnames
- Use XHTML to encode lists and tables
- Use Cascading Style Sheets to style a Web page

Most of the fundamental ideas of science are essentially simple and may as a rule be expressed in a language comprehensible to everyone.

—ALBERT EINSTEIN

WEB PAGES ARE CREATED, stored, and sent in encoded form; a browser converts them to the image we see on the screen. The Hypertext Markup Language (HTML) is the main language used to define how a Web page should look. Features like background color, font, and layout are all specified in HTML. Learning to "speak" HTML is easy. So easy, in fact, that most Web pages are not created by writing HTML directly, but by using Web authoring software; that is, by using programs that write the HTML for us automatically. Learning basic HTML, however, helps you to understand the World Wide Web, gives you experience directing a computer to do your work, and prepares you for studying other Fluency topics. When you are finished, you will speak a new "foreign" language!

This chapter begins by reviewing the concept of tags, which we discussed in Chapter 2, and we introduce the dozen most basic HTML tags from the XHTML dialect. Next comes document structuring, including details such as headings and alignment. After discussing special characters, we create an example of a text-only Web page. We decide that the page should have an image and hyperlinks, so we discuss placing images and links and how to connect them. With this knowledge we improve our sample page. After introducing the basics of lists and tables, we turn to the Cascading Style Sheet concept, an ingenious way to make Web pages attractive.

Marking Up with XHTML

HTML is straightforward: The words on a Web page are embellished by hidden formatting tags that describe how they should look. We use the XHTML dialect, the Extensible Hypertext Markup Language, which is today's WWW standard language. XHTML tags are also HTML tags, but not vice versa; there are some parts of the original HTML—think of it as slang—that are not part of XHTML.

Formatting with Tags

We recall from Chapter 2 that **tags** are words or abbreviations enclosed in angle brackets, < and >, like <title>, and that tags come in pairs, the second with a slash (/), like </title>. It's the same slash used in division. In XHTML, the tags *must* be lower case, making <TITLE>, <Title>, and <tITle> illegal. The tag pair surrounds the text to be formatted like parentheses. So a title, which every XHTML Web page has, is written as

```
<title>Tiger Woods, Masters Champion</title>
```

These two tags can be read as "this is where the title starts" and "this is where the title ends." The two forms of tag are referred to as the **start tag** and the **end tag**, and also as the *open tag* and *close tag*, emphasizing their similarity to parentheses. The title appears on the title bar of the browser (the very top of the window where the Close button is) when the page is displayed.

Say Less. The proper term for / is *slash*; it's used in division, URLs, end tags, and other functions. Its opposite, \, is a *backslash*. The opposite of a backslash is a slash, not a "forward slash."

Tags for Bold and Italic

XHTML has tags for bold text, <b> and </b>; for italic text, <i> and </i>; and for paragraphs, <p> and </p>. You can use more than one kind of formatting at a time, such as bold italic text, by properly "nesting" the tags, as in

```
<p><b><i>Veni, Vidi, Vici!</i></b></p>
```

which produces

Veni, Vidi, Vici!

It doesn't matter whether italic follows bold, or vice versa. You get the same result if you put the italic before the bold:

```
<p><i><b>Veni, Vidi, Vici!</b></i></p>
```

The key is to make sure the tags are nested correctly. All the tags between a starting tag and its ending tag should be matched. So, in the ***Veni, Vidi, Vici!*** example, between the starting paragraph tag <p> and its ending tag </p>, all other starting tags are properly nested with their matching ending tags.

Singleton tags. A few tags are not paired and so do not have a matching ending tag beginning with a /. In those cases, the closing angle bracket > of the **singleton tag** is replaced by />. One example is the *horizontal rule* <hr/> tag, which displays a horizontal line. Another example is the *break*
 tag, which continues the text on the next line and is useful for inserting blank lines within a paragraph. These tags do not surround text, so they don't need to be paired with a closing tag. (It *is* possible to write
</br>, but that's too much typing.)

More formatting tags. Documents can be formatted in many ways, and each requires its own tag, which means XHTML has many tags. But we don't have to memorize them all. Programmers and Web designers remember how to use a few kinds of tags, and then when they need one they do not use often, they just look it up; it's easier than memorizing long lists of little used tags. So, having learned how to use the <i> tag for italics, we can use any formatting tag; see Figure 4.1. Whenever we need to be reminded which tag is used to achieve a specific kind of formatting, we consult a list like www.w3schools.com/tags/default.asp.

Required Tags

Every Web page is composed of a head and a body. That means there are three XHTML tags required for every Web page: The <head> and </head>

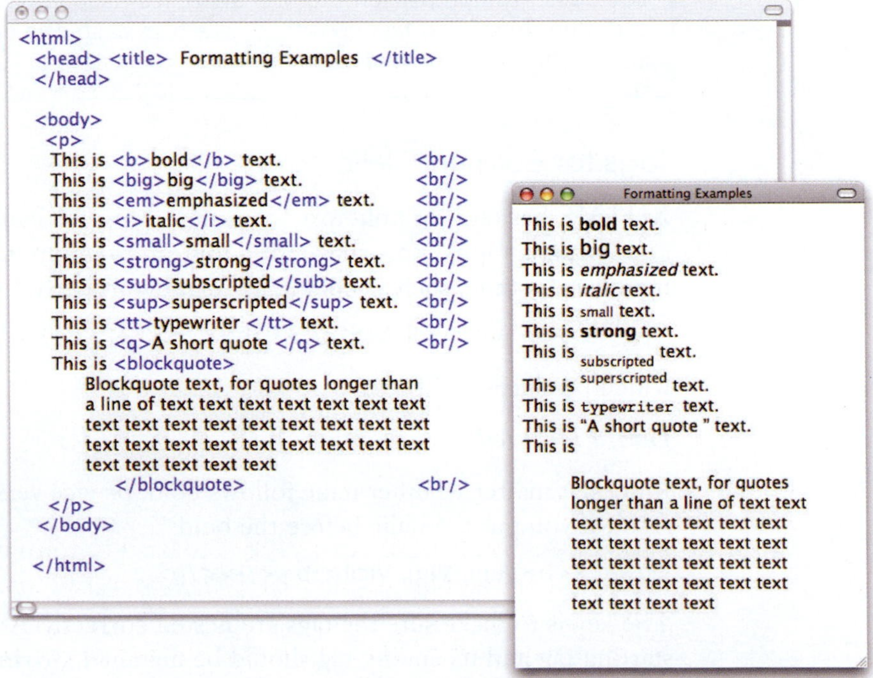

Figure 4.1 XHTML source code for formatting tags and the result (inset).

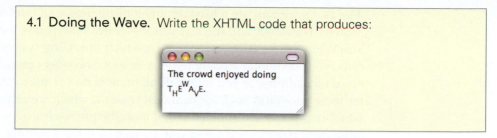

4.1 Doing the Wave. Write the XHTML code that produces:

The crowd enjoyed doing
THEWAVE.

tags to enclose the head, the <body> and </body> tags to enclose the body, and the <html> and </html> tags to enclose those two parts. This standard form is shown in Figure 4.2. The text following the letters html,

xmlns="http://www.w3.org/1999/xhtml"

specifies that the dialect is XHTML, and the part inside of the quotes must be written *exactly* as given. The *head* section, marked by the <head> and </head> tags, contains the beginning material like the title and other information that applies to the whole page; we discuss its other contents later. The body section, marked by <body> and </body>, contains the content of the page. *This form must always be followed, and all of these tags are required.*

```
<html xmlns="http://www.w3.org/1999/xhtml">
    <head>
        Preliminary material goes here
    </head>
    <body>
        The main content of the page goes here
    </body>
</html>
```

Figure 4.2 Standard form for an XHTML Web page.

There's not very much to XHTML. By the end of the next section, you will have produced your first Web page!

Lab Practice I

Fluency is a hands-on study. You have to do it to learn it. That means Fluency has a reading component and a lab component. But to become Fluent you don't need to go to a special lab. Any suitably configured computer will do. So, to help you write XHTML in this and future chapters, we "suitably configure" your computer. That just means to check that two programs are installed, and if not, to install them.

The two programs are a browser and a text editor, and both are free. The browser is Firefox, and the text editor—either Notepad++ for Windows or TextWrangler for Macs—depends on which operating system your computer runs. Your computer already has one or more browsers installed, and one or more text editors, so you might think there is no reason to change. But I prefer these programs both for technical reasons, which we can skip, and educational reasons: They are kinder and more helpful to learners; they guide you away from trouble, and when you manage to make a mistake, they help you get back on track. So we will use them both.

Firefox

Firefox is a free **open source** browser distributed by the Mozilla Foundation. Open source means that the program code is publicly available, and any programmer can contribute improvements to it. (Thousands have.) Firefox is an outstanding browser, and it is the browser referenced throughout this book. Firefox is available at www.mozilla.com/en-US/firefox/all.html. Follow the installation instructions.

Firefox Browser. Firefox is a browser from the Mozilla Project, and it is very popular because of all of its great features. When Firefox 3.0 was released in July 2008, 8,002,530 copies were downloaded in the first 24 hours—a new Guinness World Record for downloads in a day.

Text Editor

As we learned at the end of Chapter 1, a text editor is a more basic way to process text than our familiar WYSIWYG word processors such as Word and WordPerfect. Word processors, as we learned in Chapter 2, include many application-specific tags and other information in their files along with the normal characters that you type. This information confuses browsers, and so must not be part of an XHTML Web page. Because text editors do not include this extra information, they produce the sort of files that browsers like. You *must* use a text editor to write XHTML, because browsers want Web pages written only in ASCII characters. We will discuss ASCII in Chapter 8, but for now think of ASCII as the normal keyboard characters with "nothing strange." Also, when a text editor figures out what language you are writing in, it will color code your XHTML to make it easier to read. Operating systems come with text editors installed. TextEdit can be found on the Mac and Notepad comes with Windows. These are adequate for XHTML coding, but they are very basic. Better choices are available for both operating systems. If you use a Mac, then TextWrangler is your recommended text editor. If you use Windows, then Notepad++ is recommended. Get the appropriate installation at:

TextWrangler:
www.barebones.com/products/TextWrangler/download.html

Notepad++:
notepad-plus.sourceforge.net/uk/site.htm

and follow the installation instructions.

Hello, World

Assuming you have now installed Firefox and your text editor, it is time to write your first XHTML page. When programmers write their first program in a new language, they typically write a program that prints out *Hello, World,* and does nothing else. We will follow that honorable tradition.

To produce your first XHTML page, follow these instructions:

1. In the text editor, open a *New* document instance.
2. Carefully type in the text shown in Figure 4.2, making these replacements:
   - Replace *preliminary material goes here* with a title, say <title>Starter Page</title>
   - Replace *the main content of the page goes here* with the paragraph, <p>Hello, World</p>
3. Save the file as starterPage.html.
4. Open the file with the Firefox browser.

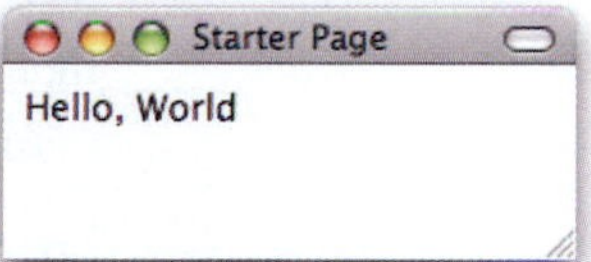

The result is a very simple Web page.

Open with Double-Click

Notice that as we write XHTML, we are working with files like starterPage.html that must be opened in two applications: the text editor, so we can make changes, and the browser, so we can see the changes we made. Obviously, we should be able to double-click on the file name to open it with the default application, but which of the two applications is the default: the editor or the browser? On this matter, the Windows and Mac OS X operating systems take different points of view.

When you double-click in Windows, the OS looks at the file extension, .html, and figures it's a Web page, and opens it by default with the browser. Of course, the default browser should be set to Firefox if you would like to use the double-clicking feature. (This is recommended.) Then to open the file in the text editor application, NotePad++, you must use the *File > Open With...* protocol.

When you double-click in Mac OS X, the OS remembers that the file was created using the TextWrangler text editor application, so it opens the file with that editor. To open the file in Firefox, you will need to use the *File > Open ...* protocol.

This is a nice example of how the two operating systems work slightly differently, but each takes a reasonable point of view. There is no "right" answer, except the one in which the OS *reads your mind*, picking the application you *think* you want when you double-click.

Save This Page

Although your first XHTML page is very simple, it will also be very useful. Because all XHTML files have the same structure as your `starterPage.html` file, you can use it as a template for *all* of your future XHTML coding. This is a timesaving way to get started on your next page.

Set up a new folder, perhaps called `xhtmlFiles`, where you will keep your XHTML files. Place the `starterPage.html` file in the new folder. Then, when you start working on a new XHTML project, make a copy of this file and rename it. Edit the title—your new page will want a better title—and replace the *Hello, World* text with the new content of your page. That way, you are sure that your future pages will always have the correct form.

Structuring Documents

The point of a markup language is to describe how a document's parts fit together. Because those parts are mostly paragraphs, headings, and text styles like italic and bold, the tags of this and the Formatting section are the most common and most useful.

Headings in XHTML

Documents tend to have headings, subheadings, and such, so HTML gives us several levels of *heading* tags to choose from: from level one (the highest) headings, `<h1>` and `</h1>`, to level two, `<h2>` and `</h2>`, all the way to level eight, `<h8>` and `</h8>`. The headings display their content in larger letters on a new line. For example,

```
<h1>Pope</h1> <h2>Cardinal</h2> <h3>Archbishop</h3>
```

appears as

> Pope
>
> Cardinal
>
> Archbishop

As you can see, the headings are bold and get less "strong" (smaller and perhaps less bold) as the level number increases.

XHTML Format Versus Display Format

Notice that although the XHTML text was run together on one line, it was displayed formatted on separate lines. This illustrates an important point: The XHTML source code tells the browser how to produce the formatted page based on the *meanings* of the tags, not on how the source instructions look.

Although the source's form is unimportant, we usually write XHTML in a structured way to make it easier for people to understand. There is no agreed upon form, but the example might have been written with indenting to emphasize the levels:

```
<h1>Pope</h1>
    <h2>Cardinal</h2>
        <h3>Archbishop</h3>
```

White Space

The two XHTML forms produce the same result. Computer experts call spaces that have been inserted for readability **white space**. We create white space with spaces, tabs, and new lines (return or enter). XHTML ignores white space. The browser turns any sequence of white space characters into a single space before it begins processing the XHTML, and then it inserts white space as needed to make the page look the way the XHTML tells it. The only exception is **preformatted** information contained within <pre> and </pre> tags, which is displayed as it appears.

The fact that white space is ignored is important when the browser formats paragraphs. All text within *paragraph* tags, <p> and </p>, is treated as a paragraph, and any sequence of white space characters is converted to a single space. So

```
<p> <b>Xeno's Paradox: </b>
Achilles and a turtle were to run a race. Achilles could
run twice as fast as the turtle. The turtle,
being a slower runner,
got a 10 meter head start, whereupon
Achilles started and ran the 10 meter distance. At that
moment the turtle was 5 meters farther. When Achilles had run
that distance the turtle had gone another 2.5 meters,
and so forth. Paradoxically, the turtle always remained
ahead. </p>
```

appears as

> **Xeno's Paradox:** Achilles and a turtle were to run a race. Achilles could run twice as fast as the turtle. The turtle, being a slower runner, got a 10 meter head start, whereupon Achilles started and ran the 10 meter distance. At that moment the turtle was 5 meters farther. When Achilles had run that distance the turtle had gone another 2.5 meters, and so forth. Paradoxically, the turtle always remained ahead.

The width of a line of text is determined by the width of the browser window. Of course, a narrower or wider browser window makes the lines break in different places, which is why HTML ignores white space and changes the paragraph's formatting to fit the space available. Table 4.1 summarizes the basic XHTML tags.

Table 4.1 Basic Tags for XHTML

Start Tag	End Tag	Meaning	Required
<html xmlns="*fn*">	</html>	XHTML document; first and last tags of XHTML; *fn* = http://www.w3.org/1999/xhtml	✓
<title>	</title>	Title bar text; describes page	✓
<head>	</head>	Preliminary material; e.g., title at start of page	✓
<body>	</body>	The main part of the page	✓
<p>	</p>	Paragraph	
<hr/>		Line (horizontal rule)	
<h1>...<h8>	</h1>...</h8>	Headings, eight levels, use in order	
<b>	</b>	Bold	
<i>	</i>	Italic	
<a href="*fn*">	</a>	Anchor reference, *fn* must be a pathname to an HTML file	
<img src="*fn*"/>		Image source reference, *fn* must be a pathname to **.jpg** or **.gif** file	
 		Break, continue text on a new line	

Brackets in HTML: The Escape Symbol

Notice that there would be a problem if our Web page had to show a math relationship such as *0<p>r*, because the browser might misinterpret *<p>* as a paragraph tag and not display it. So to show angle brackets on the page, we use an **escape symbol**—the ampersand (&)—followed by an abbreviation, followed by a semicolon. For example:

< displays as <

> displays as >

& displays as &

Note that the escape symbol, the ampersand, needs an escape, too! So, our math problem would be solved in XHTML by

<i>0<p>r</i>

Accent Marks in HTML

Letters with accent marks also use the escape symbol. The general form is an ampersand, followed by the letter (and whether it is uppercase or lowercase makes a difference), followed by the name of the accent mark, followed by a semicolon. So, for example, é displays as é, È displays as È, ñ displays as ñ, and Ö displays as Ö. Table 4.2 lists a few useful special characters for some Western European languages.

Table 4.2 Specifying accent marks for Western European language

Symbol	Text	Number	Symbol	Text	Number	Symbol	Text	Number
à	à	à	ê	ê	ê	ô	ô	ô
ä	ä	ä	î	î	î	ù	ù	ù
é	é	é	ó	ó	ó	ã	ã	ã
í	í	í	ø	ø	ø	è	è	è
ò	ò	ò	ü	ü	ü	ì	ì	ì
ö	ö	ö	â	â	â	ñ	ñ	ñ
û	û	û	ç	ç	ç	õ	õ	õ
á	á	á	ë	ë	ë	ú	ú	ú
å	å	å	ï	ï	ï			

Note: For an accent mark on an uppercase letter, make the text following the & uppercase or find the number for the uppercase letter at www.w3schools.com/tags/ref_entities.asp.

Although names like *ntilde* help Spanish speakers and others remember the escape, each special symbol can be specified by a number. Write # followed by its Unicode number; we discuss Unicode in Chapter 8. For example, `ñ` and `ñ` are equivalent. Where do you find the number? You can find a complete list at www.w3schools.com/tags/ref_entities.asp.

Although we have introduced only a few XHTML tags so far, we can already create Web pages, as shown in Figure 4.3.

Study the XHTML and notice the following points:

- The title is shown on the title bar of the browser window.
- The statement of Russell's Paradox is in bold.
- The XHTML source paragraphs are indented more than the <h2> heading lines to make them more readable.
- The line between the two paragraphs crosses the width of the browser window.
- An acute accent is used in Magritte's first name.
- The French phrase from the painting is in italics.
- The word *picture* is in italics for emphasis.

It's a simple page and it was simple to produce.

4.2 Further Explanation. Write the XHTML to produce the following text: These vowels are wearing chapeaux: â ê î ô û

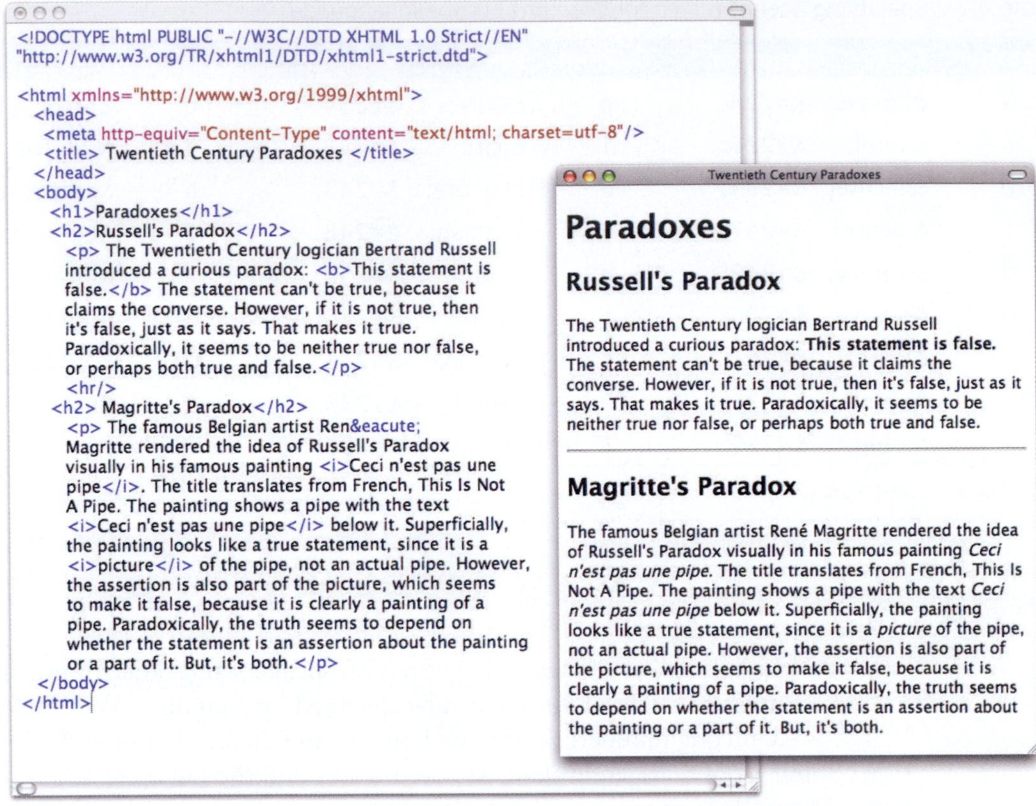

Figure 4.3 The XHTML for a simple page and the result (inset).

Lab Practice II

Programmers develop habits that help them produce correct, error-free programs easily; Web developers do the same. Our starterPage.html, a template that we've saved containing all of the *required* tags for a Web page, is an example. It saves us from having to type them fresh every time, and so helps avoid mistakes. In this section we discuss two more "tricks of the trade" that will make learning XHTML easier.

Compose and Check

Most often Web pages are created all at once—both content and form. It can be complicated because we must concentrate on two things at once: what it says *and* what it looks like. As a result, it is smart to check your typing and your tagging very often, perhaps after writing only a few tags. The reason is simple. Assume a page is okay up to a given point, and then after adding a few more tags it is wrong. It must be that the last tags added are the place to find the error. This approach greatly limits the search for errors.

A productive way to work while using the write-then-check process is to keep two windows open: your text editor and your browser. Both of them are processing the same file. After writing a few XHTML formatting tags in the editor, *Save* your file. Then check the result in the browser by a *Reload* of the source. The reload will display the updated (newly saved) page. After seeing the result, return to the editor, make a few more changes, and then repeat the *Save*, followed by the *Reload* of the browser. With this method development can proceed very fast.

Markup Validation Service

Another way to limit the mistakes you make and ensure that your Web page "works" for all Web surfers is to have it automatically *validated*. This is a service that checks to make sure your XHTML is perfectly correct. If it is wrong, the service even tells where the mistakes are and what's not proper.

Add extra information. To benefit from the automatic checking service, it is necessary to add three more lines to the starterPage.html. These are not required for the file to be a proper XHTML page, but they are needed by the checking service. Since they can always be there even when you do not need to check the file, you should insert them into your starterPage.html.

As the first two lines in starterPage.html, that is, *before* the <html ...> tag, add the lines

```
<!DOCTYPE html PUBLIC "-//W3C//DTD XHTML 1.0 Strict//EN"
"http://www.w3.org/TR/xhtml1/DTD/xhtml1-strict.dtd">
```

The cryptic text on these two lines must be typed *exactly* as given. And because many programmers and Web developers probably don't know what they mean—they just use them—we'll also treat them as a mystery. The other line that we need to add is

```
<meta http-equiv="Content-Type" content="text/html; charset=utf-8"/>
```

and it goes between the <head> tag and the <title> tag in the starterPage.html. The meaning of this line is easier to explain: It specifies that the character encoding for the Web page will be **UTF-8**, or Unicode Translation Format for bytes. In Chapter 8 we will discuss how the keyboard characters you type get represented as bytes, and this clever Unicode representation will be explained. The important point now is that the representation is *universal* and so will work all over the world.

Check my work. With the three lines added, we are ready to use the validation service. Normally, we don't validate tags until the XHTML file is stable. That is, if we use compose and check, we do not validate with each "check" (though it's okay to do so), but rather wait until we get to a "stopping place." To validate a file, go to the W3C Markup Validation Service at validator.w3.org/#validate_by_upload. The page that displays is shown in Figure 4.4. Simply browse for your XHTML file and then click **Check**.

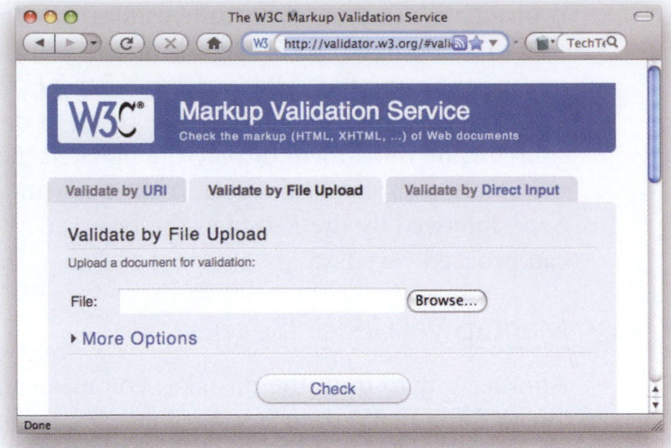

Figure 4.4 The W3C Markup Validation Service page; browse for your XHTML file and then click **Check**.

What comes back is either a green banner telling you the XHTML checks out, or a red banner and a list of errors together with an explanation of what's wrong. Don't panic if you get many errors. It's very common to get a lot of errors at the start, because we all make small mistakes. And very often one mistaken character can lead to many, many error messages.

Special Character Simplification. One benefit of including the **meta** tag with the **charset=utf-8** specification is that special characters like those shown in Table 4.2 can be typed directly into the XHTML file. Not all symbols are available in this form, which is why we learned the **&#***number*; technique, but when they are, it's handy.

Marking Links with Anchor Tags

The example shown in Figure 4.3 may be an interesting Web page, but it doesn't use hypertext at all. It would be more informative, perhaps, if it linked to biographies of Russell and Magritte. Also, it would be easier to understand if it showed Magritte's painting or linked to it.

Two Sides of a Link

In this section we discuss how to make **hyperlinks**. As you know, when a user clicks on a hyperlink, the browser loads a new Web page. This means there must be two parts to a hyperlink: the text in the current document, which is highlighted, called the **anchor text**, and the address of the other Web page, called the **hyperlink reference**.

Both parts of the hyperlink are specified in the **anchor tag**, which is constructed as follows.

- *Begin with* <a *and make sure there's a space after the* a *but not before it. The* a *is for anchor.*
- *Give the hyperlink reference using the* href *attribute* href="*filename*", *making sure to include the double quotes.*
- *Close the anchor tag with the* > *symbol.*
- *Specify the anchor text, which will be highlighted when it is displayed by the browser.*
- *End the hyperlink with the* </a> *tag.*

For example, suppose http://www.bioz.com/bios/sci/russell.html is the URL for a Web biography of Bertrand Russell; we would anchor it to his last name on our Web page with the anchor tag

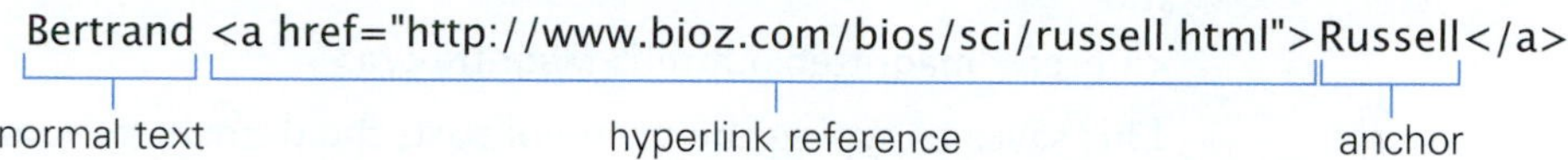

This hyperlink would be displayed with Russell's last name highlighted as

Bertrand Russell

When the browser displays the page and the user clicks on Russell, the browser downloads the biographical page given in the href. As another example, if Magritte's biography is at the same site, the text

```
<a href="http://www.bioz.com/bios/art/magritte.html">Magritte</a>
```

would give the reference and anchor for his hyperlink.

Absolute Pathnames (URLs)

In these anchor tag examples, the hyperlink reference is an entire URL because the Web browser needs to know how to find the page. Remember from Chapter 3 that the URL is made from a protocol specification, http://, a domain or IP address, www.bioz.com, and a path to the file, /bios/sci/russell .html. The files are two levels down in the directory (folder) hierarchy of the site.

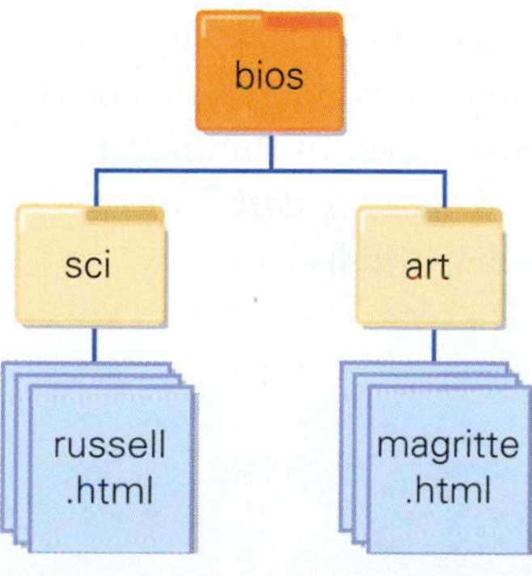

From the Russell and Magritte examples, we guess that at the Bioz Company site, the biographies have been grouped together in a top-level folder (see Chapter 3) called bios. Probably the scientists, like Russell, are grouped together in a subfolder called sci, and the artists are grouped together in a subfolder called art. Within these folders are the individual biography files: russell.html and magritte.html. The slash (/) separates levels in the directory hierarchy, and "crossing a slash" moves us lower in the hierarchy into a subfolder. Such complete URLs are called **absolute pathnames**; they are the right way to reference pages at *other* Web sites.

Relative Pathnames

Often links refer to other Web pages on the same site. Because these pages will all be stored in the same or nearby folders, their anchor tags use relative pathnames. A relative pathname describes how to find the referenced file *relative* to the file in which the anchor tag appears. So, for example, if the anchor tag is in an HTML file that is in folder *x*, and the anchor references another file also in folder *x*, only the name of the file is given, not its whole absolute path.

Suppose that we have written our own biographies for Russell and Magritte for our paradoxes.html page. If the files are named russellbio.html and magrittebio.html, and they are in the same folder as paradoxes.html, the anchor tags of the Paradoxes page can use relative references:

```
<a href="russellbio.html">Russell</a>
```

and

```
<a href="magrittebio.html">Magritte</a>
```

This saves us typing the protocol part, the domain part, and the path to the folder part, but that's not why we like relative pathnames. Relative pathnames are more flexible because they let us move Web files around as a group without having to change the references. This flexibility is important as you begin to manage your own Web page.

Going "deeper" in a folder. Relative pathnames are very simple when the file containing the anchor and the referenced file are in the same folder—we just give the file name. When the referenced file is "deeper" in the directory hierarchy, perhaps in a folder or in a folder inside another folder, we simply give the path from the current folder down to the file. For example, in the folder containing paradoxes.html we create a subfolder, biographies, which contains the two profiles. Then the anchor for the Russell bio becomes

```
<a href="biographies/russellbio.html">Russell</a>
```

because we must say how to navigate to the file from the location of the Paradoxes page. Of course, using relative pathnames means that the files for the pages must be kept together in a fixed structure, but that's the easiest solution anyway.

Going "higher" in a hierarchy. The only problem left is how to refer to folders higher up in the hierarchy. The technique for doing so, which comes from the UNIX operating system, is to refer to the next outer level of the hierarchy—that is, the containing folder—as ../ (pronounced "*dot dot slash*," of course). So if we imagine that the directory structure has the form

```
mypages
    biographies
        russellbio.html
        magrittebio.html
    coolstuff
        paradoxes.html
```

then, in paradoxes.html, the Russell biography anchor would be

```
<a href="../biographies/russellbio.html">Russell</a>
```

because the biography can't be reached by going down from the folder (coolstuff) containing paradoxes.html. Instead, we have to go up out of coolstuff to the next higher level, mypages. From there, we can navigate down to the bios through the biographies folder. We can use a sequence of dots and slashes (../../), so that each pair of dots moves the reference up one level higher in the hierarchy. For example, another page with the reference

```
<a href="../../humorpages/dumbjokes/knockknock4.html">
```

moves up to the folder containing the folder containing the page, then down through the humorpages and dumbjokes folders to the actual knockknock4 Web page.

Summarizing, hyperlinks are specified using anchor tags. The path to the file is given as the value of href in the anchor tag, and the text to be highlighted (the anchor) is given between the anchor tag and its end tag </a>. Paths can be absolute paths—that is, standard URLs—for offsite pages. Relative pathnames should be used for all onsite pages. The relative path can be just a name if the referenced file is in the same folder as the page that links to it; it can specify a path deeper, through descendant folders; or it can use the ../ notation to move higher in the directory structure. These path rules apply to images as well as hyperlinks.

fluencyBIT

Spam Buster. Analogous to <a href ...>, HTML has <mailto: ...> to link to an emailer, so users can easily reply to Web content. Although originally popular, it's not now used because crawlers look for this tag when harvesting email addresses for spam. They also look for at signs (@) and dots (.), too. To include your email address on your Web page, make a .gif of your address. It's not as convenient as mailto, but it's safer.

Including Pictures with Image Tags

Pictures are worth a thousand words, as the saying goes, so we include them in Web documents to enhance the pages. To link to a picture, that is, to enable the reader to click on a link to see a picture, we use the anchor tags as just explained. To display the picture, that is, to show it on the page, we use an image tag.

Structure of the Image Tag

An **image tag**, which is analogous to an anchor tag, specifies a file containing an image. The image tag format is

```
<img src="filename" alt="description"/>
```

where src is the abbreviation for "source" and the *filename* uses the same rules for absolute and relative pathnames as anchor tags discussed earlier. The alt value specifies an alternative form for the image, usually a textual description. It was introduced to assist persons who are partially sighted or visually impaired in some other way. For example, screen readers, which speak Web pages to blind people, don't know what the image is of, but they can say the description of the alt tag. XHTML requires alt tags, and they are good for all of us, because when an image is not available or is slow to load, browsers can display the alt information.

So, for example, if the image of Magritte's painting is stored in a file pipe.jpg, in the same folder as the Paradoxes page, we can include the image with a relative pathname

```
<img src="pipe.jpg" alt="Magritte's pipe painting"/>
```

which finds the image and places it in the document.

GIF and JPG Images

Images can come in several formats, but two of them are most important for Web pages: **GIF** (preferred pronunciation is *jif*) and **JPEG** (pronounced *JAY· peg*). GIFs (Graphics Interchange Format) are best suited for cartoons and simple drawings. **PNG** (Portable Network Graphics format) is a newer form of GIF and is also handy. JPEGs, named for the Joint Photographic Experts Group, are appropriate for high-resolution photographs and complex artwork. To tell the browser which format the image is in, the file name should have the extension .gif, .png, .jpg, or .jpeg.

Making a GIF link. We do not have to use text as the anchor. Instead, we can use an image as the anchor by combining an anchor tag with an image tag. Imagine that we have a small GIF, say this small red square, ■, called red.gif. Then we can use it as a button to link to a document, say, history_red_square.html, simply by placing the image where the anchor text would normally go:

```
<a href="history_red_square.html"><img src="red.gif" alt="Red Box"></a>
```

When the page displays, the usual highlighting that links receive will be used to mark the .gif as a link. Suppose the highlight is blue decoration. Then the box ■ has a blue frame around it, and clicking on it will load the history_red_square.html page.

fluencyALERT

Misquotes. Quotation marks are the cause of many HTML errors. Of course, quotes must match, and it is easy to forget one of the pair. But there are also different kinds of quotes: Simple quotes (" and ') are the kind HTML likes; the fancy, curved quotes, called "smart quotes" (“ ” and ‘ ’) are the kind HTML doesn't like. Check *carefully* for messed-up quotes if your HTML produces an incorrect result. Notice that your text editor should never give you smart quotes.

Attributes

So far in this chapter we have learned several tags and created two Web pages. There is only one other aspect of writing HTML to learn: attributes. **Attributes** are an additional specification that is included inside a tag. We have already seen attributes in some of the tags we have studied:

```
<a href="biographies/russellbio.html">Russell</a>
<img src="pipe.jpg" alt="Magritte's pipe painting"/>
```

The abbreviations href, src, and alt are attributes. All attributes have the form

name="*value*"

where the *name*, such as href, is the attribute, and the text in quotes, such as, biographies/russellbio.html, is the *value*. The key thing to remember is that values are *always* enclosed in quotes. Of course, the proper value for an attribute depends on what the attribute is used for. The full list of attributes is at www.w3.org/TR/html4/index/attributes.html.

The Style Attribute

Without doubt, the style attribute is the most useful attribute, because it can be used to control a huge list of properties for every feature of a Web page. **Properties** are characteristics of page components, such as color or size or position. Like other attributes, style is placed inside the tags whose contents you want to modify, and like other attributes, the value gives the change that you want to make. But because we are specifying two things—the property name *and* its specification—the value of the style has a standard form:

style = "*property_name* : *specification*"

The colon (:) separates the property name, which always appears first, from its specification. So, for example, to set the background color of a Web page to, say, black, we give the style information in the <body> tag as

```
<body style="background-color : black">
```

Similarly, we can choose a color for the text, another property of the body of the page, to be, say, green. The result

```
<body style="background-color : black; color : green">
```

sets the two properties of the page. Notice that when more than one property is set with style, the name/specification pairs are separated by a semicolon (;). Table 4.3 gives the names for the sixteen basic colors; a full list is given at www.w3schools.com/css/css_colornames.asp.

Table 4.3 Original HTML Colors

black	silver	white	gray
red	fuchsia	maroon	purple
blue	navy	aqua	teal
lime	green	yellow	olive

As another example, we can set the alignment of a heading, its typeface, and the color of its text using the style attribute

```
<h1 style="text-align : center; color : yellow; font-family : arial">
```

The heading will then be centered in the center of the page, colored yellow, and be displayed in arial font. We will have much more to say about style later. There is a huge number of style properties, making it wise to bookmark a reference list. Though the official list is at www.w3.org/TR/CSS2/propidx.html, you can probably find other lists, such as www.pageresource.com/dhtml/cssprops.htm, that are somewhat more helpful.

Attributes for Image Tags

Besides style, most tags have a set of other attributes that are set directly. For example, the attributes width and height of the image tag can be used to specify how large the image should be. So, we write

```
<img src="puffer.jpg" width="200" height="200" alt="origami puffer fish"/>
```

to specify that the photo puffer.jpg is to be 200 × 200 pixels. The browser will follow that requirement, even if the actual size of the photo is 2000 × 2000.

Normally, we want browsers to shrink images, because expanding them much above their natural size produces unsatisfactory results, as we explain in Chapter 11. When shrinking a photo, it is best to specify only the width or the height, whichever is more constrained. This is because to meet your specification the browser will shrink *that* dimension of the image by some factor *f* from its natural size. (Recall the discussion of factor of change in Chapter 1.) In the 2000 down to 200 example, $f=10$. Then, the browser can use the same factor *f* to shrink the other dimension, thereby producing the same picture, just smaller, that is, the image is not distorted. Specifying, both width and height is fine *if* they change the natural size of the image by the same factor *f*. If they do not, the browser stretches or shrinks the image to fit into the space specified. The results can be curious. The images produced from a square photo using

```
<img src="puffer.jpg" width="200" height="200" ... />
<img src="puffer.jpg" width="200" height="100" ... />
<img src="puffer.jpg" width="100" height="200" ... />
```

are shown in Figure 4.5.

Image Size. Determine the size of an image with the Windows OS by hovering over its icon; with Mac OS X, select the image in the Finder and *Get Info*. In other applications width and height are often specified, for example, as 500 × 400, but since the numbers are not labeled, it may not be obvious which is which. As a rule, width will be given first.

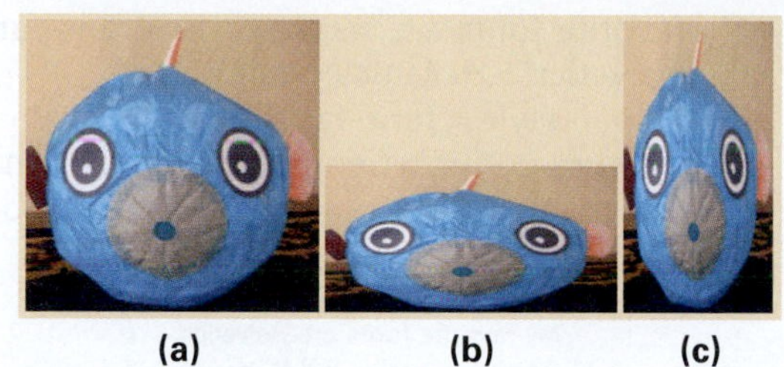

Figure 4.5 The effect of changing **width** and **height** attributes on a square image: (a) 200 × 200, (b) 200 × 100, (c) 100 × 200.

Styling position for images. Where does the image go on the Web page? To understand how images are placed, notice that text is laid out in the browser window from *left to right*, and from *top to bottom*, the same way English is written. The rule is: *Images are inserted in the page at the point in the text where the tag is specified in the XHTML, and the text lines up with the* bottom *of the image.* If the image is the same size or smaller than the letters, it is placed in line just like a letter. This is convenient for icons or smilies. If the image is larger than the letters, it appears in the text, following the rule, but the line spacing is increased to separate it from the neighboring lines.

A common and visually pleasing way to place images in text is to flow the text around them, either by positioning the image on the left with the text to its right, or vice versa. To make the text flow around the image, we use the `style` attribute in the image tag with the value `"float:left"` (shown here) or `"float:right"`. This forces the image to the left or right of the browser window. The text will continue from left to right, and from top to bottom, in the remaining space, flowing around the image.

Finally, to display an image by itself without any text around it, simply enclose the image tag within paragraph tags. That will separate it from the paragraphs above and below. Styling the paragraph to center the image

is accomplished by centering the text using the `text-align` property of the paragraph,

```
<p style="text-align : center"><img src = ... /></p>
```

even though the only "text" is simply the image.

Span. We have specified styles using the `style` attribute inside a tag, but what can we do when there is no tag handy? The answer is the `<span>` tag. Its only job is to surround text, giving a location to place styling and other attribute information. So, for example, we can write

```
My favorite fonts are <span style="font-family :
    helvetica">Helvetica</span>,
    <span style="font-family :
    century gothic">Century Gothic</span>, and
    <span style="font-family : bodoni">Bodoni</span>.
```

to get

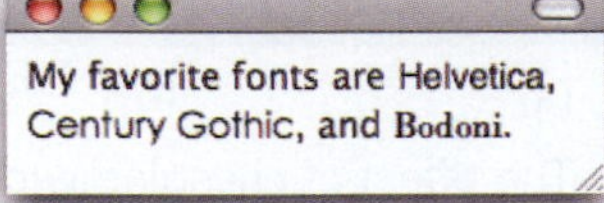

Usually there is an appropriate tag for style information, but when there isn't, <span> is available.

Applying Styling Improves the Page

With the information we have learned in the previous sections, it is possible to enhance the Paradoxes Web page shown in Figure 4.3. The result is shown in Figure 4.6. Notice the following features:

- Links with local pathnames to our own biographical profiles of Russell and Magritte.
- Special background and text colors.
- Color change of the "This sentence is false" text.
- New color styling for the headings.
- The horizontal line has been shortened to 75 percent of the window width using styling.
- The added image floating to the right of the page, and text flowing around it.

Though it is still "simple" by present-day standards of the Web, the page is much more attractive, and more informative, with a few simple styling commands and the use of attributes, such as width and height on the image. The latter was necessary because the image's natural size was three times larger in both dimensions.

Lists and Tables

Lists and tables are common features in XHTML Web pages. Often, they aren't visible to users as tables, because Web designers use them to organize information. Why this should be so will become clear in a moment. First, let's look at the basics of a list.

Lists Tags

There are many kinds of lists in HTML, the easiest being an unnumbered list. The unnumbered list tags <ul> and </ul> surround the items of the list, which are themselves enclosed in list item tags, <li> and </li>. The browser formats the list with each item bulleted, indented, and starting on its own line.

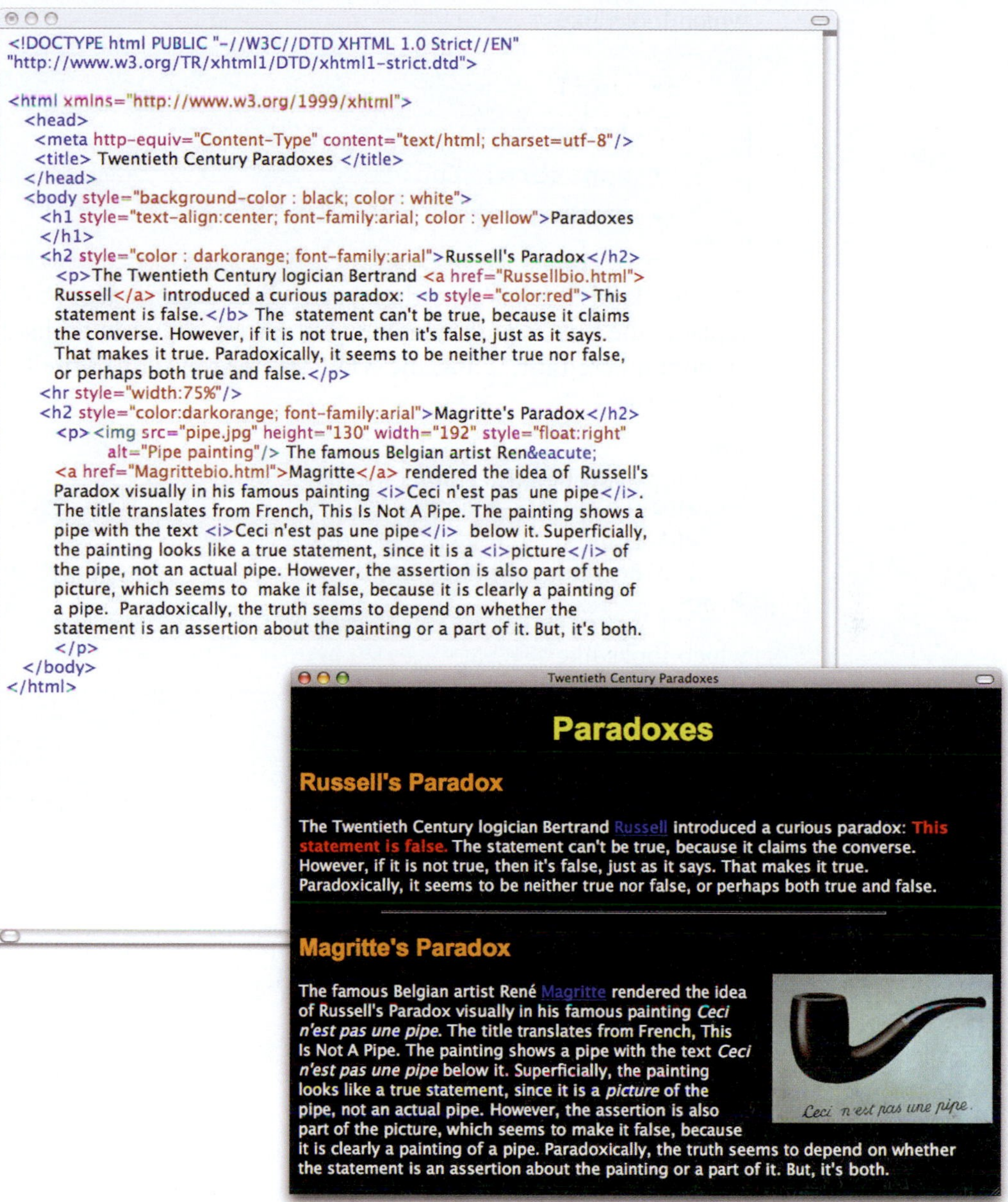

```
<!DOCTYPE html PUBLIC "-//W3C//DTD XHTML 1.0 Strict//EN"
"http://www.w3.org/TR/xhtml1/DTD/xhtml1-strict.dtd">

<html xmlns="http://www.w3.org/1999/xhtml">
  <head>
   <meta http-equiv="Content-Type" content="text/html; charset=utf-8"/>
   <title> Twentieth Century Paradoxes </title>
  </head>
  <body style="background-color : black; color : white">
    <h1 style="text-align:center; font-family:arial; color : yellow">Paradoxes
    </h1>
    <h2 style="color : darkorange; font-family:arial">Russell's Paradox</h2>
      <p>The Twentieth Century logician Bertrand <a href="Russellbio.html">
      Russell</a> introduced a curious paradox:  <b style="color:red">This
      statement is false.</b> The  statement can't be true, because it claims
      the converse. However, if it is not true, then it's false, just as it says.
      That makes it true. Paradoxically, it seems to be neither true nor false,
      or perhaps both true and false.</p>
    <hr style="width:75%"/>
    <h2 style="color:darkorange; font-family:arial">Magritte's Paradox</h2>
      <p><img src="pipe.jpg" height="130" width="192" style="float:right"
            alt="Pipe painting"/> The famous Belgian artist Ren&eacute;
      <a href="Magrittebio.html">Magritte</a> rendered the idea of  Russell's
      Paradox visually in his famous painting <i>Ceci n'est pas  une pipe</i>.
      The title translates from French, This Is Not A Pipe. The painting shows a
      pipe with the text <i>Ceci n'est pas une pipe</i>  below it. Superficially,
      the painting looks like a true statement, since it is a <i>picture</i> of
      the pipe, not an actual pipe. However, the assertion is also part of the
      picture, which seems to  make it false, because it is clearly a painting of
      a pipe.  Paradoxically, the truth seems to depend on whether the
      statement is an assertion about the painting or a part of it. But, it's both.
      </p>
  </body>
</html>
```


Figure 4.6 The Paradoxes Page: the source file and the result (inset).

As usual, though the form of the HTML doesn't matter to the browser, we write the XHTML list instructions in list form. So, for example, the XHTML for a movie list is

```
<ul>
    <li>Luxo Jr.</li>
    <li>Toy Story</li>
    <li style="font-family:courier">Monsters, Inc.</li>
    <li>WALL&#8226;E</li>
</ul>
```

which looks like

- Luxo Jr.
- Toy Story
- **`Monsters, Inc.`**
- WALL•E

Another kind of list is an ordered list, which uses the tags <ol> and </ol> and replaces the bullets with numbers. Otherwise, the ordered list behaves just like an unnumbered list. Thus, the XHTML for the start of the list of chemical elements is

```
<ol>
    <li> Hydrogen, H, 1.008, 1 </li>
    <li> Helium, He, 4.003, 2 </li>
    <li> Lithium, Li, 6.941, 2 1 </li>
    <li> Beryllium, Be, 9.012, 2 2 </li>
</ol>
```

which looks like

1. Hydrogen, H, 1.008, 1
2. Helium, He, 4.003, 2
3. Lithium, Li, 6.941, 2 1
4. Beryllium, Be, 9.012, 2 2

We can also have a list within a list, simply by making the sublists items of the main list. Applying this idea in XHTML

```
<ul>
    <li>Pear</li>
    <li>Apple</li>
        <ul>
        <li>Granny Smith</li>
        <li>Fuji</li>
        </ul>
    <li>Cherry</li>
</ul>
```

looks like

- Pear
- Apple
    - Granny Smith
    - Fuji
- Cherry

Finally, there is a handy list form called the **definitional list**, indicated by the tags <dl> and </dl>. A definitional list is usually made up of a sequence of definitional terms, surrounded by the tags <dt> and </dt>, and definitional data, surrounded by the tags <dd> and </dd>. So, for example, a definitional list is expressed in XHTML as

```
<dl>
    <dt> Man </dt>
    <dd>  <i>Homo sapiens</i>, the greatest achievement
          of evolution. </dd>
    <dt> Woman </dt>
    <dd>  <i>Homo sapiens</i>, a greater achievement of
          evolution, and clever enough not to mention it to man.
    </dd>
</dl>
```

and would be formatted by browsers as

> Man
>
> *Homo sapiens*, the greatest achievement of evolution.
>
> Woman
>
> *Homo sapiens*, a greater achievement of evolution, and clever enough not to mention it to man.

Of course, other formatting commands such as italics and bold can be used within any line items.

Handling Tables

A table is a good way to present certain types of information. Creating a table in HTML is straightforward. It is like defining a list of lists, where each of the main list items, called *rows*, has one or more items, called *cells*. The browser aligns cells to form columns.

The table is enclosed in table tags, <table> and </table>. If you want the table to have a border around it, use the attribute border inside the table tag. Each row is enclosed in table row tags, <tr> and </tr>. The cells of each row are surrounded by table data tags, <td> and </td>. So a table with two rows, each with three cells of the form

Canada	Ottawa	English/French
Iceland	Reykjavik	Icelandic

is defined by

```
<table border="1">
    <tr>
        <td>Canada</td>
        <td>Ottawa</td>
```

```
        <td>English/French</td>
    </tr>
    <tr>
        <td>Iceland</td>
        <td>Reykjavik</td>
        <td>Icelandic</td>
    </tr>
</table>
```

You can give tables captions and column headings. The caption tags are <caption> and </caption>. You place them within the table tags around the table's caption. By default, the caption is centered at the top of the table. You place the column headings as the first row of the table. In the heading row, you replace the table data tags with table heading tags, <th> and </th>, which displays the column headings in bold. The table row tags are <tr> and </tr> as usual. Thus, we can change our sample table to give it a caption and column headings:

```
<table border="1">
    <caption>Country Data</caption>
    <tr>
        <th>Country</th>
        <th>Capital</th>
        <th>Language(s)</th>
    </tr>
    <tr>
        <td>Canada</td>
        <td>Ottawa</td>
        <td>English/French</td>
    </tr>
    <tr>
        <td>Iceland</td>
        <td>Reykjavik</td>
        <td>Icelandic</td>
    </tr>
    <tr>
        <td>Norway</td>
        <td>Oslo</td>
        <td>Norwegian</td>
    </tr>
</table>
```

which will look like this:

Country Data

Country	**Capital**	**Language(s)**
Canada	Ottawa	English/French
Iceland	Reykjavik	Icelandic
Norway	Oslo	Norwegian

Notice that the first row uses the <th> tag rather than the <td> tag to specify the column headings.

Cascading Style Sheets (CSS)

We have used the style attribute to make the Paradoxes Web page more attractive. Without much effort we improved the page a lot from its original design, but we aren't yet using the full power of the styling capabilities available to us. **Cascading Style Sheets (CSS)** is the facility that is responsible for much of what is very slick on the Web pages we see everyday as we surf. It is a general styling system for documents that greatly simplifies the task of creating complex page designs. In this section we see how to use CSS.

Making Style Global

In thinking about the Web page in Figure 4.6, we notice that the style information was repeated for both level 2 headings:

```
<h2 style="color:darkorange; font-family:arial">
```

If there were twenty level 2 headings on the page, each of them would repeat this exact information. That wastes typing, of course, but that may only be a minor annoyance. Of greater concern is that if we decide later that we want to change the design—maybe we really want orangered text in Trebuchet font—we must change the specification in every one of the headings. Although this might be simply updated with a *Find/Replace All*, for any complex page, it means making each change manually.

Setting global style. The solution to the problem of repeating style information wherever it is needed is to place it in one global location inside the <head> tags, so that it applies to the whole page. We do this by placing the style information inside a pair of <style> and </style> tags. Yes, style can be used *both* as a tag and as an attribute. For example,

```
<style type="text/css">
    h2 {color : darkorange; font-family : arial}
</style>
```

The <style> tag contains a type attribute specifying the form of the style information; this should always be used *exactly* as shown here.

Within the <style> and </style> tags are specifications for each tag that should have its properties adjusted. The general syntax for these specifications is

```
elem_name { prop_name1 : spec1 ; ... ; prop_nameN : specN}
```

The text between the tag's angle brackets, known as the tag *element*, is given (h2 in the preceding example), and after that, inside curly braces ({ }), is the list of property names/specification pairs, each separated by a semicolon. The meaning is that *all* occurrences of the tag will be styled as specified. In this way a document can be given a consistent look without having to repeat the styling information every time a style tag is used.

As a further example, suppose we want to give our tables a standard form. The specification

```
<style type="text/css">
    table  {outline-style : solid; outline-color : violet}
    th {background-color : purple; font-family : courier}
    td {background-color : fuchsia; font-family : arial;
        color : white; text-align : center}
</style>
```

does that. Several properties are specified for three table elements—together—when we write

```
<tr> <th> col 1 </th>   <th> col 2 </th>   <th> col 3 </th></tr>
<tr> <td> A </td>       <td> B </td>       <td> C </td></tr>
<tr> <td> 1 </td>       <td> 2 </td>       <td> 3 </td></tr>
```

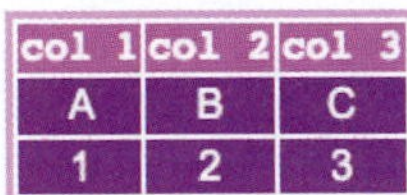

col 1	col 2	col 3
A	B	C
1	2	3

and they produce this.

The formatting is automatically applied. Of course, every table on the page will have this form.

Notice that when the style information is given inside of <style> tags, as shown here, *no* quotations marks are used.

In styling, closest wins. Global specification of style is extremely convenient and efficient, but what if there is an exception? For example, if all tables have the foregoing form, how do we make one of them have a violet cell and maybe change how the entries are aligned? Style the table data tags for that one table where it appears in the XHTML using the style attribute.

So, we might write

```
<tr> <td style="text-align : left">            1 </td>
     <td style="background-color:violet">  2 </td>
     <td style="text-align : right">           3 </td></tr>
```

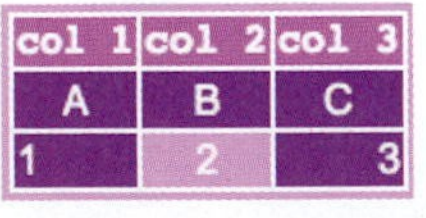

col 1	col 2	col 3
A	B	C
1	2	3

which produces this.

Notice what has happened: Only the background color in the one cell and the two alignments have changed. All of the other properties of the table—the border color, the heading background, the background of the other cells, the font face, and alignment—remain as given in the global specification in the <head>. This is exactly how we want styling information to work: We give the basic styling globally, and then if anything changes at a particular point on the Web page, we change it at that place, and we only say what is different from the default. Everything else applies as normal.

Generally, the rule with styling information is this: *The closest specification wins.* In essence, the specification closer to the site blocks the specification(s) further out. It is a very smart and flexible way to organize a system.

Adding Class to Style

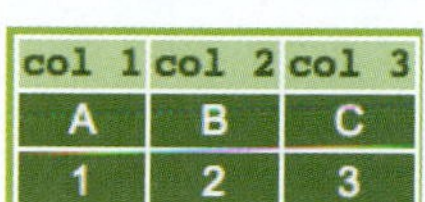

col 1	col 2	col 3
A	B	C
1	2	3

The global specification of style associated with tags gives consistent formatting, but it only simplifies our Web design as long as the tag is used in only one way. For example, suppose we want different colors for tables. How can we add class to our page by using both the preceding "spring pink" table and this summer green table? Add class.

If we want a tag, say the table tag, to be styled in several different ways, we say that we have several different *classes* of styling. A **class** is a family of styling specifications with a common name. The class is given in two places: In the style definition inside the style tags in the <head>, and at the site in the XHTML code of the <body> where we use a table of that class. For some reason, the two places work differently.

For the style definition, we give the tag's class by appending the class name (here, sum) to the tag with a dot, as in

```
<style type="text/css">
    table.sum {outline-style : solid; outline-color : lime}
    th.sum    {background-color : lightgreen; font-family : courier;
               color : darkgreen}
    td.sum    {background-color : green; font-family : arial;
               color : white; text-align:center}
</style>
```

Then, throughout the Web page, the browser knows there is a table of the class sum that has a solid lightgreen border, and table heading and data tags of the same class to go with it. As another example, the earlier spring table in the class spr would use the form table.spr.

In the <body>, when we need a table of class sum, we write

```
<table class="sum"> . . . </table>
```

to use the class attribute to specify which class of style specifications will define the table. Thus, we can write

```
<table class="sum">
    <tr> <th class="sum">col 1</th><th class="sum">col 2</th>
         <th class="sum">col 3</th></tr>
    <tr> <td class="sum"> A </td>  <td class="sum"> B </td>
         <td class="sum"> C </td>  </tr>
    <tr> <td class="sum"> 1 </td>  <td class="sum"> 2 </td>
         <td class="sum"> 3 </td>  </tr>
</table>
```

to create a summer table different from the spring table.

Class definitions are used extensively in CSS because most Web pages have many different parts that need separate styling, but the parts are built using the small set of standard XHTML tags like <table>. Obviously, style benefits greatly from class.

One More Simplification

We originally used the global style specifications of the <head> section as a way to avoid styling every use of a tag. Now, looking at the summer table specification, it seems like we're back to writing extra attributes inside the tag to get the style we want. True, it is only one attribute, class, but it quickly becomes a nuisance. Isn't there a better way? Yes.

Because all of the table data cells are to be treated in the same way in the body of the table, it should be possible to define how we want them to be for the whole table. We could put them inside the table tag specification, but that confuses the table properties with the cell properties. However, there is a table body tag, <tbody>, that encloses the rows and data of a table. It can be used to style the whole table.

Thus, we declare the fall class of the table at the beginning,

```
<style>
   table.fall {  outline-style : solid; outline-color : orangered}
   tbody.fall{  background-color : chocolate; font-family : arial;
                color : white; text-align:center}
   th.fall     {  background-color : darkorange; font-family : courier}
</style>
```

but this time we style the <tbody> tag rather than the <td> tag. This allows the fall table to be specified more simply as

```
<table class="fall">
   <tbody class="fall">
      <tr><th class="fall">col 1</th><th class="fall">col 2 </th>
         <th class="fall">col 3</th></tr>
         <tr><td> A </td><td> B </td> <td> C </td></tr>
      <tr><td> 1 </td><td> 2 </td> <td> 3 </td></tr>
   </tbody>
</table>
```

We still style the heading tags to be customized for each season, and therefore have to specify the class name for them. This is less of a nuisance than specifying the class name for every cell in the table, because the heading occurs only once per column, but it is still more typing than we want.

So, let's use the specify-the-styling-information-over-a-range idea like we used before for <tbody>. This time, notice that the headings are always in their own row, so we style a table row to handle headings. To do so, change

```
th.fall {background-color : darkorange; font-family : courier}
```

to

```
tr.fall {background-color : darkorange; font-family : courier}
```

in the global style specification. Then, at the table site in the XHTML, write

```
<tr class="fall"><th>col 1</th>< >col 2</th><th>col 3</th></tr>
```

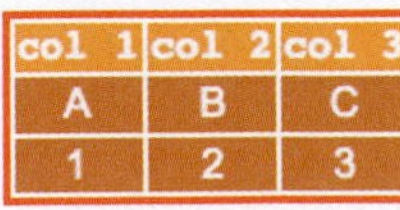

col 1	col 2	col 3
A	B	C
1	2	3

and the result is as intended.

Notice that the <tbody> tag tells how to style all cells in the table, but when we get to the <tr> tag inside, it specifies how to style that one row. It takes precedence over the specification of the <tbody> for two properties. Again, we see that the "closest style wins," but all other properties continue to apply.

Style from Files

The nice part about specifying the style information inside the <style> tags is that it is all in one place, so consistent changes can be made throughout the document very easily by modifying this one site. Reusing one's previous work is a common theme in computing, and we can apply it with CSS. All of the style information that would normally be placed inside the <head> tags can be moved to a file, and then the file name can be given with a <link> tag inside the <head>. In this way many Web pages can use the same styling information. This is how Web sites ensure that the whole site is styled in a consistent way: All pages use the same styling file(s).

Packaging the Basic Style

To illustrate this idea, suppose we have developed the American Writers' Anecdotes (AWA) page in Figure 4.7, and plan to have a series of pages about different American writers all with the same heading and styling information. We have designed a page with compatible colors and customized the links of the author tabs. Before placing the style information in a file, let's see how the links were styled.

Pseudo Classes

Normally, the default is for links to be blue and underlined. To change this, we style the anchor tag, as shown in Figure 4.7 at the end of the style section in the <head>:

```
a:link      {color : darkviolet; text-decoration : none}
a.me:link {color : gray; text-decoration : none}
a:hover    {color:red}
```

These specifications are slightly different from the styling we have used for other tags, because the anchor tag has several different states that can be styled separately. These are referred to as *pseudo classes* and are separated from the element by a colon (:). The three main states are

> link, styling for an unvisited link (anchor text)
> hover, styling when the cursor hovers over a link (see Figure 4.7)
> visited, styling for links that have been visited

In the style specification, the color is set, and text-decoration—that's the underline—is set to none. Also, notice that we have defined a class, me, that is used to "gray out" the link for the current page. Thus, the Thoreau page is classified as me and the link becomes gray.

One more very strange fact: If hover is styled, its style must come *after* link.

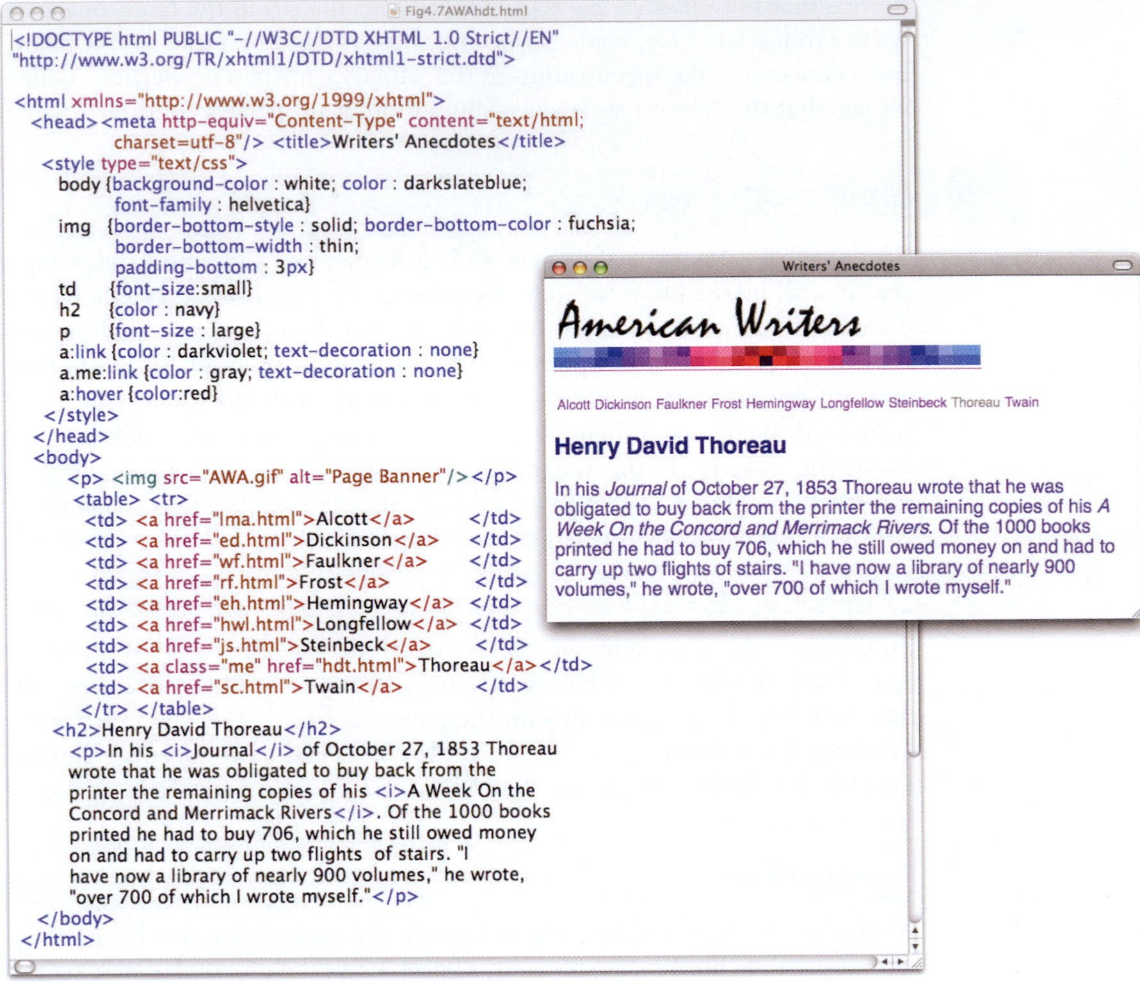

```
<!DOCTYPE html PUBLIC "-//W3C//DTD XHTML 1.0 Strict//EN"
"http://www.w3.org/TR/xhtml1/DTD/xhtml1-strict.dtd">

<html xmlns="http://www.w3.org/1999/xhtml">
  <head><meta http-equiv="Content-Type" content="text/html;
          charset=utf-8"/> <title>Writers' Anecdotes</title>
   <style type="text/css">
     body {background-color : white; color : darkslateblue;
           font-family : helvetica}
     img  {border-bottom-style : solid; border-bottom-color : fuchsia;
           border-bottom-width : thin;
           padding-bottom : 3px}
     td   {font-size:small}
     h2   {color : navy}
     p    {font-size : large}
     a:link {color : darkviolet; text-decoration : none}
     a.me:link {color : gray; text-decoration : none}
     a:hover {color:red}
   </style>
  </head>
  <body>
      <p> <img src="AWA.gif" alt="Page Banner"/></p>
       <table> <tr>
        <td> <a href="lma.html">Alcott</a>        </td>
        <td> <a href="ed.html">Dickinson</a>      </td>
        <td> <a href="wf.html">Faulkner</a>       </td>
        <td> <a href="rf.html">Frost</a>          </td>
        <td> <a href="eh.html">Hemingway</a>      </td>
        <td> <a href="hwl.html">Longfellow</a>    </td>
        <td> <a href="js.html">Steinbeck</a>      </td>
        <td> <a class="me" href="hdt.html">Thoreau</a></td>
        <td> <a href="sc.html">Twain</a>          </td>
       </tr> </table>
    <h2>Henry David Thoreau</h2>
      <p>In his <i>Journal</i> of October 27, 1853 Thoreau
      wrote that he was obligated to buy back from the
      printer the remaining copies of his <i>A Week On the
      Concord and Merrimack Rivers</i>. Of the 1000 books
      printed he had to buy 706, which he still owed money
      on and had to carry up two flights  of stairs. "I
      have now a library of nearly 900 volumes," he wrote,
      "over 700 of which I wrote myself."</p>
  </body>
</html>
```


Figure 4.7 The American Writers' Anecdotes page for Henry David Thoreau: the source and the result (inset).

Moving Style to a File

To use an external file for style information, place it into a file as a sequence of property/specification pairs. That is, place the specifications that are *inside* the `<style>` tags in the file, but don't include the `<style>` and `</style>` tags themselves.

Like XHTML files, the style file should be created with a text editor and should be plain ASCII text. The file extension—the letters that come after the last dot in the file name—should be css. We follow these rules, moving the AWA page's style information into a file that we name AWAstyle.css. It contains the information *between* the <style> and </style> tags.

To incorporate the style information of the file into a page, use the <link> tag:

```
<link rel="stylesheet" type="text/css" href="AWAstyle.css">
```

The attributes of this tag should, by now, be obvious: This link is related to the styling of the documents; the type, normally given in the <style> tag, is given here; and the file is named. After this link has been included in the program, the head section of AWA page is greatly reduced, as shown in Figure 4.8.

Moving the style information out of the way certainly shortens this section of the XHTML; notice that the head section is down to three tags. Of course, it is possible to include more global style information in the head section along with styling information in a file. The global information inside the <head> will take precedence over information in the file.

Cascading the Style Sheets

We have seen that CSS uses the rule "closest style wins." We have already seen several levels of style information, and that each can be "shadowed" by specifications closer to the site where the property applies. In fact, we can

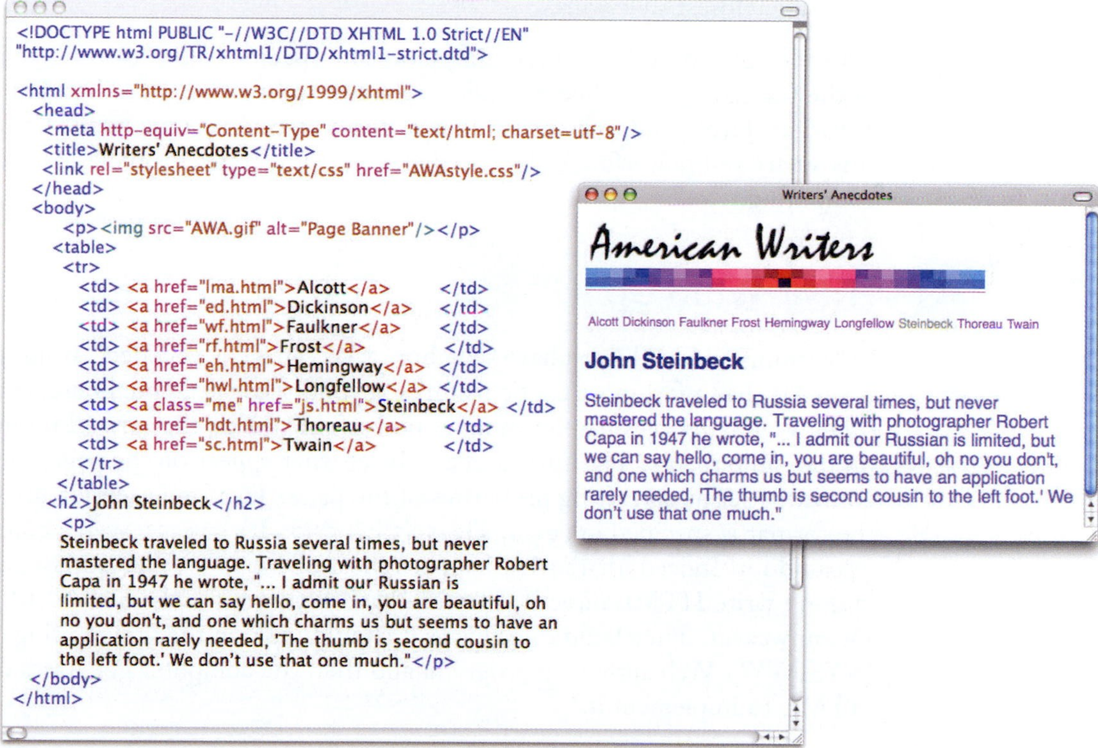

Figure 4.8 The AWA page for Steinbeck showing the <link> in the source code to the external style file AWAstyle.css and the result (inset).

identify five levels of styling information. Starting from the "farthest away," we have

Default, given by browser settings
External, given in a file
Global, given in the <head> section
Range, given in an enclosing tag
Site, given by the style attribute

Each level is broader and more general than the levels below it. Here's how we understand these levels.

At the top, the browser knows how to style the entire document based on the settings that come as a default with the browser, as modified by the user. No further information is needed. These default settings can be selectively replaced by specifications in an external file, which can be replaced by still more specifications in the global style of the head section, which can be specified further by a range and, eventually, by the tag around the information being styled. All of the style information needed at any point in the XHTML code can be found by tracing back for the closest specification. It will be found, because the default contains a specification for every styling option. The rule: closest style wins.

This idea of progressively becoming more site specific is the "cascading" idea of the Cascading Style Sheet. It allows general styling choices to be adopted at various levels, and to be overridden as the situation become better known. It is smart and powerful. And as we shall see, it illustrates many basic ideas of computing.

HTML Wrap-Up

In learning XHTML, you have seen how a Web page is encoded. Although XHTML has a few more exotic features beyond those presented here, and the other Web languages have even more powerful features, they are all variations on the same theme: Tags surround all objects that appear on the page, the context is set by specifying properties of the page's tags, and each feature of the format is specified in detail, <i>isn't it?!</i>. It's so easy, even a computer can do it! Indeed, that's what happens most of the time. Web authors usually don't write HTML directly; they use Web authoring tools, such as Adobe Dreamweaver. They build the page as it should look on the screen using a WYSIWYG Web authoring program, and then the computer generates the HTML to implement it.

Uploading. Pages are created and tested on a personal computer. To be accessed from other computers on the Internet, the HTML files, the image files, and the directory structure created for them must be uploaded (transmitted) to a Web server, a process known as **publishing**.

Summary

You learned that Web pages are stored and transmitted in an encoded form before a browser turns them into images, and that HTML is the most widely used encoding form. (Table 4.4 gives a table of the specifications that we discussed.) The chapter opened by recalling the idea of using tags for formatting and went on to introduce you to:

- A working set of XHTML tags, giving you the ability to create a Web page.
- An explanation of how links are marked with anchor tags.
- Absolute and relative pathnames. Relative pathnames refer to files deeper and higher in the directory hierarchy.
- The two most popular image formatting schemes—GIF and JPEG—and how to place them in a page.
- Lists and tables.
- Cascading Style Sheets, a general system for styling Web documents
- WYSIWYG Web authoring tools—programs that automatically create the XHTML when the page design is complete.

Table 4.4 Official W3C Web sites referenced in this chapter

Tags	www.w3schools.com/tags/default.asp
Special characters like Ö	www.w3schools.com/tags/ref_entities.asp
XHTML validation	validator.w3.org/#validate_by_upload
Attributes	www.w3.org/TR/html4/index/attributes.html
Color names	www.w3schools.com/css/css_colornames.asp
Properties	www.w3.org/TR/CSS2/propidx.html

Try It Solutions

4.1 The crowd enjoyed doing <small>T</small>_H <small>E</small>^W<small>A</small>_V <small>E</small>

4.2 These vowels are wearing chapeaux: â ê î ô û

Review Questions

Multiple Choice

1. HTML commands are called
   a. hops
   b. brackets
   c. tags
   d. tokens
2. HTML tags are words enclosed in
   a. ( )
   b. // \\
   c. { }
   d. < >
3. Which of the following would put "Kelly Clarkson — In Concert" in the title bar of a Web page?
   a. <title> Kelly Clarkson — In Concert</title>
   b. </title> Kelly Clarkson — In Concert<title>
   c. <title> Kelly Clarkson — In Concert<title/>
   d. <TITLE/> Kelly Clarkson — In Concert</TITLE>
4. Which of the following tags is not paired?
   a. <hr/>
   b. <i>
   c. <p>
   d. <html>
5. The <p> </p> tags indicate the beginning and end of a
   a. table
   b. picture
   c. paragraph
   d. preformatted text section
6. The <a...> tag is called an
   a. anchor
   b. address
   c. add
   d. append
7. The attribute specifying a blue background is
   a. bgcolor = #000000
   b. background = "blue"
   c. style = "background-color : blue"
   d. bgcolor = blue
8. The ../ notation in a relative path of hypertext reference means to
   a. open a folder and go down a folder
   b. close a folder and open the parent folder
   c. search a folder
   d. create a folder

9. To place an image on the right side of the window with the text filling the area to the left of the image, your tag would need to look like
   a. `<img src = "mountains.jpg" style="float:right"/>`
   b. `<img src align = "mountains.jpg" "right" />`
   c. `<img = "mountains.jpg" src align = "right" />`
   d. `<img "mountains.jpg" align src ="right" />`
10. The dimensions for an image on a Web page
    a. are set using the x and y attributes
    b. are set using the width and height attributes
    c. must be set to the actual size of the image
    d. are automatically adjusted by the browser to fit in the space allotted

Short Answer

1. Today most Web pages are created using ________.
2. To improve readability of HTML text, the computer experts suggest adding _______ to the source instructions.
3. The _______ tag is a way to get more than one consecutive space in a line of a Web page.
4. _______ tags are tags between other tags.
5. Specifications inside a tag are called ________.
6. _______ are usually used to link to pages on the same site.
7. A ../ in a hypertext reference indicates a(n) _______ path.
8. The src in an image tag stands for ________.
9. GIF stands for ________.
10. JPEG stands for ________.
11. To put the ten greatest inventions of all time, in order, on a Web page, you should use a(n) ________.

Exercises

1. Why learn HTML at all if authoring tools will do the work for you? Give other examples of where you are expected to learn something when there are tools available that will do the work.
2. Use XHTML to properly display the following.

General
Colonel
Major
Captain
Lieutenant
Sergeant

Corporal

Private

3. Explain why a page needs to be reloaded in a browser to see the results of editing changes made in the text editor of an XHTML document.
4. Indicate the hyperlink reference and the anchor text in this anchor tag. Then break down the hyperlink reference into the protocol, domain, path, and file name.

```
<a href="http://www.nasm.si.edu/museum/"> National Air and Space
Museum</a>
```

5. Create a calendar for the current month using a table. Put the name of the month in a caption at the top. Change the color of the text for Sunday and holidays. Make note of any special days during the month. Add an appropriate graphic to one of the blank cells at the end of the calendar.
6. Create a page with links to your favorite friends. Use one column for their names, another for their homepages, and a third column for their email addresses. Link to their homepages.
7. View and then print the source for the author's homepage. It's at

   www.cs.washington.edu/homes/snyder/index.html.

   What is the title of the page? Indicate the heading and the body for the page. Find the table. Find the list. Find the email addresses, and say how they are displayed so they are not found by a crawler. Find the absolute hyperlinks and the relative hyperlinks. How many graphics are on this page?
8. Open a new file in a text editor (Notepad++ for the Windows OS or TextWrangler for a Mac).
   a. Save the file as *YourInitialsWeb1.html*.
   b. Type in the following XHTML text, substituting your name for the items in italics.

```
<html>
   <head>
      <title>Wonderful Web page by Your Name Here</title>
   </head>
   <body>
      <h1>Your Name Here's Wonderful Web Page</h1>
      <p>This is a paragraph. It is surrounded
         by an extra blank line. </p>
      <p style="color:336600">Can you see that this
         line is in color?</p>
      <p style="color:999933">Your Name Here is a terrific
         <b>Web Page</b> designer!"</p>
      <p>This is an assignment for class. The homepage for
         the textbook <br/>
         <a href="http://www.aw-bc.com/snyder/"><i> Fluency
         with Information Technology</i></a> has student
         resources links! </p>
```

```
<p>I think I understand all of these tags! I should
   be able to create more Web pages.<br/>
   How <b>Cool</b> is that?! </p>
</body>
</html>
```

c. Save the file, and then open it with your browser. Notice how the tags changed the look of the page.

9. Open a new file in your text editor. Create your own Web page that has the following:

a. A title that is your name.
b. At least three paragraphs, two of them displayed in different colors (find the color codes in Appendix A).
c. A link to a Web site you like, but not the one site in Exercise 8.
d. At least three levels of headings that are odd numbers (1, 3, 5, 7).
e. A link to the page you made in Exercise 8.
f. At least one image or picture.

Save this file as *YourInitialsWeb2.html.*

10. Make a copy of the Web page you made in Exercise 9. (Yes, make a copy; if you edit the original, you will lose it.) Then make the following additions:

a. Add a paragraph after the first paragraph that contains a list of four of your favorite music groups. Before the list, put in this level 2 heading: *My favorite musical groups*.
b. Add a table at the bottom of the page that has two rows and three columns. In the first row, list three of your favorite restaurants; in the second row, list your favorite food at each of the restaurants in the first row.
c. Set the background color to a pastel color you think is attractive.
d. Add a link to a Web page. For example, you might want to link to your home page on a social networking site if you have one, or a Web site for one the restaurants you listed in (b).

5

chapter

Locating Information on the WWW

Searching for Truth

learning objectives

- Explain the benefits of searching in obvious places and in libraries
- Analyze how Web site information is organized
- Explain how a Web search engine works
- Find information by using a search engine
- Decide whether Web information is truth or fiction

The art of reading between the lines is as old as manipulated information.

—SERGE SCHMEMANN

A WELL-KNOWN JOKE tells of a man out for an evening walk. He meets a drunk who is on his hands and knees under a streetlight. "What are you doing?" asks the man. "Looking for my car key," replies the drunk. "You lost it here?" asks the man in conversation as he begins to help look. "No, I dropped it by the tavern." "Then why are you looking over here?" "The light's better," the drunk replies. The joke lampoons a principle—the best place to look for something is where it's likely to be found—that is key to finding information.

In this chapter we discuss searching for information and evaluating its accuracy. To find anything, we have to look where it's likely to be found. Historically, libraries have housed well-organized archives, collections, and other information resources that are good places to look. Now many of those resources are available online, so we can update the "visit the library" advice: Log in to the library. To find what we're looking for, we must also understand the hierarchical organization of information. Hierarchy speeds searching, and recognizing hierarchies when we see them helps us find information faster. Of course, using a computer to search greatly extends our reach, so we also need to understand how search engines work, how they organize the information they store, and how to interpret search results. If we are going to use search engines effectively, we need to ask the right questions, which is as important as looking in the right place. But finding information and finding truthful, accurate, insightful information are two different things. So we must be aware that deceptive information lurks on the Internet and learn to recognize accurate sources. Finally, we test our understanding by deciding whether information on a Web page is true or false.

Searching in All the Right Places

Ask a reference librarian where to find a *Scientific American*–type article on black holes and the reply will always be "*Scientific American.*" Yet many of us ask questions like that because we don't think about where to look for the information we want. Reference librarians do think about it, and we can learn from them and become better information gatherers. That's important because on the Web we don't have a librarian's help. The key to finding information is to think logically and creatively.

The Obvious and Familiar

If we're going to "look in the right place," we need to know where the information we want can be found. Like *Scientific American*, many sources are obvious and familiar if we think about it:

- To find tax information, ask the federal (IRS) or state tax office.
- To find the direction to Dover from London, look at a map of the United Kingdom.
- To find out how many shares of IBM stock are outstanding, check the company's annual report.

Many of the answers we want to find have an obvious source, so we can simply guess the online address: www.irs.gov, www.mapquest.com, and www.ibm.com, respectively.

Libraries Online

One advantage that research librarians have over most of us is that they know about many more information sources than we do. Their advantage can be our advantage if we use libraries. Libraries remain substantial information resources despite the growth of the Internet. Most college libraries and many large public libraries let you access not only the online catalog of their own collections, but also many other information resources. These libraries are just a "click away."

For example, the University of Washington's Libraries site, www.lib.washington.edu, opens with an inviting page presenting a series of links to online information resources (see Figure 5.1(a)). You can search in the UW catalog or a large number of other collections. In the Find It menu clicking on the Article & Research Databases link, transports you to a new page linking to hundreds of databases (see Figure 5.1(b)). Many of these resources are commercial databases that UW subscribes to, so only UW students and faculty can use them. However, your library probably gives you access to similar collections. Checking these sources is a quick and easy way to find information.

In addition to linking to these huge database resources, UW's librarians have helped us even more. At the bottom of the Articles & Research Databases page (Figure 5.1(b)) is the section "Starting points for research by subject."

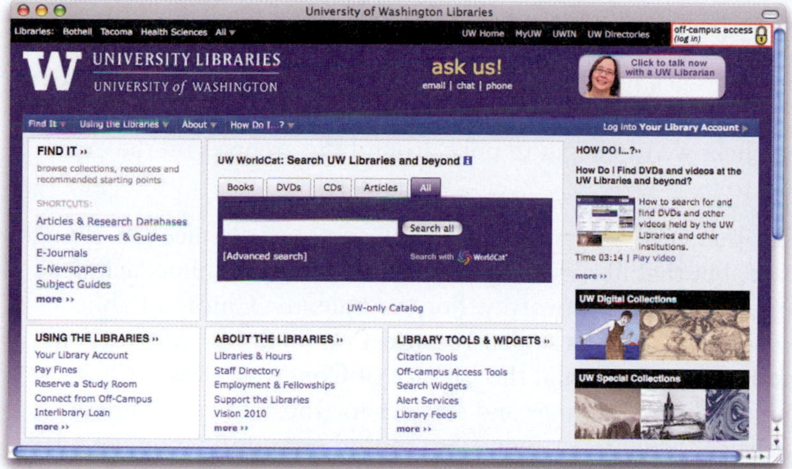

(a)

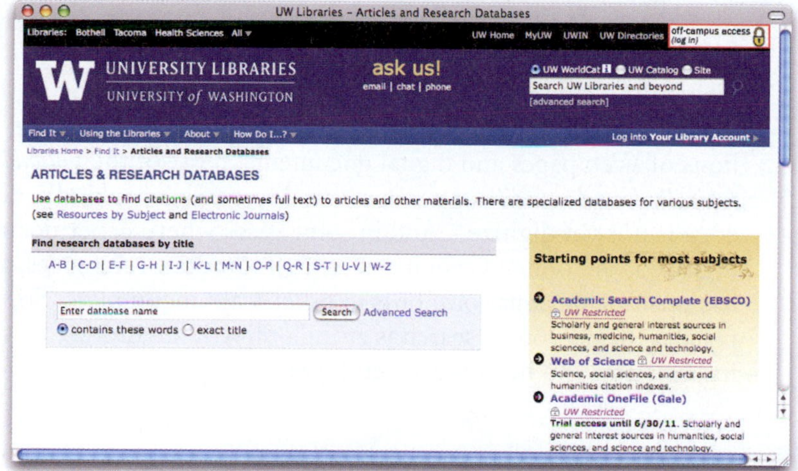

(b)

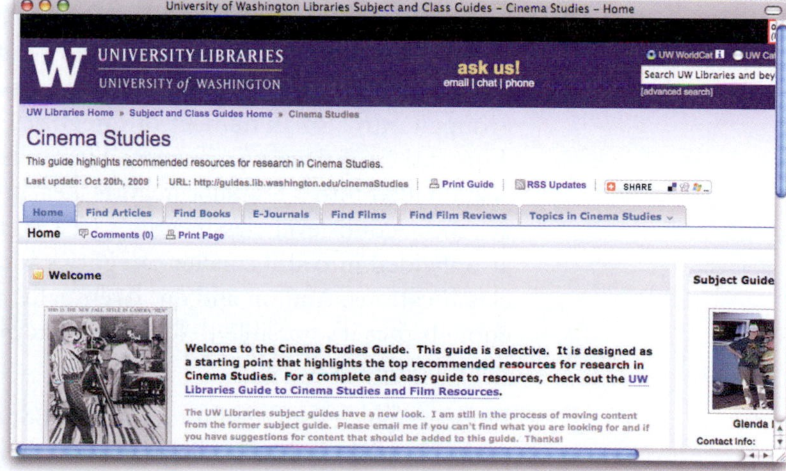

(c)

Figure 5.1 The (a) UW Libraries homepage, (b) Research Databases page, and (c) Cinema Studies page.

These are topic-specific pages that the librarians have set up. They bring together many of the library's resources on specific topics. Clicking on Cinema Studies, we see a page devoted specifically to that topic (see Figure 5.1(c)). And a little down this page is the link for "Cinema Studies e-journals, A–Z." In three clicks we can begin to poke around the archives on the exact topic of interest to us.

The point is not that UW's librarians have done an especially nice job, though I think they have, but that libraries in general provide many online facilities that are well organized and trustworthy. For example, the Chicago Public Library, www.chipublib.org, lists similar resources on its Books, Movies And More > Online Research page, and the Library of Congress, www.loc.gov/library/, has huge online collections and services for Internet users. These resources are free and open to everyone. So, to find out information, go (electronically) to the library.

Pre-Digital Information

The online digital library is not yet a substitute for going to the physical library and checking out traditional paper books and journals. Despite the billions of Web pages and digital documents, most of the *valuable information typically found in a library is not online.* Most of humankind's pre-1985 knowledge is not yet digitized. And in some cases where paper documents have been digitized, the online version is missing footnotes, references, and appendices, has unreadable equations, or is in other ways incomplete. So, while the best place to begin your research is at the online library, don't be surprised if the information you need is not yet digitally available.

How Is Information Organized?

To help us find information, librarians, archivists, Web-page designers, and others who organize collections of information give the collections a structure to make them easier to search. The process is simple: All of the information is grouped into a small number of categories, each of which is easily described. This is the top-level *classification.* Then, the information in each category is also divided into a few subcategories, each with a simple description. These are the second-level classifications (see Figure 5.2). Those subcategories are also divided into still smaller categories with brief descriptions, the third-level classifications. And on and on. Eventually, the classifications become small enough that it's possible to look through the whole category to find the information you need.

For example, a source of information about radio stations in the U.S. that carry National Public Radio might use their *geographical region* as its top-level classification, making the top-level categories:

> Northeast, Mid-Atlantic, Southeast, North Central, South Central, Mountain, Pacific

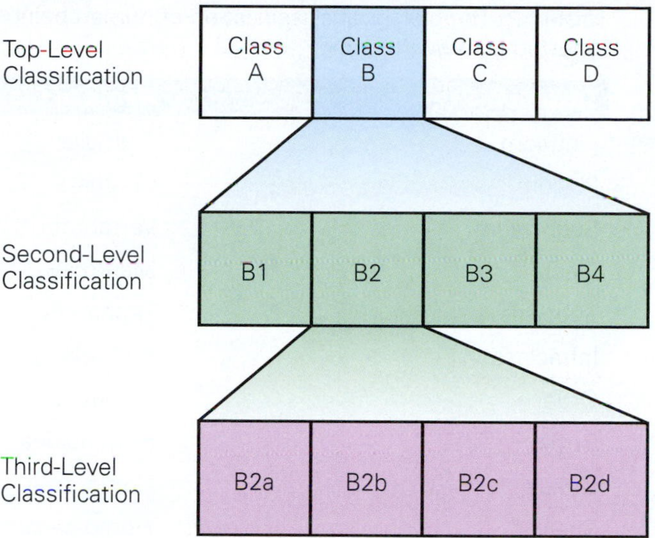

Figure 5.2 Top-level, second-level, and third-level classifications of a collection.

Within each region, the second-level classification might use the state, making the Pacific category's subcategories:

Alaska, California, Hawaii, Oregon, Washington

The third-level categories could be large cities with multiple public radio stations in populous states like California. When the final classification is small enough—Hawaii has only four public radio stations—no finer classification is needed.

There are several important properties of classifications.

- The descriptive terms must cover all of the information in the category and be easy for a searcher to apply. The breakdown of regions by country, state, and city has this property.
- The subcategories do not all have to use the same classification. So, the Pacific category could be categorized by states and the Northeast could be categorized by cities.
- The information in the category defines how best to classify it.

There is no single way to classify information.

This structure is called a *hierarchy*. As with the directory hierarchy we discussed in Chapter 3, it is a natural way to organize information. Remember that hierarchies are often drawn as trees. One very famous hierarchy is the "tree of life," the biological taxonomy of organisms. It is too large to display as a tree, but Table 5.1 shows the layers of classification for human beings, from the top-level (highest) classification—kingdom—to the last (lowest)—species. Because hierarchies are a logical way to organize information, we find them

Table 5.1 The biological classification of human beings, *Homo Sapiens*, as reported by www.itis.gov.

Taxonomic Level	Name of Classification
Kingdom	Animalia
Phylum	Chordata
Subphylum	Vertebrata
Class	Mammalia
Subclass	Theria
Infraclass	Eutheria
Order	Primates
Family	Hominoidea
Genus	Homo
Species	*Homo sapiens*

everywhere. And because they are so intuitive, we don't often consciously notice them. Our goal for the rest of this section is to recognize hierarchies when we see them because being aware of them speeds up our information discovery.

fluencyBIT

Choose to Exclude. Hierarchies work well not because of what we choose, but because of what we don't choose. For example, suppose a collection has a million items divided into 10 (roughly) equal-size categories. Picking a category eliminates from consideration the 900,000 items in the other categories. If the chosen category is also classified into 10 categories, the next choice eliminates another 90,000 items. With two choices we eliminated 990,000 items!

For example, consider the National Public Radio Web site, www.npr.org, shown in Figure 5.3. We might visit this site to find audio information about current news. The site uses hierarchical organization in several ways.

Studying the page, we first notice that the information is divided into two categories: *navigation information* at the top, and *content information* in the remainder of the page. More navigation links are scattererd throughout the content information, and at the bottom of the page. This navigation plus content structure is a standard format. The navigation links are provided for people checking the page for specific information, while the content information is for casual visitors who are browsing the latest stories NPR is covering. Notice this organization when visiting a new page.

Recognizing a Hierarchy

The navigation links define the hierarchy. The six dark topic buttons across the top of the page are the *top level* of the NPR site's hierarchy. Clicking on

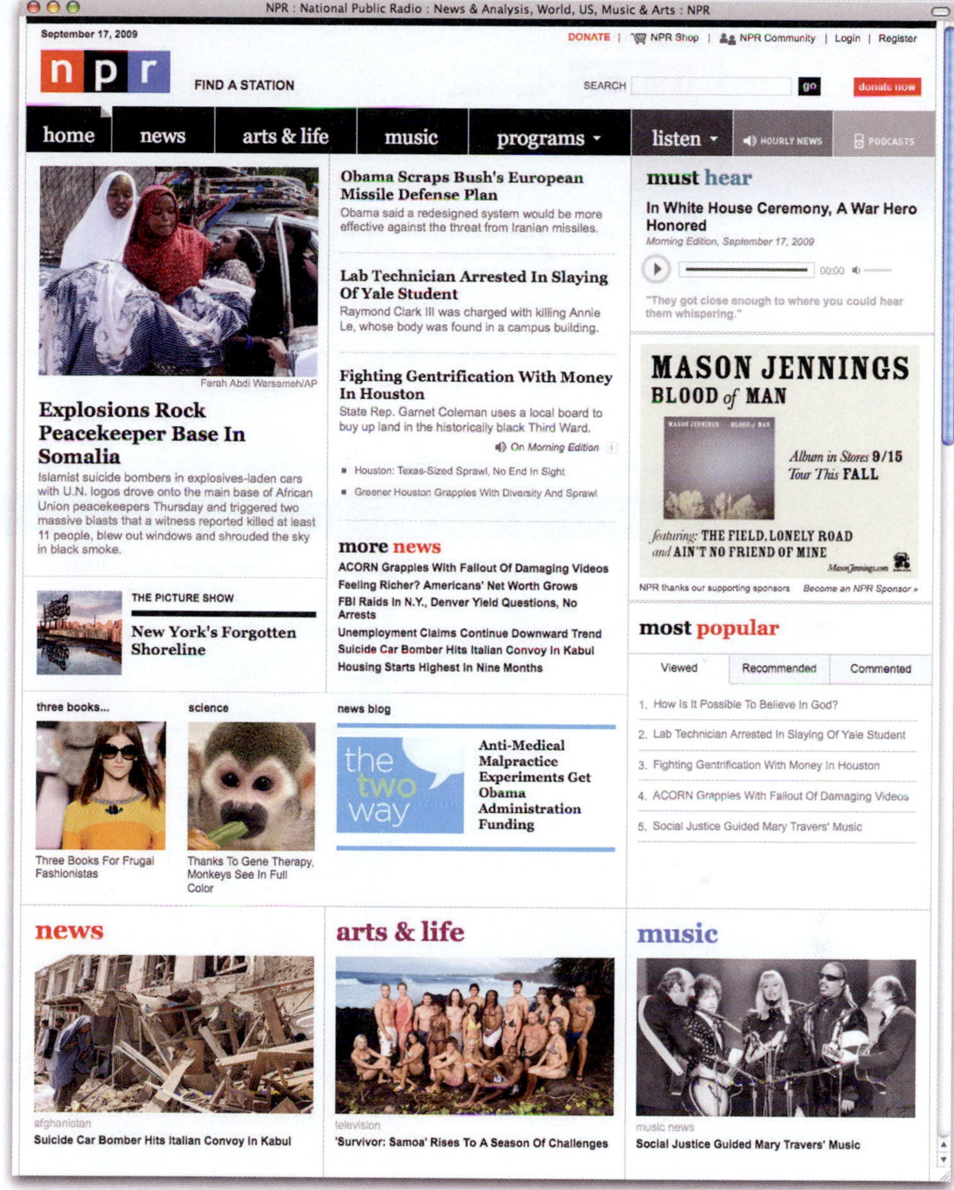

Figure 5.3 The National Public Radio (NPR) homepage http://www.npr.org.

any of these displays the links of the *second level* of the hierarchy below that top-level topic. For example, clicking on the *News* button displays a menu of nine second-level classifications:

US, *World*, *Opinion*, *Politics*, *Business*, *Technology*, *Science*, *Health* and *Sports*

Clicking on the *Programs* button, as shown in Figure 5.4(a) displays the four second-level classifications:

News/Talk, *Entertainment*, *Music* and *Special Series*

(a)

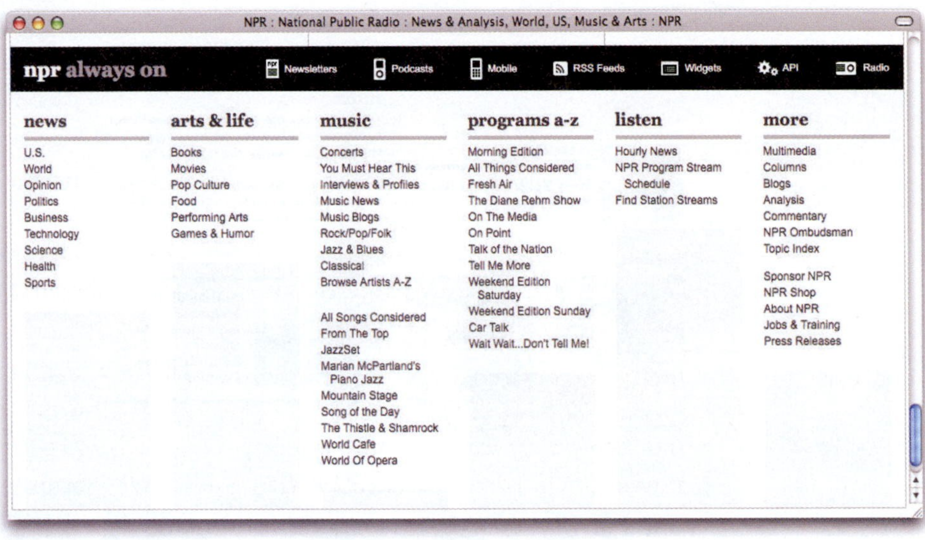

(b)

Figure 5.4 NPR site hierarchy; (a) expanded top level *programs* button to reveal four second level classifications and third level classifications below them, (b) alternative Always On classifications presented as a table.

and under each of these, third level classifications. Below each of these will be more links, specialized to the kinds of information in that part of the collection.

At the bottom of the page under "NPR Always On" is a slightly different hierarchical organization of this same information (see Figure 5.4(b)). Its structure is a large table with the top level going across and the second level going down. The difference is that the buttons at the top are designed for coverage, that is, to provide a path to all information, while the table is designed to give fast access to the most popular portions of the site.

More Structural Information

In Figure 5.3 notice that the content of the page is organized into three columns. The three columns can be filled separately. This allows the site designers to cluster related stories flexibly. For example, in the upper left corner are the breaking news stories. Halfway down the page the columns stop at the same point, a break signaling the end of the "top of the page."

At this point (shown at the bottom of Figure 5.3) the three columns resume with headings *news*, *arts & life*, and *music*. We recognize these as the three main top-level headings listed in the dark topic buttons across the top of the page. Under each of these headings are second-level headings for that topic. So, for example, the *news* column has content information for each of the second-level classifications, *US*, *world*, and so forth. Thus, the hierarchical structure of NPR's site is presented again within the content information. Such consistency not only produces an easy-to-understand site for the casual visitor, it allows the frequent visitor to become familiar with the site's structure, probably simplifying navigation.

Design of Hierarchies

Figure 5.5 shows the top two levels of the NPR site hierarchy drawn as a **tree**. At the root is the Home page, and the leaves (not shown) are either content pages or further levels of classification.

The tree is drawn on its side with the *root* (*Home*) to the left and the *leaves* (content pages, or lower hierarchical classifications) to the right (not shown). Hierarchy trees often are drawn sideways because it's more convenient to write (English) text that way. It is also common to draw trees upside down, with the root at the top. Either way, the important point is not the orientation, but the branching metaphor.

Hierarchies use a general set of rules for their design and terminology:

- Because hierarchy trees often are drawn with the root at the top, we say, "going up in the hierarchy" and "going down in the hierarchy." (Similar language—higher and deeper—was used with directory hierarchies in Chapter 3.) The terms are relative to the root being drawn at the top. So "going up" means the classifications become more inclusive; they are closer to the root. "Going down" means the classifications become more specific; they are farther from the root.
- The greater-than symbol (>) is a common way to show going down in a hierarchy through levels of classification:

  Home > Music > Browse Artists A-Z > C > The Cave Singers

A two-level hierarchy. The hierarchy shown in Figure 5.5 is a *two-level hierarchy* because there are two levels of "branching." Counting levels of a hierarchy can sometimes be a little confusing because of all the connecting lines, but it's

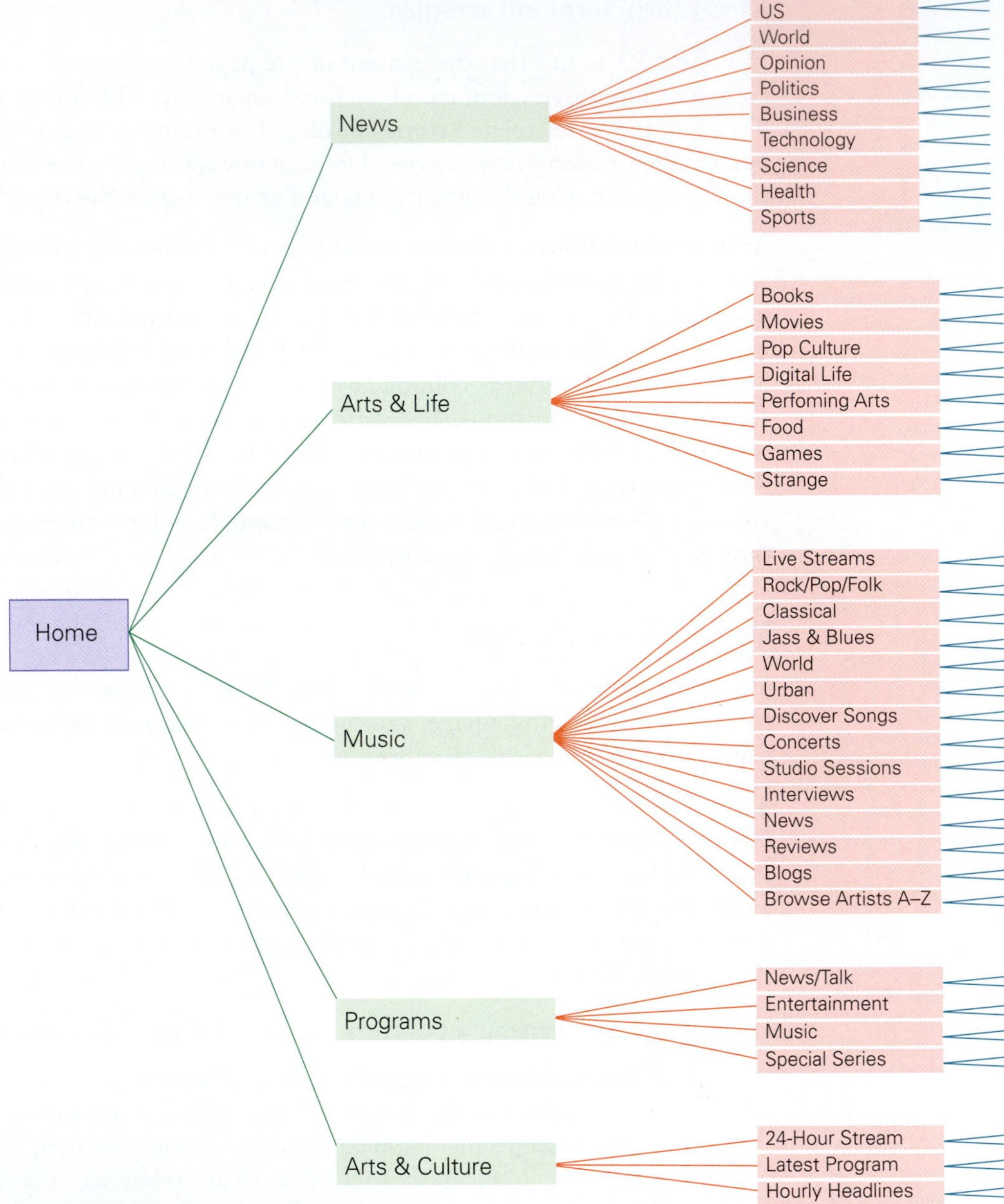

Figure 5.5 The top two levels of the NPR hierarchy tree; the root (Home) is shown at left, and the leaves (not shown) would be listed on the right under each topic.

easy if we keep two points in mind. First, the tree always has a root—the collection's name; in this case, that's *Home*. Second, all trees have leaves—the items themselves; in this case, the third-level pages, not shown. Because they exist without any hierarchy, the root and leaves do not count as levels of the hierarchy. When we ignore the root and leaves in Figure 5.5, we see two levels of classification.

Overlapping and partitioning of levels. There is not one best way to classify information; stories can be listed as a leaf more than once. For example, the story about books for fashion conscious people on a budget can be reached several ways:

Home > *Arts & Life* > *Books* > *Three Books for Frugal Fashionistas*
Home > *Listen* > *Latest Program* > *Three Books for Frugal Fashionistas*

When every leaf appears only once in the hierarchy, the groupings are called **partitionings**. The tree of life is a partitioning because every species is listed once. When groupings "overlap," meaning that an item is listed in more than one category, the leaves are repeated. Classifications that are convenient for the searcher often overlap, making such hierarchies easy to use.

Number of levels may differ. The number of classifications in a hierarchy does not need to be the same for all items. That is, the number of levels between a leaf and the root does not need to be the same for every leaf. Some groupings might require more levels of classification to reduce the group to a manageable size. For example, the *Browse Artists A-Z* under *music* asks first for the first letter of the artist's name; this makes the path at least one level longer than, say, news on the music page.

Searching the Web for Information

A **search engine** is a collection of computer programs that helps us find information on the Web. Though programs for text searching existed long before the Web, the explosion of Web-based digital information and its distribution across the planet made the invention of search engines necessary. No one organizes the information posted on the Web, so these programs look around to find out what's out there and organize what they find. It's a big task. How do search engines do it?

How a Search Engine Works

The first step, called *crawling*, looks at every page in the collection of pages to be searched. As the **crawler**—the software that does the crawling—looks through the pages, it builds an index. The index is a list of tokens (such as words) that are associated with the pages. For each token, the crawler creates a list of the URLs of pages found to be associated with that token. So, for example, we imagine that the indexed search for the word "cat" might look something like the list shown in Figure 5.6.

The second step in an indexed search is called *query processing*. The user presents tokens to the **query processor**—the software that processes the queries—that it looks up in the index. So, if you type `c-a-t` into your favorite search engine, it looks up the word in the index and returns to you the list of the pages associated with "cat" in the index.

```
       ...
  caszzzzzz:  aapaintball.com.ar/foro/archive/index.php,
              partyflock.nl/albumelement/37177026.html, ...
 caszzzzzzz:  itravelaround.com/28612.html
        cat:  www.cat.com, icanhascheezburger.com,
              en.wikipedia.org/wiki/Cat, www.cat.org.uk, ...
       cat0:  omgowned.wordpress.com/2008/06/10,
              catpointzero.com, bbs.keyhole.com/entrance.php, ...
       cat1:  www.cat1.org, en.wikipedia.org/wiki/Category_1_cable,
              www.cat1.co.uk, ...
       ...
```

Figure 5.6 Sample results of searches near the entry "cat" in an index produced by a Web crawler. Some of the lists are very long—there are over 800,000,000 URLs following *cat*.

By creating the index ahead of time, search engines are able to answer user queries very quickly, even if the original crawling takes a long time.

fluencyBIT

Three Little Words. The crawler considers almost anything followed by a space or punctuation symbol a token, except short words like *a*, *an*, and *the*. But even these words can become tokens by being part of important phrases, like *The New York Times*.

Multiword Indexed Searches

Generally, when we make a multiple-word query, we want the pages returned by the query processor to be appropriate for all of the words. That is, when we type

```
red fish blue guppy
```

we mean that each page returned should be associated with *all* of these words. (This is called an **AND-query** because it instructs the query processor to find pages relevant to the words `red` and `fish` and `blue` and `guppy`. We learn more about AND-queries and other forms of queries momentarily.)

The problem for the query processor is that there is no index entry corresponding to a *set* of tokens, just the lists for the individual words. There is no time to crawl the Web to build an index for that set of words. What is a query processor to do?

Intersecting queries. To locate pages containing these words, the query processor simply fetches the lists and **intersects** them, meaning the query processor finds which URLs are on all of the lists. To make the task of intersecting multiple lists a little easier, the URL lists might be alphabetized. This speeds up the processing because it is possible to notice easily when the same URL is on multiple lists. So, for example, for the index lists of the three tokens

token1	token2	token3
www.ab.com	www.aa.com	**www.rs.org**
www.rs.org	www.ab.com	www.zz.edu
www.ru.com	www.m.edu	
	www.rs.org	

the result of the intersection is www.rs.org, because that URL is associated with each of the three tokens as requested.

Rules for intersecting alphabetized lists. To intersect several alphabetized lists, the computer follows these simple rules:

1. Put a marker such as an arrow at the start of each list.
2. If all markers point to the same URL, save it, because all tokens are associated with the page.
3. Advance the marker(s) one position for whichever URL is earliest in the alphabet.
4. Repeat rules 2–3 until some marker reaches the end of the list.

The result is a list of the URLs saved in Step 2. Figure 5.7 illustrates this process.

5.1 Intersect Index Lists. Find the result of intersecting the following three lists using the Intersect Alphabetized Lists rules. How many steps does it take?

RED	FISH	GUPPY
en/wikipedia.org/wiki/red	en/wikipedia.org/wiki/fish	en/wikipedia.org/wiki/guppy
newsroom.urc.edu	newsroom.urc.edu	www.ifga.org
www.fullredguppy.com	www.fish.com	www.fullredguppy.com
www.red.com	www.fullredguppy.com	www.sciencedaily.com
www.sciencedaily.com	www.sciencedaily.com	www.tropicalfish.com

In summary, indexed search is very powerful because the computer takes the time to crawl the data (Web pages) and build an index first. Then all it needs to do is find the index entries for each word and intersect the lists to find the information we want. This is how a search engine like Google can look at billions of Web pages and give our answer back in one quarter of a second.

Web Books Shopping Results **1** - **10** of about **267,000** for **fluency with information technology**. (**0.25** seconds)

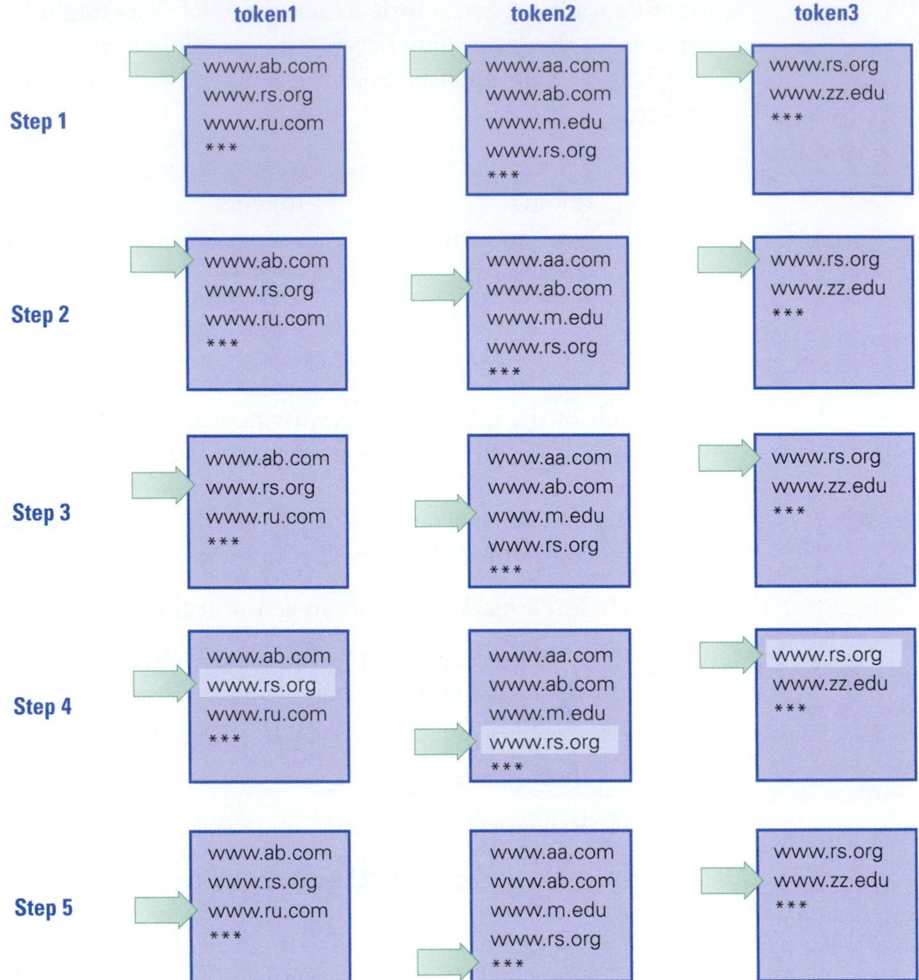

Figure 5.7 Illustrating the Intersect Alphabetized Lists rules: In each step (row of boxes) one or more arrows advance; notice Step 3 where the arrow advances in two lists in the same step because the earliest URL is on both lists.

Advanced Searches

With the index telling the query processor all of the pages containing each word, it makes sense to try to get the most out of the "crawl-then-query" idea. For this reason, query processors usually give us the option for an *Advanced Search*. Figure 5.8 shows the GUI for Google's Advanced Search, but others are similar.

Logical operators. Basic queries, including the "red fish blue guppy" query previously, are AND-queries: They require that all words given must be associated with the page for it to be a hit. A good way to think about AND-queries is that the page is a hit if

```
red AND fish AND blue AND guppy
```

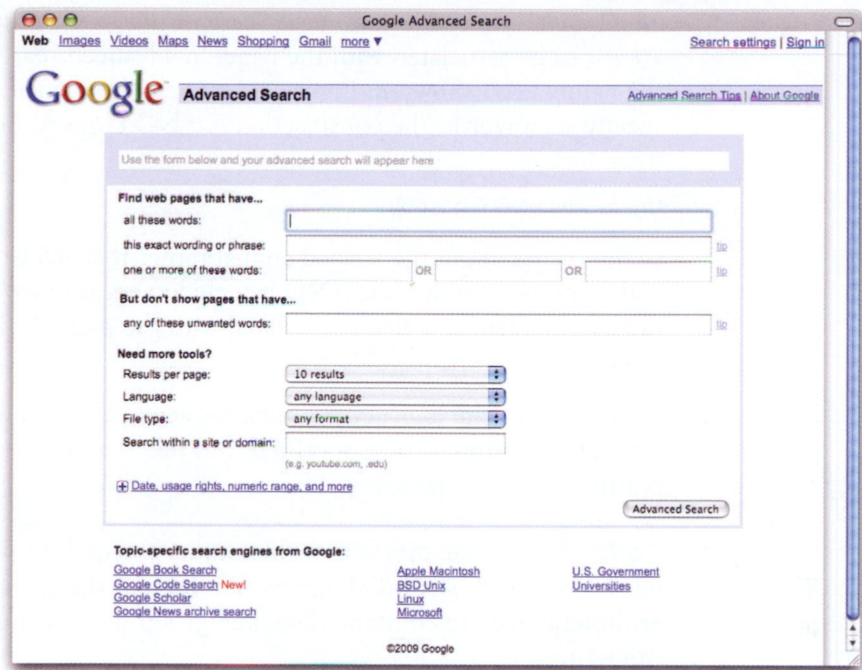

Figure 5.8 Google Advanced Search GUI: The highlighted field is for AND words, the next is for phrases, the third is for OR words, and the fourth is for NOT words.

are all associated with the page. When we write the query this way, we are using the word AND as a **logical operator**. A logical operator specifies a logical relationship between the words it connects. So, red AND fish says that the two logical tests for "Is *red* associated with the page?" AND "Is *fish* associated with the page?" must both be true. AND-queries are specified using the highlighted line of the Advanced Search GUI in Figure 5.8.

Another logical operator is OR. An **OR**-query such as

marshmallow OR strawberry OR chocolate

hits on pages that are associated with one (at least, but possibly more) of the words. Using the Advanced Search GUI in Figure 5.8, OR-queries are given on the third line. The logical operator in marshmallow OR strawberry says that one or the other (or both) of the logical tests—"Is *marshmallow* associated with the page?" OR "Is *strawberry* associated with the page?"—is true.

5.2 Once Is Enough. To answer OR-queries like **lisa OR bart OR homer**, the query processor simply combines the index list for each word. One problem is that a page associated with **bart** may also be associated with **homer**, so that page will be listed for both words. Removing such duplicates is very similar to intersecting alphabetized lists. Revise the four rules for Intersect Alphabetized Lists to create new rules that will remove duplicates.

The fourth line of the Advanced Search window is for specifying words that are *not* to be associated with the page. In advanced searches that do not use the handy GUI shown in Figure 5.8, we use the logical operator NOT to specify such words; the construction is a NOT-query. So, for example, we write

```
tigers AND NOT baseball
```

to find pages about the striped animal rather than Detroit's major league baseball team. Notice that the AND is included because we want both requirements to be true: "Is *tigers* associated with the page?" AND NOT "Is *baseball* associated with the page?"

In addition to the logical operators, the second line of the Advanced Query GUI allows phrases to be specified. But the easiest way to do this is simply to put the phrase in quotes.

Combining logical operators. Sometimes the queries we are interested in need AND, OR, *and* NOT operators. Because the logical operators work like arithmetic, we can combine them and group them using parentheses. So, we can write

```
(marshmallow OR strawberry OR chocolate) AND sundae
```

to require that one (or more) of the flavors and the word *sundae* be associated with the page. Write the OR portion of the query in parentheses so that it is clear that the flavors go together.

If the OR-terms did not use the parentheses, as in

```
marshmallow OR strawberry OR chocolate AND sundae
```

the query would be ambiguous. *Ambiguous* means that it has two or more meanings. One possible meaning is the one given above with parentheses. Another possible meaning would be parenthesized as

```
marshmallow OR strawberry OR (chocolate AND sundae)
```

which allows hits on pages associated with only the word *marshmallow* or only the word *strawberry*, because *sundae* is required only for *chocolate*.

It is usually acceptable to write queries in the form shown here using capital letters for the logical operators and parentheses to make the associations clear. In Google, it is also acceptable to use the following form in the basic search:

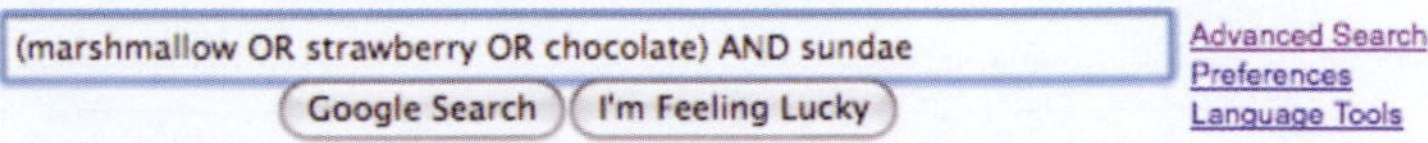

For Google, the AND is unnecessary because Google queries interpret a space to mean AND, making

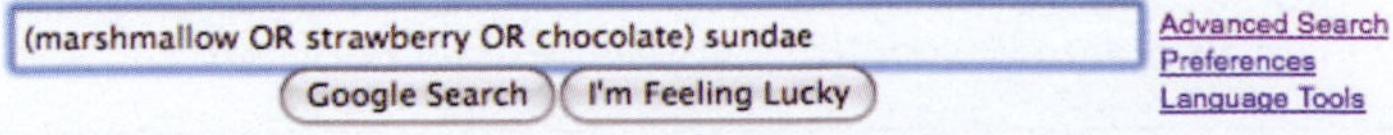

an equivalent query. But not all Advanced Search software accepts blank, so it is wise to use the AND; it is rarely a mistake.

fluencyBIT

Plus Numbers. Google ignores numbers on queries such as **rocky 3**. However, including a plus sign in front of the number tells Google not to ignore it and to use it as part of the query. Therefore, queries like **apollo +13** finds pages about that specific flight.

Google has other nice features: Minus (-) as an abbreviation for NOT; it should be snuggled up right next to the associated word. Also, if the OR-words are all grouped together they don't need to be enclosed in parentheses, assuming that what you're looking for is one of the OR-choices together with whatever the remainder of the query specifies. So we can write

```
simpson bart OR lisa OR maggie -homer -marge
```

to get data on the Simpson children.

5.3 Sunny Day Driving. Write a query for Google's basic *I'm Feeling Lucky* search window to find pages about convertibles for any of these brands: Corvette, Mazda, and Porsche.

fluencyBIT

Shortsightedness. Search engines crawl only a fraction (substantially less than half) of the Web. Because it is growing so fast, there are always new pages to be visited. Librarians call the pages not crawled, the "Invisible Web." There are other reasons that crawlers miss pages:

- No page points to it, so it never gets on the "to do" list
- The page is synthetic—that is, created on-the-fly by software for each user
- The encoding is a type the crawler does not recognize, that is, not HTML, PDF, etc.

Searching the World Wide Web

Applying your general knowledge of searching and our preceding discussion of advanced search, we are now ready to learn how to make effective queries. The two topics of importance in this section are:

- How do search engines decide whether a page is a hit?
- How do search engines decide what order to list the hits?

Knowing the answers to these two questions will help make you a much more effective searcher.

What Is a Hit?

It seems pretty obvious that a **hit** is a page that has (or doesn't have, if NOT is used) the words on it that the user gives in the query. That's nearly right, but the exact details might surprise you. So, for example, suppose you are planning to write a report on the kind of star known as a red giant, and you type

```
red giant
```

into Google. You get back 4.9 million hits. In looking at the first five (see Figure 5.9), you can already see a problem. The first hit is for a software company, and the fifth hit is for a rock band. This is not surprising. Red Giant is a good name, so we expect to hit on pages about things named "red giant" that are not stars. But we don't want to go through all those pages, either.

Looking at the Search Results

After adjusting the search to

```
red giant -software -music
```

the hits drop to 824,000, which is still ridiculously large. One thing that is interesting about the pages returned is that they all contain the words *red giant* in that order. But, an AND-query only requires that the two words appear *somewhere*; they do not have to be together, nor do they have to be in that order. Did we just get lucky? No, but we'll explain why we get all astronomy pages in a moment. Farther down in the list are pages about such things as *giant red* sculptures, squirrels, kangaroos, mustard plants, racehorses, and tropical fish. Also listed are pages in which the two words are used separately, without either modifying the other, as in a recipe for "*giant* beans baked with roasted *red* chili peppers."

But curiously, there are pages in the list that contain one word, *red*, without containing the other, *giant*. For example, the page redballproject.com/chicago/index.php contains the word *red* but not *giant*. So, why is it a hit for

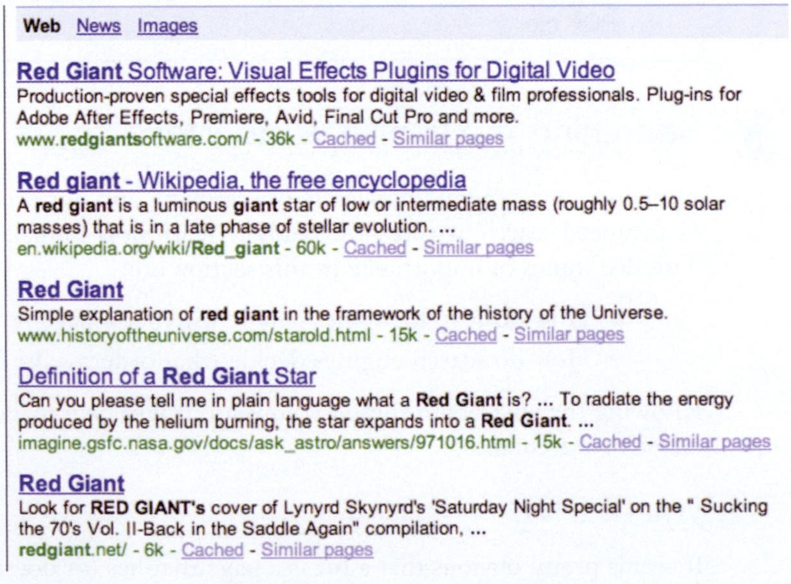

Web News Images

Red Giant Software: Visual Effects Plugins for Digital Video
Production-proven special effects tools for digital video & film professionals. Plug-ins for Adobe After Effects, Premiere, Avid, Final Cut Pro and more.
www.**redgiants**oftware.com/ - 36k - Cached - Similar pages

Red giant - Wikipedia, the free encyclopedia
A **red giant** is a luminous **giant** star of low or intermediate mass (roughly 0.5–10 solar masses) that is in a late phase of stellar evolution. ...
en.wikipedia.org/wiki/**Red_giant** - 60k - Cached - Similar pages

Red Giant
Simple explanation of **red giant** in the framework of the history of the Universe.
www.historyoftheuniverse.com/starold.html - 15k - Cached - Similar pages

Definition of a **Red Giant** Star
Can you please tell me in plain language what a **Red Giant** is? ... To radiate the energy produced by the helium burning, the star expands into a **Red Giant**. ...
imagine.gsfc.nasa.gov/docs/ask_astro/answers/971016.html - 15k - Cached - Similar pages

Red Giant
Look for **RED GIANT's** cover of Lynyrd Skynyrd's 'Saturday Night Special' on the " Sucking the 70's Vol. II-Back in the Saddle Again" compilation, ...
redgiant.net/ - 6k - Cached - Similar pages

Figure 5.9 The first five hits for the query *red giant* using Google.

the search **red giant**? The answer is that for a word to describe a page, the word doesn't actually have to be *on* the page. Specifically, the index for a word, say *red*, is not limited to pages *containing* the word. It also includes pages in which the word is used in the URL, as in www.nusantara.com/2005/08/red-ball-project-by-kurt-perschke.html (see Figure 5.10). And, most importantly, the index for a word includes pages in which the word is used in the *anchor text* of another page.

Anchor Text

Recall that when a link is used in a Web page, it has two parts: the URL and the anchor. So, if a Web page contains the following

> ... Today, in Chicago a giant red ball was sighted on Jaume Street ...

and the *giant red ball* anchor has the URL redballproject.com/chicago/index.php, then the Google crawler finds

```
... Chicago a <a href="http://redballproject.com/chicago/index.php">giant
red ball</a>
```

and assumes that the words *giant*, *red*, and *ball* all describe the page, so it adds the URL to the indexes of those three words. Although the page doesn't contain the word *giant*, the word was used in anchor text from some other page. That got the page into the index for *giant* and made it a hit for the query *red giant*.

The idea behind including a page in the indexes of any words used in anchor text is that they may be a better description for the page than the page's actual content. Imagine a page about Sarah Silverman. It might always refer to her

Figure 5.10 Photo from a page related to an art installation by Kurt Perschke in Chicago called the Red Ball Project, The pages are listed in a **red giant** search, but do not contain the word *giant*; it hits because *giant* was used in the anchor text.

as "Sarah" or use some other description for her like "the comedienne"; it may never use her whole name. But if your home page links to that page with the text

... this is the best page about Sarah Silverman that I know ...

then your link gives better information—her last name—than does the page itself. Use of the anchor text makes the crawl-then-query approach much more effective than it would be if it used just the content of the page.

Page Rank

In the 824,000 hits for the *red giant* query, the pages listed at the start are all important and relevant. How does the query processor know to list those pages first, ahead of pages about giant red squirrels, for example?

The order in which hits are returned to a query is determined by a number Google calls the **PageRank**. The higher the PageRank, the closer to the top of the list a page will be. Google pioneered the page ranking idea as a way to determine which pages are likely to be most important to you. Of course, the computer has no way of actually knowing what is important to you, but page ranking works pretty well.

Links to other pages. Although Google has not revealed the complete information about how PageRank weights sites, we do know that it works like a voting system. If page A, www.shoutOut.net/A.html, links to page B, www.celeb.com/B.html, then in the Google page ranking system, A's link adds to B's importance.

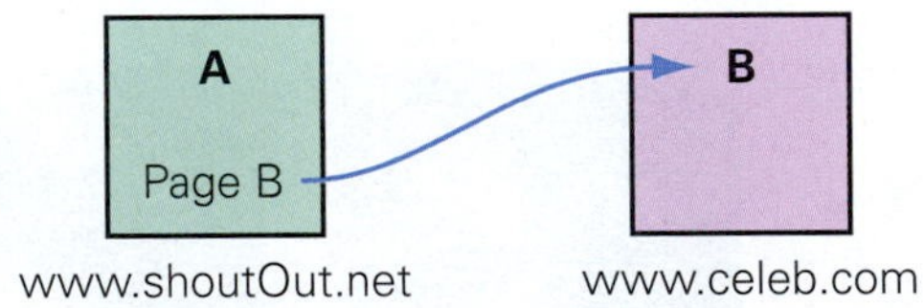

It is as if shoutOut's link is a vote for the celeb page. Pages that are linked to a lot have a higher page ranking and, therefore, are assumed to be more important. This seems to make sense.

A second important property of Google's page ranking system is that links from pages with a high page ranking are viewed as more important than links from pages with a low page ranking. So, if shoutOut has a high page ranking, its link will contribute more to celeb's rank than, say, a link from celeb.fanClub.org/myPatheticPage.html that has a low page ranking.

The PageRank is computed by the crawler, because as it looks at page A, it can notice the links to another page B and score one for B. Counting the number of links to a page is not sufficient, however, because it doesn't take into consideration that some links are more important than others. So, after the crawling is completed, the PageRank is computed and stored with each page. Then, as the query is being processed, the URLs that are found by the intersecting process can be sorted by their page ranking, highest to lowest, and returned to the user in that order.

Red giant hits. So, now we know how the order of the hits was determined. It is not surprising, therefore, that among our first half dozen hits for
red giant -software -music

en.wikipedia.org/wiki/Red_giant
www.historyoftheuniverse.com/starold.html
imagine.gsfc.nasa.gov/docs/ask_astro/answers/971016.html
hyperphysics.phy-astr.gsu.edu/Hbase/astro/redgia.html
www.daviddarling.info/encyclopedia/R/redgiant.html
nrumiano.free.fr/Estars/fading.html

there is a hit on Wikipedia. It is often listed in the first few items of a Web search, because Wikipedia must be linked to a lot, giving it a high page ranking. It also explains why a NASA site is among our top hits, and why another hit is Georgia State University. These are likely to be authoritative sites and so should have high page ranking because of many references. The historyoftheuniverse site is a page for a book, and publishers are frequently linked, raising its page ranking. Finally, the fifth and sixth hits are free online encyclopedias of science, which are probably also very popular.

But why are these (and the next several hundred that follow) all devoted to stars rather than, say, giant red squirrels or other pages that match *red* and *giant*? The answer again lies in the anchor text. As we learned earlier, the text used on one Web page to describe another is often the best descriptor of the page. So, in computing page ranking, Google gives additional PageRank importance to pages for those words used in the anchor text. This makes sense: If many people use the words *red giant* in anchor text pointing at, say, a NASA page, then it is a page that is likely to be of interest to someone making a query *red giant*, and it should appear at the top of the list for that query. It is this property that explains why pages about stars come to the top of our *red giant* list, and not pages about squirrels.

Restricting Global Search

Many sites offer the opportunity to perform a **site search**, which means looking only on their site. The site search is usually offered on the home page with a search window and a **Go** button. If you know the site has the information you want, it is advisable to go there and perform a site search. This is usually the fastest way to find the right page. Notice that for many, many sites, it is possible to guess the right URL: www.irs.gov for tax information, or www.princeton.edu for information on Princeton University, or nytimes.com for information from *The New York Times*.

Focused Searches

Often when we need information we don't care where it's found, and we ask a search engine to check the whole WWW. The result is frequently many,

many hits that take time to look through. So, when we know more about the topic we're searching for, we can direct the search by adding additional constraints; see the bottom of Google's Advanced Search page in Figure 5.8.

Constrained searches. The constraints help us pinpoint the pages we want. For example, suppose we remember seeing a video of an art school's arts festival called Manifest. It was a slick name and a great video, but you don't remember much else about it. There must be a Web site for it—can we find it?

Starting out, we search art manifest and get

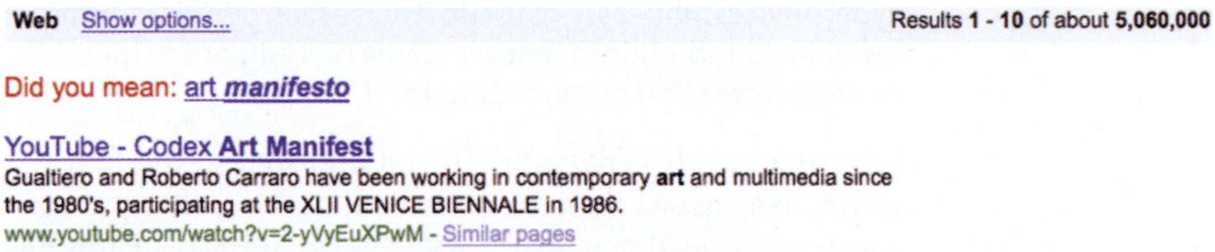

Web Show options... Results **1** - **10** of about **5,060,000**

Did you mean: art ***manifesto***

YouTube - Codex **Art Manifest**
Gualtiero and Roberto Carraro have been working in contemporary **art** and multimedia since the 1980's, participating at the XLII VENICE BIENNALE in 1986.
www.youtube.com/watch?v=2-yVyEuXPwM - Similar pages

which is kind of humorous—"Painters of the world, unite!"—but the page we are trying to find isn't in the top ten. Thinking that it's an art school, we try searching on art school manifest and get

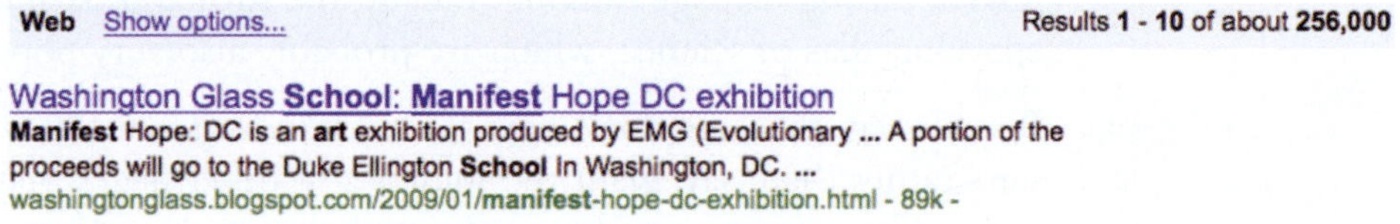

Web Show options... Results **1** - **10** of about **256,000**

Washington Glass **School**: **Manifest** Hope DC exhibition
Manifest Hope: DC is an **art** exhibition produced by EMG (Evolutionary ... A portion of the proceeds will go to the Duke Ellington **School** in Washington, DC. ...
washingtonglass.blogspot.com/2009/01/**manifest**-hope-dc-exhibition.html - 89k -

which is better, but again the page we want isn't in the top ten list.

Although that exhausts what we remember about the festival, it isn't the end of our search.

At the bottom of the Google Advanced Search GUI, we are offered the filtering options (note others under the plus sign).

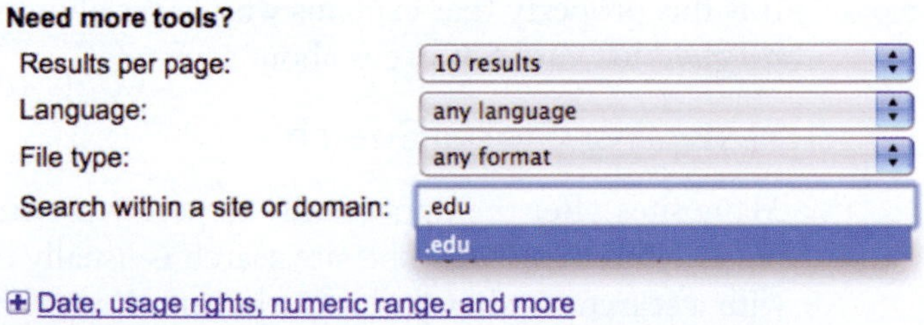

Need more tools?

Results per page:	10 results
Language:	any language
File type:	any format
Search within a site or domain:	.edu

⊞ Date, usage rights, numeric range, and more

Guessing that the school will be in the .edu domain, we limit the search to that. Now, searching only manifest with that limitation delivers the page we're looking for at the top of the top ten list.

Web Show options... Results **1** - **10** of about **1,160,000**

Manifest Urban Arts Festival is May 15, 2009
The **Manifest** Live feed is provided by Frequency TV, a student-powered station funded by the Columbia College Television Department. ...
www.colum.edu/**manifest**/ - 13k - Cached - Similar pages

That's impressive, considering the hefty list of hits for manifest. We decide to make greater use of such tools in the future, and settle back to watch the video again.

Manifest 2008

Page ranking local searches. There is one more way that these filtering tools can help. Many large sites like National Public Radio, the Internal Revenue Service, YouTube, and so forth provide a local search through their own documents. Often these searches work well, especially if the search term you're looking for is reasonably rare, and so the number of hits is small. But when it's not, and the hit list is large, the local search is often either unordered—presented in the sequence that the search engine found them—or else in some order that doesn't help you, say chronological.

In such cases, making the same search but restricting it to a specific domain—for example, www.youtube.com—works because the page ranking information orders the hits. The local search doesn't know the page ranking information and so cannot give you the advantages of that ordering. Such searches are usually very, very effective.

Finding the Needle. Narrowing the search to the right page is the first task, but finding the information can mean more searching on the page itself. Remember that browsers have a word-search facility, *Find*, under the *Edit* menu. To search on a page, use *Find*.

Web Information: Truth or Fiction?

One of the great benefits of the World Wide Web is how much it has expanded people's freedom of expression. It is possible in many countries of the world to publish anything on the Web, uncensored by companies or governments. This is a benefit, but, like all freedoms, this one carries with it some important responsibilities—not so much for the speaker, but for the reader or listener. Because anyone can publish anything on the Web, some of what gets published is false, misleading, deceptive, self-serving, slanderous, or simply disgusting. We have to be alert for this and always ask, *"Is this page legitimate, true, and correct?"* In this section we consider whether the pages we've found in our search provide reliable information.

Do Not Assume Too Much

The first thing to look for is who or what organization publishes the Web page. For example, health information from the Centers for Disease Control, the World Health Organization, or the American Medical Association is about the best you can access. These respected organizations try to publish current and correct information, so we can trust their Web pages. The published information is based on science; therefore, new discoveries might occasionally invalidate something. But we're not discussing the philosophical aspects of the *nature of truth* here. We can assume that respected organizations publish the best information available at the time, and we're unlikely to find better.

Checking the organization that publishes the information seems like overkill. After all, if the Web site's domain name is ama-assn.org, it claims to be the AMA page, and it's giving out medical information, it must be the American Medical Association, right? In fact, it is. But just because a page seems to be from a certain organization and the domain name *seems* plausible, it isn't necessarily true. Domain names are not checked. Anyone could have reserved the domain name ama-assn.org and published bogus health information. You must be wary.

To illustrate that sites are not always what they appear to be, consider the hoax perpetrated by the site www.gatt.org. The domain name looks like it is related to the General Agreement on Tariffs and Trade (GATT), the free-trade agreement of the 1990s. The site looks like the official publication of the World Trade Organization (WTO), the free-trade group that followed on from the GATT treaty. The page shows the WTO logo, gives the actual WTO address, and posts WTO-related free-trade news. However, the site is actually run by an *anti*-free-trade organization known as the Yes Men.

According to the January 7, 2001, *New York Times*, organizers of a meeting of international trade lawyers in Salzburg, Austria, sent mail to www.gatt.org inviting WTO President Moore to speak at their meeting. From www.gatt.org came an email reply declining on behalf of Mr. Moore, but offering (a fictitious) speaker, Dr. Andreas Bichlbauer, as a substitute. The meeting organizers accepted Dr. Bichlbauer who came to their October 2000 meeting and gave a very offensive speech critical of Italians and Americans. The perpetrators of the hoax even claimed that a WTO protestor threw a cream pie at Dr. Bichlbauer. They claimed that the pie contained a *bacillus,* that Bichlbauer had taken ill and was hospitalized, and that he had died. The whole hoax, which caused much embarrassment, began when someone assumed that www.gatt.org was a legitimate WTO site.

A Two-Step Check for the Site's Publisher

How can you find out if a site is legitimate? A two-step process can help.

1. The InterNIC site www.internic.net/whois.html lists the company that assigned the site's IP address (i.e., domain). Type in the domain name, such as company.com. In some instances you will receive the registration information for the domain directly. In most cases, however, the InterNIC information about the domain includes a site called a WhoIs Server maintained by the company that assigned the address. That site will tell you who owns the domain.

2. Go to the WhoIs Server site and type in the domain name or IP address again. The information returned is the owner's name and physical address.

When checking a Web site, remember to pull out the domain name from the URL.

Elaborate hoaxes like gatt.org are rare, although there have been others. A more likely situation is that information is unintentionally wrong or simply fictional. "Urban legends"—stories like alligators living in the New York City sewer system— fall into the first category. People pass along the information as true, although they don't have primary evidence or an authoritative basis for believing it. Urban myths are usually harmless, but not always. Stories in the second category, fictional and humorous, are meant to entertain us. April Fools' pages, alien spaceships visiting Seattle's Space Needle, and reports of one-ton squirrels are common and fun. Still, it's best to approach Web pages with some skepticism.

Characteristics of Legitimate Sites

What cues can alert a reader to misinformation? In a recent survey, Internet users thought that a site was more believable if it had these features:

- **Physical existence.** The site provides a street address, telephone number, and legal email address.
- **Expertise.** The site includes references, citations or credentials, and links to related sites.
- **Clarity.** The site is well organized, easy to use, and provides site-searching facilities.
- **Currency.** The site was recently updated.
- **Professionalism.** The site's grammar, spelling, punctuation, and so forth are correct; all links work.

Of course, a site can have these characteristics and still not be legitimate. A site trying to fool people can appear to be legitimate.

Check Other Sources

Finally, if the information is important to you, check more than one source. After all, it is very easy to use the Internet to find information, and it's equally easy to use it to cross-check information. Ask yourself, "If this information were true, what other source could directly or indirectly confirm it?" Of course, we must be equally skeptical about the supporting information. For example, we cannot count the number of sites referencing information as proof that it's true, because by that reasoning the alligators-in-the-sewer urban legend would seem to be supported by the 105,000 hits on `alligator AND sewer`. A better approach is to find sites that speak directly to the urban legend topic, such as `www.snopes.com`.

The Burmese Mountain Dog Page

To test our ability to assess a site, suppose we have found `burmesemountaindog.info`, a site describing the Burmese Mountain Dog (see Figure 5.11). The page looks authoritative, describing itself as the official site of the Burmese Mountain Dog Club of America. It has been posted by someone claiming DVM credentials, probably meaning doctor of veterinary medicine. There are photographs, links to the American Kennel Club, and so on. The page seems completely legitimate and meets most of the criteria that Internet users have listed as indicating authenticity. If we ask Google to find

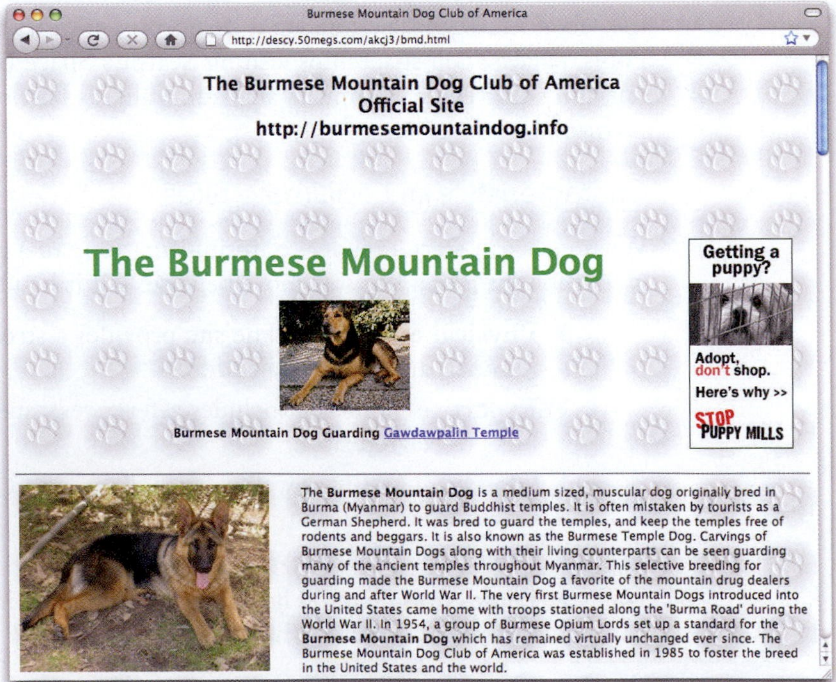

Figure 5.11 The Burmese Mountain Dog page.

burmese mountain dog, we get 604,000 hits. Many people would probably accept the page as truthful.

Because the page has a link to the American Kennel Club, akc.org, which lists all breeds the club recognizes, it's possible to check out the Burmese Mountain Dog. In the AKC's list of breeds, we find that there is no Burmese Mountain Dog, but there is a Bernese Mountain Dog, named for Berne, Switzerland. What gives? First, we ask if akc.org is legitimate by using the InterNIC WhoIs service, and we find that it is. Next, we check 50megs.com and find it is a free Web hosting site. This seems reasonable because if the Burmese Mountain Dog is not yet recognized by the AKC, perhaps an independent group of enthusiasts is behind the site. Accepting that the AKC is giving correct information about the Bernese Mountain Dog, we conclude that either the Burmese page is a fake or the Burmese Mountain Dog is not yet a recognized breed.

It is interesting that there are so many hits on Burmese Mountain Dog, but when we ask Google to look up bernese mountain dog we get 754,000 hits, so the Bernese seems to be even more popular. The similarity of names suggests that someone has made a comparison, so we check for pages citing both breeds. Searching bernese burmese mountain dog yields 26,500 hits.

The first hit is to the museumofhoaxes.com, and the next hit says, "There is no such thing as a **Burmese** mountain dog breed."

We check the site and find that that author claims Burmese Mountain Dogs are a hoax. But a few sites later in the hit list is a site with pages and pages of photos of Burmese Mountain Dogs. Who's right? A quick look at several of the pages shows photos of what the AKC calls a Bernese Mountain Dog but the photographer calls a Burmese Mountain Dog. Obviously people are mispronouncing and misspelling the name, and the two are not separate breeds. So, we visit www.burmesemountaindog.org to see a different spoof, and finally return to the original page to admire how skillful a hoax it is.

Summary

The secret to finding the information we're looking for is to look in the right place. This chapter taught us that:

- Libraries are excellent primary resource tools.
- Large public and university libraries have extensive online resources.
- Libraries not only provide information digitally, they also connect us with "pre-digital" archives—the millions of books, journals, and manuscripts that still exist only in paper form.
- We need software and our own intelligence to search the Internet effectively.

- We create queries using the logical operators AND, OR, and NOT, and specific terms to pinpoint the information we seek.
- Once we've found information, we must judge whether it is correct by investigating the organization that publishes the page, including checking the credentials of the people who write the copy.
- We must cross-check the information with other sources, especially when the information is important.

Try It Solutions

5.1 There are two intersections, www.fullredguppy.com and www.sciencedaily.com, and it takes 9 steps to find these.

5.2 The revised rules would be:

1. Put a marker such as an arrow at the start of each list.
2. If two or more markers point to the same URL, delete all but one of the URLs from the lists, moving the marker for deleted items to the next item on the list.
3. Advance the marker one position for the URL earliest in the alphabet.
4. Repeat rules 2–3 until the markers are all (but one) at the end of their lists.

5.3 The query is one of the following:

```
(corvette OR mazda OR porsche) AND convertible
(corvette OR mazda OR porsche) convertible
convertible corvette OR mazda OR porsche
```

Review Questions

Multiple Choice

1. One of the downsides of unmediated expression on the Web is
   a. a need for verification of the accuracy of the content
   b. duplication of information
   c. that very little information is available
   d. all of the above
2. Information created in ________ is likely to be digitized.
   a. 1956
   b. 1976
   c. 1996
   d. more than one of the above
3. We visit a library electronically to
   a. find information
   b. use research tools
   c. not have to whisper
   d. more than one of the above

4. A hierarchy resembles a
   a. subway map
   b. tree
   c. spoked wheel
   d. list
5. Someone searching with a search engine would use the
   a. crawler
   b. query processor
   c. index
   d. anchor
6. Most Web pages are not indexed because
   a. search engines have not crawled them
   b. pages are created on demand and those cannot be indexed
   c. other pages do not point to it
   d. all of the above
7. To omit a word from a search in Google, you would
   a. put the word MINUS in front of the word
   b. put the word in parentheses
   c. put a minus sign in front of the word
   d. put the word inside quotation marks
8. The number of results from a search using AND will likely be _______ a search using OR.
   a. no more than
   b. the same as
   c. fewer than
   d. unrelated to
9. Which of the following is not an indication of the believability of a Web site?
   a. professionalism
   b. WWW Consortium approval
   c. expertise
   d. physical existence provided by the site

Short Answer

1. Historically, the _______ has been the repository of information.
2. On the computer, you would look for information using a(n) _________.
3. _______ provide connections to specialized pages.
4. _______ are computer programs that help people find information on the Web.
5. _______ uses the keywords in the anchor link of Web pages to index its pages.
6. Counting the number of pages linked to a page helps to determine that page's _________.

7. AND, OR, and NOT are called ________.
8. Operators placed between words in a query are called ________.
9. A(n) _______ is a method of organizing information by groups.
10. If a word or phrase is enclosed in quotes in a search, the search engine will search for a(n) ________.
11. Web pages found using a search engine are called ________.
12. The _______ operator is used to exclude a word or phrase from a search.
13. In a Google search, a space is the same as using the word ________.
14. In a search, the minus (–) sign is the same as using the word ________.
15. _______ is a company that tracks information on who owns a Web site.

Exercises

1. Write down the organization chart used by Yahoo! (www.yahoo.com) for its homepage. What type of classification is it?
2. Go to InterNIC (www.internic.net/whois.html). Type in the name of a Web site and check its information. Do the same for other sites.
3. How would you find a search engine that specializes in European Web sites? Find one and use it. What do you find?
4. Create a classification scheme for clothing items. In your list, what items can be classified in more than one group?
5. Use Switchboard.com (www.switchboard.com) to look up your phone number.
6. Use MapQuest (www.mapquest.com) to look up your home address. Print the map.
7. What is the Web address for the New York Public Library?
8. Pick an issue. Find sites on both sides of the issue and analyze their content.
9. Do an ego search. Use a search engine and search for your name. How many hits were there? Classify the types of hits you found. If you are listed, how far down the list was the first listing about you?
10. Describe how the following operators can refine a Web search:
    a. Quotation marks " "
    b. AND
    c. OR
    d. NOT

11. Visit www.snopes.com and find an email hoax. Report the following information:
    a. What is the email hoax?
    b. When was it first circulated?
    c. Has it circulated as an email hoax more than once?
    d. Are there facts that Snopes offers to support their statement that it is a hoax?
12. There are several Web search engines.
    a. Use one of them to search for "search engines" and write down five different search engines.
    b. Using each of the five search engines you found, search for information about "BioWillie diesel." Record the number of hits in each of the search engines.
    c. How do you explain the difference in hit counts?
13. Now search for "Biowillie OR diesel" in the same five search engines. Record the number of hits for each. Compare your results with Exercise 12.

6
chapter

A Case Study in Online Research

Searching for Guinea Pig B

learning objectives

- Explain the advantages and disadvantages of online research
- Explain the advantages and disadvantages of primary and secondary sources in research
- Apply the case study example (R. Buckminster Fuller)
  - Use focus words to narrow an online search
  - Locate primary and secondary sources
  - Assess the authority of sources
  - Use online photos, video clips, and audio clips to enhance the research
  - Resolve controversial questions online
  - Follow up on interesting side questions
- Use the preceding skills to be able to do a curiosity-driven online research project

Sometimes I think we are alone [in the universe]. Sometimes I think we are not. In either case, the thought is quite staggering.

—R BUCKMINSTER FULLER

WE'RE ALL CURIOUS, and the IT knowledge we have developed so far is enough to help us discover the answers to questions we wonder about. Usually these questions are simple: "Is the Colorado ski area Telluride named after the chemical element Tellurium?" With a few clicks we find the answer, perhaps mention it to a friend, and that's that. The Web allows us to find the answer immediately. With the speed and convenience of the Web, we can easily add to our store of useless facts and amaze our friends.

But information technology offers us more than a simple chance to answer a single question. It allows us to investigate substantial topics that interest us and to probe deeply wherever our curiosity leads us. This is called *curiosity-driven research*. For centuries, inquisitive people who were curious about a topic would consult books, but now online research expands their opportunities.

Books do have certain advantages: They are generally authoritative, having been carefully researched, usually well written, and permanent. The disadvantages are that books contain only the information the author selects, so they give us only one point of view; they can take years to produce, so the information they offer may be dated; they are static; and despite so many titles, they cover only a limited number of topics. Books remain excellent sources of information. But the fact is, a book exists because someone was curious about a topic, researched it, and interpreted the findings. With the World Wide Web, we can choose a topic, conduct our own research, and interpret our findings. That is, our own curiosity drives the research.

In this chapter we learn to do curiosity-driven research on the Web, using the ideas introduced in earlier chapters. One goal is to explore the limits of the research that can be done on the Web, because not everything is in digital form, and not everything in digital form is worth reading. Another goal is to enjoy a tour through the life and mind of an amazing man, R. Buckminster Fuller, who described himself as both an engineer and a poet. The topic requires using different kinds of information resources. Finally, we learn to fill in the gaps in our knowledge. Although the case study covers many pages, it represents the search and research activity of a single interesting and enjoyable evening. The conclusion is that curiosity-driven research can be fun—and more interesting and rewarding than watching another rerun of *Friends*.

Getting Started with Online Research

Curiosity-driven research usually begins with a name or word we've heard or read. We wonder about it, but often at first we have too little information to begin an informed search with a search engine. In this case, we wonder about R. Buckminster Fuller, a man with a unique name. Even so, performing a Google search on

```
buckminster fuller
```

produces at least 552,000 hits (see Figure 6.1). Because we understand how searches work, we know that not all of those hits are for the person we are looking for. Some people have probably named their cat Buckminster Fuller. But even

```
buckminster fuller -cat
```

only reduces the hit count to 513,000, which is still ridiculously large.

Student Aid. Curiosity-driven research can be a random process, as different discoveries steer our search. It appears even more aimless when it's someone else's curiosity doing the driving. Though I explain why we choose the path we take, it is still possible for you to lose track of where we are. If that happens, you may want to check the summary provided at the end of the chapter in Table 6.1, which gives an overview of the research path we follow.

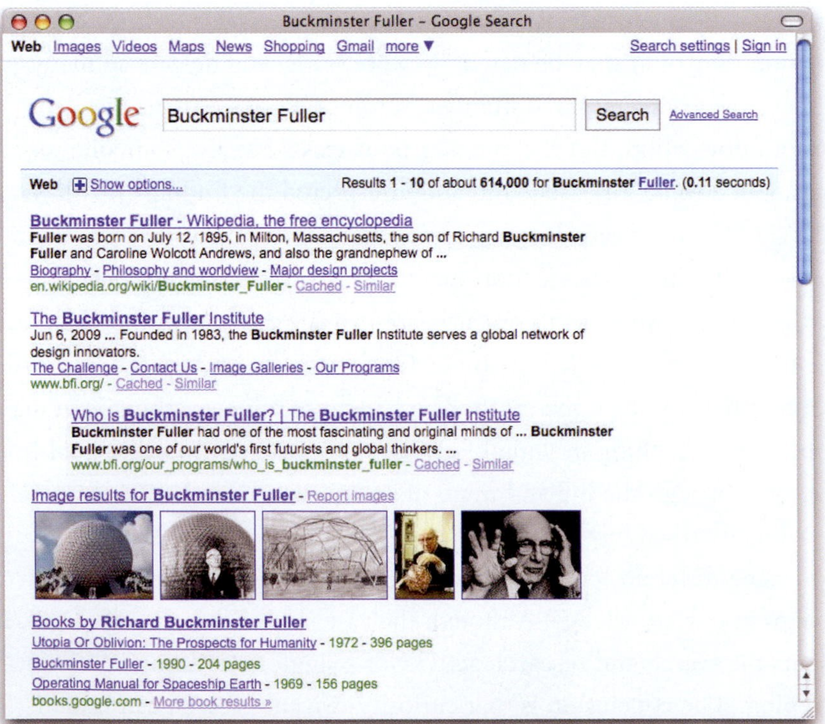

Figure 6.1 The first few hits for the **buckminister fuller** search.

To Research a Topic

We could start by reading the first hit listed by the search engine, but that's basically recreation, not research. To research a topic on the Internet, we must remember the lesson from the last chapter: that not everything we find will be true. Some sites are hoaxes, some are purposely misleading, some are humorously misleading, but many contain misinformation probably posted in the belief that it is correct, but it just isn't. We would like to find information that is true, correct, and accurate. It's a waste of time to begin reading sites without thinking about authoritativeness.

In addition to being wary of misinformation, we must also remember that page ranking, the process that orders the hits from highest to lowest, is not based on the quality of information, but on a kind of popularity—most visited and most referenced sites get the highest page rankings. This could be, and often is, because the site is authoritative; but it could also be that it's popular for other reasons. Page ranking is complicated, and it can be manipulated. Being high on the list is not a guarantee that the information is accurate.

To find what we're looking for from among this half million hits, and to reduce the risks of misinformation and placing too much importance on popularity, we take an approach that tries to find high accuracy sites. We do this by using precise search terms—call them **focus words**—that we hope will identify authoritative sites. But how do we find these precise words? Start by reading the first hit—if we're looking for focal words, it's research!

Orienting. The first hit of the `buckminster fuller` search is, as is often the case, Wikipedia, `en.wikipedia.org/wiki/Buckminster_Fuller`. Wikipedia generally is an extremely useful site for many reasons: It has wide coverage, it can be very current, the authors are often experts, it is possible to correct mistakes, and so forth. But as you know, anyone can contribute to Wikipedia, which limits the way we use it for research. It is not authoritative, but it is a great source to get us started on our research.

The Buckminster Fuller entry, shown in Figure 6.2, says first that he's R(ichard) Buckminster Fuller (1895–1983), and that he was an architect, author, inventor, designer, futurist, and visionary. So, already we know some labels that could apply to him. The text of the Wikipedia entry begins with an introduction, which mentions some of his accomplishments, but some of the terms—empheralization, Synergetics, fullerenes—are meaningless at this point, though we do recognize *geodesic dome*, which is called the best known of the inventions he developed.

Could "geodesic" be a term that will limit the search and focus us on authoritative sites? It is certainly closely linked with Fuller. But, it does not work, because when we try `buckminster fuller geodesic`, we get 576,000 hits—more than originally!

This introduction is followed by a long Biography section, a Philosophy section, and sections on Design projects, Quirks, and Practical achievements,

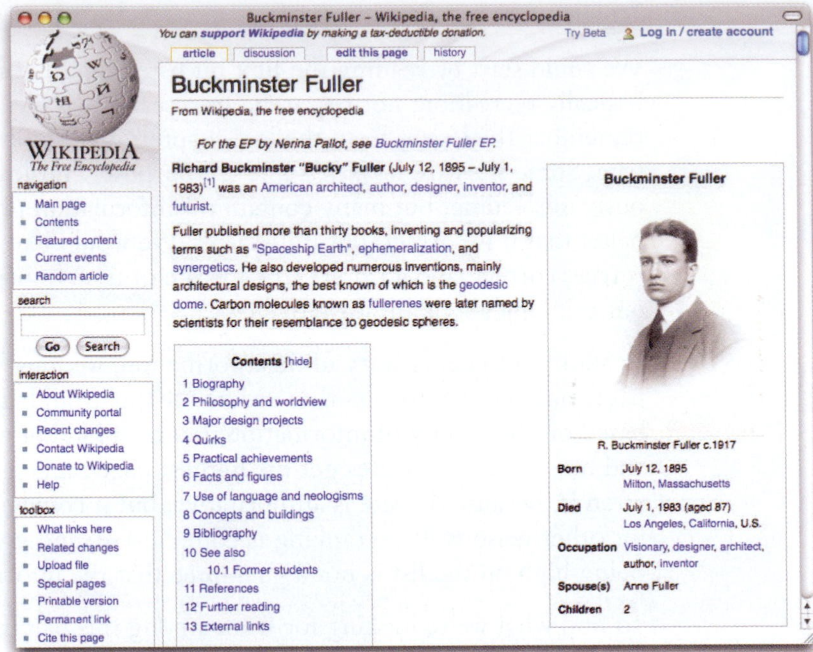

Figure 6.2 The beginning of the Buckminister Fuller Wikipedia entry.

Source: (http://en.wikipedia.org/wiki/Buckminster_Fuller) Wikipedia® is a registered trademark of the Wikimedia Foundation, Inc. (http://www.wikimediafoundation.org/), a non-profit organization. See the full terms of the GNU Free Documentation License in the Credits section at the end of this book.

most of which go into a lot of detail. There are other sections on Facts and figures, Use of language, Concepts, Bibliography, List of students, and References. It's a huge Wikipedia entry. What are the important points?

fluency ALERT

Wikipedia. Wikipedia, an encyclopedia created by Internet users, is near the top of many Google searches. It is a handy place to find the sort of information needed to start an effective search—terms unique to the topic being studied—but because anyone can edit most of the information, it is not an adequate reference. As stated on the Wikipedia site,

Wikipedia can be a great tool for learning and researching information. However, like all sources, not everything in Wikipedia is accurate, comprehensive, or unbiased. Many of the general rules of thumb for conducting research apply to Wikipedia, including:

- *Always be wary of any one single source ... or of multiple works that derive from a single source.*
- *Where articles have references to external sources (whether online or not), read the references and check whether they really do support what the article says.*
- *In most academic institutions, Wikipedia, along with most encyclopedias, is unacceptable as a major source for a research paper. Other encyclopedias, such as* Encyclopedia, Britannica *have notable authors working for them and may be cited as a secondary source in most cases.*

Accordingly, Wikipedia should always be cross-referenced.

Immediate distractions. The first sentence of the Biography section says,

> Fuller was born on July 12, 1895, in Milton, Massachusetts, the son of Richard Buckminster Fuller and Caroline Wolcott Andrews, and also the grandnephew of the American Transcendentalist Margaret Fuller.

Who's she? Is she someone we should know? Clicking on the link to her Wikipedia entry (it's longer than his), we find out (Sarah) Margaret Fuller was a nineteenth century pioneer of women's rights from Boston. She started out quietly as a magazine editor, but eventually she became a foreign correspondent in Italy for a newspaper, ended up involved with the revolution there, had a child by a marquis, and died in a shipwreck (along with the child and the marquis) off of Long Island. Apparently the Fullers are unusual people.

The second paragraph for RBF's biography begins

> ... began studying at Harvard. He was expelled from Harvard twice: first for looking at a porn troupe, and then, after having been readmitted, for his "irresponsibility and lack of interest".

So, although he entered Harvard twice, he never graduated; in fact "irresponsibility and lack of interest" sound like he might have flunked out. That's also an amazing fact, considering he's so famous for the geodesic dome.

At the bottom of the Fuller page is a long list of external links to sites outside of Wikipedia. Clicking on the first external link for, "*Everything I Know*" *Session Philly PA, 1975*, gets us to a site called *Conversations with Bucky* with copies of his 42-hour interview from 1975 (conversationswithbucky.pbworks.com). We can listen to him—it doesn't get more authoritative than that!—but before we listen to a single clip, we notice a link described as "very cool" for a mix of Crying Megamix and Buckminster Fuller—On Love at soundcloud.com/soundmind/phenomena-love-ft-buckminster-fuller-vs-edit (see Figure 6.3). This tells us nothing about Fuller, but it *is* very cool.

Distractions of this sort are extremely common in any research, whether it be at the library or on the Web. They are fun and interesting, but they don't

Figure 6.3 A mix of Crying Megamix and Buckminster Fuller's comments on love.

contribute much to a fuller understanding of Fuller. Back to the task of finding focus terms.

Focus Words

Returning to the main Wikipedia page, we noticed a photograph of a Dymaxion house, which kind of looks like a diner from an alien planet. Also, scrolling through the page we see the word *Dymaxion* several times. Not knowing what it means, we Google `define dymaxion`, and find out that the sources agree it is a trademark registered by Fuller, but there is no agreement as to what it means: Two extreme possibilities are that it's an acronym for "*dy*namic *max*imum tens*ion*," or maybe it means "doing more with less." In any case, it is closely coupled with Fuller and may be a link to his work and narrow our search to authoritative sources, making it a candidate focus term.

So, we search `buckminster fuller dymaxion` and score 39,400 hits. This is a significant reduction in the number of hits, but more importantly it focuses our attention on important sources. Reviewing the top 10 hits (Figure 6.4), we notice that these all refer to inventions Fuller created—a car, a house, a pro-

Figure 6.4 First hits for the `buckminster fuller dymaxion` search.

jection, a map—and these sites obviously discuss both the invention and the person. We notice the Wikipedia site listed as item six here. Adding *dymaxion* has narrowed the search a lot. It has served as a good focus word for the moment, but as we explore these pages, we will be on the lookout for others.

Images

Before diving into these sites, we wonder what "Bucky" looked like. There was a photo in Figure 6.2, but it was very formal and quite dated. Backing up to our original buckminster fuller search, we click on the Images link at the top of the Advanced Search window. We get 76,000 image hits—that is, .gif and .jpg files that match on these two words. They are not all pictures of him, of course, but there are plenty (see Figure 6.5). Clicking through them, there is an image with Fuller and his geodesic dome, pictures of him lecturing, and even a curious drawing of his face on a postage stamp.

Learning About Fuller

We have a list of sites that should be promising. We will spend a few minutes looking through them to familiarize ourselves with Fuller.

Fuller Biography

Clicking on the first link in the list of Figure 6.4, we get to About.com, a site that has brief signed articles. The short Fuller article (see Figure 6.6) is written by Mary Bellis. We don't know who she is, but at the moment we don't have a very clear picture of Fuller, and a brief profile is welcome. So we take a moment to skim it.

We notice two things about this article. First, when he was depressed in 1927 and was contemplating suicide, he decided, rather than following through, to dedicate his life to making the world a better place for all people. That's very inspirational. Second, in the last line it says that he called himself "Guinea Pig B" because he saw himself as a "lab animal" in the experiment of his life to make the world a better place. Perhaps "Guinea Pig B" can be another focus term. (But, we don't need one right now; we're still looking through the list from the search in Figure 6.4.)

Figure 6.5 Sample photographs from the Web found under the Images link for the **buckminster fuller** search.

Inventors are among the few people on this planet who have the ability to change life for all of us. When this ability is combined with a true love of mankind's and the planet's future, it is truly a sign of a great soul. Richard Buckminster Fuller, inventor, engineer, architect, mathematician, designer, poet, and philosopher, was a great soul and visionary who believed technology could save the World from itself, providing it was properly used.

Rebirth of an Inventor

In 1927, 'Bucky' Fuller had little reason to be optimistic about the future. The year found Bucky jobless and broke with a wife and newborn daughter Allegra to support. His first daughter, Alexandra, had died four years previous and Buckminster Fuller was still living in mourning. He had attempted suicide and was drinking heavily. In the darkness of that year, Buckminster Fuller went through a spiritual rebirth that changed the course of his life. He decided to dedicate his life to finding out how much difference one man could make in the world.

Renouncing personal and financial gain, Buckminster Fuller entered two years of seclusion to begin, in his own words: "the search for the principles governing the universe and help advance the evolution of humanity in accordance with them... finding ways of doing more with less to the end that all people everywhere can have more and more."

From 1927 on, Buckminster Fuller considered his life a living-experiment; he even gave himself the nickname 'Guinea Pig B' to denote his new life-purpose.

Figure 6.6 An **About.com** article on Buckminster Fuller, at **inventors.about.com/od/fstartinventors/a/Bucky.htm**.

6.1 Timeline. Our understanding of someone's life is often helped by a timeline correlating events with ages: How old was RBF in the Figure 6.2 photo, and in 1927 at the time of his suicidal thoughts?

Channel 13 WNET

The second site on the list is Channel 13 in New York City, WNET, a public broadcasting station (see Figure 6.7). We see first that we are at the Inventions page, and by clicking on the yellow arrows we can sweep through a slideshow of Fuller's most notable creations: Dymaxion car, Dymaxion house, geodesic dome, Synergetics, Dymaxion map, megastructures, and the Dymaxion bathroom. These are part of the companion Web site for a documentary that WNET produced on Fuller, called *Buckminster Fuller: Thinking Out Loud.*

These short, clear descriptions explain each of the ideas in a way we can understand. For example, the Dymaxion car—a three-wheeled, blimp-like vehicle—created quite a stir when Fuller introduced it. Several prototypes were built, but unfortunately one was involved in an accident, killing the driver. This is cited as the reason they were never commercially produced.

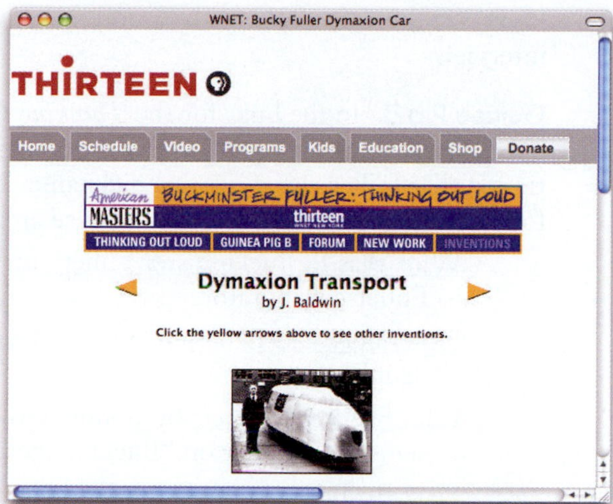

Figure 6.7 WNET page for the Dymaxion car, part of a slideshow of Fuller's inventions.

We check out the two short videos showing the car in operation; the voiceover in one points out that even in the twenty-first century, the car would be considered high performance and environmentally friendly.

Looking further at *Thinking Out Loud*. The WNET site is a goldmine of quality, understandable information. When we visit the *Thinking Out Loud* link, we get the background of the show. The page begins with the Fuller quote,

"Whenever I draw a circle, I immediately want to step out of it."

and gives helpful background about Fuller. There are a series of video quotes by experts and other important people who were probably used in the documentary. We listen to several of them.

One of the clips, www.thirteen.org/bucky/qt/1985.qt, shows Fuller describing in a speech some of his most radical ideas. He says:

> This is the real news of the last century. It is highly feasible to take care of all of humanity at a higher standard of living than anybody has ever experienced or dreamt of, to do so without having anybody profit at the expense of another—so that everybody can enjoy the whole earth—and it can all be done by 1985.

In the video clip we not only hear what he has to say, but we see the emphasis of his gestures and hear the conviction in his voice. His tone seems to say, "not only *can* we raise humanity's standard of living, we *should*." In this way, the spoken word is more powerful than the written word. The digitized information has given us valuable insight.

This observation reminds us that earlier we came across interviews with Fuller at *Conversations with Bucky*, but we got distracted by the mix track and never looked at the videos. We make a note to return to the site to listen to his interviews.

Guinea Pig B. In the links for the *Thinking Out Loud* program, we notice the one labeled "Guinea Pig B," and recall that the About.com biography mentioned that Fuller chose it as his nickname. Visiting the link, we find links to four authors writing about Fuller. These are:

Who Was R. Buckminster Fuller? by E. J. Applewhite, author and Fuller collaborator.

Experience and Experiencing by Allegra Fuller Snyder, Bucky's daughter.

Life, Facts & Artifacts by Bonnie Goldstein DeVarco, archivist and senior researcher on "Buckminster Fuller: Thinking Out Loud."

Dare To Be Naïve by Sarah Feldman. An overview of Fuller's life.

One new fact we find is that Fuller's daughter, Allegra, is apparently married to someone named Snyder. (No relation to the author of this text.)

Primary Sources

These are important essays because they are extremely reliable sources of information. Applewhite, as a collaborator, and Snyder, as Fuller's daughter, write from direct personal experience. We call them **primary sources**. We prefer information from primary sources for several reasons. First, the information is actual experience and personal impressions. Therefore, the information is unbiased, except to the degree that anything a person gathers from experience is subject to that person's ability to perceive it, motivation to be objective, and expressiveness. Primary sources are not subject to the distortion or omission that can happen when someone else reports information from a primary source. We call this "second-hand" reporting a **secondary source**. If someone reports from a secondary source, creating a tertiary source, more distortion and omission are possible. Using primary sources helps us create our own impression and point of view on the subject, and is why we have taken the time to find these pages.

Source 1—An RBF Collaborator. E. J. Applewhite, a collaborator, is considered a primary source (see Figure 6.8).

Source 2—RBF's Daughter. Buckminster Fuller's daughter, Allegra Fuller Snyder, is clearly a primary source (see Figure 6.9).

Assessing the Authenticity of Sources

Collaborators and children are easy to identify as primary sources, but our Guinea Pig B list contains two other authors.

Who Was R. Buckminster Fuller?

by E. J. Applewhite

. . . Fuller rejected the conventional disciplines of the universities by ignoring them. In their place he imposed his own self-discipline and his own novel way of thinking in a deliberate attempt—as poets and artists do—to change his generation's perception of the world. To this end he created the term Spaceship Earth to convince all his fellow passengers that they would have to work together as the crew of a ship. His was an earnest, even compulsive, program to convince his listeners that humans had a function in universe. Humans have a destiny to serve as "local problem solvers" converting their experience to the highest advantage of others. . . .

Figure 6.8 Excerpt from the Applewhite essay at the WNET "Guinea Pig B" site.

Experience and Experiencing

by Allegra Fuller Snyder

. . . My father was a warm, concerned and sharing father. As focused as he was on his own work he nevertheless included me in his experiences and experiencing. I remember with great clarity when I was about four years old. I was sick in bed and he was taking care of me. He sat down on the bed beside me, with his pencil in hand, and told me, through wonderful free-hand drawings, a Goldilocks story. I was Goldilocks and with his pencil he transported me, not to the Bear's house, but to universe, to help me understand something of Einstein's Theory of Relativity. What he was telling me was neither remote nor abstract. I was in a newly perceived universe. I was experiencing my father's thoughts and he was experiencing his own thinking as he communicated with me. It was exciting. We were sharing something together and I felt very warm and close to him in that experience. Something of this episode was later remembered in a book called Tetrascroll. . . .

Figure 6.9 Excerpt from the Allegra Fuller Snyder essay at the WNET "Guinea Pig B" site.

Source 3 — An RBF Archivist. Bonnie Goldstein DeVarco presents a fascinating account of Fuller's archive—he saved everything! Much of the content concerns specifics of the archive that are somewhat unrelated to our interest. But two paragraphs stand out in her section on Ephemeralization, quoted here (see Figure 6.10).

DeVarco's essay is based on information from the archive of Fuller's papers and artifacts, which DeVarco described as "approximately 90,000 pounds of personal history." Fuller produced this information, so it is a primary source. We presume that DeVarco, an archivist and researcher, is accurate and reliable. Though her essay is not technically a primary source, we can trust it.

Life, Facts and Artifacts

by Bonnie Goldstein DeVarco

Ephemeralization

Although the tactile pleasures of sorting through the physical artifacts of Bucky's life brings a dimension all its own to the discovery of who he was and who he shared his life with, almost the same could be done with the same body of materials available on a computer screen—from drawings, letters and manuscripts to "ephemerabilia," at the touch of a fingertip. In hundreds of letters spanning well over half a century, the love story of Bucky and Anne is told. Anne's letters carry a lilting youthful quality that punctuates even the most fatuous groupings of correspondence to be found in the Chronoofile* boxes. Her handwriting is like a beautiful victorian stenciled wallpaper and her ardent and boundless devotion gives life to the saying that behind every great man is a great woman. It is no wonder he personally deemed his most famous geodesic dome, at the 1967 Montreal Exposition, his "Taj Majal to Anne" in honor of their 50th anniversary.

... And how affecting it is to see in a letter to his mother bound into the 1928 Chronofile volume, Fuller's youthful discovery of his Great Aunt Margaret Fuller's thought and its parallels to his own as he writes, "I have been reading much by Margaret Fuller lately. I was astonished to find that some things I have been writing myself are about identical to things I find in her writings. I am terribly interested and am astounded fully that I should have grown to this age and never have read anything of her or grandfather Fuller's." . . .

*RBF kept his correspondence and other documents in a bound file organized in chronological order called the Chronofile.

Figure 6.10 Excerpt from the DeVarco essay at the WNET "Guinea Pig B" site.

Source 4 — A Content Developer and Writer. Sarah Feldman's essay has relied on the Fuller archive for its information, so it may be an excellent resource. As researchers, however, we wonder who she is. Her title or relationship to Fuller is not provided. For example, is she a scholar with academic credentials who we assume tried to be accurate, or does she write advertising copy for used car companies and perhaps embellishes the facts? We look her up in Biography.com, but her bio is not there. We go to the WNET Web site and search the site for her name. We get a link to her bio, which reads

Sarah Feldman Sarah Feldman is a consultant, teacher trainer and content developer. She has served as the National Project Director for the National Teacher Training Institute (NTTI) at Thirteen/WNET New York, and as the National Project Director for the National Teacher Training Institute for Math, Science and Technology (NTTI). She has also developed content for Thirteen's wNetStation, wNetSchool, and a variety of broadcast, multimedia, online, and videotape projects. She has also taught second grade in the South Bronx and Harlem, where she focused on students' academic and personal development.

As a director at a national teacher-training institute, content developer, and writer with access to the Fuller archive, Feldman sounds very reliable, so we are confident that her essay is also. See Figure 6.11 for an excerpt of her essay.

Dare to Be Naïve

by Sarah Feldman

Jobless, without savings or prospects, with a wife and newborn daughter to support, suicidal and drinking heavily, in 1927 Richard Buckminster Fuller had little reason to be optimistic about the future. R. Buckminster Fuller—or "Bucky," as he's affectionately known—transformed that low point in his life into a catalyst for transforming our planet's future as well as his own. ...

Renouncing personal success and financial gain, at age 32 Fuller set out to "search for the principles governing the universe and help advance the evolution of humanity in accordance with them." Central to his mission were the ideas that 1) he had to divest himself of false ideas and "unlearn" everything he could not verify through his own experience, and 2) human nature—and nature itself—could not be reformed and therefore it was the environment—and our response to it—that must be changed. Fuller entered into a two-year period of total seclusion, and began working on design solutions to what he inferred to be mankind's central problems. With his goal of "finding ways of doing more with less to the end that all people— everywhere—can have more and more," Fuller began designing a series of revolutionary structures. The most famous of these was the pre-fabricated, pole-suspended single-unit dwelling Dymaxion House. (The term Dymaxion was derived from the words "dynamic," "maximum," and "ion.") . . . Fuller's designs tended to be based [on] a geometry that used triangles, circles and tetrahedrons more than the traditional planes and rectangles. His Dymaxion Air-Ocean Map, which projected a spherical world as a flat surface with no visible distortion, brought him to the attention of the scientific community in 1943, and his map was the first cartographic projection of the world to ever be granted a U.S. patent.

A self-proclaimed "apolitical," Fuller maintained there was "no difference between [the] left and the right." Nevertheless, he admitted he struggled to "dare to be naïve," and retained an optimistic faith that "an omni-integrated, freely intercirculating, omniliterate world society" was within our grasp. A prolific writer, Fuller's magnum opus is undoubtedly "Synergetics: Explorations in the Geometry of Thinking," on which he collaborated with E. J. Applewhite in 1975. The work is considered a major intellectual achievement in its examinations of language, thought and the universe.

Though he only stood 5'2" tall, R. Buckminster Fuller looms large over the twentieth century. Though a man of incredible intellect and vision, many of "Bucky's" fans remain most impressed by the man's awe-inspiring humility—and his abiding love for his planet and his fellow human beings. "Above all," said Fuller, "I was motivated in 1927 and ever since by the most mysterious drive we ever experience—that of love. I don't think there's any influence upon my life that compares with . . . love."

Figure 6.11 Excerpt from the Feldman essay at the WNET "Guinea Pig B" site.

Assessing Our Progress

So far, we have found quotes and video clips by Fuller, and four essays (Figures 6.8 through 6.11) about him. We have assessed the reliability of these sources, and they are either from primary sources or from researchers who used the Fuller archive. This is excellent information, and is worth the time to read it. By taking the time to track down these sources, we can learn about

Fuller in a way that allows us to form our own impression, and interpret the data as we think is appropriate. The sources give us direct information—we decide what we think about it.

Notice that we do not mean that secondary or tertiary sources are of no use—we just used two from Wikipedia and About.com. They were biographical sketches that probably relied on generally available information about Fuller. We assumed they are accurate. The About.com article was signed, and a link was provided allowing us to check out the author. The point is that the secondary sources met our need for a quick introduction. Now, because we want to find the most accurate information about Fuller's life and philosophy—so that we can make up our own minds—we go to the primary source(s) ourselves.

Reading the essays gives us extraordinary insight into Buckminster Fuller; we can now describe him in our own words. He believed, according to Applewhite, that technology is not the "problem" but rather the "solution," and that deeply understanding technology is the key to individual behavior as well as to "saving" society. Snyder's essay emphasized how Fuller was a loving father. DeVarco quotes Fuller's description of the Montreal geodesic dome as the "Taj Majal to Anne" (his wife), and Feldman quotes Fuller as saying that he turned his life around in 1927, motivated by love, the greatest influence on his life. It is a personal story of a deep thinker. The geodesic dome was his "virtuoso invention" [Applewhite] and Synergetics, a "major intellectual achievement," was his greatest work [Feldman].

And our search answers questions that the short biographies cannot. Feldman, for example, confirms that Dymaxion stands for "*dy*namic," "*max*imum," and "*ion*."

Chronofile and "Everything I Know"

The third link from our Figure 6.4 list is to the Buckminster Fuller Institute. (We notice that this was the second hit in our original search, but we didn't know then that it was important.) We click on the site, which has a very impressive name and an enormous amount of information, but being impressive and enormous on the Web doesn't mean accurate. The page opens up to the Dymaxion projection (see Figure 6.12), which we'll read about in a moment, but first we go to *Home > About BFI* to check out what the Buckminster Fuller Institute is. The institute began in 1983, and among other things, the site says it

> Served as custodians for the Fuller Archive for 16 years, providing access to scholars and researchers, Fuller's exhaustive collection of papers and artifacts.

So, they kept all of Fuller's stuff for 16 years. Certainly, it should be an authoritative site. After all, this was where the material was located that DaVarco and the others used to make the WNET documentary. They have

Figure 6.12 BFI site linked to by the third hit of the **buckminster fuller dymaxion** search.

his patents here, and the books he wrote, and transcripts of *Everything I Know*, and they are leading design competitions. So, it looks like a reliable site, and we will poke around.

But first, where did Fuller's archive go? We do a Web search on buckminster fuller archive and the first hit is Stanford University Libraries R. Buckminster Fuller Archive home page. Clicking on the About the Archive link, we get the page shown in Figure 6.13. They seem to have acquired the archive the same year BFI must have relinquished it, so we will guess it went from BFI to Stanford. Reading about the archive—it contains 1,300 linear feet (about 400 meters) of papers and over 2,000 hours of recordings—it really is amazing.

In the portion headed Dymaxion Chronofile, Fuller describes recording everything he did as though it were the record of a typical "human being going through the Gay Nineties into the 20th century." The Stanford librarians call the Chronofile his "lab notebook." Fuller, it seems, was less of a "lab rat" than a pack rat, saving everything he touched throughout his life. No wonder so much is known about him.

Back at the BFI home page, we click on *Who Is Buckminster Fuller?* We find a huge amount of authoritative information, including a biography, ending with the amazing fact that *Anne* (his wife) *and Bucky died within 36 hours of one another one week before their sixty-seventh wedding anniversary!* Also, the site

About the Archive

In 1999, Stanford University Libraries acquired the archives of Richard Buckminster Fuller (1895-1983), an American polymath whose versatile career as an architect, lecturer, mathematician, writer, and social critic is documented extensively. The collection contains over 1300 linear feet of papers and manuscripts, 2000 hours of video and audio recordings, and thousands of models and other artifacts.

Image Courtesy Estate of R. Buckminster Fuller

Dymaxion Chronofile

The centerpiece of the collection, in many ways, is the Dymaxion Chronofile, an exhaustive journal of Fuller's trajectory from 1920 until his death in 1983. Fuller had been collecting clippings and artifacts since he was a child. But in 1917, he began a formal chronological file which he would later call the Dymaxion Chronofile. The Chronofile was a vast scrapbook that included copies of all his incoming and outgoing correspondence, newspaper clippings, notes and sketches, and even dry cleaning bills. Initially, the Chronofile was bound into handsome leather-backed volumes. In later years, to save space and expenses, the Chronofile was simply stored in boxes. By the end of his life, this exhaustive "lab notebook" of his life's experiment amounted to 270 linear feet.

Fuller intended for the Chronofile to be a case study of his life in context, in which his daily activities were presented in parallel with developments in technology and society. In it, he at once traced the evolution of his own thoughts, relationships, and business ventures; and documented new inventions, trends, and technologies that were emerging on the broader level.

"If somebody kept a very accurate record of a human being, going through the era from the Gay'90's, from a very different kind of world through the turn of the century--as far into the twentieth century as you might live. I decided to make myself a good case history of such a human being and it meant that I could not be judge of what was valid to put in or not. I must put everything in, so I started a very rigorous record."*

Figure 6.13 The About the Archive page from Stanford University, www-sul.stanford.edu/depts/spc/fuller/about.html.

links to the essays that we found at the Guinea Pig B page as well as others. Clicking through to Online Resources, we find a larger gold mine still, including entire books by Fuller, the Chronofile transcript, and more.

Audio Clips: *Everything I Know*

Remembering that we want to listen to some of the interviews, we wonder, what does Bucky say about Allegra? If the archive only included the 42 hours of audio clips, we would have to listen to them to find out, because audio information is not searchable. However, JoAnne Ishimine, a BFI volunteer, has transcribed the audio into text so the clips can be searched. We can search the site for Allegra. Among the resulting hits is one (session 12, clip 154) where Fuller mentions how Allegra loves to dance and then describes a conversation they had.

> And, when she was twelve, she said "Daddy," we were living in New York at that time, she said "Daddy, you were brought up in Boston with the custom that it is ill mannered for men to make gestures that the man who is properly cultivated is well in possession of his movements, and he just doesn't even move his head, he just talks and sits very motionless, beautifully disciplined to do that." And she said, "I'll tell you, I don't know if I really am a dancer, but whatever I am, my body wants to

> talk all the time." And she said, "Daddy, I like your ideas very, very much and I want them to prevail, but I think you are frustrating your ideas by your disciplining yourself to sit motionless. I think if you'd just let yourself go things would happen way better for you." She was used to my having a lot of hard luck, nobody was paying any attention to me in those days. And so she seemed so wise that I think I did everything I could to free myself up. . . . But she did make it perfectly clear, a child does move comfortably and uses his body, so I began to let myself do [*sic*] I am utterly unaware of the motions, I assure you, but I have had moving pictures taken of me I've seen myself when I've been giving a lecture and I'm practically going all over the stage like a ballet dancer.

We can see that he *is* an animated speaker in the lectures we watched from the WNET *Buckminster Fuller: Thinking Out Loud* program.

Surfing Around a Dymaxion Map

Returning to Fuller's Dymaxion map, which is how we got to the BFI Web site in the first place, we wonder what it is. The BFI site seems to concentrate on a cardboard version you can buy from them that uses the Dymaxion projection. Clicking around the site shows more information, but none that is very useful to us. So, although the BFI site was very helpful by linking us to much Fuller information, we look for other sources to find out about the map.

Recalling that the next item in our Figure 6.4 list is the Dymaxion map page at Wikipedia, en.wikipedia.org/wiki/Dymaxion_map, we click on that link. The page not only defines the Dymaxion projection, but it shows an animation of the idea. Fuller projected the globe onto an icosahedron as shown in Figure 6.14. Clicking on *icosahedron*, we link to the Wikipedia page for that geometric solid—it is a 20-sided regular solid with (equilateral) triangular faces. The page has a lot of geometry on it, but not being concerned with its

Figure 6.14 Dymaxion map showing images from Chris Rywalt's animation.

geometry, we return to the animation. Reading the Dymaxion map explanation, we get the idea of the projection: think of an icosahedron inside the earth so its "points" just touch the surface, and then imagine the earth's curved surface shrinking down onto the icosahedron's faces.

The animation then shows an icosahedron unfolding, which is extremely cool. It really gives the idea of flattening out the earth. Recalling that there is an animation at the bottom of our Figure 6.4 list, we click to it: www.westnet.com/~crywalt/unfold.html. The site is Chris Rywalt's page about programming the animation. Skipping the programming, we grab a high-resolution version of the animation to watch closely. This minimal-distortion map shows the continents in realistic proportion to one another. The specific unfolding shows the continents as one essentially contiguous island in a single sea. It's Fuller's schematic diagram for Spaceship Earth.

Resolving Questions

There is something confusing here. We knew before we started surfing the site that Fuller invented the geodesic dome, as shown in Figure 6.15. It's his "virtuoso invention." He also invented the Dymaxion map, as shown in Figure 6.14. The map page tells us that the map projects the earth onto an icosahedron. But the geodesic dome at Montreal's Expo 67 was smoother than an icosahedron. What's the difference? Are they the same idea? If not, how is a geodesic dome related to an icosahedron?

The BFI site may be the best place to find information about geodesics and the map's projection, but we didn't notice any links to such a topic in our search for a Dymaxion map explanation. There are several ways to answer questions like this. First, we can find definitions to the two terms; the answer may be apparent from the two definitions. So we search **define geodesic** and get

> the shortest line between two points on a mathematically defined surface

Figure 6.15 Geodesic dome—from the U.S. Pavilion at Montreal's Expo 67.

A geodesic is a line. We just found out an icosahedron is a solid, so they are different. But that doesn't really say how.

Another way is simply to do a search on something that approximates the question. This could get us to "answer" sites, which may or may not give us an authoritative answer. But, it's worth a try. We search difference icosahedron geodesic and get back 16,000 hits. The first two are descriptions of patents, which are useless for our investigation, but the third one is from Wolfram MathWorld, mathworld.wolfram.com/GeodesicDome.html. After showing a collection of geometric shapes—cubes, icosahedra, and so forth—there's this explanation:

> A geodesic dome is a triangulation of a Platonic solid or other polyhedron to produce a close approximation to a sphere (or hemisphere) ... Fuller's original dome was constructed from an icosahedron by adding isosceles triangles about each polyhedron vertex and slightly repositioning the polyhedron vertices.

A perfect answer: Starting with the icosahedron, simply divide each triangular face to make isosceles triangles and "pull out" the vertices to approximate the sphere's surface.

We have our answer if we can trust this site. What is wolfram.com? Clicking, we find that the company makes the math software *Mathematica*, and Steven Wolfram, the company's founder is, basically, a genius. So, we'll definitely trust this answer.

Changing Directions

One very curious point emerges from visiting the Wolfram.com site. The part that I left out of the preceding quote contains the following:

> The first geodesic dome was built in Jena, Germany in 1922 on top of the Zeiss optics company as a projection surface for their planetarium projector. R. Buckminster Fuller subsequently popularized so-called geodesic domes, and explored them far more thoroughly.

This says someone else created the first geodesic dome in Germany, and that Fuller gave it its name and pushed the concept further. This is strange. Everyone we have read so far has credited Fuller with inventing the geodesic dome. Did he work at Zeiss? The BFI biography doesn't say anything about him working at Zeiss. We decide to find out what's going on.

The next hit on our difference icosahedron geodesic search is a blog by Don Havey, www.donhavey.com/blog/tutorials/tutorial-3-the-icosahedron-sphere/, who says

> although it is generally acknowledged that [Buckminster Fuller] did not invent the shape or concept, but rather investigated and expanded upon them. Read more in the Wikipedia article on geodesic spheres.

We don't know who Havey is—his site is an interesting tutorial on transforming an icosahedron into a geodesic dome—but he's confirming Wolfram's assertion. He gives the Wikipedia link, so we click on it.

The Wikipedia page has the following explanation

> The first dome that could be called "geodesic" in every respect was designed just after World War I by Walther Bauersfeld,[1] chief engineer of the Carl Zeiss optical company, for a planetarium to house his new planetarium projector. The dome was patented, constructed by the firm of Dykerhoff and Wydmann on the roof of the Zeiss plant in Jena, Germany, and opened to the public in 1922. Some 30 years later, R. Buckminster Fuller further investigated this concept and named the dome "geodesic" from field experiments with Kenneth Snelson and others at Black Mountain College in the late 1940s. Although Fuller was not the original inventor, he developed and popularized the idea, and received a U.S. patent.

So, apparently Fuller didn't invent the geodesic dome; Bauersfeld did. He's credited with popularizing it and probably for recognizing how useful it could be. Again, we have to confirm these Wikipedia contributions from other sources.

Searching on **bauersfeld geodesic** we find over 730 hits. All the hits state that Bauersfeld built the first dome, but we don't know much about the authoritativeness of the first five sites. The sixth in the list is the home page of Princeton University physicist Tony Rothman, whom we can safely rely on, www.physics.princeton.edu/~trothman/domes.html. He gives a photo of the Zeiss dome under construction, and the Zeiss patent (see Figure 6.16). Case closed. Bauersfeld did it first; Fuller popularized it.

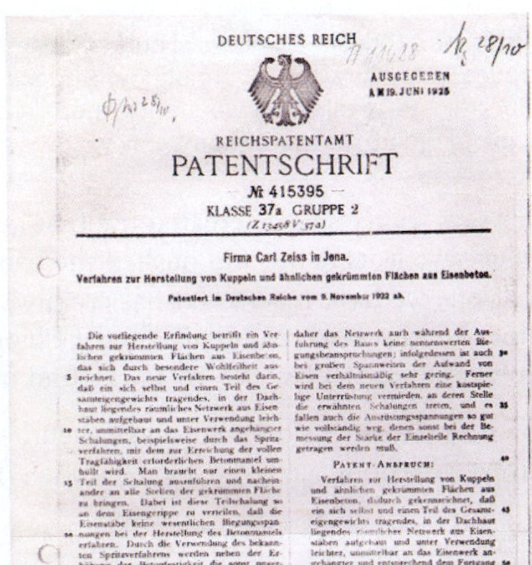

DEUTSCHES REICH

AUSGEGEBEN AM 19. JUNI 1925

REICHSPATENTAMT

PATENTSCHRIFT

№ 415395

KLASSE 37a GRUPPE 2

(Z 13458 V/37a)

Firma Carl Zeiss in Jena.

Verfahren zur Herstellung von Kuppeln und ähnlichen gekrümmten Flächen aus Eisenbeton.

Patentiert im Deutschen Reiche vom 9. November 1922 ab.

Die vorliegende Erfindung betrifft ein Verfahren zur Herstellung von Kuppeln und ähnlichen gekrümmten Flächen aus Eisenbeton, das sich durch besondere Wohlfeilheit auszeichnet. Das neue Verfahren besteht darin, daß ein sich selbst und einen Teil des Gesamteigengewichts tragendes, in der Dachhaut liegendes räumliches Netzwerk aus Eisenstäben aufgebaut und unter Verwendung leichter, unmittelbar an das Eisenwerk angehängter Schalungen, beispielsweise durch das Spritzverfahren, mit dem zur Erreichung der vollen Tragfähigkeit erforderlichen Betonmantel umhüllt wird. Man braucht nur einen kleinen Teil der Schalung auszuführen und nacheinander an alle Stellen der gekrümmten Fläche zu bringen. Dabei ist diese Teilschalung so an dem Eisengerippe zu verteilen, daß die Eisenstäbe keine wesentlichen Biegungsspannungen bei der Herstellung des Betonmantels erfahren. Durch die Verwendung des bekannten Spritzverfahrens werden neben der Erhöhung der Betonfestigkeit die sonst unver-

daher das Netzwerk auch während der Ausführung des Baues keine nennenswerten Biegungsbeanspruchungen; infolgedessen ist auch bei großen Spannweiten der Aufwand von Eisen verhältnismäßig sehr gering. Ferner wird bei dem neuen Verfahren eine kostspielige Unterrüstung vermieden, an deren Stelle die erwähnten Schalungen treten, und es fallen auch die Ausrüstungsspannungen so gut wie vollständig weg, denen sonst bei der Bemessung der Stärke der Einzelteile Rechnung getragen werden muß.

PATENT-ANSPRUCH:

Verfahren zur Herstellung von Kuppeln und ähnlichen gekrümmten Flächen aus Eisenbeton, dadurch gekennzeichnet, daß ein sich selbst und einen Teil des Gesamteigengewichts tragendes, in der Dachhaut liegendes räumliches Netzwerk aus Eisenstäben aufgebaut und unter Verwendung leichter, unmittelbar an das Eisenwerk angehängter und entsprechend dem Fortgang

Figure 6.16 German patent for the idea of the geodesic dome, but not by that name.

But, before leaving Wikipedia, we wonder who Kenneth Snelson is, and what's with Black Mountain. So, we click on the Kenneth Snelson link. He's a sculptor living in Oregon, apparently, and has created some spectacular work. His Wikipedia entry says, relative to our interest,

> Snelson claims that Buckminster Fuller, who was once his professor, took credit for Snelson's discovery of the concept of tensegrity. Fuller gave the idea its name, combining 'tension' and 'structural integrity.' The geodesic domes, which Fuller popularized, are the most commonly known structures whose composition depends on tensegrity.

Amazing. This is very odd. Did Fuller do anything but name them and popularize them? Whose claims are correct? We need to do some more looking.

Searching on snelson buckminster fuller, we immediately find an email written by Snelson to the *International Journal of Space Structures* in which he gives his side of a controversy with Fuller. He is answering an IJSS request for information for a planned special publication on tensegrity (www.grunch.net/snelson/rmoto.html). The events happened at Black Mountain College in North Carolina in the summer of 1949. Snelson, who had met Fuller at Black Mountain the previous summer, had spent an aimless year building models (or artwork—he couldn't decide whether he was an engineer or an artist) that used geometrical ideas he learned from Fuller.

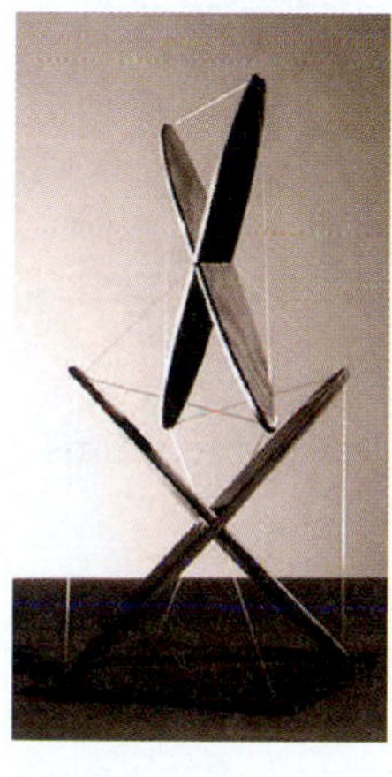

Snelson's email (which we were not permitted to reprint, but you can read at the above site) tells of his first morning at Black Mountain when he showed Fuller his plywood X-Piece. Snelson had sent Fuller photos of the sculpture, but based on Fuller's reaction, he concluded that Fuller had not understood the design. But now, Fuller turned the sculpture over and over, studying it care-fully. Finally, Fuller asked if he could keep it. Relieved that Fuller was not annoyed with him for having used Bucky's geometry for artwork, Snelson agreed, although he hadn't planned to give his work away. Later, according to Snelson, Bucky said that the sculpture had "disappeared" from his apartment.

At the core of Snelson's belief that he contributed to ideas Fuller took credit for, is Fuller's apparently slow comprehension of the X-Piece. Snelson offers a second example of proof that Fuller did not fully comprehend the implications of tensegrity. He says that on the next day, Fuller told him that the idea was clever, but that the configuration was wrong. Rather than using compression members in an X structure, they should be arranged in a tetrahedron. Snelson reports that he'd already used the tetrahedron in a mobile and had decided that the X structure was better than the tetrahedron because the X could grow along all three axes rather than the single axis of the tetrahedron. But Snelson was reluctant to challenge his teacher—students just didn't do that in 1949. Again, Snelson believes Bucky didn't fully comprehend the idea, and therefore didn't conceive it first.

Snelson says that the next day he built Bucky a model of the tetrahedral structure using adjustable metal curtain rods. He described himself as "wistful" as he watched Bucky being photographed with the model, but he didn't suspect Fuller's motives.

Fuller said in a letter to Snelson that he mentioned Snelson's role in speeches. But, according to Snelson, he never got credit in print. When in 1959, Fuller's tensegrity ideas were displayed at the Museum of Modern Art in New York City, Snelson forced Fuller publicly to admit the truth about the idea for the structure.

Searching at the Buckminster Fuller Institute for Snelson, we quickly find Fuller's version of the incident in *Everything I Know*, Vol. 8, though he incorrectly places it in 1958–1959:

> Then in the second summer at Black Mountain, Ken showed me a sculpture that he had made, and, in an abstract world of sculpture, and what he had made was a-a tensegrity structure. And he had a structural member out here two structural members out here, that were not touching the base, and they were being held together held they were in tension. And I explained to Ken that this was a tensegrity. Man, I had found, had only developed tensegrity structure in wire wheels and in universal joints. . . . When Ken Snelson showed me this little extension thing he did it was really just an arbitrary form, he saw that you could do it [tension integrity], but he was just, as I say, an artistic form or something startling to look at. And I said, "Ken, that really is the tensegrity and it's what I'm looking for because what you've done I can see relates to the octahedron and this gives me a clue of how this goes together in all the energetic geometry."
>
> So Ken opened up my eyes to the way to go into the geometry.

Fuller clearly sees Snelson as having contributed, in the form of his artwork, one more instance of tensegrity to the two that Fuller already knew. He seems not to be very defensive in his version.

Overall, Snelson's criticism of Fuller mutes the rah-rah enthusiasm of the many sites we have found. Snelson makes a case for his contribution to tensegrity. Fuller probably didn't credit him enough. But there's also more to Fuller's work than that. RBF has a solid reputation still, but it's not quite what we originally thought.

Exploring Side Questions

Finally, in terms of filling out our profile of Fuller, there is the repeated mention of buckminsterfullerenes. What are they?

They are carbon molecules. To find more, we ask Google to search on buckminsterfullerene and we find many useful links. The first link is to Wikipedia, of course, but the next is to a university research lab, www.msu.edu/~hungerf9/bucky1.html, Michigan State University's Nanotechnology Laboratory, which gives us a definition:

Buckminsterfullerene, C_{60}, the third allotrope of Carbon, was discovered in 1985 by Robert Curl, Harold Kroto, and Richard Smalley. Using laser evaporation of graphite they found C_n clusters (where $n > 20$ and even) of which the most common were found to be C_{60} and C_{70}. For this discovery they were awarded the 1996 Nobel Prize in Chemistry.

To see a fullerne, also known as a buckyball, we click "Images" on the Google Advanced Search page, and get 5,800 hits. One of them is a page from Caltech, the California Institute of Technology, eands.caltech.edu/articles/LXVIII1_2/apostolic.html, and we see that the structure fulfills the "interlocking polygons" requirement of the geodesic dome definition (see Figure 6.17).

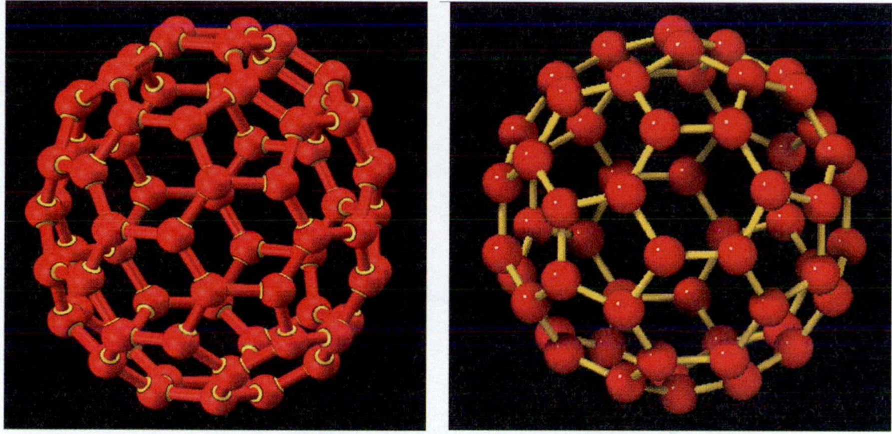

Figure 6.17 Images of buckminsterfullerenes, C_{60} and C_{70} (also known as fullerenes or buckyballs).

Checking the online dictionary, we find that *allotrope* means "structural form of" (making buckyballs different from graphite and diamond forms of carbon). We now know that a fullerene is a stable molecule of carbon composed of 60 or 70 atoms in the shape of a geodesic sphere. However, the discovery of fullerenes piques our curiosity, and we decide to go to the Nobel Prize site to learn more about the discovery.

Recalling that all countries have a country extension, and that Sweden is the home of the Nobel Prize, we guess that the site is www.nobel.se, which redirects us to the correct site, nobelprize.org. There we click Nobel Prizes > Nobel Prize in Chemistry > All Nobel Laureates in Chemistry > 1996 to find the page shown in Figure 6.18. From there we can read the "illustrated presentation" explaining the equipment and experiment that Curl, Kroto, and Smalley used to produce buckyballs and win the Nobel Prize. As it happens, C_{60} has the same structure as a soccer ball: 12 pentagons and 20 hexagons.

The mention of soccer gets us to wondering how the A. C. Milan team is doing, so we click up. ...

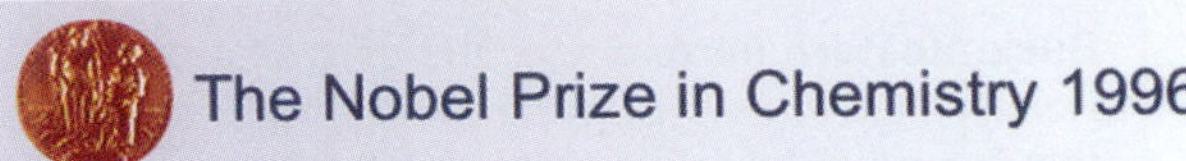

"for their discovery of fullerenes"

Figure 6.18 The Nobel Prize site for the discovery of the buckminsterfullerene.

Case Study Wrap-Up

We explored Buckminster Fuller's life because he was an interesting person. We're finished, at least for the moment, so we can put the computer to sleep and get some sleep ourselves. But often the next step is to use the information for some other purpose, say, to write a report. In that case, before turning off the computer we should create a summary file containing:

- Bookmarks from the sites we visited—they can be copied from the browser as a group
- Notebook entries of the search terms used with the search engines
- Brief notes on our impressions from the information we found—interesting discoveries, most useful sites, why we followed up on some topics and skipped others, and so forth

This information is our record of the research process, which we can refer to for writing our report. We should write down our impressions right away because they fade. The amazement of new discoveries wears off, we forget things, and time changes our attitude about the content. It is important to have time to digest what we've learned and to organize it in our minds, but the excitement of learning something new gives a fresh quality that we cannot reconstruct later.

The Process

The goal of this chapter was to illustrate curiosity-driven research using the Web, and we have been quite successful (see a summary of our efforts in Table 6.1). The two main themes of this tour through Buckminster Fuller's life were the process of finding the information and the methods of deciding whether the information was authoritative. We tried to use the "right" source for the type of information we wanted.

Searching for Guinea Pig B: The Buckminster Fuller Research Path

The entries in Table 6.1 describe the research path followed in this chapter. Most lines represent an access to a WWW document, image, audio or film clip, and so on. Indenting indicates subsidiary actions.

To make the search effective, we wanted to learn enough to ask the right questions. So, we started by checking the Wikipedia biography, but we wanted more authoritative information. We tried a search on **buckminster fuller geodesic** and had more hits than when we started. But in the biography we learned that Fuller had invented something called a Dymaxion house, so we decided to search for information containing **dymaxion**. This greatly reduced the hits. In the same way, clicking on the **"Guinea Pig B" link at the WNET site** led to a rich set of links mostly of primary sources. Later on, "buckminsterfullerene," with its narrow technical meaning, led us to that information quickly. We didn't do a Web search each time we wanted information; instead, we sometimes went directly to a likely source—dictionary, WNET personnel, the RBF Institute, the Nobel Prize page—based on the type of information we wanted. This saved us from "aimless wandering" around the Web.

Table 6.1 Record of the case study search

Begin with a Google search **buckminster fuller** and get many hits
Start reading first one—Wikipedia—to find some characterizing focal term
Finding **geodesic** as a candidate, search **buckminster fuller geodesic**, but it doesn't limit search
Learn basic facts about RBF's life, including that he is related to Margaret Fuller
Check Wikipedia biography of Margaret Fuller—nineteenth-century feminist thinker, died in shipwreck
Learn RBF entered Harvard twice, and exited twice, involuntarily, without a degree
Click on "Conversations with Bucky," but rather than listening to him, check a mix track at Sound Cloud
Find **dymaxion** as candidate focal term; check definition—trademark with widely different meanings
Google **buckminster fuller dymaxion** and get Figure 6.4 hit list, reducing number greatly
Return for a moment to **buckminster fuller** search to click on "Images" to find photos of him
Start reading **About.com** bio, discover suicide thoughts, redirected life to helping mankind; called self Guinea Pig B
Make note to use **guinea pig b** as focus term when we need another one

(continues)

Table 6.1 Record of the case study search (continued)

- Check WNET site from *Thinking Out Loud*; study slideshow of inventions including Dymaxion car videos
- Click thru WNET site, view Fuller passionately arguing world hunger/housing woes can be eliminated by 1985
  - Make note to watch other Fuller clips from *Everything I Know*
- Find four WNET essays: Applewhite, Snyder, DeVarco, and Feldman
  - Assess sources—Applewhite and Snyder are primary, DeVarco is archivist, Feldman not stated
- Read Applewhite's essay for professional assessment—great intellect, creative, influential
- Read Snyder's essay for RBF as father—warm, loving, deeply believed in primary experience
- Read DeVarco's essay—the "ephemera" of RBF's life; he called Expo dome "Taj Majal to Anne"
  - Check on Feldman, first at biography site, then WNET personnel; writer with access to papers
- Read Feldman's essay—threads RBF facts with personal aspects of success, tragedy, and family
- Summarize our impressions of essays
- Visit Buckminster Fuller Institute site
  - Check BFI's authenticity—kept all of Fuller's stuff for sixteen years
    - Wonder what happened to Fuller archive BFI doesn't have; search **buckminster fuller archive**
    - Locate it at Stanford University; read archivists description of it—it's huge—he kept everything
  - Review Basic Chronology—married to Anne; two children, one died; many jobs, many awards
  - *Discover Everything I Know* transcript—a searchable record of the 42 hours of conversations
  - Find Fuller describing how Allegra asked him to become more animated
- At BFI site, try to understand Dymaxion map
  - Discover Dymaxion map site at Wikipedia and watch animation
    - Check Wikipedia link for icosahedron—it's a regular 20-sided solid with triangular faces
    - Check Chris Rywalt's site—programmer of the animation—to get a higher resolution copy
- Wonder how icosahedron and geodesic dome relate
  - Check dictionary definitions by searching **define geodesic**—unsatisfactory
  - Search **difference icosahedron geodesic**, get to Wolfram MathWorld with a good explanation
    - Check **wolfram.com**—it's a company making math software; founder Steven Wolfram a genius
- MathWorld site says Fuller did not build 1st geodesic dome; it was German, 1922; Fuller popularized the idea
- The next hit on **difference icosahedron geodesic** is a blog repeating claim; links to Wikipedia
  - Check Wikipedia; confirms Bauersfeld built it for planetarium in Jena DE; also controversy with Ken Snelson
    - Search **bauersfeld geodesic**; first hits confirm Bauersfeld inventor
    - Seek authoritative site; find 6th hit is Princeton professor giving German patent and photo
  - Return to other controversy over the originality of Fuller's ideas: Snelson
    - Check Ken Snelson, he's a sculptor from Oregon
    - Check the *International Journal of Space Structures* page giving Snelson's view of discovery
    - Return to BFI's site to search *Everything I Know* transcripts for Fuller's view; he acknowledges Snelson
  - Conclude that our knowledge of Fuller is reasonably complete and balanced for a start
- Wonder what a buckminsterfullerene is, and use Google to find citations
  - Find a definition and the discoverers' names from Nanotechnology Lab
  - Find using Google Images graphic renderings of C_{60} and C_{70}—geodesic spheres, not domes
    - Look up a dictionary definition of *allotrope* and infer the difference from graphite and diamond
- Navigate to the Nobel site and find short biographies of the discoverers

When we found information, we were always concerned with its authoritativeness. In some cases, it didn't matter much, such as when we checked the Wikipedia biography to find words like *Dymaxion*. In other cases, we looked for primary sources, knowing that they are the purest forms of information about a topic because they are based on direct experience. For secondary sources, we checked the author's credentials. Secondary sources were valuable because they could both fill in gaps in our knowledge and show us how others interpreted the same information. Our goal was to learn as much as possible from primary sources so that we could interpret the information ourselves, and then to read secondary sources for more viewpoints and information. This strategy helped us to differentiate other people's opinions from the facts.

Too Fussy About the Facts?

We focused on how authoritative the information is, but our experience throughout is that when we found a fact—for example, Fuller was depressed in 1927 and was thinking of suicide, but decided instead to turn his life around—it was confirmed over and over again by every source we looked at carefully. That's not surprising, because we insisted on authoritative sources, but it seems reasonable to wonder if checking everything is really unnecessary.

Rather than depending on my assertion that it is necessary, we can find out. It is possible to test the presence of faulty information on the Web by making careful searches. For example, in clicking around sites that mention RBF, one quickly sees a claim that he produced over 2,000 patents in his lifetime. In fact, he has 28 patents—still an awesome achievement for anyone—and they are all listed at the BFI site at bfi.org/node/75, shown in Figure 6.19; this list

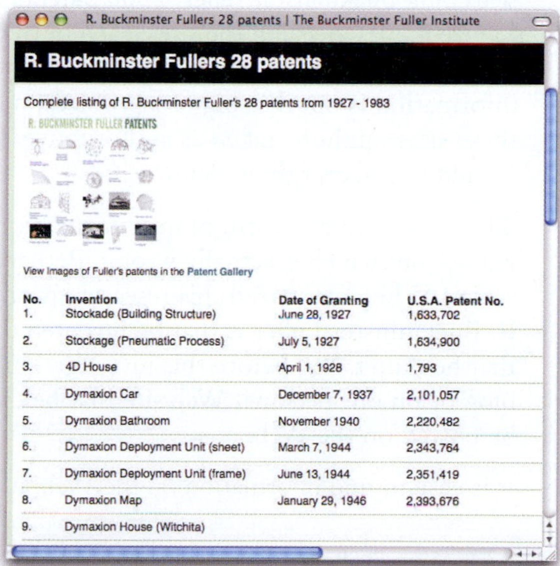
R. Buckminster Fullers 28 patents | The Buckminster Fuller Institute

R. Buckminster Fullers 28 patents

Complete listing of R. Buckminster Fuller's 28 patents from 1927 - 1983

R. BUCKMINSTER FULLER PATENTS

View images of Fuller's patents in the Patent Gallery

No.	Invention	Date of Granting	U.S.A. Patent No.
1.	Stockade (Building Structure)	June 28, 1927	1,633,702
2.	Stockage (Pneumatic Process)	July 5, 1927	1,634,900
3.	4D House	April 1, 1928	1,793
4.	Dymaxion Car	December 7, 1937	2,101,057
5.	Dymaxion Bathroom	November 1940	2,220,482
6.	Dymaxion Deployment Unit (sheet)	March 7, 1944	2,343,764
7.	Dymaxion Deployment Unit (frame)	June 13, 1944	2,351,419
8.	Dymaxion Map	January 29, 1946	2,393,676
9.	Dymaxion House (Witchita)		

Figure 6.19 The first entries on a list of RFB patents from bfi.org/node/75.

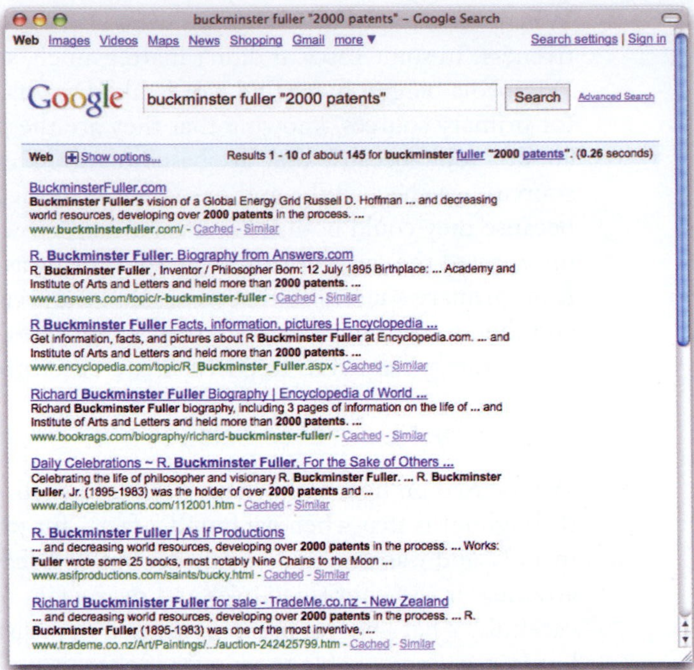

Figure 6.20 First hits for the search **buckminster fuller "2000 patents"** CAUTION: He did not have 2,000 patents.

can be checked at the U.S. Patent and Trademark Office Web site. Anyone can find this fact out, and find it quickly.

We can find out how many sites might have this erroneous information by searching buckminster fuller "2000 patents". The first few hits are shown in Figure 6.20. Checking the sites, each of them actually states that he held 2,000 patents. There are about 100 such sites. But before concluding that misinformation is not that big of a problem, notice by the URL's how many of these sites might be taken as authoritative. On this point they are wrong. Would you accept their claim?

The most common form of misinformation online is information that we "all know," but which is actually wrong. Perhaps the best example of this is ourselves! When we started this research, probably the only thing we knew about R. Buckminster Fuller is that he invented the geodesic dome. We found out that he didn't. Yet, before this investigation, we might have written in our blog or on our personal Web site that he did, causing more misinformation to be posted on the Web.

It is easy to find information on the Web; it's just as easy to check that it's right.

6.2 Who Believes? Give a search query that you could try that would hit on sites that assert Buckminster Fuller invented the geodesic dome.

Summary

We began the chapter by noting that for research, the Web is better in many ways than reading a book. In a short time we found interesting and definitive information about our topic, Buckminster Fuller.

- We accessed primary data from Fuller, his colleagues, and his family.
- We read short biographies, looked at photographs and film clips, heard audio clips, consulted the dictionary, watched animations, and used many other types of reference material.
- Multimedia resources gave us the chance to form our own opinions based on more than printed words.
- Computer searches, including global Google searches, site searches, and page searches, accelerated our discovery process.
- Information we gleaned from several authors' essays on Fuller connected us to additional sources.
- We discovered Buckminster Fuller based on our own curiosity.

Try It Solutions

6.1 Ages: 22 in photo, 32 when he turned his life around.

6.2 `buckminster fuller ("invented the geodesic" OR "inventing the geodesic")` hit more than 1,570 times.

Review Questions

True/False and Multiple Choice

1. A tertiary source draws directly from personal experience.
2. Each step away from a primary source increases the likelihood of error and omissions.
3. Books have limited research value because they
   a. take a long time to produce
   b. contain only information the author selects
   c. contain only a single point of view
   d. all of the above
4. Advantages of the Web over a book include
   a. the Web can be easily updated
   b. easier access
   c. dissemination of information is faster and cheaper
   d. all of the above

5. A primary source is
   a. the only source on a topic
   b. a source with personal experience
   c. a source that has been verified
   d. all of the above
6. Secondary sources are valuable for all of the following reasons except
   a. refuting primary sources
   b. organizing information
   c. providing interpretation
   d. filling in gaps
7. Which of the following is not an advantage of online research?
   a. the ability to quickly scan multiple sources
   b. the ability to view multimedia contents such as photographs, audio, and video
   c. the unerring reliability of information found online
   d. the speed with which a search can be conducted
8. What type of inconsistencies can be found in online information?
   a. misspellings
   b. gaps and inconsistencies
   c. bias and outright lies
   d. all of the above
9. Page ranking is based on
   a. accuracy
   b. last update
   c. size
   d. hits
10. _______ is a Web site created and maintained by Internet users.
    a. Google
    b. Yahoo
    c. Wikipedia
    d. eBay
11. Which of the following would probably be the most accurate resource for information on a famous person?
    a. About.com
    b. Biography.com
    c. a fan site dedicated to the individual
    d. Wikipedia

Short Answer

1. _______ is research for the sake of learning.
2. To look for pictures on the Web, you could do a Google search for _______.

3. Information that comes directly from the source is called a(n) ________.
4. _______ are used to save the name and address of a Web site for future reference.
5. A _______ is someone who reports information from a primary source.

Exercises

1. Find Buckminster Fuller's birthday. Who does he share it with?
2. Do a search for "Thomas Jefferson." Find a list of his inventions. Narrow the search to sites on Jefferson and one of those inventions.
3. Play "Six Degrees of Kevin Bacon" and pick two starts to see how many related hits you can find for both of them. Limit the search by ignoring topics such as reviews and books.
4. Perform a search for "Buckminster" and "Dymaxion" to see how many hits there are.
5. Do a search for "Ernest Hemingway." Locate a primary source, a secondary source, and two tertiary sources. Do the sites agree or are there inconsistencies?
6. Do a search for "Richard Nixon" and his dog, "Checkers." Then limit the search until there are fewer than 100 hits.
7. Do a search for "Alaska" and "coffee plantation." Then limit the search until there are fewer than 100 hits.
8. Organize the *Favorites* folder on your computer. Arrange the *Favorites* into classifications. Create additional folders as needed to organize the files. Copy the *Favorites*, if needed, so that they can be listed in more than one place.
9. Do a search for "Grace Murray Hopper." Find a picture of the first computer bug. Read the stories behind it.
10. Why is Wikipedia considered a poor primary resource for a research paper?
11. Differentiate between primary, secondary, and tertiary sources. Use examples from the chapter and from your own research.
12. Do a search on the term "singularity." Find sources for "gravitational singularity" and "technological singularity." List your sources, and identify if they are primary, secondary, or tertiary. Finally, explain what technological singularity is and how you think it will affect society.
13. Using online research, investigate the history of the term "computer bug." Find and list
    a. At least three primary sources
    b. At least three secondary sources
    c. Check the Wikipedia entry. Is it correct?

INTERVIEW

with

Vinton G. Cerf

Vinton G. Cerf is widely known as one of the "fathers of the Internet." He is the co-designer of the architecture of the Internet and the TCP/IP protocols, the process that sends data over the Internet. While working at the U.S. Department of Defense's Advanced Research Projects Agency (DARPA) from 1976 to 1982, Vint played a key role leading the development of Internet and Internet-related data packet and security technologies. From 1982 to 1986, he led the engineering of the first commercial email service to be connected to the Internet while at MCI.

Vint has been vice president and chief "Internet evangelist" for Google since 2005. He is honorary chairman of the IPv6 Forum, a group advocating the 16-digit IP addressing solution, and is also a distinguished visiting scientist at NASA's Jet Propulsion Laboratory, where he is working on the design of an interplanetary Internet. Among Vint's numerous awards and honors are the Turing Award (the computer science equivalent of the Nobel Prize), the U.S. National Medal of Technology, and the Presidential Medal of Freedom. He holds a B.S. in Mathematics from Stanford University and M.S. and Ph.D. degrees in Computer Science from UCLA.

How did you get started in all of this?

My interest in computing was piqued by a visit arranged by my father to System Development Corporation in 1958 where the Semi-Automated Ground Environment (SAGE) system was housed. This was a tube-based computing system developed by the RAND Corporation and spun out as System Development Corporation in 1957 to program and operate for the U.S. Air Force. I was fascinated by the idea that radar information from the Distant Early Warning system located in northern Canada could be transmitted electronically to the SAGE system and analyzed to detect Russian bombers coming over the North Pole. I was 15 at the time.

In 1968, the U.S. Defense Advanced Research Projects Agency (then called ARPA, now DARPA) released a Request for Quotation for an Interface Message Processor (IMP) with which to implement the ARPANET. Professor Leonard Kleinrock [at UCLA] concurrently proposed to create and operate a Network Measurement Center that would be used to compare measured performance of the ARPANET with the queuing theoretic models that Kleinrock and his students were developing. I became the principal programmer for that effort. In the meantime, Stephen Crocker became the head of the Network Working Group (NWG) that included graduate students from at least a dozen universities whose computer science departments were supported by ARPA. Crocker led the effort to create the protocols used to allow host computers on the ARPANET to communicate with one another, despite the wide variations in computer hardware and operating systems that existed at that time. I participated with others in this work.

During the time I worked on the Network Measurement Center, Robert Kahn, a senior member of the staff at Bolt, Beranek and Newman (BBN, the maker of the IMP) and one of his colleagues, David Walden, came to visit UCLA after the first IMPs were installed at UCLA, Stanford Research Institute (SRI), University of California at Santa Barbara, and University of Utah. This four-node network formed the nascent ARPANET.

By the fall of 1973, we had developed an architecture and protocol (Transmission Control Protocol or TCP) that would form the basis of the Internet design. The Institute of Electrical and Electronic Engineering (IEEE) published our paper in May 1974. By December of 1974, my students and I had fleshed out the details of the TCP design and we began experimental implementations in 1975, working with BBN and University College London. These implementations demonstrated various flaws and the protocol continued to evolve, finally being split into the basic Internet Protocol (IP) and a revised version of the TCP. The suite of protocols that grew up around these basic components became known as the TCP/IP protocol suite.

The actual roll out of the Internet occurred on January 1, 1983, when all the hosts on the ARPANET were converted to run only TCP/IP protocols.

Did you imagine that the Internet protocol would become as pervasive as it is today when you first designed the protocol?

At the time that Bob Kahn and I were working on open networking in 1973, our research community had had several years of experience with the ARPANET, its host-to-host protocol (NCP for Network Control Program), and several application protocols including file transfer protocol (FTP), telecommunications network protocol (TELNET), and electronic mail protocol (eventually the Simple Mail Transport Protocol or SMTP). TELNET was in use to allow remote access to any time-sharing system on the ARPANET. Files were exchanged using FTP, and networked email, which had been invented by Ray Tomlinson at BBN and elaborated upon by several of the NWG participants, was in use.

I don't think I fully appreciated what would happen when nearly 2 billion people got online and the World Wide Web (WWW) application became a dominant force. The latter was invented in 1989 by

Tim Berners-Lee and Robert Cailliau at the European Particle Physics Laboratory CERN, and spread rapidly after the first commercial browser, Netscape Navigator, was developed by Marc Andreessen, who had worked with his colleague, Eric Bina, at the National Center for Supercomputer Applications (NCSA) on an earlier graphical WWW browser they called Mosaic. The availability of commercial Internet service did not emerge until 1989, and personal computers were around only since about 1984.

And what do you now envision for the future of the Internet?

It is clear that an increasing amount of access to the Internet will take place by way of mobile systems. Many sensor networks will be connected to the Net as will appliances around the house, the office, in the car, and things we carry with us. Higher speed access will enable increasing amounts of audio, video, and interactive applications, including a considerable amount of collaborative entertainment games as well as scientific and business collaboration with online instruments and shared documents (word processing, spreadsheets, presentations, etc.). More scientific instruments (telescopes, electron microscopes, spectrometers, particle accelerators, and so on) will be placed online, allowing for rapid access to scientific data. Increasing fractions of published material will be available and searchable online, and retrospective digitization will make much of the world's information discoverable in fractions of a second. Translation of written languages is improving, making ever-more information accessible. Spoken interactions with Internet applications are also improving with time. Perhaps some day we will be able to have conversations with Internet-based systems that will help us find what we need. One can readily anticipate that more transactions of all kinds will take place online. There is already strong evidence that social networking is creating new forms of personal interactions in the general population.

What challenges do you face?

At Google, the biggest challenges have to do with keeping up with the rapid influx of information in the World Wide Web, the increasing demand for streaming audio and video applications, the increasing use of collaborative interactions, and the need for language translation. Capturing all the world's written material and indexing it to make it discoverable is a daily challenge. The basic Internet design, now about 36 years old, needs further adaptation for meeting the demand for increased numbers of devices on the Net. A new version of the Internet Protocol, version 6 (IPv6), must be deployed before the present version (IPv4) runs out of unique address space.

There are many vulnerabilities in the system (especially the hosts at the edges of the Internet) that must be remedied. Privacy is a major concern and new techniques are needed to insure it.

Do you have any advice for students studying IT?

Information technology continues to thrive as a field in which new ideas can still be transformative. Just a brief look at the last 15 years illustrates the point. During that time we have seen the rise of Yahoo, Google, eBay, Amazon, Skype, YouTube, Facebook, MySpace, and a host of other new companies whose founders have taken ideas and turned them into reality through the magic of networked software. The network has no limits—it is an endless software frontier. If you can imagine it, you can program it and make it accessible on the network.

What do you think about an Interplanetary Internet?

In 1998, I met with a small group of engineers from the Jet Propulsion Laboratory hosted by the California Institute of Technology. We began to explore what might be needed in the way of networked communication resources if manned and robotic exploration of the solar system continued to accelerate. We asked ourselves what might the solar system be like in 100 years, by which time perhaps some forms of colonization or at least persistently manned laboratories might be found on the surface of planets or their moons, or in orbit around them. We concluded that it would be useful to design a set of protocols that could operate across the solar systems with the same degree of interoperability that the terrestrial Internet provides. We quickly discovered that the traditional TCP/IP protocol suite would not work well at interplanetary distances, and that disruption of communication caused by normal celestial motion or by solar storms or even local mobility (like the rovers on Mars) dictated a new design. We developed something we called the Bundle Protocol, which is the interplanetary equivalent of the Earth's Internet Protocol.

Dr. Cerf's full interview can be found at www.aw.com/snyder.

2

PART

Algorithms and Digitizing Information

chapter

PART 2

Introduction

NOW THAT YOU are more skilled with information technology, it's time to learn a few of the underlying concepts that make computing possible. Like black holes in astronomy or natural selection in ecology, the underlying computing phenomena are interesting to learn about. The difference is, computing concepts can have direct applicability to your daily IT use.

In Part 2 you will learn how information is represented—from basic bits, through sound and video, to virtual reality. We explain what a transistor is, and how a few million of them can process information. And we introduce the fundamental idea of an algorithm, though you've already encountered several in Part 1. At the end of Part 2 you will have an intuitive idea of what's happening inside a computer and how it stores information.

In your experience so far, you have known the frustration that comes when some aspect of IT does not work the way you want. So, you know that figuring out what's wrong is one of the most important capabilities a computer user can possess. We can't give you a guaranteed, works-every-time algorithm to debug your problems, but we can provide useful guidelines that will help you solve IT mysteries faster.

An Introduction to Debugging

To Err Is Human

learning objectives

- Explain how ordinary precision differs from precision required in computing
- Describe the six-step strategy for debugging
  - Explain the purpose of each step
  - Give an example of each step
- Apply the six-step strategy for debugging the XHTML code for a Web page
  - State what changes you made during debugging
  - State what changes were unnecessary
- Learn how to approach debugging when you don't understand the system
- Appreciate the problems of making perfectly reliable computing systems

One item could not be deleted because it was missing.

—MAC OS SYSTEM 7.0 ERROR MESSAGE

You are not thinking. You are merely being logical.

—NEILS BOHR TO ALBERT EINSTEIN

A COMMON SAYING among computer users is "To err is human, but to really foul things up takes a computer." One characteristic that makes a computer so useful—and sometimes so frustrating—is that it does exactly what it is told to do, and nothing more. Because it follows each instruction "to the letter" and continually checks itself, it operates almost perfectly. So, in truth, the computer doesn't foul things up at all. We humans—those of us who write the software and those of us who use it—are not perfect, and that combination can really foul things up. So we have to learn how to troubleshoot what's wrong and to get ourselves out of trouble. Learning debugging techniques—the subject of this chapter—is perhaps the best way to deal successfully with mistakes and errors, and to avoid the foul-ups in the first place.

The first goal of this chapter is to recognize that the greatest, most common source of problems is our lack of precision. Computers don't understand what we *mean*, only what we *say*. So we must say exactly what we mean. The next objective is to understand what debugging is in modern IT systems. We introduce the debugging process using a student/parent scenario. This lets us analyze the process as the student/parent interaction unfolds. The next goal is to abstract the debugging principles from the story. These principles do not give a mechanical procedure guaranteeing success, but rather a reliable set of guidelines. We apply the principles to debugging a faulty Web page design. This detective work won't reveal *who*dunit—because we are the obvious "perps"—but rather *what*dunit, our error. Then we show how to approach a seemingly impossible task: debug a system when we have no idea how the system works. Finally, we discuss the possibility of bug-free software.

Precision: The High Standards of Computing

When using information technology, we must be precise. The standard of accuracy in IT is extremely high, much higher than our everyday precision level.

Precision in Everyday Life

In normal conversation, for example, when giving telephone numbers, many North Americans will say "oh" rather than "zero," as in "five-five-five-oh-oh-one-two" for 555-0012. Of course, the listener knows that phone numbers are numeric, and simply makes the mental conversion. A computer does not know this unless it has been specifically programmed to know it and to make the conversion. To a computer, the "oh" and "zero" are different (bit sequences). So, if we type "oh" for "zero," a computer will simply accept the input, try to use it literally, and cause an error.

fluencyBIT

Merrily Mistaken. Sometimes we purposely and humorously exploit this confusion, as in Canada's alternating letter-numeral postal code for Santa Claus, H0H 0H0.

The "oh" for "zero" substitution is used by North Americans because it is easier to say, having only one syllable. (Other English speakers say "*naught*" for "*zero.*") It is probably not the sort of error we would make if we were asked to type a phone number into a database system or other software. And, even if it were, the software might catch the error, because some software systems *have* been programmed to know that phone numbers are numeric. Rather than converting "oh" to "zero," however, they usually just object to receiving non-numeric input. But there are many cases in which the computer cannot help us when we make an error.

Exactly How Accurate Is "Precise?"

New computer users often type in an incorrect email address or URL. A common error is the confusion of "oh" and "zero," or "el" and "one," though there are many other similar mistakes new users make. If computers can catch mistakes like "oh" for "zero" in databases, why can't they catch them in email addresses and URLs? The reason is simple: Although "oh" and "el" are illegal in all phone numbers, they are not illegal in all email addresses and URLs. For example, `flo@exisp.com` and `f10@exisp.com` are both legitimate email addresses. If the software made "zero" for "oh" and "one" for "el" substitutions, poor Flo would never get any email. So, computers must accept the letters or numbers as typed for email addresses and URLs. Users must be precise when entering the information.

fluencyALERT

Be Sensitive. Be alert to case sensitivity—the difference between lowercase and uppercase—in email addresses and URLs. To computers, C and c are different, so we must type the case exactly. Sometimes computers are programmed to ignore case. For example, case does not matter in Internet domain names—flo@exisp.com and flo@ExISP.COM are the same—because case is normalized for DNS lookup. But frequently the path information in URLs—that is, the text after / symbols—is case sensitive because it is processed by the destination Web server. So, www.exisp.com/flo/home/ and www.exisp.com/FLO/HOME/ may be different. When in doubt, assume that case matters and try lowercase first.

Lexical Structures

We call the kinds of inputs just discussed **field inputs** because they are the sorts of information that are entered into boxes on forms that are used for names, code numbers, user IDs, files, folder names, and so on. All field inputs are governed by some **lexical structure**, rules about the legal form for input fields. The lexical structure limits the symbols that can be used in specific positions; possibly how many symbols can be used (i.e., a length limit); and possibly which punctuation symbols can be used. Lexical constraints can be very restrictive. For example, the lexical structure for inputting course grades is limited to two symbols: the first symbol must be chosen from {A, B, C, D, F} and the second symbol must be chosen from {+, –, ƀ}. (The ƀ denotes *blank*.) So, A+ is acceptable, but C++ is wrong. Lexical constraints can be loose, too, allowing any sequence of symbols of any length. Computers check to see that the lexical constraints are met, preventing lexical errors. But if the lexical structure permits alternatives of a commonly confused symbol, no check can be made. Both alternatives are legal, as in the flo and f10 UserIDs. Precision is essential.

Spacing Out. The ƀ represents blank or space. This solves the problem that spaces must be visible in some cases so that we know that they're there. "Multiplication dots," ·, are used by word processors (see Chapter 2), but when they are easily confused with other symbols, we use ƀ to represent blank.

Because we have to be accurate when supplying input to a computer, we can avoid considerable grief by being as exact as possible. It's faster and less frustrating to enter information exactly the first time, than to be sloppy, discover our mistake, and reenter it correctly.

Debugging: What's the Problem?

Debugging is the method of figuring out why a process or system doesn't work properly. Debugging is usually applied to computer or communication systems, especially software, but the techniques are the same whether the systems are mechanical, architectural, business, and so on. Though debugging relies on logical reasoning and is usually "learned from experience," there are general debugging principles and effective strategies that you can learn. Knowing these techniques is important because in IT, a major part of using a system is knowing how to figure out why things are not working properly.

Debugging in Everyday Life

People debug or **troubleshoot** all the time. When their cars don't start, they figure out whether the battery is dead or whether the fuel tank is empty. Faults and failures in everyday life usually involve otherwise correct, working systems with a broken or worn-out part. That is, the system is properly designed and constructed, but some part failed. The car's dead battery keeps it from starting, for example. When the part is replaced, the system works.

Debugging in Information Technology

Debugging an information system is slightly different. In information systems, we might have entered wrong data or wrong configuration information in a working system. When it's corrected, the system works. Another possibility is the system might have a *logical design error*. An analogy in car design is when the backup lights, which should only work when the car is in reverse gear, also come on when we step on the brakes. This is a design or construction error. In software, such logical errors are quite possible even in commercial software, and users must be aware that they may not be using a correct, working system. Despite this fact, we will always begin by assuming a "correct, working system."

Whose Problem Is It?

When debugging an information system, remember that *we* are almost always part of the problem: We command the computer to do tasks and we input the information. When the computer is in an error state despite our thinking that everything should have worked perfectly, two of the three possible problems—wrong data, wrong command, or broken system—involve us. Furthermore, since the hardware and software have been tested thoroughly, the two possibilities that involve us are the two most likely possibilities. Our commands or data probably led to the problem, so we'll have to fix them. Computers cannot debug themselves.

Because people don't knowingly make errors, we think that what we did is right, and that it's the computer's fault that something has gone wrong. It might be—both hardware and software errors do happen—but they are much, much rarer than human errors. If our checking doesn't quickly reveal a small typographical error or the like, then we usually assume that the problem is with the computer or software. But we should consider one more possibility: It may be that we *think* we did everything right because we misunderstand the system and how it works, and so maybe we really did make a mistake. It's hard to admit, sometimes, that we've made a mistake, but at least the computer can't change its opinion of us!

Computer Pioneer Grace Hopper. Rear Admiral Grace Murray Hopper, a computer pioneer, coined the term *bug* for a glitch in a computer system while she was working on the Harvard Mark computers in the 1940s. When the Mark II computer had a moth jammed in one of its relays (electro-mechanical switches), bringing the machine down, technicians taped the bug into the machine's logbook (see Figure 7.1).

Hopper was one of the inventors of a kind of software known as a compiler, which translates a programming language into machine instructions (see Chapter 9), and she greatly influenced the development of the programming language Cobol. Conscious of the physical limitations on computing, Hopper used a length of copper wire (approximately one foot long) to illustrate a "nanosecond" (1/1,000,000,000th of a second), because it is approximately the distance electricity can travel in that time.

A Navy ship was named in her honor.

Figure 7.1 The Harvard Mark II logbook noting "First actual case of bug being found."

Using the Computer to Debug

Not only is the computer unable to debug itself, we can't debug it directly, either. That is, the error, even if it's our mistake, is internal to the computer, either in the stored data or the software logic. To get information about the error, we have to ask the computer to tell us what data it has stored, to run the faulty software, and so forth. We are one step removed from the failure and what's causing it, and we need the computer to help us find the problem.

Though there may be a bug in our software, most of it works correctly. A computer version of the 1960s slogan "If you're not part of the solution, you're part of the problem" is: "If it's not part of the solution, it can't be part of the problem." That is, if you can find a solution to your task that does not use a problem (faulty) part of the system, you've achieved your goal. Bypassing an error with an alternative approach is called a **workaround**. Workarounds are essential when we use commercial software. Bugs in commercial systems are usually not fixed until the updated version is released, so we have to work around them until then.

A Dialog About Debugging

Consider the following scenario:

You and your friends make a video spoofing college life. You show it to your cluster in the dorm and everyone thinks it's hilarious. You upload it to YouTube, where you expect it to receive many, many views. You send your parents email with the URL, and anxiously await their praise of your cleverness. But there is no response. Eventually you phone them to ask if they read their mail. "Yes. We tried the link a moment ago, but something's wrong." Your impulse is to say, "Pathetic!" but you ask brightly, "What's wrong?"

You are about to debug your parents' interactions with the Internet. What you know is that they have a high-speed connection, they use the Firefox browser, software like Flash is reasonably up-to-date, because you upgraded them at the last break, and they are better with the computer than most of your friends' parents. That's all the information you have, and it's typical.

Debugging is solving a mystery. Just as we watch detectives solve mysteries in whodunits, we should watch ourselves solve mysteries when debugging. Why? Because this approach will probably reach a solution faster than if we aimlessly "try stuff." By purposely asking questions such as, "Do I need more clues (inputs)?"; "Are my clues reliable?"; and "What is a theory to explain the problem?" we focus better and will discover a solution faster.

The first step in debugging is to check that the error is reproducible. Computers are deterministic, which means that they will do exactly the same thing every time if given the same input. But there is a tiny possibility that a one-time transient glitch caused the problem. So, start by trying to reproduce the problem.

You ask your parents,

> "Can you try the link again?"
>
> "Sure. Hold on, I just paid the credit card bill. Don't you love online banking?"
>
> "I'm sure I would if I had any money to bank."

And, as the scenario unfolds, your parent says,

> "OK. It says, 'Cannot Connect.' and it has that little yellow triangle with the exclamation point."
>
> "Is that what happened last time," you ask?
>
> "I don't think so, but maybe."
>
> "Can you try it again?"
>
> "Yes. Same thing."

The next step is to be sure that you know exactly what the problem is. Mystery novels usually have a dead body, making the problem clear. The mystery is who murdered the person, not why the dead person failed to show up for work the next morning. But in computing, the computer may perform a sequence of operations *after* an error, and they must be eliminated first as the focal point of the debugging. For example, the reason there are no mailing labels coming out of your printer may be due to a printer problem, but it could be due to a problem with the word processor or database that is sending the labels to the printer, or it could be that the file containing the addresses is empty; that is, there are no addresses to print. We don't want to debug the printer when the problem is an empty file.

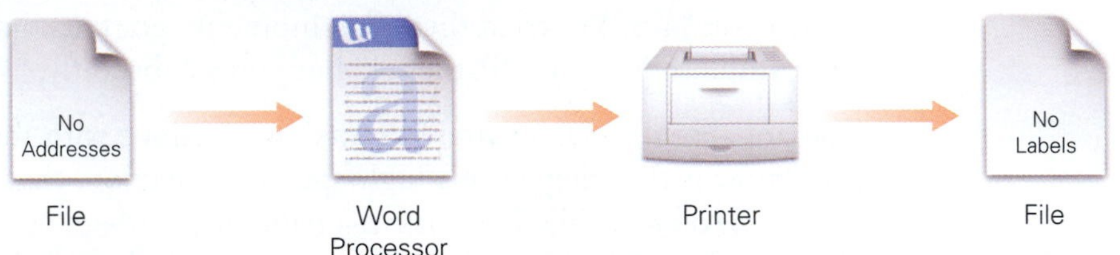

Determining what exactly is the problem is critical.

> "Is there more explanation on the error message?"
>
> "Yes. It says, 'FireFox can't establish a connection to the server www.youtube.com.' "

A standard next step is to check all of the "obvious" error sources. Of course, if the error were all that obvious, you wouldn't be debugging—you'd have already fixed the problem. What kinds of errors are obvious depends on the problem, naturally, but checking inputs, connections, links, and so on is standard.

Ask your parents to check all of the obvious causes.

> "Did you just click on the URL I put in my email?"
>
> "No. It was on two lines in your email, so I cut it and pasted it into the slot."
>
> "Both parts?"
>
> "Yes."
>
> "Can you read it to me?"
>
> "Yes. It's www.youtube.com/watch?v= followed by the letters capital Q, small j, capital A, five, capital SHZ, small w, eight, small a, capital E'. Is that it?"
>
> "Sounds like it. I wonder if YouTube is down?"

Clearly your folks understand enough about the World Wide Web to get the URL typed in correctly. Except it isn't playing your hilarious video.

It's now time to apply a basic strategy of debugging: Isolate the problem by dividing the operation into those parts that are working and those that are not. This means theorizing about where the problem is located and possibly gathering more information. At this point you should take nothing for granted. Limit the number of untested assumptions you make. The error could be anywhere.

The goal is to eliminate as many possibilities as you can, or to focus on the failing part.

In the case of your parents' browser, there could be a problem at either end. You quickly use your computer to click up the video, proving that the YouTube site is up. You ask your parents,

> "Is your computer running?"
>
> "Sure, I just paid the credit card bill."

So, both ends of the connection are working. And there are no other parts.

Everything seems to check out. This is a common situation when debugging. You analyze the problem, perhaps getting more data, and conclude that everything is okay. Except it's not. There's a bug somewhere. It's natural to become frustrated, but the best response is to review your analysis. You've made some assumptions, gathered data, made some tests, interpreted the results, and made some deductions. Ask yourself: "Is there a wrong assumption?" "Did I misunderstand the data?" "Did I make a wrong deduction?" It's important at this point to think objectively about the process. *A good approach is to step through the process from beginning to end, comparing what should be happening with what is happening.*

So, starting from the beginning, you ask your parents to go to a different site.

> "Can you try another site, like NPR or the *New York Times*?"

You know they have ready access to those sites, being news junkies.

> "What's happening?" you ask.
>
> "Nothing; `npr.org` is not responding."
>
> "Meaning what?"
>
> "The little spinner is going around."

So they can't connect to NPR, either. At this point you have a prediction—NPR ought to work—that doesn't match the facts. That's what you're looking for. How could banking work but not NPR?

> "Whoa!"
>
> "What?"
>
> "I gave up on NPR and tried `nytimes.com`, and got a different error message, saying something about a security certificate. Should I cancel?"

And now you know the problem. Browsers worry about security certificates when they're trying to make secure connections for activities like banking. Sites like YouTube, NPR, and the *New York Times* don't need secure connections or certificates, but your parents' computer is still asking for one. Nonsecure sites respond to the request in different ways. Your parents must have left the `https://` in the location window and just added the URLs after it.

"Does the location window say https?"

"Yes!"

"Delete the 's' and try my site again. You're gonna love the video!"

Debugging Recap

The key point of the debugging illustration is that there is a semi-organized process to follow to find out what's wrong. The key points are:

- Make sure that you can reproduce the error.
- Determine exactly what the problem is.
- Eliminate the "obvious" causes.
- Divide the process, separating out the parts that work from the part that doesn't.
- When you reach a dead end, reassess your information, asking where you may be making wrong assumptions or conclusions; then step through the process again.
- As you work through the process from start to finish, make predictions about what should happen and verify that your predictions are fulfilled.

This is not a guaranteed-to-work process, but it is a useful set of guidelines. Debugging requires tough, logical reasoning to figure out what's wrong. But, it's possible to do, and though it is not as entertaining as deducing whodunit from the clues in a mystery novel, there is a certain satisfaction to figuring out the answer.

fluencyBIT

> **Closer Examination.** Watching yourself debug as if you were a mystery detective is important. It helps you be more objective—is the debugger (you) chasing the wrong lead?—and it helps you separate yourself from the process, reducing frustration. Thinking about what you are doing is a good idea generally, of course. After all, Socrates said, "The unexamined life is not worth living."

Butterflies and Bugs: A Case Study

To illustrate the debugging principles in action, imagine that we've developed a simple page in XHTML. Our goal page is shown in Figure 7.2, but the results we're getting are shown in Figures 7.3–7.5. Obviously, there is an error somewhere. The XHTML code we've written is shown in Figure 7.6. We can study the XHTML very, very closely and "brain out" where the error is, or we can use the debugging strategy. You can follow along online with our debugging process at www.aw.com/snyder/.

As we begin watching ourselves debugging the XHTML, we recall that the first step is to be sure we can reproduce the error.

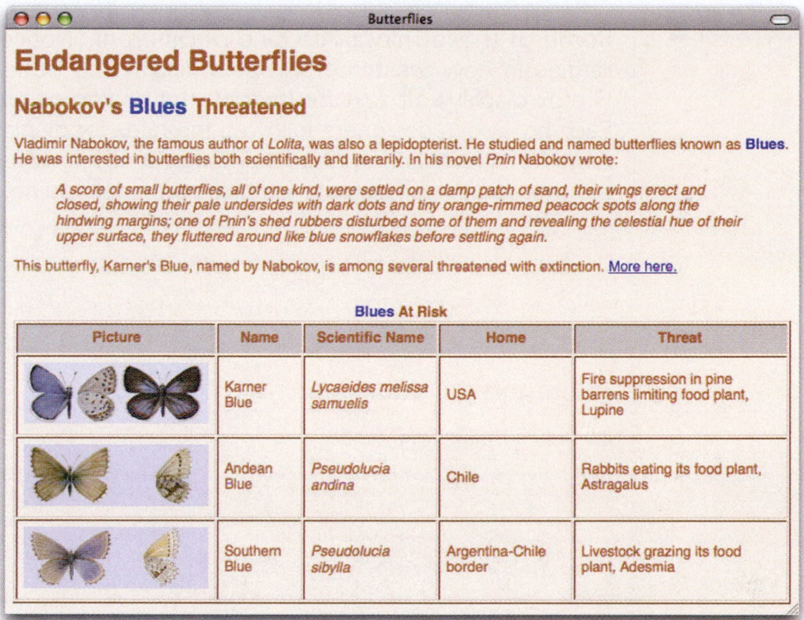

Figure 7.2 The intended Web page.

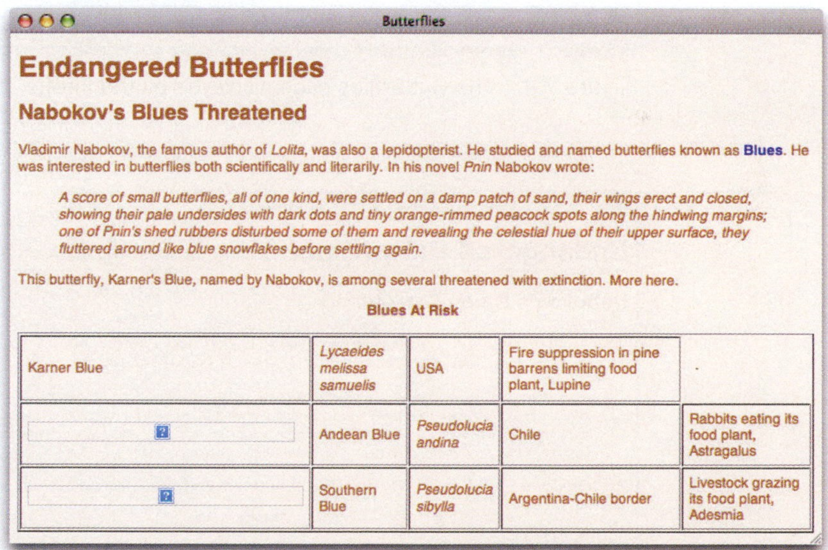

Figure 7.3 The Butterflies page displayed by the Safari browser.

Reproduce the Error. So, we close our browser and reopen our file using a "fresh" copy. Unfortunately, the results are the same. In fact, the browsers produce somewhat different but equally incorrect results. There is definitely a problem with our XHTML.

fluencyBIT

Some of These Things Are Kind of Different. Notice the differences and similarities in how the three browsers display the Butterflies page; for example, Firefox displays **alt** text for (two of) the broken pictures, but the others don't. Each browser's designers followed the rules for displaying XHTML, but there is room for different interpretation. Though annoying when we are planning a page, the differences can sometimes help when debugging.

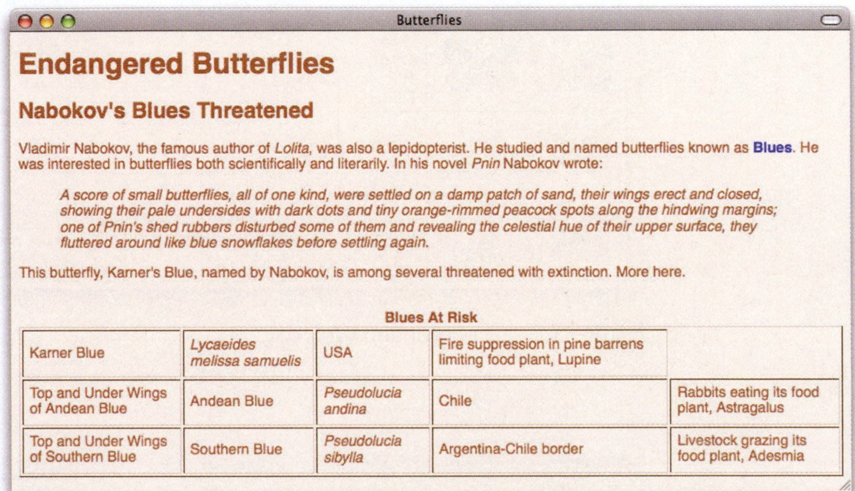

Figure 7.4 The Butterflies page displayed by the Firefox browser.

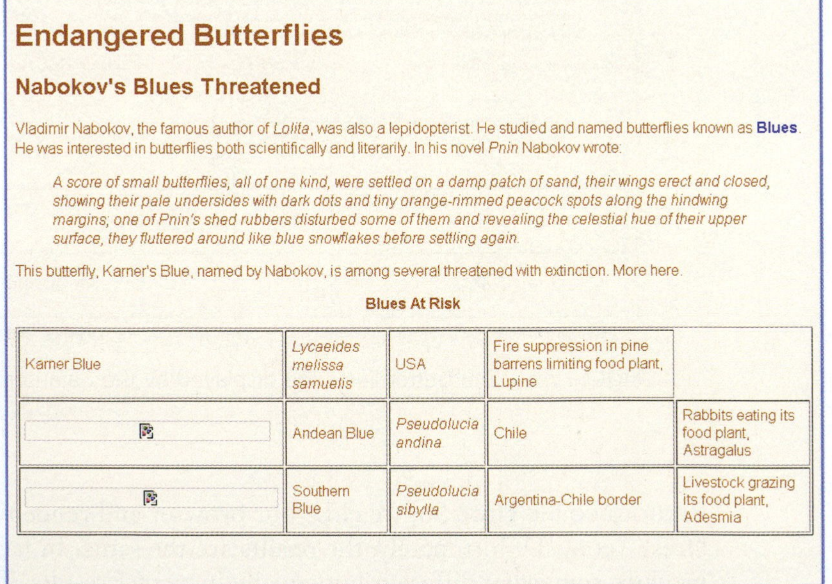

Figure 7.5 The Butterflies page displayed by the Chrome browser.

```
<!DOCTYPE html PUBLIC "-//W3C//DTD XHTML 1.0 Strict//EN"
"http://www.w3.org/TR/xhtml1/DTD/xhtml1-strict.dtd">

<html xmlns="http://www.w3.org/1999/xhtml">
 <head>
  <meta http-equiv="Content-Type" content="text/html; charset=utf-8"/>
   <title>Butterflies</title>
    <style type="text/css">
       body {background-color : linen; color : sienna; font-family : helvetica}
       span.b {color ; blue}  td, th  {padding : 6px}
    </style>
 </head>
 <body>
   <h1> Endangered Butterflies</h1>
   <h2>Nabokov's <span class="b">Blues</span> Threatened</h2>
   <p>Vladimir Nabokov, the famous author of <i>Lolita</i>, was also a lepidopterist.
      He studied and named butterflies known as <b style="color:blue">Blues</b>. He
      was interested in butterflies both scientifically and literarily. In his novel
      <i>Pnin</i> Nabokov wrote:</p><blockquote><p><i>A score of small butterflies, all
      of one kind, were settled on a damp patch of sand, their wings erect and closed,
      showing their pale undersides with dark dots and tiny orange-rimmed peacock spots
      along the hindwing margins; one of Pnin's shed rubbers disturbed some of them and
      revealing the celestial hue of their upper surface, they fluttered around like blue
      snowflakes before settling again.</i></p></blockquote><p> This butterfly, Karner's
      Blue, named by Nabokov, is among several threatened with extinction.
      <ahref="http://www.libraries.psu.edu/nabokov/endan2.htm"> More here.</a></p>
   <table border="1">
      <caption style="margin-top : 15px"><b><span class="b">Blues </span>At Risk</b>
         </caption>
      <tr style="background-color : silver"> <th>Picture</th> <th>Name</th> <th>Scientific
         Name</th> <th>Home</th> <th>Threat</th></tr>
      <tr><td><img src="lmeli.jpg" alt="Top and Under Wings of Karner Blue"/></td>
         <td> Karner Blue</td>
         <td><i>Lycaeides melissa samuelis</i></td>
         <td>USA</td>
         <td>Fire suppression in pine barrens limiting food plant, Lupine</td></tr>
      <tr><td><img src="pandi.jpg" alt="Top and Under Wings of Andean Blue"/></td>
         <td> Andean Blue</td>
         <td><i>Pseudolucia andina</i></td>
         <td>Chile</td>
         <td>Rabbits eating its food plant, Astragalus</td></tr>
      <tr><td><img src="psiby.jpg" alt="Top and Under Wings of Southern Blue"/></td>
         <td> Southern Blue</td>
         <td><i>Pseudolucia sibylla</i></td>
         <td>Argentina-Chile border</td>
         <td>Livestock grazing its food plant, Adesmia</td></tr>
   </table>
 </body>
</html>
```

Figure 7.6 Faulty HTML text for the Butterflies page.

Determine the problem exactly. The next step is to determine the problem exactly. In the case of debugging HTML, identifying the problem is simple: just look at the displayed page. We see we have a faulty table with no pictures; also, the table entries are skewed in the first row; the word *Blues* in the heading and table caption are not blue. As we look closer, we also notice that the "More here." link is not highlighted, as it should be. Since these errors seem to be related to different parts of the page, we can assume they are caused by different mistakes in the XHTML. It is common when debugging to be looking for more than one bug, but usually we don't know it. Here, at least, we suspect multiple bugs.

Eliminate the obvious. Once we know what the problem is, we look for the "obvious" errors. The most obvious XHTML error is to forget to close a tag; that is, to forget the matching "slash-tag." Checking the XHTML, however, we see that every tag is matched. So that simple tactic fails.

Our next idea might be to ask the Validator what's wrong; see Figure 7.7. It's a good idea, but it doesn't work for two reasons.

Errors found while checking this document as XHTML 1.0 Strict!		
Result:	18 Errors, 14 warning(s)	
File :	Browse... *Use the file selection box above if you wish to re-validate the uploaded file butterfly.html*	
Encoding :	utf-8	(detect automatically)
Doctype :	XHTML 1.0 Strict	(detect automatically)
Root Element:	html	
Root Namespace:	http://www.w3.org/1999/xhtml	

Figure 7.7 The Validator report returned for the Endangered Butterflies page.

The main reason is that the Validator only critiques how we write XHTML, and it is quite possible to write correct XHTML that does not achieve our design goals. The other reason is that although we might get lucky and make a mistake that is both wrong XHTML and messes up the design, the tactic only works for one or two errors. If there are too many errors, the Validator just gets confused and starts having issues with everything: There are not 18+14=32 mistakes in this code. We have to make progress reducing the errors first, and then maybe we try the Validator again.

Looking at the faulty pages, the most glaring problem is that the word "Blues" is not colored. The most likely reason for this is that we specified the color incorrectly. So we look at the color specification

```
span.b {color ; blue}
```

and the error is immediately apparent. In the `class="b"` form of `span`, we used a *semicolon* rather than a *colon* to separate the property (`color`) from its value (`blue`). When we change to a colon, both uses of Blues are displayed in blue.

With one bug swatted, we focus on another obvious error: Why is the "More here." link not highlighted? Again, the obvious answer is that we messed up the anchor tag, perhaps giving the wrong URL. Looking at the anchor tag

```
<ahref="http://www.libraries.psu.edu/nabokov/endan2.htm">More
here.</a></p>
```

we again see immediately what's wrong: The anchor tag is given by the single letter `a`, and `href` is an attribute; therefore, a space should follow the `a`. As we expect, when we insert the space, the link is highlighted.

Two bugs down and one to go, we think. Turning to that last one, we wonder why the table is messed up. The colored bar in the first row is peculiar. No "obvious" cause for it comes to mind, unless it is related to the fact that the images are not displaying. There is an obvious possible cause for this: A mistake in the <img src= .../> specification. We check the names of the three image files: lmeli.jpg, pandi.jpg, and psiby.jpg against the three files (see Figure 7.8), and we notice that there is a difference. The file names in the HTML are lowercase, but the file names themselves are uppercase. Sometimes this matters and sometimes it doesn't. Not remembering whether it's important for our computer, we capitalize the names in the XHTML file to make them match, but there is no change. That "obvious" idea fails. So, we Undo the change and move on to the next step.

Divide Up the Process. The next step is to separate those parts of the system that work from the part that does not. This is not always possible to do perfectly, but we should try. In the present case most of the page is fine, so we focus on the first row of the table. When we carefully compare the intended solution with the faulty solution, we immediately notice that there is a whole row missing: The table is supposed to have a top row, shown in silver, with the column headings. Perhaps whatever is messing up the headings is messing

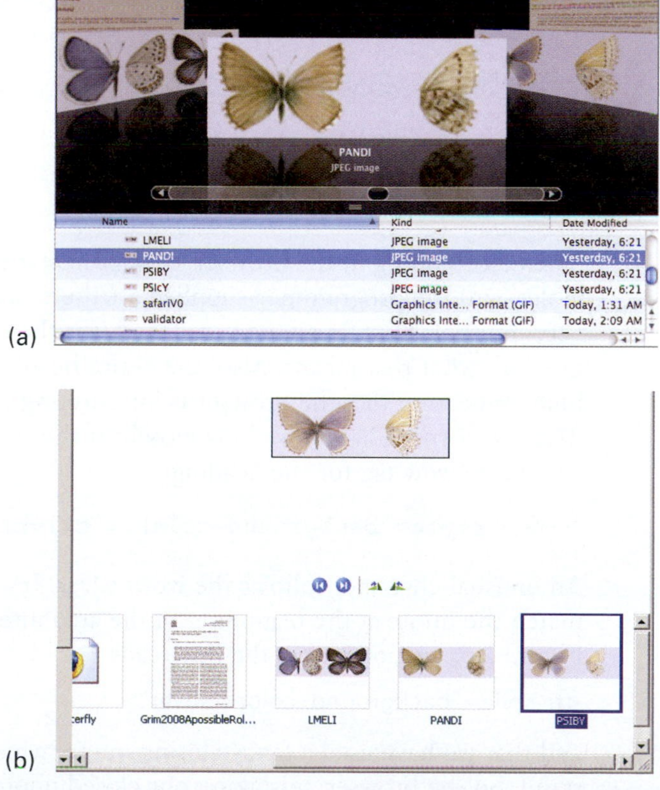

Figure 7.8 The image files for (a) Mac OS X and (b) Windows.

up the first row, too. So, we focus on the heading row and the first data row of the table.

When we look back at Figure 7.6, both rows look perfect. What can the problem be? We can pore over the XHTML closely looking for errors, but we need some help. It would be great if the browser software could tell us how it is interpreting our code, because we might spot where it's getting into trouble. Browsers and debugging systems for HTML *can* give us a color-coded version of the HTML showing how it's being interpreted. Figure 7.9 shows the Firefox browser's Source View display for the table (choose *View* > *Page Source*).

```
    <table border="1">
       <caption style="margin-top : 15px"><b><span class="b">Blues </span>At Risk</b>
          </caption>
       <tr style="background-color : silver▯><th>Picture</th><th>Name</th><th>Scientific
          Name</th><th>Home</th><th>Threat</th></tr>
       <tr><td><img src="lmeli.jpg" alt="Top and Under Wings of Karner Blue"/></td>
          <td> Karner Blue</td>
          <td><i>Lycaeides melissa samuelis</i></td>
          <td>USA</td>
          <td>Fire suppression in pine barrens limiting food plant, Lupine</td></tr>
       <tr><td><img src="pandi.jpg" alt="Top and Under Wings of Andean Blue"/></td>
          <td> Andean Blue</td>
          <td><i>Pseudolucia andina</i></td>
          <td>Chile</td>
          <td>Rabbits eating its food plant, Astragalus</td></tr>
       <tr><td><img src="psiby.jpg" alt="Top and Under Wings of Southern Blue"/></td>
          <td> Southern Blue</td>
          <td><i>Pseudolucia sibylla</i></td>
          <td>Argentina-Chile border</td>
          <td>Livestock grazing its food plant, Adesmia</td></tr>
     </table>
  </body>
</html>
```

Figure 7.9 The Source View displayed by the Firefox browser for the start of the table.

The color-coding in the browser shows the text colored in black, the tags in violet, and the programmer-supplied attribute data in blue. But the coloring is very unusual: First, lmeli.jpg is red, and it is the only content that is, but we're not sure what that means. Also, the entire heading line of the table is colored blue, indicating that the browser is interpreting it as part of a single attribute. That's incorrect. When we look closely at the start of the attribute, we see it is part of the row tag for the heading,

```
<tr style="background-color : silver▯>
```

An unusual character follows the word silver. It's supposed to be a quote to match the quote at the beginning of the attribute value. When we recheck Figure 7.6, we notice that the line reads

```
<tr style="background-color : silver”>
```

and that we have used a fancy closing quote, which browsers do not understand. So the browser, mistaking our closed quote for some other bizarre character, keeps looking for a closing quote. It eventually finds one in the image tag at the beginning of the next table row. So, the browser considers the background color to be everything from the beginning of the word silver up to the start of the file name lmeli.jpg, as it shows us in blue. Obviously, this isn't a color, and it explains what happened to the heading row—it was misinterpreted as part of the color specification. Replacing the fancy (smart) closed quote with the plain quote, which is required by all browsers, gives us a table with a heading row and three data rows, as shown in Figure 7.10. Narrowing the focus of our search to the first part of the table works.

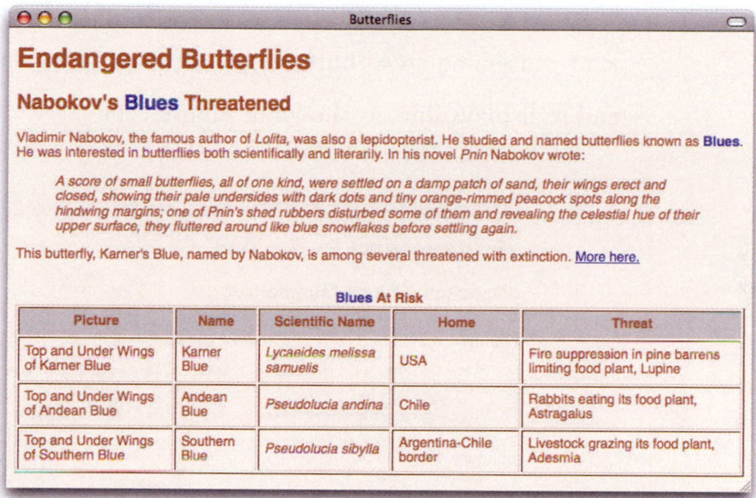

Figure 7.10 The Butterflies page after correcting the heading color.

Unfortunately, our debugging effort is not complete, because the pictures still do not display. We now focus our attention on the image tags in each row. We noticed earlier that lmeli.jpg was red, and we assumed that was significant, but after correcting the closing quote, it was changed to blue in the Page Source display. That indicates it is being interpreted correctly by the browser.

7.1 Where *Are* We? Of six debugging guidelines given earlier, which have we tried, and which one are we working with at the moment for the Butterflies page?

Reassess. We seem to be stuck. We've narrowed the problem down to the image tags, checked them, and determined that they are well structured. We have made the names uppercase to match the file names but that didn't help, and we've verified that the browser is interpreting the text properly. Everything looks correct. Frustration seems like the next step.

More constructively, we acknowledge that the XHTML can look perfect *to us* and still not work. What we *think* is true leads us to the wrong conclusion. So, we reassess to figure out what mistake we're making in our understanding of the XHTML. In this process we ask ourselves such questions as "What wrong assumptions am I making?" and "What wrong conclusions am I drawing?" Eventually, we may have to consider the possibility that the software we are using is broken, but that's usually the last possibility. Finding the answers to these questions usually locates the bug, but it will take some hard thinking and some experimentation.

In the present case we wonder, "Are the images really okay?" They looked fine in the file check of Figure 7.7, so we assume, "yes," the images are okay. Next, we ask, "Is there something wrong with the JPEG specification?" So, we make a little GIF file named butterfly.gif and change the first row figure to

```
<tr><td><img src= "butterfly.gif" alt= "..."/></td>
```

and it displays fine, as shown in Figure 7.11.

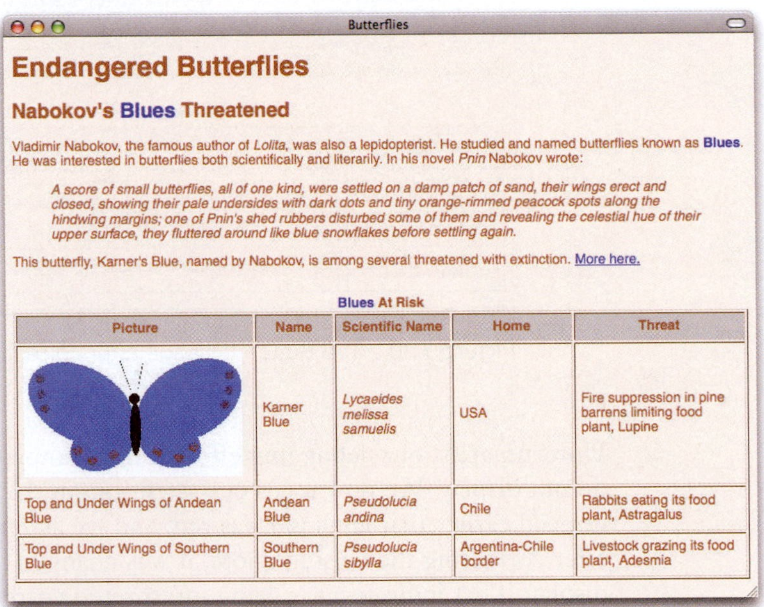

Figure 7.11 The table from the Butterflies page after revising with a new file.

This is an important development because it proves that the browser can display our pictures, but not the JPEG figures we want. Maybe there's another odd character in the image tag that we didn't notice. Some text editors can look for illegal characters—for example, in TextWrangler, the facility is called Zap Gremlins—allowing us to clean up a file when we suspect odd characters. But we don't need it. We can simply delete the file name lmeli.jpg and type it in again, but it still doesn't work. So, the problem isn't a bad character in the original image tag. It must be a problem with the file name, because that is all we changed when we displayed the GIF. What have we assumed that isn't true? To check the name, we open the LMELI file with the browser, since it shows the complete file name in the Location window. The window shows

```
.../Endangered/LMELI.JPEG
```

indicating that the file's extension is .JPEG, not .JPG as we have been using in the image tags. (We recall from Chapter 4 that browsers understand both .JPEG and .JPG as image files, but the operating system must still have the exact name for the file.) We probably would have noticed this immediately if the file extensions were being displayed, so even before we fix the XHTML, we go to the Help menu to find out how to direct our operating system to display file extensions.

We can fix this by correcting the image attributes or changing the names of the files. When we revise the image attributes as in

```
<tr><td><img src="LMELI.JPEG" alt= "..."/></td>
```

the result is identical to Figure 7.2. We've solved it!

Butterflies and Bugs: A Postmortem

We have found the bugs in the XHTML of the Butterflies page. In the process of tracking them down we made a series of conjectures, tried different changes to the program, ran a couple of experiments, and drew conclusions. How did we do? Certainly the result turned out fine.

Changes made. For the record, we made the following changes to the XHTML during the debugging process.

1. Replaced a semicolon with a colon in the blue color specification.
2. Placed a space between a and href to make the link active.
3. Changed the image tags to capitalize the file names; then reverted.
4. Fixed the quote following silver.
5. Replaced the file name LMELI.JPG with the butterfly.gif.
6. Restored LMELI.JPG reference.
7. Corrected the file extensions from .JPG to .JPEG.

Unnecessary changes. Of these seven changes, only 1, 2, 4, and 7 were necessary to fix the problem. The other changes were unnecessary: change 3 was not necessary because the file names are not case sensitive on the computers we used; change 5 was an experiment to force the browser to display a figure; and change 6 reversed change 5, repeating the "JPG error." The unnecessary changes were introduced when we made wrong conjectures about the cause of the error or were experimenting. Making changes that are unnecessary is quite typical, because making incorrect conjectures is also quite typical. Luckily these changes didn't make the situation worse, but it is possible to introduce new errors when following the wrong logical path or experimenting.

Hiding other errors. When we first described the errors, we thought we had three: a bad caption, a bad link, and a broken table. Because there were two things wrong with the table—messed up heading line and wrong file names specified—we actually had four errors.

The table errors were complicated to analyze because with one of the figures missing, we couldn't be sure whether the two problems were independent, as they turned out to be. Perhaps the missing figure was causing both errors—the missing heading line and the missing images. It is common for one error to hide another, so we always have to suspect that there is more than one error.

In Which Case. Generally, file references for Windows and Mac are not case sensitive, but UNIX systems are. Because you do not know which operating system will host your Web page, it is essential to make the case of the file references match the names.

Viewing the Source. Notice that the most effective technique in our debugging exercise—after thinking logically—was to use the browser's *Source View* feature. (Unfortunately, the Validator didn't help.) Seeing the color- and font-coded XHTML source told us how the browser interpreted our page. This revealed an error directly. In general, one of the most powerful debugging techniques is to find ways for the computer to tell us the meaning of the information it stores or the effects of the commands it executes. Having the computer stipulate how it's interpreting our instructions can separate the case in which we give the right command, but mess up expressing it, with giving the wrong command. This is an important difference for finding a bug.

Little Errors, Big Problems. Finally, the errors in the XHTML code were quite tiny: a semicolon instead of a colon, a missing space, a wrong quote, and three missing *e* characters in the file extensions. Of the 1,119 noncontent, nonblank characters in the original file, the six wrong characters represent about one-half of 1 percent of the XHTML programming. The conclusion: We must be extremely precise.

No Printer Output: A Classic Scenario

Debugging HTML is possible because we know and write HTML, but we don't create most computer systems, and they are extremely complex, way beyond our understanding. A standard personal computer and its software are more complex than the space shuttle in several ways. As users, we have little idea how something so complex works; how is it possible to troubleshoot a system we don't understand?

Of course, we cannot debug software and information systems at the detailed level used by programmers or engineers. If there is a basic, conceptual error in the system, we probably won't find it. But we don't have to. Before we come in contact with a system, it is tested extensively. This testing doesn't eliminate all errors, but it probably means that the "standard operations" used by "average" users are run through their paces many times. Systems should be bug-free, and we should be able to depend on the software.

fluencyBIT

Putting It to the Test. As noted in Chapter 2, "getting out and getting back in" often works when an application is not operating correctly. The reason this method works is related to how software is tested. Beginning with a fresh configuration, the testing proceeds "forward" into the application, with the common operations getting the most attention. So the most stable part of a system is the part that is reachable from an initial configuration—the part you first meet when you're "getting back in."

To illustrate debugging a system without understanding it, consider a classic debugging scenario: You try to print a document and nothing comes out of the printer. This problem happens often to all users. What you know about the context of the problem is a cable connects the computer/printer system, part of the system is mechanical, the flow of information is from one device to the other, and the system has worked in the past.

Applying the Debugging Strategy

The printing problem is solved just like the earlier problems were solved: *reproduce the error*, *understand the problem*, and *check the obvious causes*. These steps include checking the printer's control panel, the paper, the cartridges, the cable connections, the file to be printed, the installation of the printer driver (that the correct printer dialog box comes up when the *Print* command is issued), whether others can print if this is a shared printer, and whether you can print a different document. If these steps do not solve the problem, you may think it's time to ask for help. You've already gone further than most users, so it's not embarrassing, but you can do more.

Pressing On

Take the next step in the debugging strategy: *Try to isolate the problem*. This is daunting because you don't really understand how printing works. Not to worry. It's still possible to make progress.

Because you have printed before, you know your computer is configured correctly. You try to print a simple document like a text file, but it's the same story: The printer driver's dialog box comes up, asks how many copies you want, and so forth—you reply 1, click **Print**, and the machine appears to compute for a moment. But when you check the printer, nothing's there. What is happening to your output?

Thinking through what you imagine to be the process, you guess that when you click **Print**, the printer driver must convert the file into the form suitable for the printer. Because the computer runs briefly after you click **Print**, it's a safe bet that it's doing something like a conversion. Then your computer must send the converted file to the printer. Does it go? Surely, if the computer tried to send the file to the printer and the printer didn't acknowledge getting it, the computer would tell you to plug in the printer. Or would it? Suppose you unplugged the printer from the computer and tried again to print. You run this experiment and the same thing happens! The printer can't even receive the converted file, and there are no complaints. What's happening? Where is the file?

Perhaps the computer is saving the converted file. Why? Shouldn't it print if it's told to print? This is a little odd, because it's not asking you to plug in the printer. Could the other files you tried to print be waiting too, even though the printer was plugged in earlier? So, you start looking around for the stranded file(s). You locate the printer driver's printing monitor (*Start* > *Settings* > *Printers* on the PC; among the active programs on the Mac). When you open this monitor, you find a list of all the files you've tried to print recently. They're not printing—they're just listed.

The Print Queue

You have discovered the **print queue** for your machine, a place where printing tasks wait before being processed. You didn't even know that computers *have* print queues, but apparently they do. It's obvious that your file is stalled in the printing queue. As described in Chapter 2 under "Clicking Around," you explore the monitor application, discovering that the queue is "turned off" or possibly "wedged." (The actual description for "turned off" varies from system to system; for the PC it is *Use Printer Offline*, which is set under *File*; for Macs the Print Queue button is configured to *Start Print Queue*; shared printers are different still.) Though machines are different, the situation is the same: The computer's settings tell it to queue your converted files rather than print them immediately. How it got into this state you may never know. The best approach is to cancel or trash all of the jobs in the queue, because there are probably many duplicates, and restart the queue. That is, configure the printer so that it tries to print your files immediately rather than queuing them. Your printing problem may be solved! Or have you forgotten to reconnect the cable to your printer?

7.2 No Response. Another possibility when discovering the print queue with a long list of files is not that it has accidentally been turned off, but that the monitor reports the printer is not responding. What should you do then?

Calling Tech Support?

Summarizing the situation, you boldly tried debugging the printing operation in spite of the fact that it's complicated and you know almost nothing about how computers print. You aptly assumed that the software is okay. You discovered that computers use a print queue, though it's a mystery why. The queue can stop or stall, but by using the print monitor you can restart it. Locating the problem involved the standard debugging strategy applied with courage and common sense, and the results were successful. Obviously, there are many problems that are not solved using this approach—those that actually require some technical knowledge—but you should always assume that the standard debugging strategy will work. Only when you've applied it without complete success, is it time to call Tech Support.

fluencyBIT

Sleep on It. Professionals know that when they can't find a bug, it's time to take a break. Whether our minds continue to work on the problem subconsciously or that returning refreshed to the problem clears our thinking, briefly getting away from the problem helps.

Ensuring the Reliability of Software

Anyone who uses information technology regularly knows that software contains bugs, and that even catastrophic errors—crashes—are frustratingly frequent. Most of these errors are just an annoyance. But computers control life-support systems and other medical apparatus, airplanes, nuclear power plants, weapons systems, and so on. Errors in these systems are potentially much more serious—"crash" is not a metaphor. How do we know the software running safety-critical systems is perfect? We don't! It's a sobering thought.

Safety-Critical Applications

Any system, whether mechanical or electronic, that supports life or controls hazardous devices or materials should work flawlessly. Accepting anything less seems reckless. But it is easier to say that we want perfection than it is to achieve it.

Hardware Failures. To understand the issues, distinguish first between hardware failures and software failures. In general, hardware failures can be resolved using techniques such as **redundancy**. For example, three computers can perform all the computations of a safety-critical system and make decisions based on majority vote. If a failure in one computer causes it to come up with a different answer, the other two overrule it. The chance that the identical error would happen in each computer simultaneously is infinitesimally small. Another technique, dubbed *burn in*, exploits the so-called "infant mortality" property of computer hardware failures caused by manufacturing problems: Most errors show up after only a few hours of operation. A computer that has a record of successful operation is likely to continue to operate successfully. Overall, such techniques give us confidence that the hardware will work properly.

Software Failures. Software is another matter. Compared with mechanical and electronic systems, software is amazingly complex. The number of possible configurations that a typical program can define grows exponentially and quickly becomes unimaginably large even for small programs. All states that the software can get into, known as **reachable configurations**, cannot be examined for their correctness. This reality poses a serious problem for programmers and software engineers: How can they be sure their programs work correctly?

Like all engineers, programmers begin with a **specification**—a precise description of the input, how the system should behave, and how the output should be produced. The specification doesn't say how the behavior is to be achieved necessarily, just what it should be. Using various design methods, programmers produce the program. The program can be tested with sample inputs, and the outputs can be checked against the specification. If they do not match, there is a bug and the program must be fixed. *A program is said to be correct if its behavior exactly matches its specification.*

Though we have a tidy definition for correctness, there are two problems to achieving it, and both are showstoppers. First, it is not possible to know if the specification is perfect. Second, even if it were, it is not possible to establish correctness by testing. These two facts mean that we cannot *know* whether a program is correct, even if it is. Programmers and software engineers have developed many ingenious tools and technologies, including testing, to locate bugs and improve software. These can and do give us confidence that the program closely approximates its specification. But confidence, not certainty, is the best we can do.

fluencyBIT

Hard Fact of Software. Programming pioneer Edsger Dijkstra first stated this fundamental fact: Program testing reveals only the presence of bugs, never their absence.

The Challenge. What can we do about the fact that we can't prove that the software we use is correct? There are two aspects to consider.

- We must accept that software may contain bugs despite Herculean efforts of programmers and software engineers to get it right. So, we must monitor our software usage, be alert to unusual behavior that can indicate bugs, and be prepared to limit the harm that they can do.
- Because programmers and software engineers are aware of the challenge to produce correct software, poorly tested software is simply unprofessional; users should demand high-quality software, refuse buggy software, and be prepared to change to better software.

Thus we must be cautious and informed users and take our business to those who produce the best product.

Fail-Soft and Fail-Safe Software

Returning to the problem of software that controls safety-critical systems, what should the standard of quality be? The software may be perfectly correct, but we can't be sure. We *can* limit the harm that may result from using imperfect software. If we know that software is safe—that the life-support system does not cause patients to die, and the nuclear power plant software will not cause a meltdown—then perhaps we are less concerned about bugs. The idea of **safe software** changes the focus from worry about program correctness to concern about the consequences of errors in the software.

Testing and other techniques can give us confidence that software works "under normal circumstances," so safety focuses on what happens in unusual circumstances. It is difficult to test software under unusual circumstances, as when an earthquake damages a nuclear power plant. So, there are two design strategies: fail-soft and fail-safe. **Fail-soft** means that the program continues to operate, providing a possibly degraded level of functionality. **Fail-safe** means that the system stops functioning to avoid causing harm. The basic strategy, therefore, is to continue to operate as long as productive service is safely provided, but when that isn't possible, to avoid negative outcomes by stopping entirely.

Perfectly safe software is just as impossible as correct software, since the only way for the software to avoid all harm is not to do anything at all—not even start the nuclear power plant. Using software to control potentially dangerous systems means taking a risk, just like crossing a bridge or riding an elevator.

Summary

This chapter began by emphasizing why being precise is important when using computers. The standard of precision is higher than in most other situations, so being careful and exact makes using computers easier. We learned:

- What debugging is and why we need to know how to do it.
- Basic debugging strategy, including the whys and hows of debugging.
- To debug a Web page, using the *Source View* of the document that shows how the computer interprets the HTML.
- How to analyze our debugging performance, noting that debugging involves both correct and incorrect conjectures.
- That it's possible to debug a sophisticated system like a computer printer with little more than a vague idea of how it works, by using our standard debugging strategy applied with common sense and courage.
- That it is practically impossible to have bug-free software. This doesn't mean that we must quit using computers or accept bugs, but we must watch for unusual behavior that might indicate bugs and take precautions to limit the harm that they can cause.

Try It Solutions

7.1 We have tried the first four guidelines—reproduce the error, determine the problem, eliminate the obvious causes, and divide working from non-working parts. We are about to start to reassess our information.

7.2 The printer's software seems to be "wedged," so cycling power for the printer—turning it off for five seconds and then turning it back on—is the best response.

Review Questions

Multiple Choice

1. An example of an understanding error is a
   a. memory error
   b. data entry error
   c. design error
   d. none of the above
2. The best way to solve an understanding error is to
   a. restart the system
   b. change software
   c. try again
   d. all of the above
3. The first step in debugging is to
   a. check for obvious errors
   b. try to reproduce the problem
   c. isolate the problem
   d. find exactly what the problem is
4. The debugging process can be described as a
   a. guaranteed-to-work process
   b. road map
   c. set of guidelines
   d. list
5. The last step in the debugging process is to
   a. look again to identify the mistake
   b. reproduce the problem
   c. divide up the process
   d. determine the exact problem
6. Most software
   a. contains bugs
   b. is bug-free
   c. contains no known bugs
   d. works exactly as it should in every circumstance

Short Answer

1. _______ are information that is entered into boxes on a form.
2. A(n) _______ is a set of rules that determines what is legal for field input.
3. Use a _______ to represent a space on the computer.
4. _______ and debugging mean essentially the same thing.
5. A glitch in a computer system is called a(n) _______.
6. A(n) _______ is an error in the way a system was developed.
7. An alternative approach to get around a problem is called a(n) _______.
8. All the possible states in which a piece of software can exist are its _______.
9. A(n) _______ program continues to operate when there is a problem, although its efficiency may be degraded.
10. A(n) _______ program shuts down to avoid causing problems.

Exercises

1. You walk into a room and flip the light switch. Nothing happens. Describe the debugging process you use to solve the problem.
2. What advantages does an organized approach have over a trial-and-error approach?
3. Draw a schematic of the debugging process. Apply this to the debugging process for Exercise 1.
4. How would you say "Room 309"? Did you say "zero" or "oh"? How about a ZIP code? Try 57026.
5. What is the lexical structure for entering dates into the computer? Use the standard American format for a two-digit month, a separator, a two-digit day, a separator, and a four-digit year.
6. Devise a lexical structure for entering a phone number into the computer. What characters are allowed and when? Do the same thing for ZIP codes.
7. Think "outside the box" to solve a problem. You have a quiz in an hour and you're stranded. You must contact the professor before the quiz or you won't pass the course. How do you contact the professor? List multiple alternatives.
8. You've been doing debugging since you learned how to check your math back in grade school. Check the math on this problem.

   $N = -((12 + 6) - 7 \times 4 + ((9 - 2) \times 3) / 7)$
   $N = 18 - 7 \times 4 + 7 \times 3 / 7$
   $N = 11 \times 4 + 21 / 7$
   $N = 44 + 25 / 7$
   $N = 49 / 7$
   $N = 7$

9. Design several workarounds for the computer printing error. Pretend it's your term paper and it has to be printed. How would you get around the problem that the computer and the printer aren't printing?

10. Here is the XHTML for a simple Web page. Find the errors in it and get the page to display properly. Test the page to be sure it works properly.

```
<html>
<head>
<title>My Favorites</title>
</head>
<body>
<ol>
  <li>Movies</li>
</ol>
<ul>
  <li><i>Grease</i></li>
  <li><i>Knocked Up</i></li>
  <li><i>Transformers</i></li>
</ul>
<ol>
  <li>Shows</li>
  <li><i>Survivor</i></li>
  <li><i>American Idol</i></li>
  <li><i>Mad Men</i></li>
  <li>Stars</li>
</ol>
<ol>
  <li>Owen Wilson</li>
  <li>Kate Hudson</li>
  <li>January Jones</li>
</ol>
</body>
</html>
```

11. Your car won't start. Go through the debugging process for getting it started.

12. Describe fail-soft and fail-safe systems on your computer and with your software. Approach the problem from a nontechnical, user standpoint. What safeguards are in place to keep you from damaging or destroying your system, programs, and data?

13. Take a major system such as a commercial airliner or a hydroelectric power plant and describe the fail-soft and fail-safe system they might have.

14. Describe the concept of lexical structure. Give three examples different from those in the chapter.

15. Suppose your friend's personal music player (such as an iPod) isn't playing any songs. Explain the process you would go through to debug the problem. List at least eight questions you would ask, and explain how each is an application of the debugging guidelines.

Representing Information Digitally

Bits and the "Why" of Bytes

learning objectives

- Explain the link between patterns, symbols, and information
- Compare two different encoding methods
- Determine possible PandA encodings using a physical phenomenon
- Give a bit sequence code for ASCII; decode
- Explain how structure tags (metadata) encode the *Oxford English Dictionary*

Ancora imparo. ("I am still learning.")

—MICHELANGELO, MOTTO

MOST PEOPLE know that computers and networks record and transmit information in *bits* and *bytes*. From basic English, you can guess that bits probably represent little pieces of information. But what are bytes? And why is "byte" spelled with a *y*? In this chapter we confirm that bits do represent little pieces of information, we define bytes, and, by the end, we explain the mysterious *y*. But the chapter is much more fundamental than these basic concepts. It describes how bits and bytes—the atoms and molecules of information—combine to form our virtual world of computation, information, and communication. (Multimedia is covered in Chapter 11.) We even explain how information exists when there is nothing, as when Sherlock Holmes solves the mystery using the information that "the dog didn't bark in the night."

The first goal of this chapter is to establish that digitizing doesn't require digits—any set of symbols will do. You will learn how pattern sequences can create symbols, and discover that symbols can represent information. The next goal is to learn the fundamental patterns on which all information technology is built: the presence and absence of a phenomenon. Called the PandA encoding here, this meeting of the physical and logical worlds forms the foundation of information technology. We then define bits, bytes, and ASCII. Finally, we describe the digitization of the *Oxford English Dictionary* to show how metadata is added to content so computers can help us use it.

Digitizing Discrete Information

The dictionary definition of *digitize* is to represent information with digits. In normal conversation, *digit* means the ten Arabic numerals 0 through 9. Thus, digitizing uses whole numbers to stand for things. This familiar process represents Americans by Social Security numbers, telephone accounts by phone numbers, and books by ISBN numbers. Such digital representations have probably been used since numerals were invented. But this sense of *digitize* is much too narrow for the digital world of IT.

fluencyBIT

> **Digital Man.** The first person to apply the term *digital* to computers was George Stibitz, a Bell Labs mathematician. While consulting for the U.S. military, he observed that "pulsed" computing devices would be better described as digital because they represent information in discrete (that is, separate) units.

Limitation of Digits

A limitation of the dictionary definition of *digitize* is that it calls for the use of the ten digits, which produces a whole number. But in most cases the property of being numeric is unimportant and of little use. Numbers quantify things and let us do arithmetic, but Social Security numbers, phone numbers, and ISBN numbers are not quantities. You are not better than someone else is if you have a larger telephone number. So, when we don't need numbers, we don't need to use digits. But what else can we use to digitize?

Alternative Representations

Digitizing in computing can use almost any symbols. For example, the North American telephone number `888 555 1212` could be represented as *** %%% !@!@. This encoding, rather than using {1, 2, 3, 4, 5, 6, 7, 8, 9, 0}, uses the symbol set {!, @, #, $, %, ^, &, *, (,)}. These symbols are simply the uppercase digit characters on a keyboard. If we use the symbol set { ▶, ▼, ◀, ▶▶, ■, ◀◀, ▶▶|, ▲, |◀◀, ❚❚ } the phone number is represented as: ▲ ▲ ▲ ■ ■ ■ ▶ ▼ ▶ ▼. This could be called *player encoding* because it uses the standard symbols from music players. These symbols work just as well as the digits as long as the telephone keypad is relabeled, as shown in Figure 8.1. The reason the encoding works is that a phone number's digits simply tell us which sequence of keys to press. Any ten distinct symbols will work as long as the keypad is labeled properly.

Symbols, Briefly

One practical advantage of digits over other less familiar symbols is that digits have short names. Imagine speaking your phone number as "asterisk, asterisk, exclamation point, closing parenthesis, exclamation point . . ." In fact, as IT

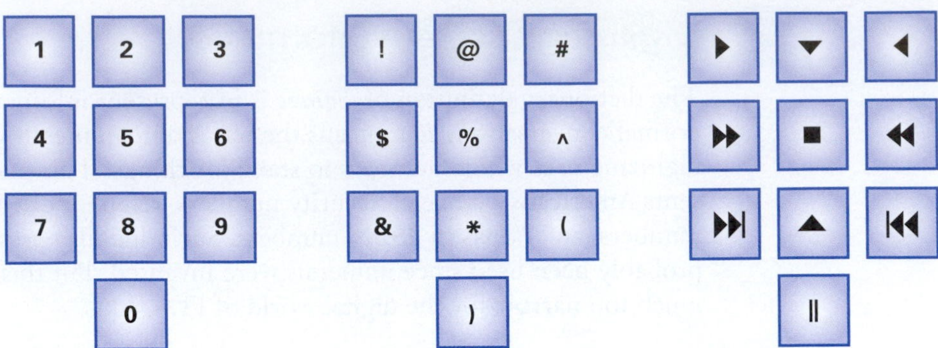

Figure 8.1 Three symbol assignments for a telephone keypad.

has adopted these symbols, the names are getting shorter. For example, computer professionals often say exclamation point as *bang* and asterisk as *star*. Instead of saying "eight, eight, eight, five, five, five, one, two, one, two" we could say "star, star, star, per, per, per, bang, at, bang, at," which is just as brief. So, the advantage of brevity is not limited to digits.

Ordering Symbols

One other advantage of digits for encoding information like telephone numbers is that the items can be listed in numerical order. This feature is rarely used for the kinds of information discussed here; for example, telephone books are ordered by the name of the person rather than by the number. But sometimes ordering items is useful.

To place information in order by using symbols (other than digits), we need to agree on an ordering for the basic symbols. This is called a **collating sequence**. In the same way that the digits are ordered

$0 < 1 < 2 < 3 < 4 < 5 < 6 < 7 < 8 < 9$

the player symbols could be ordered

∥ < ▶ < ▼ < ◀ < ▶▶ < ■ < ◀◀ < ▶▶| < ▲ < |◀◀

Then, two coded phone numbers can be ordered based on which has the smaller first symbol, or if the first symbol matches, then on which has the smaller second symbol, or if the first two symbols match, which has the smaller third symbol, and so on. For example,

▲ ∥ ∥ ■ ■ ■ ▶ ▼ ▶ ▼ < ▲ ▲ ▲ ■ ■ ■ ▶ ▼ ▶ ▼

Today, **digitizing** means representing information by symbols—not just the ten digit symbols. But which symbols would be best? Before answering that question, we should consider how the choice of symbols interacts with the things being encoded.

Fundamental Information Representation

The fundamental patterns used in IT come into play when the physical world meets the logical world. In the physical world, the most fundamental form of information is the presence or absence of a physical phenomenon.

- Does matter occupy a particular place in space and time, or not?
- Is light detected at a particular place and time, or not?
- Is magnetism sensed at a particular place and time, or not?

The same goes for pressure, charge, flow, and so on. In many cases, the phenomena have a continuous range of values (discussed in Chapter 11). For example, light and color have a smooth range of intensities

while others like clicking and drumming are discrete.

From a digital information point of view, the amount of a phenomenon is not important as long as it is reliably detected—whether there is some information or none; whether it is present or absent.

In the logical world, which is the world of thinking and reasoning, the concepts of *true* and *false* are important. Propositions such as "Rain implies wet streets" can be expressed and combined with other propositions such as "The streets are not wet" to draw conclusions such as "It is not raining." Logic is the foundation of reasoning, and it is also the foundation of computing. *By associating "true" with the presence of a phenomenon and "false" with its absence, we can use the physical world to implement the logical world. This produces information technology.* This section describes that association.

The PandA Representation

PandA is the name we use for the two fundamental patterns of digital information based on the presence and absence of a phenomenon. PandA is the mnemonic for "**Presence and Absence**." A key property of the PandA representation is that it is black and white; that is, the phenomenon is either present or it is not; the logic is either *true* or *false*. Such a formulation is said to be **discrete**, meaning "distinct" or "separable"; it is not possible to transform one value into the other by continuous gradations. There is no gray.

A binary system. The PandA encoding has just two patterns—Present and Absent—making it a **binary system**. The names Present and Absent are not essential to our use in digitization, so we often associate other words with them that suggest the discrete, black-and-white nature of the two patterns (see

Table 8.1). The assignment of these names to the two patterns is also arbitrary: There is no law that says that in all cases *On* means "Present" and *Off* means "Absent." We could agree to assign the names the other way around; engineers deep into a circuit design often do. As long as all of the information encoders and decoders agree, any assignment works. The associations given in Table 8.1 seem reasonable, however, and they are probably the most common. But the entries are only names for the two fundamental patterns.

Table 8.1 Possible interpretations of the two PandA patterns

Present	Absent
True	False
1	0
On	Off
Yes	No
+	–
Black	White
For	Against
Yang	Yin
X	Y
. . .	. . .

Bits form symbols. In the PandA representation, the unit is a specific place (in space and time), where the presence or absence of the phenomenon can be set and detected. The PandA unit is known as a **bit**, which can assume either of the two PandA patterns, Present or Absent. *Bit* is a contraction for "binary digit." (The term *bit* was originally adopted because early computer designers interpreted the two patterns as 1 and 0, the digits of the binary number system; they are more economical to say and write than "present" and "absent," so we continue to use them.) Though bit sequences can be interpreted as binary numbers, the key idea is that groups of bits form **symbols**. Encoding numbers is a particularly useful application of symbols, but the idea is more general.

fluencyBIT

Coincidence? Though *bit* means "small piece" in English, the term actually derives from a contraction of *binary* and *digit*. Of course, bits represent small pieces of information, suggesting the choice may not have been a coincidence.

Encoding Bits on a CD-ROM. The compact disc read-only memory (CD-ROM) is the technology of the familiar audio CD applied to storing programs and data. Developed jointly by the Phillips and Sony Corporations, the CD was originally intended only for recorded audio and video. But the two companies engineered the technology so cleverly that CDs are almost error free, making them perfect for storing data and software. Here's how CDs work.

CDs are made of clear plastic that is forced into a round mold, something like a round waffle iron, having a smooth bottom and a bumpy top. When the plastic hardens and is removed from the mold, the topside bumpy pattern is covered with aluminum to make it shiny. A protective layer is put over the aluminum and the "label" is printed on the top.

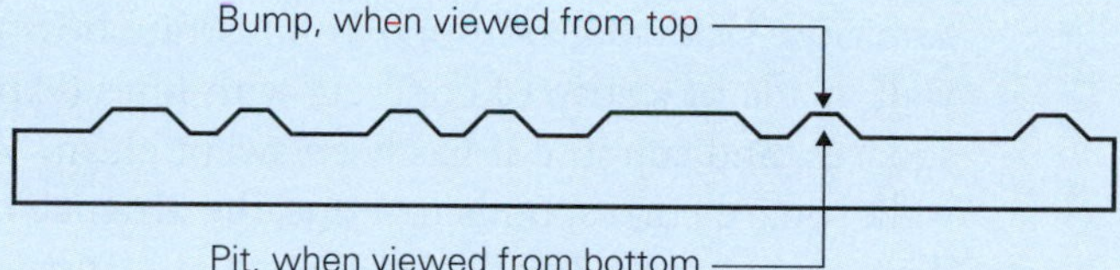

The bumps encode the information. Because they are read from the bottom of the CD, the bumps are called *pits*. The region between the pits is called the *land*. A laser beam is focused up through the CD onto the pitted surface. The beam reflects off of the aluminum and back to a sensor that detects whether the beam is striking a pit, a land, or a diagonal in between.

The pits are arranged in a line that begins at the *inner* edge of the CD and spirals out to the *outer* edge. (Notice that inside-out is the opposite of vinyl records.) The first part of the spiral is used for calibrating the laser reading device, then comes an index (track list) for locating specific positions on the CD, and finally the actual information (music or software) is stored in binary.

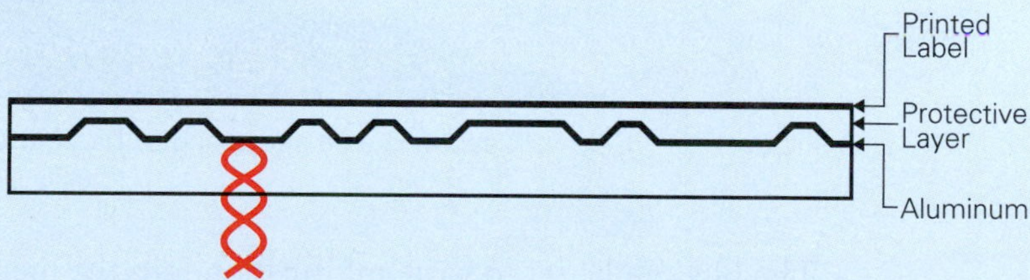

In addition to CDs and DVDs, which are manufactured with the information already stored on them—it's a pattern in the mold—there are CD Recordable (CD-R) discs and CD Rewriteable (CD-RW) discs. Both types are blank to begin with and use somewhat different materials. CD-R disks can be written to once and only read thereafter; CD-RW disks can be written to and rewritten to.

fluencyBIT

Positive Presence. The use of physical phenomena to represent information sometimes poses problems because there might be more than two alternatives. For example, a magnetic material might not be magnetized at all, or it can have positive polarity or negative polarity; that is, there are three possibilities. In such situations, engineers adopt one state such as positive polarity to mean "present" and all other states to mean "absent."

Bits in Computer Memory

Memory is arranged inside a computer in a very long sequence of bits. That is, places where the physical phenomenon encoding the information can be set and detected.

Analogy: sidewalk memory. To illustrate how memory works, imagine a sidewalk made of a strip of concrete with lines (expansion joints) across it forming squares, and suppose it has been swept clean. We agree that a stone on a sidewalk square corresponds to 1 and the absence of a stone corresponds to 0. This makes the sidewalk a sequence of bits (see Figure 8.2.) Sidewalk memory can encode information just like computer memory—it's just not as economical with space!

Figure 8.2 Sidewalk sections as a sequence of bits (1010 0010).

The bits can be set to write information into the memory, and they can be sensed to read the information out of the memory. To write a 1, the phenomenon must be made to be present; for example, put a stone on a sidewalk square. To write a 0, the phenomenon must be made to be absent; for example, sweep the sidewalk square clean. To determine what information is stored at a specific position, check whether the phenomenon is present or absent. So, if a stone is on a square, the phenomenon is present (1); otherwise, it is absent (0).

Alternative PandA encodings. There is no limit to the number of ways to encode two states using physical phenomena, of course. Remaining in the world of sidewalks, we can use stones on all squares, but use white stones and black stones for the two states. We can choose black as present and not black as absent. Or, we can use multiple stones of two colors per square, saying that more white stones than black means 1 and more black stones than white means 0. (We must take care that the total number of stones on each sidewalk square is always an odd number.) Or we can place a stone in the center of the square for one state and off center for the other state. And so forth. These are all PandA encodings, provided the "phenomenon" is chosen properly: presence of black, presence of majority of white, and presence of a centered stone.

fluencyBIT

No Barking. Sherlock Holmes uses one bit of information to solve the disappearance of a prize racehorse in the story "Silver Blaze." In the vicinity of the stable during the night (place and time), the phenomenon (barking watchdog) was not detected (absent), implying to Holmes the dog knew the thief, who had to be Simpson, the owner. Holmes reasons that barking "present" implies the thief is not known to the household; barking "absent" implies the opposite. There is information present even though the phenomenon is absent.

Combining bit patterns. The two bit patterns alone give us a limited resource for digitizing information. That is, we can represent things with only two values: votes (*aye*, *nay*), personality types (*A*, *B*), baseball games (*won*, *loss*). Usually the two patterns must be combined into sequences to create enough symbols to encode the intended information. When there are $p = 2$ patterns as there are in the PandA representation, arranging them into n-length sequences, creates 2^n symbols. Table 8.2 relates the length of the bit sequence to the number of possible symbols. The 16 symbols of $n = 4$ length bit sequences are shown in Table 8.3.

Table 8.2 Number of symbols when the number of possible patterns is two

n	2^n	Symbols
1	2^1	2
2	2^2	4
3	2^3	8
4	2^4	16
5	2^5	32
6	2^6	64
7	2^7	128
8	2^8	256
9	2^9	512
10	2^{10}	1,024

Table 8.3 Sixteen symbols of the 4-bit PandA representation

Symbol	Binary	Physical Bits	Hex	Symbol	Binary	Physical Bits	Hex
AAAA	0000		0	PAAA	1000		8
AAAP	0001		1	PAAP	1001		9
AAPA	0010		2	PAPA	1010		A
AAPP	0011		3	PAPP	1011		B
APAA	0100		4	PPAA	1100		C
APAP	0101		5	PPAP	1101		D
APPA	0110		6	PPPA	1110		E
APPP	0111		7	PPPP	1111		F

The PandA encoding is the fundamental representation of information. By grouping bits together, we can produce enough symbols to represent any number of values. By creating symbols using the two PandA patterns, we can record and transform information using resources from the physical world. Information and computation are abstract concepts without physical form, but with the miracle of IT they can become real. Our lives are simplified when machines and networks do the work.

Hex Explained

Before using PandA to represent text, let's solve a mystery from Chapter 4. Recall that when we specified colors in HTML, we said that one form a color specification could take was using hex digits, as in #FF8E2A for pumpkin color. These **hex digits**, short for hexadecimal digits, are base-16 numbers. We didn't explain hex at the time, but cited `www.w3schools.com/css/css_colorsfull.asp` as a source where color and numbers could be correlated.

The reason for using hexadecimal is as follows. When we specify an RGB color or other encoding using bits, we must give the bits in order. The bit sequence might be given in 0's and 1's, as in

color : #111111110011000111000101010 *Illegal Style Definition*

but writing so many 0's and 1's is tedious and error prone. Computer professionals long ago realized that they needed a better way to write bit sequences, so they began to use hexadecimal digits.

The 16 Hex Digits

The digits of the **hexidecimal** numbering system are 0, 1, … , 9, A, B, C, D, E, F. Because there are 16 digits—maybe we should call them *hexits*—they can be represented perfectly by the 16 symbols of 4-bit sequences. In Table 8.3, the binary and hex are given for each value. So bit sequence 0000 is hex 0, bit sequence 0001 is hex 1, and so forth, up to the bit sequence 1111, which is hex F. (This is simply a numeric interpretation of the bits, which will be explained in Chapter 11.)

Changing Hex Digits to Bits and Back Again

Because each hex digit corresponds to a 4-bit sequence, and vice versa, we can translate between hex and binary easily: given hex, write the associated groups of 4 bits. Given a sequence of bits, group them into sequences of four, and write the corresponding hex digit. Therefore,

0010 1011 1010 1101 = 2BAD

and

FAB4 = 1111 1010 1011 0100

So, in HTML when we specify the color white as #FFFFFF, we effectively set each bit of the RGB specification bits to 1.

8.1 What's the Beef? What is ABE8 BEEF as a bit sequence? To find the answer, use Table 8.3.

Digitizing Text

The two earliest uses of the PandA representation—or binary representation—were to encode numbers and keyboard characters. These two applications are still extremely important, but now representations for sound, images, video, and other types of information are almost as important. In this section we talk about how text is encoded; we'll discuss how the other forms of information are encoded in Chapter 11.

Remember that the number of bits determines the number of symbols available for representing values: n bits in sequence yield 2^n symbols. And, as you've learned, the more characters you want encoded, the more symbols you need. Roman letters, Arabic numerals, and about a dozen punctuation characters are about the minimum needed to digitize English text. We would also like to have uppercase and lowercase letters, and the basic arithmetic symbols like +, –, *, /, and =. But, where should the line be drawn? Should characters not required for English but useful in other languages, like German (ö), French (é), Spanish (ñ), and Norwegian (ø), be included? What about Czech, Greek, Arabic, Thai, or Cantonese? Should other languages' punctuation be included, like French (« ») and Spanish (¿)? Should arithmetic symbols include degrees (°), pi (π), relational symbols (≤), equivalence (≡), and for all (∀)? What about business symbols: ¢, £, ¥, ©, and ®? What about unprintable characters like backspace and new line? Should there be a symbol for smiley faces (☺)? Some of these questions are easier to answer than others. We want to keep the list small so that we use fewer bits, but not being able to represent critical characters would be a mistake.

Assigning Symbols

The 26 uppercase and 26 lowercase Roman letters, the 10 Arabic numerals, a basic set of 20 punctuation characters (including blank), 10 useful arithmetic characters, and 3 nonprintable characters (new line, tab, and backspace) can be represented with 95 symbols. Such a set is enough for English and is accessible using the keys on a basic computer keyboard. To represent 95 distinct symbols, we need 7 bits because 6 bits gives only $2^6 = 64$ symbols. Seven bits give $2^7 = 128$ symbols, which is more than we need for the 95 different characters. Some special control characters, used for data transmission and other engineering purposes, must also be represented. They are assigned to the remaining 33 of the 7-bit symbols.

An early and still widely used 7-bit code for the characters is **ASCII**, pronounced AS·key. ASCII stands for American Standard Code for Information Interchange. The advantages of a "standard" are many: computer parts built by different manufacturers can be connected, programs can create data and store it so that different programs can process it later, and so forth. In all cases, there must be an agreement as to which character is associated with which symbol (bit sequence).

Extended ASCII: An 8-bit Code

As the name implies, ASCII was developed in the United States. By the mid-1960s, it became clear that 7-bit ASCII was not enough because it could not fully represent text from languages other than English. So IBM, the dominant computer manufacturer at the time, decided to use the next larger set of symbols, the 8-bit symbols, as the standard for character representation. Eight bits produce $2^8 = 256$ symbols, enough to encode English and the Western

European languages, their punctuation characters, and a large set of other useful characters. The larger, improved encoding was originally called Extended ASCII, as shown in Figure 8.3; today it is known by the curious name of **ISO-8859-1**. The original ASCII is the "first half" of Extended ASCII; that is, 7-bit ASCII is the 8-bit ASCII representation with the leftmost bit set to 0. Though Extended ASCII does not handle all natural languages, it does handle many languages that derived from the Latin alphabet; the ASCII of Figure 8.3 is also known as *Latin-1*. Handling other languages is solved in two ways: recoding the second half of Extended ASCII for the language's other characters, and using the multi-byte Unicode representation.

ASCII	0000	0001	0010	0011	0100	0101	0110	0111	1000	1001	1010	1011	1100	1101	1110	1111
0000	NU	SH	SX	EX	ET	EQ	AK	BL	BS	HT	LF	YT	FF	CR	S0	SI
0001	DL	D1	D2	D3	D4	NK	SY	EΣ	CN	EM	SB	EC	FS	GS	RS	US
0010		!	"	#	$	%	&	'	(	)	*	+	,	-	.	/
0011	0	1	2	3	4	5	6	7	8	9	:	;	<	=	>	?
0100	@	A	B	C	D	E	F	G	H	I	J	K	L	M	N	O
0101	P	Q	R	S	T	U	V	W	X	Y	Z	[	\	]	^	_
0110	`	a	b	c	d	e	f	g	h	i	j	k	l	m	n	o
0111	p	q	r	s	t	u	v	w	x	y	z	{	|	}	~	DT
1000	80	81	82	83	IN	NL	SS	ES	HS	HJ	YS	PD	PV	RI	S2	S3
1001	DC	P1	PZ	SE	CC	MM	SP	EP	Q8	QQ	QA	CS	ST	OS	PM	AP
1010	AO	¡	¢	£	¤	¥	¦	§	¨	©	ª	«	¬	-	®	¯
1011	°	±	^{2}	^{3}	´	µ	¶	·	¸	^{1}	º	»	¼	½	¾	¿
1100	À	Á	Â	Ã	Ä	Å	Æ	Ç	È	É	Ê	Ë	Ì	Í	Î	Ï
1101	Ð	Ñ	Ò	Ó	Ô	Õ	Ö	×	Ø	Ù	Ú	Û	Ü	Ý	Þ	β
1110	à	á	â	ã	ä	å	æ	ç	è	é	ê	ë	ì	í	î	ï
1111	ð	ñ	ò	ó	ô	õ	ö	÷	ø	ù	ú	û	ü	ý	þ	ÿ

Figure 8.3 ASCII, the American Standard Code for Information Interchange.

Note: The original 7-bit ASCII is the top half of the table; the whole table is known as Extended ASCII (ISO-8859-1). The 8-bit symbol for a letter is the four row bits followed by the four column bits (e.g., A = 0100 0001, while z = 0111 1010). Characters shown as two small letters are control symbols used to encode nonprintable information (e.g., BS = 0000 1000 is backspace). The bottom half of the table represents characters needed by Western European languages, such as Icelandic's eth (ð) and thorn (þ).

IBM's move to 8 bits was bold because it added the extra bit at a time when computer memory and storage were extremely expensive. IBM gave 8-bit sequences a special name, **byte**, and adopted it as a standard unit for computer memory. (Octet is used as a synonym for byte.) Bytes are still the standard unit of memory, and their "8-ness" is noticeable in many places. For example, recent computers are "32-bit machines"—not 30-bit or 35-bit—so their data paths (the part that processes most instructions) can handle 4 bytes at a time.

fluencyBIT

The Ultimate. Although ASCII and its variations are widely used, the more complete solution is a representation, called *Unicode*. It uses more than one byte (up to four) to encode about 100,000 symbols, enough for *all* languages. The actual encoding into bytes is given by the Unicode Translation Format or UTF-8.

ASCII Coding of Phone Numbers

Let's return to the phone number 888 555 1212, whose representation concerned us at the start of the chapter. How would a computer represent this phone number in its memory? Remember, this is not really a number, but rather, it is a keying sequence for a telephone's keypad represented by numerals; it is not necessary, or even desirable, to represent the phone number as a numerical quantity. Because each of the numerals has a representation in ASCII, we can express the phone number by encoding each digit with a byte. The encoding is easy: Find each numeral in Figure 8.3 and write down the bit sequence from its row, followed by the bit sequence from its column. So the phone number 888 555 1212 in ASCII is

```
0011 1000 0011 1000 0011 1000
0011 0101 0011 0101 0011 0101
0011 0001 0011 0010 0011 0001 0011 0010
```

You can use Figure 8.3 to check this encoding. This is exactly how computers represent phone numbers. The encoding seems somewhat redundant because each byte has the same left half: 0011. The left halves are repeated because all of the numerals are located on the 0011 row of the ASCII table. If only phone numbers had to be represented, fewer bits could be used, of course. But there is little reason to be so economical, so we adopt the standard ASCII.

Notice that we have run all of the digits of the phone number together, even though when we write them for ourselves we usually put spaces between the area code and exchange code, and between the exchange code and the number. The computer doesn't care, but it might matter to users. It's easy to add these spaces and other punctuation.

fluencyBIT

Two Bits, Four Bits. The term *byte* has motivated some people to call 4 bits—that is, half a byte—a *nibble*.

8.2 Numbers as Letters. Encode the phone number (888) 555-1212 in ASCII, including the punctuation. (Notice that there is a space before the first 5.)

To find the answer, locate each character in Figure 8.3 and write the four bits at the left of the row and the four bits at the top of the column. For example, the open parenthesis—(—is in the third row and corresponds to 0010 1000.

NATO Broadcast Alphabet

Finally, although we usually try to be efficient (e.g., use the shortest symbol sequences) to minimize the amount of memory needed to store and transmit information, not all letter representations should be short. The code for the letters used in radio communication is purposely inefficient in this sense, so they are distinctive when spoken amid noise. The NATO broadcast alphabet, shown in Table 8.4, encodes letters as words; that is, the words are the symbols, replacing the standard spoken names for the letters. For example, *Mike* and *November* replace "em" and "en," which can be hard to tell apart. This longer encoding improves the chances letters will be recognized when spoken under less-than-ideal conditions. The digits keep their usual names, except nine, which is frequently replaced by *niner*.

Table 8.4 NATO broadcast alphabet designed not to be minimal

A	Alpha	H	Hotel	O	Oscar	V	Victor
B	Bravo	I	India	P	Papa	W	Whiskey
C	Charlie	J	Juliet	Q	Quebec	X	X-ray
D	Delta	K	Kilo	R	Romeo	Y	Yankee
E	Echo	L	Lima	S	Sierra	Z	Zulu
F	Foxtrot	M	Mike	T	Tango		
G	Golf	N	November	U	Uniform		

It's Greek to Me. There are dozens of phonetic alphabets for English and many other languages. The NATO alphabet, used for air traffic control, begins with "alpha," raising the question, "What is the first letter of the Greek phonetic alphabet?" Alexandros.

The *Oxford English Dictionary*

Representations like ASCII encode text directly, 8 bits per letter. But most documents have more than just text. For example, one might need to format information, such as font, font size, justification, and so on. We could add formatting characters to ASCII, but this is a poor idea for several reasons. The most serious problem is that it mixes the content (i.e., the text) with the description of its form. The descriptive information (**metadata**) specifies the content's formatting or structure, and it should be kept separate from the text. So, we specify metadata by using tags, as we have seen in the searching discussion (see Chapter 2) and HTML (see Chapter 4). Tags use the same character representation as the content itself, which simplifies the encoding, and they are much more versatile. In this section, we illustrate how tags encode the structure of a document, by describing the digitization of the *Oxford English Dictionary*.

Using Tags to Encode

The *Oxford English Dictionary* (*OED*) is the definitive reference for every English word's meaning, etymology, and usage. Because it is comprehensive, the *OED* is truly monumental. The printed version is 20 volumes, weighs 150 pounds, and fills 4 feet of shelf space. In 1857, the Philological Society of London established the goal of producing a complete list of all English words. They expected that the completed dictionary would comprise 6,400 pages in four volumes. By 1884, with the list completed only up to *ant*, it became clear to James Murray, the lexicographer in charge, that the effort was much more ambitious than they originally thought. The first edition, completed in 1928, long after Murray's death, filled 15,490 pages and contained 252,200 entries. In 1984, the conversion of the *OED* to digital form began.

Now imagine that you have typed in the entire *OED* as a long sequence of ASCII characters from A through the end of the definition for *zyxt*, the last word in English. That task would take one person about 120 years. The result would be a digitized dictionary, but in the form of a very long sequence of ASCII characters. Would a computer be able to help us use it?

Suppose we want to find the definition for the verb *set*, which is notable for having the longest entry in the *OED*. The searching software—as described in Chapter 2—would look for *s-e-t* and find it thousands of times. This is because *set* is part of many words, like clo*set*, hor*set*ail, and *set*tle, and *set* is used in many definitions, for example, "*match-point* in tennis is the final score ending the present game, *set*, and match."

We can solve the first problem—avoiding *s-e-t* within words—by ignoring all occurrences that do not have a punctuation character or space before and after the *s-e-t*. The software can do that. But how does it find the definition for *set* among the thousands of true occurrences of the word *set* in other definitions? The software processing the text file, unable to understand the dictionary's contents, would have no clue which one it is.

People use a number of cues to find information in the dictionary, such as alphabetic order and the fact that a new definition begins on a new line, and the defined word is printed in bold. Though we could insert HTML-like tags for new lines or boldface type, a better solution is to use the tags to describe the *structure* of the dictionary's content. That is, incorporate metadata.

Structure Tags

A special set of tags was developed to specify the *OED*'s *structure*. For example, <hw> is the *OED*'s tag for a *headword*, the word being defined. As usual, because tags surround the text like parentheses, there is a closing *headword* tag, </hw>. Thus, the place in the *OED* where the verb *set* is defined appears in the tagged text file of the dictionary as

```
<hw>set</hw>
```

Other tags label the pronunciation <pr>, the phonetic notations <ph>, the parts of speech <ps>, the homonym number <hm> for headwords that sound the same, and so forth. There are also tags to group items, such as <e> to surround an entire entry and <hg> to surround a head group (that is, all of the information at the start of a definition). In the *OED* the first entry for the verb *set* begins

set (sɛt), *v.*[1]

giving the word being defined, the pronunciation, the part of speech (verb), and the homonym number (1). We expect it must be tagged as

```
<e><hg><hw>set</hw> <pr><ph>s&epsilont</ph></pr>,
<ps>v</ps>.<hm>1</hm></hg>
```

Notice the use of the escape code (&epsilon) for the epsilon character in the pronunciation, which is similar to the use of & for accented letters in HTML (Chapter 4). Also, the </e> is not shown because it must be at the very end of the entry.

With the structure tags in the dictionary, software can find the definition of the verb *set* easily: Search for occurrences of <hw>set</hw>, which indicate a definition for set, check within its head group for <ps>v</ps>, which indicates that it is a verb form of set being defined, and then print out (formatted) all of the text within the <e> and </e> tags.

Of course, the tags do not print. They are included only to specify the structure, so the computer knows what part of the dictionary it is looking at. But in fact, structure tags are very useful for formatting. For example, the boldface type used for headwords can be automatically applied when the dictionary is printed based on the <hw> tag. In a similar way, the italics typeface can be applied in the part of speech. The parentheses surrounding the pronunciation and the superscript for the homonym number are also generated automatically. Thus, knowing the structure makes it possible to generate the formatting information.

The opposite is not true. That is, formatting tags do not usually tell us enough about a document to allow us to know its structure. In the *OED* example, though boldface is used for headwords, it is also used for other purposes, which means that just because a word is boldface does not mean it is a headword. In fact, because some formatting information, like italics, has both structural and nonstructural occurrences, the *OED* digitization includes some formatting information with the structural information. The structure is more important, but most complex documents use both types of tags.

Sample *OED* Entry

Figure 8.4 shows the entry for *byte*, together with its representation, as it actually appears in the file of the online *OED*. At first the form looks very cluttered, but if you compare it with the printed form, you can make sense of the tags. The tags specify the role of each word of the dictionary. So, for example, to find the first time the word *byte* was used in print, the software searches for `<hw>byte</hw>`, then looks for the quote date tags, `<qd>` and `</qd>`, to find that the first use of the word was in 1964. Structure tags help the software help the user.

byte (baIt). *Computers.* [Arbitrary, prob. influenced by bit sb.[4] and bite sb.] A group of eight consecutive bits operated on as a unit in a computer.

1964 ***Blaauw*** & ***Brooks*** in *IBM Systems Jrnl.* III. 122 An 8-bit unit of information is fundamental to most of the formats [of the System/360]. A consecutive group of *n* such units constitutes a field of length *n*. Fixed-length fields of length one, two, four, and eight are termed bytes, halfwords, words, and double words respectively. **1964** *IBM Jrnl. Res. & Developm.* VIII. 97/1 When a byte of data appears from an I/O device, the CPU is seized, dumped, used and restored. **1967** ***P. A. Stark*** *Digital Computer Programming* xix. 351 The normal operations in fixed point are done on four bytes at a time. **1968** *Dataweek* 24 Jan. 1/1 Tape reading and writing is at from 34,160 to 192,000 bytes per second.

```
<e><hg><hw>byte</hw> <pr><ph>baIt</ph></pr></hg>. <la> Computers</la>. <etym> Arbitrary,
prob. influenced by <xr><x>bit</x></xr> <ps>n.<hm>4</hm></ps>and <xr><x>bite</x>
<ps>n.</ps></xr></etym> <s4>A group of eight consecutive bits operated on as a unit in a
computer.</s4><qp><q><qd>1964</qd><a>Blaauw</a> &amp. <a>Brooks</a><bib>in</bib>
<w>IBM Systems Jrnl.</w> <lc>III.122</lc> <qt>An 8-bit unit of information is fundamental to most
of the formats <ed>of the System/360</ed>.&es.A consecutive group of <i>n</i> such units
constitutes a field of length <i>n</i>.&es.Fixed-length fields of length one, two, four, and eight are
termed bytes, halfwords, words, and double words respectively. </qt></q><q><qd>1964</qd>
<w>IBM Jrnl. Res. &amp. Developm. </w> <lc>VIII. 97/1</lc> <qt>When a byte of data appears
from an I/O device, the CPU is seized, dumped, used and restored.</qt></q><q><qd>1967</qd>
<a>P. A. Stark</a> <w>Digital Computer Programming</w> <lc>xix. 351</lc> <qt>The normal
operations in fixed point are done on four bytes at a time.</qt></q> <q><qd> 1968</qd> <w>
Dataweek</w> <lc>24 Jan. 1/1</lc> <qt>Tape reading and writing is at from 34,160 to 192,000
bytes per second.</qt></q></qp></e>
```

Figure 8.4 The OED entry for the word byte (top panel), together with the representation of the entry in its digitized form with tags (bottom panel).

Because the tag characters are included with the content characters, they increase the size of the file compared with plain text. The entry for *byte* is 841 characters, but the tagged code is 1,204 characters, almost a 50 percent increase.

Why "Byte"?

As informative as the *OED* definition is, it doesn't answer that nagging question: Why is *byte* spelled with a *y*? To understand the charming nature of the answer, we need to know that computer memory is subject to errors (a zero changing to a one, or a one to a zero), caused by such things as cosmic rays. Really. It doesn't happen often, but often enough to worry computer engineers, who build special circuitry to detect and correct memory errors. They often add extra bits to the memory to help detect errors—for example, a ninth bit per byte can detect errors using parity.

Parity refers to whether a number is even or odd. To encode bytes using **even parity**, we use the normal byte encoding, for example, *1010 0010*, and then count the number of 1's in the byte. If there is an even number of 1's, we set the ninth bit to 0; if there is an odd number, we set the ninth bit to 1, for example, *1010 0010 1*. The result is that all 9-bit groups have even parity, either because they were even to begin with and the 0 didn't change that, or they were odd to begin with, but the 1 made them even. Any single bit error in a group causes its parity to become odd, allowing the hardware to detect that an error has occurred, although it can't detect which bit is wrong.

So, why is *byte* spelled with a *y*? The answer comes from Werner Buchholz, the inventor of the word and the concept. In the late 1950s, Buchholz was the project manager and architect for the IBM supercomputer, called Stretch. For that machine, he explained to me, "We needed a word for a quantity of memory between a bit and a word." (A "word" of computer memory is typically the amount required to represent computer instructions; on modern computers, a word is 32 bits.) Buchholz continued, "It seemed that after 'bit' comes 'bite.' But we changed the 'i' to a 'y' so that a typist couldn't accidentally change 'byte' into 'bit' by the single error of dropping the 'e'." No single letter change to *byte* can create *bit*, and vice versa. Buchholz and his engineers were so concerned with memory errors that he invented an *error-detecting name* for the memory unit!

Summary

We began the chapter by learning that digitizing doesn't require digits—any symbols will do. We explored:

- PandA encoding, which is based on the Presence and Absence of a physical phenomenon. Their patterns are discrete; they form the basic unit of a bit. Their names (most often 1 and 0) can be any pair of opposite terms.

- 7-bit ASCII, an early assignment of bit sequences (symbols) to keyboard characters. Extended or 8-bit ASCII is the standard.
- How documents like the *Oxford English Dictionary* are digitized. We learned that tags associate metadata with every part of the *OED*. Using that data, a computer can easily help us find words and other information.
- The mystery of the *y* in *byte*.

Try It Solutions

8.1. 1010 1011 1110 1000 1011 1110 1110 1111

A B E 8 B E E F

8.2. 0010 1000 0011 1000 0011 1000 0011 1000 0010 1001

0010 0000 0011 0101 0011 0101 0011 0101 0010 1101

0011 0001 0011 0010 0011 0001 0011 0010

Review Questions

Multiple Choice

1. A good example of a collating sequence that you learned in school is
a. PandA
b. i before e
c. ABCs
d. all of the above

2. How many characters could be represented by two dice?
a. 12
b. 16
c. 36
d. 256

3. Which of the following doesn't need to be quantified?
a. ZIP codes
b. locker numbers
c. ID numbers
d. all of the above

4. What is the correct interpretation for **!!@@?
a. star, star, one, one, two two
b. as, as, bang, bang, hit, hit
c. star, star, bang, bang, at, at
d. star, star, hit, hit, bang, bang

5. Which of these is not digital?
   a. a clock with hands
   b. a calendar
   c. a checkbook balance
   d. a television channel
6. PandA is a combination of
   a. true and false
   b. on and off
   c. yes and no
   d. all of the above
7. Finish this: I like cats. Fluffy is a cat. Therefore
   a. Fluffy is not a dog
   b. I don't like dogs
   c. Cats don't like dogs
   d. I like Fluffy
8. A binary system
   a. consists of only two possible items
   b. uses discrete data
   c. can be represented by PandA
   d. all of the above
9. The medium used for storing data on a CD is made from
   a. iron
   b. plastic
   c. magnetism
   d. light
10. On the computer, the word PandA is represented by
    a. 1 and 0
    b. 0 and 1
    c. bytes
    d. off and on

Short Answer

1. If bits are to atoms, bytes are to ______.
2. To ______ is to represent information with digits.
3. PandA is short for ______.
4. When data are ______, they are separate and distinct and cannot be transformed into another value by gradations.
5. A(n) ______ is an agreed upon order for basic symbols.
6. ______ bits are needed to represent a space in ASCII.
7. Four bits is often called a(n) ______.
8. All the values in a PandA formulation are ______.

9. ______ is short for binary digit.

10. The ______ of a bit is its storage pattern in the physical world.

11. ______ is short for hexadecimal.

12. Base-16 is also called ______.

13. Letters, numbers, and symbols are represented on the computer using the ______.

14. All computer systems share a(n) ______ set of symbols used to represent characters.

Exercises

1. Make a list of the numbers you use that are not treated as numbers. (For example, you do not perform math on them.)

2. What is a bit and how was the word created?

3. What does PandA stand for and what does PandA name?

4. Come up with a list of ten different PandA encodings.

5. What North American telephone number is: ▲ ⏸ ⏸ ◀ ◀ ■ ▲ ⏮ ⏸ ⏸ ?

6. Encode (800) 555-0012 in ASCII, including punctuation.

7. You bought a mosaic coffee table in Santorini, Greece, last summer called "Animals of Atlantis." While listening to a boring story about your friend's visit home, you notice the table is eight tiles across, which could be the bits of a byte. What ASCII message did the Greeks encode, using the obvious PandA encoding?

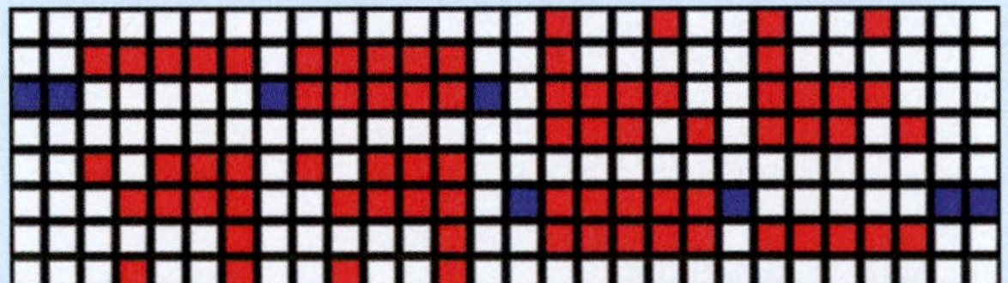

8. The Hawaiian alphabet has 18 symbols. Discuss the symbols you would use for their character set and how many bits would be needed for it.

9. Translate the following hexadecimal into binary and then into English.

   68 65 78 61 64 65 63 69 6D 61 6C

10. Change the letters of the sentence "THE APPLE LOGO HAS A BYTE MISSING" into NATO broadcast code (ignore spaces in all cases) and then represent the result with ASCII. How many bytes are required for each?

11. Explain the idea of PandA encoding. Give five PandA encodings that could apply in a cafeteria.

12. In recalling a childhood memory of walking to school with a friend who came from a different direction, a grandparent noted that the children needed a way to know if the other person had already reached the rendezvous point and gone on, or had not yet reached it and needed to be waited for. The recalled solution was: "If I get here first, I will put this rock on that fence post. If you get here first, you knock it off." Is it a PandA solution? Why or why not? Does it work?

13. You have discovered the following string of binary ASCII code; figure out what they mean.

    01010111 01100001 01111001 00100000 01110100 01101111 00100000 01100111 01101111 00100001

Principles of Computer Operations

Following Instructions

learning objectives

- Describe how the Fetch/Execute Cycle works, listing the five steps
- Explain the function of the memory, control unit, ALU, input unit and output unit, and program counter
- Explain why integration and photolithography are important in integrated circuits
- Discuss the purpose of an operating system
- Describe how large tasks are performed with simple instructions

Where ... ENIAC is equipped with 18,000 vacuum tubes and weighs 30 tons, computers in the future may have 1,000 vacuum tubes and perhaps weigh just one-half ton.

—POPULAR MECHANICS, 1949

There is no reason why anyone would want to have a computer in their home.

—KEN OLSEN, PRESIDENT OF DIGITAL EQUIPMENT CORPORATION, 1977

THIS CHAPTER introduces two key inventions in information technology that rank among the top technological achievements of all time: computers and integrated circuits (ICs). They are both complex and sophisticated topics, so specialized, in fact, that a Ph.D. degree is *not* sufficient training to understand current technologies fully. Making today's computers and chips requires large teams of specialists. If an individual expert can't completely understand computers or integrated circuits, is there hope for the rest of us?

Both topics are based on easy-to-understand ideas. Pushing the basic ideas to their limits makes the technology complex and sophisticated, and that is definitely beyond our needs. But we should learn the main ideas, because the same basic instruction execution processes used by computers are applied in many different computing situations. Web browsers process Web pages using instruction execution that is just like a computer's operation. Spreadsheets use the same ideas. You operate as an instruction executer when you prepare your income taxes. This idea is fundamental to processing information and a key concept of IT.

First, we discuss the Fetch/Execute Cycle. Second, we describe the parts of a computer, how they're connected, and, briefly, what each does. Then we outline how these parts execute instructions. We give a detailed example that shows that computers operate straightforwardly. Next, we discuss software and operating systems to explain how a computer's primitive abilities can achieve impressive results. Finally, we explain the "big ideas" behind integrated circuits and how semiconductor technology works.

Instruction Execution Engines

Before dissecting a computer, consider what a computer actually does. The obvious answer, "It computes," doesn't say very much, because "computing" mostly involves software, not hardware.

What Computers Can Do

Computers deterministically perform or execute instructions to process information. We can describe a computer as an "instruction execution engine." The most important aspect of this definition is that a computer does what it is told—it follows instructions—so someone or something else must decide what those instructions are. Programmers do that, of course. If the instructions don't work, it's not the computer's fault because the computer simply follows the programmed instructions.

What Computers Can't Do

A key feature of the definition is the term *deterministically*. When it's time for the computer to determine which instruction to execute next, it's required by its construction to execute a specific instruction based only on the program and the data it's been given. It has no options. As compared to people, computers are very methodical.

- Computers have no imagination or creativity.
- Computers have no intuition.
- Computers are literal, with no sense of irony, subtlety, proportion, or decorum.
- Computers don't joke or have a sense of humor.
- Computers are not vindictive or cruel. (Some frustrated users will find these assertions far-fetched.)
- Computers are not purposeful.
- Computers have no free will.

Computers only execute instructions. Deterministically. Consequently, rerunning a program with the same data produces exactly the same result every time.

World Domination. During the 1950s and 1960s, as computers were leaving the lab and entering business, there was concern in the popular press about "computers taking over the world." People worried because computers could do some tasks amazingly well; for example, they could add 100,000 numbers in one second. There were grim stories of tyrannical computers enslaving people. But when it finally happened—when life as most people knew it *depended* on computers—no one apparently noticed.

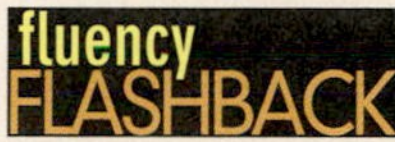

No. 1 Computer. Credit for inventing the first electronic computer is in dispute, but most people give the credit to J. Presper Eckert and John Mauchly of the University of Pennsylvania. Named ENIAC for Electronic Numerical Integrator And Calculator, the Eckert/Mauchly machine was built for the U.S. Army in 1946. ENIAC is in many ways the intellectual antecedent of current computers. Another academic, John V. Atanasoff of Iowa State University, developed ideas used by Eckert and Mauchly, and at about the same time, built the Atanasoff-Berry Computer (ABC), with graduate student Clifford E. Berry. In an epic patent infringement lawsuit, Judge Earl Larson decided on October 19, 1973, that Atanasoff's prior invention invalidated the Eckert/Mauchly patent.

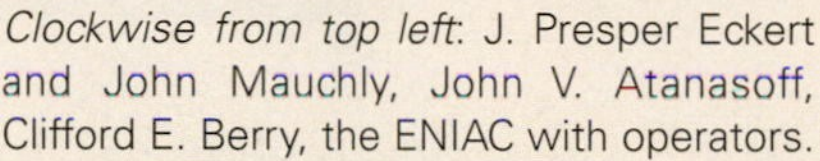

Clockwise from top left: J. Presper Eckert and John Mauchly, John V. Atanasoff, Clifford E. Berry, the ENIAC with operators.

The Fetch/Execute Cycle

Calling a computer an "instruction execution engine" suggests the idea of a machine cycling through a series of operations, performing an instruction on each round. And that's pretty much the idea. Computers implement in hardware a process called the **Fetch/Execute Cycle**. The Fetch/Execute Cycle consists of getting the instruction, figuring out what to do, gathering the data needed to do it, doing it, saving the result, and repeating. It's a simple process, but repeating it billions of times a second accomplishes a lot.

A Five-Step Cycle

The five steps of the Fetch/Execute Cycle have standard names, and because these operations are repeated in a never-ending sequence, they are often written with an arrow from the last step to the first showing the cycle (see Figure 9.1). The step names suggest the operations described in the previous paragraph. But the Fetch/Execute Cycle is a little more complicated than that. What is an instruction like? How is the next instruction located? When instructions and data are fetched, where are they fetched from, and where do they go?

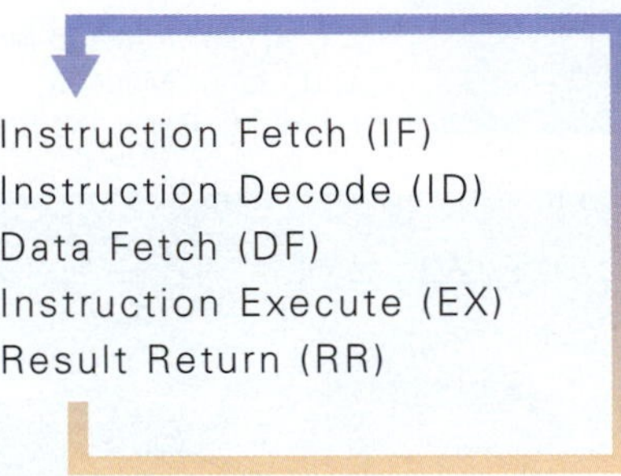

Figure 9.1 The Fetch/Execute Cycle.

Anatomy of a Computer

To understand how the Fetch/Execute Cycle works, you must understand how a computer's parts are arranged to fetch and execute instructions. All computers, regardless of their implementing technology, have five basic parts or subsystems: memory, control unit, arithmetic/logic unit (ALU), input unit, and output unit. These are arranged as shown in Figure 9.2. *Note*: It is just a coincidence that there are five steps to the Fetch/Execute Cycle and five subsystems to a computer—they're related, of course, but not one-to-one.

The five subsystems of a computer have the characteristics described in the following sections.

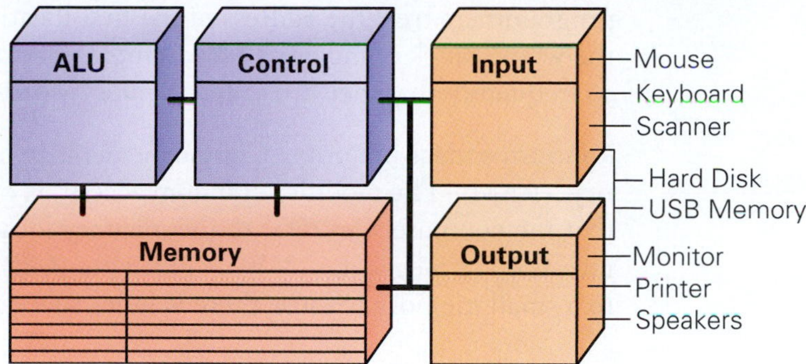

Figure 9.2 The principal subsystems of a computer.

Memory

Memory stores both the program while it is running and the data on which the program operates. Memory has the following properties.

- **Discrete locations.** Memory is organized as a sequence of discrete locations, like apartment building mailboxes. In modern memory, each location is composed of 1 byte (that is, a sequence of 8 bits).
- **Addresses.** Every memory location has an address, like a mailbox, although computer memory addresses are whole numbers starting at 0.
- **Values.** Memory locations record or store values, like a mailbox holds a letter.
- **Finite capacity.** Memory locations have a finite capacity (limited size), so programmers must keep in mind that the data may not "fit" in the memory location.

Byte-size memory location. These properties are displayed in Figure 9.3, which shows a common visualization of computer memory. The discrete locations are represented as boxes. The address of each location is displayed above the box, and the value or contents of the memory locations are shown in the boxes.

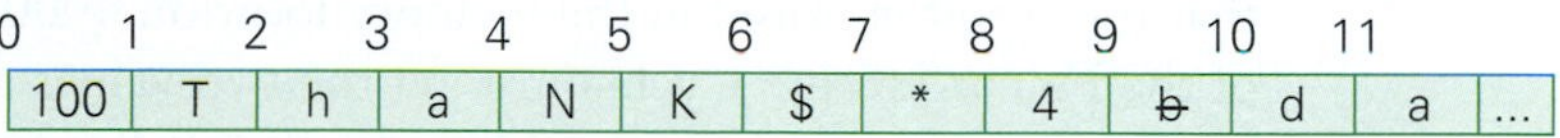

Figure 9.3 Diagram of computer memory illustrating its key properties.

The 1-byte size of a memory location is enough to store one ASCII character (letter, numeral, or punctuation symbol), or a number less than 256. Therefore, a single computer memory location has very limited capacity. To overcome this limitation, programmers simply use a sequence of memory locations, and ignore the fact that they all have separate addresses; that is, programmers treat the address of the first location as if it were the address of the whole block of memory. For example, blocks of 4 bytes are used as a unit so frequently that they are called memory words.

Random access memory. Computer memory is called **random access memory** (RAM). The modifier "random access" is out-of-date and simply means that the computer can refer to the memory locations in any order. RAM is measured in megabytes (MB) or gigabytes (GB). A large memory is preferable to a small memory because there is more space for programs and data.

fluencyBIT

Free Memory. *Mega-* is the prefix for "million," so a megabyte should be 1,000,000 bytes of memory. In fact, a megabyte is 1,048,576 bytes. Why such a weird number? Computers need to associate 1 byte of memory with every address. A million addresses require 20 bits. But with 20 bits, $2^{20} = 1{,}048{,}576$ addresses are possible with binary counting. So, to ensure that every 20-bit address is associated with 1 byte of memory, the extra 48,576 bytes are included "free." All memory includes bonus memory.

In summary, memory is like a sequence of labeled containers known as locations: The address is the location's number in the sequence; the value or the information stored at the location is the container's contents; and only so much can fit in each container.

Control Unit

The **control unit** of a computer is the hardware implementation of the Fetch/Execute Cycle. Its circuitry fetches an instruction from memory and performs the other operations of the Fetch/Execute Cycle on it.

Computer instructions are much more primitive than the commands we give computers from GUIs. A typical machine instruction has the form

```
ADD 4000, 2000, 2080
```

which appears to command that three numbers, 2,000, 2,080, and 4,000, are added together, *but it does not*. Instead, the instruction asks that the two numbers stored in the memory locations 2000 and 2080 are added together, and that the result is stored in the memory location 4000. So the Data Fetch step of the Fetch/Execute Cycle must get the two values at memory locations 2000 and 2080, and after they are added, the Result Return step stores the answer in memory location 4000.

fluencyTIP

Large Numbers. Fitting these three operand addresses—4000, 2000, 2080—into one instruction word is not literally possible because they require at least 36 bits to represent them. I have simplified this example. Computers actually use separate load and store instructions, which solve the apparent "problem," and need not concern us further.

This fundamental property of computer instructions bears repeating: The instruction

```
ADD 4000, 2000, 2080
```

does *not* command the computer to add the numbers 2000 and 2080. Rather, the instruction commands the computer to add the numbers *stored in memory locations* 2000 and 2080, whatever those numbers are. Because different values could be in those memory locations each time the computer executes the instruction, a different result can be computed each time. The concept is that computer instructions encode the memory addresses of the numbers to be added (or subtracted or whatever), not the numbers themselves, and so they refer to the values *indirectly*. The indirection means that a single instruction can combine any two numbers simply by placing them in the referenced memory locations (see Figure 9.4). Referring to a value by referring to the address in memory where it is stored is fundamental to a computer's versatility.

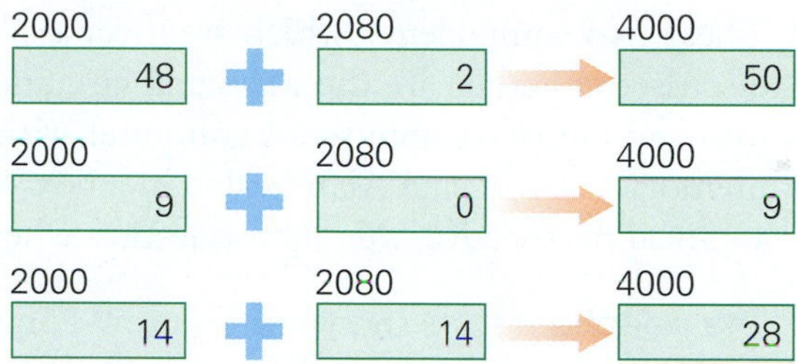

Figure 9.4 Illustration of a single ADD instruction producing different results depending on the contents of the memory locations referenced in the instruction.

Arithmetic/Logic Unit (ALU)

As its name suggests, the **arithmetic/logic unit (ALU)** performs the "math." The ALU is the part of the computer that generally does the work during the Instruction Execute step of the Fetch/Execute Cycle. So, for the sample instruction

```
ADD 4000, 2000, 2080
```

the ALU does the actual addition. A circuit in the ALU can add two numbers—an amazing capability when you think about it. There are also circuits for multiplying two numbers, circuits for comparing two numbers, and so on. You can think of an ALU as carrying out each machine instruction with a separate circuit, although modern computers are so sophisticated that they can combine several operations into one circuit.

9.1 Same Data, Different Operations. Using the data from Figure 9.4, execute the multiply instruction **MUL 4000, 2000, 2080** and (read this carefully) the subtract instruction **SUB 4000, 2080, 2000**.

Most computer instructions perform some kind of math, that is, most instructions transform data. But information processing also includes moving data, that is, some instructions transfer data without changing it. Instructions for data transfer don't usually use the ALU. Computers have instructions for both transforming and transferring information.

For instructions that use the ALU, it is clear what the Data Fetch and Result Return steps of the Fetch/Execute Cycle must do. Data Fetch gets the values from memory that the ALU needs to perform operations like ADD and MULTIPLY. These values are called **operands**. The instruction includes the addresses where the data is to be found. The Data Fetch step delivers these values to the ALU. When the ALU completes the operation, producing a sum or product or other value, the Result Return step moves that answer from the ALU to the memory at the address specified in the instruction.

Input Unit and Output Unit

These two components, which are inverses of each other, and therefore easily discussed together, are the wires and circuits through which information moves into and out of a computer. A computer without input or output—that is, the memory, control, and ALU sealed in a box—is useless. Indeed, from a philosophical perspective, we might question whether we can say it "computes."

The peripherals. As shown in Figure 9.2, many kinds of devices—called **peripherals**—connect to the computer **input/output (I/O)** ports, providing it with input or receiving its output. The peripherals are not considered part of the computer; they are specialized gadgets that encode or decode information between the computer and the physical world. The keyboard encodes our keystrokes into binary form for the computer. The monitor decodes information from the computer's memory and displays it on a lighted, color screen. In general, the peripherals handle the physical part of the operation, sending or receiving the binary information the computer uses.

The cable from the peripheral to the computer connects to the input unit or the output unit. These units handle the communication protocol with the peripherals. As a general rule, think of the input unit as moving information from the peripheral into the memory, and the output unit as moving information from the memory and delivering it to the outside world.

Portable memory and hard drives. Some peripherals, such as USB memory and hard disks (hard drives), are used by computers for both input and output. They are storage devices, places where the computer files away information when it is not needed (an output operation) and where it gets information when it needs it again (an input operation). The hard disk is the *alpha-peripheral*, being the most aggressively engineered and tightly linked device to the computer. The hard disk is essential because although programs and their data must reside in the computer's memory when programs run, they reside on the hard disk the rest of the time because the hard disk provides more (permanent) storage space. In that sense, the hard disk is an extension of the computer's memory, even though typically it is a hundred times larger and several thousand times slower.

A device driver for every peripheral. Most peripheral devices are "dumb" because they provide only basic physical translation to or from binary signals. They rely on the computer for further processing, which is almost always required to make the peripheral operate in an "intelligent way." So, as I type the letters of this sentence, signals are sent from the keyboard to the computer indicating which keys my fingers press. When the computer receives information that I've pressed the *w* and the Shift key simultaneously, the computer—not the keyboard—converts the *w* keystroke to an uppercase *W*. Similarly, keys like Ctrl and Backspace are just keys to the keyboard. Added processing by a piece of software called a **device driver** gives the keyboard its standard meaning and behavior. Every device needs a device driver to provide this added processing. Because the peripheral device has unique characteristics, a device driver is specialized to one device only.

New Toys. Many users are excited about purchasing a new peripheral such as a printer or scanner. They plug it into their computer, but forget that it needs a device driver to run. Computers often come loaded with standardized or popular device drivers, so users don't know, or forget, that peripherals require them. Peripherals should come with device driver(s); if not, they can be downloaded from the manufacturer's Web site.

The Program Counter: The PC's PC

The final question is how a computer determines which instruction to execute next.

Address of the Next Instruction

Recall that when the Fetch/Execute Cycle executes a program, the instructions are stored in the memory. That means every instruction has an address, which is the address of the memory location of the first byte of the instruction. (Instructions of current computers use 4 bytes, or one word.) Computers keep track of which instruction to execute next by its address. This address, stored in the control part of the computer, should probably be called the *next instruction address*, but for historic reasons it is actually known by the curious term **program counter**, abbreviated PC. *(For the rest of this chapter,* PC *refers to program counter, not personal computer.)*

The Instruction Fetch step of the Fetch/Execute Cycle transfers the instruction from memory at the address specified by the program counter to the decoder part of the control unit. Once the instruction is fetched, and while it is being processed by the remaining steps of the cycle, the computer prepares to process the next instruction. It assumes that the next instruction is the next one in sequence. Because instructions use 4 bytes of memory, the next instruction must be at the memory address PC + 4, that is, 4 bytes further along in sequence. Therefore, the computer adds 4 to the PC, so that when the Fetch/Execute Cycle gets around to the Instruction Fetch step again, the PC is "pointing at" the new instruction.

Branch and Jump Instructions

This scheme of executing instructions in sequence seems flawed: Won't the Fetch/Execute Cycle blaze through the memory executing all the instructions, get to the last instruction in memory, and "fall off the end of memory," having used up all of the instructions? This won't happen unless the program has a bug, because computers come with instructions called *branch* and *jump* that change the PC. After the control unit prepares for the next instruction in sequence by adding 4 to the PC, the Instruction Execute step of the current (branch or jump) instruction resets the PC to a new value. This overrides the selection of the next instruction in sequence and makes the PC address some other instruction in memory. The next instruction is fetched from that memory location on the next round of the Fetch/Execute Cycle.

Instruction Interpretation

The process of executing a program is also called **instruction interpretation**. The term derives from the idea that the computer interprets our commands, but in its own language.

To illustrate the idea of interpreting instructions, let's follow the execution of a typical ADD instruction. Figure 9.5 shows the situation before the Fetch/Execute Cycle starts the next instruction. Notice that some of the memory locations and the program counter (PC) are visible in the control unit.

The process of instruction execution begins with **Instruction Fetch (IF)**, which moves the instruction at the address given by the PC from the memory

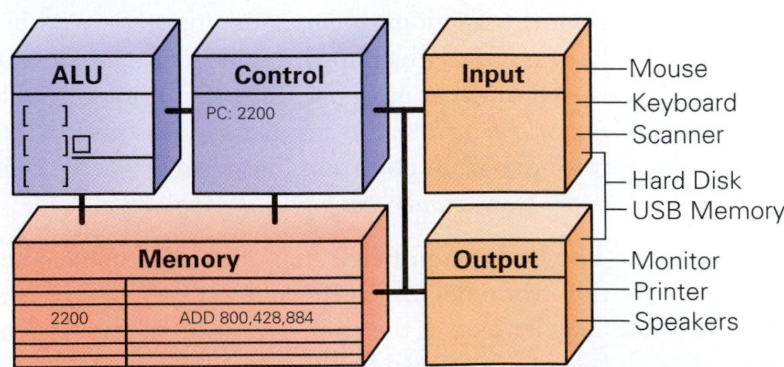

Figure 9.5 Computer before executing an ADD instruction.

unit to the control unit. (See Figure 9.6, where the instruction address is 2200 and the sample instruction is ADD 800, 428, 884.) The bits of the instruction are placed into the decoder circuit of the control unit. Once the instruction is fetched, the PC can be readied for fetching the next instruction. For today's computers whose instructions are 4 bytes long, 4 is added to the PC. (The updated PC value is visible in the Data Fetch configuration, as shown in Figure 9.8 and those that follow.)

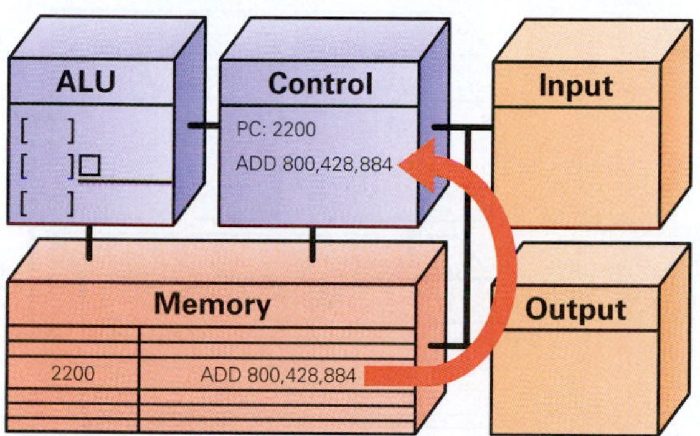

Figure 9.6 Instruction Fetch: Move instruction from memory to the control unit.

Figure 9.7 shows the **Instruction Decode (ID)** step, in which the ALU is set up for the operation in the Instruction Execute step. Among the bits of the instruction, the decoder finds the memory addresses of the instruction's data, the *source operands*. Like ADD, most instructions operate on two data values stored in memory, so most instructions have addresses for two source operands. These two addresses (428, 884) are passed to the circuit that will fetch the operand values from memory during the next (Data Fetch) step. Simultaneously, the decoder finds the *destination address*, the place in memory where the answer will be sent during the Result Return step. That address (800) is placed in the RR circuit. Finally, the decoder figures out what

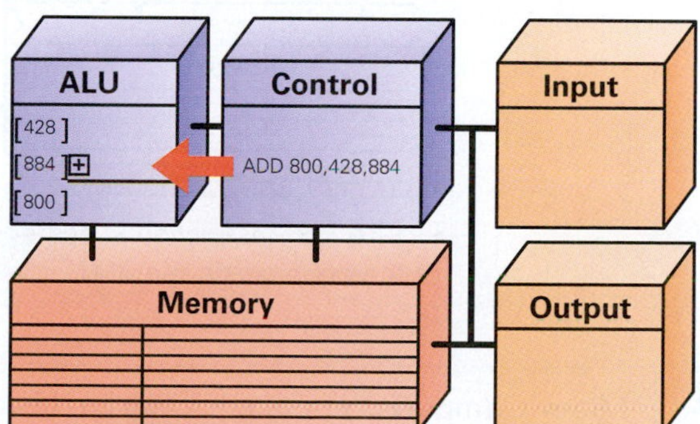

Figure 9.7 Instruction Decode: Pull apart the instruction, set up the operation in the ALU, and compute the source and destination operand addresses.

operation the ALU should perform on the data values (ADD) and sets up the ALU appropriately for that operation.

Figure 9.8 shows the **Data Fetch (DF)** step. The data values for the two source operands are moved from the memory into the ALU. These values (12, 42) are the data that the instruction will work on in the next (Instruction Execute) step.

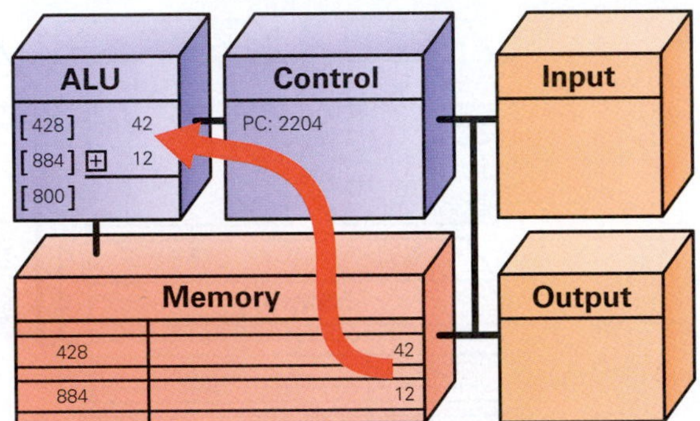

Figure 9.8 Data Fetch: Move the operands from memory to the ALU.

Instruction Execution (EX) is illustrated in Figure 9.9. The operation—set up during the Instruction Decode step—performs the computation. In the present case, the addition circuit adds the two source operand values to produce their sum (54). This is the actual computation.

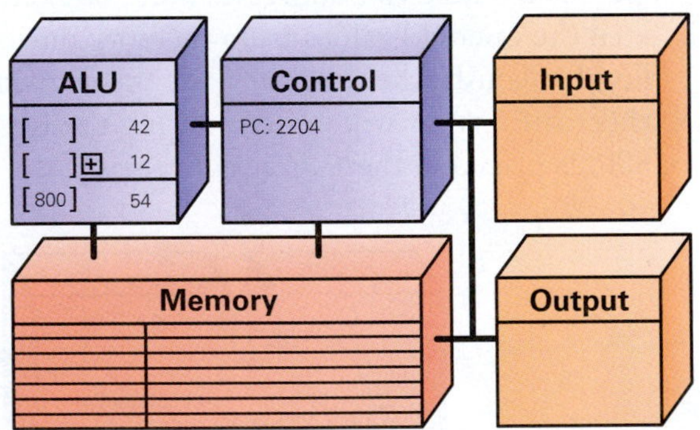

Figure 9.9 Instruction Execute: Compute the result of the operation in the ALU.

fluencyBIT

> Micro Computer. In our presentation, Instruction Execution—the "compute" part of the Fetch/Execute Cycle—accounts for only 20 percent of the time spent executing an instruction; it averages even less on real computers. Measured by silicon area, the ALU—the circuitry that does the computing—takes up less than 5 percent of a typical processor.

Finally, the **Result Return (RR)** step, shown in Figure 9.10, returns the result of Instruction Execution (54) to the memory location specified by the destination address (800) and set up during Instruction Decode. Once the result is returned, the cycle begins again.

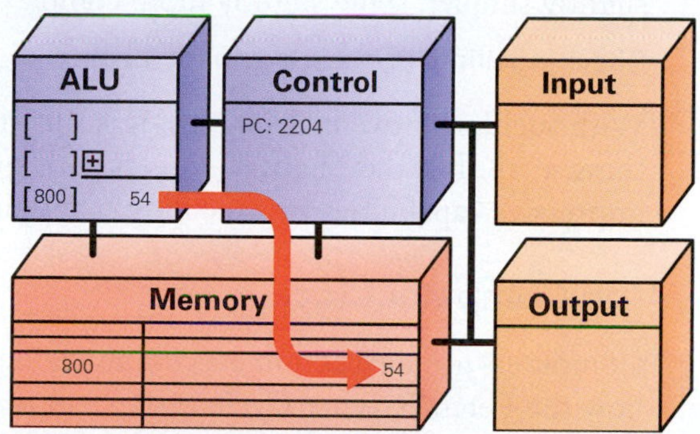

Figure 9.10 Result Return: Store the result from the ALU into the memory at the destination address.

Many, Many Simple Operations

Computers "know" very few instructions. That is, the decoder hardware in the controller recognizes, and the ALU performs, only about 100 or so different instructions. And there is a lot of duplication. For example, different instructions are used for different kinds of data: one instruction adds bytes, a different instruction adds whole words (4 bytes), a third adds "decimal" numbers, and so on. Altogether, there are only about 20 different kinds of operations. *Everything* that computers do must be reduced to some combination of these primitive, hardwired instructions. They can't do anything else.

The ADD instruction has average complexity, and MULT (multiply) and DIV (divide) instructions are at the screaming limit of complexity. Examples of other instructions include:

- Shift the bits of a word (4 bytes) to the left or right, fill the emptied places with zeros, and throw away the bits that fall off the end.
- Compute the logical AND, which tests if pairs of bits are both true, and the logical OR, which tests if at least one of two bits is true.
- Test if a bit is zero (or nonzero), and jump to a new set of instructions based on the outcome.
- Move information around in memory.
- Sense the signals from input/output devices.

Computer instructions are very primitive.

fluencyBIT

Stop! If the Fetch/Execute Cycle is an infinite loop, how does a computer stop? Early computers actually had Start and Stop buttons, but modern computers simply execute an "idle loop" when there's nothing to do. The instructions keep checking to see if there's anything to do, like process a mouse click or keystroke.

Cycling the Fetch/Execute Cycle

Using ADD, we have illustrated how a computer is able to execute instructions. ADD is representative of the complexity of computer instructions—some are slightly simpler, some slightly more complex. There are no instructions like

```
Check_spelling_of_the_document_beginning_at_memory_location 884
```

With such primitive instructions, it is surprising that computers can do anything at all. But they achieve success with speed. Computers manifest their impressive capabilities by executing many simple instructions per second.

The Computer Clock

Computers are instruction execution engines. You have just studied in detail how the Fetch/Execute Cycle carries out one ADD instruction. Since the computer does one instruction per cycle, the speed of a computer—the number of instructions executed per second—depends on the number of Fetch/Execute Cycles it performs per second. The rate of the Fetch/Execute Cycle is determined by the computer's **clock**, and it is measured in **megahertz**, or millions (mega) of cycles per second (hertz). Computer clock speeds have increased dramatically in recent years, resulting in speeds measured in 1,000 MHz. A 1,000 MHz clock ticks a billion (in American English) times per second, which is one **gigahertz** (1 GHz) in any language. (See Figure 9.11 for terms; "giga" is pronounced with hard g's.) Clock speeds are a common feature of computer advertisements, but how important are they?

Beauty of Prefixes. Prefixes "change the units" so that very large or small quantities can be expressed with numbers of a reasonable size. A well-known humorous example concerns Helen of Troy from Greek mythology "whose face launched 1,000 ships." The beauty needed to launch one ship is one-thousandth of Helen's, that is, 0.001 Helen, or 1 MilliHelen.

1000^1	kilo-	$1024^1 = 2^{10} = 1{,}024$	milli-	1000^{-1}
1000^2	mega-	$1024^2 = 2^{20} = 1{,}048{,}576$	micro-	1000^{-2}
1000^3	giga-	$1024^3 = 2^{30} = 1{,}073{,}741{,}824$	nano-	1000^{-3}
1000^4	tera-	$1024^4 = 2^{40} = 1{,}099{,}511{,}627{,}776$	pico-	1000^{-4}
1000^5	peta-	$1024^5 = 2^{50} = 1{,}125{,}899{,}906{,}842{,}624$	femto-	1000^{-5}
1000^6	exa-	$1024^6 = 2^{60} = 1{,}152{,}921{,}504{,}606{,}876{,}976$	atto-	1000^{-6}
1000^7	zetta-	$1024^7 = 2^{70} = 1{,}180{,}591{,}620{,}717{,}411{,}303{,}424$	zepto-	1000^{-7}
1000^8	yotta-	$1024^8 = 2^{80} = 1{,}208{,}925{,}819{,}614{,}629{,}174{,}706{,}176$	yocto-	1000^{-8}

Figure 9.11 Standard prefixes from the Système International (SI) convention on scientific measurements. Generally a prefix refers to a power of 1000, except when the quantity (for example, memory) is counted in binary; for binary quantities the prefix refers to a power of 1024, which is 2^{10}.

One Cycle per Clock Tick

A computer with a 1 GHz clock has one billionth of a second—one nanosecond—between clock ticks to run the Fetch/Execute Cycle. In that short time, light travels about one foot (30 cm). Is it really possible to add or multiply that fast? No. In truth, modern computers try to *start* an instruction on each clock tick. They pass off completing the instruction to other circuitry, like a worker on an assembly line. This process, called *pipelining*, frees the fetch unit to start the next instruction before the last one is done. As shown in Figure 9.12, if the five steps of the Fetch/Execute Cycle take a nanosecond *each*—which is still extremely fast—it's possible to finish one instruction on each clock tick as long as there is enough circuitry for five instructions to be in process at the same time. That way the computer finishes instructions at the starting rate of one per tick. Of course, to execute 1,000 instructions in a five-stage pipeline takes 1,004 clock cycles—1,000 to start each instruction, and 4 more for the last 4 steps of the last instruction. So it is not quite true that 1,000 instructions are executed in 1,000 ticks, but it's probably close enough.

A Billion Instructions per Second?

So, does a computer with a 1 GHz clock execute a billion instructions per second? Computer salespeople would like you to believe it's true, but it's not. We said that computers *try* to start an instruction on each clock tick, but there is a long list of reasons why it's not always possible. If the computer cannot start

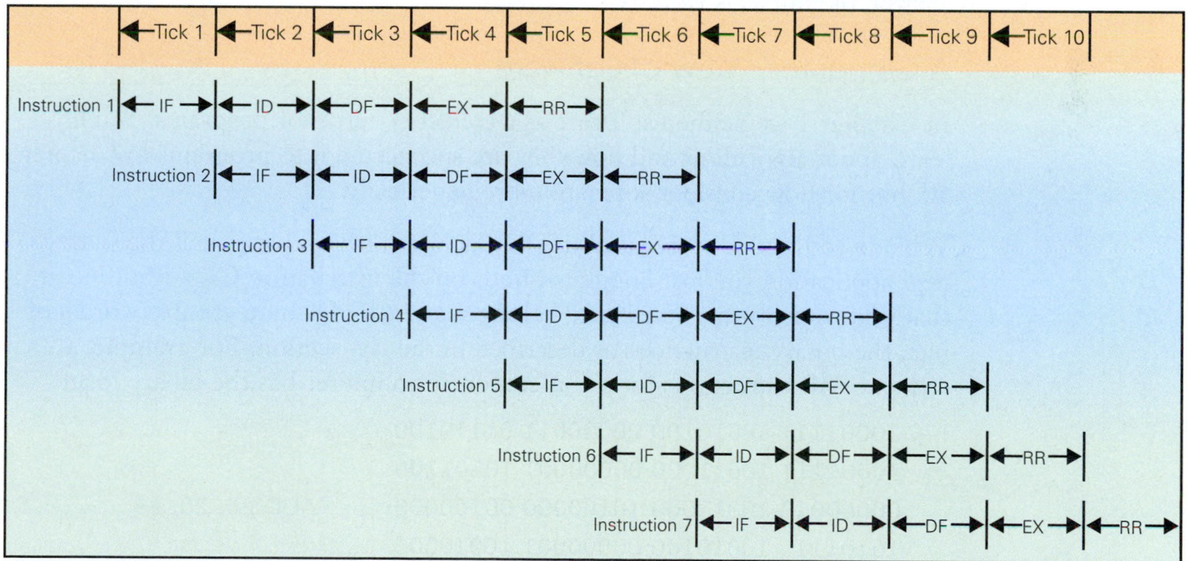

Figure 9.12 Schematic diagram of a pipelined Fetch/Execute Cycle. On each tick, the IF (Instruction Fetch) circuit starts a new instruction, and then passes it along to the ID (Instruction Decode) unit; the ID unit works on the instruction it receives, and when it finishes, it passes it along to the DF (Data Fetch) circuit, and so on. When the pipeline is filled, five instructions are in process at once, and one instruction is finished on each clock tick, making the computer appear to be running at one instruction per tick.

instructions on each clock tick, its execution rate falls *below* 1 billion instructions per second. But the situation is even more complicated. Computer engineers have figured out how to start more than one instruction at a time, even though instructions are supposed to be finished before the next one starts. If several instructions can be started at the same time often enough, they can make up for not starting instructions at other times. Thus the rate can be *more than* 1 billion per second. It is extremely difficult—even for experts—to figure out how fast a modern computer runs. As a result, the one-instruction-per-cycle guideline—which was once dependable—is no longer correct.

fluencyBIT

Multicore Computers. In recent decades the rule *each computer chip contains one computer processor* has been true. Now, chips contain a few **processor cores**, a processor (control and ALU) with a tiny amount of memory (called a level 1 cache). Each of these is an instruction execution engine, and they share the memory unit and I/O units.

Software

You have studied what computer hardware can do, and what you have learned is "not very much." That is, while computers are very fast, the operations they can perform at each step are extremely simple. How can all of the amazing things computers do—video games, Photoshop, grammar checks, Google searches, and on and on—be done with such primitive instructions? The answer, of course, is *software*.

A Computer's View of Software

In Chapter 1 we defined software as a collective term for programs. You'll learn about algorithms and how they are specialized into programs in Chapter 10, but for now consider software more generically.

When a computer "sees" software, that is, when it's told to install the snazzy new application you just bought, it finds on the installation CD (or online, if that was your source) an extremely long sequence of 4-byte groups (words) of bits, the binary instructions as described in the last section. For example, a sequence of instructions for a contemporary computer has the binary form:

```
. . . 10001111 10010100 00000011 01110100
      10001111 10011000 00000001 10101100
      00000010 10011000 10100000 00100000  ↔  ADD 20, 20, 24
      10101111 10010100 00000001 10010000 . . .
```

This sequence, the **binary object file**, or simply the **binary**—can be hundreds of thousands to millions of words long. Once installed on the hard disk, the computer runs the software by copying the binary instructions into the RAM and interpreting them using the Fetch/Execute Cycle. It does whatever the instructions tell it to do.

Assembly Language

Although the binary object file is the only form in which a computer can be given software, it is anything but user-friendly. It's not really human readable. Humans can decode it, of course, but it's so difficult that understanding even a handful of words can take hours, motivating people to do anything to avoid it. And humans don't want to produce it either. In fact, people are so error prone that it's essentially impossible for us to manually produce 100 words of correct binary (3,200 bits). Binary object code is a form of software only a computer can love.

Luckily, computers can be programmed to translate software expressed in other forms into the binary form they like. The process, shown in Figure 9.13, has two steps; we'll focus first on the second step: *Assembling*.

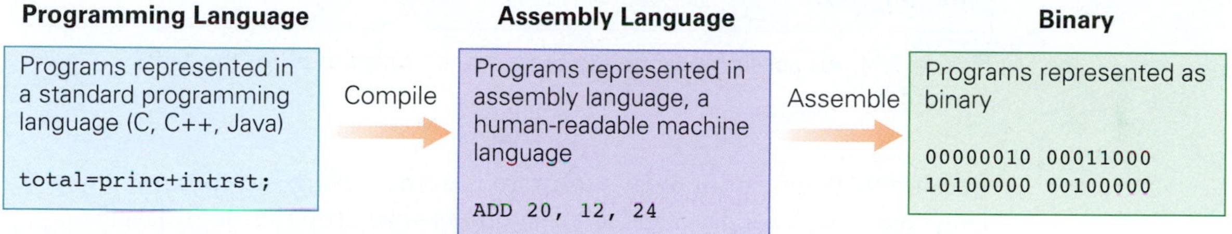

Figure 9.13 The three primary forms of encoding software: programming language, assembly language, and binary machine language.

Assembly language is simply an alternative form of machine language expressed using letters and normal numbers so people can understand it. It was invented almost immediately after the invention of computers, because working with binary is so brutal. The translation process to binary is straightforward: The computer scans the program written in assembly code, and as it encounters words like ADD, it looks them up in a table to find how to encode them in binary; it converts all numbers to binary, and then *assembles* the binary pieces into an instruction. Assembly language is the "lowest" software level—meaning the most primitive—that humans work with, and then only rarely. Mostly, assembly language is the output of the more complex process of *compiling*. Figure 9.14 shows the computation of *n*-factorial (*n*!) written in the assembly language of the MIPS computer architecture.

Programming Languages

Virtually all software today is written in a **high-level programming language**, where the "high-level" phrase differentiates the language from assembly language and binary, which are technically also programming languages—notations used to express computation. Programs written in a high-level language are **compiled**, that is, translated, into assembly language programs, which are then assembled into binary. A program, therefore, is a computation that is represented in three different forms.

```
factorial:
bgtz  $a0, doit              # Argument > 0
li    $v0, 1                 # Base case, 0! = 1
jr    $ra                    # Return
doit:
subi  $sp,8                  # Allocate stack frame
sw    $s0,($sp)              # Position for argument n
sw    $ra,4($sp)             # Remember return address
move  $s0, $a0               # Push argument
sub   $a0, 1                 # Pass n-1
jal   factorial              # Figure v0 = (n-1)!
mul   $v0,$s0,$v0            # Now multiply by n, v0 = n*(n-1)!
lw    $s0,($sp)              # Restore registers from stack
lw    $ra,4($sp)             # Get return address
addi  $sp,8                  # Pop
jr    $ra                    # Return
```

Figure 9.14 An assembly language program to compute *n*! for the MIPS computer.

Because 99.9 percent of today's software is written using such programming languages—C, C++, Java, and a dozen others—we drop the "high-level" phrase; it adds little. These languages are preferred because unlike assembly language, they have special statement forms that help programmers describe the complicated tasks they want computers to do. For example, computations frequently test whether or not some situation exists, so programming languages have if statements to help to create the test. An if statement has three parts:

- a yes/no question (the test)
- instructions the computer should perform if the test is true
- instructions the computer should perform if the test is false

Figure 9.15 shows a fragment of program text; lines 7–10 illustrate the programmer's use of an if statement. Lines 4–6 illustrate a for statement, a specialized statement form that causes instructions to be repeated. Programming languages have many other specialized capabilities to help programmers. When the programming language statements are compiled and assembled into binary, a few lines of program usually result in many, many machine instructions.

Operating Systems

Computers are capable of doing so few things independently, that without software, they can't even start up. The start-up process (booting) is one of a long list of basic operations that are necessary to effectively use a computer, but which are not built into the hardware. The programs for these basic tasks are collectively called the **operating system (OS)**. The three most widely used operating systems are Microsoft's Windows, Apple's Mac OS X, and

```
var j, frame = -1, duration = 150, timeout_id = null;
var images = new Array(20);
function advance( ) {
    for (j = 0; j < 19; j++) {
        document.images[j].src = document.images[j+1].src;
    }
    if (frame == -1)                                         test
        document.images[19].src = pics[randNum(8)].src;      true instructions
    else
        document.images[19].src = pics[frame].src;           false instructions
    timeout_id = setTimeout("animate( )", duration);
}
```

Figure 9.15 A fragment of program text written in the high-level language JavaScript.

UNIX, which has variations including Linux. None is best—each has its triumphs and tragedies. They all fill the gap between the limited capabilities of the hardware and the needs of a useful working environment.

In addition to booting, operating systems perform memory management. Examples include keeping track of where programs are stored on the hard disk and copying them into the RAM when you (click on the icon to) run them. The OS doesn't copy the whole program into RAM initially, because you might not need every feature. As you use more features, the memory manager finds and loads the software for them without you knowing it. Operating systems manage all of the I/O devices such as the keyboard, mouse, screen, hard drive, printer, and so on. They also manage the computer's Internet connection, but the browser is not part of the OS. In general, operating systems perform tasks needed by all other software, making computers much more useful than they are as raw hardware.

User applications draw on OS facilities. For example, the OS provides the file system, so when you save your work in an application, the software asking you to specify the file name and the folder into which it should be stored is a facility provided by the OS.

Programming

In addition to using powerful languages, programmers use another technique that makes their difficult job easier: They build on previously developed software. Consider the analogy of house building. Strictly speaking, a house "begins" with trees, sand, rocks, and so on, but no one actually starts construction at such a low level; we build with nails, lumber, and glass, materials that have been transformed from their original natural form to simplify construction. These materials are further transformed into more complex components, such as ceiling trusses, windows, cabinets, and such before carpenters put them together into a house. Software works the same way: The basic operations and facilities from the OS are used to construct useful, but primitive, functions.

Programming Pioneers. The first programmers, those who wrote and ran the programs on the ENIAC, were women: Kathleen McNulty Mauchly Antonelli, Jean Jennings Bartik, Frances Snyder Holberton, Marlyn Wescoff Meltzer, Frances Bilas Spence, and Ruth Lichterman Teitelbaum. They were recruited from the ranks of "computers," humans who used mechanical calculators to solve complex mathematical problems before the invention of electronic computers.

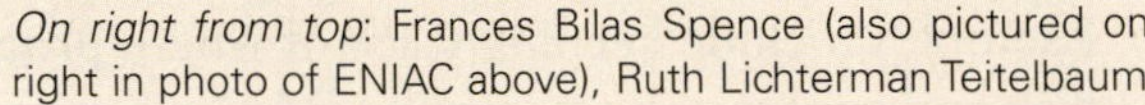

Clockwise on left from top: Kathleen McNulty Mauchly Antonelli, Jean Jennings Bartik, Frances Snyder Holberton, Marlyn Wescoff Meltzer

On right from top: Frances Bilas Spence (also pictured on right in photo of ENIAC above), Ruth Lichterman Teitelbaum

These are combined to make more complex operations, which are further combined to create still more sophisticated facilities, and on and on.

For example, all of the software for a GUI—the frame around the window, the slider bars, buttons, triangle pointers, menus, and such are packaged for programmers and provided with the operating system. This is why GUIs for an OS are so similar. (In Chapter 2 we implied that programmers use consistent interfaces to help users learn their software quickly—and it's true—but it's also true that it's easy for programmers to make use of the library of standard GUI parts, which helps them make applications look alike.) For example, the `setTimeout` operation in line 11 of Figure 9.15 applies software someone else wrote—and it was almost certainly written by a programmer who applied other software from the operating system that someone else wrote, and so on. The ability to create software by combining other software is known as **functional composition**, and is discussed more completely in Chapter 20.

fluencyBIT

Great Composition. When Microsoft's Vista operating system was released in January 2007, it reportedly contained 40 million lines of program.

There is an important point about powerful programming language and its easy ability to build on other programmers' work: Programmers can easily create extremely complex systems providing tremendously useful capabilities to many users. The situation is different from the "construction analogy" in a significant way. To own a house, you must pay for the know-how to build it *and* the materials that go into it; to own software, you only need to pay for the know-how to build it, because no (significant) materials or time are needed to replicate software. Creating software is expensive; copying it is (essentially) free. This means that many benefit from the expertise and hard work of others. True, programming is difficult and programmers are well paid, but because there are almost no "replication costs," using their work is easy. One of the best characteristics of computers is that it is so easy to apply and benefit from other people's intellect.

Install Software

The software sold with a computer is only the beginning. There is a profusion of commercial and open source (see Chapter 12) software to help with the tasks we want to do. We just find the software we need, make sure it runs on our computer and operating system, and install it.

During the process of installing software, the operating system places it on the hard disk with the other applications, and sets it up to be ready to run.

Software that comes on a CD-ROM is easy to install: Put the CD in the drive, click on it, and after you accept the End User License Agreement (EULA), it basically installs itself.

Software downloaded from the Internet is usually installed in a two-step process. The first step, decompressing the downloaded file, either happens automatically or happens when you click on it. The file is usually decompressed into a folder by itself, and clicking on that installer program starts the actual installation. After accepting the EULA, there are often several steps, but these usually don't require you to do anything. When it has finished installing, the software is ready to use and you can delete the downloaded file.

Integrated Circuits

Integrated circuits (ICs) are important because the technology allows extremely complex devices to be made cheaply and reliably. Two characteristics of ICs make this possible: integration and photolithography. Oh, yes. Integrated circuits are also very small.

Miniaturization

Modern computer clocks can run at GHz rates because their processor chips are so tiny. The farthest electrical signals can travel in a nanosecond is about one foot, and in a computer much more has to happen to the signals than simple transmission. Early computers, which filled whole rooms, could never have run as fast as modern computers because their components were farther apart than one foot. Making everything smaller has made computers faster by allowing for faster clock rates.

Integration

But the real achievement of microchip technology is not miniaturization, but **integration**. It is impossible to overstate its significance. T. R. Reid, in his book *The Chip*, called the invention "a seminal event of postwar science: one of those rare demonstrations that changes everything."

To appreciate how profound the invention of integrated circuitry is, understand that before integration, computers were made from separate parts (discrete components) wired together by hand. The three wires coming out of each transistor, the two wires from each resistor, the two wires from each capacitor, and so on, had to be connected to the wires of some other transistor, resistor, or capacitor. It was very tedious work. Even for printed circuit boards in which the "wiring" is printed metallic strips, a person or machine had to "populate" the board with the discrete components one at a time. A serious computer system would have hundreds of thousands or millions of these parts and at least twice as many connections, which were expensive and time consuming to produce, error prone, and unreliable. If computers were still built this way, they would still be rare.

The "big idea" behind integrated circuits is really two ideas working together. The first idea is that the active components—transistors, capacitors, and so forth—and the wires that connect them, are manufactured from similar materials by a single (multistep) process. So, rather than making two transistors

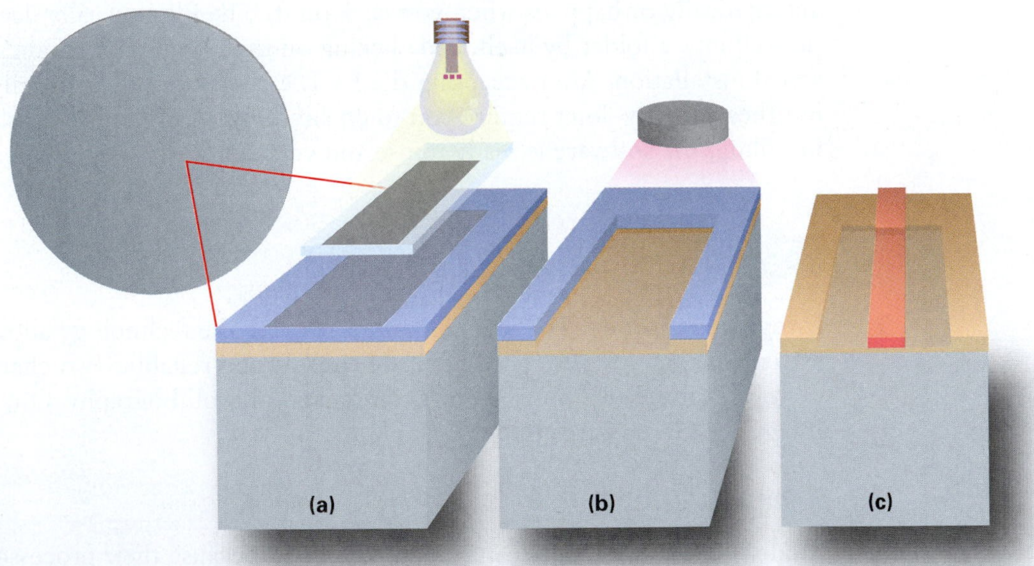

Figure 9.16 Early steps in the fabrication process. (a) A layer of photoresist (blue) is exposed to UV light through a pattern mask (light blue), hardening the exposed areas; (b) after washing away the unexposed photoresist, hot gases etch away (nearly all of) the exposed layer; (c) the remaining resist is washed away and other layers are created by repeating the patterning and etching processes. In later stages of the fabrication process, (d) "impurities" (green) such as boron are

and later connecting them by soldering a pair of their wires together, IC technology places them side by side in the silicon, and at some stage in the fabrication process—perhaps while some of the transistor's internal parts are still being built—a wire connecting the two is placed in position. The crux of integration is that the active and connective parts of a circuit are built together. Integration saves space (promoting speed), but its greatest advantage is that it produces a single monolithic part for the whole system all at once without hand wiring. The resulting "block" of electronics is extremely reliable.

Photolithography

The second idea behind integrated circuits is that they are made with **photolithography**, a printing process. Here's how it works. Making a chip is like making a sandwich: Start with a layer of silicon and add layers of materials to build up the transistors, capacitors, wires, and other features of a chip. For example, wires might be made of a layer of aluminum. But the aluminum cannot be smeared over the chip like mayonnaise covers a sandwich; the wires must be electrically separated from each other and connected to specific places. This is where photolithography comes in.

Transistors and other features of a chip are created in a series of steps that begin by depositing a layer of material on the silicon (see Figure 9.16). That layer is covered by a light-sensitive material called **photoresist**, and a mask is placed over it. The mask (like a photographic negative) has a pattern

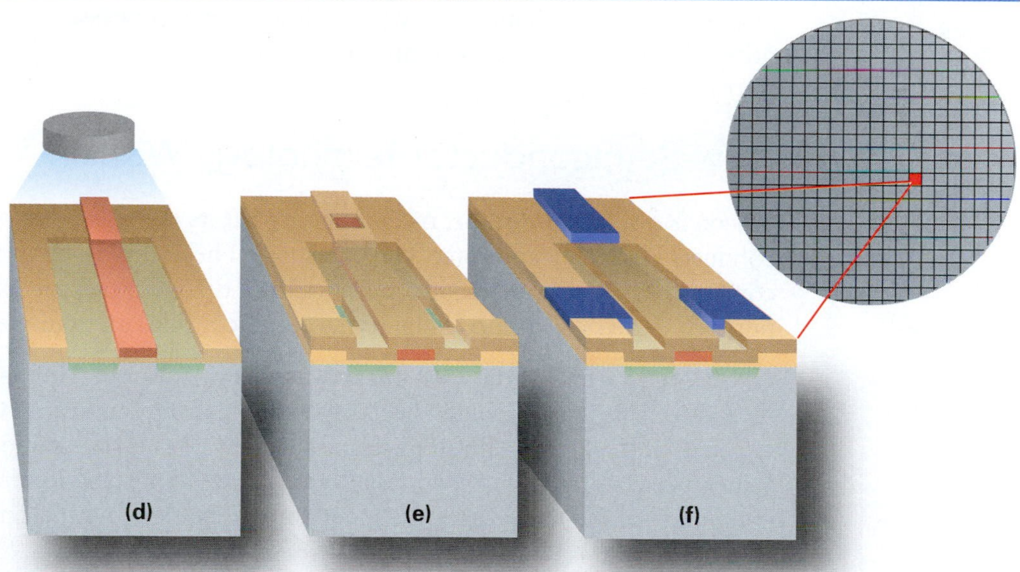

diffused into the silicon surface in a process called doping, which improves the availability of electrons in this region of the silicon. (e) After additional layering, etching exposes contact points for metal wires, and (f) a metal (dark blue) such as aluminum is deposited, creating "wires" to connect to other transistors. Millions of such transistors form a computer chip occupying a small square on the final fabricated wafer.

IC Man. Jack Kilby shared the 2000 Nobel Prize in Physics for inventing the integrated circuit. Kilby worked for the electronics firm Texas Instruments. New to the staff, Kilby hadn't accrued summer vacation time, so while the other employees were away on their holidays, he invented integrated circuits.

Using borrowed and improvised equipment, he conceived of and built the first electronic circuit in which all of the components, both active and connective, were fabricated in a single piece of semiconductor material. On September 12, 1958, he successfully demonstrated the first simple microchip, which was about half the size of a paper clip. Kilby went on to pioneer applications of microchip technology. He later co-invented both the hand-held calculator and a thermal printer used in portable data terminals.

corresponding to the features being constructed. Exposure to (ultraviolet) light causes open areas to harden; unexposed areas do not and can be washed away leaving the pattern. Hot gases etch the original layer, and when the remaining photoresist is removed, the pattern from the mask—and the new features—remain.

The key aspect of photolithography is that regardless of how simple or complicated the wiring is, the cost and amount of work involved are the same. Like a page of a newspaper, which costs the same to print whether it has 5 or 5,000 words, the cost of making integrated circuits is not related to how complicated they are. Thanks to the photolithographic process, computers and other electronics can be as complicated as necessary.

How Semiconductor Technology Works

Silicon is a **semiconductor**, meaning just what its name implies—it sometimes conducts electricity and sometimes does not. The ability to control when semiconductors do and don't conduct electricity is the main process used in computer construction. To understand this point, consider an example.

In Chapter 5 we used the AND operation when we searched for red giant to find Web pages that included both keywords. During our search Google tested to see if "red" was on a given page and if "giant" was on the same page too. When the results of those two tests were known, an instruction in the Google computer ANDed them together. How can that be done with electricity?

The On-Again, Off-Again Behavior of Silicon

Imagine that we have a wire with two gaps in it. We fill each gap with specially treated semiconducting material (see Figure 9.17). We send an electrical signal along the wire, which we will interpret as yes, both "red" and "giant" appear on the page. At the other end of the wire we detect whether the "yes" is present or absent, an application of the PandA encoding from Chapter 8. In

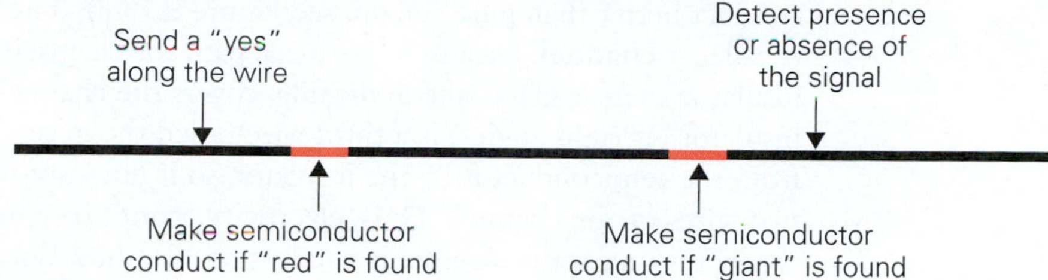

Figure 9.17 Computing **red AND giant** using a semiconducting material.

between we control the conductivity of the semiconducting material using the outcomes of the two tests. We make the material in the first gap conduct if "red" is found, and the material in the second gap conduct if "giant" is found. If the material conducts electricity, the signal can pass to the other end of the wire. So, if "yes" is detected at the output end, both gaps must be conducting; that is, both outcomes are true. If "yes" is not detected, then one or the other (or possibly both) of the two semiconducting points must not be conducting, which means "red" and "giant" are not both found.

This simple principle—the setting up of a situation in which the conductivity of a wire is controlled to create the logical conclusion needed—is the basis of all the instructions and operations of a computer. In the hardware of the computer where this test is done, the two semiconducting points of the AND circuit are not limited to the specific question of whether "red found" AND "giants found" is true; instead, the circuit computes x AND y for any logical values x and y. Such a circuit is part of the ALU of Google's computer (and yours), and it performs the Instruction Execute step of all the AND instructions.

9.2 OR Circuitry. Suppose the search was "marshmallow" OR "strawberry". Use a split wire (—[ ]—) to show the arrangement analogous to Figure 9.17 for determining the outcome using a semiconductor.

The Field Effect

So how do we control the conductivity of a semiconductor? We use the *field effect*. As we all know from combing our hair with a nylon comb on a dry day, objects can be charged positively or negatively. The comb strips off electrons from our hair, leaving the comb with too many electrons and our hair with too few. Because like-charges repel, our hair "stands on end" as each hair pushes away from its neighbors; but opposites attract, so the comb pulls the hair toward it. This effect that charged objects have on each other without actually touching is called the field effect. The field effect controls a semiconductor.

The ends of the two wires are specially treated (doped) to improve their conducting and nonconducting properties, that is, when they conduct, they conduct better than pure silicon; see Figure 9.18(a). The part between the ends is called a **channel**, because it creates a path for electricity to travel on. An insulator such as glass, silicon dioxide, covers the channel. Passing over the insulator (at right angles) is a third wire called the **gate**. The gate is separated from the semiconductor by the insulator, so it does not make contact with the two wires or the channel. Thus, electricity cannot be conducted between the two wires unless the channel is conducting. But how does the channel conduct?

The silicon in the channel can conduct electricity when it is in a charged field. The conductivity is the result of electrons being attracted or repelled in the silicon material, depending on the type of treatment on the ends (see Figure 9.18). So, charging the gate positively creates a field over the channel; electrons are attracted from the silicon material into the channel, causing it to conduct electricity between the two wires. If the field is removed, the electrons disperse into the silicon, the channel doesn't conduct, and the two wires are isolated. Of course, the gate is simply another wire, which is or is not conducting (charged) under the control of other gates, and so on.

Transistors

The example in Figure 9.18 illustrates a **field effect transistor**. A **transistor** is simply a connector between two wires that can be controlled to allow a charge to flow between the wires (conduct) or not. The transistor described is a **MOS (Metal Oxide Semiconductor)** transistor. These three terms refer to the materials in the cross-section of the transistor from top to bottom: the gate is metal, the glass insulator is oxide, and the channel is the semiconductor. Modern computers are developed with **CMOS** technology, which stands for "complementary MOS" and means two different, but complementary, treatments for the channels.

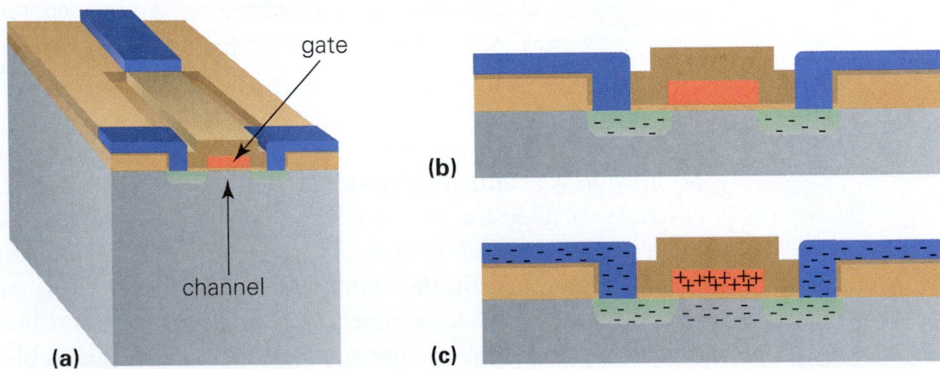

Figure 9.18 Operation of a field effect transistor. (a) Cross-section of the transistor of Figure 9.16(f). (b) The gate (red) is neutral and the channel, the region in the silicon below the gate, does not conduct, isolating the wires (blue); (c) charging the gate causes the channel to conduct, connecting the wires.

Combining the Ideas

Let's put these ideas together. We start with an information-processing task. The task is performed by an application implemented as a large program written by a programmer in a programming language like C or Java. The program performs the specific operations of the application, but for standard operations like *Print* or *Save*, the application program uses the OS. The program's commands, written in the programming language, are compiled into many simple assembly language instructions. The assembly instructions are then translated into a more primitive binary form (the machine instructions), which the computer understands directly.

The application program's binary instructions are stored on the hard disk. When we double-click on the application's icon, the OS copies the first part of the program's instructions into the computer's RAM and tells the computer to begin to execute them. When more instructions are needed, the OS brings them in.

The Fetch/Execute Cycle, a hardwired sequence of five steps that are repeated over and over, executes the instructions (see Figure 9.1).

- **IF** Fetch the instruction stored at the memory location specified by the program counter and place it in the control part of the computer. The PC is advanced to reference the next instruction after the fetch.
- **ID** Decode the instruction. That is, decide what the operation is, where the data values (operands) are, and where the result should go.
- **DF** Fetch the data from memory while the arithmetic/logic unit is set up to perform the operation.
- **EX** Execute; the ALU performs the operation on the data values.
- **RR** Store the result back in memory.

The cycle is repeated endlessly.

All of the computer's instructions are performed by the ALU circuits. The AND instruction, for example, is implemented with MOS technology by breaking a wire in two places and filling the gaps with the semiconducting material of a field effect transistor forming channels connecting the wire pieces. An oxide insulator and a metal gate cover each semiconductor channel. If, for example, the instruction is

```
AND 4040, 4280, 2020
```

then the data value fetched from memory location 4280 would control the gate on the first MOS transistor, and the data value fetched from memory location 2020 would control the gate on the second MOS transistor. A true operand value creates a field, causing the channel to conduct, and a false operand value is neutral, preventing the channel from conducting. An electrical signal interpreted as "yes" is sent down the wire. If the "yes" is detected at the output end of the wire, both transistors are conducting, and the result is true; otherwise, the result is false. Either way, the result is returned to memory location 4040.

That's it, from applications to electrons. It is a sequence of interesting and straightforward ideas working together to create computation. No single idea is *the* key idea. They all contribute. The power comes from applying the ideas in quantity: Application programs and operating systems are composed of millions of machine instructions, the control unit executes billions of cycles per second, memories contain billions of bits, processors have hundreds of millions of MOS transistors, and so on in an impressive process.

Ours has been a simple but accurate description of a computer. This description mirrors the design and operation of many early computers built in the days before silicon technology advanced to the microprocessor stage; that is, before everything in Figure 9.2 fit on a chip. Once silicon technology matured to that stage, computer architects—the engineers who design computers—became very aggressive. By applying integrated circuitry to its fullest, they optimized the Fetch/Execute Cycle and the simple structure of Figure 9.1 almost beyond recognition. To achieve their impressive speeds, today's computers are dramatically more complex than explained here. But the abstraction—the logical idea of how a computer is organized and operates—is as presented.

Summary

This chapter began by describing the Fetch/Execute Cycle, the instruction interpretation engine of a computer system. You learned that:

- The repeating process fetches each instruction (indicated by the PC), decodes the operation, retrieves the data, performs the operation, and stores the result back into the memory.
- This process is hardwired into the control subsystem, one of the five components of a processor.
- The memory, a very long sequence of bytes, each with an address, stores the program and data while the program is running.
- The ALU does the actual computing.
- The input and output units are the interfaces for the peripheral devices connected to the computer.
- Machine instructions do not refer to the data (operands) directly, but rather indirectly. Thus, different computations can be done with an instruction, just by changing the data in the referenced memory locations each time the instruction is executed.
- Programmers must create complex computations by software layers, building up simple operations from the base instructions, more complex operations from the simple ones, and so forth.

- Programmers use sophisticated programming languages to create operating systems as well as complex applications software.
- The basic ideas of integrated circuits are integrating active and connective components, fabrication by photolithography, and controlling conductivity through the field effect.

Try It Solutions

9.1. Only the contents of location 4000 changes; for multiply, 96, 0, 196; for subtract, –46, –9, 0.

9.2.

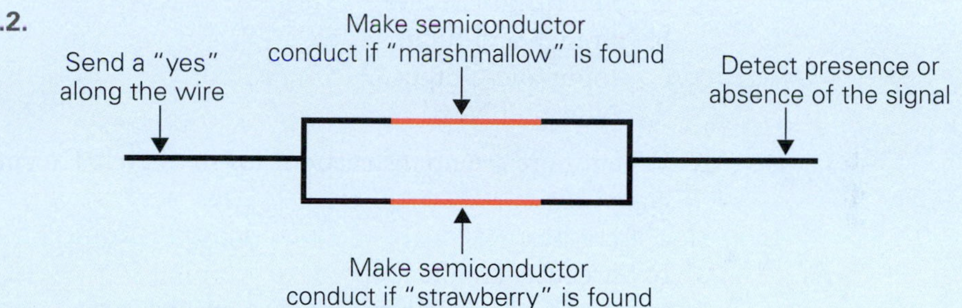

Review Questions

Multiple Choice

1. Which of the following is a characteristic of a computer?
   a. literal
   b. free will
   c. creativity
   d. intuition
2. There are ______ steps in the Fetch/Execute Cycle.
   a. 3
   b. 4
   c. 5
   d. 6
3. The Fetch/Execute Cycle operates
   a. once a second
   b. thousands of times a second
   c. hundreds of thousands of times a second
   d. hundreds of millions of times a second
4. One byte of memory can store
   a. any number
   b. one word
   c. one character
   d. one block

5. The ALU is used in the
   a. Instruction Fetch
   b. Instruction Execution
   c. Result Return
   d. Instruction Decode
6. Which of the following is used for input and output?
   a. keyboard
   b. hard disk
   c. mouse
   d. printer
7. The program counter is changed by instructions called
   a. Fetch and Execute
   b. Branch and Jump
   c. Input and Output
   d. Now and Next
8. When there are no instructions for the Fetch/Execute Cycle, the computer
   a. crashes
   b. executes an idle loop
   c. sends an empty instruction to processing
   d. always has instructions to execute
9. From smallest to largest, the correct order is
   a. giga, kilo, mega, tera
   b. kilo, mega, giga, tera
   c. tera, kilo, mega, giga
   d. kilo, mega, tera, giga
10. Modern computers know
    a. only a handful of instructions
    b. a couple of dozen instructions
    c. about a hundred instructions
    d. thousands of instructions
11. Which of the following is not a high-level programming language?
    a. Java
    b. C
    c. Assembly
    d. Visual Basic

Short Answer

1. _______ deterministically execute instructions to process information.
2. Computers operate under a set of operations called the _______.
3. _______ is an acronym for the name of the location where computer programs run and data is stored.
4. The _______ part of the computer is the hardware part of the Fetch/Execute Cycle.

5. Computers operate _______, that is, they follow instructions exactly based on the program and data they have been given.
6. The math in the computer is done by the _______.
7. Transferring and transforming information is called _______.
8. _______ are the devices that connect to the computer.
9. The _______ encodes keystrokes into binary form for the computer.
10. The computer's clock is measured in _______.
11. _______ is the task of creating complex instructions for the computer to follow from a set of simple instructions.
12. Computers keep track of the next instruction to execute by its _______.
13. _______ is the technical term for the process of executing a program.
14. A(n) _______ sometimes conducts electricity and sometimes doesn't.
15. The flow of electricity in a channel in a semiconductor is controlled by a(n) _______.
16. _______ is a long list of words, more accurately, a long series of 0's and 1's that make up a computer program.
17. Today, most software is written using a(n) _______ programming language.

Exercises

1. Break the process of brushing your teeth into separate steps. Be as specific as possible.
2. How many bits in a kilobyte? megabyte? terabyte?
3. Find out how much memory your computer has. Calculate exactly how many bytes it has.
4. If a 1 GHz computer can start four instructions per cycle and can start a new instruction on 80 percent of its cycles, how many instructions can it complete in a second? in a minute?
5. If the mouse cable is five feet long, how long does it take the current generated by a mouse click to travel from the mouse to the computer?
6. If the cable connecting the hard disk to the computer is six inches long, what effect would it have on performance if the length was reduced by half? doubled?
7. Explain why the keyboard and the mouse are input devices and the monitor is an output device.
8. Explain how a complicated process like driving can be accomplished as a series of simple steps.
9. Explain how a system that can do only a limited number of very simple tasks can accomplish an almost unlimited number of complicated tasks.

10. Do an online search to find an explanation of how computer circuits are made.
11. Locate a computer circuit and take a close look at it. Describe what it looks like.
12. Using the Fetch/Execute Cycle, describe how you'd answer a true/false question.
13. Most of the cost of a new drug is tied up in research and testing. The actual production and distribution of the medication is only a small part of the cost. Explain how this parallels software development.
14. List the five steps in the Fetch/Execute cycle, and describe each. Can you think of how these steps might correspond to eating at a restaurant?
15. List ten devices that can be connected to a computer, and classify each as "input," "output," or "I/O" if it is both.
16. Using the WWW, explain where the unit "hertz" originated. Give at least four examples of places where that word is used, either correctly or incorrectly, that are not directly related to computers.

Algorithmic Thinking

10 chapter

What's the Plan?

learning objectives

- List the five essential properties of an algorithm
- Explain the difference between an algorithm and a program
- Use the *Alphabetize CDs* algorithm to illustrate algorithmic thinking:
  - Follow the flow of the instruction execution
  - Follow an analysis to pinpoint assumptions
  - Explain the function of loops and tests
- Demonstrate algorithmic thinking by being able to:
  - Explain what the *Beta* sweep abstraction does
  - Explain what the *Alpha* sweep abstraction does

The most beautiful thing we can experience is the mysterious. It is the source of all true art and science.

—ALBERT EINSTEIN, 1930

The process of preparing programs for a digital computer is especially attractive, not only because it can be economically and scientifically rewarding, but also because it can be an aesthetic experience much like composing poetry or music.

—DONALD E KNUTH, 1970

AN ALGORITHM is a precise, systematic method for producing a specified result. We know algorithms as recipes, assembly instructions, driving directions, business processes, nominating procedures, and so on. Algorithms are key to processing information, of course, and you've already met several in this book. There are three main reasons to learn more about algorithms. First, we must create algorithms so that other people or computers can help us achieve our goals. To be successful, our algorithms must "work." This chapter explains how to create effective algorithms. Second, we will follow algorithms created by others. If we know the "dos" and "don'ts" of algorithm design, we can pay better attention to the details and be alert to errors in other people's instructions. Finally, learning about algorithms completes the study we began in Chapter 8 of how computers solve problems. Understanding this process makes us better computer users, better debuggers, and better problem solvers—that is, more Fluent.

The goals of this chapter are to understand what algorithms are and to learn to think algorithmically. We begin by looking at everyday algorithms. Next, we introduce and illustrate the five fundamental properties of algorithms. We explain the role of *language* in specifying algorithms and the value of a formal language. Then, we discuss the relationship between algorithms and programs. Guidelines—useful when writing out driving directions—help us understand the role of context in executing algorithms. We create an algorithm for alphabetizing our audio CD collection, which helps us discover how and why algorithms are structured the way they are. We execute the algorithm; that is, we sort a five-slot rack of our favorite CDs, watching the progress of the algorithm. Then, perhaps most important, we analyze the algorithm to extract key concepts in algorithmic thinking.

Algorithm: A Familiar Idea

In Chapter 1 we defined an algorithm as a precise and systematic method for producing a specified result. Algorithms are familiar—we've already seen several of them in this book.

- **Recognition of a button click.** In Chapter 1, after describing how computers draw buttons on the screen (an algorithm itself), we explained how the button is "clicked." The systematic method described how, when the mouse is clicked, the computer can look through the list of buttons it has drawn on the screen, and for each button check to see if the cursor is inside the square defining the button.
- **Placeholder technique.** In Chapter 2 we described a three-step process to eliminate short letter sequences (for example, new lines), which can also be parts of longer strings (for example, double new lines), without also eliminating them in the longer strings.
- **Hex to bits.** In Chapter 8 we used algorithms to convert back and forth between hexadecimal digits and bits.

fluencyBIT

Weird Word. *Algorithm* seems to be an anagram of logarithm, but it comes from the name of a famous Arabic textbook author, Abu Ja'far Mohammed ibn Mûsâ al-Khowârizmî, who lived about A.D. 825. The end of his name, al-Khowârizmî, means *native of Khowârism* (today Khiva, Uzbekistan). It has been corrupted over the centuries into *algorithm*.

We use algorithms every day. The arithmetic operations—addition, subtraction, multiplication, and division—we learned in elementary school are algorithms. Making change is an algorithm, as are looking up a number in a telephone book, sending a greeting card, and balancing a checkbook. Changing a tire is algorithmic, too, because it is a systematic method to solve a problem (replace a flat tire). Usually, though, *algorithm* means a precise method used in information processing.

Algorithms in Everyday Life

Most of the algorithms that we know, like arithmetic, we learned from a patient teacher or we figured out for ourselves, like how to look up a phone number. Because we are the ones performing the operations, we don't think much about algorithms as an explicit sequence of instructions. We simply *know* what to do. Other algorithms—recipes, bicycle assembly instructions, driving directions to a party, or income tax filing rules—are written out for us. Written algorithms interest us because we want to be able to think up an algorithm, write it out, and have some other agent—person or computer—perform its instructions successfully.

The specification of an algorithm must be "precise." The algorithms mentioned from the earlier chapters, though possibly clear enough for a person to follow, are not precise enough for a computer. Computers, as we saw in Chapters 7 and 9, are so clueless and literal that every part of a task they perform must be spelled out in detail. To write a precise algorithm, we need to pay attention to three points.

- **Capability.** Make sure that the computer knows what and how to do the operations.
- **Language.** Ensure that the description is unambiguous—that is, it can be read and understood one way only.
- **Context.** Make few assumptions about the input or execution setting.

These issues are crucial not only when algorithms are written for computers, but also when they're written for people. We expect people to use their heads and compensate for weaknesses in our descriptions, but sometimes humans are clueless and literal, too, especially when dealing with unfamiliar situations. So, it's always best to make our instructions precise, avoid ambiguity, be sure users know what to do, and minimize assumptions, no matter what or who performs the algorithm.

Five Essential Properties of Algorithms

An algorithm that is specified well enough for a computer to follow must have five essential properties:

- Input specified
- Output specified
- Definiteness
- Effectiveness
- Finiteness

Input specified. The **input** is the data to be transformed during the computation to produce the output. We must specify the type of data, the amount of data, and the form that the data will take. Suppose the algorithm is a recipe. We must list the ingredients (type of input), their quantities (amount of input), and their preparation, if any (form of input), as in, "1/4 cup onion, minced."

Output specified. The **output** is the data resulting from the computation, the intended result. Often the description is given in the name of the algorithm, as in "Algorithm to compute a batting average." As with input, we must specify the type, amount, and any form of the output. A possible output for some computations is a statement that there is no output—that is, there is no possible solution. Recipes specify their output too, giving the type, quantity, and form of food, as in, "3 dozen 3-inch chocolate chip cookies."

Definiteness. Algorithms must specify every step. **Definiteness** means specifying the sequence of operations for transforming the input into the output.

Details of each step must be spelled out, including how to handle errors. Definiteness ensures that if the algorithm is performed at different times or by different agents (people or computers) using the same data, the output is the same. Similarly, recipes should be definite, but because they often rely on the judgment, practicality, and experience of the cook, they can be much less definite than computer algorithms and still be successful. And where they are not definite—"salt and pepper to taste"—it's usually a good thing.

Effectiveness. It must be possible for the agent to execute the algorithm mechanically without any further input, special talent, clairvoyance, creativity, help from Superman, and so on. Whereas definiteness specifies which operations to do and when, **effectiveness** means that they are doable. Examples of ineffective instructions abound: "Enter the income you would have received this year if you had worked twice as hard," "Print Alexander the Great's blood type," and "Say whether the coin toss at the next Super Bowl is heads."

Finiteness. An algorithm must have **finiteness**; it must eventually stop, either with the right output or with a statement that no solution is possible. If no answer comes back, we can't tell whether the agent is still working on an answer or is just plain "stuck." Finiteness is not usually an issue for noncomputer algorithms because they typically don't repeat instructions. But, as you will see, computer algorithms often repeat instructions with different data. Finiteness becomes an issue because if the algorithm doesn't specify when to stop the repetition, the computer continues to repeat the instructions indefinitely.

A process with these five properties is called an algorithm.

fluencyBIT

Work without End. "Long" division is an algorithm in which finiteness is important. For example, divide 3 into 10. As we add each new digit (3) to the quotient, the computation returns to the same situation. When should the algorithm stop?

```
    3.33
3)10.00
   9
   1 0
     9
    10
    ...
```

Language in Algorithms

Because algorithms are developed by people but executed by another agent, they must be written in a language that is understood by both. The person who creates the instructions and the agent that performs them must interpret the instructions the same way.

Natural language. If the agent is a person, we use a natural language, such as English. We assume that all speakers understand every sentence of a language similarly, but it's not true. In fact, it's probable that no two people understand a language exactly the same way. An instruction may mean one thing to the writer and something else to the agent. Ambiguity is very common in natural languages, but alternate interpretations are not to blame as much as the fact that natural languages are not very precise. For example, although recipe writers choose specific words like *fold in* or *beat* rather than *stir*; most of us mix the ingredients differently. Generally, a natural language is an extremely difficult medium in which to express algorithms.

Programming language. Since natural languages don't work well, we use programming languages when the executing agents are computers. Programming languages are **formal languages**, designed to express algorithms. They are precisely defined. Programming languages are rarely ambiguous; their precise definition ensures that the programmer and the computer agree on what each instruction means; we will see the programming language JavaScript in Part 4. Programmers know that what they tell the computer to do is exactly what it will do. Of course, programmers make mistakes, but at least they are sure that if the computer does something wrong, the problem is with their algorithmic design, not with the computer's interpretation.

The Context of a Program

A program can fulfill the five properties of an algorithm (input specified, output specified, definiteness, effectiveness, and finiteness), be unambiguous, and still not work right because it is executed in the wrong *context* (the assumptions of the program are not fulfilled). For example, a form that asks you for your *Last Name* may mean your family name or surname, as is the case for Western names. The request produces the right result in the United States, but perhaps not in countries like China where the family name is given first. Good algorithm designers reduce the dependence on context by asking for *Family Name* rather than *Last Name* and *Given Name* rather than *First Name.*

Context Matters: Driving Instructions. Consider driving directions, another example where context matters. For example, the instruction

From the Limmat River go to Bahnhof Strasse and turn right

seems reliable, but it may not be. The "turn right" instruction assumes that you are traveling in a specific direction. If you are traveling east, perhaps, the instruction works, because you are in the context the instruction writer assumed (see Figure 10.1). But if you are traveling west, the instruction doesn't work because you need to turn left on *Bahnhof Strasse*. You are following the instructions in a context the writer didn't expect. Turning right will send you north if you approach from one direction and send you south if you approach from the other direction.

You must consider the context in which to apply the algorithm—in this case, the point of departure. You can write such conditions as input conditions or you can simply avoid them. The best solution is not to use words like *right* that depend on orientation until you've established it. Terms like *north*, which are orientation independent, are better.

Travel directions are an example of the kind of everyday algorithm that goes wrong because of context—usually because the writer assumes too much. There are simple guidelines for writing better travel directions.

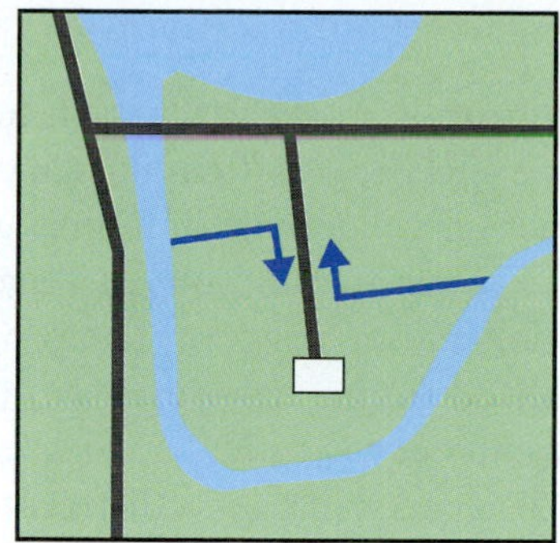

Figure 10.1 Diagram of approaching a street (Bahnhof Strasse) from different directions, giving the "turn right" instruction different meanings.

Travel Directions: To give better travel directions, follow these rules to reduce the dependence on context.

- *Give the starting point: "From Place de la Concorde...."*
- *State the direction of travel: "Going west on Route 66...."*
- *Give landmarks, especially when turning: "Turn left; you'll see a temple (Todai-ji) on your right...."*
- *Give measured distances (2.3 miles) instead of blocks, cross streets, or traffic lights, which can be ambiguous.*
- *Include an* "overshot" test: *"If you cross Via Giuseppi Verdi, you've gone too far."*

10.1 Better Directions. Mapping software, such as Google Maps, generally gives helpful maps and directions, but they can often be improved. The route from the White House Visitor Center to the National Air and Space Museum has these three instructions. Analyze the main turn (Step 2) in the route and say what additional information the directions could give that would help a visitor.

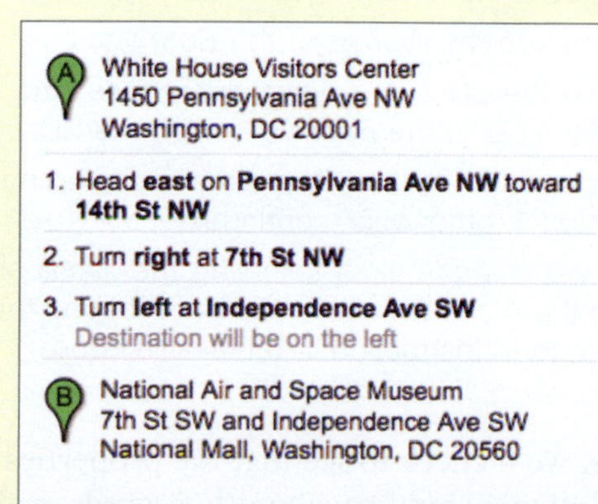

A White House Visitors Center
1450 Pennsylvania Ave NW
Washington, DC 20001

1. Head **east** on **Pennsylvania Ave NW** toward **14th St NW**
2. Turn **right** at **7th St NW**
3. Turn **left** at **Independence Ave SW**
   Destination will be on the left

B National Air and Space Museum
7th St SW and Independence Ave SW
National Mall, Washington, DC 20560

©2009 Google. Map data ©2009 Google.

Program Versus Algorithm

A **program** is an algorithm that has been customized to solve a specific task under a specific set of circumstances in a specific language. Making change—subtracting an amount of money, *x*, from a larger amount paid, *y*, and returning the result as coins and currency—is an *algorithm*, but making change in U.S. dollars is a *program.* The program uses the "making change" algorithm specialized to the denominations of coins (1¢, 5¢, 10¢, 25¢, 50¢, $1) and paper currency ($1, $2, $5, $10, ...) of the United States. Making change in New Zealand dollars is a different program; it also uses the making change algorithm but with the New Zealand coins (5¢, 10¢, 20¢, 50¢, $1, $2) and paper currency ($5, $10 $20, ...). From our point of view, whether the method is general (algorithm) or specialized (program) makes no difference. They're both algorithms and the issues are the same.

An Algorithm: *Alphabetize CDs*

It's time for a sample algorithm. Though most of the algorithms in later chapters use a programming language to ensure precision, our first algorithms are written in English.

Imagine that your CD collection, which fills a large, slotted rack, is completely disorganized. You've decided it's time to get organized, so you want to alphabetize your CDs by the name of the group, the performing musician, or perhaps the composer. How would you go about solving this problem?

Here is an algorithm for alphabetizing your CDs:

Alphabetize CDs

Input: An unordered sequence of CDs filling a slotted rack
Output: The same CDs in the rack in alphabetical order
Instructions:

1. Use the term *Artist_Of* to refer to the name of the group, musician, or composer on a CD.
2. Decide which end of the rack is the beginning of the alphabetic sequence and call the slot at that end the *Alpha* slot.
3. Call the slot next to the *Alpha* slot the *Beta* slot.
4. If the *Artist_Of* the CD in the *Alpha* slot comes later in the alphabet than the *Artist_Of* the CD in the *Beta* slot, swap the CDs.
5. If there is a slot following the *Beta* slot, begin calling it the *Beta* slot and go to Instruction 4; otherwise, continue.
6. If there are two or more slots following the *Alpha* slot, begin calling the slot following the *Alpha* slot *Alpha* and begin calling the slot following it the *Beta* slot, and go to Instruction 4; otherwise, stop.

In the next sections, we'll check to see that the properties of definitiveness, effectiveness, and finiteness hold true; in other words, we'll check that we truly have an algorithm.

How does this algorithm work? Follow Figure 10.2 as we go through the process.

Instruction 1. *Use the term* Artist_Of *to refer to the name of the group, musician, or composer on a CD.* This instruction gives a name to the operation of locating the name used for alphabetizing. (*Artist_Of* is shorthand for extracting the name of the performer, simplifying Instruction 4; it could be eliminated at the expense of a wordier Instruction 4.)

Instruction 2. *Decide which end of the rack is the beginning of the alphabetic sequence and call the slot at that end the* Alpha *slot.* The purpose of this instruction is to give the process a starting point. It also gives the initial meaning to the word *Alpha*. In the algorithm, *Alpha* refers to slots in the rack. At the start, *Alpha* refers to the first slot in the alphabetic sequence. As the algorithm progresses, it refers to successive slots in the rack.

Instruction 3. *Call the slot next to the* Alpha *slot the* Beta *slot.* This instruction gives the word *Beta* its initial meaning. The names *Alpha* and *Beta* have no inherent meaning; the programmer needs to name slots in the rack and chose these words.

Instruction 4. *If the* Artist_Of *the CD in the* Alpha *slot comes later in the alphabet than the* Artist_Of *the CD in the* Beta *slot, swap the CDs.* This is the workhorse instruction of the algorithm. It compares the names of the recording artists of the CDs in the slots *Alpha* and *Beta* and, if necessary, exchanges them so that they are in the proper order. It may not be necessary to swap if the CDs are already positioned properly. But either way, when this instruction is done, the alphabetically earlier CD is in the *Alpha* slot.

Instruction 5. *If there is a slot following the* Beta *slot, begin calling it the* Beta *slot and go to Instruction 4; otherwise, continue.* This instruction gives a new definition for the *Beta* slot so that it refers to the next slot in the sequence, if there is one. With this new definition of *Beta*, Instruction 4 can be executed again, comparing a different pair of CDs. One of the pair, the CD in the *Alpha* slot, was compared the last time Instruction 4 was executed, but because *Beta* refers to a new slot, the pair of CDs is "new." If all slots have been considered—that is, there is no next slot for *Beta* to refer to—the algorithm continues to Instruction 6 instead of returning to Instruction 4.

Instruction 6. *If there are two or more slots following the* Alpha *slot, begin calling the slot following the* Alpha *slot* Alpha *and begin calling the slot following it the* Beta *slot, and go to Instruction 4; otherwise, stop.* By the time we get to this instruction, the alphabetically earliest CD is in the *Alpha* slot, thanks to the combination of Instructions 4 and 5. The idea is to advance *Alpha* to the next slot and to sweep through the last of the rack, again locating the alphabetically earliest CD with the Instruction 4–5 combination, and now it's the alphabetically next earliest. Then *Alpha* moves again, the Instruction 4–5 combination is repeated again, and so on. Each time, the CDs in slots up to and including *Alpha* are alphabetized. When there are no longer enough slots to call a new one *Alpha* and the next one *Beta*, the whole rack is alphabetized and the algorithm stops.

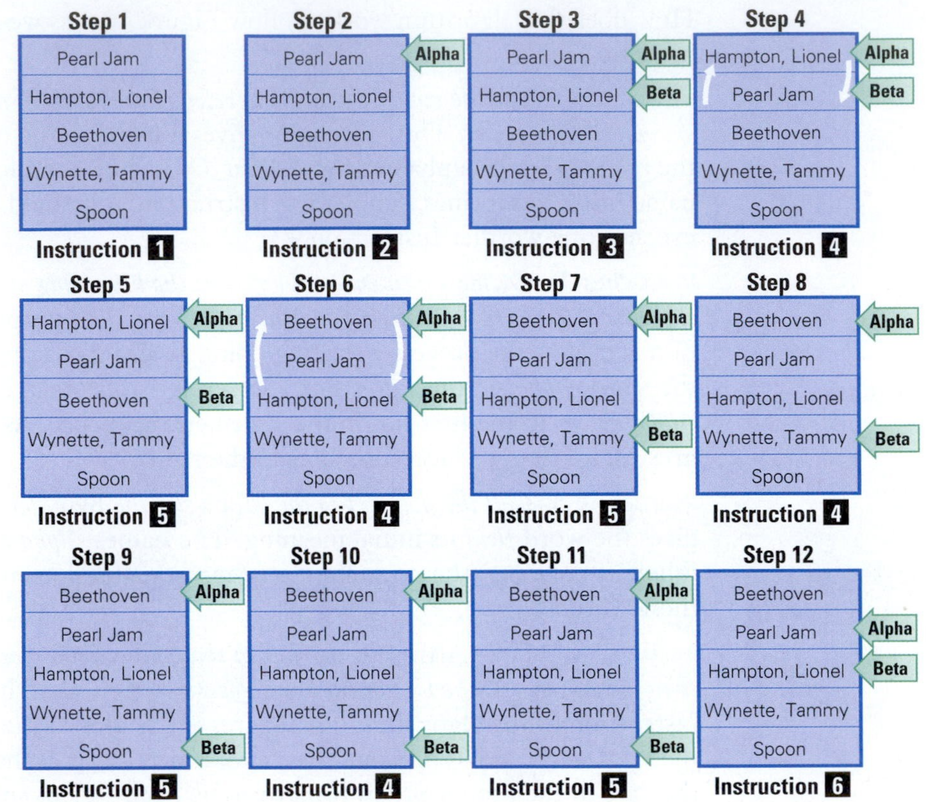

Figure 10.2 The steps of the *Alphabetize CDs* algorithm. A snapshot of the CD rack is shown at the completion of each instruction. Notice how *Beta* sweeps through all of the slots following *Alpha*. After the first 11 steps, the alphabetically earliest CD, Beethoven, is in the *Alpha* slot.

The *Alphabetize CDs* approach is better than dumping the CDs on the floor and trying to return them to the rack in order. Keeping the CDs in the rack while it orders them is not the property that makes *Alphabetize CDs* an algorithm, however. It could be rewritten to work with the CDs spread out on the floor. Rather, it is the fact that *Alphabetize CDs* uses a method to find the alphabetically first CD, then the next, then the next after that, and so forth until the alphabetically last CD is found. That is, *Alphabetize CDs* is systematic.

Analyzing the *Alphabetize CDs* Algorithm

The *Alphabetize CDs* example illustrates the five basic properties of algorithms. The input and output are specified. Each instruction is described

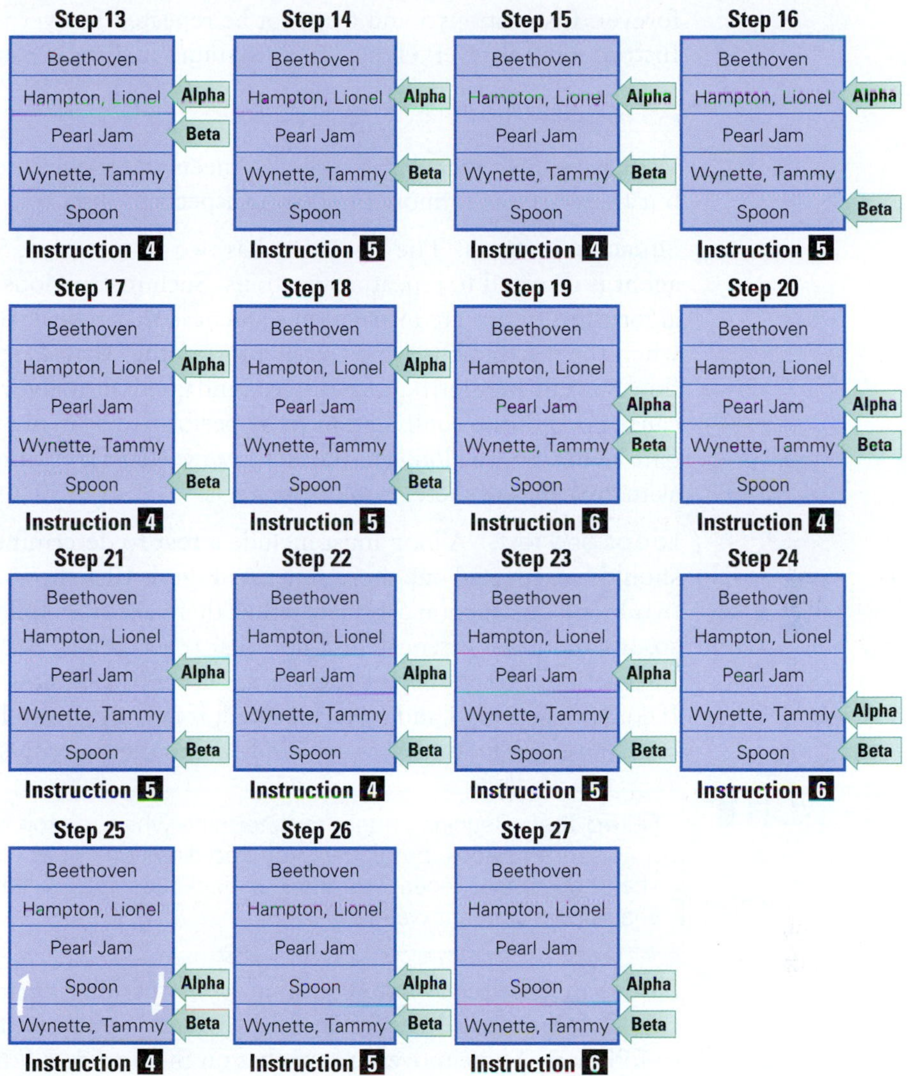

(b)

precisely—or as precisely as English allows—fulfilling the definiteness requirement. The operations of the algorithm are effective because actions like selecting the next slot and counting to see if there are at least two slots left are simple and mechanically doable. The most complicated operation, deciding which of two artists' names is earlier in the alphabet, is also a completely mechanical process. We only need to compare the first two letters of the names; the one closer to *A* is the earlier. If those two letters are the same, we compare the second letters, and so forth. So, our algorithm has the effectiveness property. Finally, the algorithm is finite. Because Instructions 4, 5, and 6 are repeated, this property is not so obvious. However, notice that each time Instruction 4 is repeated, *Alpha* and *Beta* refer to a different pair of slots that has not previously been considered together. Because slots can be paired in a rack in a finite number of *different* ways, Instruction 4 cannot be repeated forever. Instructions 5 and 6 cannot be repeated forever without repeating Instruction 4 forever. Hence, the program satisfies the finiteness property.

A Deeper Analysis

We have shown that *Alphabetize CDs* meets the requirements of an algorithm, but there are other, more interesting aspects to discover.

Structural features. The algorithm has two instructions, 5 and 6, in which the agent is directed to repeat instructions. Such instructions create *loops* in the algorithm. Loops are instruction sequences that repeat; they are more obvious when the instructions are given in a form other than English. Consider the flowchart in Figure 10.3. Loops are fundamental to algorithms because they cause parts of the computation to be performed as many times as there are data items. So, the loops in the *Alphabetize CDs* algorithm repeat instructions as many times as there are slots, or CDs.

Loops and tests. A loop must include a **test** to determine if the instructions should be repeated one more time. As Figure 10.3 shows, *Alphabetize CDs* has two loops. Instruction 5 tests whether there are slots following the *Beta* slot; if so, Instruction 4 is repeated; if not, that repetition of the inner loop ends. Instruction 6 tests whether there is at least a pair of slots after the *Alpha* slot. If so, Instructions 4 and 5 are repeated; if not, the outer loop ends. These tests cause the loop to complete and ensure the finiteness property.

fluencyBIT

Failed Test. Requiring a test to determine when to stop repeating instructions may seem obvious, but some shampoo directions read: "Wet hair, massage in shampoo, rinse, repeat," failing the finiteness test. What runs out first—the shampoo or the hot water?

Notice that for the loop to continue at Instruction 5, *Beta* must move to the next slot. Similarly, Instruction 6 moves *Alpha* to the next slot and resets *Beta* to follow it. These moves ensure that on the next test *Beta* and *Alpha* refer to different slots. If there are no changes between the two consecutive tests, the outcome is the same and the loop never stops.

Assumptions. Assumptions are made in specifying *Alphabetize CDs*. First, we assume (and state in the Input specification) that the CD rack is full. This matters because the instructions do not handle the case of empty slots. (For example, if *Beta* were an empty slot, how would Instruction 4 operate?) The algorithm requires that the *Artist_Of* two CDs are compared, but if one or both of the slots are empty, the agent might not know what to do. The specification is correct because it states that it expects a full CD rack as input. A better solution would explain what to do if the rack is not full. Then the "full" requirement could be dropped.

"Following" an assumption. When the *Beta* slot is first set in Instruction 3, only one slot is next to *Alpha* because in Instruction 2 *Alpha* is chosen to be an end slot. This ensures that there is a unique slot *following Alpha* for *Beta* to refer to, and so the specification is effective. There is an assumption in the use

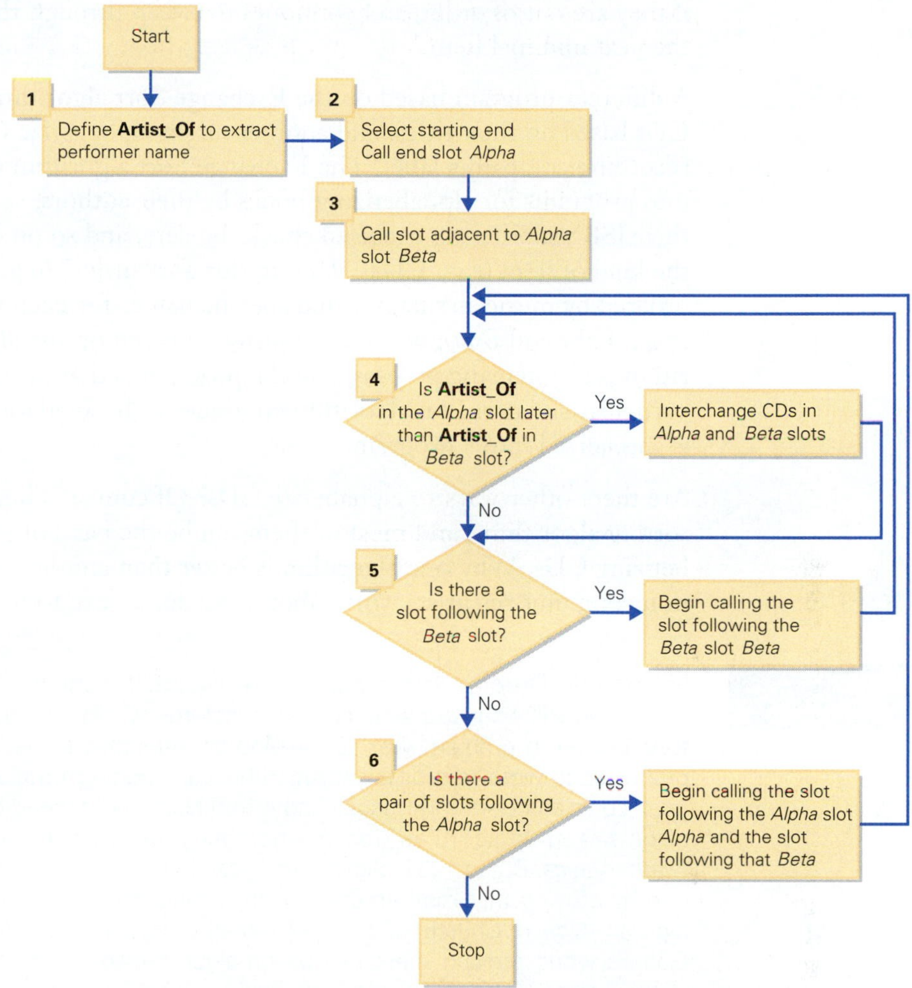

Figure 10.3 Flowchart of *Alphabetize CDs*. Operations are shown in rectangles; decisions are shown in diamonds. Arrows indicate the sequencing of the operations.

of the term *following* in Instructions 5 and 6. Instruction 5 refers to a slot "following" *Beta*, which means a slot farther from the end chosen in Instruction 2. Similarly, Instruction 6 refers to a pair of slots "following" *Alpha*, meaning the slots farther from the end chosen in Instruction 2. But, nowhere is the term *following* defined. This makes the orientation of the term *following* an assumption. The orientation can be defined—and would have to be for a computer to execute the algorithm—but people know what "following" means.

The Exchange Sort Algorithm

The *Alphabetize CDs* example illustrates a standard algorithm called **Exchange Sort**. In the *Alphabetize CDs* example, we used the Exchange Sort algorithm to alphabetize CDs based on the names of the musicians. The Exchange Sort algorithm compares pairs of items chosen in a particular way, exchanges them if they are out of order, and continues to sweep through the items to locate the next minimal item.

A different program based on the Exchange Sort algorithm might alphabetize CDs based on their titles, and another might alphabetize CDs based on their recording company's label. The Exchange Sort algorithm can be specialized into programs for alphabetizing books by their authors, sequencing books by their ISBNs, ordering canceled checks by date, and so on. When we choose the kind of item (e.g., CDs), the criterion for "order" (e.g., alphabetically ordered by musician's name), and specific names for keeping track of the items (e.g., *Alpha* and *Beta)*, we create a program based on the algorithm. The algorithm is a systematic process, and the program is that process formulated for a particular situation. An algorithm continues to be an algorithm even when it is specialized into a program.

Are there other ways to alphabetize CDs? Of course. There are dozens of sorting algorithms, and most of them can be the basis of programs for alphabetizing CDs. Why one algorithm is better than another is the sort of question computer scientists worry about. We don't have to be concerned.

Impossible Dream. At the start of the twentieth century, German mathematician David Hilbert listed several great problems worthy of study in the new century. His tenth problem was to develop an algorithm to decide whether logical propositions were true or false. Algorithmically testing truth seemed like a great goal. Logicians Bertrand Russell and Alfred North Whitehead began setting down axioms and logic rules for mathematics in their three-volume *Principia Mathematica*. But in 1931, Slovak-American logician Kurt Gödel astonished everyone by proving that mathematical truth testing wasn't possible. Soon American logician Alonzo Church and English mathematician Alan M. Turing extended Gödel's work, proving there can be no algorithm to decide truth and laying the foundation for theoretical computer science.

Abstraction in Algorithmic Thinking

The *Alphabetize CDs* example may seem very complicated when described in so much detail, but it's easier to understand than it first appears because we can think of parts of the algorithm's behavior as whole units rather than as individual instructions. This is abstraction, as defined in Chapter 1.

The idea of treating parts of the algorithm's behavior as a unit—not the instructions themselves, but the behavior the instructions define—is key to algorithmic thinking. We want to discipline ourselves to think about algorithms this way.

Know the Score. Try the *Alphabetize CDs* algorithm on five or six of your favorite CDs. Doing so simplifies the ideas in this section.

Beta Sweep Abstraction

Instructions 4 and 5 illustrate the idea of an abstract computational unit. We call it ***Beta* sweep**. It's the operation of considering in order all CDs following a specific *Alpha*. The sweep tick-tick-ticks through those slots, comparing artists, and swapping them when necessary. More precisely,

Beta Sweep: While *Alpha* points to a fixed slot, *Beta* visits each slot following *Alpha*, in sequence, comparing its CD with the CD in the *Alpha* slot, and swapping them when necessary.

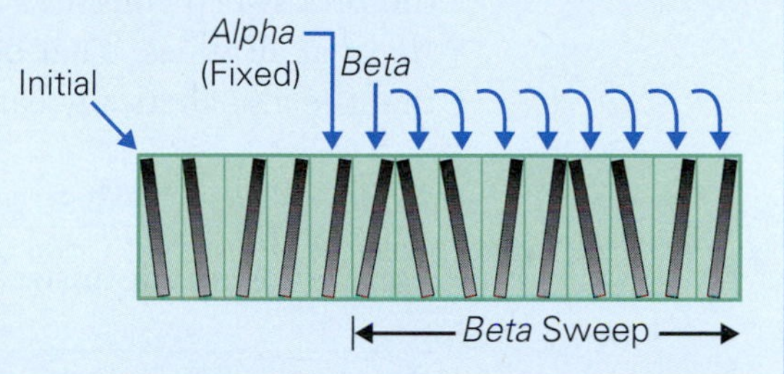

By thinking of *Beta* sweeping through the CDs as a single computational unit, we recognize that it has the effect of finding the next CD in order and moving it to the *Alpha* slot.

Properties of *Beta* sweep abstraction. When we think of the *Beta* sweep abstraction, we recognize some of its important properties. The *Beta* sweep is

1. **Exhaustive.** It considers all CDs from the *Alpha* slot to the end of the rack, making sure that none is left out.
2. **Nonredundant.** It considers each slot following *Alpha* only once. It never considers the same pair of CDs twice, which ensures that the sweep will stop.
3. **Progressive.** At any given time, the alphabetically earliest CD seen so far in this sweep is in the *Alpha* slot.
4. **Goal-achieving.** After the sweep completes, the alphabetically earliest CD among all CDs considered in this sweep (including *Alpha*) is in *Alpha*.

These are not general properties of all algorithms; these are only specific properties of the *Beta* sweep abstraction of the *Alphabetize CDs* program. (They are also properties of the "inner loop sweep" of the Exchange Sort algorithm if we make them general, not referring to "CDs," "slots," "*Alpha*," "*Beta*," etc.)

Where did the four properties of the *Beta* sweep abstraction come from? We noticed them when we analyzed how the *Alphabetize CDs* algorithm works (see the Analyzing the *Alphabetize CDs* Algorithm section earlier in this chapter). They are examples of features we should notice about the behavior of an algorithm when we study how it operates. Why? Because these properties (together with the *Alpha* sweep properties described next) will convince us that the algorithm actually works, that it achieves its goal of alphabetizing.

10.2 Sweeping Up. Say that a *Beta* sweep is a sequence of Instruction 4 and Instruction 5 pairs. Referring to Figure 10.2, say which steps define each of the *Beta* sweeps.

To see how the properties of the *Beta* sweep can convince us that the algorithm works, first note that properties 1 through 3 imply property 4. That is, the *Beta* sweep considers all CDs once and keeps the alphabetically earliest in *Alpha* at all times. That behavior after processing all CDs in a sweep ensures that the alphabetically earliest CD is in *Alpha*, which is part of the answer.

Alpha Sweep Abstraction

For the rest of the answer, consider the ***Alpha* sweep** abstraction.

Alpha Sweep: *Alpha* sweeps from the slot where the alphabetization begins through all slots (except the last), performing the *Beta* sweep instructions each time.

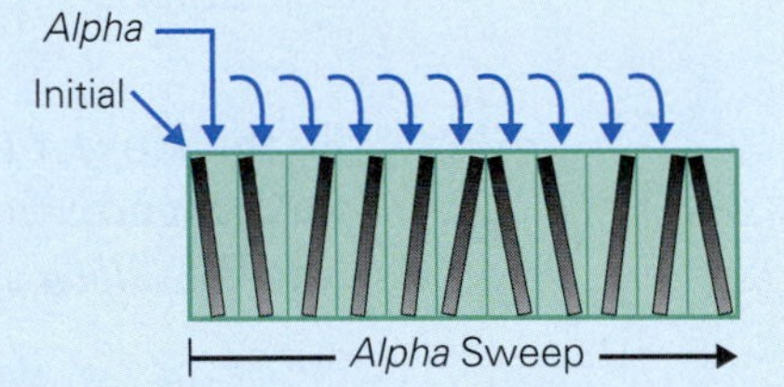

Properties of *Alpha* sweep abstraction. We can list properties that we notice about the *Alpha* sweep abstraction. The *Alpha* sweep is

1. **Exhaustive.** It considers all CDs from first to (but not including) last.
2. **Nonredundant.** No slot is assigned to *Alpha* more than once, so the process stops if the *Beta* sweep stops, and it does, by property 2 of the *Beta* sweep abstraction.
3. **Progressive.** At the end of each *Beta* sweep, the alphabetically next earliest CD is in *Alpha*.
4. **Complete.** When the last *Beta* sweep is completed, the CD in the last slot is later in the alphabet than the CD in the next-to-last slot because the last *Beta* sweep involved these last two slots—property 3 of the *Beta* sweep. (Refer to Figure 10.2, Step 25.)
5. **Goal-achieving.** The alphabetically earliest CD is in the first slot at the end of the first *Beta* sweep, by its property 4 and the fact that all CDs are considered; thereafter, in every new position for *Alpha*, the *Beta* sweep assigns the next earliest CD. The program alphabetizes the rack.

Property 5 of the *Alpha* sweep says this program works. We stated that it did originally, but by noticing these properties of the two abstractions—*Beta* sweep and *Alpha* sweep—we can see *why* it works. When we create computer solutions, knowing why our solution works is the only way to be sure the solution does work, achieving our computing goal. Algorithmic thinking involves inventing algorithms that achieve our goals and understanding why they work.

Abstracting for Other Algorithms and Programs

We must emphasize that the *Alpha* sweep and *Beta* sweep abstractions are *specific* to the Exchange Sort algorithm and to programs like *Alphabetize CDs* derived from it. Other algorithms and programs exhibit different behaviors and require different abstractions based on the way they solve their problems. Those abstractions will have properties different from (but analogous to) the four properties of the *Beta* sweep and the five properties of the *Alpha* sweep. Every situation is different, but the approach—abstracting the behavior and understanding the properties—is always the same.

Looking to the Future

This chapter introduced several new ideas. The reward for the reader who has reached this point with an understanding of these concepts is the satisfaction of having seen nearly all of the basic ideas underlying algorithms and programming. With perhaps two exceptions, every programming idea covered in this book appears in this chapter. So, there is not that much to algorithms and programming—all that's left is elaborating on these ideas and mastering them. That's plenty, of course, but it doesn't require many more ideas.

Because we have spent a lot of time understanding these ideas, it is worth it to spend a moment naming them, especially since we will run into them again in later chapters.

- **Variables**. *Alpha* and *Beta* are variables in the *Alphabetize CDs* program.
- **Locations**. The slots in the CD rack are like a computer's memory locations.
- **Values**. The CDs are the values stored in the locations.
- **Function**. *Artist_Of* is a function for locating the name of the group or performer on a CD (a value).
- **Initialization**. Instructions 2 and 3 initialize the variables *Alpha* and *Beta*, respectively.
- **Loops**. The Instructions 4 and 5 form a loop; the Instructions 4 through 6 also form a loop.
- **Array**. The rack is a (linear) array.

We will study these terms more completely in upcoming chapters.

Summary

In this chapter we introduced algorithms, one of the most fundamental forms of thinking. You now understand that:

- Everyday algorithms (e.g., recipes) can be ineffective because we write them in an imprecise natural language.
- Algorithms have five fundamental properties.
- *Alphabetizing CDs* in a filled rack is an algorithm. The six-instruction program named two slots, *Alpha* and *Beta*, and made repeated sweeps over the remaining CDs.
- *Alphabetize CDs* is a program built using the Exchange Sort algorithm.
- Processing *Alphabetize CDs* involves two interacting behaviors: the *Beta* sweep and the *Alpha* sweep. These abstractions have several properties, which explain why the algorithm produces an alphabetized sequence.
- Abstractions and their properties are the essence of algorithmic thinking. Algorithmic thinking can become second nature, making us effective problem solvers.

Try It Solutions

10.1 Notice that 8th St. does not cross Pennsylvania Ave., so after you cross 9th St., 7th is your next right.

10.2 Sweep 1: 4–11, Sweep 2: 13–18, Sweep 3: 20–23, Sweep 4: 25–26.

Review Questions

Multiple Choice

1. An algorithm has ______ basic requirements.
   a. three
   b. four
   c. five
   d. seven
2. An algorithm must be
   a. precise
   b. approximate
   c. concise
   d. general

3. Which of the following does not fit?
   a. natural language
   b. formal language
   c. synthetic language
   d. programming language

4. A computer program must
   a. complete a specific task
   b. work in a specific set of circumstances
   c. be written in a specific language
   d. all of the above

5. Which instructions are repeated in the *Alphabetizing CDs* algorithm on pages 286–287?
   a. all of them
   b. 4 and 5
   c. 4 to 6
   d. 3 to 5

6. If you saw a monitor, keyboard, mouse, printer, and CPU, you would assume these parts formed a computer. This is an example of
   a. abstraction
   b. encapsulation
   c. utilization
   d. algorithm

7. You notice that the only item in alphabetical order after the first *Beta* sweep of *Alphabetize CDs* is the first item. This is an example of
   a. abstraction
   b. encapsulation
   c. utilization
   d. algorithm

8. In the *Alphabetize CDs* algorithm
   a. the *Alpha* sweep points to every slot except the last
   b. the *Beta* sweep points to every slot on every sweep
   c. the *Alpha* points to the first slot of the sweep and the *Beta* points to the rest
   d. the *Alpha* points to the first slot and the *Beta* points to the last slot

9. Following an *Alpha* sweep, how many items are you sure are in the correct order?
   a. 0
   b. 1
   c. 2
   d. all of them

10. Input includes the
    a. type of data
    b. amount of data
    c. form of the data
    d. all of the above

11. Output
    a. is the intended result
    b. is the user's contribution to an algorithm
    c. must include the type, amount, and form of the result
    d. is more than one of the above

Short Answer

1. An explicit set of instructions is a(n) ______.
2. A programming language is a(n) ______ language because it is precisely defined.
3. A(n) ______ is a generalized method while a(n) ______ is a specialized solution.
4. The ______ of an algorithm defines the setting for its use.
5. A(n) ______ finds the item in a list that is next in order to the *Alpha* item.
6. In a *Beta* sweep, the ______ property makes sure every item in the list is considered.
7. In a *Beta* sweep, the ______ property makes sure the sweep is finite.
8. The *Alpha* and the *Beta* in the *Alphabetize CDs* program are called ______.
9. A(n) ______ is the computer term for a set of instructions that repeat.
10. The memory locations of a computer stores items, but the contents of these locations contain the ______ of the items.

Exercises

1. Describe the process for subtracting a four-digit number from a five-digit number.
2. Why aren't natural languages such as English good for programming?
3. Using the *Alphabetize CDs* algorithm, illustrate the five properties of an algorithm.
4. Does the instruction "go downhill" have the same problems as "go right"? Explain.
5. What is the purpose of the *Artist_Of* operation in Step 1 of the *Alphabetize CDs* algorithm?

6. Given the following artists, write down the instructions and steps to put these in order.

   Newton-John, Olivia
   Hill, Faith
   Incubus
   Chapman, Steven Curtis
   Mendelssohn, Felix

7. What would you need to do to arrange the CDs in reverse order instead of alphabetical order? What would you need to do to arrange them in order by copyright?

8. Discuss what you would need to add to the *Alphabetize CDs* algorithm to alphabetize the CDs of Juice Newton, Wayne Newton, and Olivia Newton-John.

9. Explain why *Alpha* doesn't have to reference the last slot.

10. Write a version of the Exchange Sort algorithm to alphabetize CDs in a slotted rack, from last to first order; that is, that has the same result as *Alphabetize CDs*, but from the back end forward.

11. Define "algorithm" and explain its essential properties. List five noncomputer examples of algorithms you have used in the past week. Be specific.

12. Using *Alphabetize CDs* as an example, create an algorithm to sort the following names into alphabetical order.

   Natalie Attired
   Emmanuel Transmission
   Candi Cane
   Sandi Banks
   Lefty Banks
   Candi Bar
   Your Name

13. Using the WWW, determine how a binary search works (www.NIST.gov has a good explanation). Use the binary search algorithm to find your name from the list you just alphabetized in the Exercise 12. Write down the steps you follow.

11 chapter

Representing Multimedia Digitally

Light, Sound, Magic

learning objectives

- Explain how RGB color is represented in bytes
- Change an RGB color by binary addition
- Explain the meaning of "computing on a representation"
- Explain concepts related to digitizing sound waves
- Explain the meaning of the Bias-Free Universal Medium Principle
- Explain the difference between "bits" and "binary numbers"

Blue color is everlastingly appointed by the Deity to be a source of delight.

—JOHN RUSKIN, 1853

Science will never be able to reduce the value of a sunset to arithmetic.

—DR LOUIS ORR, 1960

A TYPICAL DAY at college involves so many forms of digital information that few of us notice: There's sending email with an attached photo to your folks, texting friends, downloading MP3 tunes from the Web, watching online videos, having the required EKG to try out for the swim team, admiring your roommate's new iPhone, using the smart ID card from your work, and researching with the ever-popular database, the library's Online Catalog. Though these examples seem to be much more complicated than the digital representations we've seen so far—well, maybe not the catalog—they are not. As you'll see in this chapter, all these common multimedia devices build on the basic ideas you've already learned.

From the earlier discussions you learned that discrete things—things that can be separated from each other—can be represented by bits. We begin this chapter by looking closer at RGB color, which has been mentioned several times before. You will learn how a color is encoded in bits, and how you can make the colors darker or lighter. This process—a basic part of digital photo software—is little more than doing arithmetic on binary numbers. Changing the color of an image and performing other modifications illustrates these concepts. Next, we discuss JPEG and MPEG and the need for compression techniques for images and video. We go on to discuss optical character recognition to emphasize the advantages of encoding information in digital form. The discussion of virtual reality that follows helps to clarify how well computers can create synthetic worlds. And finally, the whole topic of digital representation is summarized in one fundamental principle.

Digitizing Color

In Chapter 8 we discussed the binary encoding of keyboard characters to create the ASCII representation, but we (and the creators) didn't pay much attention to which bit patterns are associated with which characters. It's true that in ASCII the numerals are encoded in numeric order, and the letter sets are roughly in alphabetical order, but the assignment is largely arbitrary. The specifics of the keyboard character encoding don't matter much (as long as everyone agrees on them) because the bytes are used as units. We rarely manipulate the individual bits that make up the pattern for the characters. For other encodings, however, manipulating the individual bits is essential.

RGB Colors: Binary Representation

Recall that giving the intensities for the three constituent colors—red, green, and blue (RGB)—specifies a color on the monitor. Each of the RGB colors is assigned a byte (8 bits) to record the intensity of that color. But the color intensities are not assigned arbitrarily, like the letter characters in ASCII. Instead, color intensity is represented as a quantity, ranging from 0 (none) through 255 (most intense); the higher the number, the more intense the colored light. When we want to change the intensity, we just add to or subtract from the values, implying that the encoding should make it simple to perform arithmetic on the intensities. So, RGB intensities are encoded as binary numbers.

Binary numbers compared with decimal numbers. Binary numbers are different from decimal numbers because they are limited to two digits, 0 and 1, rather than the customary ten digits, 0 through 9. The number of digits is the **base** of the numbering system—2 or 10—but that is really the only difference. The other features distinguishing binary from decimal relate to that one difference.

For example, in decimal numbers, we use a **place value** representation, where each "place" represents the next higher power of 10, starting from the right. In binary, it's the same idea, but with higher powers of 2.

Place value in a decimal number. Recall that to find the quantity expressed by a decimal number, the digit in a place is multiplied by the place value and the results are added. So, in Table 11.1, for example, the result is one thousand ten, found by adding from right to left: the digit in the 1's place (0) multiplied by its place value (1), plus the digit in the 10's place (1) multiplied by its place value (10), and so on: $0 \times 1 + 1 \times 10 + 0 \times 100 + 1 \times 1{,}000$.

Table 11.1 The decimal number 1,010 representing one thousand ten = 1,000 + 10

10^3	10^2	10^1	10^0	Decimal Place Values
1	0	1	0	Digits of Decimal Number
1×10^3	0×10^2	1×10^1	0×10^0	Multiply place digit by place value
1,000	0	10	0	and add to get a decimal 1,010

Place value in a binary number. Binary works in exactly the same way except that the base of the power is not 10 but 2, because there are only two digits, not ten. Therefore, instead of the decimal place values, 1, 10, 100, 1,000, ..., resulting from the successive powers of 10, the binary place values are 1, 2, 4, 8, 16, ..., resulting from the successive powers of 2.

Power	Decimal	Binary
0	$1 = 10^0$	$1 = 2^0$
1	$10 = 10^1$	$2 = 2^1$
2	$100 = 10^2$	$4 = 2^2$
3	$1{,}000 = 10^3$	$8 = 2^3$
4	$10{,}000 = 10^4$	$16 = 2^4$
. . .	. . .	. . .

Thus, if we are given a binary representation, we can find the (decimal equivalent) value if we multiply the digit times the place value and add the results. See Table 11.2, which shows that 1010 in binary has the value ten in decimal: $0 \times 1 + 1 \times 2 + 0 \times 4 + 1 \times 8$.

Table 11.2 The binary number 1010, representing the decimal number ten = 8 + 2

2^3	2^2	2^1	2^0	Binary Place Values
1	0	1	0	Bits of Binary Number
1×2^3	0×2^2	1×2^1	0×2^0	Multiply place bit by place value
8	0	2	0	and add to get a decimal 10

fluencyBIT

2nd Base. The "base" of a numbering system, 10 for decimal and 2 for binary, is also called its **radix**.

Because powers of 2 don't increase as fast as powers of 10, binary numbers need more places than decimal numbers to represent the same amount. So, for example, representing one thousand ten as a binary number requires ten bits, as shown in Table 11.3. Compare Table 11.3 with Table 11.1.

Table 11.3 Binary representation of the decimal number one thousand ten = 11 1111 0010

2^9	2^8	2^7	2^6	2^5	2^4	2^3	2^2	2^1	2^0	Binary Place Values
1	1	1	1	1	1	0	0	1	0	Bits of Binary Number
1×2^9	1×2^8	1×2^7	1×2^6	1×2^5	1×2^4	0×2^3	0×2^2	1×2^1	0×2^0	Multiply place bit by place value
512	256	128	64	32	16	0	0	2	0	and add to get decimal 1,010

Converting a binary number to a decimal number. Because the bit is either 0 or 1, the "multiply the digit times the place value" rule is especially easy in binary—a 1 means include the place value and a 0 means "forget it." So, to convert a binary number to its decimal equivalent, just add the place values for the places with 1's. Thus, in Table 11.3, if we start with the highest place value, we have 512 + 256 + 128 + 64 + 32 + 16 + 2 is decimal 1,010.

Spacing Out. When writing long decimal numbers, North Americans usually separate groups of three digits with a comma for readability. Binary numbers, which are usually even longer, are grouped in four-digit units, separated by a space, as in, "The binary number 11 1111 0010 represents the decimal number 1,010."

11.1 Alternating. What decimal number is the binary number 1 0101 0101?

Black and White Colors

Returning to the representation of color, the fact that a byte—8 bits—is allocated to each of the RGB intensities means that the smallest intensity is 0000 0000, which is 0, of course, and the largest value is 1111 1111. To figure out what decimal number this is, we add up the place values for the 1's,

$$\begin{aligned}1111\ 1111 &= 2^7 + 2^6 + 2^5 + 2^4 + 2^3 + 2^2 + 2^1 + 2^0 \\ &= 128 + 64 + 32 + 16 + 8 + 4 + 2 + 1 \\ &= 255\end{aligned}$$

which explains why the range of values is 0 through 255 for each color.

As you learned in Chapter 1, black is the absence of color,

0000 0000	0000 0000	0000 0000	*RGB bit assignment for black*
red byte	green byte	blue byte	

whereas white

1111 1111	1111 1111	1111 1111	*RGB bit assignment for white*
red byte	green byte	blue byte	

has full intensity for each color. Between these extremes is a whole range of intensity.

Changing a Decimal Number to a Binary Number

As you've seen, to convert a binary number to decimal representation you add up the powers of 2 corresponding to 1 bits. Converting a decimal number into a binary representation is only slightly harder, and is essentially the opposite process. We proceed by filling in the following table, which works for numbers less than 1,000.

Number being converted										
Place value	512	256	128	64	32	16	8	4	2	1
Subtract										
Binary Number										

Start by placing the number to be converted, say 200, in the first cell.

Number being converted	200									
Place value	512	256	128	64	32	16	8	4	2	1
Subtract										
Binary Number										

Then we work across the table performing one of the following operations in each column depending on how large the number being converted is compared to the place value.

> **Smaller:** If the number being converted is smaller than the place value below it, copy the number into the next cell to its right; enter a 0 as the binary digit.
>
> **Equal or Larger:** If the number being converted is equal to or larger than the place value below it, subtract the place value from the number and copy the result into the first cell of the next column; enter a 1 as the binary digit.

Thus, the first step in converting 200 to binary is

Number being converted	200	200								
Place value	512	256	128	64	32	16	8	4	2	1
Subtract										
Binary Number	0									

and the completed table

Number being converted	200	200	200	72	8	8	8	0	0	0
Place value	512	256	128	64	32	16	8	4	2	1
Subtract			72	8			0			
Binary Number	0	0	1	1	0	0	1	0	0	0

indicates that the result is 1100 1000. Like decimal representation, we can drop any leading zeros.

11.2 86 Confusion. What is the binary representation of the decimal 86? (Use the table if you wish.)

Lighten Up: Changing Color by Addition

Returning to our discussion of color representation, the extreme colors of black and white are easy, but what color does the following represent?

1100 1000	**1100 1000**	**1100 1000**
red byte	green byte	blue byte

First, notice that each byte contains the decimal value 200, which you recognize from the conversion just explained. So the mystery color is the color produced by the specification RGB (200, 200, 200). Like black and white, the mystery color has equal amounts of red, green, and blue, and it is closer to white than black. In fact, it is a medium gray ■. All colors with equal amounts of RGB are gray if they are not black or white. It's just a question of whether they're closer to black or white.

To Increase Intensity: Add in Binary

To make a *lighter* color of gray, we obviously change the common value to be closer to white. Suppose we do this by increasing each of the RGB values by 16—that is, by adding 16 to each byte—as shown in Figure 11.1.

1100 1000	binary representing decimal number	200
+ 1 0000	binary representing decimal number	16
1101 1000	binary representing decimal number	216

Figure 11.1 Adding 16 to an RGB value.

The result in Figure 11.1 is found by simply setting the 16's place value—that is, changing it from 0 to 1. When the increase is applied to each color, the result is

1101 1000	**1101 1000**	**1101 1000**
red byte	green byte	blue byte

which is a lighter shade of gray ■. By the way, we can add or subtract any amount as long as the result is not less than 0 or greater than 255.

Lighter Still: Adding with Carry Digits

Imagine that we want the color lighter still by another 16 units of intensity for each RGB byte. Adding another 16 isn't quite as easy this time. The 16's position in the binary representation 1101 1000 of decimal 216 is already filled with a 1. So we "carry" to the next higher place. Thus,

1	carry digit	
1101 1000	binary representing decimal number	216
+ 1 0000	binary representing decimal number	16
1110 1000	binary representing decimal number	232

So our color intensities are

1110 1000	**1110 1000**	**1110 1000**
red byte	green byte	blue byte

Notice that if we'd simply added 32 to 200 originally, we'd have ended up with the same result—the gray with each intensity set at 232 .

We just illustrated the binary addition process. As with other aspects of binary, binary addition is similar to decimal addition. We work from right to left, adding corresponding digits in each place position and writing the sum below. Like decimal addition, there are two cases. Sometimes, we can add the two numbers in a place and the result is expressed as a single digit. That was the case the first time we added 16 to the RGB byte: we added 1 + 0 in the place and the result was 1. Other times, when we add two digits in a place their sum is larger than can be expressed by a single digit, so we must carry to the next higher place. That was the case the second time we added 16 to the RGB byte: we added 1 + 1 in the place, which is 10 in binary, and wrote a 0 in the place and carried a 1 to the next higher digit. Because there may be a carry involved, it is best to think of adding as involving three digits in each place: the two digits being added plus (possibly) a carry.

The rules for binary addition can be learned using an example for each case.

The first example—called the "no carry-in" case—adds A + B when A is the binary number 1100, which is 12 in decimal, and B is 1010, which as you know is 10 in decimal.

```
 ↓↓↓↓ ——— Illustrates the "no carry-in" cases
1 0000  ← Carry, shown explicitly
  1100  ← A
+ 1010  ← B
------
1 0110  ← Sum
```

This illustrates the four no carry-in cases of adding binary digits—all combinations of 0 and 1. In each case there is no *carry-in*—that is, no carry from the previous place. The only interesting case is 1 + 1. Of course, in decimal 1 + 1 = 2, which is 10 in binary, so we put down the 0 in the place and carry the 1 to the next higher position. The carry to the next higher digit is called a *carry-out*, and we notice that the carry-out of one place becomes the carry-in of the next higher place. (Verify that the sum is the binary representation of 22 = 12 + 10.)

The next example, the "carry-in" case, adds A + B when A is 1011, which is 11 in decimal, and B is 111, which is 7 in decimal. Leading 0's are shown to complete the picture, and the rightmost place adds 1 + 1 to get the "carrying process" started.

```
↓ ↓↓↓ ── Illustrates the "carry-in" cases
  1 1110  ← Carry, shown explicitly
  0 1011  ← A
+ 0 0111  ← B
--------
  1 0010  ← Sum
```

The four cases illustrate adding binary digits with a carry-in. Three of the four have the property that the sum of the two digits and the carry are too large to be expressed by a single binary digit, so there is a carry-out to the next higher place. Only the leftmost case, 0 + 0 with a carry-in, can be expressed by a single digit, 1. The new case is the second from right position, which adds 1 + 1 with a carry-in yielding the decimal 3 or binary 11. We write down the 1 in the place and carry a 1 to the next higher position. (Verify that the sum is the binary representation of 18 = 11 + 7.)

The rules from these examples are summarized in Table 11.4. We can now apply the rules to add the binary numbers 110 1001 and 110 0011. (What decimal numbers are these?) This time, we follow the usual procedure of showing only the nonzero carries.

```
  11     11   ← Carry
   110 1001   ← A
 + 110 0011   ← B
 ----------
  1100 1100   ← Sum
```

Table 11.4 Summary of the rules for binary addition. The carry-in is added to the two operands, A and B, to give the place digit and carry-out.

Carry-in	0	0	0	0	1	1	1	1
A	0	1	0	1	0	1	0	1
B	0	0	1	1	0	0	1	1
Place digit	0	1	1	0	1	0	0	1
Carry-out	0	0	0	1	0	1	1	1

Binary addition is so easy, even computers can do it.

One and One. Sometimes we rhetorically ask if a clueless person knows that 1 + 1 = 2.

How clueless are computers?

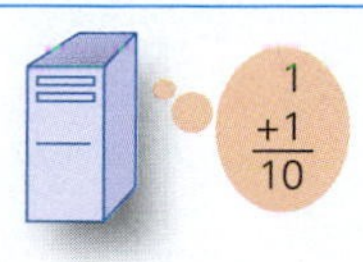

Overflow

Because computers use fixed-size bit sequences (for example, a byte is 8 bits long), an interesting question is what happens when there is a carry-out of the most significant bit—that is, the leftmost bit. For example, 255 + 5 in binary is

```
    1111 1111
  + 0000 0101
  -----------
  1 0000 0100
```

But 260 needs 9 bits, one bit too many to fit into a byte. Such situations are called **overflow exceptions**. Computers report them when the computation they're told to perform overflows; it's up to programmers to recover from the error. Usually programmers try to avoid the situation by choosing large bit fields that will not overflow.

11.3 Summing Up. Add these two binary numbers:

```
  1 0101 0111
+   111 0110
```

Computing on Representations

Though we have focused on binary representation, conversions between decimal and binary, and binary addition, the previous sections have also introduced another fundamental concept of digital representation: the idea of *computing on representations*. When we made gray lighter, we showed how digital information—for example, the RGB settings of a pixel—can be changed through computation. For a better understanding of the idea, consider the more involved example that follows.

Changing the Colors of a Moon Photo

Suppose you have scanned a beautiful black-and-white photo of the moon into your computer, similar to Figure 11.2(a). Unfortunately, it misses the gorgeous orange of the close-to-the-horizon moon that you and your friends saw the previous weekend. As a memento for them, you decide to colorize it yourself.

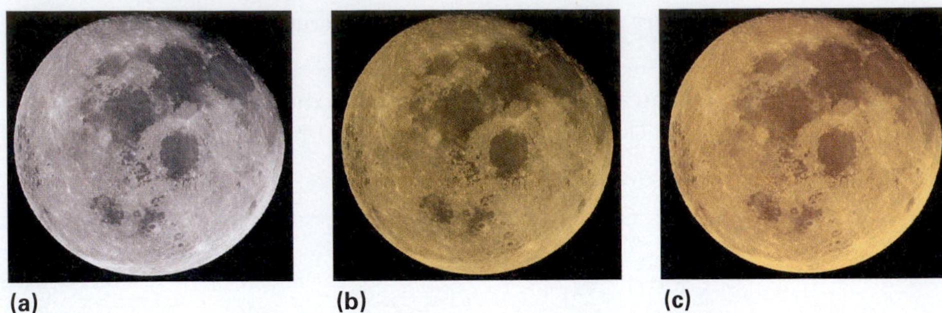

Figure 11.2 Moon photos. (a) The original black-and-white picture, (b) tinted version of original, (c) with boosted highlights.

In the computer, the pixels of your photo form a long sequence of RGB triples. What values do they have? Because they are all black, white, or gray, it's easy to guess. There is the (0,0,0) of the black night sky, the (255,255,255) of the brightest part of the moon, some light gray values very close to white—for example, (234,234,234)—of the craters and *marae* (dry oceans) of the moon, and some dark gray values in the corner very close to black—for example, (28,28,28)—from a smudge left on the glass of your scanner. How can you colorize it?

Removing the smudge. To create the picture, you must remove the smudge and transform the pixels of the black-and-white image into the colors that you remember. The first task is easy because any value "close" to black can be changed to true black by replacing it with (0,0,0). But what does *close* mean? The sample dark gray value (28,28,28) is represented in binary as

0001 1100 0001 1100 0001 1100

Though other dark gray values may be somewhat larger or smaller, it is a safe guess that any dark gray pixel will have the most significant (leftmost) 2 bits of each of its RGB bytes set to 00. That's because, from the binary representation, a byte whose most significant two bits are 00 is less than 64—that is, less than one quarter of the magnitude of full intensity—and any pixel, all of whose colors are less than a quarter magnitude, must be a darker color.

To change the smudge to pure black, the process is to go through the image looking at each pixel and testing to see if the first 2 bits of each of its bytes are 00. If they are, set each byte to 0. Recalling our substitution arrow from Chapter 2, we describe this operation as

00xx xxxx 00xx xxxx 00xx xxxx ← 0000 0000 0000 0000 0000 0000

where *x* is a standard symbol for a "don't care digit" or "wildcard"—that is, a symbol matching either 0 or 1. So the substitution statement says, "Any three RGB bytes, each of whose first 2 bits are 00, are replaced with all zeros." Making that substitution throughout the image removes the digitized smudge. (Notice that this is an algorithm.)

Making the moon orange. Similarly, shifting the color of the moon to orange involves changing the white pixels (255,255,255). You decide that the orange of the moon ( ) must be about the color represented by (255,213,132). Changing all of the white pixels to this orange color requires the substitution

255 255 255 ← 255 213 132

or, in binary,

1111 1111 1111 1111 1111 1111 ← 1111 1111 1101 0101 1000 0100

to produce an orange moon. But it will not change the gray of the craters, because they are not pure white and therefore won't be modified by this replacement. If, like changing the dark gray to black, the very light gray were changed to this orange too, all of the beautiful detail of the craters would be lost. How do we change the white to orange and change the gray to the appropriate orange-tinted gray?

Light gray into orange tint. There are many very sophisticated ways to adjust color; we'll change light gray into orange in three steps:

- Red byte—leave unchanged
- Green byte—subtract 42 from the green value; that is, reduce the green slightly
- Blue byte—subtract 123 from the blue value; that is, reduce the blue quite a bit

Thus, the light gray color (234,234,234) is changed into (234,192,111), and the slightly darker light gray (228,228,228) is changed into (228,186,105), a slightly grayer orange. These numbers are computed by noting how white (255,255,255) changed into the chosen orange (255,213,132): the red byte was unchanged, the green byte was reduced by 42, and the blue byte was reduced by 123. If all pixels having the most significant bit of each RGB byte equal 1 (that is, the white pixels and all the light gray pixels) are changed by this three-step process, the white areas would become orange and the gray parts would become grayish orange.

You have cleaned up the smudge and colorized the moon, as shown in Figure 11.2(b).

Boosting the red. Now you inspect your work and decide that the gray parts of the moon are really not as luminous as you remembered. So, you decide to boost the red. If the red in all of the orange pixels is shifted to 255, the moon's craters look too red and "unnatural." But a compromise is to "split the difference." That is, if the current value of the red byte in an orange tint is 234, say, half the difference between it and pure red—(255 – 234)/2 = 10.5—could be added to get 244. (You need whole numbers, so drop the "point 5.") Thus, the two sample tints (234,192,111) and (228,186,105) become (244,192,111) and (241,186,105), respectively. This process brightens the craters, as demonstrated in Figure 11.2(c), without making them appear unnatural. The resulting image looks great, and you can attach it to your email to your friends.

Image Processing Summary

We have computed on a digital representation. We scanned a real photograph into the computer and created an artificial image. First, we improved it by removing the smudge from the scanning process. Then, we colorized it by changing white and light gray into orange and corresponding shades of orange-gray. Finally, we boosted the red in the orange-gray tints to make it a little brighter. We discussed these changes as if you were programming them, which you could do, but image processing software like Photoshop accomplishes these modifications through menu choices like changing *Saturation*, *Brightness*, *Hue*, and so forth. Such software manipulates the pixels with transformations like those described here, as well as in much more sophisticated ways. The result is not the photograph of the moon as it might have been taken last weekend, but rather a different image, a synthetic image closer to what you remember or prefer. It is definitely not reality . . . because we can just as easily make "the man in the moon" smile.

Digitizing Sound

In this section we discuss digitizing, though this time we focus on digitizing sound rather than images because it is slightly easier and equally interesting. The principles are the same when digitizing any "continuous" information.

An object—think of a cymbal—creates sound by vibrating in a medium such as air. The vibrations push the air, causing pressure waves to emanate from the object, which in turn vibrate our eardrums. The vibrations are transmitted by three tiny bones to the fine hairs of our cochlea, stimulating nerves that allow us to sense the waves and "hear" them as sound. The force, or intensity of the push, determines the volume, and the **frequency** (the number of waves per second) of the pushes is the pitch. Figure 11.3 shows a graph of a pure tone sound wave. The horizontal axis shows time and the vertical axis shows the amount of positive or negative sound pressure.

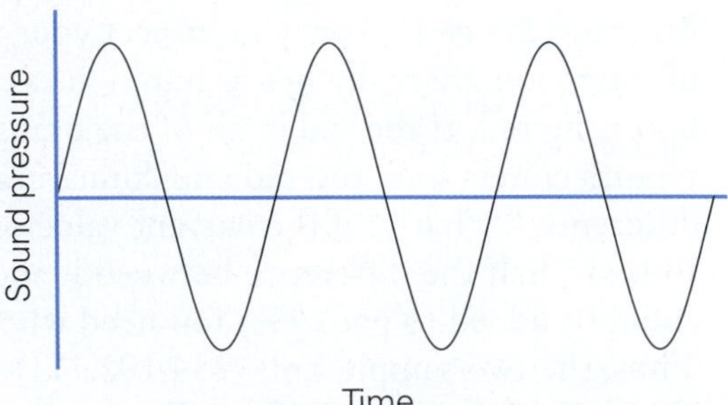

Figure 11.3 Sound wave. The horizontal axis is time; the vertical axis is sound pressure.

From a digitization point of view, the key is that the object vibrates *continuously*, producing a continuously changing wave, which is called **analog** information. As the wave moves past, say, a microphone, the measured pressure changes smoothly. When this pressure variation is recorded directly, as it was originally by Thomas Edison with a scratch on a wax cylinder, and then later with vinyl records, we have a continuous (**analog**) representation of the wave. In principle, all of the continuous variation of the wave is recorded. Digital representations work differently.

Analog to Digital

To digitize continuous information, we must convert to bits. For a sound wave, we can record with a binary number the amount by which the wave is above or below the 0 line at a given point on our graph, that is, the amount of positive or negative sound pressure. But at what point do we measure? There are infinitely many points along the line, too many to record every position of the wave.

Sampling. So, we **sample**, which means we take measurements at regular intervals. The number of samples in a second is called the **sampling rate**, and the faster the rate, the more accurately the wave is recorded (see Figure 11.4).

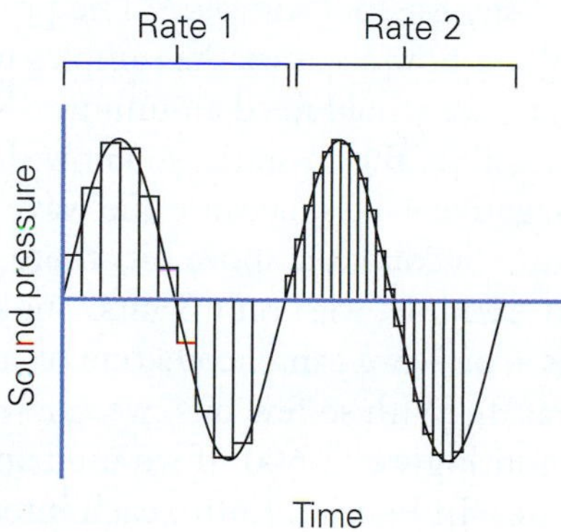

Figure 11.4 Two sampling rates; the rate on the right is twice as fast as that on the left.

How fast a sampling rate? To get a good recording of the wave, we need a sampling rate that is related to the wave's frequency. For example, if a sampling were too slow, sound waves could "fit between" the samples and we'd miss important segments of the sound.

Fortunately, we have guidelines for the sampling rates. In electrical engineering, the **Nyquist rule** says that a sampling rate must be at least twice as fast as the fastest frequency. And what is the fastest frequency we can expect? Because human perception can hear sound up to roughly 20,000 Hz, a 40,000 Hz sampling rate fulfills the Nyquist rule for digital audio recording. For technical reasons, however, a somewhat faster-than-two-times sampling rate was chosen for digital audio, 44,100 Hz.

ADC, DAC. The digitizing process works as follows: Sound is picked up by a microphone (called a *transducer* because it converts the sound wave into an electrical wave). This electrical signal is fed into an **analog-to-digital converter (ADC)**, which takes the continuous wave and samples it at regular intervals, outputting for each sample binary numbers to be written to memory.

The process is reversed to play the sound: The numbers are read from memory into a **digital-to-analog converter (DAC)**, which creates an electrical wave by interpolation between the digital values—that is, filling in or smoothly moving from one value to another. The electrical signal is then input to a speaker, which converts it into a sound wave, as shown in Figure 11.5.

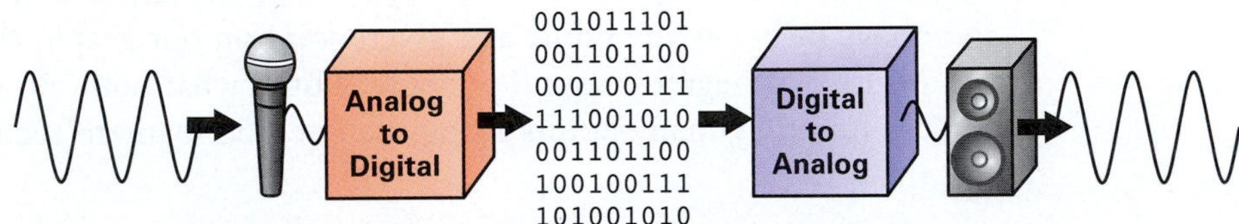

Figure 11.5 Schematic for analog-to-digital and digital-to-analog conversion.

How many bits per sample? The problem of digitizing is solved except for describing how accurate the samples must be. To make the samples perfectly accurate, we would need an unlimited number of bits for each sample, which is impossible. But to start, we know that the bits must represent both positive and negative values, because the wave has both positive and negative sound pressure. Second, the more bits there are, the more accurate the measurement is. For example, with only 3 bits, one of which is used to indicate whether the sign is + or –, we can encode one of four positions in either direction (they align at 0). With so few bits, we can only get an approximate measurement, as shown in Figure 11.6(a). If we used another bit, the sample would be twice as accurate. (In Figure 11.6(b), each interval is half as wide, making the illustrated crossing in the "upper" half of the interval.)

Using more bits yields a more accurate digitization. The digital representation of audio CDs uses 16 bits, meaning that 2^{16} = 65,536 levels are recorded, 2^{15} = 32,768 for positive values and 32,768 for negative values.

fluencyBIT

Unforgiving Minute. How many bits does it take to record a minute of digital audio? There are 60 seconds of 44,100 samples of 16 bits each, times 2 for stereo. That's 84,672,000 bits, or 10,584,000 bytes, more than 10.5 megabytes. An hour is 635 MB!

Advantages of Digital Sound

A key advantage of digital information (as demonstrated in the last section) is that we can compute on the representation.

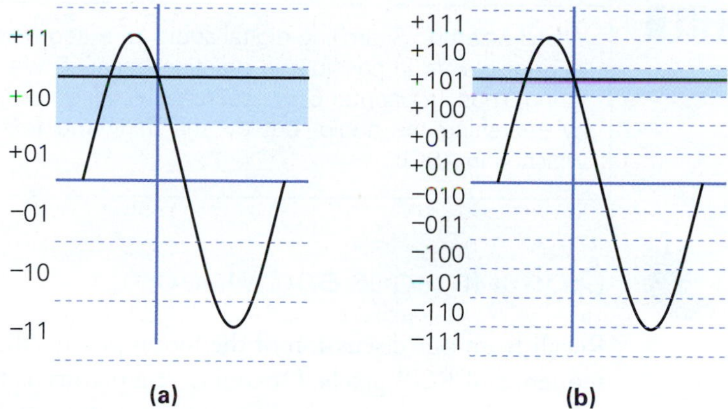

Figure 11.6 (a) Three-bit precision for samples requires that the indicated reading is approximated as +10. (b) Adding another bit makes the sample twice as accurate.

MP3 compression. One computation of value is to *compress* the digital audio; that is, reduce the number of bits needed to represent the information. For example, an orchestra produces many sounds that the human ear can't hear—some are too high and some too low. Our ADC still encodes these frequencies—not to annoy our dog, but simply as part of the encoding process. By computing special functions on the digital audio representation, it's possible to remove these waves without harming the way the audio sounds to us. This is the sort of compression used for MP3. In MP3 we typically get a **compression ratio** of more than 10:1, which means that the number of bits is reduced to less than one-tenth of what it was. So a minute of MP3 music typically takes less than a megabyte to represent. This makes MP3 popular for Internet transmission, because it has lower bandwidth requirements. We discuss bandwidth—the rate at which bits are transmitted—shortly.

Another computation is to "fix" a recording in the same way we "fixed" our moon picture. If someone coughs during a quiet moment of Verdi's *Requiem*, we can remove the offending noise from the recording. Performances can be sped up or slowed down without affecting pitch, volume, and so on.

fluencyBIT

MP3. The "sound track" of a digital video in the MPEG representation is known as MPEG level 3, or MP3.

Reproducing the sound recording. Another key advantage of digital representations over analog is that they can be reproduced exactly. We can copy the file of bits that make up an audio performance without losing a single bit of information. When the original and the copy are played by the same system, they sound exactly the same. With analog representation, the copy is never as exact as the original, and because of wear, a second (or third or hundredth) playing of the same version is never as good as the first. Digital recordings never have these problems as long as the bits remain stable.

fluencyBIT

Word Search. Searching digital audio for a segment of sound, though possible in principle, is impossible in practice because we have to specify the search string. Thus, in Chapter 6, we searched Fuller's *Everything I Know* recordings not by searching the audio, but by searching the textual transcript of the audio, which is in ASCII.

Digital Images and Video

Recall from our discussion of the moon picture that an image is a long sequence of RGB pixels. Of course, the picture is two-dimensional, but we think of the pixels stretched out one row after another in memory, which is one-dimensional. How many pixels are there? For an 8 × 10 image scanned at 300 pixels per inch, there are 80 square inches, each requiring 300 × 300 = 90,000 pixels for a grand total of 7.2 megapixels. At 3 bytes per pixel, it takes 21.6 MB of memory to store one 8 × 10 color image. That's more memory than personal computers came with not so long ago. Sending such a picture across a standard 56 Kb/s phone connection—that's kilo*bits* per second—would take at least 21,600,000 × 8/56,000 = 3,085 seconds, or more than 51 minutes (longer than the average college class). So, how can people without fast connections see screen-size pictures in seconds when surfing the Web?

Image Compression

First, a typical computer screen has fewer than 100 pixels per inch (ppi), not 300, so storing the picture digitized at 100 ppi is a factor of 9 savings immediately. Hand-held devices have even smaller screens. But this isn't quite the simplification we need, first because a 100 ppi picture that size still takes more than five and a half minutes to send, and second because once received, we might want to print the picture, requiring the resolution again. Luckily, electrical engineers invented the JPEG compression scheme. JPEG stands for "Joint Photographic Experts Group," a nickname for an International Standards Organization (ISO) team that guides the development of digital representation of still photographs.

Compression means to change the representation in order to use fewer bits to store or transmit information. For example, faxes are usually long sequences of 0's and 1's that encode where the page is white (0) or black (1). Rather than sending all the 0's and 1's, we can use run-length encoding to take advantage of the fact that the sequences of 0's and 1's tend to be long. **Run-length encoding** uses binary numbers to specify how long the first sequence (run) of 0's is, then how long the following sequence of 1's is, then how long the following sequence of 0's is, and so on. This works best for long, not short, sequences of 0's and 1's, and most of the time run-length compression is a big win.

Run-length encoding is a **lossless compression** scheme, meaning that the original representation of 0's and 1's can be perfectly reconstructed from the compressed version. The first number says how many 0's to write down, the second number says how many 1's to write down next, the third number says how many 0's to write down next, and so forth. The opposite of lossless compression is **lossy compression**, meaning that the original representation cannot be exactly reconstructed from the compressed form. MP3 is lossy because the high notes cannot be recovered—but it doesn't matter since we can't hear them anyway.

fluencyBYTE

Color Table
1 FF 00 00
2 FF FF FF
3 00 FF 00
. . .

Hungary

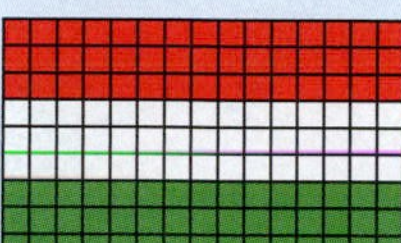

Italy

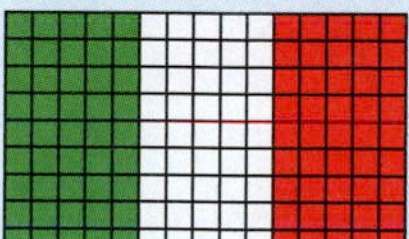

GIF Encoding. The Graphics Interchange Format (GIF) is the recommended encoding for icons, cartoons, and simple art. GIF (pronounced *jif*, according to the inventors, but both soft and hard g are heard) is a lossless encoding scheme that pushes the idea of run-length encoding beyond the runs-of-0s and runs-of-1s idea. There are three ideas that make GIF encodings work. First, the number of colors is limited to 256, which is plenty for simple art. (Transparent is also allowed so the background can show through.) The use of 256 allows for the second idea: Do not represent colors as 3-byte RGB triples, but make a table of colors, put the RGB into the table, and refer to the colors by their one-byte index—their number in the table (see the table at the left). These two ideas give a simple encoding, which records runs of colors.

For example, the file **huFlag**, which gives the size of the image in pixels followed by the list of runs expressed as *length:color* pairs (lc-pairs), where *color* is an index into the table

```
huFlag: [15×9]  45:1, 45:2, 45:3
```

can be decoded into a 15 × 9 pixel Hungarian flag. The flag's first three rows are each 15 consecutive red pixels, making a run—when we stretch out the pixels into a sequence—of 45; the white and green bands are similar. Italy's flag, however, is not encoded as succinctly.

```
itFlag: [15×9]  5:3,5:2,5:1,5:3,5:2,5:1,5:3,5:2,5:1,
                5:3,5:2,5:1,5:3,5:2,5:1,5:3,5:2,5:1,
                5:3,5:2,5:1,5:3,5:2,5:1,5:3,5:2,5:1
```

and requires groups of three of the *length:color* pairs to encode a row in the flag, implying that it needs nine groups of three. This illustrates GIF's preference for horizontal bands of color rather than vertical bands. Computing the costs we have

Direct pixel encoding	9 × 15 pixels × 3 RGB bytes	= 405 bytes
Hungarian Flag	3 lc pairs × 2 bytes + 12 bytes (table)	= 18 bytes
Italian Flag	9 × 3 lc pairs × 2 bytes + 12 bytes (table)	= 66 bytes

showing the advantage of even this simple scheme. (A table entry is 4 bytes.)

The third idea is to add Lempel-Ziv-Welch (LZW) compression, which looks for pixel patterns like 5 green, followed by 5 white, followed by 5 red, and encodes them into the table so the pattern can be indexed, just like the colors. This idea gets the Italian flag to an encoding approximating that of the Hungarian flag. LZW is rather involved, but the idea will obviously help, especially with vertical bands like the Italian flag.

The Portable Network Graphics (PNG) format is emerging as a more advanced lossless replacement for GIF.

JPEG compression is used for still images. Our eyes are not very sensitive to small changes in hue (chrominance), but we are quite sensitive to small changes in brightness (luminance). This means we can store a less accurate description of the hue of a picture (fewer bits) and, although this compression technique is lossy, our eyes won't notice the difference. With JPEG compression we can get a 20:1 compression ratio, compared to an uncompressed still image, without being able to see a difference. For example, the digital image in Figure 11.7(a) has been compressed 45:1 in Figure 11.7(b) with almost no detectable difference on a computer screen; but at 125:1 compression in Figure 11.7(c) the image is ruined—or perhaps is art of a new form.

The idea behind JPEG compression is visible in Figure 11.7(c), which has purposely been excessively compressed. Large areas of similar hues are "lumped together" as the same hue, so a whole area can be colored with a single set of RGB values. If the differences are slight, compression is not noticeable, but if the differences are significant and the regions are large, the quality of the image degrades.

Figure 11.7 Detail from a 493 × 527 image compressed using JPEG. (a) Essentially full resolution (b) 45:1 compression, (c) 125:1 compression. View images at www.aw.com/snyder.

The repeated values can be run-length compressed to reduce the memory required even further. The handy feature of JPEG compression is that we can control the amount of compression: Image compression software gives us a control—a slider or dial, say—so we can choose the amount of compression we want. Fiddling with the control allows us to determine visually how much more compression can be applied without seriously affecting the look of the image.

MPEG Compression Scheme

MPEG, the compression scheme of the Motion Picture Experts Group of the ISO, is the same idea applied to motion pictures. On the one hand, it seems like an easier task because each image—each frame—is not seen for very long, so we should be able to get away with even greater levels of single-image compression. On the other hand, the problem seems more difficult because it takes many stills to make a movie. In MPEG compression, JPEG-type compression is applied to each frame, but then "interframe coherency" is used. Because two consecutive video images are usually very similar, MPEG compression only has to record and transmit the "differences" between frames. This results in huge amounts of compression. So, MPEG and other compression schemes only need moderate amounts of bandwidth, allowing us to watch videos on YouTube and Vimeo.

Optical Character Recognition

On certain toll roads, computers watch cars pass, read their license plates, find the "car's" account in a database, and deduct the toll from its account. It sure beats stopping every few miles to pay another toll! The interesting aspect of this technology is that there is no bar code or electronic transponder; a computer simply recognizes the letters of the license plate. Reading license plates is very easy for humans, but it's a big deal for computers.

Consider some of the difficulties. First, the computer must capture an image of the license plate, but the camera points at the highway and picks up many images that are not license plates—the scene, parts of cars, trailers, litter, road-kill before it is road-kill, and so on. An electronic device called a **frame grabber** recognizes when to "snap" the image and send it to the computer for processing. Assuming a frame with a license plate in it has been snapped, the computer must figure out where in the image it is, because there is no standard location for a license plate on a vehicle, and even if there were, the vehicle could be changing lanes. Looking for letters and numbers doesn't work, because some vehicles display bumper stickers or advertising. Once the license plate is found, recognizing its characters is the most significant challenge, because they're not yet characters, but thousands of pixels.

License plate colors are chosen because of their high contrast (for example, dark letters on a light background). The computer scans groups of pixels looking for edges where the color changes and it forms these into features. A **feature** is a part of a character to be recognized. For example, a *P* might be described by the features of a "vertical stroke" and a "hole" at the top of the stroke, because lines and holes are patterns that can be recognized by noting where color changes. Given the features, a **classifier** matches the features to the alphabet to determine which are close, perhaps finding a strong correlation with *P*, a weaker one with *9*, and an even weaker one with *D*. Finally, after picking the most likely characters, an optical character recognizer checks the context, trying to decide if the combination makes sense; for example, if a license plate exists with that combination of letters. Finding the number in the database, the computer determines that it has read the plate correctly and debits the owner's account.

Ray Kurzweil with the Kurzweil Personal Reader, a 1988 version of his invention.

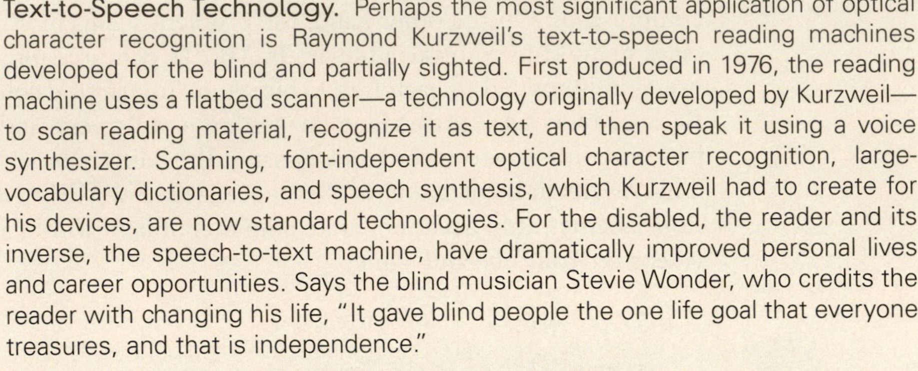

Text-to-Speech Technology. Perhaps the most significant application of optical character recognition is Raymond Kurzweil's text-to-speech reading machines developed for the blind and partially sighted. First produced in 1976, the reading machine uses a flatbed scanner—a technology originally developed by Kurzweil—to scan reading material, recognize it as text, and then speak it using a voice synthesizer. Scanning, font-independent optical character recognition, large-vocabulary dictionaries, and speech synthesis, which Kurzweil had to create for his devices, are now standard technologies. For the disabled, the reader and its inverse, the speech-to-text machine, have dramatically improved personal lives and career opportunities. Says the blind musician Stevie Wonder, who credits the reader with changing his life, "It gave blind people the one life goal that everyone treasures, and that is independence."

Raymond Kurzweil received the National Medal of Technology and the Lemelson-MIT Award for Innovation, which is like a Nobel Prize for inventors. (See the interview following this chapter for observations by Ray Kurzweil.)

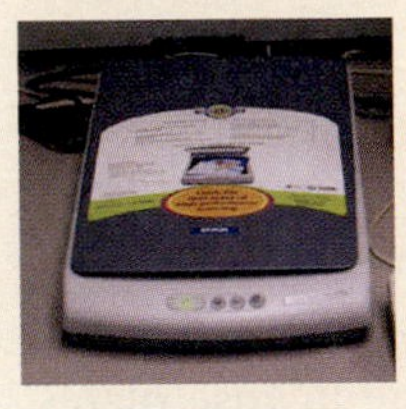

Today's Kurzweil readers utilize flatbed scanners and software running on a personal computer.

fluencyBIT

Beginning Reader. In 1954, J. Rainbow demonstrated an optical character reader that could recognize uppercase typewritten characters at the rate of one letter per minute.

OCR Technology

Optical character recognition (OCR) is a very sophisticated technology that enables a computer to "read" printed characters. OCR's business applications include sorting mail and banking. The U.S. Postal Service uses a system that locates the address block on an envelope or card, reads it in any of 400 fonts, identifies its zip code, generates a nine-digit bar code, sprays the bars on the envelope, sorts it, and, with only a 2 percent error rate, processes up to 45,000 pieces of mail per hour. In banking, the magnetic numbers at the bottom of the check have been read by computers since the 1950s; now OCR is used to read the *handwritten* digits of the numeric check amount to verify that a data entry person has interpreted the amount correctly. That is, the computer checks the person.

Human Character Recognition. As you probably know, those "fuzzy, wiggly" text-deciphering problems we must solve to access some Web sites are called **captchas**. They are there to keep out "spambots," the programs that post ads, bait visitors to malware sites, and deliver other undesirable junk. As annoying as captchas are, they successfully protect sites most of the time.

But it is a battle of wits. While some programmers work hard to make captchas easy for humans to recognize but difficult for computers, the hackers who write spambot programs are working hard to recognize them. It's a war in which the advantage shifts back and forth. Reports say some spambot programs can answer 35 percent of first-generation captchas right. Captchas have gotten "fuzzier" to keep the spambots at bay, but before they get so fuzzy even people can't read them, sites are implementing a new system called **reCaptcha**.

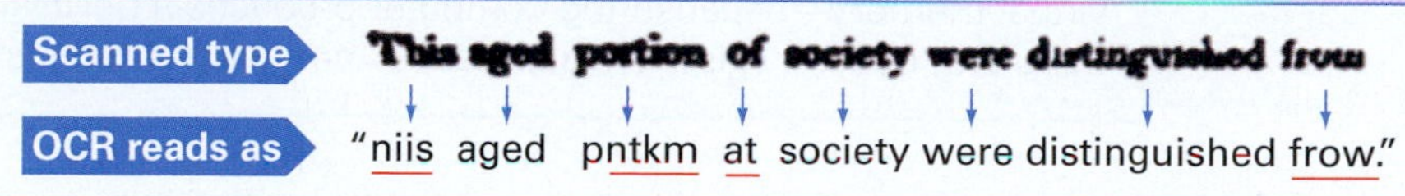

This idea works as follows: Instead of purposely creating fuzzed-up words, reCaptcha uses words from real books with poor printing that OCR systems can't figure out and have problems interpreting. The reCaptcha system asks a group of people two words—one known and one unknown. If those who got the known word right generally agree on the unknown word (a few errors are okay), they are allowed to enter the site, and the reCaptcha can add that word to its "known" word list. This process then helps the digitized book to be corrected.

Virtual Reality: Fooling the Senses

The ultimate form of digital representation is to create an entire digital world. The idea has become known as **virtual reality (VR)**. So far, VR has less to do with representing the world and more to do with fooling our senses into perceiving something that doesn't exist.

Rapidly displaying still images is a standard way to fool our eyes and brain into seeing motion. Virtual reality applies that idea to our other senses and tries to eliminate the cues that keep us grounded in reality. For example, when we see a TV scene of a train coming toward us, we know by various cues, such as peripheral vision, that we're watching a TV; we see the motion but we're not fooled. However, if we're wearing a helmet with a TV in front of each eye that shows the train in a complete scene, gives us three-dimensional vision, and fills in our peripheral vision as well, so that when we move our head we can look at other parts of the scene, the cues are reduced or eliminated. Add high-quality audio in each ear and a treadmill so that we seem to be walking or running through the scene, and it's easy to imagine how a computer can effectively fool us into thinking the train is chasing us.

Haptic Devices

Certain deceptions are more useful. **Haptic devices** are input/output technology for interacting with our sense of touch and feel. For example, a haptic glove enables a computer to detect where our fingers are and to apply force against them. When we bring our fingers close enough together, the glove stops their movement, and leaves us with the feeling of holding something. With haptic gloves and the VR helmet, a computer can depict Legos in space, which, when we grab them, gives us the sensation of holding them and makes us think we are assembling them. When the glove pulls down on our fingers, we think the Legos are heavy, perhaps made of metal. The world is virtual, but credible. Such technology is used to train surgeons for complex operations.

fluencyBIT

Virtual Meaning. The term *virtual* is used often in computing—for example, virtual memory—because the computer produces a believable illusion of something that doesn't exist. **Virtual** means "not actually but just as if."

The Challenge of Latency

The challenge with virtual reality and other sophisticated output devices like video, is for the system to operate fast enough and precisely enough to appear natural. When still images are presented too slowly in an animation, the illusion of motion is lost. When that happens in a VR system—when we turn our head but the scene doesn't smoothly change—we can get dizzy, maybe even sick. Our sensation of touch and feel actually operates faster than the 30 Hz standard for visual perception, closer to 1,000 Hz. Therefore, for the illusion to work, when we "see" our virtual hand going to pick up a virtual Lego, we must "feel" that we've touched it before we "see" that we've touched it.

This phenomenon is called **latency**—the time it takes for information to be delivered. We are familiar with long latencies, such as when Web pages are not delivered instantly, but the phenomenon arises wherever information is generated or transmitted. In most cases, as with Web pages, long latencies just make us wait, but in video, VR, voice communication, and so on, long latency can ruin the medium. Reducing latency is a common engineering goal, but there is an *absolute limit* to how fast information can be transmitted—the speed of light. Eventually, the virtual world is constrained by the physical world.

The Challenge of Bandwidth

Closely related to latency is **bandwidth**—a measure of how much information is transmitted per unit time. Bandwidth is related to latency in that a given amount of information (for example, 100 KB) transmitted with a given bandwidth (for example, 50 KB/s) determines the (best) latency by dividing the amount by the bandwidth; in this case, 100/50 = 2, or 2 seconds of latency. Other delays can extend the latency beyond this theoretical best. Higher bandwidth usually means lower latency. (The rule eventually fails for speed-of-light and switching-delay reasons.) So, faster modems mean that Web pages load faster.

VR is a developing technology. It is still challenged by both latency and bandwidth limitations—it takes many, many bytes to represent a synthetic world. Creating them and delivering them to our senses is a difficult technical problem. Nevertheless, it is an exciting future application of computing.

Bits Are It

Looking back over this and previous chapters, you have seen that 4 bytes can represent many kinds of information, from four ASCII keyboard characters to numbers between zero and about 4 billion. This is not an accident, but rather a fundamental property of information, which we summarize in this principle:

Bias-Free Universal Medium Principle: *Bits can represent all discrete information; bits have no inherent meaning.*

Bits: The Universal Medium

The first half of the principle—all discrete information can be represented by bits—is the universality aspect. Discrete things—things that can be separated from each other—can be represented by bits. At the very least, we can assign numbers to each one and represent those numbers in binary. But, as we saw with color, it's possible to be much smarter. We assigned the RGB colors so the intensity could be increased or decreased using binary arithmetic. This representation of color is much more organized than simply saying, "Black will be 0, purple will be 1, yellow will be 2," and so on. As a result of organizing the representation in a sensible way, we can *easily* compute on it, making changes like brightening the image. Of course, if the information is continuous—that is, if it is analog information like sound—it must first be made discrete by an analog-to-digital conversion. But once digitized, this information, too, can be represented by bits.

Bits: Bias-Free

The second half of the principle—bits have no inherent meaning—is the bias-free aspect. Given a bit sequence

```
0000 0000 1111 0001 0000 1000 0010 0000
```

there is no way to know what information it represents. The meaning of the bits comes entirely from the **interpretation** placed on them by us or by the computer through our programs. For example, the 4 bytes could be a zero byte followed by the RGB intensities (241,8,32) ■. Or, the 4 bytes could be an instruction to add two binary numbers. As a binary number, the bits work out to 15,796,256.

So, bits are bits. What they mean depends on how the software interprets them, which means they work for any kind of information. Storage media need to store one pair of patterns only: 0 and 1. The principle explains why, for example, a single transmission medium—the TCP/IP packet—is all that's needed to deliver any kind of digital information across the Internet to your computer: text, photos, or MP3 tunes. It delivers bits and that's enough.

Bits Are Not Necessarily Binary Numbers

Since the public first became aware of computers, it has been "common knowledge" that computers represent information as binary *numbers*. Experts reinforce this view, but it's not quite right. Computers represent information as bits. Bits can be *interpreted* as binary numbers, as you've seen, which is why the experts are not wrong. But the bits do not always represent binary numbers. They can be interpreted as ASCII characters, RGB colors, or an unlimited list of other things (see Figure 11.8). Programs often perform arithmetic on the bits, as you saw when we modified the moon image; but often they do not, because it doesn't make sense with the intended interpretation of the information. Computers represent information with bits. They are an amazing medium.

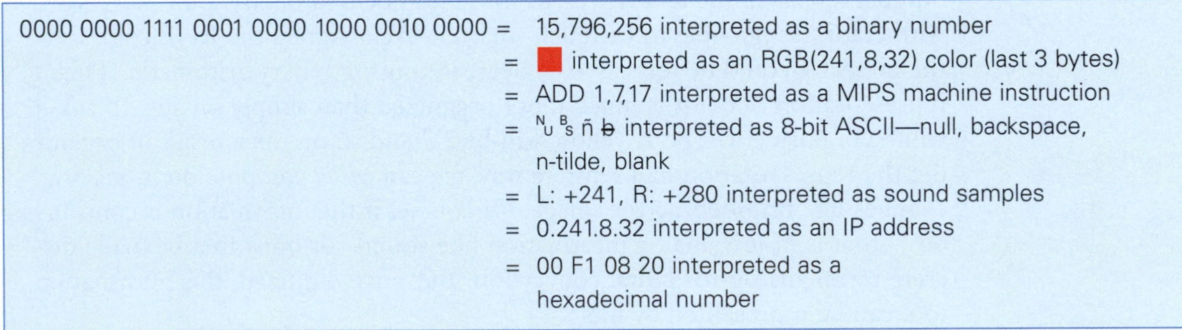

Figure 11.8 Illustration of the principle that "bits are bits." The same 4 bytes shown can be interpreted differently.

Summary

In this chapter we considered how different forms of information are represented in the computer. You learned that:

- With RGB color, each intensity is a 1-byte numeric quantity represented as a binary number.
- Binary representation and binary arithmetic are like they are for decimal numbers, but they are limited to two digits.
- The decimal equivalent of binary numbers is determined by adding their powers of 2 corresponding to 1's.
- We can use arithmetic on the intensities to "compute on the representation," for example, making gray lighter and colorizing a black-and-white picture of the moon.
- When digitizing sound, sampling rate and measurement precision determine how accurate the digital form is; uncompressed audio requires more than 80 million bits per minute.

- Compression makes large files manageable: MP3 for audio, JPEG for still pictures, and MPEG for video. These compact representations work because they remove unnecessary information.
- Optical character recognition is a technology that improves our world.
- Virtual reality illustrates the complexities of conveying information to all of our senses simultaneously.
- The Bias-Free Universal Medium Principle embodies the magic of computers through universal bit representations and unbiased encoding.

Try It Solutions

11.1 The binary number 1 0101 0101 is 256 + 64 + 16 + 4 + 1 = 341.

11.2 The decimal number 86 is `1 0 1 0 1 1 0`.

11.3 The sum is `1 1100 1101`.

Review Questions

Multiple Choice

1. Each RGB color intensity ranges from
   a. 0–15
   b. 0–255
   c. 1–16
   d. 1–256
2. The RGB setting for blue is (0 is off, 1 is on)
   a. 0000 0000 0000 0000 0000 0000
   b. 1111 1111 0000 0000 0000 0000
   c. 0000 0000 1111 1111 0000 0000
   d. 0000 0000 0000 0000 1111 1111
3. Analog information is
   a. discrete
   b. continuous
   c. random
   d. digital
4. According to the Nyquist rule, the sampling rate of sound is roughly
   a. half of what humans can hear
   b. the same as what humans can hear
   c. twice what humans can hear
   d. three times what humans can hear

5. The accuracy of a digitized sound is determined by
   a. the sampling rate
   b. the precision of the sample
   c. the size of the digitized file
   d. all of the above

6. A digital-to-analog converter
   a. changes digital information to analog waves
   b. converts continuous sound to digital sound
   c. converts sound to an electrical signal
   d. sets approximated values

7. MP3 is the sound information of
   a. MPEG movies
   b. all digital movies
   c. all computer sound
   d. all digital computer sound

8. Jessica Simpson's "A Little Bit" is 3 minutes 47 seconds long. How many bits is that?
   a. 1,411,200
   b. 40,042,800
   c. 84,672,000
   d. 320,342,400

9. OCR is used in all of the following areas except
   a. text-to-speech recognition
   b. ZIP code recognition
   c. supermarket checkout
   d. bank account recognition

10. Raymond Kurzweil is known as the inventor of
   a. OCR
   b. text-to-speech recognition
   c. image compression
   d. virtual reality

Short Answer

1. When all the RGB color settings are set to 0, the color displayed is _______.
2. The first digit of a binary number is always _______.
3. _______ is the term used when digital values are converted to create an analog sound.
4. _______ sound removes the highest and lowest samplings as part of its compression algorithm.
5. A(n) _______ is used to convert analog sound to digital values.

6. _______ is a compression scheme for digital video while _______ is the scheme for digital images.
7. _______ is the group that oversees the development of digital media standards.
8. On the computer, _______ means to store or transmit information with fewer bits.
9. A process that allows the computer to "read" printed characters is called _______.
10. Conversion of the written word to speech is called _______.
11. The creation of a digital representation of the world is called _______.
12. JPEG is to still images what _______ is to motion pictures.
13. _______ are used with computers to control a person's sense of touch.
14. _______ is the time it takes information to be delivered.
15. The _______ states that bits can represent all discrete information even though the bits have no meaning of their own.
16. GIF stands for _______.

Exercises

1. Write the algorithm for converting from decimal to binary.
2. Write the algorithm for converting from binary to decimal.
3. Add 1492 and 1776 in binary and display the answer in binary.
4. In binary, add 1011, 1001, 110, and 1100.
5. Convert RGB 200, 200, 200 to hex C8C8C8 by converting it to binary and then to hex.
6. Add 168 and 123 in binary. How many bytes does it take to represent each number? How many bytes are needed for the answer? What happens if there aren't enough bytes to store the answer?
7. Software is now in use that can let you "try on" a dress virtually. What process would be used to change that bright red, taffeta dress into a soft pink? What would be needed to change it to sea foam (light green)? What would it take to turn it into a color to match your eyes?
8. Explain how a picture at 300 pixels per inch could be converted to a picture with 100 pixels per inch.
9. Most music is now sold on CD-ROM. Explain how a singer's voice in the recording studio goes to the earphones on your computer. Why are both processes needed for this to succeed?
10. Digitally, what would need to be done to raise (or lower) a singer's voice an octave?
11. Why are JPEG, MPEG, and MP3 considered algorithms?

12. Convert the following binary numbers to decimal:
    a. 10100101
    b. 11011011
    c. 00100100
    d. 10000000
    e. 11111111
13. Convert the following decimal numbers to binary:
    a. 106
    b. 9
    c. 202
    d. 123
    e. 255
14. Explain RGB as it applies to flat-panel displays. Explain why mixing equal proportions of paint and light produce different results. What do they produce?
15. Give the ASCII symbol corresponding to the binary numbers in Exercise 12. What principle does this question illustrate?

INTERVIEW

with

Ray Kurzweil

Inventor, author, and futurist Ray Kurzweil is a modern-day Thomas Edison. He was the principal developer of many break-through innovations: the first omni-font optical character recognizer, the first print-to-speech reading machine for the blind, the first flatbed scanner, the first text-to-speech synthesizer, the first music synthesizer capable of recreating the grand piano and other orchestral instruments, and the first commercially marketed large-vocabulary speech recognition system. Ray has successfully founded and developed businesses in optical character recognition, music synthesis, speech recognition, reading technology, virtual reality, financial investment, medical simulation, and cybernetic art. His Singularity prediction about rapid technological change is the subject of both his book and movie entitled *The Singularlity Is Near*. In addition to scores of other national and international awards, Ray received the 1999 U.S. National Medal of Technology, the nation's highest honor in technology; was inducted into the National Inventors Hall of Fame in 2002; and received the Arthur C. Clarke Lifetime Achievement Award in 2009. Ray's Web site, **KurzweilAI.net**, is a leading resource on artificial intelligence.

Do you have a "favorite story" to tell about one of your inventions?

We announced the Kurzweil Reading Machine, which was the first print-to-speech reading machine for the blind, on January 13, 1976. I remember this date because Walter Cronkite, the famous news anchor for CBS News, used it to read his signature sign-off that evening "And that's the way it was, January 13, 1976." It was the first time that he did not read this famous phrase himself.

I was subsequently invited to demonstrate this new reading machine on the *Today Show*. We only had one working model and we were nervous about demonstrating it on live television since there was always the possibility of technical glitches. They responded that it was live or nothing.

We arrived at the *Today Show* studio very early in the morning and set up the reading machine. Sure enough, it stopped working a couple of hours before show time. We tried various easy fixes that failed to rectify the problem. So our chief engineer frantically took the machine apart. With electrical pieces scattered across the studio floor, Frank Field, who was to interview me, walked by and asked if there was a problem. We said that we were just making a few last minute adjustments.

Our chief engineer put the machine back together, and it still was not working. Then, in a time-honored tradition of repairing delicate technical equipment, he picked up the machine and slammed it into the table. It worked perfectly from that moment on, and the live demonstration and interview went without a hitch.

Stevie Wonder happened to catch me on the broadcast, and called our office wanting to stop by and pick up his own reading machine. Our receptionist did not believe it was really the legendary musical artist, but she put him through anyway. We were just finishing up our first production unit, so we rushed that to completion. Stevie stopped by, stayed several hours to learn how to use it, and went off with his new Kurzweil Reading Machine in a taxi. That was the beginning of a [more than] thirty-year friendship that continues to this day. A few years later, Stevie was instrumental in my launching Kurzweil Music Systems, Inc.

Your inventions range from the Kurzweil 250 to a nutritional program that cured you of type 2 Diabetes. Is there a tie that binds your many inventions?

My original, and still primary, area of technology interest and expertise is a field called "pattern recognition," which is the science and art of teaching computers to recognize patterns. It turns out that the bulk of human intelligence is based on our remarkable ability to recognize patterns such as faces, visual objects, speech, and music. Most of my technology projects are related to recognizing patterns, for example, character recognition and speech recognition. Even my work in music synthesis was influenced by pattern recognition. We had to answer the question as to what patterns cause humans to recognize sounds as coming from a particular type of instrument, such as a grand piano.

I quickly realized that timing was important for my inventions, and began to develop mathematical models of how technology develops over time. This endeavor took on a life of its own. By using these models, I was able to make predictions about technologies ten to thirty years into the future, and beyond. From these efforts, I realized that the twenty-first century was going to be an extraordinary time in advancing human civilization. This insight has been a major motivation for me to find the means to live long enough, and in good health, to experience this remarkable century.

I also realized that one of the areas of technology that is accelerating is health and medical technology. Therefore the tools we will have to keep ourselves healthy will grow in power and sophistication in the years ahead. It is important, therefore, to keep ourselves healthy using today's knowledge so that we are in good shape to take advantage of the full flowering of the biotechnology revolution, which is now in its early stages.

Many of your past predictions about the future of technology have "come true." How is it that you are able to make such specific and accurate predictions?

Most futurists simply make predictions without a well-thought-out framework or methodology. I have been studying technology trends for more than a quarter century, and have been developing detailed mathematical models of how technology in different fields evolves. I have a team of people gathering data to measure the key features and capabilities of technologies in a wide array of fields, including computation, communications, biological technologies, and brain reverse engineering. From this work, it has become clear that technologies, particularly those that deal with information, are growing at a double exponential rate (that is, the rate of exponential growth is itself growing exponentially). Typically, an information-based technology at least doubles its capability for the same unit cost every year.

The other important issue is that very few people realize that the pace of technical change, what I call the paradigm shift rate, is itself accelerating. We are doubling the pace of technical change every decade. I once spoke at a conference celebrating the fiftieth anniversary of the discovery of the structure of DNA. We were all asked what changes we foresaw for the next fifty years. With very few exceptions, the other speakers used the amount of change in the last fifty years as a guide to the amount of change we will see in the next fifty years. But this is a faulty assumption. Because the rate of change is accelerating, we will see about thirty times as much change in the next fifty years as we saw in the last half century.

In your book *The Age of Spiritual Machines,* you foresee a future where computers have exceeded human intelligence. How and when do you expect this to come about?

We can separate this question into two questions: When will computers have the computational capacity (the "hardware" capability) of the human brain? Secondly, when will we have the content and methods (the "software") of human intelligence?

In my book *The Age of Spiritual Machines*, which came out in 1999, I said we would achieve the computational capacity of the human brain for about $1,000 by 2019. I estimate this capacity to be about 100 billion neurons, times about 1,000 interneuronal connections per neuron, times 200 calculations per second per connection, or about 20 million billion calculations per second. This was considered a controversial projection in 1999, but there has been a sea change in perspective on this issue since that time. Today, it is a relatively mainstream expectation that we will have sufficient computational resources by 2019. Computers are at least doubling their speed and memory capacity every year, and even that rate is accelerating.

The more challenging issue is the software of intelligence. A primary source of what I call the "templates" of human intelligence is the human brain itself. We are already well along the path of reverse engineering the brain to understand its principles of operation. Here also we see exponential advance. Brain scanning technologies are doubling their resolution, bandwidth, and price-performance every year.

Knowledge about the human brain, including models of neurons and neural clusters, is doubling every year. We already have detailed mathematical models of several dozen of the several hundred regions that comprise the human brain. I believe it is a conservative projection to say that we will have detailed models of all the regions of the brain by the mid-2020s.

By 2029, we will be able to combine the subtle powers of pattern recognition that the human brain excels in, with several attributes in which machine intelligence already exceeds human capabilities. These include speed, memory capacity, and the ability to instantly share knowledge. Computers circa 2029, possessing human levels of language understanding, will be able to go out on the Web and read and absorb all of the available literature and knowledge.

Will these computers of the future have human emotions?

Indeed, they will. Emotional intelligence is not a side issue to human intelligence. It is actually the most complex and subtle thing we do. It is the cutting edge of human intelligence. If a human had no understanding of human emotions, we would not consider that person to be operating at a normal human level. The same will be true for machines. Already, there is significant interest in teaching computers about human emotions: how to detect them in humans and how to respond to them appropriately. This is important for the next generation of human-machine interfaces. As we reverse engineer the human brain, and understand how the different regions process information, we will gain an understanding of what our emotions mean. A very important benefit of this endeavor will be greater insight into ourselves.

What drawbacks do you foresee for the future you envision?

Technology is inherently a double-edged sword. All of the destruction of the twentieth century (for example, two world wars) was amplified by technology. At the same time, we are immeasurably better off as a result of technology. Human life expectancy was 37 years in 1800 and 50 years in 1900. Human life was filled with poverty, hard labor, and disease up until fairly recently.

We are now in the early stages of the biotechnology revolution. We are learning the information processes underlying life and disease, and are close to developing new treatments that will overcome age-old diseases, such as cancer, heart disease, and diabetes. This same knowledge, however, can also empower a terrorist to create a bioengineered pathogen. There is no easy way to separate the promise from the peril, as both stem from the same technology. We will see similar dilemmas with nanotechnology (technology in which the key features are less than 100 nanometers) and with artificial intelligence.

The answer, I believe, is to substantially increase our investment in developing specific defensive technologies to protect society from these downsides. We can see a similar battle between promise and peril in the area of software viruses. Although we continue to be concerned about software viruses, the defensive technologies have been largely successful. Hopefully we will be able to do as well with biotechnology and other future technologies.

Could you offer some advice to students with regard to keeping pace with information technology and perhaps with regard to inventing it?

This is a very exciting time to be embarking on a career in science and technology. The pace of change and the expansion of new knowledge is greater than at any time in history, and will continue to accelerate. The impact of science and technology goes substantially beyond these subjects themselves. Ultimately, new technological advances will transform every facet of human life and society.

I would advise students to:

1. Obtain a strong background in math, as this is the language of science and technology. Math also represents a way of thinking that leads to discovery and understanding.
2. Become an ardent student of technology and technology trends. Build your inventions for the world of the future, not the world you see in front of you today.
3. Focus on a particular area of science or technology that particularly fascinates you. The days when one person could master all of science and technology are long gone. However, as you focus, don't put on the blinders to what is going on in fields around you.
4. Follow your passion.

3

PART

Data and Information

Chapter

3 PART

Introduction

OUR UNDERSTANDING of information technology deepens as we become more versatile users. With greater knowledge and wider experience, it's wise to consider the bigger picture, noticing how IT can be used and abused. In Part 3 we discuss topics such as netiquette (etiquette for network users), viruses, and passwords.

We will focus on spreadsheets and databases—how they store, structure, and deliver information that interests us. Knowing how to create our own databases helps us organize our own information, but it also makes us more effective at accessing other databases.

Two important topics covered in Part 3 are especially active in the "public debate" about IT: privacy and security. We present the technical description of each topic, as well as both sides of the debate. Every IT user is personally interested in privacy and security. It is important to be informed.

Social Implications of IT

Computers in Polite Society

12

chapter

learning objectives

- Describe several tips associated with netiquette and explain the benefits of following them
- Explain the phrase "expect the unexpected" and how that advice helped in handling an email bug
- List some ways your computer can become infected with malicious software
- Name three permitted/not permitted uses of licensed software
- Explain what rights are granted to material that is copyrighted

While modern technology has given people powerful new communications tools, it apparently can do nothing to alter the fact that many people have nothing useful to say.

—LEE GOMES, *SAN JOSE MERCURY NEWS*

THIS CHAPTER concerns the use of computers in social settings, but it's not going to discuss the basics of cell phones, text messaging, email, video chat (iChat, Skype), blogs, YouTube and Flickr, Facebook, MySpace, Twitter, rating sites (Digg, del.icio.us), or other such activities. You are using them already; no explanation is necessary. We *will* discuss how to use email well and other guidelines to be good online citizens, habits that are known collectively as netiquette. And we discuss how to protect your online privacy. As you enjoy the social benefits of the Internet, however, others in the online society do not share your interest in friendship and fun. They have goals like burying you in spam, spying on your sensitive information, taking over your computer, defrauding you, and other decidedly anti-social behavior. This chapter is concerned with dealing with those hazards, so the social use of computing continues to be very enjoyable.

The original developers of the Internet envisioned it as an important tool for commerce, government, education, the military, and public service. (Recall that the first top-level domain names were .com, .gov, .edu, .mil, .int, .org, and .net.) The developers formed a tightly knit community of a few hundred people in which the members were respectful, trustworthy, and interdependent; there was little abuse or bad behavior. Of course, they used the Internet for social purposes, and they played games online. Nevertheless, they were probably all shocked to see the explosion of social applications that evolved on the Internet when the user community expanded from hundreds to hundreds of millions of people. With the expansion, things had to change.

Out on Good Behavior

In normal society, people learn proper behavior from their families, relatives, religion, and community. Acting badly offends others and makes them mad. They remember the bad behavior, and punish the offenders in large and small ways. "Acceptable behavior" evolves to smooth social interactions. It's easier to live with people who recognize a basic level of courtesy and respect. It's social pressure, and it works.

The online world we live in today is different in many ways. First, our range of interactions is much broader than it was when we lived in villages; we may never meet face-to-face with the people we interact with online. Second, our families and relatives influence our online behavior very little, and many of our families are not well equipped to teach good online behaviors. Third, we can be anonymous on the Internet. If no one knows who we are, we can behave as badly as we want. Right?

It is true that people can get away with very bad behavior on the Internet with few consequences. But there are two reasons not to "be as bad as we can be." First, we are not entirely anonymous online. Law enforcement can use legal means to gain access to the identities of people who are committing crimes on the Internet. It is possible with the help of Internet service providers (ISPs) and companies like Microsoft to figure out who's who online. Second, we all want to enjoy the benefits the Internet gives us. So in the same way that the need to live together socially caused us to develop standards of civilized behavior, our daily uses of the Internet also encourage us to behave within bounds of reasonable behavior.

Netiquette

Etiquette—guidelines for proper behavior in social situations—applies to our social interactions on the Internet, too. It's called **netiquette**. It was originally developed for email use, but now it is interpreted more broadly to be civilized behavior in any of the social settings on the Internet. Table 12.1 gives some standard guidelines.

Netiquette matters because the people we interact with online are mostly our friends, family, and coworkers. These are the people we normally treat well in nonelectronic situations, so it is wise to be aware of how our digital interactions might be misinterpreted or have an adverse impact.

Specific Guidelines for Email

Our personal use of electronic communication (SMS, Twitter, Facebook) can be guided by the persona we wish to project to our friends. But at work, we should follow rules of respect and good behavior so as to meet general business practice. Here are some additional habits to adopt.

Ask about one topic at a time. An email message requiring a response from the receiver should treat only one topic. For example, don't ask your boss when your raise begins in the same email that you ask if you left your brown sweater in his office. Because most of us handle one matter at a time, the reader of a one-topic message can respond to the matter and then delete or archive the mail. With multiple topics, it is likely that one or more will be dropped or ignored. For example, you'll find out you did forget the sweater, but your request for a start date of your raise might be ignored. The subject line of the email can describe that one topic. Email is cheap; it costs no more to send two messages than one. But managing one-topic messages is much easier for everyone.

Table 12.1 Guidelines for responsible behavior on the Internet

Guidelines	Responsible Behaviors
Act as if you are there in person	Display your best side: In online interactions don't say or do things that you wouldn't say or do to the person face-to-face.
Remember that you aren't there in person	In face-to-face conversation, facial expressions, pauses, volume, emphasis, body language, and so on convey meaning that is not available in email or messaging. Explain yourself more completely. Avoid writing that can be misunderstood—"I can't praise her cooking enough"—and use notations like smilies—**emoticons**—to flag humor. Before sending or posting very emotional content, sleep on it.
One-on-one talks	Never forward email without the sender's permission.
Email isn't private	Your school, company, or ISP may have access to your email. Email can be subpoenaed for court; only put in email what you'd write on a postcard.
Delete doesn't remove content	Because copies are kept (to recover from crashes), most Net content is still accessible after it has been deleted. Watch what you post—your boss or your next boss may see it. Think especially of MySpace and Facebook pages.
Don't waste your Net friend's resources	Sending long rambling "musings" or huge image files wastes your friend's time and slows network connections or possibly server space. Be thoughtful. Don't send at all or warn about the size in the Subject line.
Avoid flame wars	**Flame wars** are nasty email exchanges in which a few people fight, but cc a group of others. Don't continue a flame war; contact a flamer separately.
Confirm addressees	Before clicking **Send** on an email, check that the "To" list is correct. If you accidentally send a personal reply to a group—you clicked **Reply All** when you wanted **Reply**—follow up immediately with an apology.
It's a different time there	Don't expect immediate responses; the recipient may live in another time zone and may be busy with other activities, like sleeping. When reading email, remember that the sender might have sent several messages. Check the message list before replying; there may be a "forget it" message.

Include context. An all too common email reply, unfortunately, is "Yes." We all like to get positive email, of course, but the unfortunate part is we've forgotten the question. The subject line is no help; it reads, *Re: Question*.

Any email-reading software worth two bits gives you a way to include the original message in a reply. Including the question with the reply is a courtesy. It provides the context for your answer, so you can give a short reply without leaving the receiver clueless. To avoid the email history becoming large, it's courteous to limit the context to the most recent message or to the most relevant point.

Use an automated reply. When you are unable to answer your email for a few days, it is polite to set up an **automated reply** saying you are away, and perhaps indicating when you expect to read your email again. The automated reply, called a **vacation message** in the earliest mailers, is generally available from your mail server. The benefit of using the vacation message is that readers know why you're not responding. Otherwise, they may think you are lazy or that they are being ignored or snubbed.

Answer a backlog of emails in reverse order. When we keep up with reading our email, we usually answer messages in the order they're received. But if we haven't answered our email for a while and our inbox is brimming, it's best to answer email in *reverse* order of its arrival. Many of the oldest messages will have "timed-out." That is, we may not have to answer a message because a more recent follow-up message supersedes it. Or we may receive a "forget it" message sent by someone who received our vacation message and realized they couldn't wait for a reply. Not answering such email saves time and saves our correspondent aggravation. For example, when your boss sends a message asking for everyone's availability for a future meeting, it is unnecessary and somewhat embarrassing to reply when a later message sets the time for the meeting. Answering email in reverse time-order allows us to read these resolution messages before we read the original. There's only one caution: Avoid the temptation to quit and never finish reading the backlog.

Clarifying ownership of email. As a general rule, most people assume that when they send email, it is private. It is impolite and inconsiderate to forward email without getting the sender's permission. Asking permission to forward email gives the sender a chance to review the message to decide if there is something in it that should not be passed along. The sender's opinion is important because although the mail may look innocent to you, other readers may react differently and the sender may know that. Notice that most email in the United States is *not* a private conversation. Companies, colleges, or other organizations can (under most circumstances) review emails sent or *received* by the members of their organization; that is, *your* personal email account might be private, but your readers' may not be (see Chapter 13).

Use targeted distribution lists. There are many good reasons, such as changing your address, for sending the same email message to many recipients. But keeping a single list of all people you've ever exchanged email with and then forwarding the latest lame Internet joke is just a bad idea. Offices often have standard email lists for different business units, but if not, you should set up lists for those units that you must send group mail to.

By observing the following rules and general courtesies, your email can be more pleasant and effective.

- ✓ *Ask about one topic at a time.*
- ✓ *Include context.*
- ✓ *Use an automated reply.*
- ✓ *Answer a backlog of email in reverse order.*
- ✓ *Get the sender's permission before forwarding email.*
- ✓ *Use targeted distribution lists.*

Expect the Unexpected

Expecting the unexpected is a valuable survival skill in life and in computing. When something unexpected happens, we should not only notice it, but also we should ask ourselves "Why did that happen?" or "What's going on?" By wondering about the unexpected event and analyzing what might have caused it, we may discover an advantage, avoid harm, learn something new, or, perhaps most important, save ourselves from looking like total dummies! Because it is difficult to discuss "the unexpected" in general terms, consider a specific situation in which analyzing the unexpected is beneficial.

A Mailing List Handler Has a Bug

Occasionally—meaning every year or so in my experience—a mailing list application for a large (1,000 names or more) mailing list fails. (Another name for a mailing list application is a **list-server**.) The problem could be a bug in the mailing list software, but more likely the list's **moderator**—the person responsible for deciding what is sent out to the mailing list—could have misconfigured it. Whatever the cause, there is a more-or-less typical sequence of messages to everyone on that mailing list that reveals that some people don't expect the unexpected.

The event begins innocuously enough with a message such as

From: "Sue Marie Acker" <smacker@thermalmail.com>
Subject: Re: Topic of most recent mailing to this list
To: Mondo_list

Remove me from this list, please.

A few similar messages of this sort follow. This is an unexpected event. Mailing lists are for sending information from one source, say, an organization, to many receivers. This kind of mail looks like communication from a *receiver* back to the source, and then back to all receivers. Unexpected.

Though there are many systems for managing mailing lists, and we probably don't understand how they work, no software for handling mailing lists should send requests for removal from the list to the entire list. They should probably be sent to the moderator or intercepted by someone else managing the list. Something is wrong here. It could be in the protocol for removing from the list, or it could be something else. *Everyone* on the mailing list should have noticed this and given it some thought. The moderator, especially, should have noticed it, fixed it, and sent a short apology.

But because he or she didn't fix it, the next message is

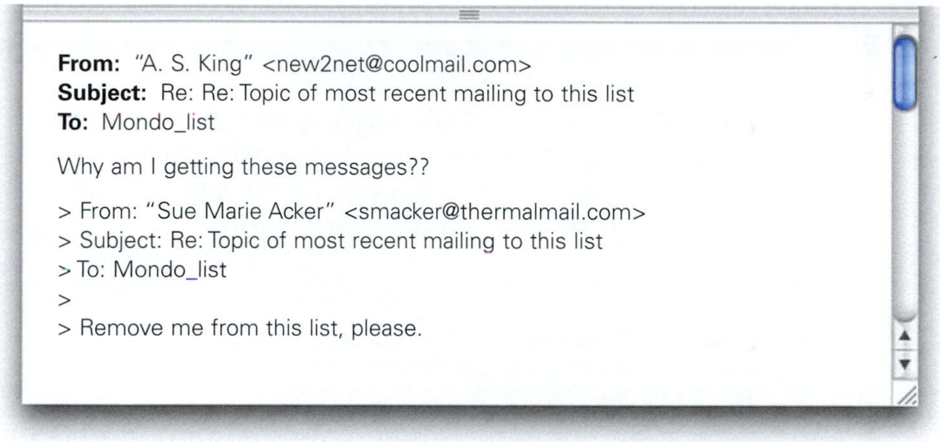

From: "A. S. King" <new2net@coolmail.com>
Subject: Re: Re: Topic of most recent mailing to this list
To: Mondo_list

Why am I getting these messages??

> From: "Sue Marie Acker" <smacker@thermalmail.com>
> Subject: Re: Topic of most recent mailing to this list
> To: Mondo_list
>
> Remove me from this list, please.

From this mail we can conclude that the problem is not simply with the "unsubscribe" feature, the facility that removes people from a mailing list. (The fault might have been limited to "unsubscribe" because all previous mail concerned that issue.) Now it is clear that the mailing list handler is reflecting all of the mail it receives. If we send anything to this list, everyone will get it. The moderator is not intercepting replies to the list. So, until someone fixes the problem, the only way to avoid getting more email is if everyone stops sending to this list.

At this point everyone should have figured out the situation, and there should be no further traffic. That is what would happen if everyone were expecting the unexpected. (It would be good if a civic-minded individual sent a private email to the moderator pointing out the problem.) Nevertheless, there follow several more messages of the form

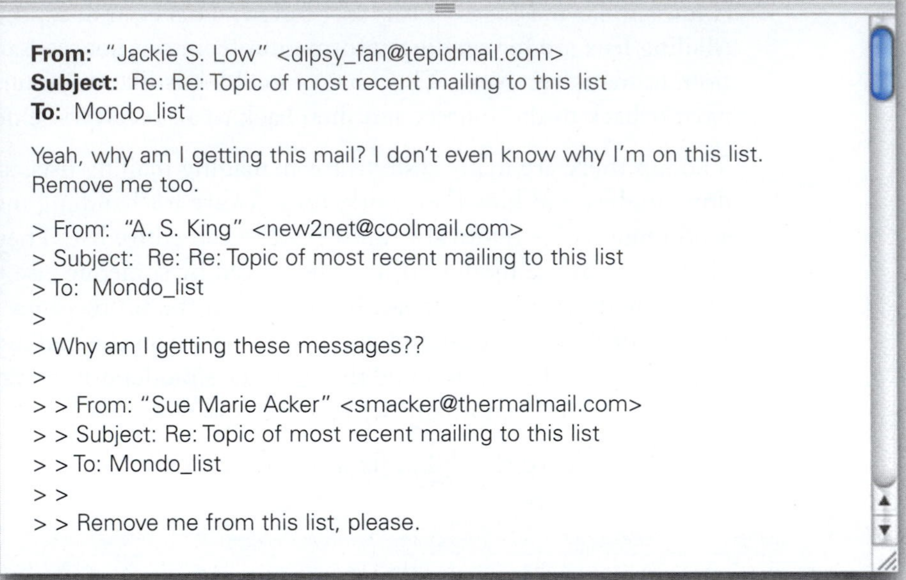

From: "Jackie S. Low" <dipsy_fan@tepidmail.com>
Subject: Re: Re: Topic of most recent mailing to this list
To: Mondo_list

Yeah, why am I getting this mail? I don't even know why I'm on this list. Remove me too.

> From: "A. S. King" <new2net@coolmail.com>
> Subject: Re: Re: Topic of most recent mailing to this list
> To: Mondo_list
>
> Why am I getting these messages??
>
> > From: "Sue Marie Acker" <smacker@thermalmail.com>
> > Subject: Re: Topic of most recent mailing to this list
> > To: Mondo_list
> >
> > Remove me from this list, please.

After a dozen of these "Yeah, what's up with this?" types of messages, someone gets completely frustrated with those who don't seem to be figuring out that continuing to send email to the list prolongs everyone's agony. That person—actually there are usually several—writes

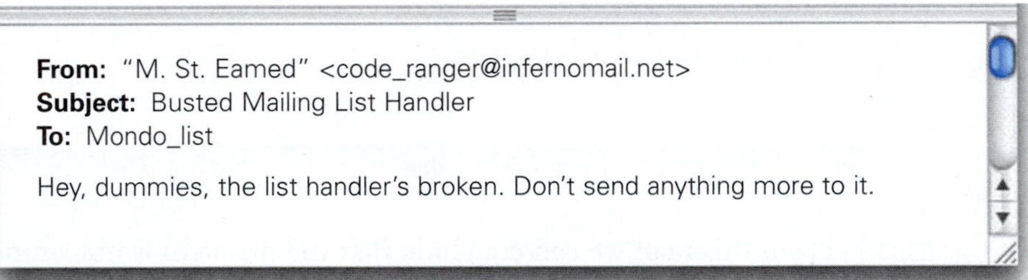

From: "M. St. Eamed" <code_ranger@infernomail.net>
Subject: Busted Mailing List Handler
To: Mondo_list

Hey, dummies, the list handler's broken. Don't send anything more to it.

This will be immediately followed by a message of the form

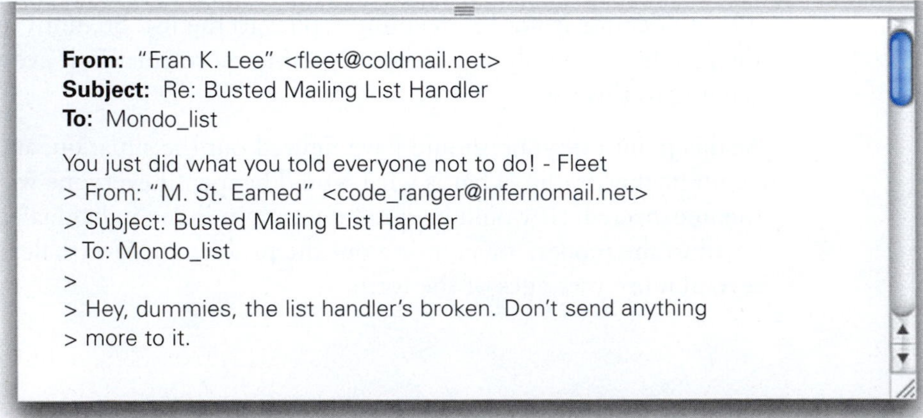

From: "Fran K. Lee" <fleet@coldmail.net>
Subject: Re: Busted Mailing List Handler
To: Mondo_list

You just did what you told everyone not to do! - Fleet
> From: "M. St. Eamed" <code_ranger@infernomail.net>
> Subject: Busted Mailing List Handler
> To: Mondo_list
>
> Hey, dummies, the list handler's broken. Don't send anything
> more to it.

Or perhaps the message will read, "I find it offensive getting messages calling me a dummy." Then other frustrated people will jump in with comments pointing out that any person who sends email to a broken email list claiming to be offended at being called a dummy probably is a dummy, and so on. This can go on for dozens of messages before the person responsible for the mailing list finally gets it fixed. Keep in mind that the people sending these messages are on the mailing list because they have something in common, which means that they probably know each other. How embarrassing!

The point about this email history is that it should have been obvious very quickly (with A. S. King's message, or earlier) that something unusual was happening. With a moment's thought, people should have realized how to act in a rational manner even though they had no way of knowing exactly what was wrong. Clearly most of the people involved in the event did so; otherwise there would have been *much more* such email.

The lesson to be learned is not simply to be alert to mailing list handler bugs, but to be alert to unusual events of any kind at any time. Then, think about them. At the very least, it could save you some embarrassment.

fluency ALERT

Unexpectedly Flaky. Occasionally a familiar application that you use a lot will do something strange, such as slowing down, "forgetting" changes, misaligning the cursor, or failing in other ways. Such behaviors are unexpected, and often immediately precede a crash. When you notice your software "acting strange," act immediately: save *to a new file name*, exit, and restart. The problem is usually just with the software, but it could be with the instance; a new file name avoids overwriting your previously saved version.

Creating Good Passwords

One day electronic hardware may reliably detect who we are when we come in contact with a computer, and there will be no need for **passwords**. Meanwhile, passwords are a key part of our daily interaction with computers. This section considers selecting, changing, and managing passwords as well as password principles that can make your daily computer usage easier. Chapter 13 deals with the related topic of computer security.

The Role of Passwords

The point of a password, of course, is to limit computer or software system access to only those who know a not-likely-to-be-guessed sequence of keyboard characters. So, obviously, it is necessary to select such a sequence. We'll discuss how to choose an effective password momentarily.

Breaking into a computer without a password. But couldn't one computer break into another if we program it to try all passwords algorithmically until it finds the true password? Computers are surely fast enough, but they're not that dumb. Or, rather, the software running on them won't let potential users (other computers) try zillions of passwords. The software for the login protocol may include a delay when notifying the user that the password is wrong. The delay is not particularly noticeable to a human user, but it slows down the login protocol to the point that it is too slow to try zillions of passwords. Alternatively, software may notice long sequences of failed attempts to type the correct password and take some action. Of course, humans sometimes produce a sequence of failed attempts because they are agitated or groggy or try to log in using a pencil held in their teeth while holding a coffee cup in one hand and a Danish pastry in the other. So, login protocols allow several password failures before deciding that someone is trying to break in.

Forgetting a password. Another curiosity about passwords is that if we forget ours and ask the system's administrator to find out what it is, he or she can't usually tell us. How can that be? Don't they have complete access—known as **superuser** or **administrator** status—to all of the computers, and so aren't they able to look up passwords? Yes, but the actual password is not stored on the computer.

When a new password is created, it is scrambled or encrypted and then stored in that form. The new password is thrown away. Then, at login, the password is scrambled using the same algorithm used originally when the new password was set. The two scrambled sequences are then compared. If they are the same, the right password must have been given. If not, the password must have been wrong. This technique is used so that passwords are not stored as "clear text" that someone can steal. How the scrambling is done is explained in Chapter 13. When you ask for your forgotten password, the superuser creates a new password and forces its scrambled form to replace the old one. You then use the new password.

Guidelines for Selecting a Password

When we receive a new computer account, we are usually given an automatically generated password that is a scramble of letters and digits and possibly special characters: `rU4Uw2?gR8`. And we are told to change it so that we'll select something we can remember. Changing it to our girlfriend's name wouldn't be a good idea because that's too easily guessed, at least by our friends. But what is a good choice?

Passwords are better if they are longer, at least eight characters, and if they contain a mix of uppercase and lowercase letters, numbers, and, if allowed, punctuation characters. It's better to pick a sequence that is not found in dictionaries and has no "obvious" personal association, such as your name. And passwords are better if they are easy to remember. These may seem like difficult constraints to fulfill, but it's still pretty easy to think of a good password in only a few minutes.

Guidelines for Creating Good Passwords, heuristics (pretty good rules) that tend to produce effective passwords.

- *Select a personally interesting topic, such as a parent, favorite movie, or best travel destination, and always select passwords related to that topic. Because you will use many passwords, selecting from one topic helps you to remember them.*
- *Develop a password from a phrase rather than a single word. The phrase must be memorable to you. It will be compressed according to the next rule.*
- *Encode the password phrase, trying to make it short (8–12 characters) by abbreviating, and by replacing letters or syllables with alternative characters, spellings, or encodings that include numbers and uppercase letters.*

The goal is to create letter strings (consisting of a mixture of numbers and letters) that are not in dictionaries.

For example, if you are using your father as the topic and your chosen phrase is his alma mater, Oxford University, then:

Oxford University	→ OxfordU	Shorten standard abbreviation
	→ Ox4dU	Replace *for* with "4"
	→ Ohx4dyou	Replace *O* with "Oh," U with "you"

The result doesn't make much sense to someone who hasn't seen the construction process, but it wouldn't be difficult for you to remember.

If your topic is your favorite movie, *Gone with the Wind*, you might use the following process to construct a password:

Gone with the Wind	→ GWTW	Shorten, standard abbreviation
	→ G2uTW	Replace *W* with "2u"
	→ G2uT2U	Replace *W* with "2U"
	→ G2uTdosU	Replace 2 with Spanish "dos"

The last replacement is not really needed because the password is already pretty obscure, but it illustrates a way to make passwords longer. And the use of Spanish emphasizes that passwords can build on any part of your knowledge, heritage, or background.

Finally, if you are using your vacation to Australia as your topic, and your phrase is *Surfing In Australia*, you might come up with this:

Surfing In Australia	→ SurfingInOz	Australia is often abbreviated "Oz"
	→ SurfinInOz	Drop *g* as in slang
	→ Surf2inOz	Replace *inIn* with "2in"
	→ sirf2inOz	Replace *Sur* with "sir"
	→ sirF2inOz	Introduce a capital for variety

It is possible to be too clever, so it's smart to stop the process before your password gets too obscure. After all, you must be able to remember it!

Total Recall. It might seem that remembering such obscure passwords is difficult, but it usually is not. If you type them daily, they come to mind quickly. It's almost as if your "fingers memorize them." If you use them, say, only monthly for your credit card account, following these heuristics will help you remember how you made them.

Notice the importance of the topic. The topic provides context to narrow the possibilities for us personally, serving as a memory aid. If we're changing from having used G2uT2U for a year, a password based on phrases like "Frankly, my dear" or "Rhett and Scarlet," suitably transformed, should be easy to remember. And even if (foolishly) we tell someone our password, and (more foolishly) explain what it means, and (most foolishly) describe the topic from which we select passwords, the topic is probably rich enough that we can still use it. There are most likely enough phrases and enough variations that we can still create obscure passwords.

This process is intended to produce an obscure password (not in a dictionary) that should be easy to recall without having to write it down. But should it be written down anyway? It's a personal choice. Some people are not comfortable unless their password is written down somewhere. Others are sure they'll remember it under any circumstances, even after an all-night party at a brewery.

12.1 Create a Password. Using transformations like those in the examples, change the word *password* into a good password. Limit yourself to three transformations.

Changing Passwords

Passwords should be changed periodically. Organizations often have a policy as to how often a password must be changed, and sometimes there are security intrusions that cause administrators to ask that passwords be changed. Whether you should change your password depends on how likely it is that the password has become known and how important it is to keep the information secure. If you haven't changed your password in a year, it may be time to consider changing it.

Every system that uses passwords has software to change them, though we usually don't notice it when we don't need it. Check the GUI where you enter your password for the option to change it. If that doesn't work, do a search for "password" with the online *Help* facility. These systems typically ask for your current password, your new password, and a second copy of your new password. The second copy is simply a way of checking for a typing error. If they match, the password is changed.

Managing Passwords

People who make extensive use of computers may have to present passwords in dozens of situations. Obviously, if each password is different, it can become a serious challenge to remember them all. But using a single password might create a different headache. If some of them must change often, there is the hassle of having to visit all accounts frequently to update to a new password. One strategy is to have two current passwords, only one of which you change often. Then you only have to try three or four times to get the right password: the slowly changing one, the quickly changing one, and perhaps the last version of each one in case you hadn't yet gotten around to updating it.

Finally, it is possible to recycle passwords in two ways. First, if you have a good, easy-to-remember password, change it slightly using the process described above to create a new one. So, if you've been using the *Gone with the Wind* password `G2uT2U` and need to change it, go for the Spanish version, `G2uTdosU`. This works well for routine changes, but if there is a security concern related to your password, you should pick a totally new one from your topic area. Second, if you have several good passwords, it is probably safe to reuse them over time, especially if they are not variants of each other. Security experts do not like this idea, but most of us don't have top-secret files on our computers. Just use good judgment when choosing and managing your passwords.

fluencyTIP

Risk Assessment. Use judgment when choosing passwords. For a personal computer kept at home that only you use, even a single-letter password is probably too much. For your online bank account, a password of the type discussed here is a good idea. Assess the risk in each case. Even your boyfriend's name can work in some instances.

Spam

Unsolicited commercial email (UCE), popularly known as **spam**, is a serious annoyance for regular computer users. Without doing anything to provoke it, a person can be sent more than a hundred spam messages a day. There are laws against spam in many places, but it still persists.

fluencyBIT

Unwanted Input. The term *spam* is widely believed to derive from a *Monty Python* skit in which the word "spam" was chanted by Vikings to drown out restaurant conversation, humorously showing that unwanted input impedes legitimate communication.

A **spam filter**, software that separates legitimate mail from spam, gives excellent protection against the problem. Examples include SpamAssassin, spamBusters, and PureMessage. In most cases the service that provides your email account—your school or company, for example—already has a spam filter installed; it may even be working and you don't even know it.

The spam filter software processes email messages as they arrive, separating the spam from the legitimate mail, which it places in your inbox. Because a program cannot possibly understand the content of the email—see our discussion of the Turing test in Chapter 23—determining if email is spam is really just a program's best guess. The program scans the email and assigns a score that measures how many properties typical of spam are also properties of the email. If the score is above the user threshold, the email is considered spam and moved to a separate folder, called the *spam quarantine*. Users can check the quarantine to be sure no legitimate mail is being stopped.

fluencyBYTE

How Spam Filtering Works A spam filter is usually created from several filters working together. Each filter is applied to every email. Each filter checks for a specific feature of spam, and if it finds one, it adds a point to the email's score. At the end, all scores are added, and if the total is too high, the mail is considered spam. Mail from friends typically gets a low score.

Some features a spam filter checks for are

- **Forged header information.** Headers are the mailer's part of email that is often visible as gibberish at the beginning of a message; spammers often change headers to hide their identity and filters detect that.
- **Suspicious content.** The email body may mention specific words like "sex" or phrases like "why pay more?" or other telltale signs of spam. Each occurrence earns the email points. More generally, filters check if the email looks like certain types of spam, like a mortgage ad or announcement of a lottery win; these also earn additional points.
- **No text, just an image.** Some spammers try displaying their spam as an image, because spam filters cannot understand images. Filters fight back by assigning many points to image-only emails.
- **Foreign language email.** Messages not written in your native language get points.
- **Fonts and caps.** Messages all in uppercase, or having very large or small fonts, or text in bright red are all indicators of being spam.

Find a typical list of tests at **spamassassin.apache.org/tests.html**.

When using a spam filter, check the spam quarantine folder occasionally to verify that it is catching only spam. If some of your email—say mass mailings from your club or other organization—are being wrongly flagged as spam, you can add their addresses to a "permitted" list in the spam filter; then, when the filter encounters mail from those sites, it will be delivered to your inbox.

Controlling Spam

After the spam filter scores the email, it is delivered to your inbox if the score is below your spam threshold. Because determining whether email is spam or not is only a guess, some mistakes are inevitable. Setting the threshold lets you control how to handle the "close calls." Because messages are assigned more points when they have more properties typical of spam, a lower threshold amounts to saying, "I will call a message spam based on fewer properties." Raising the threshold amounts to saying, "I want more evidence that a message is spam before it's quarantined." Table 12.2 summarizes the effects of these choices.

Table 12.2 How spam thresholds affect email delivery

Change Threshold	Effect on Legitimate Messages	Effect on Spam
Higher	Fewer legitimate messages quarantined	More spam gets through to inbox
Lower	More legitimate messages quarantined	Less spam gets through to inbox

As a general rule, once you have found the threshold you're comfortable with, you will rarely have to adjust it again.

Comfort Range. When using a new spam filter, check the quarantine faithfully for legitimate messages for the first few weeks. The best case is no good messages in the quarantine and little spam getting through to the inbox; the threshold is set just right. Otherwise, adjust the threshold up or down and continue to check the quarantine until satisfied.

Not All Unsolicited Email Is Spam

Companies that have sold us products online want to tell us about new offers by email. And often, we want to know about those offers. Usually, when we are buying a product for the first time and are in the process of checking out, we are shown a checkbox that we can click—usually it is already checked—that says it's okay for the company to send email about products. If we check that box, then commercial email sent by that company is not spam, but commercial email that we have approved.

If we decide later that we do not want to receive any more mail from the company, we can usually stop it by one of two ways. The first and easiest way is to **unsubscribe**. Reputable companies include at the bottom of every email an *unsubscribe* link (admittedly, in very small print). Clicking on the link sends a notification to the company that you no longer want to receive their email notices. Unsubscribing effectively cancels the original approval for the email. The company will acknowledge having received the request to unsubscribe. (The actual removal from the list may take 24 hours.)

The second way is to go to the company's site (or possibly the bottom of an email) and locate their privacy policy. (Privacy policies are explained in Chapter 13.) It will tell you how the company is using the information it has recorded in your account. One of these uses will be to send you offers via email. There will be a chance to "opt out" of the email, which is a second means to cancel your original approval.

There is one other case where unsolicited email is not spam. People who work together in an office are usually on an email list together. This is very handy for office business, and it might be okay with the boss to request information occasionally from your coworkers on nonwork topics. This is very useful when you're not sure who, if anyone in the office, has the information you would like. So, as a courtesy to them, specify in the Subject line of the email that it is spam and give the topic. For example, a request for a restaurant recommendation for an after-game dinner with relatives could use this as the subject:

SPAM: Post-game restaurant recommendations?

Then, anyone who doesn't know can simply delete the mail unread. That minimizes the annoyance of nonwork-related use of the office mailing list.

Scams

Many things people want to do are easy to do with computers: find information (Google), keep up with friends (Twitter), buy merchandise (Amazon), and so forth. Another thing some people want to do—cheat others—is also easy using computers. Scams are common in our online life, so we must be aware of them.

Nigerian Widow Scam

The Nigerian Widow scam is so common that it has become a widely understood reference in popular culture (see Figure 12.1). The scam is technically known as an **advance-fee fraud**, but most international law enforcement officials refer to it as the **419 fraud** after its section number in Nigerian Criminal Code.

The 419 scam works like this:

- Someone you never heard of claims to have great wealth that they cannot access ($25,000,000).
- They ask your help in transferring the money, usually out of their country.
- For your help, they intend to give you a large share (20 percent) of the money.
- They emphasize that the operation is confidential—tell no one.
- After you agree to help, things go wrong with the transfer.
- They need some money to bribe officials or pay various fees before they can get the money out.
- You give them the money thinking you will get much more in the future. This is the "advance fee" part.
- The scammers need more and more money as time passes.
- Eventually you threaten them, and they disappear.

The scam has many, many variations—search the Web for the latest variations—but they all require urgency, secrecy, and your money.

fluencyBIT

Just the Facts, Lady. Reading the 419 scam in Figure 12.1, one might wonder if there really was a Sani Abacha from Nigeria or a Munirat Abacha. In fact, Sani Abacha was a Nigerian dictator who died in 1998, apparently of a heart attack. His wife was Mariam Jidah; there is no evidence he had a second wife. Munirat Abacha seems to be a name made up for these scam letters.

SUBJECT: URGENT RESPONSE

DEAR SIR

IT IS WITH HEART FULL OF HOPE THAT I WRITE TO SEEK YOUR HELP IN THE CONTEXT BELOW. **I AM MRS. MUNIRAT ABACHA THE SECOND WIFE OF THE FORMER NIGERIA HEAD OF STATE, LATE GENERAL SANI ABACHA,** WHOSE SUDDEN DEATH OCCURRED ON 8TH OF JUNE 1998.

HAVING GOTTEN **YOUR PARTICULARS FROM THE FAMILY LIBRARY**, I HAVE NO DOUBT ABOUT YOUR CAPACITY AND GOOD WILL TO ASSIST US IN RECEIVING INTO YOUR CUSTODY (FOR SAFETY) THE SUM OF US$20MILLION WILLED AND DEPOSITED IN MY FAVOUR BY MY LATE HUSBAND, PLUS 24 CARAT GOLD DUST WORTH USD5M.

THE **MONEY AND THE GOLD IS CURRENTLY KEPT IN GLOBAL SECURITIES WITH A WEST AFRICAN SUB-REGIONAL GLOBAL TRUST DEPOSIT A/C AND FINANCE.** AS LEGALLY REQUIRED IN THE ADMINISTRATION OF MY LATE HUSBAND PROPERTY UNDER THE AUTHORITY OF THE FAMILY LAWYER'S NAMED BARRISTER IKE OFUOBI HOWEVER, THE DEMOCRATIC GOVERNMENT HAS ON ASSUMPTION OF OFFICE SET UP A PANEL OF ENQUIRY TO PROBE THE FINANCIAL ACTIVITIES OF MY LATE HUSBAND (FORMER HEAD OF STATE) WITH A DECISION TO SEIZE ALL HIS ASSETS RESPECTIVELY. THE INVESTIGATION TEAMS HAVE SUBMITTED THEIR REPORT; PRESENTLY SOME CASH ASSETS HAVE BEEN FOUND AND SEIZED.

FORTUNATELY, OUR FAMILY LAWYER HAD SECRETLY PROTECTED THE PERSONAL WILL OF MY HUSBAND FROM THE NOTICE OF THE INVESTIGATIONS AND HAVE STRICTLY ADVISED THAT THE WILLED MONEY BE URGENTLY MOVED INTO AN **OVERSEAS ACCOUNT OF A TRUSTED FOREIGN FAMILY FRIEND** WITHOUT DELAY, FOR SECURITY REASONS. THE GOVERNMENT HAD EARLIER PLACED FOREIGN TRAVEL EMBARGO ON ALL OUR BUSINESS EMPIRE.

THE SITUATION HAS BEEN SO TERRIBLE THAT WE ARE **VIRTUALLY LIVING ON THE ASSISTANCE OF WELL-WISHERS.** IN VIEW OF THIS PLIGHT THEREFORE, I EXPECT YOU TO BE TRUSTWORTHY AND KIND ENOUGH TO RESPOND TO THIS CALL (S.O.S) TO **SAVE ME AND MY CHILDREN FROM A HOPELESS FUTURE.**

I HEREBY AGREE TO COMPENSATE YOUR SINCERE AND CANDID EFFORT IN THESE REGARDS WITH 20% OF THE FUND WHEN FINALLY RECEIVED IN YOUR LOCAL BANK ACCOUNT. THE ATTORNEY HAS PERFECTED **ARRANGEMENT WITH THE BANKERS TO EFFECT COMPLETE LODGMENTS** OF THIS MONEY INTO YOUR ACCOUNT WITHIN A WEEK OF THE RECEIPT OF YOUR RESPONSE THROUGH MY LAWYER'S MAIL. THEY HAVE EQUALLY GUARANTEED 100% RISK FREE AND SMOOTH TRANSFER. PLEASE ALL CONTACTS MUST BE MADE THROUGH MY LAWYER BARR. IKE OFUOBI. VIA HIS E-MAIL BOX: OFUOBICHAMBARS@YAHOO.COM. OR DIRECT FAX NO. 234-1-7594263.

REGARDS,

MRS. MUNIRAT ABACHA

Figure 12.1 A typical "Nigerian Widow" scam email.

Unfortunately, the 419 scam has been extremely successful for the scammers. The U.S. Secret Service claims Americans lose tens of millions of dollars every year to this scam. There are whole Web sites dedicated to combating the Nigerian Widow scam (www.419scam.org), but it continues to thrive. In a recent variation, the email says that you have won a lottery in a foreign country. This should sound very suspicious: How many foreign lotteries do you usually enter? How often do people hit the jackpot in lotteries? But, people continue to take the bait.

Obviously, any email that appears to give you something for nothing can safely be deleted. The world just doesn't work that way.

fluencyBIT

Different Story, Same Fraud. The Nigerian Widow scam is not new. The same fraud, known as the Spanish Prisoner scam, was used extensively in the 1920s. The story was that an extremely wealthy man was locked in a Spanish jail, and his family promised riches in gratitude to anyone who helped him escape. Of course, the helper would pay for one failed attempt after another.

Phishing

If someone walked up to you and said, "Give me your Social Security number, your driver's license number, the passwords to all of your computer accounts, credit card numbers, . . . ," you would laugh. You are not about to give such sensitive information to any random person. If the person is wearing a nice blue suit and has a badge in his or her pocket indicating an agent from the FBI, you still wouldn't give that data, at least not until you verified that they really were from the FBI, and on what legal authority they are asking for all of this information.

But everyday people voluntarily give up such personal information. It is a mystery why they would be so skeptical in person, but so trusting online.

The term for the social engineering process of convincing trusting people to voluntarily give up personal data is **phishing**, short for *password harvesting fishing*. The scam works as follows.

Spam email is sent out designed to look like it comes from a reputable organization, such as a bank, PayPal, eBay, and so forth. The mail uses actual content from the reputable organization's site, such as logos, images, and fonts. Some go to such extremes as to use the actual Help Line 1-800 phone number. It's easy to be taken in—see how realistic Figure 12.2 appears.

The text of the message makes one of several claims on behalf of the reputable organization:

- Your account has been accessed by unauthorized people
- Your account has experienced unusual activity
- There has been a security breach, which they are trying to fix
- They are performing an audit and find possible problems with your account

The list could go on and on. They ask that you log on to resolve the issue. If you click on most of the links in the email, you get to a bogus site that will look like it might be from the reputable organization, but it will be a phishing site. It asks you to give your account numbers, password, and other private information. The scammers simply collect the data that's entered.

12.2 Some of These Things Are Kind of Bogus. Some of these things are probably okay. In the email in Figure 12.2, which of the four links probably go to a phishing site, if any, and which may be legitimate (if any)?

Phishing scams begin to look familiar (and pretty lame) after a while. Banks and other reputable organizations do not send you email to discuss your account. If you do think there really may be a problem with your account at some reputable organization, contact them directly. To do so, *manually* type in the URL for their home page, or Google the organization. Click on the contact link on their home page to get phone numbers or snail mail addresses.

Subject: Bank of America Alert: Update Your Account
From: Bank Of America <update@boa.com>
Reply-To: no-reply@boa.com
Date: 12/29/2006 5:40 AM

Online Banking Alert

Need additional up to the minute account information?
Sign In »

Your Online Banking is Blocked

We recently reviewed your account, and suspect that your Bank Of America account may have been accessed by an unauthorized third party. Protecting the security of your account and of the Bank Of America network is our primary concern. Therefore, as a preventative measure, we have temporarily limited access to sensitive account features.

To restore your account access, please take the following steps to ensure that your account has not been compromised:

https://www.bankofamerica.com/cgi-bin/ias/GotoReset

We apologize for any inconvenience this may cause, and appreciate your assistance in helping us maintain the integrity of the entire Bank Of America system.

Thank you.

Because your reply will not be transmitted via secure e-mail, the e-mail address that generated this alert will not accept replies. If you would like to contact Bank of America with questions or comments, please sign in to Online Banking and visit the customer service section.

Bank of America, N.A. Member FDIC. Equal Housing Lender
© 2006 Bank of America Corporation. All rights reserved

Figure 12.2 An example of a fraudulent email phishing attempt claiming to be from Bank of America.

The risk in phishing scams is identity theft, which is discussed in the next chapter.

Viruses and Worms

Among the unsavory critters that you can encounter in the social world of computing, viruses and worms are very common. They can be quite destructive, but they are easy enough to protect against. First, what are they?

Viruses and **worms** are small programs that can make copies of themselves. If that were all they did, they wouldn't be much of a problem. But malicious programmers can include additional instructions that can harm your computer, phone, or other computer-based device. They can modify or delete files, fill up your memory and disk with copies of itself, watch your keystrokes looking for passwords, or take over your computer to launch other unwanted activities elsewhere. This malicious code can be the source of serious problems.

The difference between a virus and a worm is that the virus program "rides along" with other software, while the worm can actually send itself to other devices on the Internet. This difference doesn't matter too much to us, because we can be attacked in many ways by both critters.

A **Trojan program**, which takes its name from the Trojan horse of Greek legend, is a program with software hiding inside, performing operations unbeknownst to the user. Technically it is a virus, but rather than spreading itself to other computers, it gathers data. For example, Trojans can record keystrokes to get passwords, record other sensitive data, and load other malicious software.

fluencyBYTE

First Malicious Worm. In the 1950s, computer scientists noticed that it was possible to write a program that makes exact copies of itself; it wasn't a particularly useful fact and they mostly forgot about it. Then, on November 2, 1988, Robert Tappan Morris, Jr., a computer science graduate student, apparently lost control of such a program, and the general public learned for the first time that programs could replicate. Morris' program was supposed to replicate itself once on each computer and send itself along to others—making it a worm. But due to an unfortunate bug, it kept reproducing itself, filling up the computer's memory and hard disk. It infected 6,000 computers—10 percent of the Internet at the time—before it was stopped. The damage had to be cleaned up by hand, costing millions of dollars. Morris was convicted under the U.S. Computer Fraud and Abuse Act of 1986; he received a sentence of three years' probation, 400 hours of community service, and a $10,000 fine.

Though the Morris worm caused considerable harm, it also demonstrated how vulnerable the Internet was from erroneous or malicious software. In November 1988, DARPA—the developers of the Internet—formed CERT, an organization that monitors the security of the Internet (see www.cert.org).

Vectors of Attack

CERT was originally set up to combat network-based **malware**: software intended to do harm to a computer connected to the Internet. But as computer technology has spread, so have the opportunities to be mischievous. Today, we must worry about our phones as much as our computers, and worry about file sharing as much as email. The mode in which a virus, worm or other malware gets into your computer is called the **vector of attack**. We consider five methods that are by now considered standard vectors of attack.

Email attachments.

Mechanism	An infected file is attached to an email.
Behavior to Avoid	Clicking on the attachment to open it.
Result	The malware (usually a worm) runs, sending copies of the email and the attachment to the names in your email address book.
Protect Yourself	Don't automatically open attachments; find out (from the sender) why it was sent and what it is for.

Clicking on the file causes your computer to run a program associated with the file, which releases the virus or worm. The famous Melissa virus in 1999 was of this type; it was part of a Microsoft Word document. When the unsuspecting recipient clicked on the attached file, LIST.DOC, a Word macro ran and the damage was done. Melissa cost an estimated $80 million to repair, and it was widely described in the press. (The author, David L. Smith, got 20 months in prison.) So you might think the public would avoid impulsively clicking on attachments, but a year later the I Love You virus worked exactly the same way, and again it infected millions of computers! The lesson: Don't automatically click on attachments.

A key part of protecting yourself is to notice the file type of the attachment. As you know, the **file type**, indicated by the **file extension**, the letters following the last dot in the file name, describes the kind of information in the file. In the Melissa virus, .DOC is the file extension indicating that the type of information in the file is a Microsoft Word document. Table 12.3 gives a list of the file extensions for files considered to be capable of delivering viruses and worms via an attachment. Of these, the worst is probably .exe, the file type for executable programs for the Windows operating system. Always be alert for the .exe file extension, and click on it only when you are *completely sure* that it is safe to do so.

See It All. Operating systems offer the option of hiding file extensions, but hiding them is a bad idea. By selecting to show file extensions, you can see the complete file name and recognize hazardous attachments. For example, the harmless looking newCar.jpg might actually be an executable worm file newCar.jpg.exe with its extension hidden. Being duped like this can cause a lot of grief. For instructions on how to set your OS to display file extensions, search under *Help* for "show file extensions."

Not all attachments are dangerous. For example, media files such as .gif, .png, .jpg (.jpeg), .tif (.tiff), .mpg (.mpeg), and .mp3 are usually safe. Operating systems allow extensions to be hidden (they are there for the computer, not for you), but *you must display them to practice safe computing*.

Spoofed links.

Mechanism	A hyperlink in an email has been changed to point to a different site.
Behavior to Avoid	Clicking on the link to jump to it.
Result	Several alternatives could occur at the target site—it could be a phishing site, or it could be a setup to install infected software.
Protect Yourself	Avoid clicking on links from email or Web pages that you are uncertain about. Also, *Copy/Paste* URLs into the location window to be sure you know the site you are visiting.

Table 12.3 File extensions for file types capable of carrying viruses or worms

.386	Virtual Device Driver (Windows 386 enhanced mode)
.3gr	VGA Graphics Driver/configuration files
.add	Adapter Driver file
.ade	Microsoft Access project extension
.asp	Active Server Page
.bas	Microsoft Visual Basic class module
.bat	Batch file
.chm	Compiled HTML Help file
.cmd	Microsoft Windows NT command script
.com	Microsoft MS-DOS program
.cpl	Control Panel extension
.crt	Security certificate
.dbx	Database Index
.dll	Dynamic Link Library
.exe	Program file
.fon	Font file
.hlp	Help file
.hta	HTML program
.inf	Setup information
.ins	Internet Naming Service
.isp	Internet communication settings
.js	JavaScript file
.jse	JavaScript encoded-script file
.lnk	Shortcut
.mdb	Microsoft Access program
.mde	Microsoft Access MDE database
.msc	Microsoft Common Console document
.msi	Microsoft Windows Installer package
.msp	Microsoft Windows Installer patch
.mst	Microsoft Windows Installer transform
.ocx	Microsoft Object Linking
.pcd	Corel Adaptec CD Creator image file
.pif	Shortcut to MS-DOS program
.reg	Registration entries
.scr	Screen saver
.sct	Windows Script Component
.shb	Shell Scrap object
.shs	Shell Scrap object
.url	Internet shortcut
.vb	Visual Basic Script file
.vbe	Visual Basic Script-encoded file
.vbs	Visual Basic Script file
.vxd	Microsoft Windows Virtual Device Driver
.wsc	Windows Script Component
.wsf	Windows Script File
.wsh	Windows Script Host Settings file

As you will recall, hyperlinks have two parts: the part you read and the part the computer reads. To spoof a link is to fake what the link points to. A common trick is to show blue anchor text like www.goodSite.com that looks okay, but the computer is directed to another site by the href attribute, for example, to www.badSite.com. When you click on the link, the computer simply jumps to the site it has been given.

One way to check where the computer will go when you click the link is to look at the status bar at the bottom of the browser. (You're using Firefox, right?) When you move your cursor over the link and the gloved pointer appears, the address in the status bar is the one the computer will use if you click on the link. This is one quick test to protect yourself against spoofed links. So, like file extensions, the status bar should be enabled.

There are other, more insidious ways to spoof a link, so the approach just described is not guaranteed. It is useful only when you're pretty sure everything is safe. The best policy is not to click on links unless you have a good reason to trust the email or the site where they appear. And your trust should be informed by how you got to the site. If you reached the site by

- clicking on a link at a trusted site, or
- clicking on a link resulting from a Yahoo or Google or other search, or
- typing in the URL yourself,

then you know where you are. If you got to a site by clicking from a questionable site, it may be questionable, too.

This discussion might seem overly cautious, but look at the next vector.

Social engineering.

Mechanism	A user is presented with an opportunity to visit an unknown link, often from spam or comments at a social networking site.
Behavior to Avoid	Clicking on the link and then "updating" software.
Result	The computer is seriously compromised.
Protect Yourself	Don't install software offered to you from a site you don't trust; get all software from the creators.

Social engineering is the term used for a relatively recent technique used by predators to install malware on your machine. The technique works as follows. *Bots*—programs that perform computer operations humans might also perform—visit social networking sites and post comments that include a tantalizing URL. After taking the bait by clicking on the link, the user is told to upgrade some standard software they probably already have running. For example, a recent version of this technique asked users to install the next version of the Flash Player. But the software offered by the site is actually a bogus version of the standard software with the virus inside. Once it is installed, the damage is done, and all because the user was so trusting.

Whenever you are asked to upgrade software, go to the source—in this case, Adobe—by typing in the correct URL. (You can guess it (www.flash.com) if you have visited the site before.) Legitimate companies distributing software *always* make it very easy to install their software. If you can't remember the URL for the company that makes the software, Google it. It is extremely likely to be the first hit.

P2P file sharing.

Mechanism	Files are transferred containing infected software or spyware.
Behavior to Avoid	Installing sharing software and files from unreliable sites.
Result	Computer is seriously compromised; possible loss of personal information including passwords; possible copyright violation.
Protect Yourself	Avoid P2P sharing from unreliable sites; protect your computer with a firewall and *up-to-date* anti-virus software.

Peer-to-peer (**P2P**) file sharing is a widely used means of sharing files, especially music files. Though it can be extremely convenient, it can also be quite risky.

Peer to peer refers to the relationship between computers connected by the Internet. The computers share files by each being a "file server" of its files for the others. It is a convenient arrangement. However, predators can set up sites, often using pirated music, to attract unsuspecting users. Once the users install the software to become a peer (usually software from the predator's site containing the malware, not legitimate P2P software from sites like Gnutella or BitTorrent), the damage is done.

Though installing infected P2P software has the usual problems associated with viruses and worms, it has the added problem that it is easy for the predator to acquire personal information you have stored on your computer. P2P is a valuable technology, but it requires care to use safely.

Bluetooth and MMS file transfers.

Mechanism	Files are received from nearby computers by Bluetooth or MMS.
Behavior to Avoid	Approving software installation.
Result	Computer (phone) is seriously compromised.
Protect Yourself	Install only software you have purposely acquired.

Much of our discussion has focused on risks in the context of email and the Web, but there are concerns with smartphones and other hand-held mobile devices. They are computers, too, of course, running operating systems such as Symbian. They can be targets of malware.

As with the preceding examples, avoiding installing software from unknown sources is the main issue. The software often arrives via Bluetooth communication from an infected device. The files for applications often have the extension .sis for the Symbian operating system; when you are asked if you want to install the program you are also warned that it cannot be trusted. If you didn't purposely get the application from a reputable source, the answer to the "Install?" question is, obviously, **Cancel**.

A new, more worrisome development is the use of media files, that is, files with extensions like .jpg, .mp3, and .rm. We normally think of media files as passive, and therefore not good candidates for viruses. These files also arrive via Bluetooth and MMS file transfer and they look very plain. After clicking on them, however, they don't play or display like they should, but rather they ask installation-related questions. Since media files don't need any installation, the proper response, again, is **Cancel**.

fluencyBYTE

"Rap Sheet" on an Email Worm: MyDoom.BB The MyDoom.BB worm is typical of hundreds of email worms and viruses that have been tracked in recent years; a current list of those still alive on the Internet is at **www.f-secure.com/virus-info/wild.html**. People continue to click on infected attachments years after their creation, keeping them alive. At the time of this book's publication, MyDoom.BB was still the third most active virus/worm.

Name: MyDoom.BB.

Aliases: MyDoom.M, Email-Worm.Win32.Mydoom.m, W32/Mydoom.bb@MM, W32/MyDoom-O, W32.Mydoom.AX@mm, Mydoom.AU, WORM_MYDOOM.BB.

DoB: February 17, 2005.

Lineage: A hacked variant of MyDoom.M.

MO: The worm infects the computer as **java.exe**, and sets up a backdoor communication link (port 1034) to listen for further instructions.

Spread: After installation, the worm sends email to all addresses that can be found on the infected machine. The email fakes an "unable to deliver" message typical of mail servers.

Subject Lines: One of the following subject lines is randomly selected:

hello	Message could not be delivered
error	Mail System Error - Returned Mail
status	Delivery reports about your e-mail
test	Returned mail: see transcript for details
report	Returned mail: Data format error
delivery failed	

Message Body: A variety of message bodies are created, each saying in some way that the message the user sent couldn't be delivered, and asking them to check for details in an attached file.

Attached File Name: One of the following: readme, instruction, transcript, mail, letter, file, text, attachment, or document.

File Extensions: The infected file has one of the following file extensions: .bat, .cmd, .com, .exe, .pif, or .scr. *Notice that each of these file extensions is in Table 12.3.*

With the popularity of mobile devices increasing at an amazing rate, matched only by their increase in performance and applications, we can expect many more attempts by predators to exploit such devices in the future.

Protecting Yourself

Surviving in a world full of viruses and worms requires vigilance. First, compute safely. In the earlier discussion of vectors of attack, methods for avoiding problems were described. Following those behaviors is smart.

You Got the Virus. Not. Not all virus reports are real. While some people are busy creating viruses, other people are creating virus hoaxes, trying to social-engineer you into some kind of action. If you get mail saying you have to take some action in response to a virus, be skeptical. It might be a hoax. Before doing anything, check McAfee's list of known hoaxes at vil.mcafee.com/hoax.asp.

The second point, and by far the most important, is to install an anti-virus program. There are numerous vendors (search on "anti-virus software"), and considering how valuable the protection is, their prices are reasonable. Whatever the cost, however, anti-virus software is mandatory. This applies to your smartphone as much as to your computer.

Computer Security Tips. Many security Web sites give guidelines on how to protect your computer's security, and they serve as a good summary to this section. Thanks to the IT staff at Iowa State University for this list.

1. Install anti-virus software and keep it up-to-date. Organizations have site licenses; individuals can find anti-virus software vendors on the Web.
2. Install an anti-spyware program. You can find vendors for PC software on the Web. Note that spyware is not an issue for Macintosh computers.
3. Keep your operating system and browser software current. System software vulnerabilities are usually found and fixed quickly by vendors, and are included in updates.
4. Do not download files from an unknown source. Be suspicious of sites eager to send you files.
5. Use a password of the type described in this chapter. It should be at least 8 characters long.
6. Do not open email attachments from unknown sources.
7. Use file sharing only from trusted sites. Protecting your computer is a good reason not to download pirated music.
8. Run only those services you need. Installed software you do not use, such as IIS (Microsoft's Web server) and UPNP (universal plug and play), can be vectors for malware.
9. Protect your computer from Internet intruders with a firewall, which is available from your operating system vendor.
10. Back up your computer regularly. If malware does infect your computer, your losses will be minimized.

Because new viruses are created every day, virus software needs to be updated. So keeping the software up-to-date is another obligation for the intelligent computer user.

Protecting Intellectual Property

Like land or Rover or a Land Rover, information is something that can be owned. Information, including photographs, music, textbooks, and cartoons, is the result of the creative process. The act of creation gives the creator ownership of the result in the United States and most of the world. Sometimes there are multiple forms of ownership. If on her new CD Norah Jones sings a song written by Paul Simon, he owns the words and music, and she owns the performance. If a person creates something while working for a company, the company generally owns the information. All such human creations are called **intellectual property** to distinguish them from real estate, pets, cars, and other stuff that can be owned.

The two aspects of intellectual property that we are interested in here are software and copyright on the Web. Each affects how you can use information technology.

Licensing of Software

When you buy software, you load it onto your machine without giving much attention to the legal mumbo jumbo that you agree to by opening the package or downloading the file. (Sure, lawyers probably read the fine print, but the rest of us don't.) If you were to read it, you'd discover a remarkable fact: You didn't buy the software—you actually leased it. That is, **software licenses** tend to give you the use of the software, but the ownership remains with the company that is marketing it. (Of course, every license is different, forcing us to discuss the topic generally. To be sure about your particular agreement, check your software license.) We are not interested in why this is the case; rather, we want to know how such agreements constrain our behavior.

Use of the software. If the agreement allows us to use the software, we can use it on at least one computer, and we may be permitted to use it on all of the computers we own. The fact that we use it personally generally means that we use one instance at a time. Installing several instances for convenience may be okay. But, if the number of computers it can be installed on is restricted, then we should explore purchasing an alternative license—the family plan—to cover other computers.

Don't sell it or give it away. Because you don't *own* commercial software, you cannot give it to your friend. If you do, you would violate the terms of the contract that you agreed to when you opened the software package. But even if you simply bought software from a friendly programmer you met in the computer lab, you probably still can't give it away. The programmer created the software—it's his or her intellectual property—and the programmer has full copyright protection. Like a photographer who creates a stunning picture, the programmer's ownership of the software allows copies to be made and sold to people like you. You buy a photograph to frame and enjoy; you buy software to run and enjoy. Unless the programmer gives you the explicit right to copy and distribute the software, you cannot sell it or even give it away.

Try before you buy. Finally, there is **shareware**, which is software that is usually distributed over the Internet. You can download a copy for free, and you can copy it and give it to your friends. The idea of shareware is that you can try out the software, and if you like it and use it, you pay the person who created it. (The price is listed.) It's a great system because it gives craftsman programmers a chance to distribute their often well-built and effective software, and because you can try it before you purchase it. But it is an honor system. If you use the software, you should pay for it. It is unethical to download software on the implied promise of paying for it if you use it, and then to use it without paying. Prices are generally very modest, and the software is often exceptionally good.

Open Source Software

Software from vendors like Microsoft and Adobe is *proprietary*, meaning the vendors keep the source code (program) private; when you get a copy to install, you receive only the binary code for your computer model and operating system (see Chapter 9). The other kind of software—software for which the program is publicly available —is known as **open source** software. For example, the Mozilla browser software is open source, and Firefox, SeaMonkey, Epiphany, MozBraille (Web page rendering for the visually impaired), and other browsers are built on top of it. As a result, personal copies of Firefox, for example, are free. Many, many useful programs are open source.

Open source seems not to make sense: Who pays for the technology and how can a company make money if the product is publicly available? Companies developing technology often make their products open source to promote wide distribution; they make their money selling specialized versions to corporate clients, providing customer support, and selling other software that interfaces to it. Advocates of open source point out that if the software is publicly available, other people work on it and improve it, a point that is repeatedly borne out. After all, who would have the resources to build a Braille browser from scratch? When looking for new software, find out what open source software is available for your application.

Copyright on the Web

When a person writes a term paper, builds a Web page, or creates a sculpture, he or she automatically owns the **copyright** on that "work" in the United States and most nations of the world. The creator typically owns the copyright, unless the creation is "work for hire," in which case the owner is the person who paid the creator, usually a company. For example, if you create a personal Web page, you own the copyright, but if you build a Web page as part of your job, the company owns it. Posting information on the Web is a form of publishing, and though Internet copyright and other law is not fully developed yet, it is a good assumption that information on the Web is owned by someone.

fluencyBIT

No © 'em. At one time, to claim copyright, you had to include the phrase "© Copyright *dates* by *author/owner*. All Rights Reserved." That's no longer necessary for works produced after March 1, 1989. However, the copyright notice is still used as a reminder and reference.

What rights are included in a copyright? Obviously the right to copy it, but surprisingly, there are others. Copyright protects the owner's right to

- Make a copy of the work
- Use a work as the basis for a new work, called *creating a derivative work*
- Distribute or publish the work, including electronically
- Publicly perform the work, as in music, poetry, drama, or to play a video or audio recording
- Publicly display the work, as in displaying an image on a computer screen

It is the very act of creating the intellectual property that creates these rights. No application or approval is required. The work doesn't require the © symbol. It's copyrighted the moment it's finished.

Notice the second item in the list: using the work to create a derivative work. This is an important aspect of copyright because it prevents someone from, for example, changing each of the *Simpsons* characters in some small way—aging, perhaps—and then claiming to have created a new dysfunctional cartoon family. Only their creator, Matt Groening, has the right to change the characters. You might be tempted to bypass copyright law by restating a work in your own words, but if your creation is too much like the original, you've produced a derivative work rather than new intellectual property. Thus, for example, if someone restates this book in different words, I can sue them—and I might.

Free personal use. Of course, just because someone else owns a work doesn't mean that you can't use and enjoy it. Obviously, the fact that they've published it on the Web means that you are free to read, view, or listen to it as you wish. Printing it so that you can read it on the bus is okay, as is filing away a copy on your computer for future *personal* enjoyment. You can mail the URL to your friends—the URL, not the content—notifying them of the information. Such applications are why the information was published on the Web in the first place.

When is permission needed? Many sites have a written copyright policy. Often the information is placed in the **public domain**, meaning that it is free for anyone to use, in any form. This is convenient because it means that you can treat the information as your own. You can even sell it if you have a buyer. Sometimes owners state that the information can be republished or used in other forms, as long as you cite the source. They retain ownership, but you get to use it. All you have to do is follow their guidelines. And, of course, some sites—those that don't state otherwise—retain all rights to the Web-published information under the applicable copyright laws. Generally, this means that if you want to use works from such a site in one of the five ways listed earlier, you must get permission from the owners of the information. Using such copyrighted property without permission is illegal, of course. But the fact that a site retains the rights to its information should not keep you from asking for permission. Many sites routinely give permission; their purpose in requiring you to ask for it is to control the distribution of their works. It takes only a little effort to ask.

The concept of fair use. Between the free personal use and the need to get permission is a gray area in which limited use of copyrighted materials is allowed without getting permission. This is known as the concept of "fair use." **Fair use** is recognized in copyright law to allow the use of copyrighted material for educational or scholarly purposes, to allow limited quotation of copyrighted works for review or criticism, to permit parody, and a few other uses. For example, I can quote Stanley Kubrick's *2001: A Space Odyssey* in the following way

One of the most widely known computer instructions is David Bowman's command, "Open the pod bay doors, HAL."

without getting the permission of the present owner (Warner Brothers), because I am using the quotation for the educational purpose of instructing you about fair use. This is true even though this book is a commercial application of the quoted material. And you would be allowed to use similar brief quotations in class assignments, for example. Indeed, fair use provides many opportunities for using copyrighted material for socially beneficial purposes. The problem is that it can be very unclear just when fair use applies.

When is it fair use? The following four questions are applied to determine whether a given use of copyrighted information constitutes fair use.

- What is the planned use?
- What is the nature of the work in which the material is to be used?
- How much of the work will be used?
- What effect would this use have on the market for the work if the use were widespread?

What constitutes fair use is complex and subject to disagreements by fair-minded Web users, lawyers, and even judges. Indeed, in 1997 a two-year Conference on Fair Use (CONFU) struggled mightily with the interpretations and failed to clarify the matter fully. It is beyond the scope of this section to delve into the nuances of deciding fair use. But the University of Texas publishes a very useful guideline; when in doubt, check it out: www.utsystem.edu/ogc/INTELLECTUALPROPERTY/cprtindx.htm.

No Harm in Asking. When asking for copyright permission, state what works you are interested in, such as "the photograph on your page ... /greatpix/elvis/"; how you would like to use the works, such as "put copies on my personal Web page at . . . "; and any other relevant information, such as "I want to colorize his suede shoes so they are actually blue."

To:

Date:

I am writing to you to request permission to use the material described below. This material will be posted on a Web site that receives approximately ________ hits per month. The URL is

____

The material will be posted on July 1 and will remain on the Web site for an indefinite period. I am asking permission for the nonexclusive, worldwide right to publish this material.

Description: Include the title and author of the work, the source (if from a book, give the ISBN; if from a Web site, give the complete URL), and a copy of the work if possible (the text or art you want to use).

Full credit will be given to the source. A release form appears below, along with space for indicating your desired credit line.

If you do not control these rights in their entirety, please let me know to whom else I must write. Thank you.

Sincerely,

Your name

Your contact information

I warrant that I have the right to grant the permission to republish the material specified above.

Permission is granted by: ____________________________

Title: ____________________________

Address: ____________________________

Date: ____________________________

Preferred acknowledgment: ____________________________

Violating the Copyright Law

Many people say that it is all right to use copyrighted material for noncommercial purposes, but that's false. You break the law whether you sell the material or not, though commercial use usually results in larger fines or damages when you're sued. Because the penalties for copyright infringement are substantial—up to $100,000 per act—it pays to be careful. By far the best approach is to think up your own material—that is, create intellectual property with your own intellect. You're not required to ask for anyone else's permission, and you enjoy copyright protection too!

Uncopyrightable Fact. Facts cannot be copyrighted. For example, "*Uncopyrightable* is the longest English word without repeated letters" is a fact, and so is uncopyrightable.

Plan of Action

In the previous sections we have revealed the main "bad boys" of computer security. Unfortunately, that's not the end of the story, because as more technology is created, more ways to abuse it will undoubtedly be developed. But for the moment, these are our main concern. The last matter, then, is to consider what to do about them.

The following is a brief plan of action that applies the information in the previous sections (and assumes that you have done nothing to protect yourself so far). After we have presented the steps, we consider what to do as an ongoing activity.

The plan is to address security in three different areas:

- Installing protective systems
- Tuning the installed protections
- Behaving to avoid difficulties

If in your computing you observe these guidelines, you should have few remaining security concerns.

Installing Protective Systems

The first rule of security is to set up a barrier, so your computer needs security protection systems such as a firewall, anti-virus software, anti-spyware protection, and possibly a rootkit scanner.

Firewall. A **firewall** is a barrier between two networks, or in the "personal" firewall case, between the Internet and your computer. Generally, firewalls filter network traffic that is trying to cross the barrier. It allows through only those messages with a destination in the protected area. If you are running a modern operating system, windows XP or newer, or Mac OSX, a firewall is already operating. Otherwise, installing personal firewall software is essential (search "personal firewall" for commercial and free options).

Virus protection. Anti-virus software must be operating at all times to protect against the worms, viruses, and Trojans that flow in during everyday computer usage. If you use a campus or business computer, the administrators have probably already protected you, but your own computer is your responsibility. Install virus protection software immediately and keep it current (search "anti-virus software").

Anti-spyware. **Spyware** is software that snoops on your private information, causes advertising pop-ups, and monitors your Internet behavior for advertising purposes. Anti-spyware protection is often bundled with anti-virus software, and finding a package that includes both is smart (search "anti-spyware software").

Rootkit detection. A **rootkit** is malware that directly manipulates the operating system data structures to hide its presence. It does this, for example, by removing itself from the list of active programs that users see. Rootkits have become a much more serious problem in recent years for those visiting certain kinds of sites, such as gaming sites, gambling sites, pornography, and similar "not-G-rated" destinations. If your computer has been used to visit such sites, install a rootkit detector (search "rootkit detection software").

Once this software is installed, a periodic review to make sure it is up-to-date is wise. The company or shareware site that provided the software will have information on updates or newer versions.

Tuning Installed Protections

The barrier is your first line of defense; the next step is to tune up the other software you are using. This begins with your operating system.

Staying up-to-date. Keeping your operating system current is essential. Recent versions of Windows have automatic OS updates, and because these very frequently deliver security "patches," it is essential that the process be allowed; browsers also depend for their effectiveness on automatic updates. Most other applications automatically check for updates, giving you the opportunity to install them. They should be installed, too. Why run old, buggy software?

Browser sense. Firefox is the required browser for the "lab" exercises in this book, and using it as your default browser is smart; Opera and Safari are other good options. The browser is the main entry point for external information, and so its security is critical. Firefox is sound, and responsive in the face of new security threats. The key point, however, is not to use the security-plagued older versions of Internet Explorer.

Emailer sense. The developers of Firefox also distribute a great email program, Thunderbird. Switching from your current mailer to Thunderbird is not difficult, and like Firefox, Thunderbird is responsive to the contemporary security issues.

Spam filter. It is probably wise to check your spam quarantine to be sure that you are not missing email. If spam is getting through, consider adjusting its threshold.

WiFi protection. If your computer is using a wireless connection to the Internet, then it is receiving and sending all of its information by radio broadcast, which any computer can listen to. That includes passwords. An essential requirement is that you encrypt the transmissions so others cannot observe them. The **wired equivalent privacy WEP2** is *required* at a minimum; WEP is *not* secure enough. Other protocols can offer even greater security.

Disable file sharing. Though file sharing can be convenient, it is a risky facility to leave running in large wireless network situations such as a college campus; snoopers can be poking around. Leave it turned off until you absolutely need it, and then leave it on the minimum amount of time in such cases.

As before, once configured in a security-sensitive way, little needs to be done except periodic reviews.

Behaving to Avoid Difficulties

As in other aspects of our lives, we can adopt certain computer usage habits that help us avoid difficulties.

Download cautions. The greatest security risk to your computer is installing compromised software. But a computer is useless without software, implying that you must download it. Thus, removing the "compromised" modifier is the only choice; that is, only install the good stuff.

There are two points: First, never install software without thinking about it beforehand, especially if the request to install is unexpected. When the computer asks if you want to install some software, you shouldn't be thinking, "Huh? Where did that come from?" but rather, "Yes, that's what I'm trying to do." Second, you should know the source of the software you are installing. If a Web site says you need a newer version of Flash (or some other software) to run their software, type in www.flash.com to get it; don't take the version offered. It could be fine, but the copy from flash.com is *definitely* good. For shareware, that is, free software, trust sites like SourceForge, ZDNet,V3.

Careful with attachments. As we explained, open email attachments only when you are expecting them. Otherwise, contact the sender to find out what the attachment was about, especially if it has one of the "watch list" file extensions listed in Table 12.3.

Password protection. Adopt a set of passwords as described earlier—standard, rarely changed, and another that you willingly change when requested—all based on the one theme. Naturally, you will use strong passwords for sensitive uses such as online banking, but the passwords discussed earlier can be easy enough to use and remember that several will cover most of your applications. Password-protecting your computer is smart, too; probably more people have access to it than you think.

By setting such a plan in motion, you can have the confidence that your computer is protected. Then, only casual attention to the "latest" in security news and the occasional review of your plan are probably all you need to keep the "bad guys" away.

Summary

The chapter began with a discussion of the weaknesses of email and the importance of netiquette. You learned that thoughtful email users limit messages requiring an answer to one topic, include context, and do not forward private messages or broadcast email indiscriminately. We continued our discussion about:

- "Expecting the unexpected" as a useful survival skill. The challenge is to think about the unexpected event and correctly determine whether and how to respond.
- Creating an easy-to-remember password. The approach emphasized selecting passwords that are connected to a common topic. It is smart to choose simple passwords when little security is needed and to choose more obscure passwords when there is greater risk.
- The damage caused by viruses and worms. We can reduce the chance of infection by installing and running anti-virus software. We must be aware of hoaxes and phishing scams. Copyright infringement poses a legal risk, so we shouldn't share software or pirate copyrighted material from the Web.
- We have learned how to implement a plan of action to ensure that our personal computers remain private and secure.

Try It Solutions

12.1 There is no single answer. Possible answers include:
`password` → `pa2sword` → `pa2s2uord` → `pa2s2uORD`
`password` → `tossword` → `2ssword` → `2sSabres`
`password` → `noFword` → `properword` → `4perWord`
`password` → `pass2uord` → `pass2uOhare` → `ATCOhare`

12.2 The Sign In >>, the https, and sign in to Online Banking links go to the phishing site. The Equal Housing Lender link is probably okay.

Review Questions

Multiple Choice

1. A list moderator does all of the following except
   a. configures the list-server for its members
   b. edits all messages sent to the list
   c. maintains a list of members subscribed to the list-server
   d. handles errors and problems for the list-server
2. When you forget your password
   a. you must apply for a new one
   b. the system administrator looks up your password
   c. the system administrator unscrambles your password and gives it to you
   d. the system administrator assigns a new password for you to use
3. Computer viruses and worms have been around since
   a. the early days of computers
   b. the early days of the Internet
   c. the late 1980s
   d. the late 1990s
4. Computer viruses are typically spread by
   a. copying software from an infected computer
   b. receiving email from an infected computer
   c. opening email from an infected computer
   d. sending email to an infected computer
5. Copyrighted material may be used
   a. only in nonprofit instances
   b. only when written permission is granted
   c. if proper credit is given to the owner
   d. without permission in limited circumstances

Short Answer

1. _______ is etiquette for the Internet.
2. A(n) _______ is a programmed response to your email that's sent when you are away.
3. A(n) _______ is the person who controls a list-server.
4. The individual who controls access to a computer system, including logins and passwords, is called a(n) _______.
5. A(n) _______ is a program that embeds itself in another program, copies itself, and spreads to other computers.
6. A(n) _______ is a program that copies itself from one machine to another across a network.

7. _______ is nonmaterial, human creations that people can claim ownership to.
8. New work created from an existing work is called a(n) _______.
9. Information in the _______ is free for anyone to use.
10. _______ is the illegal use of email to scam users into surrendering their personal information, usually items like Social Security numbers, bank account numbers, and credit card numbers.

Exercises

1. What is this password: BH9oH2won0? (*Hint*: It was a popular 1990s TV show.)
2. Devise a year's worth of passwords based on a common theme.
3. Go to www.wildlist.org. Check the current list to see how many viruses are currently considered "in the wild."
4. For each of the following, determine whether the practice is legal, illegal, or iffy. Defend your answer.
   a. You sell a copy of a computer game to your friend.
   b. You exchange computer games with your friend.
   c. You sell your old PC with the software still on it, but you keep the original copies of the software.
   d. You download a piece of shareware but don't pay for it.
   e. You frequently use a piece of shareware but don't pay for it.
   f. You install your company's software on your home computer.
   g. You frequently play a freeware game.
   h. You install software on your computer and the laptop of your college-bound child.
   i. You make a backup CD of a set of originals.
   j. You buy one license but install it throughout a lab.
5. For each of the following, determine whether the practice is legal or illegal.
   a. You create a comical, big-eared cartoon rodent.
   b. You publish a Web page without using the copyright notice.
   c. You write a sequel to *Titanic*.
   d. You include a link to a Web page in your term paper.
   e. You include a paragraph from the *Fluency* text in your term paper.
   f. You put your favorite band's picture on your Web site.
   g. You scan the autographed picture of your favorite band and put it on your Web site.
   h. You put a sound bite from a movie on your answering machine.
   i. You put a sound bite from a movie into your class presentation.
   j. You use parts of your friend's term paper from last semester in your term paper.

6. How many possible eight-character passwords can be created using only uppercase letters and numbers?
7. Use the Web to find rules on netiquette. From these, develop your own list of rules.
8. Describe how computer viruses and worms are like the living kind of viruses. In these same terms, describe how to protect your computer from these synthetic viruses.
9. Describe five ways to protect yourself and your personal information from phishing.
10. Explain how vendors make a profit from open source software.

Privacy and Digital Security

Shhh, It's a Secret

13
chapter

learning objectives

- Explain what is meant by privacy; discuss the issues surrounding privacy of information
- List and explain the meaning of the OECD Fair Information Practices
- Compare privacy in the United States to the European Union privacy practices
- Discuss the issues of disagreement concerning privacy: Opt-in/Opt-out and compliance/enforcement
- Explain the security methods used in public key cryptosystems (PKCs), in particular, in the RSA system
- Perform simple encryption from cleartext to cipher text and perform the reverse decryption

I've never looked through a keyhole without finding someone was looking back.

—JUDY GARLAND, COMMENTING ON HER LACK OF PRIVACY, 1967

PRIVACY is a fundamental human right. The United Nations Universal Declaration of Human Rights recognizes privacy in Article 12. The constitutions of Australia, Hungary, and South Africa, among others, state a right to privacy. Though privacy is not explicitly mentioned in the U.S. Constitution, the U.S. Supreme Court has accepted privacy as a right implied by other constitutional guarantees. And privacy is a right that matters to us all. No matter how exemplary our lives may be, there are aspects of it we would prefer to keep secret. And they are no one else's business. When those aspects interact with information technology, the issues of electronic privacy and security become important. There is much more than our passwords that we want to keep to ourselves.

In this chapter we discuss privacy and security. To begin, we consider a business transaction as a basis for understanding the topic of privacy and for considering who has an interest in private information. We consider different definitions of privacy, adopting a clear but abstract definition. We look at how private information can be kept private, and we list the principles of privacy, including the principles from the Organization for Economic Cooperation and Development. Then we explore the differences between how the principles are followed in the United States and in other countries, including a disagreement between the United States and the European Union over these principles. Next we consider how cookies can be abused to compromise Web users' security. Finally, we discuss the problem of identity theft.

The next topic is encryption. After learning encryption vocabulary, we study a simple encryption example. Public key cryptosystems (PKCs) are studied as a means of achieving more convenient security for Internet-related situations. PKC systems seem at first to offer almost no protection, and then they seem to offer so much protection that it's impossible to decrypt what was encrypted. This dilemma is resolved for the RSA public key system. We explore the matter of compromising RSA's security, with the outcome that 100 billion computers wouldn't really help!

Finally, we consider how to keep your information secure from computer failures.

Privacy: Whose Information Is It?

Buying a product at a store generates a transaction, which produces information. The merchant can gather the date and time of the purchase, the product, the cost, and possibly information about other products in the same "market basket." Is this information connected to a specific customer? Paying with cash generally ensures anonymity; that is, the buyer is not connected with the purchase, though cash payments in small towns or even in neighborhood stores where "everyone knows everyone" probably aren't anonymous. However, other transactions can definitely link the purchase with the customer:

- Paying by check, credit card, or debit card
- Purchasing through mail order or on the Internet
- Providing a "preferred customer" number
- Buying a product that must be registered for a service agreement or warranty

If you're buying socks, you probably don't care if this information is recorded. If you're buying *Dating for Total Dummies*, you probably do. You want your purchase of the book to be private.

But what is private? It's not easy to define; we'll give a formal definition later. For now, we'll examine the *Dating for Total Dummies* transaction.

How Can the Information Be Used?

The book merchant, who accepts your credit card for *Dating for Total Dummies*, can reasonably claim that gathering the transaction information is a normal part of conducting business (keeping a record until the payment clears), and so the information belongs to the store, or at least doesn't belong to you alone. If the bookstore decides, based on the information from this transaction, to send you an advertisement—"*Improve Your Love Life* Spring Sale"—the store is using the information for the standard business practice of generating more business. You may even be happy to receive the advertisement. But even if you're not, using "customer information" is so established—it's probably been used since merchandising began—that few would claim the store misused the information. If the merchant sells your name and lovelorn status to the local florists, movie theaters, restaurants, cosmetic surgeons, and so forth, has the information been misused? They are only trying to generate more business, too. Is it misused if the information gets to the campus newspaper, where it is published? Has the store broken the law? (The United States differs from Europe in this respect.) Can't you just be left alone to upgrade your dating skills in peace?

Modern Devices and Privacy

Supreme Court Justice Louis D. Brandeis would have sympathized with your wish. He described privacy as the individual's "right to be left alone." He also wrote (with Samuel D. Warren) in the *Harvard Law Review*:

> *The narrower doctrine [of privacy] may have satisfied the demands of society at a time when the abuse to be guarded against could rarely have arisen without violating a contract or a special confidence; but now that* ***modern devices*** *afford abundant opportunities for the perpetration of such wrongs without any participation of the injured party, the protection granted by the law must be placed upon a broader foundation. [Emphasis added]*

This argues that, in the past, it was hard for people's privacy to be violated without their knowledge, but using *modern devices*, people's privacy can be violated without their knowing it. The amazing thing about Warren and Brandeis' comments is that they were written in 1890. The modern devices they referred to were the first portable cameras and the faster film permitting short exposure photographs. They continued,

> *While, for instance, the state of the photographic art was such that one's picture could seldom be taken without his consciously "sitting" for the purpose, the law of contract or of trust might afford the prudent man sufficient safeguards against the improper circulation of his portrait; but since the latest advances in photographic art have rendered it possible to take pictures surreptitiously, the doctrines of contract and of trust are inadequate to support the required protection.*

What would Warren and Brandeis have thought about phone cameras, the ever-present surveillance camera, Flickr, or YouTube? Their important point is that your image—and more generally, information about you—deserves "sufficient safeguards against improper circulation." It's a nineteenth-century formulation of a twenty-first-century concern.

Controlling the Use of Information

The *Dating for Total Dummies* problem comes down to, "Who controls the use, if any, of the transaction information?" There is a spectrum spanning four main possibilities.

1. **No Uses.** The information ought to be deleted when the store is finished with it (for example, when the payment has cleared), because there is no further use of it.
2. **Approval or Opt-in.** The store can use it for other purposes, but only if you approve the use.
3. **Objection or Opt-out.** The store can use it for other purposes, but not if you object to a use.
4. **No Limits.** The information can be used any way the store chooses.

This spectrum, which ranges from No Uses to No Limits, includes other intermediate points, too.

There is also a fifth possibility, call it *Internal Use*, where the store can use the information to conduct business with you, but for no other use. "Conducting business with you" might mean keeping your address on file so that they can send you announcements about book readings. It would not include giving or selling your information to another person or business, but it may not require your approval either.

fluencyBIT

Another Perspective. The Preamble to the Australian Privacy Charter states, "A free and democratic people requires respect for the autonomy of individuals, and limits on the power of both state and private organizations to intrude on that autonomy.... Privacy is a basic human right and the reasonable expectation of every person."

If the transaction took place in Europe, New Zealand, Australia, Canada, Hong Kong, or several other countries, the law and standards would place it between (1) and (2) on the spectrum, but very close to (1). If the transaction occurred in the United States, the law and standards would place it between (3) and (4) on the spectrum, but very close to (4). Perhaps of greater concern, many Americans apparently *assume* that there is a privacy law that is close to the fifth case, internal use. We will return to these different standards in a later section, but first we must understand the concept of privacy.

A Privacy Definition

As important as it is, privacy is difficult to define. It is more than Brandeis' right "to be left alone." Generally, privacy concerns four aspects of our lives: our bodies, territory, personal information, and communication. Of these only the last two concern us here. We adopt this definition:

Privacy: *The right of people to choose freely under what circumstances and to what extent they will reveal themselves, their attitude, and their behavior to others.*

This definition emphasizes first that it is the person who decides the "circumstances" and the "extent" to which information is revealed, not anyone else. The person has the control. Second, it emphasizes that the range of features over which the person controls the information embodies every aspect of the person—themselves, their attitudes, and their behaviors. Adopting such an inclusive definition is essential for covering situations of importance. For example, buying *Dating for Total Dummies* was an act, covered by behavior, included in our privacy definition. Notice that it doesn't automatically imply the No Uses classification. We may decide that the fact that the book was paid for with a credit card rather than cash—that is, with an identifying form of payment as opposed to an anonymous one—was evidence of a willingness by the buyer to reveal the fact of the purchase. Or we could decide that the form of payment has no bearing on whether the information should be revealed; permission to reveal it must be explicitly given.

Enjoying the Benefits of Privacy

When other people decide to reveal our information, the consequences can be disastrous. Consider Star Wars Kid. He was a pudgy 15-year-old Quebec high school student who in 2002 made a video of himself in his school's A/V Lab in which he waved a golf-ball retriever around pretending it was a Star Wars lightsaber. Other students at the school found the video and made a copy that they posted on Kazaa, the file sharing site. *They did the revealing, not him.* The video became an instant hit, but because the student is clumsy and nonprofessional, he was ridiculed. Many spoofs were made parodying his video. He was jeered and taunted at school. Eventually, he sought therapy. One source estimates that by 2006, it had been viewed hundreds of millions of times, making his video, which he probably wished to keep to himself, the most watched video of all time.

Sometimes we want publicity, and sometimes we don't. Strong privacy laws insure that we control the dissemination of our information. (Canada has strong privacy laws, but that was not the subject of the Star Wars Kid court case.) The benefits to us personally are obvious.

Threats to Privacy

Now that we have the definition, what are the threats to privacy? There are only two basic threats: government and business. A third threat, snooping or gossiping private parties, will be handled by security, that is, by keeping the information private. Historically, the governmental threat—a regime spying on its citizens—worries people the most, probably because when it happens the consequences are so serious. The business threat is a more recent worry, and its IT aspects even newer still. There are two types of business threats: surveillance of employees and the use of business-related information, including transaction information, for other purposes.

Voluntary Disclosure

A person can in principle enjoy perfect privacy by simply deciding not to reveal anything to anyone; that is, to be a hermit, though that probably would mean living alone on a remote island, surviving on coconuts and clams. But most of us interact with many people and organizations—businesses, our employer, and governments—to whom it is in our interest to reveal private information. That is, we freely choose to reveal information in exchange for real benefits.

- We tell our doctors many personal facts about ourselves so they can help us stay healthy.
- We allow credit card companies to check our credit record in exchange for the convenience of paying with a card.
- We permit our employer to read email we send at work, understanding that we are using the employer's computer, Internet connection,

and time; that the email system is there for us to use on the job; and that we have no need or intent to send personal email.

- We reveal to the government—though not in the United States—our religion, our parents' names and birthplaces, our race and ethnicity, and so on for the purposes of enjoying the rights of citizenship.

How private can we be when we reveal so much about ourselves, our attitudes, and our behavior?

Social Networking. Today, the most common way to share personal information is on social networking sites: Twitter, Facebook, Flickr, YouTube, and the like. We voluntarily reveal ourselves to be a friend, to make friends, to share with our friends. Of course, it's publicly available for everyone to see—friends, relatives, employers, and government investigators to name a few. As we will learn at the end of the chapter, the information may survive forever despite our best efforts to delete or remove it. So, it is wise to consider what to post on a social networking site. As they say, "If you wouldn't publish it in the paper, don't publish it on the Web."

Fair Information Practices

It is possible to reveal information about ourselves and still enjoy considerable privacy, but it depends on what happens to the information after we've revealed it to other people and organizations. If they keep the information confidential, use it only for the purposes for which they gathered it, and protect it from all threats, our privacy is not seriously compromised. We receive the benefits and preserve our privacy. It's a good deal.

But if those people or organizations are free to give or sell the information to anyone else, they are also revealing information about us. Our privacy is compromised. It's not enough to trust the people we give the information to. There must be clear guidelines adopted for handling private information, so that we have standards by which to judge whether the trust is warranted. For that we have the Fair Information Practices principles.

OECD Fair Information Practices

In 1980 the Organization for Economic Cooperation and Development (OECD)—an organization of currently 30 countries concerned with international trade—developed an eight-point list of privacy principles that became known as the Fair Information Practices. They have become a widely accepted standard, forming a reasonably complete solution to the problem of keeping information private while at the same time revealing appropriate information to businesses and governments. The public has an interest in these principles becoming law. The principles also give a standard that businesses and governments can meet as a "due diligence test" for protecting citizens' rights of privacy, thereby protecting themselves from criticism or legal action. The OECD principles are a practical implementation of privacy protection.

The OECD Fair Information Practices principles are as follows.

- **Limited Collection Principle:** There should be limits to the personal data collected about anyone; data should be collected by fair and lawful means; and it should be collected with the knowledge and consent of the person whenever appropriate and possible.
- **Quality Principle:** Personal data gathered should be relevant to the purposes for which it is used, and should be accurate, complete, and up-to-date.
- **Purpose Principle:** The purposes for collecting personal data should be stated when it is collected, and the uses should be limited to those purposes.
- **Use Limitation Principle:** Personal data should not be disclosed or used for purposes other than stated in the Purpose Principle, except with the consent of the individual or by the authority of law.
- **Security Principle:** Personal data should be protected by reasonable security measures against risks of disclosure, unauthorized access, misuse, modification, destruction, or loss.
- **Openness Principle:** There should be general openness of policies and practices about personal data collection, making it possible to know of its existence, kind, and purpose of use, as well as the identity and contact information for the data controller.
- **Participation Principle:** An individual should be able to (a) determine whether the data controller has information about him or her, and (b) discover what it is in a timely manner, in an understandable form, and at a reasonable charge (if any). If the inquiry is denied, the individual should be allowed to find out why and be able to challenge the denial. Further, the individual can challenge the data relating to him or her, and if successful, have the data erased, completed, or changed.
- **Accountability Principle:** The data controller should be accountable for complying with these principles.

An important aspect of the OECD principles is the concept that the **data controller**—the person or office setting the policies—must interact with individuals about their information, if any, and must be accountable for those policies and actions.

Comparing Privacy Across the Atlantic

Despite being a fundamental human right, privacy is not enjoyed in much of the world at the OECD standard for both government- and business-held information. This is somewhat surprising because privacy is well understood, its IT implications are clear, and all that's left is to enact laws and enforce them. What's the problem?

Privacy often comes in conflict with private or governmental interests. For example, the United States has not adopted the OECD principles, despite being a major player in the OECD and having created earlier principles on which the Fair Information Practices are based. It can be presumed that this is because many U.S. companies profit by gathering and collating information, or by buying and using information in ways that are inconsistent with the OECD principles. Similarly, the Chinese government isn't going to protect the right to privacy when it denies other basic human rights. The rights to privacy for these countries' citizens are thus diminished. Globalization may change that.

In 1995, in a landmark advancement for privacy, the European Union issued the European Data Protection Directive, a benchmark law incorporating the OECD principles. The member countries have enacted this law giving everyone in the EU the same high level of privacy.

Many non-EU countries, such as Australia, New Zealand, Canada, Hong Kong, and non-EU European countries, have adopted laws based on OECD principles. This is important because one provision in the EU Directive requires that data about EU citizens be protected by the standards of the law even when it leaves their country. Non-EU countries that want information on EU citizens must show that they have privacy laws consistent with the OECD principles. Switzerland, a non-EU country, applied and was approved. The United States applied and was not. What sorts of laws protect U.S. privacy?

U.S. Laws Protecting Privacy

The United States passed the Privacy Act of 1974, a strong limit on the government's ability to invade people's privacy. (The U.S. Patriot Act of 2002 and its reauthorization in 2005 has seriously weakened its protections.) This covers half of the privacy problem—interactions with *government*. But the reason the United States failed to meet the requirements of the EU Directive concerns information stored by *businesses*.

By contrast to the "omnibus" solution of adopting the OECD list, the United States uses an approach called "sectoral," meaning that it passes laws to deal with specific industries (business sectors) or practices. Examples include:

- Electronic Communication Privacy Act of 1986
- Video Privacy Protection Act of 1988
- Telephone Consumer Protection Act of 1991
- Driver's Privacy Protection Act of 1994
- Health Insurance Privacy and Accountability Act of 1996

To illustrate, the Driver's Privacy Protection Act makes it illegal for motor vehicle registration departments to make information publicly available. Mass marketers once used motor vehicle information to create mailing lists. (Driving an expensive car might imply that you have a large income.) Now, the DMV must *get permission from the registrant* before making the information available for any purpose other than registering cars.

fluencyBIT

Don't Ask. When the Supreme Court upheld the constitutionality of the Driver's Privacy Protection Act, the *Wall Street Journal* quoted a mass marketing industry spokesman as saying it was "death to us . . . If you can't use information about a person without permission, that generally means you're not going to have a list of any great substance." That is, using information without permission is essential to mass marketing.

The sectoral approach, though it often provides very strong privacy protections in specific narrow cases, leaves much information unprotected. By contrast, an omnibus solution provides consistent protection to all information. Citizens do not have to wonder whether specific information is safe.

Privacy Principles: European Union

The differences in privacy laws between the U.S. and the EU are a serious problem for multinational companies and Internet and Web-based businesses. A company cannot move data from an EU country to the United States until the United States meets the OECD principles. (Non-EU states subscribing to the OECD principles would probably object, too.)

The Federal Trade Commission (FTC) and the EU have been negotiating for years to solve this problem. A tentative agreement was founded on a concept called a Safe Harbor, which means a U.S. company that follows the rules of the agreement can receive information from the EU. The FTC Safe Harbor guidelines are much weaker than the OECD principles. There are two glaring points of disagreement—Opt-in/Opt-out and compliance/enforcement—that are causing most of the difficulties.

Opt-in/Opt-out refers to the approval and objection aspects of privacy as illustrated in our *Dating for Total Dummies* example. That is, when can an organization use information it collects for one purpose for a different purpose? "Opt-in" means the business cannot use it unless the person explicitly allows the new use. "Opt-out" means the business can use it unless the person explicitly prohibits the new use. Privacy principles as far back as 1972 have consistently required Opt-in for all changes in use, because otherwise the person does not control the use of private information. (Opt-in is actually a longer-standing principle than stated. Warren and Brandeis' 1890 concept of a "special confidence" between photographers and their subjects protecting their privacy amounts to Opt-in. That is, the photographer would violate the confidence unless he or she asked for and received permission from the subject first.) It was the Opt-in requirement of the motor vehicle registration act that caused predictions of "death" by the mass marketing spokesman. The FTC guidelines, however, require Opt-in only for highly sensitive information like medical data; Opt-out is the standard in the U.S.—and opposite of the OECD guidelines.

Compliance/Enforcement refers to how organizations meet their obligations under the principles, that is, how the role of the data controller is implemented. The EU and other OECD-subscribing countries have introduced offices to perform the duties of the data controller. There is no such person or office in the United States. The FTC proposes that U.S. companies "comply voluntarily" as a result of "market pressure." Private firms like TRUSTe and private agencies like the Better Business Bureau would do the monitoring. These private agencies and firms would then report violations to the FTC, but privacy advocates point out that such a voluntary process amounts to no enforcement at all. The EU apparently agrees.

These privacy issues are important to both sides. Without Opt-in and enforcement, the OECD principles are badly eroded. But with those requirements, industries like direct marketing are, by their own description, mortally affected. At last check, the stalemate continues.

fluencyBIT

Voluntary Compliance? Privacy consultant Richard M. Smith discovered in November 1999 that Real Networks' JukeBox software was gathering music taste profiles based on users' unique IDs. The company had a privacy policy, but it did not mention the unique ID or the profiling activity, *until he caught them.* Further, Real Networks had hired the audit firm TRUSTe.

A Privacy Success Story

Americans' electronic privacy has become dramatically worse since 2000 with spam, spyware, identity theft, exploits, phishing, and the like, but there is a success story. Unfortunately, the story also illustrates that, in the context of privacy, "voluntary compliance" doesn't work.

Consider the history of the Do-Not-Call List. In the 1990s households would receive numerous calls every evening from telemarketers trying to sell products. Though Americans hated the calls and heaped criticism and scorn on telemarketers, the calls only got worse. Nothing was done about it. Why? Because the "industry self-policing" mechanism was a little-known system requiring a person either (a) to write a letter to the industry association—you couldn't even call, despite the fact it was a *tele*marketing association—or (b) to opt-out online by paying a fee using a credit card. That is, people had to pay to stop being harassed by the telemarketers! And even then, these actions only stopped the telemarketers that belonged to that association. Despite these difficulties, five million households put their phone numbers on the list.

Finally, the problem got so bad that the U.S. government set up the Do-Not-Call List, a central place where people could simply give their phone number—by phone or online—to stop telemarketers. The list was an instant success! Ten million households opted-out on the first day of operation.

Today more than 175,000,000 phone numbers are on the Do-Not-Call List. And, of course, the telemarketing business has largely collapsed.

Partial Success. Voluntary compliance has succeeded in getting Web sites to publish privacy policies. It's a small accomplishment, because the privacy policies don't imply any assurance of privacy, as the Real Networks example shows. An Annenberg survey (2003) found that 57 percent of those polled thought (mistakenly) that a site with a privacy policy does not share data with other organizations. But privacy policies are all different. Some are strong; others simply explain that information *is* shared with other organizations, often in terms that make it sound like that's exactly what you would like them to do. So, read the policies carefully, or for quicker results, search for "opt" to find the place where they tell you how to opt-out of their data "sharing."

There was no economic incentive for telemarketers to make it easy for people to opt-out, though history proves it was easy to do. So, rather than setting up a way for Americans to be left alone—as Brandeis wished—to enjoy dinner without the interruption of telemarketing calls, the industry association "voluntarily complied" by making it difficult and ineffective to opt-out. There is no reason to think Internet information gatherers are any different.

The Cookie Monster

Cookies are a standard computer science concept originally used by Netscape engineers to connect the identity of a client across a series of independent client/server events. Here's the problem cookies solve.

Recall the Web server's view of the client/server relationship, as shown in Figure 13.1. Imagine this is your bank's server, and you are paying bills online, which makes you a client. The server is helping many clients at once, and to know who's who, the server stores a **cookie**—a record containing seven fields

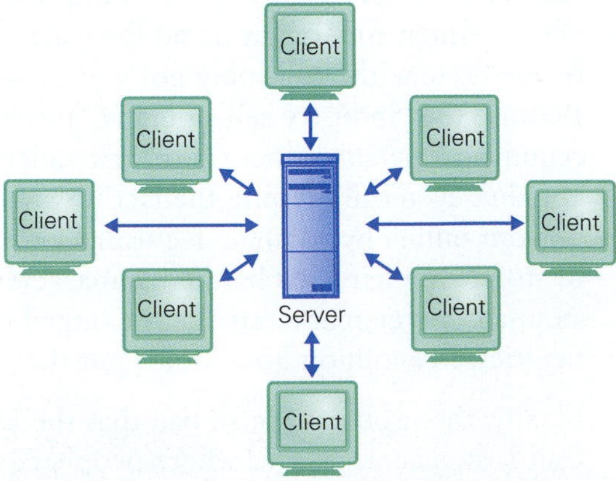

Figure 13.1 Server's view of the client/server relationship.

of information that uniquely identify a customer's session—on your computer. Many sites use cookies, even when the interaction is not intended to be as secure as a bank transaction. For example, the National Air and Space Museum sent me this cookie

```
www.nasm.si.edu   FALSE / FALSE   2052246450   CFTOKEN   89367880
```

while I was writing Chapter 3. The meaning of the fields is unimportant, except to note that the first is the server and the last is the unique information identifying my session. Cookies are exchanged between the client and the server on each transmission of information, allowing the server to know which of the many client computers is sending information. Cookies are an elegant way for servers to give clients the illusion they are the only one being served.

Finding Cookies. Modern browsers let you control the cookie policy for your computer—a good reason to run a modern browser. They show you the cookies you have stored and delete them at your request. Cookie control is usually found as a security or privacy tab under browser preferences. For Firefox, navigate *Preferences > Privacy > Show Cookies . . .* or check Help.

The reason users need to know about cookies is that they can be abused using a loophole called a **third-party cookie**. In principle, a cookie is exchanged between the client and the server making the interaction private. This privacy is enforced because browsers don't allow servers to check to see what other cookies are stored on your computer. Why would a server want to know? An online business might want to know if a customer has visited other similar businesses in the last few minutes to evaluate its competition and see how often it's the first place customers visit.

But there is a loophole. If the Web site includes advertisements on its page, it often contracts with an ad company to create and place the ads. While the browser is setting up your page, the server directs it to link to the ad company—a third party—to deliver the ad. At that moment, your computer is in a client/server relationship with the ad company, and can allow it to place a cookie on your computer. You may have never heard of the ad company or be aware that it's placing information on your computer. If you visit a different server that uses the same ad company, it will also exchange cookies when it places its ads. Since the ad company gets the same cookie from your computer that it placed moments before for a different company, it knows that you visited the other company. By this means it is possible to log considerable information about a user's behavior. Is that bad? It's up to you to decide.

fluencyBIT

Many Double Clicks. In June 2000 Richard M. Smith, the privacy consultant, testified before Congress that in the previous six months his computer had logged 250,000 Internet transactions, roughly 10 percent of which was traffic to a single Web advertising company, DoubleClick, allowing them to track the URLs of the sites he visited.

So, cookies are useful and essential for Web interactions with online banks and brokers. But, they can be abused. What can be done? All modern browsers allow users to control how cookies are processed. One possibility is to turn them off entirely, forcing the browser to ask you every time a server wants to send you a cookie whether you will accept it. Though it may be annoying, it is also very interesting to turn off cookie acceptance for a while to see how many cookies are sent, and from what servers. You'll be surprised. Turning cookies off prevents you from being able to bank online, but you can turn cookie acceptance back on when you want.

Browsers also allow users to automatically accept cookies from the servers they visit, but not to automatically accept them from third parties. Such a setting allows cookies to work as they were originally intended, since we are usually willing to accept cookies from a site we choose to visit. Though cookies are not the worst computer privacy risk users take, it is also easy to manage the risk by simply setting your browser's cookie policy at your own comfort level.

Identity Theft

We have focused most on the Use Limitation Principle of the Fair Information Practices, wherein a person decides whether to allow a use (Opt-in) that is different from the original use for which information was collected. But the Security Principle has become at least as important. The Security Principle states that those who hold private information are obligated to maintain its privacy against unauthorized access and other hazards. Americans do not enjoy protection from this principle either.

In February of 2005 the information broker ChoicePoint announced that personal data it holds on 145,000 Americans had been, in the company's words, "viewed by unauthorized parties." ChoicePoint keeps data on people's credit rating, and initially they only admitted that information on 32,000 people had been compromised. This smaller number apparently referred only to the Californians on the list, because California has a law requiring notification of security violations. Public pressure forced ChoicePoint to admit to and notify the larger population.

The Electronic Privacy Information Center (EPIC), a privacy watchdog, stated the situation more plainly: "ChoicePoint, which recently admitted it sold personal information on 145,000 Americans to identity thieves, also sold such information on at least 7,000 people to identity thieves in 2002." In an unrelated incident in March 2005, it was discovered that information about thousands of season-pass holders to Disney Japan had been stolen.

How can this private information be used? One possibility is **identity theft**—the crime of posing as someone else for fraudulent purposes. Because information from a company like ChoicePoint includes credit card numbers, Social Security numbers, bank account numbers, and employers, a thief has no more difficulty applying for a credit card or a loan than does the person whose information it actually is. It's the victim, however, who ends up with a ruined credit rating and large debts.

Over 800 identity thefts have been reported from the ChoicePoint event. Though the Federal Trade Commission resolved the matter with ChoicePoint by negotiating $10 million in civil fines and $5 million in consumer redress, it is likely that identity theft will remain an issue for some time.

fluencyBIT

Identity Crisis. Chipmaker Intel introduced a unique ID for each Pentium III processor chip, but removed it under intense criticism. The ID would have greatly simplified the task of matching Web-collected data—it's like all .COMs using the same cookie on a given machine.

Managing Your Privacy

Unfortunately, our brief discussion about privacy threats has touched only a few high points. What's a user to do about privacy?

The main obligation is to understand that in the U.S., protecting your privacy is *your* job; the laws are completely inadequate. Constructive actions can be recommended, however:

- Purchase up-to-date virus checking software, as described in Chapter 12, to minimize the unsavory critters that arrive by email.
- Adjust your cookie settings in your browser—they're under *Preferences* > *Privacy* in Firefox—to match your comfort level.
- Read the privacy statement of any site to which you will give personally identifying information *before* you give it, including credit card information for a purchase. Though you may want to assume they will not share the information, a better assumption is that they will, until you see the place in their privacy policy where they say they do not. Sites that do not share make this *very* obvious.
- Review the phishing protections given in Chapter 12 to avoid scams, since being a victim of a phishing scam can make you vulnerable to identity theft.
- Patronize reputable companies for music, software, DVDs, and other downloaded files; file sharing is thought to be a major vector for spyware and other privacy-compromising software.
- Be skeptical. Paranoia isn't necessary, but skepticism is.
- Stay familiar with the current assaults on privacy; they're often announced in the national media, but it's a simple matter to find them at sites like EPIC (www.epic.org).
- As a final action item, perhaps Americans should be lobbying for U.S. adoption of OECD's Fair Information Practices.

fluencyBIT

Making Privacy Public. Some Web companies are addressing issues of privacy. For example, Facebook recently held open forums to discuss its proposed Statement of Rights and Responsibilities for its site. Issues discussed included the ownership of the content, limitations on use, opt-in, deletion and removal, and other privacy-related topics.

Encryption and Decryption

The best way to keep electronic information secret is to **digitally encrypt** it—that is, to transform the representation so it is no longer understandable.

Encryption Terminology

In Chapter 12 you saw encryption applied to passwords. We noted that if we forget our password, the superuser usually cannot tell us what it is because the software stores it in encrypted form—what we called *scrambled*. In a **cryptosystem**—a combination of encryption and decryption methods—the password is the **cleartext** or **plaintext**, that is, the information before encryption. The encrypted password is the **cipher text**, the encrypted form. Passwords use a **one-way cipher**—an encryption technique that cannot be easily reversed—because there's really no need to decrypt them: The system encrypts the password the user enters and compares it to the stored version, which is also encrypted. If they don't match as cipher text, they don't match as cleartext either. So, for password scrambling, the simple one-way encryption works.

Information is encrypted so it can be safely transmitted or stored. Transmitting or storing unencrypted information makes it vulnerable to snooping. Eventually, the cleartext must be recovered by reversing the encryption process, or **decrypting** the cipher text. In the diagram of the cryptosystem shown in Figure 13.2, the sender and receiver agree on a key, K_{SR}. The sender uses the key to encrypt the cleartext, and the receiver uses it to decrypt the cipher text. The key can be applied to the letters of the cleartext in various ways.

A common way is as follows: ASCII letters are treated as numbers using their bit representation and transformed by some mathematical operation with an inverse, say, multiplication, to produce the cipher text bits. That is, a few letters of the ASCII text are multiplied times the key and the resulting number is sent or stored. The cleartext can be recovered by applying the inverse operation (division by the key, in this case).

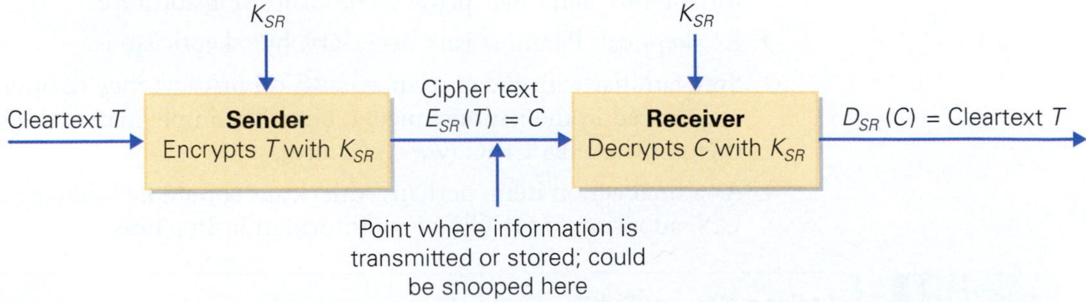

Figure 13.2 Schematic diagram of a cryptosystem. Using a key K_{SR} known only to them, the sender encrypts the cleartext information to produce a cipher text, and the receiver decrypts the cipher text to recover the cleartext. In the middle, where the content is exposed and can be snooped, it is unintelligible.

XOR: An Encryption Operation

Exclusive OR, known as XOR, is an interesting way to apply a key to cleartext. XOR, which can be described as "*x* or *y* but not both," is written like an addition symbol in a circle, ⊕. It combines two bits by the rule: If the bits are the same, the result is 0; if the bits are different, the result is 1. Thus, if 0101 is the cleartext and 1001 is the key, then

	0101	Cleartext
⊕	1001	Key
	1100	Cipher text

XOR produces `1100` for the cipher text. Applying the key to the cipher text again with XOR produces the original cleartext:

	1100	Cipher text
⊕	1001	Key
	0101	Cleartext

Thus XOR is its own inverse.

Encrypting a message. To illustrate encryption, imagine two students who have been writing messages to each other on the white board in the computer lab, but now they're worried that other people may be reading them, and so they decide to encrypt them. They agree on the key `0001 0111 0010 1101`, and plan to encode pairs of ASCII letters by transforming them with the key using XOR. Here's what they do (see Figure 13.3).

Using the cleartext `Meet@12:15@Joe's`, they first write down the ASCII representation of these letters in pairs. (The ASCII representation is shown in Figure 8.3.) Next, they XOR each of these 16-bit sequences with their key sequence to produce the cipher text, which in this case has the ASCII equivalent of ZHrYW$^{F}_{S}$%$^{E}_{\Sigma}$&$^{C}_{N}$WgxH0_. This is the cipher text—a very strange sequence that should be secure to the casual observer in the computer lab. The cipher text can be easily decrypted using the same technique, because

Cleartext			Key	Cipher Text	
Me	0100 1101 0110 0101			0101 1010 0100 1000	ZH
et	0110 0101 0111 0100			0111 0010 0101 1001	rY
@1	0100 0000 0011 0001			0101 0111 0001 1100	W$^{F}_{S}$
2:	0011 0010 0011 1010	⊕	0001 0111 0010 1101 =	0010 0101 0001 0111	%$^{E}_{\Sigma}$
15	0011 0001 0011 0101			0010 0110 0001 1000	&$^{C}_{N}$
@J	0100 0000 0100 1010			0101 0111 0110 0111	Wg
oe	0110 1111 0110 0101			0111 1000 0100 1000	xH
's	0010 0111 0111 0010			0011 0000 0101 1111	0_

Figure 13.3 Encrypting the cleartext `Meet@12:15@Joe's`, using ASCII encoding of letter pairs, the key `0001 0111 0010 1101`, and the operation of exclusive OR to produce the cipher text ZHrYW$^{F}_{S}$%$^{E}_{\Sigma}$&$^{C}_{N}$WgxH0_. (Decryption works in the opposite direction, as if the "⊕" and " = " symbols of the figure were exchanged.)

XOR is its own inverse: XOR each of the ASCII equivalents of the cipher text with the key to produce the cleartext bits of the pairs. Then, look up the letters in the ASCII table. We can see that this scheme must always work by reviewing Figure 13.3 and using two facts:

- If any bit sequence is XORed with another bit sequence (the key) and the result is also XORed again with the key, that result is the original bit sequence.
- With XOR, it makes no difference whether the key is on the left or the right.

These facts mean that encrypting is moving from left to right in the figure, whereas decrypting would move from right to left.

13.1 Unusual Name. Find the ASCII encoding of your name (refer back to Figure 8.3), and use the students' key XOR encryption from Figure 13.3 to encrypt it.

Breaking the code. How secure is the code? Probably not too secure, though being a cipher text containing only 16 characters, a code cracker has very little to work with. The longer the text, the easier it is to decode, because once enough letters have been used, it's possible to notice what bit patterns show up frequently. Even in our short message there are two H's in the second position, corresponding to e's, and two W's in the first position, corresponding to @'s. Repeated W's are not very likely in a longer text, but repeated H's are.

As you know, *e* is the most common letter in English. Seeing these patterns and guessing that they correspond to *e* bytes, we can begin to figure out the cleartext from the cipher text by replacing each occurrence with *e*'s. (Naturally, r in the first position—the encoding of *e* with the first half of the key—will show up with the same frequency.) In English, the 12 most common letters are e, t, a, o, i, n, s, h, r, d, l, and u. (Curiously, most people who remember this sequence do so by pronouncing it!) Other languages are different, of course. These dozen letters represent about 80 percent of the letters in the average English text. Using these letters, we can replace the dozen most frequently occurring (left and right) patterns. Decrypting that many letters of a cipher text would make decrypting the remainder a simple *Wheel-of-Fortune* endgame. We would have broken the code without ever knowing that the two students had used XOR as the encryption operation, or what the key was. The only property we used was that the students' code consistently replaced each letter with one of two patterns. Clearly they had better be smarter next time!

fluencyBIT

Tse Beht of Tnmeh. The frequency count for English is not fixed, of course. Different sources produce somewhat different results, even for large documents. For example, *A Tale of Two Cities* contains more than half a million letters that are distributed from greatest to least frequency: e, t, a, o, n, i, h, s, r, d, l, and u. That is, *n* and *i* are swapped, and *s* and *h* are swapped from the standard distribution.

Being smarter about byte-for-byte substitutions is easy to do. For example, grouping more than two bytes will help our student encoders. The harder problem is that the sender and the receiver have to agree on the key *ahead of time*. That is, they had to meet or at least communicate for the purpose of selecting the key. If they don't meet, but communicate instead, that communication isn't secure because there is no agreed upon key yet. Key exchange would be a showstopper for applications like Internet commerce, where credit card numbers should be kept secret, but the customer and the company cannot meet, perhaps because they are on opposite sides of the planet. The problem is beautifully solved using public key encryption.

Public Key Cryptosystems

In a **public key cryptosystem (PKC)**, people who want to receive secure information publish a key that senders should use to encrypt messages. For example, the key could be published on a Web page. Imagine that the key is 129 digits long and the senders are told to cube 32-byte groups of ASCII letters—yes, treat the bits like a 256-bit number and raise it to the third power—divide the result by the key, and send the remainder (that is, the bits smaller than the key that are left over from the division). The key was chosen so that the receiver, but not the general public or a code cracker, can decrypt it. If we change Figure 13.2 to a public key encryption, we get Figure 13.4.

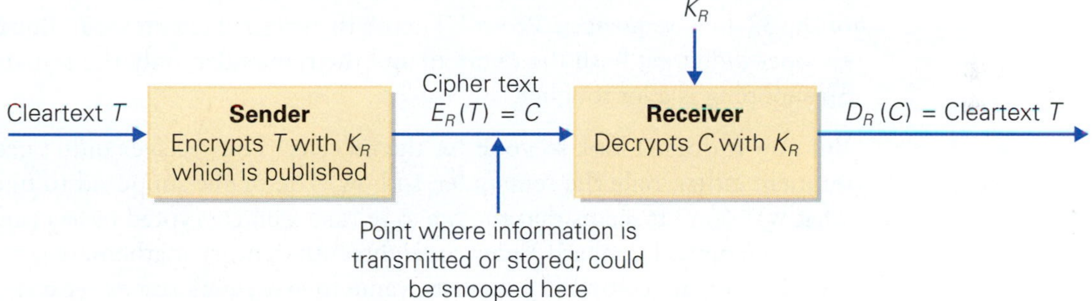

Figure 13.4 Public key cryptosystem. The sender uses the receiver's public key K_R to encrypt the cleartext, and only the receiver is able to decrypt it to recover the cleartext.

fluencyBIT

Public Spirited. Computer scientists Whitfield Diffie and Martin Helman invented public key cryptosystems in 1976.

Code Cracker's Problem

The bad guy who is trying to snoop on the communication by intercepting the cipher text and decrypting it knows the key, too, because it's published on the Web page. And it would seem the bad guy has the same ability to perform arithmetic on the cipher text that the receiver does. How much security can there be when so much information is known?

But cracking the code isn't so easy. All that was sent was the **remainder**—the bits that were left over from the division.

Recall from middle school that the definition for division, *a/b*, is to satisfy the equation

$$a = b \cdot c + d$$

for *divisor b*, *quotient c*, that is, the result of the division, and *remainder d*. Further, *d* will be smaller than *b*. For example, 30/8 becomes

$$30 = 8 \cdot 3 + 6$$

which is the same as saying, "30 divided by 8 is 3 with a remainder of 6." This is called the **quotient-remainder form of division**. Substituting the variables of our encryption situation, the equation becomes

$$T^3 = K_R \cdot c + d$$

for cleartext T and some quotient c that doesn't interest us. Only d, the remainder, is sent.

Snooping and Decrypting

If the code cracker had the quotient *c and* the remainder *d*, he or she could simply multiply the quotient by the key ($K_R \cdot c$) and add in the remainder to produce T^3. Using a calculator to find the cube root gives the binary number of the 32-byte sequences. Presto! There's the original cleartext, *T*. But the snooper didn't get both the quotient and the remainder, only the remainder. So snooping is a lot tougher.

But now it doesn't look so good for the receiver. The receiver didn't get the quotient either, only the remainder, so how is he or she supposed to figure out what was sent? It seems that the message is so well encrypted *no one* can figure it out! Happily, Leonhard Euler, an eighteenth-century mathematician, and a few enterprising computer scientists, came to everyone's rescue—except, of course, the cracker.

RSA Public Key Cryptosystem

The **RSA public key cryptosystem** is the best known of the PKC systems. Named for its inventors, Ron Rivest, Adi Shamir, and Len Adleman, the RSA scheme is basically the same as the PKC scheme we just described. We need to learn enough about how it works to retrieve the original cleartext. *Why* it works relies on very deep mathematics and computer science that will not be described here. But it does work. It has withstood formidable attacks and will continue to as computers get faster. We'll describe the assaults on RSA after we give it a try.

fluencyBIT

> **Secret Prize.** Rivest, Shamir, and Adleman were awarded the 2003 Turing Award by the Association for Computing Machinery, computing's Nobel Prize, for their creation of the RSA cryptosystem.

The RSA scheme relies on prime numbers. Recall from middle school that **prime numbers** can only be divided evenly—that is, without a remainder—by 1 and themselves. So, the first few prime numbers are 2, 3, 5, 7, 11, 13, 17, 19, 23, 29, 31, ...

Mathematicians adore prime numbers because they have amazing properties. The rest of us only know that prime numbers are the basic "atoms" of a whole number: Any number can be **factored** into primes in only one way. The factors of a number x are just whole numbers that when multiplied together give x. So, factors of 30 are

$1 \times 30 = 30$
$2 \times 15 = 30$
$3 \times 10 = 30$
$5 \times 6 = 30$
$2 \times 3 \times 5 = 30$

but only {2,3,5} are the prime factors of 30.

Choosing a Key

The secret of the RSA scheme, of course, is that the receiver didn't publish any random 129-digit sequence as the public key, K_R. The key has some special properties. Specifically, the public key must be the product of two different prime numbers, p and q,

$K_R = pq$

Because multiplying two numbers of roughly equal size produces a number twice as long, p and q must be about 64 or 65 digits long to produce the 129-digit public key of the example. Additionally, p and q, besides being long enough and prime, must also be 2 greater than a multiple of 3. It's a rather strange requirement, but essential, as you'll see in a moment. Many primes have this property. For example, 5 and 11 are 2 larger than multiples of 3, namely, 3 and 9. As a running example, take

$p = 5$
$q = 11$
$K_R = pq = 55.$

Encrypting a Message

To encrypt a cleartext, divide it into blocks—we'll use 6-bit blocks of the ASCII encoding for the running example, but they're usually many bytes long—cube the blocks, divide them by the public key, and transmit the remainders from the divisions. (We use 6-bit blocks just to keep the numbers small.)

Thus, to encrypt the amount of a credit card transaction,

```
****$0.02
```

the ASCII characters are expressed in their byte representation

```
0010 1010 0010 1010 0010 1010 0010 1010 0010 0100 0011 0000
0010 1110 0011 0000 0011 0010
```

and grouped into 6-bit blocks,

```
0010 1010 0010 1010 0010 1010 0010 1010 0010 0100 0011 0000
0010 1110 0011 0000 0011 0010
```

shown in white and blue.

Recalling from Chapter 11 that bits can be interpreted in any way that is convenient, our groups are interpreted as numbers

$T = 10, 34, 40, 42, 10, 34, 16, 48, 11, 35, 0, 50$

Cubed, they are

$T^3 = 1000, 39304, 64000, 74088, 1000, 39304, 4096, 110592, 1331, 42875, 0, 125000$

and divided by the key $K_R = 55$ and expressed in quotient, remainder form they are as follows

$1000 = 55 \cdot 18 + 10$
$39304 = 55 \cdot 714 + 34$
$64000 = 55 \cdot 1163 + 35$
$74088 = 55 \cdot 1347 + 3$
$1000 = 55 \cdot 18 + 10$
$39304 = 55 \cdot 714 + 34$
$4096 = 55 \cdot 74 + 26$
$110592 = 55 \cdot 2010 + 42$
$1331 = 55 \cdot 24 + 11$
$42875 = 55 \cdot 779 + 30$
$0 = 55 \cdot 0 + 0$
$125000 = 55 \cdot 2272 + 40$

And finally, only the remainders are kept to yield the cipher text

$C = 10, 34, 35, 3, 10, 34, 26, 42, 11, 30, 0, 40$

These numbers are the encrypted message to be sent. (The apparent coincidence that some of the cipher text numbers happened to be the same as their corresponding cleartext occurs because our sample numbers (55) are so small. The result is still incomprehensibly scrambled.)

The Decryption Method

How does the receiver reconstruct the cleartext? First, we must compute the quantity

$s = (1/3)[2(p - 1)(q - 1) + 1]$

For our running example, this curious number is

$s = (1/3)\ (2 \cdot 4 \cdot 10 + 1) = 81/3 = 27$

To make s come out right, we added the requirement of "2 greater than a multiple of 3" when choosing p and q.

The amazing fact is that if the cipher text numbers C are each raised to the s power, C^s—that's right, C^{27} in our example—and divided by the key K_R, the remainders are the cleartext! That is, for some quotient c that we don't care about,

$C^s = K_R \cdot c + T$

which is *truly* the key to the RSA scheme.

Decrypting: $C = 10$. To demonstrate this amazing fact, take the first number of our cipher text

$C = 10$

and compute

$C^s = C^{27} = 10^{27} = 1{,}000{,}000{,}000{,}000{,}000{,}000{,}000{,}000{,}000$

which is not a binary number, but the huge decimal number of 1 followed by 27 zeros. Divide by $K_R = 55$ and express the result in the quotient-remainder form

$1{,}000{,}000{,}000{,}000{,}000{,}000{,}000{,}000{,}000$
$= 55 \cdot 18{,}181{,}818{,}181{,}818{,}181{,}818{,}181{,}818 + 10$

Thus, $T = 10$, so the first 6 bits of the cleartext must be 10 in binary, 001010, as can be checked.

Decrypting: $C = 3$. The numbers can get very large for us—encryption algorithms actually use several techniques, such as modular arithmetic, to avoid the large intermediate numbers—but let's try another example. The fourth term of the cipher text is

$C = 3$

which we can raise to the 27th power with a calculator to get

$3^s = 3^{27} = 7{,}625{,}597{,}484{,}987$

Dividing by the public key K_R and expressing the result in the quotient-remainder form yields

$7{,}625{,}597{,}484{,}987 = 55 \cdot 138{,}647{,}226{,}999 + 42$

implying that the fourth block of the text is binary for 42, or 101010, as can be verified. As a third example, we notice that everything works out right for the cipher text $C = 0$.

Why does the RSA work? Euler proved the following theorem in 1736. (This is the only occurrence of higher mathematics in this book. It isn't necessary to understand it. Simply accept that Euler's formula makes the RSA scheme work out.)

Theorem: Let p and q be distinct primes, $K = pq$, $0 < T < K$, and $r > 0$. If $T^{r(p-1)(q-1)+1}$ is divided by K, the remainder is T.

For our use of Euler's formula, $r = 2$, because

$$\begin{aligned}(T^3)^s &= (T^3)^{(1/3)[2(p-1)(q-1)+1]} \\ &= T^{2(p-1)(q-1)+1}\end{aligned}$$

Thus, when the cipher text—that is, the remainders—is raised to the s power and divided by the key, the cleartext is recovered.

Summarizing the RSA System

To summarize, (our sample version of) the RSA public key crypto scheme follows these steps:

1. **Publishing**. Select two different prime numbers, p and q, which are 2 larger than a multiple of 3, and define $K_R = pq$, the public key. Compute $s = (1/3)[2(p-1)(q-1)+1]$. Keep p, q, and s secret. Publish K_R where senders can find it.
2. **Encrypting**. Get the public key from the receiver, and break the cleartext bit-sequence into blocks according to the receiver's instructions, but less than K_R. Cube each block, divide each of the cubes by K_R, and send the remainders to the receiver as the cipher text.
3. **Decrypting**. Using the secret value s, raise each number in the cipher text to the s power, divide each result by K_R, and assemble the remainders into the blocks of the bit sequence of the cleartext.

Of course, humans don't do these calculations. Software does. And though the software is extremely sophisticated to perform these operations fast, the principles that the programs implement are embodied in these three steps.

RSA security challenge. Can RSA withstand attacks? Can anyone actually break the code? As far as is known, scientifically, a code cracker would have to figure out what s is to break the code. Constructing s is easy if the two primes p and q are known.

Factoring the key. The problem of finding s reduces to factoring the public key K_R to discover p and q. But factoring large numbers is a computationally difficult problem, even for the world's fastest computers. It is the fact that factoring large numbers is so difficult that keeps the public key encryption schemes secure. Put another way, if the key is large enough, it can be published because there is no known way to factor it into its two prime components in any reasonable amount of time.

Strong Encryption Techniques

Public key encryption techniques are known as **strong encryption**. The term is intended to convey the fact that a communicating party can use the tech-

RSA's Challenge. In 1977, shortly after inventing their scheme, Rivest, Shamir, and Adleman issued a challenge to the world: Break the small cipher text they encrypted with their public key RSA129—the 129 refers to the number of digits of their key—and win $100. This was a bold challenge because, although there was no known way to factor a 129-digit key quickly, maybe someone could invent a better factoring algorithm. The best known method at the time wasn't much better than the grammar school technique of dividing consecutive prime numbers into the number, looking for one that divides evenly. If computer scientists were clever enough to come up with public key encryption in the first place, they could probably come up with better ways to factor.

In fact, in 1981 Carl Pomerance did invent a new factoring method that gave some hope, though all the while other computer scientists were trying to prove that the factoring process could never be improved much. Pomerance's algorithm was better, but it didn't crack the code. Eventually, Arjen Lenstra and Mark Manasse organized an effort, which in 1994, using better algorithms, the Internet, and the improved speed of computers, cracked the RSA129 cipher. Their strategy took eight months and used nearly a thousand computers from around the world. But this wasn't the end of public key cryptosystems—it only revealed the factors of a *single* public key.

Most of us don't have a thousand computers or eight months to spend trying to snoop a single credit card transaction. Even if the secret is extremely important—a missile code, for example, or the outcome of the final episode of a TV series—and the code cracker has the resources of the U.S. government, the RSA scheme is still secure because all it takes to make things harder for code crackers is to increase the size of the key.

The difficulty of factoring increases dramatically as the key length grows. It has been estimated that increasing the key to 250 digits—that is, doubling its length—would increase the cracking time 100,000,000 times. Keys can be increased to 300 or 400 digits or more if one hundred million times harder is not enough. Larger keys do not seriously complicate the problem for the encryption and decryption processes compared to their impact on increasing the factoring time.

When RSA129 was cracked—an effort dubbed the largest computation of all time—everyone was waiting breathlessly to know what the secret message was. It turned out to be THE MAGIC WORDS ARE SQUEAMISH OSSIFRAGE.

nology to protect their communication so that no one else can read it. Period. From a national defense or crime-fighting perspective, complete secrecy is of great concern. Agencies that protect society from internal and external threats have routinely snooped on those people and organizations that may cause harm. Because surveillance would be impossible if the "bad guys" got such technology, the U.S. government has fought a long-running battle since the invention of PKC technology to keep it contained and out of the hands of "bad guys." This has never been a very realistic goal because papers describing the scientific foundations of the technology—including Diffie and Helman's original paper, "New Directions in Cryptography" (*IEEE Transactions on Information Theory* IT(22):644–654)—are published in scientific journals, which anyone with a respectable computer science education can read to build his or her own encryption software. On the other hand, security professionals probably have a point. It could be valuable to spy on people who are in the process of planning crimes or attacks.

Of course, most people don't write their own software—they buy it—and that probably includes most "bad guys." If cryptography software vendors had to give government agencies and law enforcement officials a way to break such codes, perhaps we could have both security and a defense against the "bad guys." How could that be? Doesn't breaking the code require earth-shaking discoveries in factoring? Not from the software vendor's point of view.

Two techniques that could be used are known as **trapdoor** and **key escrow**.

- **Trapdoor.** While the software is encrypting the cleartext, ways might be provided to bypass the security. When the cipher text is sent, the cleartext could also be sent to law enforcement or security officials. The trapdoor would work like a telephone wiretap in that the "bad guys'" encryption software would be configured without their knowledge. Legal safeguards (a court-approved warrant) would be required to do so. Other trapdoor techniques exist.
- **Key Escrow.** Knowing the key makes breaking the code easy, so a key escrow system would require encryption software to register the key (actually, the two prime numbers from which the key is created) with a third party, who would hold the primes in confidence. Then, if there is ever a need to break a code—law enforcement personnel having a court-approved warrant, for example, or your computer being toasted in a fire—the escrow agent could provide the two primes.

These two schemes could also be abused: Couldn't anyone with (legal or illegal) access to your computer open the trapdoor? Wouldn't the escrow company be a tantalizing target for criminals because it contains everyone's PKC keys? Neither of these schemes has satisfied security and other experts.

Redundancy Is Very, Very, Very Good

As the saying goes, "Life is uncertain; eat dessert first." Uncertainty poses physical security challenges for networking and computer use generally.

Uncertainty results from lightning strikes that cut power, earthquakes and other natural disasters, terrorist attacks, accidents, and simple entropy—the tendency of things to "run down." To the list of physical risks, add the potential logical problems of program bugs, operator errors—*How could I have done that?!*—computer viruses, worms, backdoor assaults, and many more. Each of us would like to avoid such disasters. Life is uncertain, so it makes sense to take precautions.

Businesses whose success depends on computers—that is, most businesses—archive files daily and store these backups off-site so the disaster that zaps the original information doesn't also zap the backup. These companies have a system recovery team to clean up after a disaster strikes. And often they have system redundancy, that is, multiple computers performing the same work, so that when one fails, another—a *hot spare*—is up and running.

Alternate Superstition. People can be superstitious, believing, for example, that thinking about a disaster can make it happen. Naturally, repressing such thoughts is sensible. But believing a different superstition—that taking precautions against disasters, like saving often, prevents them—may make more sense in computing. They're both superstitions, of course, but the second one reduces the harm when it turns out to be wrong, which it will.

A Fault Recovery Program for Business

Preparing to recover information after a disaster is quite technical, beyond the scope of this book, but the basic idea is easy.

Start by keeping a complete copy of everything written on the system as of some date and time. This is a **full backup**. After that, create **partial backups** of the changes since the last full (or partial) backup. "Changes" means to keep a copy of any files or folders that have been created or modified. Having the full backup and a copy of the changes allows the current version to be reconstructed by using the changes to update the earlier full backup.

Eventually there will have been so many partial backups that another full backup should be made. How often partial backups are performed is usually decided by the cost, and grief, of losing all of the information since the last partial backup. It would be easier to have full backups every few minutes, but that's too much information to copy and save. However, too many partial backups can make reconstruction extremely tedious, so regular full backups are a good idea.

After a disaster, recover by installing the last full backup copy. Then recreate the state of the system by making the changes saved in the partial backups in order. Continue with each partial backup until the most recent. That's as close to "full recovery" as it's possible to get. All of the information since the most recent backup (full or partial) has been lost.

13.2 Backup Plan. Imagine that a computer with the following file structure is backed up for the first time:

```
FOLDER: Desktop
  newCarPhoto.jpg
  FOLDER: Stuff
    oldCarPhoto.jpg
    ChrisLetter.doc
```

Then, the ChrisLetter document is edited, the oldCarPhoto image is deleted, and a new file, insurance.pdf, is added. Say what information the archiving software would copy in a partial backup.

Backing Up a Personal Computer

Backups aren't just for businesses. If you work on a computer system that is managed by a professional staff (like most college systems), there is little need to worry about backups. The support staff nearly always takes care of backups, though you should check to be sure. However, backing up your own personal computer is your responsibility. There are two important points to think about regarding backups.

How and what to back up. First, to back up your own computer, you need a place to keep the copy, and you need software to make the copy.

The two easiest "places" to keep the copy are on an external hard disk or "in the cloud," which is an online storage server. The price of external disks is low enough that anyone who can afford a computer can afford an external disk, which can also be used as permanent storage for large collections such as videos. The "cloud" solution works like free email accounts such as Yahoo! and Gmail: The company's computers store the information for you and they take responsibility of keeping it available to you. When making a backup, you upload the files you need to archive.

Software for making a backup to an external device like a hard disk comes with modern operating systems. For Windows Vista, it is the Backup and Restore Center facility, and for the Mac OSX, it is the Time Machine facility. The best advice is to follow the guidelines offered by the software.

fluencyALERT

A Three-Line Sermon. Disasters don't just happen to someone else. (I had disk meltdowns while writing each of the previous editions of *Fluency*.) Backups are truly important. Backup today. Amen.

Of course, in exceptional cases—when you are traveling, perhaps—you can back up manually by simply copying your directories and files to a CD. Remember, you don't have to back up information that:

- Can be recreated from some permanent source, such as software
- Was saved before but has not changed—last year's email archive, for example
- You don't care about, like your Web cache or old versions of term papers

Most of us do not have much to back up if we do so every two or three months.

How Often? No rule says when to back up. Organizations must follow a fixed schedule, but individuals can simply assess the risk of losing everything. Hard use makes laptops more likely to fail than desktops; very new and very old equipment is more likely to fail than a middle-aged system. There is always risk.

Recovering deleted information. The second thing about backups is that they prevent "delete from deleting." Here is why. An organization's support staff backs up files regularly, usually daily. They keep the information safe so fires and earthquakes will not harm it. And, they often keep it for a very long time so people can go back to find information that they deleted long ago. If you accidentally delete important files, file restoration is a very desirable and helpful service. So, deleting a file that is in the archive means that it is not truly gone. For example, in Try It 13.2, notice that oldCarPhoto.jpg is still in the full backup, and so could be recovered even though it was deleted.

Of course, backups can save evidence of crimes or other inappropriate behavior, too. Computer users have hastily tried to delete incriminating files in hopes of covering up undesirable activity only to learn later that the files like oldCarPhoto.jpg can be completely recreated from the backups. Unlike paper files, digital copies of files are easy to create and cheap to store, so it can be difficult to eradicate all copies of digital information.

Email is especially dangerous if you're trying to hide inappropriate behavior, but it's especially helpful if you're trying to discover it: Two copies of email are produced immediately when the **Send** button is clicked—one in the sender's sent mail directory, and one somewhere else, which is probably impossible for the sender to delete. Further, if that email is around for more than a few hours, it will probably be backed up. Of course, your own backups have this same permanence property. Perhaps the Information Age will promote better behavior.

fluencyBIT

Gone, but Not Forgotten. Emptying trash on a personal computer is another example when delete does not truly delete. Computers keep a *free list* of available disk storage blocks, and they take blocks from it whenever they write data. Emptying trash usually adds the trashed files' blocks to the free list, allowing them to be reused but without changing their contents. Until the blocks are overwritten, experts can recover the information. Choose "Secure" *Empty Trash* to completely remove files.

Summary

After discussing a privacy scenario, we defined privacy as the right of individuals to choose freely under what circumstances and to what extent they will reveal themselves, their attitudes, and their behaviors. We learned that:

- Revealing personal information can be beneficial, so the people and organizations that receive the information must keep it private. The guidelines for keeping data private have been created by several organizations, including the Organization for Economic Cooperation and Development.
- Guidelines often conflict with the interests of business and government, so some countries like the United States have not adopted

them. Because the U.S. takes a sectoral approach to privacy, adopting laws only for specific business sectors or practices, much of the information collected on its citizens is not protected by OECD standards.

- There have been long-running negotiations between the EU and the United States regarding privacy standards. The dispute's two main sticking points are Opt-in/Opt-out and compliance/enforcement.
- The "third-party cookie" loophole allows companies to gather information; identity theft is an unresolved problem. The best way to manage privacy in the Information Age is to have OECD-grade privacy laws.
- Public key cryptography (PKC) is a straightforward idea built on familiar concepts.
- Computer scientists have not yet proved the invincibility of the RSA scheme, but it can be "made more secure" simply by increasing the size of the key. This has little effect on the encryption and decryption processes, but it greatly increases the problem of finding the prime factors that make up the key.
- Strong encryption methods worry defense and law enforcement officials, but the conflict between balancing those concerns with the interests of peaceful, law-abiding citizens has not been reconciled.
- Backing up computer files is an essential safeguard. It ensures that your files will survive for a long time, even if you don't want them to.

Privacy and security topics have not been fully resolved in the public forum, and both pose daunting challenges. Laws and policies are still under construction. Privacy seems to be waiting for the broad adoption of the OECD safeguards for both business and government information gathering. Security seems to be waiting for a way for parties to communicate securely by mechanisms fully within their control, yet that can be compromised in extraordinary circumstances of public importance.

Try It Solutions

13.1 Assume your name is Barack Obama. The following would be the ASCII representation and XOR encryption of your first name:

name:	0100 0010	0110 0001	0111 0010	0110 0001	0110 0011	0110 1011
	B	A	R	A	C	K
⊕ key:	0001 0111	0010 1101	0001 0111	0010 1101	0001 0111	0010 1101
	key		key		key	
cipher:	0101 0101	0100 1100	0110 0101	0100 1100	0111 0100	0100 0110
	U	L	e	L	t	f

13.2 ChrisLetter.doc, insurance.pdf, Stuff_file_list, and Desktop_file_list would be backed up.

Review Questions

Multiple Choice

1. For a business, the least restrictive use of private information is called
   a. No Uses
   b. Approval
   c. Objection
   d. No Limits

2. An individual faces the fewest potential invasions of privacy from the policy called
   a. No Uses
   b. Approval
   c. Objection
   d. No Limits

3. Which of the following is an example of identity theft?
   a. taking a test for someone else
   b. using your older sibling's ID
   c. posing as someone you're not to vote
   d. all of the above

4. The Code of Fair Information Practices lacked
   a. methods for correcting mistakes
   b. legal penalties
   c. protection for children
   d. rules for gaining access to your own data

5. You discover that credit information on you is inaccurate. Which principle does this violate?
   a. Limited Collection
   b. Quality
   c. Security
   d. Openness

6. Which Fair Information Practice provides for ways to correct your faulty credit record?
   a. Quality
   b. Purpose
   c. Participation
   d. Accountability

7. Data on EU citizens is
   a. not as secure as data on Americans
   b. protected even outside of the EU
   c. not protected by OECD principles
   d. protected in Europe but not outside of it

8. The Driver's Privacy Protection Act
   a. prevents departments of motor vehicles from releasing private information
   b. prevents departments of motor vehicles from charging for information
   c. prevents departments of motor vehicles from releasing information without permission
   d. allows departments of motor vehicles to sell information, provided the buyer discloses how the information will be used
9. Information from people in EU countries can be shared outside of the EU, providing the business or government follows the principles of
   a. Don't ask, don't tell
   b. Safe Harbor
   c. Fair Information Practices
   d. Opt-in/Opt-out
10. If the cleartext is 1101 and the XOR key is 1001, the cipher is
   a. 1011
   b. 0100
   c. 0110
   d. 1110
11. XOR can be described as
   a. *x* and *y* or *x* or *y*
   b. *x* or *y*
   c. *x* or *y* but not both
   d. none of the above
12. Digital encryption is
   a. only used for passwords
   b. easily broken by computer experts
   c. the use of math to make communication unreadable to snoops
   d. all of the above
13. Social networking
   a. is not private
   b. can be viewed by potential employers
   c. allows members to present themselves to others and to interact with them
   d. all of the above

Short Answer

1. _______ is the right of people to choose freely under what circumstances and to what extent they will reveal themselves, their attitude, and their behavior to others.
2. In regard to information technology, privacy is primarily concerned with _______ and _______.
3. _______ is an anonymous form of payment.
4. The _______ serve as a guideline for protecting personal privacy in regard to international trade.

5. The _______ provides a benchmark by which businesses can measure how well they are protecting the privacy of individuals.
6. A(n) _______ is responsible for maintaining personal information and is held accountable for it.
7. The _______ is the European Union's law incorporating the OECD principles.
8. In the United States, _______ offers more protection than _______ for protecting personal information.
9. A(n) _______ is a combination of encryption and decryption.
10. _______ or plaintext is information before it is encrypted.
11. Passwords generally use a(n) _______ because it's hard to reverse and there's little need to decrypt it.
12. The _______ cryptosystem is the best-known public key cryptosystem.
13. _______ is the crime of posing as someone else for fraudulent purposes.
14. _______ is software that monitors and records details of computer usage.
15. A(n) _______ is an incremental backup of all changes since the last backup.
16. A(n) _______ is the listing of available blocks that can be used to store files.
17. _______ is the posting of personal information on publicly viewable space.

Exercises

1. What are the two types of business threats regarding privacy?
2. There are several national "sweepstakes" that deliver big prizes to the winners. To be a part of these contests, you must register and provide your address (so they can deliver your check on national TV!). What potential privacy concerns are involved with such contests?
3. Credit card companies track your transactions. How can they abuse this?
4. What flaws exist in a sectoral approach to privacy?
5. Based on existing legislation, who appears to have more influence, business or individuals?
6. Explain how a simple serial number stored in a cookie can be used to store personal information.
7. Is compliance without enforcement effective?
8. Discuss the different approaches to privacy taken by the European Union and the United States.
9. Discuss the loopholes between compliance and enforcement.
10. Using XOR and 10110110, determine the cipher for the ASCII text for THE MAGIC WORDS ARE SQUEAMISH OSSIFRAGE.

14 chapter

The Basics of Spreadsheets

Fill-in-the-Blank Computing

learning objectives

- Explain how data is organized in spreadsheet software
- Describe how to refer to spreadsheet rows, columns, and cell ranges
- Explain relative and absolute references
- Apply concepts of relative and absolute references when filling a formula
- Explain the concept of tab-delimited input and output

There are 10 kinds of people in the world: Those who know binary and those who don't.

—ANONYMOUS

FROM THE VERY beginning of mankind's use of symbols and writing, we have arranged information to make it more useful. Organized information is easier to understand, easier to remember, and easier to navigate. With the invention of information technology, there is a further reason to organize information: Computers can process it for us. This is a bonus we gain for very little effort, especially when we use spreadsheets.

In this chapter we introduce the basic ideas of spreadsheets. Because they make computer users so effective, especially in business, spreadsheets have become very sophisticated. This chapter introduces you to the basic ideas, making them personally useful. If you need more power, you'll have a great foundation for learning more; if not, you'll be acquainted with a very versatile tool.

We begin by introducing the basics of spreadsheet use, including constructing lists, sorting them, naming cells, and controlling the format of the entries. Next we add numeric information to the spreadsheet and learn how to manipulate it, which teaches you about formulas, relative and absolute references, and functions. Computing new numbers from numbers already in the table is what spreadsheets do best and, happily, it is an extremely easy facility to learn and use. After learning these basic concepts, we practice them on "everyday" problems; that is, tasks of personal interest: We build a 1-minute calendar for our weekly schedule, set up a transportation schedule so we don't miss the bus so often, make a "cheat sheet" for computing discounts at the music store, and develop data for helping decide how much to borrow for a "big ticket" purchase like a car or sound system. None of these tasks is so difficult as to require a computer, but since we're using a computer anyway, we can solve them quickly to our personal satisfaction. Finally, we use the Best Movie list to practice manipulating data in a spreadsheet.

Arranging Information

Commonly, textual information is organized into lists, as we know from making shopping lists, invitation lists, "to do" lists, class lists, and many others. As a running example, we'll use a list of migratory birds:

Short-tailed shearwater
Swainson's hawk
Wheatear
Arctic tern
Willow warbler
Long-tailed skua

Looking at the list, you see that it contains six bird names even though you may not be too familiar with birds. You probably figured it out because you know that hawks and warblers are birds and the items appear on separate lines. The names themselves are quite diverse as text: single word names, double word names, hyphenated names, and even a possessive. Since the computer doesn't have your knowledge, it needs to be told the extent of each entry, that is, how much text there is in each entry. The separate line cue helps, but if the entries were very long, they would spill to another line, and that cue wouldn't work.

Kinda the Same. Spreadsheet software is available from many sources. The content of this chapter applies generally to Microsoft Excel, OpenOffice, AppleWorks, Lotus 1-2-3, Quattro Pro, and others. Every system is different, however, because menus and defaults are particular to each system. With a moment's exploration, you should be able to perform any operation in this chapter on your system.

An Array of Cells

To help us create a list, spreadsheets give us an array of **cells** that we fill in to set up our list.

I20 fx

◇	A	B	C	D	E
1					
2		Short-tailed shearwater			
3		Swainson's hawk			
4		Wheatear			
5		Arctic tern			
6		Willow warbler			
7		Long-tailed skua			
8					

The lines are part of the graphic user interface; they help us and the computer agree on what an item is and how the positions of items are related to each other.

Notice that four of the six items in the list do not fit within the lines provided. Even though it takes more space to display the entry than the computer provides, entries do not straddle cells. Each occupies only the cell into which it is typed, as is shown when we enter test data in the cells to their right.

G22 | fx

◇	A	B	C	D	E
1					
2		Short-tailed sh	*Test data*		
3		Swainson's ha	*to see*		
4		Wheatear	*what happens*		
5		Arctic tern	*when long*		
6		Willow warbler	*entries can't*		
7		Long-tailed sk	*spill*		
8					

The test data, which blocks the long entries from spilling to the empty cells on the right, indicates that entries that are too long are clipped. (Items only spill when the cells to their right are unused.) We can either let the entries be clipped, or make the cells wider, as explained later in Table 14.1. We choose the latter.

Sorting the Data

A common operation on any list, especially when it gets long, is to alphabetize or sort it. Spreadsheet software makes sorting easy. We must specify which items to sort, so naturally, we must select the list. We select the list by dragging the cursor across the cells; the resulting selection is indicated with highlighting.

B2 | fx Short-tailed shearwater

◇	A	B	C	D	E
1					
2		Short-tailed shearwater			
3		Swainson's hawk			
4		Wheatear			
5		Arctic tern			
6		Willow warbler			
7		Long-tailed skua			
8					

All of the items inside the blue box are selected, including the white item, which is a different color only because it was the first cell selected, that is, it's the place where the dragging began. The *Sort ...* operation is found among the menu items, and is often shown as an icon somewhere in the GUI. It allows us to choose ascending or descending order. The software uses an algorithm like the one we discussed in Chapter 10 to sort audio CDs. Sorting our list of birds in ascending order produces the following result.

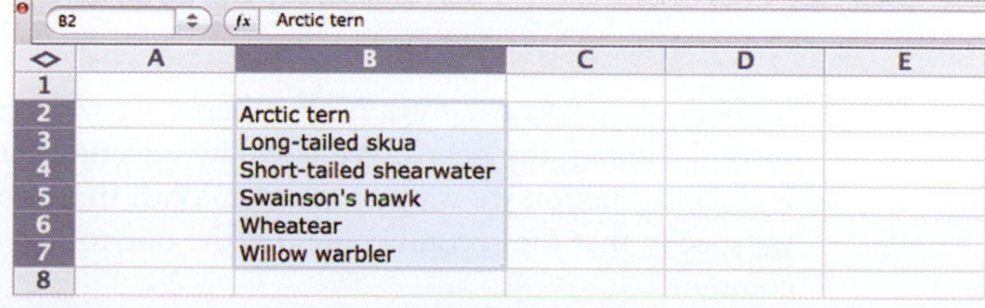

B2 | fx Arctic tern

◇	A	B	C	D	E
1					
2		Arctic tern			
3		Long-tailed skua			
4		Short-tailed shearwater			
5		Swainson's hawk			
6		Wheatear			
7		Willow warbler			
8					

Notice that the sorting software orders the list alphabetically on the first letter of the entry, not on the type of bird, for example, "hawk." This is consistent with the spreadsheet view that the cell entries are "atomic" or "monolithic" from the computer's point of view, meaning that the computer does not consider any of their constituent parts. If the list contained both Swainson's hawk and Swainson's warbler, they would appear together in sorted order. But if we wanted those birds to be grouped with the hawks and the warblers respectively, then it would be necessary to sort on the second part of the name. That would require the type of the bird (e.g., "hawk" or "warbler") to be in a separate cell—in its own column.

Adding More Data to the List

Our list is not so complete. We will leave the common names in a single column, but we'll add the scientific names using two columns, one for genus and one for species.

F12

	A	B	C	D	E
1					
2		Arctic tern	Sterna	paradiasaea	
3		Long-tailed skua	Stercorarius	longicaudus	
4		Short-tailed shearwater	Puffinus	tenuirostris	
5		Swainson's hawk	Buteo	swainsoni	
6		Wheatear	Oenanthe	oenanthe	
7		Willow warbler	Phylloscopus	trochilus	
8					

As you know, scientific names are usually written in italics. Spreadsheets give us the ability to format cell entries with the kinds of formatting facilities found in word processors, such as italics, bold, font styles, font sizes, justification, colored text and backgrounds, and so on. Naturally, the formatting facilities are found under the *Format* menu. We italicize the scientific names and right justify the genus name so it looks like it is paired with the species name.

F12

	A	B	C	D	E
1					
2		Arctic tern	*Sterna*	*paradiasaea*	
3		Long-tailed skua	*Stercorarius*	*longicaudus*	
4		Short-tailed shearwater	*Puffinus*	*tenuirostris*	
5		Swainson's hawk	*Buteo*	*swainsoni*	
6		Wheatear	*Oenanthe*	*oenanthe*	
7		Willow warbler	*Phylloscopus*	*trochilus*	
8					

Naming rows and columns. Now suppose we want to alphabetize on the second column, the genus. We begin by selecting the whole list because that is the information we want to reorder. With three columns selected, how do we specify that the second column is the one to sort on rather than the first column?

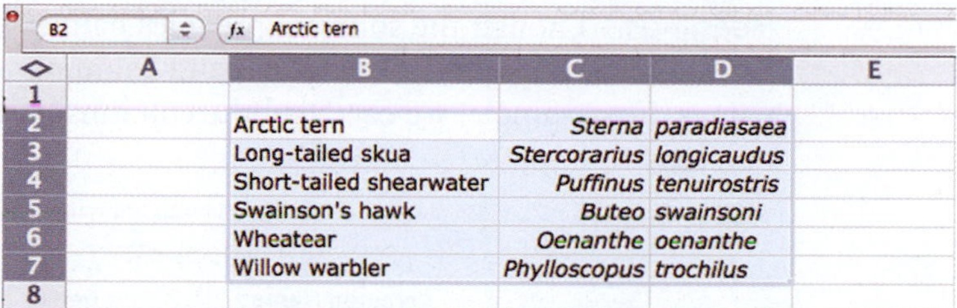

B2 | fx Arctic tern

	A	B	C	D	E
1					
2		Arctic tern	Sterna	paradiasaea	
3		Long-tailed skua	Stercorarius	longicaudus	
4		Short-tailed shearwater	Puffinus	tenuirostris	
5		Swainson's hawk	Buteo	swainsoni	
6		Wheatear	Oenanthe	oenanthe	
7		Willow warbler	Phylloscopus	trochilus	
8					

Spreadsheet programs automatically provide a naming scheme for referring to specific cells. The columns are labeled with letters and the rows are labeled with numbers. This allows us to refer to a whole column, as in column C, or to a whole row, as in row 4, or to a single cell by specifying both the column letter and the row number, as in B2. Thus, when we request to sort the entries, the sorting software displays a *Sort* GUI.

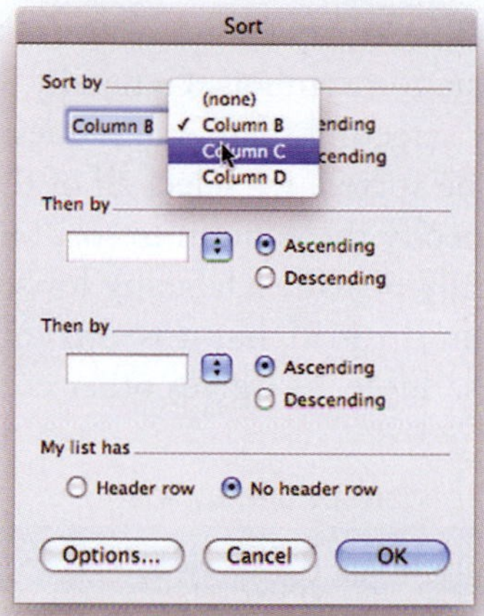

We choose to sort the selected rows based on entries in column C (which contains our *genus* entries) by clicking on the directional arrows. This produces the following result.

B2 | fx Swainson's hawk

	A	B	C	D	E
1					
2		Swainson's hawk	Buteo	swainsoni	
3		Wheatear	Oenanthe	oenanthe	
4		Willow warbler	Phylloscopus	trochilus	
5		Short-tailed shearwater	Puffinus	tenuirostris	
6		Long-tailed skua	Stercorarius	longicaudus	
7		Arctic tern	Sterna	paradiasaea	
8					

Note that the naming scheme allows us to refer to a group of cells, by naming the first cell and the last cell and placing a colon (:) in between, as in "the cells B2:D7 are highlighted in the figure." This kind of reference is called a **cell range**.

14.1 New Range. What is the cell range for the scientific names of the birds whose common name includes "-tailed"?

Headings. Though the software provides names for referring to cells, it is convenient for us to name the rows and columns with more meaningful names. For example, we can label the columns with the type of information entered.

F16 fx

	A	B	C	D	E
1		**Common Name**	***Genus***	***Species***	
2		Swainson's hawk	*Buteo*	*swainsoni*	
3		Wheatear	*Oenanthe*	*oenanthe*	
4		Willow warbler	*Phylloscopus*	*trochilus*	
5		Short-tailed shearwater	*Puffinus*	*tenuirostris*	
6		Long-tailed skua	*Stercorarius*	*longicaudus*	
7		Arctic tern	*Sterna*	*paradiasaea*	
8					

Summarizing, spreadsheets are made up of cells that are displayed to the user as rectangles in a grid. Information is entered in a cell and treated as an elemental piece of data no matter how long it is or if it contains spaces or other punctuation symbols. Generally, we build a list of items that can be sorted simply by selecting them and requesting the sorting operation. If multiple columns must be sorted, we select all of the information to be reordered, request *Sort*, and specify the column to sort on when the GUI asks for it. Spreadsheets automatically provide a labeling for specifying the column/row position of any element in the grid, but it is also convenient to add our own, more meaningful names. Table 14.1 gives other common operations useful for lists.

Table 14.1 Common spreadsheet operations

Operation	Using Excel...	Using Open Office...
Change column width manually	Place cursor at right side of column name, then drag	Place cursor at right side of column name, then drag
Change column width automatically	*Format > Column > Autofit Selection*	*Format > Column > Optimal Width ...*
Cut, copy, paste contents	Standard: ^X, ^C, ^V	Standard: ^X, ^C, ^V
Fancy formatting	*Format > Cells ...*	*Format > Cells ...*
Clear cells	*Edit > Clear > All*	*Edit > Delete Contents ...*
Delete columns, rows	*Edit > Delete ...*	*Edit > Delete Cells ...*
Hide a column	*Format > Column > Hide*	*Format > Column > Hide*

Note: All spreadsheet applications provide these common operations; explore your system.

Computing with Spreadsheets

Though spreadsheets don't have to contain a single number to be useful, their most common application is to process numerical data. Numerical data is usually associated with textual information, too, so most spreadsheets have both. For example, suppose our migratory bird spreadsheet has been further filled out, as shown in Figure 14.1.

◇	B	C	D	E	F	G
1	**Common Name**	***Genus***	***Species***	**Migration**	**Distance(Km)**	**Body Len(m)**
2	Swainson's hawk	*Buteo*	*swainsoni*	USA-Argentina	13500	0.52
3	Wheatear	*Oenanthe*	*oenanthe*	Alaska-E Africa	13500	0.16
4	Willow warbler	*Phylloscopus*	*trochilus*	Chukotka-S Africa	15500	0.11
5	Short-tailed shearwater	*Puffinus*	*tenuirostris*	Tasmania-Bering Strait	12500	0.43
6	Long-tailed skua	*Stercorarius*	*longicaudus*	N Greenland-Southern Ocean	16000	0.51
7	Arctic tern	*Sterna*	*paradiasaea*	Greenland-Antarctic	19000	0.35
8						

Figure 14.1 Bird migration spreadsheet.

The Migration column gives the end points of the bird's semiannual migration route, the Distance column gives the approximate length of that flight in kilometers, and Body Len gives the size of the bird (length) in meters. In the following discussion the Genus, Species, and Migration columns will be hidden.

Writing a Formula

Suppose we want to find out how far the Swainson's hawk flies in miles rather than kilometers. Because one kilometer is 0.621 miles, we must multiply the value in cell F2 by 0.621 to find out. We can perform this specific computation with a calculator, but we will probably want to know the distances in miles for all of the migration flights. So, we decide to create a new column for the distance in miles and instruct the spreadsheet how to compute it.

◇	B	F	G	H	I
1	**Common Name**	**Distance(Km)**	**Body Len(m)**	**Distance(Mi)**	
2	Swainson's hawk	13500	0.52		
3	Wheatear	13500	0.16		
4	Willow warbler	15500	0.11		
5	Short-tailed shearwater	12500	0.43		
6	Long-tailed skua	16000	0.51		
7	Arctic tern	19000	0.35		
8					

What entry do we want in position H2? We'd like it to be equal to F2 $\times$ 0.621, so we type

=F2*0.621

which appears in the H2 window and the *Edit Formula* window on the edit bar above.

SUM | fx =F2*0.621

◇	B	F	G	H	I
1	**Common Name**	**Distance(Km)**	**Body Len(m)**	**Distance(Mi)**	
2	Swainson's hawk	13500	0.52	=F2*0.621	
3	Wheatear	13500	0.16		
4	Willow warbler	15500	0.11		
5	Short-tailed shearwater	12500	0.43		
6	Long-tailed skua	16000	0.51		
7	Arctic tern	19000	0.35		
8					

Notice that we use an asterisk (*) for the multiplication symbol rather than a cross or dot. When we press Enter or Return, the value in H2 is the result of the computation, that is, 8,383.5 miles.

H3 | fx

◇	B	F	G	H	I
1	**Common Name**	**Distance(Km)**	**Body Len(m)**	**Distance(Mi)**	
2	Swainson's hawk	13500	0.52	8383.5	
3	Wheatear	13500	0.16		
4	Willow warbler	15500	0.11		
5	Short-tailed shearwater	12500	0.43		
6	Long-tailed skua	16000	0.51		
7	Arctic tern	19000	0.35		
8					

We have just instructed the spreadsheet software to compute the value in cell H2 by telling it what the cell should equal. We did this by typing a formula into the cell. Formulas, which begin with an equal sign (=), define the value for the entry based on the values of other entries. We used numbers (0.621), cell references (F2), and standard arithmetic operations (*) as found on a calculator. If we ever change our estimate of the distance Swainson's hawks migrate, that is, change the value in F2, then the spreadsheet software will *automatically change* the value in H2 to reflect the revision.

Equal Opportunity. When we type characters into a cell, the spreadsheet software needs to know if we are giving it data that should be stored, or if we are giving it a formula saying how to compute information for that cell. The equal sign (=) is the indicator: It's a formula if it starts with =; otherwise it's data.

Consider the formula a bit more. We entered the formula =F2*0.621 into cell H2. The cell contains this formula, not 8383.5. We can prove this by clicking on H2 and checking the *Edit Formula* window.

H2 | fx | =F2*0.621

◇	B	F	G	H	I
1	**Common Name**	**Distance(Km)**	**Body Len(m)**	**Distance(Mi)**	
2	Swainson's hawk	13500	0.52	8383.5	
3	Wheatear	13500	0.16		
4	Willow warbler	15500	0.11		
5	Short-tailed shearwater	12500	0.43		
6	Long-tailed skua	16000	0.51		
7	Arctic tern	19000	0.35		
8					

Then, by temporarily changing the value in F2 from 13,500 to, say, 14,000, we notice that H2 automatically increases to 8,694.

By specifying this formula, we have defined an equation

$$H2 = F2 \times 0.621$$

just as we would in algebra. Recall that such an equation means that both sides of the equal sign refer to the same value. So, entering the formula into H2 means that we want the cell to have the value of F2 * 0.621 now and forever. Because F2 presently contains the data 13,500, cell H2 displays as 8383.5. When we change the value of F2, the value of H2 must change, because the equality must be preserved. Thus, when we put a formula into a cell (the right side of the equation), the computer does the math and displays its value (the left side of the equation).

14.2 **One Size.** A meter is equal to 100 centimeters. Write the formula for converting the body length of Swainson's Hawk to centimeters.

Repeating a Formula

We can specify a similar computation for cell H3 and the other cells in that column by entering them in the same way.

Copy/Paste. Thinking about it, however, we might guess that *Copy/Paste* will work to replicate the equation to other cells. So, we select cell H2, which, in Excel, is indicated by an animated highlight (the dashes revolve around the box). Other spreadsheet software simply shows a solid box around the item.

H2 | fx =F2*0.621

	B	F	G	H	I
1	Common Name	Distance(Km)	Body Len(m)	Distance(Mi)	
2	Swainson's hawk	13500	0.52	8383.5	
3	Wheatear	13500	0.16		
4	Willow warbler	15500	0.11		
5	Short-tailed shearwater	12500	0.43		
6	Long-tailed skua	16000	0.51		
7	Arctic tern	19000	0.35		
8					

The cell's contents are shown in the *Edit Formula* window. We *Copy* this cell (^C), select the remaining cells in the column by dragging the mouse across them, and *Paste* (^V). The result shows all of the distance values computed. This is quite a bit of computation for very little effort on our part.

H3 | fx =F3*0.621

	B	F	G	H	I
1	Common Name	Distance(Km)	Body Len(m)	Distance(Mi)	
2	Swainson's hawk	13500	0.52	8383.5	
3	Wheatear	13500	0.16	8383.5	
4	Willow warbler	15500	0.11	9625.5	
5	Short-tailed shearwater	12500	0.43	7762.5	
6	Long-tailed skua	16000	0.51	9936	
7	Arctic tern	19000	0.35	11799	
8					

Notice that in the *Edit Formula* window the equation shows as F3*0.621. This corresponds to the computation for the cell H3, the first of the highlighted cells (white) into which we pasted the formula. And we notice a curious thing: Whereas the formula we pasted was F2*0.621, the formula was transformed into F3*0.621 when it was pasted into H3; it was transformed into F4*0.621 for H4, and so on. This is exactly what we want for this column, namely that the value in column H is based on the corresponding values in column F. The software makes this transformation for us automatically. (This is explained later in the Transforming Formulas section.)

Filling. It's possible for these computations to be performed even more easily! Let's go back and redo them from the point where we had just entered the formula for the Swainson's hawk,

G	H	I
Body Len(m)	Distance(Mi)	
0.52	8383.5	
0.16		

Notice in the image that the highlighted cell H2 is outlined in color, but there is also a small box or tab beyond the cell's lower right corner (near the cursor). This is called its **fill handle**. We can grab this handle with the cursor and "pull" it down the column, applying the operation we just performed on H2 to those cells.

H2 fx =F2*0.621

	B	F	G	H	I
1	Common Name	Distance(Km)	Body Len(m)	Distance(Mi)	
2	Swainson's hawk	13500	0.52	8383.5	
3	Wheatear	13500	0.16	8383.5	
4	Willow warbler	15500	0.11	9625.5	
5	Short-tailed shearwater	12500	0.43	7762.5	
6	Long-tailed skua	16000	0.51	9936	
7	Arctic tern	19000	0.35	11799	
8					

This process is known as **filling**. It's automated copying and pasting! Filling is a shortcut that allows us to replicate, that is, *Copy/Paste*, the contents of the cell with the fill handle, saving us from explicitly setting each cell in the column or manually using the *Copy/Paste* operations. Whenever the fill handle is visible on a highlighted cell, the contents can be replicated by filling.

14.3 Give an Inch. Suppose we would also like to see the birds' body lengths measured in inches. Using the fact that a meter is 39.37 inches, what steps do we perform to add this information in column I of the spreadsheet?

Transforming Formulas: Relative Versus Absolute

The software automatically transforms the formulas as it pastes them or fills them into a cell because we used a **relative cell reference** when we wrote F2. Spreadsheets allow two kinds of cell references—relative and absolute—and we must be careful which we use. The **absolute cell** reference to this cell is $F$2; it tells the software never to change the reference when filling or pasting. Here's what's happening.

Relative means "relative position from a cell." When we pasted the formula =F2*0.621 into H2, the software noticed that cell F2 is two cells to the left of H2. That is, the formula refers to a cell in the same row, but two cells to the left.

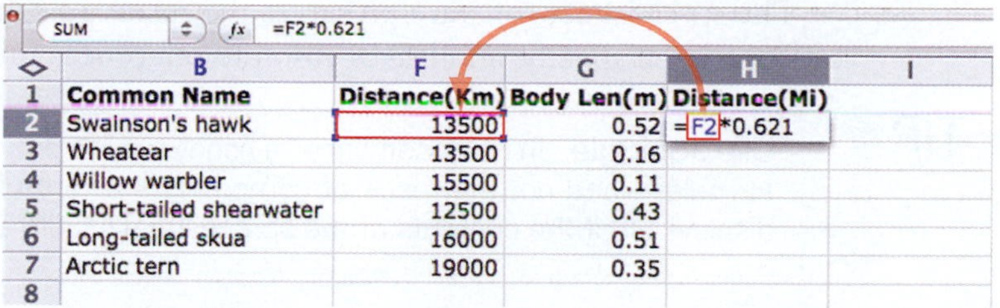

SUM | =F2*0.621

	B	F	G	H	I
1	Common Name	Distance(Km)	Body Len(m)	Distance(Mi)	
2	Swainson's hawk	13500	0.52	=F2*0.621	
3	Wheatear	13500	0.16		
4	Willow warbler	15500	0.11		
5	Short-tailed shearwater	12500	0.43		
6	Long-tailed skua	16000	0.51		
7	Arctic tern	19000	0.35		
8					

Since this is a relative reference, the software preserves the relationship of "two cells to the left in the same row" between the position of the referenced cell and the cell where the formula is pasted. So, when we *Paste* or fill this same formula into H3, the software transforms the formula so it still refers to the cell two cells to the left in the same row; that is, the formula is changed to =F3*0.621. Similarly, this occurs whenever a relative formula is pasted or filled.

J20

	B	F	G	H	I
1	Common Name	Distance(Km)	Body Len(m)	Distance(Mi)	
2	Swainson's hawk	13500	0.52	=F2*0.621	
3	Wheatear	13500	0.16	=F3*0.621	
4	Willow warbler	15500	0.11	=F4*0.621	
5	Short-tailed shearwater	12500	0.43	=F5*0.621	
6	Long-tailed skua	16000	0.51	=F6*0.621	
7	Arctic tern	19000	0.35	=F7*0.621	
8					

An absolute reference always refers to the fixed position—the software never adjusts it.

Because there are two dimensions in spreadsheets—columns and rows—there are actually two ways a formula can be relative. This makes four cases:

F2—column and row are both relative

$F2—absolute column, but relative row

F$2—relative column, but absolute row

$F$2—column and row are both absolute

For example, assume cell A1 contains 1. When the formula =A$1+1 is filled from A2 down column A into new rows, the formula is untransformed and 2's are computed, because the cell's row reference ($1) is absolute and the column reference, though relative, didn't change as we filled down the column into new rows. All cells refer to the same cell, A1. But when that formula is filled from B1 across row 1 into new columns, the relative column reference (A) is transformed, =B$1+1, =C$1+1, =D$1+1, and so on, and the numbers 2, 3, 4, … are computed.

B1 | =A$1+1

	A	B	C	D	E
1	1	2	3	4	5
2	2				
3	2				
4	2				
5	2				
6	2				

The spreadsheet software preserves the relative position in whichever dimension(s) you specify, and leaves absolute references unchanged.

Use Squiggle. In Microsoft Excel, a handy way to prove that cells actually contain formulas—and not the result of computing the formula—is to type Ctrl-~. This displays all of the contents of the spreadsheet's cells, including the formulas.

Cell Formats

Although it is amazing that the migratory birds fly so far twice a year, it is perhaps even more impressive that the smaller birds do it. One analysis that a biologist might make to take both distance and size into consideration is to divide the bird's size into the distance flown. This *flying score* measures each bird in a way that allows a more equal comparison.

We will use the distance in kilometers (column F) and length in meters (column G) so that the "meters" cancel out giving a "unitless" score. As before, we define a new column and enter the equation into the first cell. After finding the hawk's score, we fill the column with the formula, computing the results.

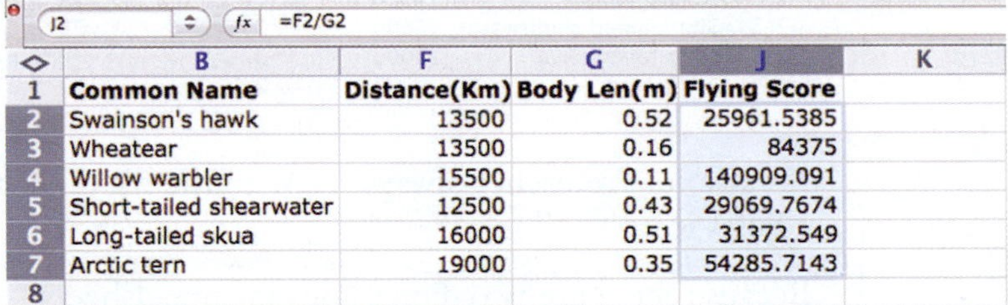
J2 fx =F2/G2

	B	F	G	J	K
1	Common Name	Distance(Km)	Body Len(m)	Flying Score	
2	Swainson's hawk	13500	0.52	25961.5385	
3	Wheatear	13500	0.16	84375	
4	Willow warbler	15500	0.11	140909.091	
5	Short-tailed shearwater	12500	0.43	29069.7674	
6	Long-tailed skua	16000	0.51	31372.549	
7	Arctic tern	19000	0.35	54285.7143	
8					

The scores are somewhat difficult to read because they have too many digits, or as a mathematician might say, more digits than are significant. For the numbers to be useful, we need to format them, say, by making them whole numbers.

All spreadsheet software provides control over the format of the information displayed. For example, Excel displays this GUI for formatting cells.

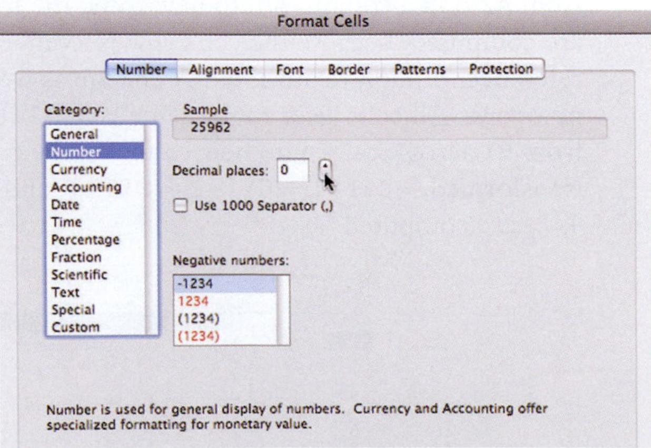

This GUI gives us control over the types of information in the fields (*Category*); control over the number of decimal digits for the *Number* category chosen; control over setting the "1000s" separators (commas for North America); and control over the display of negative numbers.

When we reduce the number of decimal digits to 0, that is, specify whole numbers only, we get this result.

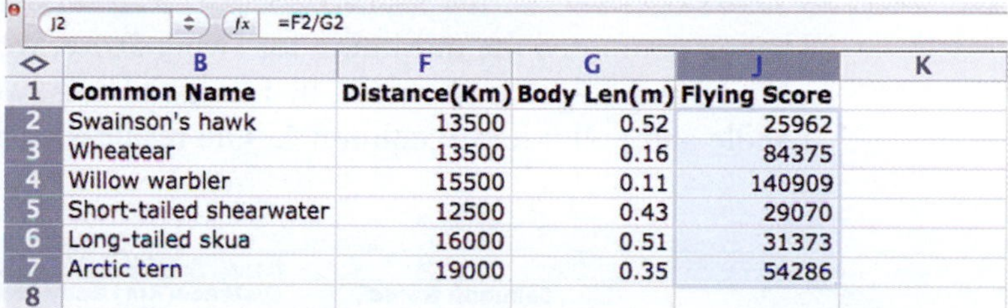

J2 =F2/G2

	B	F	G	J	K
1	Common Name	Distance(Km)	Body Len(m)	Flying Score	
2	Swainson's hawk	13500	0.52	25962	
3	Wheatear	13500	0.16	84375	
4	Willow warbler	15500	0.11	140909	
5	Short-tailed shearwater	12500	0.43	29070	
6	Long-tailed skua	16000	0.51	31373	
7	Arctic tern	19000	0.35	54286	
8					

This confirms our intuition that smaller birds score higher even if their distances flown are not the largest.

Functions

Picking the Willow warbler as the most amazing flier is based on its being the maximum value in the Flying Score column. Visually finding the maximum for this column is easy to do, but it's somewhat harder to do for the other columns because the entries have the same number of digits; also, the list could be much longer. So we set up the spreadsheet to compute the maximum.

Finding the Maximum

Spreadsheet software provides **functions** for computing common summary operations such as totals (sum), averages, maximums (max), and many others. To use these functions, we give the function name and specify the cell range to be summarized in parentheses after it. So, for example, we write

=max(J2:J7)

in a cell at the bottom of column J, and label that row with the "Maximum:" caption.

SUM =max(J2:J7)

	A	B	F	G	J	K
1		Common Name	Distance(Km)	Body Len(m)	Flying Score	
2		Swainson's hawk	13500	0.52	25962	
3		Wheatear	13500	0.16	84375	
4		Willow warbler	15500	0.11	140909	
5		Short-tailed shearwater	12500	0.43	29070	
6		Long-tailed skua	16000	0.51	31373	
7		Arctic tern	19000	0.35	54286	
8						
9	Maximum:				=max(J2:J7)	
10						

The formula directs the software to find the largest value in the cell range J2:J7, that is, the Flying Score column. There is a full list of function names under *Insert > Insert Function....*

The Easy Case. Functions and column letters are not case sensitive in spreadsheets, so we can type them however we wish. The software stores the result as uppercase, which is how it's displayed after its initial entry.

Having computed the maximum for Flying Score, we can figure the maximum of the other columns as before, by filling. That is, we grab the J9 cell by its fill handle and pull it left to column F. The result is curious.

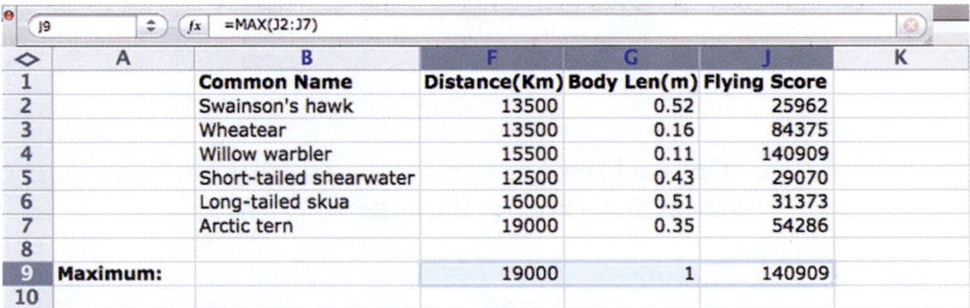
J9 =MAX(J2:J7)

	A	B	F	G	J	K
1		Common Name	Distance(Km)	Body Len(m)	Flying Score	
2		Swainson's hawk	13500	0.52	25962	
3		Wheatear	13500	0.16	84375	
4		Willow warbler	15500	0.11	140909	
5		Short-tailed shearwater	12500	0.43	29070	
6		Long-tailed skua	16000	0.51	31373	
7		Arctic tern	19000	0.35	54286	
8						
9	Maximum:		19000	1	140909	
10						

The "1" in the Body Len column is a whole number rather than 0.52, the largest of the two-decimal-digit fractions in column G. Why? Because the maximum value computation in the Flying Score column inherits the whole number setting from before. When we drag it across to the other columns, it brings its formatting with it. So, the software looks for the largest value in Body Len, finds that it is 0.52, and then rounds it to a whole number, that is, 1. Formatting this cell so that it displays numbers with two decimal digits fixes the problem.

For completeness, let's also compute the average for each column using the average function. The result requires some additional formatting in the last two columns.

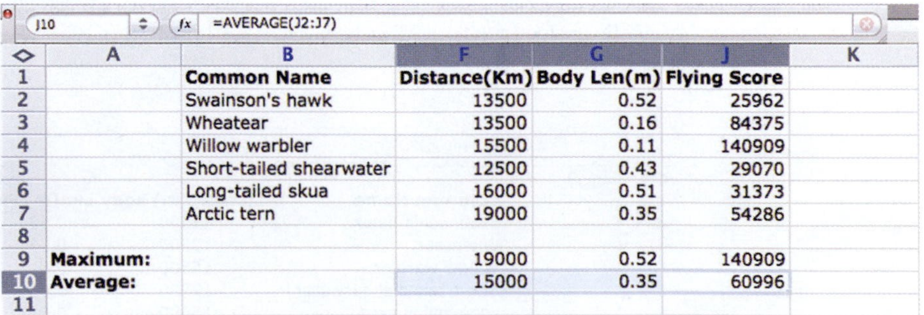
J10 =AVERAGE(J2:J7)

	A	B	F	G	J	K
1		Common Name	Distance(Km)	Body Len(m)	Flying Score	
2		Swainson's hawk	13500	0.52	25962	
3		Wheatear	13500	0.16	84375	
4		Willow warbler	15500	0.11	140909	
5		Short-tailed shearwater	12500	0.43	29070	
6		Long-tailed skua	16000	0.51	31373	
7		Arctic tern	19000	0.35	54286	
8						
9	Maximum:		19000	0.52	140909	
10	Average:		15000	0.35	60996	
11						

Filling Hidden Columns

Perhaps unexpectedly, we have computed more than is visible in this image. Notice that we have two hidden columns between G and J, the columns that we used earlier for converting from metric to English units. When we "unhide" these columns we see that by dragging the cell definitions across the rows, we have computed the maximum and average of the previously hidden columns, too.

This makes sense because these columns are part of our spreadsheet; they just were not displayed previously. Of course, if we no longer wanted the English conversion columns, we could delete them. The final spreadsheet, slightly adjusted in formatting, is shown in Figure 14.2.

L28 | fx

	A	B	C	D	E	F	G	H	I	J
1		**Common Name**	**Genus**	**Species**	**Migration**	**Distance(Km)**	**Body Len(m)**	**Distance(Mi)**	**Body Len(in)**	**Flying Score**
2		Swainson's hawk	*Buteo*	*swainsoni*	USA-Argentina	13500	0.52	8383.5	20.47	25962
3		Wheatear	*Oenanthe*	*oenanthe*	Alaska-E Africa	13500	0.16	8383.5	6.30	84375
4		Willow warbler	*Phylloscopus*	*trochilus*	Chukotka-S Africa	15500	0.11	9625.5	4.33	140909
5		Short-tailed shearwater	*Puffinus*	*tenuirostris*	Tasmania-Bering Strait	12500	0.43	7762.5	16.93	29070
6		Long-tailed skua	*Stercorarius*	*longicaudus*	N Greenland-Southern O	16000	0.51	9936	20.08	31373
7		Arctic tern	*Sterna*	*paradiasaea*	Greenland-Antarctic	19000	0.35	11799	13.78	54286
8										
9	**Maximum:**					19000	0.52	11799	20.47	140909
10	**Average:**					15000	0.35	9315	13.65	60996
11										

Figure 14.2 Final spreadsheet for the migratory birds.

Charts

The spreadsheet organizes our data and computes new values, but it is often helpful to see the results graphically when comparing values. Spreadsheet software makes creating charts remarkably easy.

The process is to select the values to be plotted and then click on *Chart...* under the *Insert* menu. A wizard walks us through the graphing process. To see what happens, let's select the items in the Flying Score column. When we click on *Chart...*, the wizard gives us a choice of graph styles, as shown across the top of the GUI in Figure 14.3. To get an idea of what the graph will look

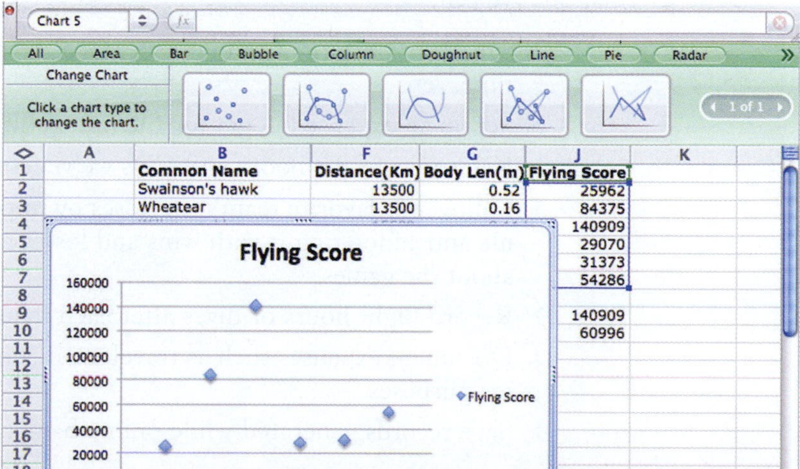

Figure 14.3 The Excel charting wizard after choosing the XY-Scatter Plot from the style menu, and "points" from the template display.

like with our data, we select the "points" form and get the completed chart. Notice that the wizard, detecting that the column has a heading (how does it know?), uses the heading to label the point as a key to the right.

Clicking on any part of the graph displays a pop-up window that offers editing options; choosing a background fill and changing the font results in the chart in Figure 14.4.

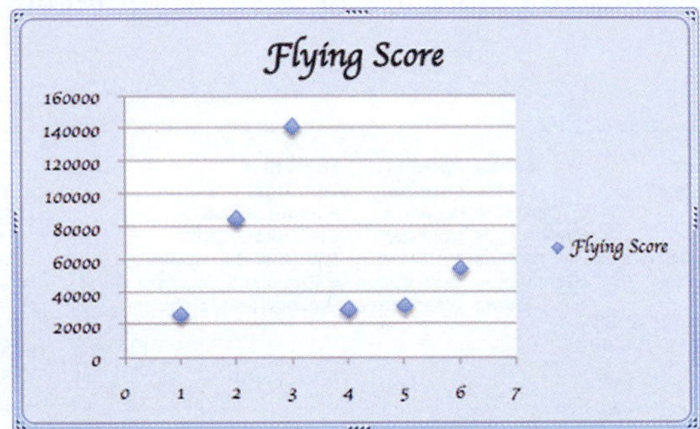

Figure 14.4 The final formatted chart displaying the Flying Score.

Daily Spreadsheets

Some people use computers all day and never use a spreadsheet; others use spreadsheets constantly. The rest of us are somewhere in between: Spreadsheets are convenient and versatile tools that simplify computing. In this section we look at a few personal applications as a way to gain a bit more experience with using spreadsheets.

Many opportunities exist to use spreadsheets to organize our personal information. We can

- Track our performance in our personal exercise program—distances, time, reps
- Set up an expense budget for the next term
- Keep a list of the books and CDs we've lent to others
- Follow our favorite team's successes by importing the season schedule and annotating it with wins and losses and our own comments about the games
- Record flight hours or dives after each flying or scuba lesson
- Document expenses such as travel, or income such as tips for income tax purposes
- Save records generated while online banking

Spreadsheets can even serve as an address book or recipe file.

Here are more ways to apply spreadsheets in personally relevant ways.

Calendar

Calendars are everywhere, and computers come with calendar software, so making a calendar with a spreadsheet hardly seems like an important application. But you would be surprised. Some people find calendar software clumsy; some people want to restructure their week, beginning, say on Wednesday; some people want a mix of larger/smaller appointment timeslots; workers with "2-on-1-off" jobs want double week calendars; and so on. At a meeting, you might set up a schedule for room or equipment usage or for a team's practices; it's often convenient to present information as a calendar, such as espresso sales by hour and day. Making a custom calendar solves these problems, and it only takes a minute. Really!

The calendar—and many other tasks—are easy because spreadsheet software, when it fills certain types of data such as days, dates, times, and such, *automatically increments*, that is, automatically adds 1 as it fills each cell. This feature is known as **series fill**. The spreadsheet knows that "adding 1" to Sunday results in Monday, and "adding 1" to January 31 results in February 1. Some systems assume, when they see values like Sunday, that it's not just text data, but rather it's one of these special data types, and they use series fill; in all systems series fill is available in the menus: *Edit > Fill > Series....* If you type in `Sunday` and you want to copy the word *Sunday*, that is, you don't want to treat it as a special type of data, then don't use series fill. Or simply *Copy/Paste*.

A convenient way to use series fill is to enter the first two items of the series into adjacent cells, select the two cells, and then pull on the handle to fill either the row or column. This double-cell fill indicates a series, where the amount of increment between successive items is not necessarily +1, but the difference between the pair. We use series fill extensively in the calendar construction.

To begin we enter a day of the week into a cell in the spreadsheet, say `Sunday`, and format it as we like it, perhaps with bold letters and a background color. Depending on which software we are using, we either drag the fill handle across the next six columns to fill in the successive days of the week, or we request such a fill operation using the menus.

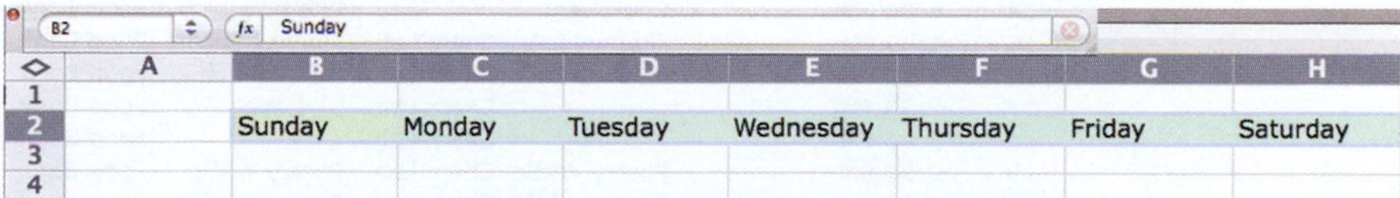

B2 | fx Sunday

	A	B	C	D	E	F	G	H
1								
2		Sunday	Monday	Tuesday	Wednesday	Thursday	Friday	Saturday
3								
4								

The result should be enhanced by the day of the month. So, we enter a date, say January 28, in the row below, format it, and fill it across.

B3 | fx 1/28/2009

	A	B	C	D	E	F	G	H
1								
2		Sunday	Monday	Tuesday	Wednesday	Thursday	Friday	Saturday
3		28-Jan	29-Jan	30-Jan	31-Jan	1-Feb	2-Feb	3-Feb
4								

That result is ready for the times of day. We enter 8:00 AM into cell A4, format it to taste, including bold and color. We want half hour appointment slots, but normally the time fill increments by hours rather than half hours. We could figure out how to change the increment, but instead we enter 8:30 AM in cell A5.

A5 | fx 8:30:00 AM

	A	B	C	D	E	F	G	H
1								
2		Sunday	Monday	Tuesday	Wednesday	Thursday	Friday	Saturday
3		28-Jan	29-Jan	30-Jan	31-Jan	1-Feb	2-Feb	3-Feb
4	8:00 AM							
5	8:30 AM							
6								

Using this pair of cells we fill down the column to 8:00 PM; this achieves the desired half hour appointment times.

This double-cell fill is an easy way to cause the spreadsheet software to count by a specific amount. Note that entering 8:00 without the "AM" results in an international or military time fill.

The result is shown in Figure 14.5 with sample contents.

The point is not that we've created a spectacular appointment calendar, but that the spreadsheet software makes it easy to create one. We did almost no typing: We entered Sunday and filled; we entered January 28 and filled; we entered 8:00 AM and 8:30 AM and filled the pair. We were done! It's possible to do this in under a minute. We have a custom calendar exactly matching our needs.

J31 | fx

	A	B	C	D	E	F	G	H
1								
2		Sunday	Monday	Tuesday	Wednesday	Thursday	Friday	Saturday
3		28-Jan	29-Jan	30-Jan	31-Jan	1-Feb	2-Feb	3-Feb
4	8:00 AM							
5	8:30 AM							
6	9:00 AM							Work
7	9:30 AM		Fluency		Fluency		Fluency	Work
8	10:00 AM		Fluency		Fluency		Fluency	Work
9	10:30 AM		Intl Conflicts		Intl Conflicts		Intl Conflicts	Work
10	11:00 AM		Intl Conflicts		Intl Conflicts		Intl Conflicts	Work
11	11:30 AM							Work
12	12:00 PM							Work
13	12:30 PM		Chemistry		Chemistry		Chemistry	Work
14	1:00 PM		Chemistry		Chemistry	Food Bank	Chemistry	Work
15	1:30 PM		Fluency Lab	Chem Lab	Fluency Lab	Food Bank		Work
16	2:00 PM		Fluency Lab	Chem Lab	Fluency Lab	Food Bank	Work	Work
17	2:30 PM			Chem Lab		Food Bank	Work	Work
18	3:00 PM			Chem Lab		Food Bank	Work	Work
19	3:30 PM		Poetry WkSp	Chem Lab	Poetry WkSp	Food Bank	Work	Work
20	4:00 PM		Poetry WkSp	Chem Lab	Poetry WkSp	Food Bank	Work	Work
21	4:30 PM		Poetry WkSp		Poetry WkSp	Food Bank	Work	Work
22	5:00 PM						Work	Work
23	5:30 PM						Work	Work
24	6:00 PM		Volley Ball		Dinner w/Boink		Work	Work
25	6:30 PM		Volley Ball				Work	Work
26	7:00 PM		Volley Ball				Work	Work
27	7:30 PM		Volley Ball				Work	Work
28	8:00 PM							Jimmy's
29								

Figure 14.5 Calendar spreadsheet with entries added.

Discount Table

Let's get further practice with series fill, and with relative and absolute cell references.

Because downloading music for MP3 players is so popular, music stores that sell CDs try to compete by offering "store credit" discounts, that is, discounts on future purchases at the store. One store offers

- $1.00 store credit for each $10.00 spent plus
- $3.00 store credit for every two CDs purchased (one CD earns only $1.00 credit)

To help you to figure your credits, you can construct a table, which you can print out and take to the store, showing the various discounts. This is another very easy spreadsheet application.

To begin, we decide on the axes for the table: The left column is the "dollars spent" column, showing $10.00 increments, and the top row is the "CDs purchased" row, showing 1 CD increments. These are both number series, but the spreadsheet software doesn't automatically provide series fill for numbers. So we must choose it, or fill in the series using formulas, which is also possible, of course. For the top row, we fill the first and second cells with 1 and 2 and then fill across.

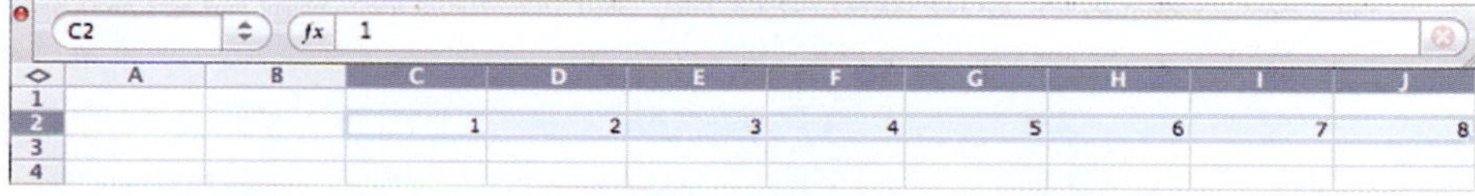

For the left column, we enter the first two items, `$10.00` and `$20.00`, select the pair, and fill down.

B3 | fx 10

	A	B	C	D	E	F	G	H	I	J
1										
2			1	2	3	4	5	6	7	8
3		$10.00								
4		$20.00								
5		$30.00								
6		$40.00								
7		$50.00								
8		$60.00								
9		$70.00								
10		$80.00								
11		$90.00								
12		$100.00								
13		$110.00								
14		$120.00								
15		$130.00								
16		$140.00								
17		$150.00								
18										

The software figures out that we want to increment by $10.00. All that remains is to specify the table entries. For that, we write a formula.

For each $10.00 spent the store gives a $1.00 credit. So, part of the formula is to divide the item in column `B` by 10. For example

```
=$B3/10
```

To ensure that the number we are dividing is always in column B, we make the column reference absolute. The row reference should be relative because we want the calculation to apply to whatever row the formula is in.

The store also gives $3.00 credit for every two CDs purchased. The easiest way to apply this rule is to multiply the CD axis entry (in row 2) by 3/2.

```
=(3/2)*C$2
```

which is the right answer when the number of CDs is even, but for an odd number of CDs it is too much by half. For example, 1*3/2 is 1.5, that is, $1.50, but the store only gives $1.00 credit. The solution is to throw away any fractional digits, that is, to truncate the number. Spreadsheets have a function, trunc, for this purpose,

```
=trunc((3/2)*C$2)
```

As with the first rule, we use an absolute reference and a relative reference. Row 2 is absolute so that all entries refer to it, but the column should be relative, so that the computation applies to the column that the formula is in.

The combined formula for both discount rules is

```
=$B3/10 + trunc((3/2)*C$2)
```

which we enter into cell C3. This yields the right answer: $2.00 ($1.00 for the amount paid plus $1.00 for the single CD).

C3 | fx =$B3/10+TRUNC((3/2)*C$2)

	A	B	C	D	E	F	G	H	I	J
1										
2			1	2	3	4	5	6	7	8
3		$10.00	$2.00							
4		$20.00								
5		$30.00								
6		$40.00								
7		$50.00								
8		$60.00								
9		$70.00								
10		$80.00								
11		$90.00								
12		$100.00								
13		$110.00								
14		$120.00								
15		$130.00								
16		$140.00								
17		$150.00								
18										
19										

Filling the formula down the column and then across the rows produces the final table.

L19 | fx

	A	B	C	D	E	F	G	H	I	J
1										
2			1	2	3	4	5	6	7	8
3		$10.00	$2.00	$4.00	$5.00	$7.00	$8.00	$10.00	$11.00	$13.00
4		$20.00	$3.00	$5.00	$6.00	$8.00	$9.00	$11.00	$12.00	$14.00
5		$30.00	$4.00	$6.00	$7.00	$9.00	$10.00	$12.00	$13.00	$15.00
6		$40.00	$5.00	$7.00	$8.00	$10.00	$11.00	$13.00	$14.00	$16.00
7		$50.00	$6.00	$8.00	$9.00	$11.00	$12.00	$14.00	$15.00	$17.00
8		$60.00	$7.00	$9.00	$10.00	$12.00	$13.00	$15.00	$16.00	$18.00
9		$70.00	$8.00	$10.00	$11.00	$13.00	$14.00	$16.00	$17.00	$19.00
10		$80.00	$9.00	$11.00	$12.00	$14.00	$15.00	$17.00	$18.00	$20.00
11		$90.00	$10.00	$12.00	$13.00	$15.00	$16.00	$18.00	$19.00	$21.00
12		$100.00	$11.00	$13.00	$14.00	$16.00	$17.00	$19.00	$20.00	$22.00
13		$110.00	$12.00	$14.00	$15.00	$17.00	$18.00	$20.00	$21.00	$23.00
14		$120.00	$13.00	$15.00	$16.00	$18.00	$19.00	$21.00	$22.00	$24.00
15		$130.00	$14.00	$16.00	$17.00	$19.00	$20.00	$22.00	$23.00	$25.00
16		$140.00	$15.00	$17.00	$18.00	$20.00	$21.00	$23.00	$24.00	$26.00
17		$150.00	$16.00	$18.00	$19.00	$21.00	$22.00	$24.00	$25.00	$27.00
18										

We can print out the table and take it with us to the store to help strategize our purchases to get the biggest discount. For example, we might trade CD purchases with a friend to get a larger combined discount, which we then share.

The table was easy to construct. We used two series, one for the dollars and one for the CDs, to create the axes. The table entries used a single formula that referenced the axis entries with one absolute and one relative coordinate so that the entry for the column/row position was computed correctly. This technique is common whenever we have two axes.

Paying Off a Loan

Suppose you are considering a large purchase, which may or may not have woofers. Your uncle has agreed to lend you the money, but ever the businessman, he's charging you 5 percent interest. To decide how much to spend, you want to create a table of the monthly payments required for different amounts borrowed for different times. The table setup follows the strategy of the last section: Fill a row across the top with different numbers of payments, and fill a column with different amounts.

	A	B	C	D	E	F	G
1							
2		Payments	6	12	18	24	
3		$1,000					
4		$1,500					
5		$2,000					
6		$2,500					
7		$3,000					
8		$3,500					
9		$4,000					
10		$4,500					
11		$5,000					

Among the functions available with spreadsheets is the "payment" computation, PMT. When we click on it under the *Insert > Function…* menu, a GUI is displayed for PMT.

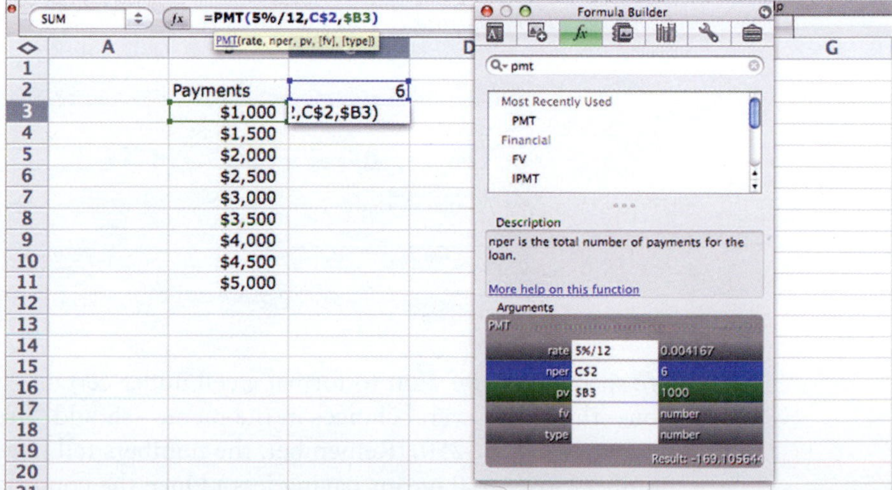

The inputs to the function are the monthly interest Rate, which is 1/12th of the annual rate your uncle is charging, so the proper entry is 0.05/12. The number of payments (Nper) is the amount in row 2 for this column, and the present value, or the amount of the loan (Pv), is the amount in column B for this row. We enter the numbers. As with the discount table in the previous section, the inputs mix absolute and relative references to refer to the row and column entries. So, Nper is C$2 because we always want to reference row 2, and Pv is $B3 because we always want to reference column B. The formula result, shown at the bottom of the GUI, is the amount required to repay $1,000 in six payments. Notice that the result is negative, because the payment is a cost to you.

Filling the formula down the column and across the rows results in a table with red, parenthesized values, which is the default display form for negative numbers.

C3 | fx =PMT(5%/12,C$2,$B3)

	A	B	C	D	E	F	G
1							
2		Payments	6	12	18	24	
3		$1,000	($169.11)	($85.61)	($57.78)	($43.87)	
4		$1,500	($253.66)	($128.41)	($86.67)	($65.81)	
5		$2,000	($338.21)	($171.21)	($115.56)	($87.74)	
6		$2,500	($422.76)	($214.02)	($144.45)	($109.68)	
7		$3,000	($507.32)	($256.82)	($173.34)	($131.61)	
8		$3,500	($591.87)	($299.63)	($202.23)	($153.55)	
9		$4,000	($676.42)	($342.43)	($231.12)	($175.49)	
10		$4,500	($760.98)	($385.23)	($260.01)	($197.42)	
11		$5,000	($845.53)	($428.04)	($288.90)	($219.36)	
12							

If we don't like the parentheses, we can reformat the entries, say leaving them red.

Perhaps, because the table is intended to help us decide how much to borrow, the best way to display the entries is to display them in two colors: Green for those within our budget and red for those over our budget. Deciding that a payment of $250 per month is a comfortable limit, we click on *Format > Conditional Formatting…* and get this GUI.

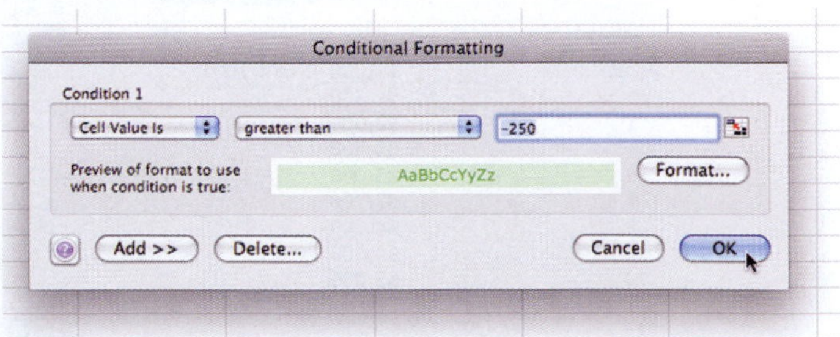

We specify that we want to format a cell under certain conditions. The condition—there are several choices in the menu—should "fire" for cells greater than or equal to –250. (Remember, the numbers tell how much we *pay*, so a number closer to 0 means paying less.) Once the condition is set up, we click on the **Format...** button in the Conditional Formatting dialog box, and pick a font color and a cell color. The final result makes it visually easy to decide how much to borrow.

H21 *fx*

	A	B	C	D	E	F	G
1							
2		Payments	6	12	18	24	
3		$1,000	($169.11)	($85.61)	($57.78)	($43.87)	
4		$1,500	($253.66)	($128.41)	($86.67)	($65.81)	
5		$2,000	($338.21)	($171.21)	($115.56)	($87.74)	
6		$2,500	($422.76)	($214.02)	($144.45)	($109.68)	
7		$3,000	($507.32)	($256.82)	($173.34)	($131.61)	
8		$3,500	($591.87)	($299.63)	($202.23)	($153.55)	
9		$4,000	($676.42)	($342.43)	($231.12)	($175.49)	
10		$4,500	($760.98)	($385.23)	($260.01)	($197.42)	
11		$5,000	($845.53)	($428.04)	($288.90)	($219.36)	
12							

Importing Data

Much of the data we are interested in comes from some other source, that is, we didn't produce it. This probably means it has already been organized, and so may already exist in a spreadsheet or in a table in another application. Call this **foreign data**—data from another application that we want to import into a spreadsheet. Though importing previously formatted data into a spreadsheet can be tricky, there are some guidelines to make it easier.

Tab-Delimited Data

As a rule, spreadsheets prefer to import foreign data as **tab-delimited text**. "Text" means ASCII text, that is, files with .txt extensions. Because they are text files, numbers like *100* are represented as three numeral characters rather than as a single binary number. This allows the spreadsheet software to convert the ASCII form into whatever internal number representation it prefers. "Tab-delimited" means that each cell's entry is **delimited** (ends with) a tab in the file, and each row is delimited with a return (the symbol that results from pressing Return or Enter on the keyboard). Other delimiters are recognized, too, such as spaces and commas. Spreadsheets can output their lists as tab-delimited text. Copying and pasting tab-delimited text is a simple way to import foreign data.

Lists with some other form can often be converted into the preferred tab-delimited form by copying the foreign data into a text editor or word processor and editing it using *Search/Replace*, possibly using the placeholder technique introduced in Chapter 2. The goal is to substitute a tab or other preferred delimiter for a delimiter in the file that the spreadsheet software doesn't understand. Writing the result to a text file eliminates any formatting characters from the word processor.

Another important source of data is the World Wide Web. The information is already in text form—so that condition is fulfilled—and often it is formatted with HTML table tags, as described in Chapter 4. It seems it should be possible to *Copy* a table from HTML and *Paste* it into a spreadsheet. For some browser-spreadsheet combinations it works, but for others it doesn't. It all depends on how the browser delimits "copies" taken from the source. If you try to *Copy/Paste* table data from the Web and it doesn't work, try another browser before beginning the tedious task of reformatting the foreign data by other means. You'll probably get lucky.

✓checkLIST Guidelines for importing foreign data:

- ✓ *When possible, save foreign data as tab-delimited ASCII text in a file with a* .txt *extension.*
- ✓ *When foreign data comes from the Web, select a browser that supports* Copy/Paste *of tagged tables.*
- ✓ *When the foreign data format is messed up, use a text editor with* Search/Replace, *apply the placeholder technique, and write the revised data with a* .txt *extension. Import the resulting file.*

For example, suppose you want to print out a custom bus schedule. Transportation schedules often include more data than we need, so if we grab a copy of the whole schedule from the Web, we can trim and edit it to match our needs in a spreadsheet. Visiting the city's Web page, we locate the bus schedule and *Copy* it, as shown in Figure 14.6, and then *Paste* it into the spreadsheet.

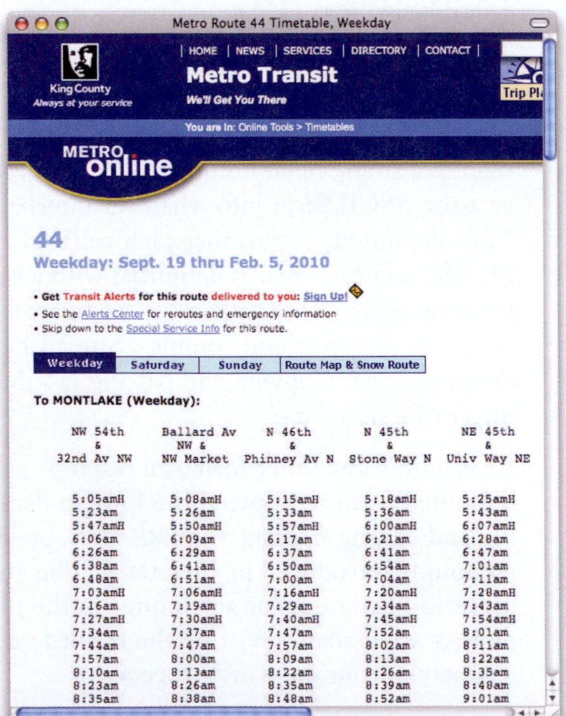

NW 54th & 32nd Av NW	Ballard Av NW & NW Market	N 46th & Phinney Av N	N 45th & Stone Way N	NE 45th & Univ Way NE
5:05amH	5:08amH	5:15amH	5:18amH	5:25amH
5:23am	5:26am	5:33am	5:36am	5:43am
5:47amH	5:50amH	5:57amH	6:00amH	6:07amH
6:06am	6:09am	6:17am	6:21am	6:28am
6:26am	6:29am	6:37am	6:41am	6:47am
6:38am	6:41am	6:50am	6:54am	7:01am
6:48am	6:51am	7:00am	7:04am	7:11am
7:03amH	7:06amH	7:16amH	7:20amH	7:28amH
7:16am	7:19am	7:29am	7:34am	7:43am
7:27amH	7:30amH	7:40amH	7:45amH	7:54amH
7:34am	7:37am	7:47am	7:52am	8:01am
7:44am	7:47am	7:57am	8:02am	8:11am
7:57am	8:00am	8:09am	8:13am	8:22am
8:10am	8:13am	8:22am	8:26am	8:35am
8:23am	8:26am	8:35am	8:39am	8:48am
8:35am	8:38am	8:48am	8:52am	9:01am

Figure 14.6 Bus schedule from the Web selected for copying.

We only want the departure time from our stop and the arrival time at campus. By deleting columns we can create a simple two-column schedule. Adding the two columns for the return trip produces a custom schedule, as shown in Figure 14.7, that can be printed and kept in a wallet, a purse, or cached on a mobile device.

	A	B	C	D	E	F
3		5:23am	5:43am	5:46am	6:05am	
4		5:47amH	6:07amH	6:01am	6:21am	
5		6:06am	6:28am	6:16am	6:37am	
6		6:26am	6:47am	6:27amH	6:49amH	
7		6:38am	7:01am	6:38am	7:00am	
8		6:48am	7:11am	6:46amH	7:09amH	
9		7:03amH	7:28amH	6:52am	7:22am	
10		7:16am	7:43am	7:06am	7:31am	
11		7:27amH	7:54amH	7:19am	7:44am	
12		7:34am	8:01am	7:25am	7:57am	

Figure 14.7 Customized schedule with "to campus" in white, "from campus" in purple.

Arranging Columns

Spreadsheets are designed to manipulate rows and columns of information easily. Most other applications are good with rows, but not columns. For example, it is common in word processing to present a list of information, one item per line, as in this 81-line list of Best Picture winners, which includes Oscar awards / nominations, director, and year.

> *Slumdog Millionaire*, 8 / 10, Danny Boyle, 2008
> *No Country for Old Men*, 4 / 8, Joel & Ethan Coen, 2007
> *The Departed*, 4 / 5, Martin Scorsese, 2006
> *Crash*, 3 / 6, Paul Haggis, 2005
> *Million Dollar Baby*, 4 / 7, Clint Eastwood, 2004
> *Lord of the Rings: Return of the King*, 11 / 11, Peter Jackson, 2003
> ...

Though the lines may not be intended as a table, when each one contains the same information in the same order, we naturally align it into a table in our minds. Adding new rows is easy. Inserting or rearranging the columns is a headache. Spreadsheets can help.

To manipulate columns in an application not well-suited to the task, we must create a consistently delimited text file of the data, and import it into a spreadsheet, as described earlier. (Most entries are delimited with commas, so only the slash (/) presents a problem.) We then manipulate the list and write out the file as text. After being revised in the spreadsheet, the file can be returned to the application. We will illustrate this idea by rearranging the columns of the movie list.

For example, suppose we want to reorder the columns so the year follows the movie, and change the *awards / nominations* data so it reads, for *Slumdog Millionaire*, "8 of 10 Oscars."

To begin:

- Make a file containing only the list
- Use *Search/Replace* to replace every space-slash-space (" / ") with a comma (","), so that the numbers get separate columns.
- Import the file into the spreadsheet

The result is shown in Figure 14.8.

A1 | fx

	A	B	C	D	E	F	G
1							
2		Slumdog Millionaire	Danny Boyle	8	10	2008	
3		No Country for Old Men	Joel & Ethan Coen	4	8	2007	
4		The Departed	Martin Scorsese	4	5	2006	
5		Crash	Paul Haggis	3	6	2005	
6		Million Dollar Baby	Clint Eastwood	4	7	2004	
7		Lord of the Rings: Return	Peter Jackson	11	11	2003	

Figure 14.8 The movie list imported into a spreadsheet.

Using *Cut* and *Paste* we move the last column to become the second column.

C1 | fx

	A	B	C	D	E	F	G
1							
2		Slumdog Millionaire	2008	Danny Boyle	8	10	
3		No Country for Old Men	2007	Joel & Ethan Coen	4	8	
4		The Departed	2006	Martin Scorsese	4	5	
5		Crash	2005	Paul Haggis	3	6	
6		Million Dollar Baby	2004	Clint Eastwood	4	7	
7		Lord of the Rings: Return	2003	Peter Jackson	11	11	

We also use a new column to combine the awards and nominations into one phrase. The formula uses an operation called **concatenate**, which means to join pieces of text together, one after the other. We will join four pieces of text together: the number of awards, the text " of " (ƀofƀ), the number of nominations, and the text " Oscars" (ƀOscars); where ƀ is our symbol for a space.

awards "of" *nominations* " Oscars"

This is expressed by the formula

```
=concatenate(e2," of ",f2," Oscars")
```

For the movie *Slumdog Millionaire*, the formula produces

G2 =CONCATENATE(E2," of ",F2," Oscars")

	A	B	C	D	E	F	G	H
1								
2		Slumdog Millionaire	2008	Danny Boyle	8	10	8 of 10 Oscars	
3		No Country for Old Men	2007	Joel & Ethan Coen	4	8		
4		The Departed	2006	Martin Scorsese	4	5		

The function concatenate can join any number of text pieces, and is a handy tool for combining words and numbers.

14.4 Director's Cut. Write the spreadsheet formula to be placed in H2, that would produce the contents "Danny Boyle, director" and that could be filled down column H to apply to all directors. (Ignore the plural for the Coen brothers.)

The result, after filling into column G, is shown in Figure 14.9(a). This revised column converts two columns of data to a phrase that can replace them. We move the two numerical columns to the end of the table (we need to keep them or the concatenate formula won't work) and reorder the columns as we intend (see Figure 14.9b).

(a) G2 =CONCATENATE(E2," of ",F2," Oscars")

	A	B	C	D	E	F	G
1							
2		Slumdog Millionaire	2008	Danny Boyle	8	10	8 of 10 Oscars
3		No Country for Old Men	2007	Joel & Ethan Coen	4	8	4 of 8 Oscars
4		The Departed	2006	Martin Scorsese	4	5	4 of 5 Oscars

(b) A1

	B	C	D	E	F	G	H
1							
2	Slumdog Millionaire	2008	Danny Boyle		8 of 10 Oscars	8	10
3	No Country for Old Men	2007	Joel & Ethan Coen		4 of 8 Oscars	4	8
4	The Departed	2006	Martin Scorsese		4 of 5 Oscars	4	5

(c) E2 — Paste Special

Paste: All, Formulas, Values, Formats, Comments, Validation, All except borders, Column Widths, Formulas and number formats, Values and number formats

Operation

		E	F	G	H
1					
2	Slur		8 of 10 Oscars	8	10
3	No (... Coen		4 of 8 Oscars	4	8
4	The ... se		4 of 5 Oscars	4	5
5	Cras		3 of 6 Oscars	3	6
6	Milli ... d		4 of 7 Oscars	4	7
7	Lorc ... ı		11 of 11 Oscars	11	11

(d) A1

	B	C	D	E	F	G	H
1							
2	Slumdog Millionaire	2008	Danny Boyle	8 of 10 Oscars			
3	No Country for Old Men	2007	Joel & Ethan Coen	4 of 8 Oscars			
4	The Departed	2006	Martin Scorsese	4 of 5 Oscars			
5	Crash	2005	Paul Haggis	3 of 6 Oscars			
6	Million Dollar Baby	2004	Clint Eastwood	4 of 7 Oscars			
7	Lord of the Rings: Return	2003	Peter Jackson	11 of 11 Oscars			

Figure 14.9 Revising the movie list. (a) Constructing the phrase, (b) reordering the main columns, (c) creating the text form of the phrase with *Paste Special...*, (d) the completed table.

To complete the table, we want to *Cut* and *Paste* the Oscars column into column E and throw away the last two data columns. But if we do that, the data that the Oscars column depends on will be gone. What we must do is *Paste* the Oscars as *values*, that is, as text, into column E. So, we use *Edit > Paste Special...* and select *Values*. This converts the Oscars column from formulas to text (see Figure 14.9c) so that it no longer depends on the data columns. Now, the "working columns" can be removed producing the final result (see 14.9(d)).

This completes our revisions, and we can copy the final results from our spreadsheet to our document.

> *Slumdog Millionaire*, 2008, Danny Boyle, 8 of 10 Oscars
>
> *No Country for Old Men*, 2007, Joel & Ethan Coen, 4 of 8 Oscars
>
> *The Departed*, 2006, Martin Scorsese, 4 of 5 Oscars
>
> *Crash*, 2005, Paul Haggis, 3 of 6 Oscars
>
> *Million Dollar Baby*, 2004, Clint Eastwood, 4 of 7 Oscars
>
> *Lord of the Rings: Return of the King*, 2003, Peter Jackson, 11 of 11 Oscars
>
> ...

The result achieves our intended columnar modifications. When we explain the process in complete detail it seems complicated, but it takes only a few minutes to put it into a spreadsheet, fix it, and copy the reformatted text into the document.

Summary

In this chapter we explored the basic ideas of spreadsheets. We found that:

- Spreadsheets present an array of cells, each of which is capable of storing one data item: a number, a letter sequence, or a formula.
- Numbers and text can be formatted so that they display as we prefer—proper font, correct number of digits, and so on.
- The power of spreadsheets comes from entering formulas that calculate new values based on the values in other cells.
- The formula is one side of an equation, which the computer solves for us, preserving the equality whenever the numbers that the formula depends on are changed and displaying the new value in the cell.
- In addition to performing arithmetic on the cells, we can apply functions to individual items or to whole cell ranges.
- Both relative and absolute references to cells are needed depending on the circumstances.
- In addition to sorting, there are functions for finding totals, averages, the maximum or minimum, and others.

- Spreadsheets are a practical tool for routine computing.
- It's easy to teach ourselves more about spreadsheets simply by trying them with courage.
- Spreadsheets may be the most useful software for personal computing.

Try It Solutions

14.1 The cell range is C5:D6, because the two birds with "-tailed" in their names are in rows 5 and 6, and the scientific names span columns C and D.

14.2 The formula is =G2*100.

14.3 *Step 1.* The recommended first step is to label the next column, I, with an appropriate heading, though it is not actually required.

Step 2. Enter the formula =G2*39.37 in cell I2, which computes the length of Swainson's hawks in inches; it's 20.28 inches.

Step 3. Click once on cell I2 to select it, and drag the fill handle down the column to fill in the lengths of the other birds.

14.4 The formula is =concatenate(D2, ", director").

Did you remember the space after the comma?

Review Questions

True/False

1. Text too wide to fit into a cell is truncated.
2. Cells in a spreadsheet are 10 characters wide.
3. Spreadsheets are most commonly used to process numerical data.
4. *Copy/Paste* will duplicate a formula, but it won't utilize relative and absolute cell references.
5. The small box or handle in a selected cell's lower right corner is used to move the contents of a cell.
6. A cell reference cannot contain relative and absolute references at the same time.
7. To change a relative cell reference to an absolute reference, you should use the ampersand (&).
8. Spreadsheet columns can be hidden but rows cannot.
9. Text files are generally stored in ASCII format.
10. A spreadsheet can import any kind of data.

Multiple Choice

1. A series of cells is called a(n)
   a. tuple
   b. group
   c. array
   d. sheet
2. Respectively, rows and columns are designated with
   a. numbers, letters
   b. letters, numbers
   c. numbers, numbers
   d. names, numbers
3. Which of the following is a valid range of cells?
   a. D1:D4
   b. C3:D5
   c. A1:E1
   d. all of the above
4. Which of the following is not a valid range of cells?
   a. A1>A5
   b. C3-C8
   c. 3B:6B
   d. all of the above
5. How many cells are in the range B2:D7?
   a. 6
   b. 12
   c. 18
   d. unknown
6. Spreadsheet formulas start with
   a. +
   b. =
   c. @
   d. !
7. The results of a calculation in a spreadsheet cell are displayed in
   a. the cell to the right
   b. the cell immediately below
   c. the cell where the formula is written
   d. front of the formula
8. Filling is also known as
   a. moving
   b. formatting
   c. replicating
   d. clearing

9. Which of the following is a completely relative cell reference?
   a. J4
   b. $J4
   c. J$4
   d. $J$4

10. If the formula =$B$3 * .062 is copied from cell B4 to B5, the result will be
    a. =$B$4 * .062
    b. =$B$3 * .062
    c. =B5 * .062
    d. an error

11. If $G5 appeared in a formula, you'd know
    a. the G is absolute and the 5 is relative
    b. the G is relative and the 5 is absolute
    c. both are relative
    d. both are absolute

12. _______ is the character used to create an absolute cell reference.
    a. @
    b. =
    c. *
    d. $

13. You generate a carriage return when you press
    a. Spacebar
    b. Tab
    c. Return
    d. Shift

Short Answer

1. Cell entries are _______, that is, the computer will not consider any of their constituent parts.
2. A(n) _______ is the vertical arrangement of cells in a spreadsheet.
3. A(n) _______ is the horizontal arrangement of cells in a spreadsheet.
4. A group of one or more cells is called a(n) _______.
5. The small box in the lower right corner of a selected cell (or range of cells) is called the _______.
6. A(n) _______ cell reference automatically transforms a formula when it is pasted or filled.
7. A(n) _______ cell reference retains a reference to a fixed position when it is pasted or filled.
8. _______ are formulas built into a spreadsheet to make it easier to create calculations.

9. Use the _______ function to find the largest number in a range of cells.
10. Use the _______ function to find the smallest number in a range of cells.
11. A _______ is a range of cells filled with increments of a certain type of data.
12. Use the _______ function to find only the integer portion of a number.
13. The _______ function should be used to determine loan payments.
14. _______ is useful data that exists in a form that was created by a different application.
15. _______ means "to join together."

Exercises

1. Look through the list of functions for a spreadsheet. Make a list of 10 functions and how you could use them.
2. Use a spreadsheet to create a checkerboard. Resize the rows and columns of a spreadsheet to make 8 rows and 8 columns of equal size. Color alternate squares red and black. Print it in color.
3. Take a bag of M & M's. Count the number of each color. Create a spreadsheet from this. Write down each color and put the number of M & M's of that color in the cell next to it. Change the color of the cells to match the color of the M & M's. Write a formula to find the total. If you want, create a pie chart for this. Select the colors and the numbers. Create a chart and select pie chart. Edit it as needed.
4. Find the number of rows in your spreadsheet. Click on a cell and hold down the ↓ key until it stops. Find the number of columns in your spreadsheet. Click on a cell and hold down the → key until it stops. Columns are labeled with letters. Once you get to column Z, numbering starts over with AA. Calculate the number of columns. Then use the spreadsheet to calculate the number of cells in the spreadsheet. Use one cell for the number of rows. Use another for the number of columns. Write the formula to display the answer in another cell.
5. Create a spreadsheet to display the classes in your plan of study. Use a column for each semester and enter the classes below it.
6. Modify the spreadsheet for Paying Off a Loan. Change it so you can enter the interest in a cell and have the cell in your formula. Test it to see how changes in the interest rate affect your ability to repay the loan.
7. Go to www.tides.info/. Select a location and get the tide charts for the current month. Copy the data and paste it into a spreadsheet. Change the formatting of it to suit your tastes.
8. Create a spreadsheet to calculate the future value of an investment. Use the FV function for this. Future value is the value of a monthly investment at a certain rate over a period of time. You could use it for calculat-

ing your retirement nest egg. Enter the number of years in a row near the top. Start with 5 and go to 40 by fives. On the side enter the amount you're willing to invest each month. Start with $100 and fill it to $2,000.

In the cell above the $100, enter the interest rate you expect to earn on the investment. In the first cell of the table (where the 5 and $100 intersect), enter your formula. Use FV. The first one is the interest rate. Enter that cell. The second one is the years. Enter that cell. The last one is the amount. Enter that cell. When you fill using this cell, the formulas won't work—you'll need to modify them to always stay in the interest rate cell.

You'll need a $ in front of the row and column. For the years, you'll need the $ in front of the column. For the amount, you'll need the $ in front of the row. You'll then be able to copy it. The numbers will be negative. To make them positive (after all, it's money you're saving), use the absolute value function (ABS).

9. Create a personal budget. Put income in its own column. Total it. Put expenses in another column. Total it. The more accurate you are, the closer your budget will be. There should be at least a little money left over at the end of the month!
10. Create a GPA calculator. Enter your classes in one column. Next to it enter the number of credits. Next to that enter the grade points earned for that class. (Usually it's one point per credit for a D, two per credit for a C, three per credit for a B, and four per credit for an A.) Total the credits and the grade points. The GPA is grade points divided by credits.
11. Create a spreadsheet of your expected annual income. Put the year into a column and fill it up until the year you expect to retire. Next to the first year, enter your expected annual income. In the next cell, enter a formula to add three percent to the first year's income. Fill this formula for the rest of the years. If you put the percentage increase in a cell of its own and then use that in the formula, you'll be able to change the annual salary increase to see how that affects your pay.

15
chapter

Advanced Spreadsheets for Planning

"What If" Thinking Helps

learning objectives

- State the two basic design criteria for creating effective spreadsheets
- Explain how conditional formatting of spreadsheet entries applies an interpretation to spreadsheet information
- Explain conditional formulas, and their components and behavior
- Perform "what if" analysis with a spreadsheet
- Use AutoFiltering and advanced filtering to customize spreadsheet lists
- Explain the importance of symbolic naming of spreadsheet cells

One man's constant is another man's variable.

—ALAN PERLIS, 1968

THE INTRODUCTION to spreadsheets in the last chapter taught only the most basic operations. Based on that explanation you could be excused for wondering how it is that spreadsheets are the "most useful general-purpose computer application." They seem so limited. But you'll soon see that's not the case; in this chapter we introduce advanced spreadsheet techniques. This chapter's study shows that spreadsheets not only help us organize our data and analyze it, but they also allow us to explore possibilities that might arise and to work out strategies for reacting to those changes. These advanced spreadsheet concepts are just as easy to learn as the basic topics of the last chapter were, and they allow us to look into the future.

Spreadsheets are often taught using business applications, but we use a "running example" with more personal interest: a spreadsheet to plan a driving holiday. Perhaps you are the sort of person who likes spontaneous travel and thinks a detailed plan spoils the fun. Or maybe you like to have a carefully plotted itinerary. Either way, the plan helps us to understand important constraints on our travel, such as time and money. Once we know those limits, the trip can be either spontaneous or scheduled.

So far the spreadsheets we have created have been used only once, rather than being saved and used again and again. When a spreadsheet becomes a basic tool of our everyday work or recreation, it must be as useful and convenient as possible. That means good design, and we will present a short list of design guidelines in this chapter.

The advanced features we discuss concern using spreadsheets conditionally. These include adjusting the formats or values of cells based on various circumstances; for example, we may wish to flag values that are "out of bounds." We will also *filter* our spreadsheets, including or excluding data as our analysis requires. Another analytical tool supports "what if" experimentation; that is, the spreadsheet helps us examine alternatives and see the consequences of various decisions.

Designing a Spreadsheet

When we make a spreadsheet to find an answer and then delete it, it hardly matters what form it has as long as the computation is right. When a spreadsheet is used repeatedly, it doesn't only give answers, it becomes a tool of planning, analysis, and decision-making. To be effective, the spreadsheet must be well designed, being as informative and flexible as possible. We give design guidelines that further these goals after we describe what data we will use in our sample spreadsheet.

The Trip

The data we use in our example is about two friends, Pat and Alex, who know that it's not possible to drive to the North Pole, but wonder if it's possible to drive to the Arctic Circle. Turning to the Web, they find the following.

- There is an Arctic Circle Street in Rockford, Illinois (a false start).
- A highway crosses the Arctic Circle in the Yukon Territory of Canada, between Dawson and the Northwest Territories settlement of Inuvik.
- The trip to Inuvik is 3,663 miles from their home in Chicago, and takes 3 days and 8 hours of driving time (see Figure 15.1).
- The highway is unpaved over several hundred miles of the distance.

Obviously, the given driving time is continuous, which they do not plan to do. So they decide to make a spreadsheet to figure out how long it will take and how much it will cost. We use their spreadsheet as our example in this chapter.

Traveling Companion. Read the following sections at a computer and build the spreadsheets along with the text; it is an extremely effective way to learn these concepts. Moreover, when finished, you will have a spreadsheet to use to plan your travels. Find all the necessary files at www.aw.com/snyder/.

Design Guidelines

We adopt two basic principles for setting up effective spreadsheets. The first rule is:

Focus on Form: *Make the form logical, the layout clean, and the entries clear and understandable.*

Because the spreadsheet is not for the computer but for people to use in solving problems, it must be easy to understand and easy to work with. This makes the form of the presentation of data key. Arrange the data logically, which for English speakers generally means that

- descriptive information should be on the top and left sides, and
- summary information should be on the bottom and right sides.

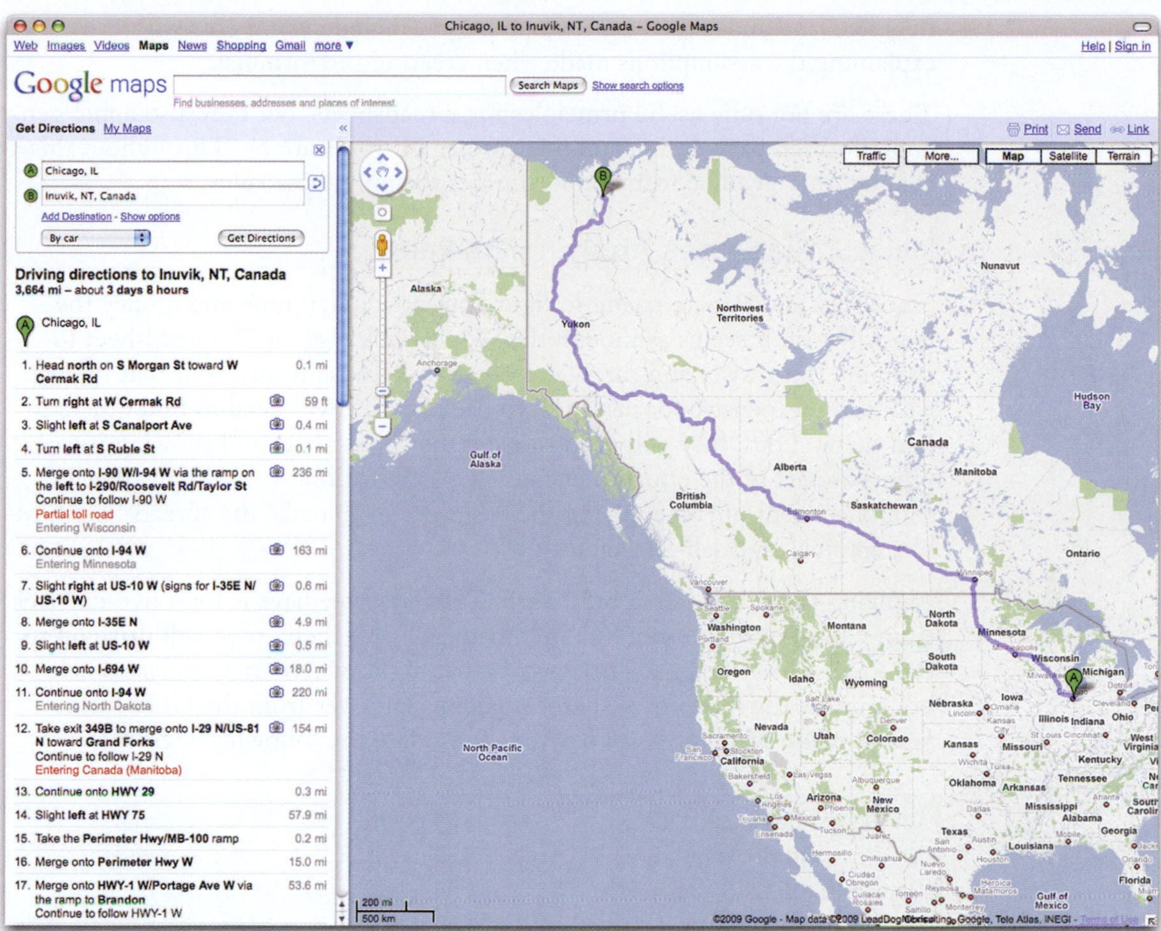

Figure 15.1 Google map directions for a trip from Chicago, Illinois (A green pin), to Inuvik, Northwest Territories (B green pin).

Fonts should be clear, possibly different for headings and data. Colors—for both font and fill—should be used in moderation, so that they attract attention to the important aspects of the sheet and aren't a distraction. Use a separate sheet for each table—multiple sheets don't cost more to use and individual sheets make working with mutiple tables more manageable. Hiding information that isn't needed in the current context is also a key way to make a spreadsheet clear and understandable.

The second rule is:

Explain Everything: *It should be possible to know immediately what every cell means.*

Initially, the rule implies that we say where the data comes from, and to include meaningful column headings and identifying information about the rows. Cells and ranges are assigned symbolic names (explained later) so the content becomes meaningful. For summary information cells, choose modifiers like *total* and *largest*. For computations, include comments with the cells explaining the assumptions made when creating the formulas.

These are not only useful principles for spreadsheets, but they also apply generally to Web page design and many other IT applications. Throughout this chapter, there will be many opportunities to apply these rules.

Initial Spreadsheet: Applying the Rules

Since Alex and Pat are trying to figure out how much time and money the trip will cost, it seems as though they could click together a spreadsheet to compute the answer and throw it away. But, because it turns out that the trip will be too expensive for just the two friends, they will need to find others to join them. Thus, they will keep revising the spreadsheet and showing it to others as part of the effort to encourage participation. Accordingly, they should concentrate on applying the design rules to make the spreadsheet flexible, credible, and self-explanatory.

Applying the rules is straightforward. The data they have is for a five-day trek from Chicago to Dawson, Yukon Territory. From there, they will drive up to the Arctic Circle and back to Dawson that night, where they expect to celebrate in the town's renovated 1890s saloons left over from the Gold Rush. Using online mapping software, they formulate the following segments.

Chicago to Carrington, ND:	778 miles,	12 hrs, 2 minutes
Carrington to Battleford, SK:	620 miles,	11 hrs, 6 minutes
Battleford to Fort St. John, BC:	648 miles,	11 hrs, 26 minutes
Fort St. John to Watson Lake, BC:	555 miles,	10 hrs, 17 minutes
Watson Lake to Dawson, YK:	601 miles,	11 hrs, 55 minutes
Round-trip Dawson to Arctic Circle:	484 miles,	14 hours

The friends are interested in how much the trip will cost, so they add a column for fuel costs, which they find on the Web (www.gasbuddy.com). Part of the trip is through the U.S., of course, where gas is priced by the gallon in U.S. dollars, and part of the trip is through Canada, where petrol (gas) is priced by the liter in Canadian dollars, so the spreadsheet lists where the price estimate comes from, as shown in Figure 15.2.

Trip to the Arctic Circle
by Pat and Alex; competed 23. June.2009

Segment	Time Est.	Miles	Fuel Price Report	Fuel Price
Chicago to Carrington ND	12:02	778	US Chicago	$3.59
Carrington to Battleford SK	11:06	620	US Moorehead MN	$2.96
Battleford to Fort St. John BC	11:26	648	CA Moose Jaw SK	$1.09
Fort St. John to Watson Lake YK	10:17	555	CA Medicine Hat AB	$1.01
Watson Lake to Dawson YK	11:55	601	CA Mi 54 AK Hiway BC	$1.21
Dawson to Dawson via AC	14:00	484	CA Mi 54 AK Hiway BC	$1.21

Figure 15.2 Initial spreadsheet for the Arctic Circle road trip.

The principle of "focus on form" is evident in a variety of places. The spreadsheet in Figure 15.2 has a title listing the authors and stating the completion date. Columns are assigned clear headings. The heading row is filled with a soft color that separates it from the content, which is preferable to intense colors that can distract. A clean, sans serif font presents the data justified in the cells, so the columns align and give a clean, neat appearance.

The principle of "explain everything" is illustrated by three comments, which explain the data sources. Comments are like sticky notes that can be added to cells. Their presence is denoted by the red triangle in the cell's upper right corner (see the headings in Figure 15.2). Hovering the cursor over the cell displays the comment.

Miles
Pat: US prices in gallons
CA prices in liters; each in
local currency.
778
620 US Moorehead MN $2.96

To insert a comment in Excel, select the cell and then navigate *Insert > Comment*. The author's name is automatically placed at the beginning of the comment. To edit it, select the cell and navigate *Insert > Edit Comment*. To remove a comment, find it as an option for *Clear*, that is, navigate *Edit > Clear > Comments*.

These two design principles will be exhibited throughout the remainder of the spreadsheet development.

Conditional Formatting

Another technique to make a spreadsheet more effective is to conditionally format the cells. In Chapter 14 you saw conditional formatting for calculating loan payments, where monthly payments within the budget were displayed in green and payments exceeding the budget were displayed in red. **Conditional formatting** allows us to *apply an interpretation to the data*—payments within budget, payments over budget—and express that interpretation in an easy to perceive manner.

Cell Value Is Specifications

The Arctic Circle road trip spreadsheet has a variety of opportunities to use conditional formatting to help the friends understand the data. One observation about the trip is that there is considerable variance in how long they must travel on each segment; some days are much longer than others. To emphasize the long days, Pat and Alex decide to apply conditional formatting to the Time Estimate column: Any segment over 12:00 hours of driving is interpreted as "long" and will be displayed in bold. They select the Time Estimate entries, and choose *Format > Conditional Formatting…* to arrive at the following dialog window.

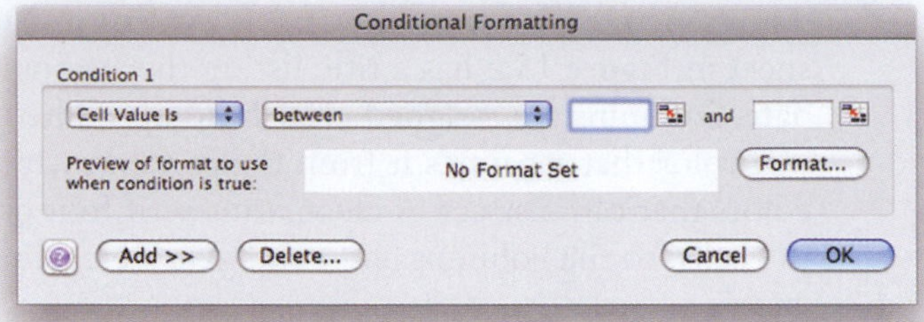

This window lets users specify one or more conditions. If the program finds that these conditions apply to the cell, it formats the entry in the manner specified under *Format*. Users specify the condition by picking one of a set of relationships and filling in the limits. The default condition, *between*, is shown, but the travelers want the *greater than* condition. So, clicking the menu selection button to the right of *between*, they select *greater than*.

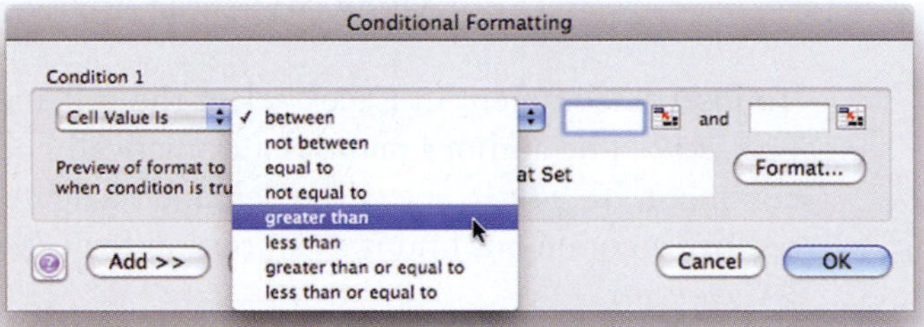

After entering the 12:00 hour time threshold and selecting bold formatting, they click **OK**, creating the result shown in Figure 15.3.

Studying the result, the friends notice that the formatting has had the effect of marking the Chicago to Carrington segment as long, but not marking the Watson Lake to Dawson segment, which is only seven minutes shorter. Perhaps rather than having the long day defined by some absolute bound like 12:00 hours, they should define "long day" as "any day that is longer than the average." Conditional formatting allows formulas to be used rather than absolute limits like 12:00 hours. Revising the conditional formatting specification to compare to the formula

```
=average(b$2:b$7)
```

Trip to the Arctic Circle
by Pat and Alex; competed 23. June.2009

Segment	Time Est.	Miles	Fuel Price Report	Fuel Price
Chicago to Carrington ND	**12:02**	778	US Chicago	$3.59
Carrington to Battleford SK	11:06	620	US Moorehead MN	$2.96
Battleford to Fort St. John BC	11:26	648	CA Moose Jaw SK	$1.09
Fort St. John to Watson Lake YK	10:17	555	CA Medicine Hat AB	$1.01
Watson Lake to Dawson YK	11:55	601	CA Mi 54 AK Hiway BC	$1.21
Dawson to Dawson via AC	**14:00**	484	CA Mi 54 AK Hiway BC	$1.21

Figure 15.3 The Arctic Circle road trip spreadsheet with conditional formatting for "long days."

results in

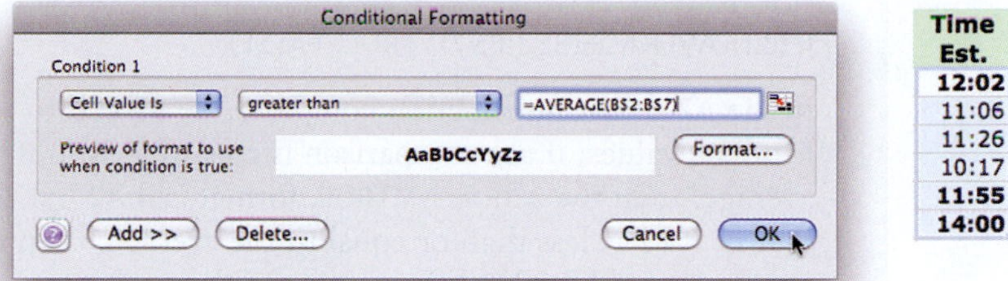

which achieves their goal.

The absolute references in the range specification (B$2:B$7) are essential, because the friends are formatting a column of cells, and the spreadsheet software, as usual, adjusts relative cell references. The result is that the longer days are highlighted, where “longer” now means “greater than average.”

15.1 Minimum Criterion. Using the min( ) function, give the entry for each item of the top row in the Conditional Formatting window to format the cell with the shortest distance.

Formula Is Specifications

Although the large drive time *defines* a long segment, it is the travel—the segment—that is causing the long day. The friends want to highlight the information in the first column (A), Segment. It’s possible to format those items based on the AVERAGE(B$2,B$7), but there is a problem: The value that must be compared to the average is B2, not A2. That is, making a comparison with some cell other than the one being formatted is not possible using the *Cell Value Is* facility in the Conditional Formatting window. The alternative to *Cell Value Is* is *Formula Is*, and that is the facility the friends want.

Selecting the *Formula Is* option causes the window to be redisplayed as

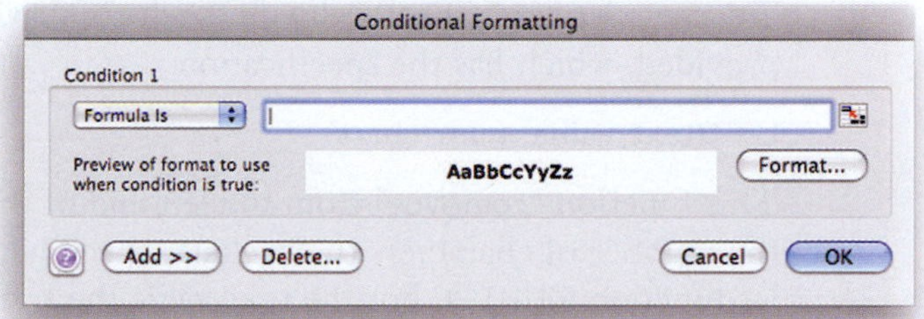

The friends need a formula that is true when the entry is to be formatted and false otherwise. The function they use to decide this condition is the IF( ) function, which has this general specification:

IF(condition, action_on_true_outcome, action_on_false_outcome)

They need to specify the format of the IF( ) function for the A2 cell, so they place

```
IF(B2>AVERAGE(B$2:B$7), TRUE, FALSE)
```

in the A2 cell. This function compares the B2 cell to the average of the Time Estimate values; if the comparison is true, that is, if B2 is greater than the average, then the action is "TRUE, format cell A2"; if the comparison is false, that is, if B2 is less than or equal to the average, then the action is "FALSE, do not format cell A2."

To implement highlighting the Segment, the friends clear the conditional formatting of the Time Estimate column, select the Segment entries of column A, and enter the formula. The result is shown in Figure 15.4.

Trip to the Arctic Circle
by Pat and Alex; competed 23. June.2009

Segment	Time Est.	Miles	Fuel Price Report	Fuel Price
Chicago to Carrington ND	12:02	778	US Chicago	$3.59
Carrington to Battleford SK	11:06	620	US Moorehead MN	$2.96
Battleford to Fort St. John BC	11:26	648	CA Moose Jaw SK	*$1.09*
Fort St. John to Watson Lake YK	10:17	555	CA Medicine Hat AB	*$1.01*
Watson Lake to Dawson YK	11:55	601	CA Mi 54 AK Hiway BC	*$1.21*
Dawson to Dawson via AC	14:00	484	CA Mi 54 AK Hiway BC	*$1.21*

Figure 15.4 Conditional formatting to highlight trip Segments, whose Time Estimate is greater than average.

Distinguish Between the U.S. and Canada

Figure 15.4 illustrates one more instance of conditional formatting: The prices in the Fuel Price column given in Canadian dollars are italicized. Like the Segment formatting just considered, the Fuel Price formatting requires an IF( ) function in a formula. The complication, however, is determining when a price is in Canadian dollars, because it's not possible to determine that from the amount in the cell. However, the Fuel Price Report column has the property that it lists the source of the price quote in the first two letters of the cell, so whenever the country is CA, the price should be italicized.

To access letters of a cell value for such comparisons, the function LEFT( ) is provided, which has the specification

```
LEFT(text_value, num_chars)
```

This function "removes" from the left end of the letter sequence (text_value) the number of characters (num_chars) specified; of course, there is also a similar function RIGHT( ). For the text_value the friends use D2, the Fuel Price Report; for the second parameter, they use 2. So, to do the match requires the formula

```
LEFT(D2, 2)="CA"
```

as the condition for the IF( ) function. Note that quotes are required around CA because it must be treated as a letter string. In words, the expression says,

"Take the first two characters from the left end of the text in cell D2 and compare them to the letters "CA"." Placing the expression in an IF( ) function as the condition

IF(LEFT(D2, 2)="CA", TRUE, FALSE)

produces the formatting decision: If the text and the string are equal, then format the cell—because the fuel price estimate is in Canadian dollars; if they are not equal (false), do not format the cell. So, to italicize the entries, the friends select the Fuel Price entries, request *Format > Conditional Formatting...*,

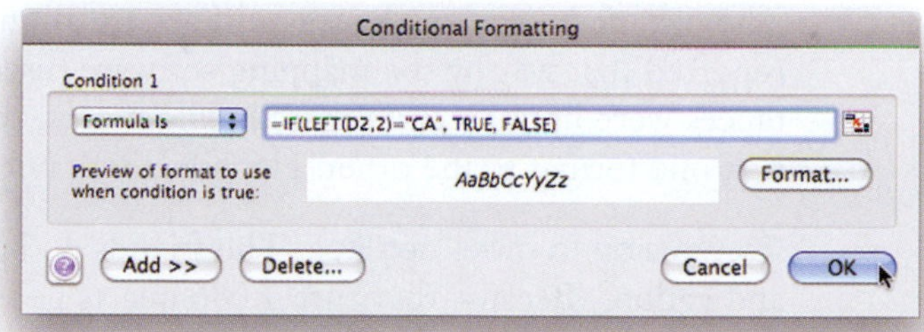

enter the IF( ) function into the formula window, and click **OK**, which yields the result shown in Figure 15.4. Notice that there was no change in formatting of the first two entries of Fuel Price because the first two letters in column D were not "CA" and so their formatting wasn't changed.

Finally, they add a comment to Segment explaining that highlighting means the estimated driving time is above average, and a comment to Fuel Price explaining that italic means the price is given in Canadian dollars for a liter of petrol.

15.2 Relaxing Vacation. Give the entry for the top row of the Conditional Formatting window that will format the Segment text for the day with the shortest traveling distance. Which column does this conditional formatting rule apply to?

Conditional Formulas

In the same way that the friends used an IF( ) function to change the formatting in response to certain conditions, they can make the entire computation of a cell contingent on the outcome of a condition using **conditional formulas**. This is essential for Pat and Alex, because they are using fuel measured in gallons and liters, and money measured in U.S. dollars and Canadian dollars. Figuring how much a tank of fuel costs requires precision. In this section we explain how spreadsheets can compute conditional factors and show how to use this capability to figure out the cost of each segment of the trip. The new column will be called Amount Paid. Before considering how to compute it, let's figure out exactly what they need to do.

Figuring the Amount Paid

First, we need to know how far the car typically goes on a unit of fuel, that is, its average mileage. Most drivers have some idea what their mileage is, and Alex's old Subaru averages 22 miles per gallon (mpg) of gas. So, they figure the cost of the fuel as

*cost = price * distance/mpg*

and add a comment to the Amount Paid column stating that the assumed mpg is 22.

The distances listed in the spreadsheet are all in miles because they were reported that way by the mapping software (used from the U.S.). If some distances were in miles and others in kilometers, the friends would have to convert one format to the other. Happily, that's not necessary.

Conversion to miles per liter. The friends do have to convert between liters and gallons. Because there are 1.056 quarts per liter, and four quarts in a gallon, they know they can go only 1/4 as far on a quart of fuel as on a gallon of fuel, meaning the Subaru's 22 mpg is really 22/4 = 5.5 mpq (miles per quart). But a liter is a little bit more than a quart, so a liter of fuel should carry them a little bit farther, by that amount. That is, 5.5 mpq is really 5.5*1.056 miles per liter (mpl), which is 5.8 mpl.

We can check this: If we buy 4 liters, we can go 23.2 miles based on the 5.8 mpl. How much more is that than if we bought 4 quarts? Four quarts gets us 22 miles, so it's 23.3/22, or a factor of 1.056 more, when we account for round-off errors. So, we know the mpl. If this sort of thinking gives you "brain-fry," simply look up the conversion on the Web (mpl = mpg/3.788).

Applying two cases, conditionally. So, for cases where the two travelers know the price in gallons, they multiply it times distance/mpg; when they know the price in liters, they multiply it times distance/mpl. Obviously, this is a job for the IF( ) function. Like the previous conditional formatting example, the friends will test on the first two letters of the Fuel Price Report field. If the data is from the U.S., they use the first computation, otherwise they use the second. The appropriate equation is

```
=IF(LEFT(D2,2)="US", E2*C2/22, E2*C2/5.8)
```

Notice that unlike before, this formula compares to "US". The result is an estimate of the total of the amounts paid for the fuel purchased for each segment, assuming the price of fuel is the average price of the location listed and the vehicle's mileage is 22 mpg. These assumptions are recorded in a comment. The entry is U.S. dollars in the U.S. and Canadian dollars in Canada, so the friends format Amount Paid with italics, as before. These results are shown in Figure 15.5.

Trip to the Arctic Circle
by Pat and Alex; competed 23. June.2009

Segment	Miles	Fuel Price Report	Fuel Price	Amount Paid
Chicago to Carrington ND	778	US Chicago	$3.59	$126.96
Carrington to Battleford SK	620	US Moorehead MN	$2.96	$83.42
Battleford to Fort St. John BC	648	CA Moose Jaw SK	*$1.09*	*$121.78*
Fort St. John to Watson Lake YK	555	CA Medicine Hat AB	*$1.01*	*$96.65*
Watson Lake to Dawson YK	601	CA Mi 54 AK Hiway BC	*$1.21*	*$125.38*
Dawson to Dawson via AC	484	CA Mi 54 AK Hiway BC	*$1.21*	*$100.97*

Figure 15.5 Arctic Circle spreadsheet with Amount Paid column added. Notice that Time Estimate has been hidden, and that a comment noting the assumption of 22 mpg has been added to Amount Paid heading.

Cost in One Currency

We give one more illustration of conditional formulas. For the friends to know the total cost estimate for their trip, it is essential to know the expenditures in one currency. Being Americans, they choose U.S. dollars. Therefore, they add a column, Cost. It will contain a copy of the Amount Paid cell when that's reported in U.S. dollars, and it will contain the U.S. dollar equivalent when the Amount Paid is reported in Canadian dollars. The computation uses the same ideas described earlier and will again use the IF( ) function.

Checking on the Web, Pat finds the exchange rate for Canadian currency to U.S.; it states that a Canadian dollar is worth $0.948 in U.S. dollars. Therefore, for each spreadsheet price given in Canadian dollars, they simply multiply the price times $0.948 to get the price in U.S. dollars.

Developing the IF( ) function needed for the Cost column (column G), they test column D as usual to determine if the price is in U.S. or Canadian dollars. The test for G2 is LEFT(D2,2)="CA". If it is Canadian, then they want F2*0.948, and if it is not, then they simply want F2, because it is already in U.S. dollars. The whole expression,

```
=IF(LEFT(D2,2)="CA", F2*0.948, F2)
```

results in an amount expressed in U.S. dollars. They fill the computation down the column and inspect to see that italicized amounts become slightly smaller in the Cost column.

Finally, the friends enter the data for the return trip by the same route—not their first choice, but maybe the quickest and cheapest way home. After doing so, they add a SUM( ) function to compute the total cost of the trip. The result is shown in Figure 15.6.

The friends are surprised that it's so expensive—and they have only accounted for the fuel cost. They still need to eat, they need to sleep somewhere besides the Subaru, and they need to buy treats and souvenirs. They need a couple of friends to help share the costs!

Trip to the Arctic Circle
by Pat and Alex; competed 23. June.2009

Segment	Miles	Fuel Price Report	Fuel Price	Amount Paid	Cost
Chicago to Carrington ND	778	US Chicago	$3.59	$126.96	$126.96
Carrington to Battleford SK	620	US Moorehead MN	$2.96	$83.42	$83.42
Battleford to Fort St. John BC	648	CA Moose Jaw SK	*$1.09*	*$121.78*	$115.45
Fort St. John to Watson Lake YK	555	CA Medicine Hat AB	*$1.01*	*$96.65*	$91.62
Watson Lake to Dawson YK	601	CA Mi 54 AK Hiway BC	*$1.21*	*$125.38*	$118.86
Dawson to Dawson via AC	484	CA Mi 54 AK Hiway BC	*$1.21*	*$100.97*	$95.72
Dawson to Watson Lake YK	601	CA Mi 54 AK Hiway BC	*$1.21*	*$125.38*	$118.86
Watson Lake to Fort St. John BC	555	CA Medicine Hat AB	*$1.01*	*$96.65*	$91.62
Fort St. John to Battleford SK	648	CA Moose Jaw SK	*$1.09*	*$121.78*	$115.45
Battleford to Carrington ND	620	US Moorehead MN	$2.96	$83.42	$83.42
Carrington to Chicago IL	778	US Chicago	$3.59	$126.96	$126.96
				Total:	$1,168.33

Figure 15.6 Arctic Circle spreadsheet completed to the point of producing an estimate for fuel costs.

15.3 Gas Tax. Suppose a gas tax has been levied in Minnesota, that is, the places whose right-most letters are "MN." Define a formula for a **Fuel Surcharge** column in which 10 percent is added to any fuel quotations from Minnesota, and all other quotations remain unchanged.

Naming: Symbolic Reference

In their development of conditional formatting and conditional formulas, the friends have referred, as usual, to B2, D2, E2, and so on. But this could lead to problems later on. Suppose they insert a column in the spreadsheet. Will the references adjust? Certainly, the earlier *comment* referring to column D will not adjust, thwarting their effort to make the spreadsheet clear. Additionally, they have embedded several assumptions—gas mileage, currency exchange rate—into the formulas. These quantities can change: Exchange rates change by the minute, and they might find another car with better gas mileage to drive. The spreadsheet has become too dependent on the specific positions and data used at the moment. If the goal is to use the spreadsheet repeatedly, they must be more insulated from such changes.

Defining Names

A helpful design methodology is to give names to the components of our spreadsheets. Computer scientists say it is better to refer to cells *symbolically*—that is, by name—than to refer to them *literally*—that is, by their explicit column/row position reference. A *name* is a word or phrase assigned to a cell or range of cells. Once the name has been assigned, it can be used wherever cell references would normally be used, such as formulas. Using names reduces the chance of messing up range specifications, and minimizes the likelihood errors will creep in when columns and rows are added later.

We illustrate this idea by revising the friends' spreadsheet to use names. After choosing *Insert > Name > Define …* , we are presented with the Define Name window, shown in Figure 15.7(a). The range is automatically filled in for us based on our selection prior to choosing the command. Enter a name—it generally cannot contain spaces—and the software assigns that range of cells that name. But this action has only *defined* a name; it is so far unused. Now, choosing *Insert > Name > Apply …* allows us to use the name, as shown in Figure 15.7(b). Clicking **OK** tells the software to look through the formulas, and wherever it finds a reference for the cells bound to a selected name—that is, in the range C2:C12 in this example—the symbolic name replaces the literal position in the formula.

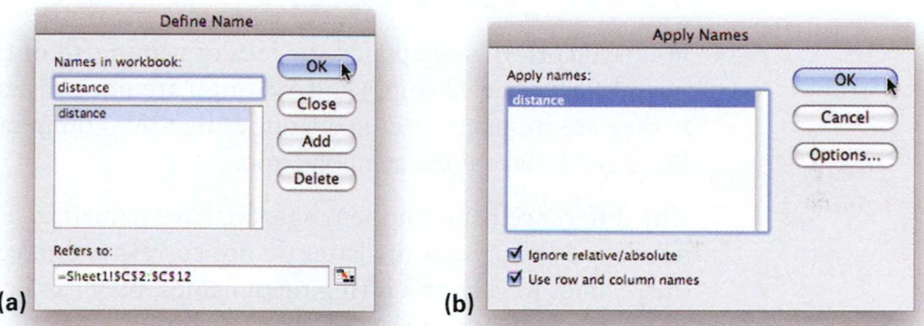

Figure 15.7 Name windows: (a) the *Define Name* window and (b) the *Apply Names* window.

Notice that we have chosen to name the column headed Miles with the range name of distance, because that is a somewhat better description. The point is that names are separate from the labels that we assign, though often we use the same word.

Applying Names

After clicking **OK** in the Apply Names dialog, the name distance is applied to the spreadsheet formulas. We can look at cells, for example F2, in which we have used the distance value, C2. We see the entry

```
=IF(LEFT(D2,2)="US", E2*distance/22,E2*distance/5.8)
```

in the formula bar, indicating that the name has been applied to this formula. In addition to being safer, it is easier to read and understand the formula when symbolic names are used.

To see how we could apply this idea to other parts of the spreadsheet, let's define some more symbolic names. We choose

```
priceSrc    D2:D12
fuelPrice   E2:E12
amtPaid     F2:F12
cost        G2:G12
```

Then we apply the names to the formulas. When the process is complete, the formula in F2 has the form

```
=IF(LEFT(priceSrc,2)="US", fuelPrice*distance/22,fuelPrice*distance/5.8)
```

which is much easier to understand.

Using symbolic names is an excellent idea, and we could adopt a design rule that says to always use symbolic names, but we do not have to. It is already implied by the rule Explain Everything. When users select cell F2, for example, they should see in the formula bar a formula that makes sense. Symbolic names are easier for people to understand (and the computer doesn't care).

Make Assumptions Explicit

We haven't *completely* applied the idea of naming all of the quantities in the spreadsheet. The 22 (mpg) and 5.8 (mpl) are not constants of the universe like π; they are instance-specific quantities that our computation depends upon. We should make them symbolic, too.

The difference between the ranges we have named so far and these parameters to the formulas is the latter do not correspond to cells. But, by assigning their values to cells and giving them names, they can be used to explore travel alternatives, as you will see in the next section.

Alex and Pat have established an area below the Segments entries where they listed their assumptions. They identified the three parameters used so far: mileage in gallons, mileage in liters, and exchange rate. An additional assumption, the number of travelers, doesn't show up in any formula, but they are pretty sure that the number of travelers will change, so they decided to add a cell for that number, too. Their assumptions area has the form

Assumptions:	
Miles per gallon:	22
Miles per liter:	5.81
US-Canadian Exchange Rate:	0.948
Travelers	2

The friends assign names to the values to make it easier to replace in the formulas. The names are mpg, mpl, xchRate, and buddies. The mpl value is computed using the formula

```
=mpg/3.788
```

implying that it is not independent of mpg.

Finally, the constants used in the Amount Paid formula must be changed manually. We cannot use the *Insert > Name > Apply…* command, because the reference in the formula is to 22, not to a cell containing 22. So, we manually replace 22 by mpg in the formula bar, and fill the new formula into the other cells of the column. Of course, mpl and xchRate must also be changed manually as well. The modifications are visible in F2, which completes the naming.

```
=IF(LEFT(priceSrc,2)="US", fuelPrice*distance/mpg,fuelPrice*distance/mpl)
```

Once we name the bottom line fuelCost, we have revised the spreadsheet to name the relevant cells and ranges, an improvement that has taken a few minutes. Had the names been introduced as the entries were being developed, which is the way they should be used, the cost of using them would have been unnoticed.

"What If" Analysis

Pat and Alex are a little surprised that driving to the Arctic Circle and back is going to cost them roughly $1,200 for gas alone. They will need to find some friends to travel with them to help defray the cost, but before doing that they need a better idea of what the whole trip will cost them, and whether there are ways to control costs. Because spreadsheets recalculate everything whenever a number is changed, they are ideal for speculating on the consequences of change. Make a change, and notice what happens to the "bottom line."

Direct Experimentation

With their present spreadsheet, Alex and Pat can do some of this speculative analysis directly. It involves changing cells, looking to see what happens, and then undoing the change. It's cumbersome, but it's quick.

For example, they wonder if

- The Subaru could be tuned up to get 25 mpg, how would that affect fuel costs?
- With more people and therefore more weight in the vehicle, maybe 22 mpg is too high. What is the effect of 20 mpg?
- A friend with a 30 mpg vehicle offered to drive, how would that change fuel costs?

By changing mpg, the friends discover that these assumptions change fuel costs to be $1,028, $1,284 and $856, respectively. Obviously, the cost of the trip is very sensitive to the efficiency of the vehicle. Using the same technique, they also discover that the trip is not very sensitive to the currency exchange rate, at least not within the range in which it is likely to fluctuate. So, waiting for the U.S. dollar to strengthen against the Canadian dollar won't help much.

The problem with experimenting directly with the spreadsheet is that it risks making permanent changes to the data and formulas that have been so carefully entered. Fortunately, there is a better way to experiment with a spreadsheet.

Scenarios

The speculative or **what if analysis** that the friends just performed is nicely supported in spreadsheet software by a tool called Scenarios. A **scenario** is a named alternative to a spreadsheet based on different inputs. A scenario is an aid to understanding changes in plans, like changes in gas mileage. Let's see how the friends can use a scenario.

Tune-up scenario. Selecting the mpg cell, because we are exploring alternatives to the current mileage of 22, we navigate *Tools > Scenarios...* and arrive at the Scenario Manager window, as shown in Figure 15.8(a). This window is the principal interface to the Scenario facility: It is the place to define new scenarios, edit them, and request summaries. Initially, there are no scenarios defined, of course, so we click on **Add...**.

The Add Scenario window (Figure 15.8(b)) is the place to name a scenario. In addition, the software fills in the cell(s) that will change, and a comment as to who created it and when the scenario was defined. Clicking **OK** takes us to the Scenario Values window (Figure 15.8(c)), where we enter the alternative value for mpg. Notice that the symbolic name is used for the field, now that we have named the cells. Clicking **OK** takes us back to the Scenario Manager window (Figure 15.8(d)), where the newly added scenario can be seen in the list. We have created a scenario and archived it.

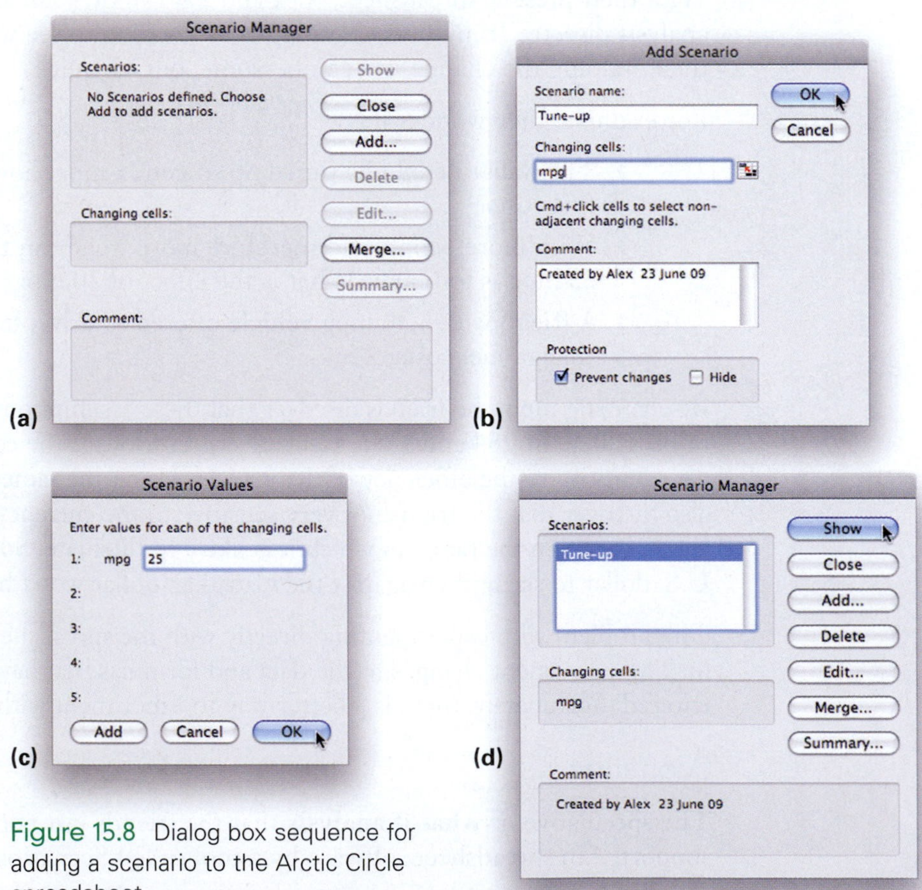

Figure 15.8 Dialog box sequence for adding a scenario to the Arctic Circle spreadsheet.

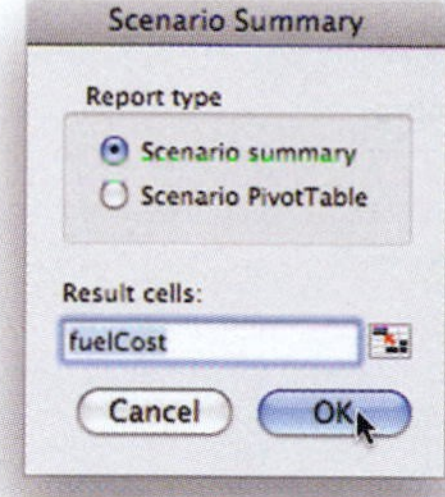

Having taken some effort to define the scenario, we can run it. Notice at the bottom of the Scenario Manager window (Figure 15.8(d)), there is a **Summary...** button. When we click it, a dialog box appears asking what cell we consider the "bottom line" of the computation. That is, supposing the scenario came to pass, what value are we most interested in? The software predicted that G14, which is our fuelCost, is the summary information we want to know about. We click **OK**, and are presented with the Scenario Summary sheet shown in Figure 15.9. The sheet nicely summarizes the base case (Current Values column) and the "bottom line" of our Tune-up scenario. (The analysis implies that a tune-up is beneficial if it costs less than $140, though it's probably a good idea to tune up a car before any long trip!)

Scenario Summary		
	Current Values:	*Tune-up*
Changing Cells:		
mpg	22	25
Result Cells:		
fuelCost	$1,167.32	$1,027.24

Notes: Current Values column represents values of changing cells at time Scenario Summary Report was created. Changing cells for each scenario are highlighted in gray.

Figure 15.9 The Scenario Summary sheet showing the result of the Tune-up scenario.

The time required for the Tune-up scenario setup may not seem like it is worthwhile, compared to simply changing the mpg cell and looking to see what happens. But, the benefits are coming.

Traveling companions scenario. Because Pat and Alex want to consider the advantages of taking along one or more friends, they add, below their FuelCost cell, another cell with the cost per person, as in

Total:	$1,167.32
Cost Each:	$583.66

which is implemented by the formula =FuelCost/buddies. They name the per person fuel cost cell ppFuel. Then, they construct another pair of scenarios.

The extra passenger scenario follows the same protocol used for the Tune-up scenario. Figure 15.10 shows the key steps. Notice first that in the Edit Scenario window, Figure 15.10(a), two fields are specified by name as varying, mpg and buddies. Having two fields changing means that in the Scenario Values window, Figure 15.10(b), both values are listed with value fields. They set buddies to 3 and drop mpg to 21 because of the extra weight. Then, in the Scenario Summary window, Figure 15.10(c), they specify G16, the ppFuel cell, as the one they are most interested in. Finally, in the Scenario Summary sheet, Figure 15.10(d), the new scenario is presented with the earlier scenario and the base case. As expected, having another person along helps with costs, even if it harms mileage a bit.

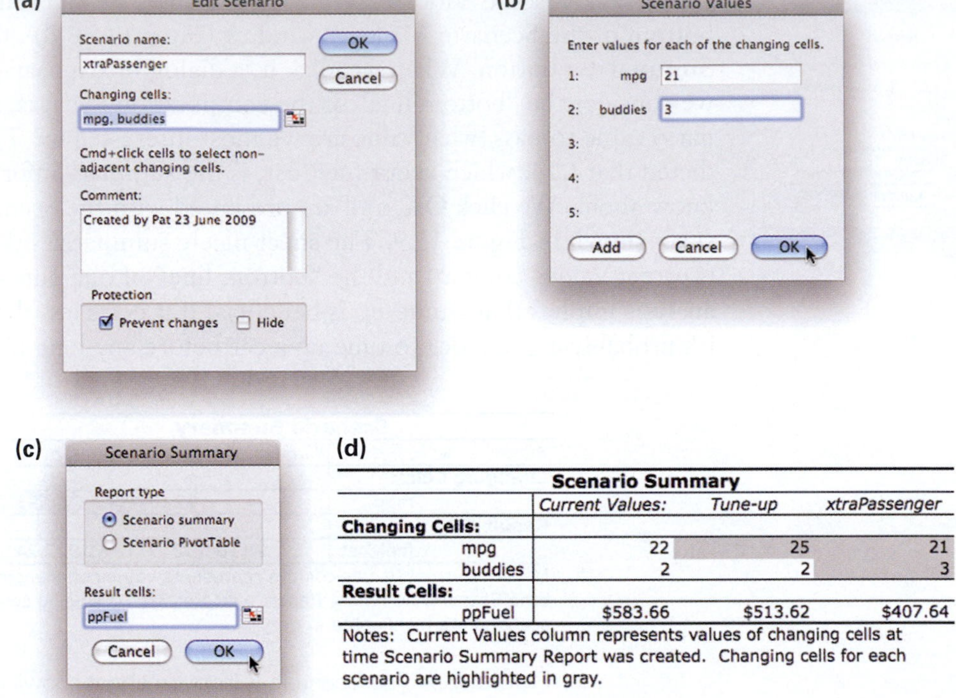

Scenario Summary	Current Values:	Tune-up	xtraPassenger
Changing Cells:			
mpg	22	25	21
buddies	2	2	3
Result Cells:			
ppFuel	$583.66	$513.62	$407.64

Notes: Current Values column represents values of changing cells at time Scenario Summary Report was created. Changing cells for each scenario are highlighted in gray.

Figure 15.10 The Extra Passenger scenarios and their effect on ppFuel.

Obviously, the "high mileage" scenario develops in the same way.

Analyzing a Model

The travelers have a good estimate of the fuel costs for their trip and the cost benefits of taking others along. But how much will the trip actually cost them? To answer the question, they build a model that accounts for all of the foreseeable costs of the trip, and how these combine with fuel costs to produce the bottom line expense for going to the Arctic Circle. Here's what they do.

Formulating a model. To start, they think a little harder about the costs. To save lodging expenses, they decide to camp, which is sensible because they are headed into the wilderness and they own camping equipment. A few moments on the Web reveals that they can camp at public campgrounds, provincial parks, and, once they are in the wilderness, the wilderness itself. On the next page of their spreadsheet, they click together another table, shown in Figure 15.11.

In the Lodging table, there is an entry for each night the travelers spend on the road, saying where they are staying and how many people are covered by the Price. They will stay in a hostel in Dawson on the night they arrive and the next night, and because the price is given "per bed," the occupancy is listed as 1. In the other cases, it is listed as buddies. The lodging expense entries are computed as

```
=price*buddies/occupancy
```

Trip to the Arctic Circle
by Pat and Alex; competed 23. June.2009

Lodging	Occupancy	Price	Lodging Expense	Contin-gencies	Just In Case
Campground	2	25	25	Base Cost	$100
Provincial Park	2	20	20	Tires	$160
Provincial Park	2	20	20		
Wilderness	2	0	0		
Hostel@$20	1	20	40		
Hostel@$20	1	20	40		
Wilderness	2	0	0		
Provincial Park	2	20	20		
Provincial Park	2	20	20		
Campground	2	25	25		
Total:			210		260
Total Per Person			105		130

Figure 15.11 The lodging and contingency data for the Arctic Circle road trip.

which yields the total lodging expense, ppLodging, when summed at the end of the column. Each person's share is found by dividing by buddies.

Regarding contingencies, ppContin, there are tolls and probably an oil change at some point, but they decide that although "stuff happens," it will only total about $100. There is concern about the tread on the rear tires of the Subaru, and they decide to budget some new tires if needed. They compute the total of the entries and divide by buddies.

The model. Finally, with more complete data available, the friends make one more table.

Trip to the Arctic Circle
by Pat and Alex; competed 23. June.2009

Costs	Amount Per Person
Fuel	$583.66
Lodging	$105.00
Contingency	$130.00
Total	$818.66

This table summarizes the per person expenses of the spreadsheet. This is their model: It shows ppFuel, ppLodging, and ppContin subcomputations, and computes the grand total, called estTotal. It doesn't contain a food charge, because the friends decide that they would eat even if they stayed at home, so food isn't a direct cost of the trip.

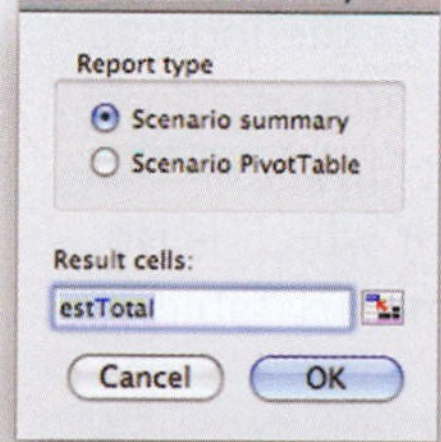

Reusing scenarios. Having set up the scenarios earlier, it is possible to rerun them again to see how the total cost changes as the number of travelers increases. They navigate to the Scenario Manager and click on **Summary...** again. When the Scenario Summary window appears, they change the "bottom line" to the estTotal cell, which is the one that matters now.

After clicking **OK**, they get the following report summarizing the model.

Scenario Summary			
	Current Values:	*1 Extra*	*2 Extra*
Changing Cells:			
mpg	22	21	20
buddies	2	3	4
Result Cells:			
estTotal	$818.66	$577.64	$458.51

Notes: Current Values column represents values of changing cells at time Scenario Summary Report was created. Changing cells for each scenario are highlighted in gray.

The model predicts the expenses to the extent that the estimates are correct. It is very convenient.

A change in plans. Pat and Alex quickly find the first friend interested in the Arctic Circle trip, provided they get the tires before they go. The next person they speak to is concerned about camping in country famous for bears, and prefers instead to stay at hostels. It seemed silly to stop at a hostel each night, drop off the friend, and the other three continue on to the campground. So they decide to run another scenario to see how staying in hostels would change the cost of the trip.

The Hostel Upgrade scenario requires a new field, camping.

Total:			210
Total Per Person			105
Camping	Yes		

This Yes/No field controls the occupancy of the lodging table. That is, the occupancy data, which was previously defined to be the number of people who would stay in the campsite (buddies), becomes

```
=IF(camping="Yes", buddies, 1)
```

This formula specifies that everyone either stays in the campsite (Yes) or has a bed at the hostel (No). They add a comment describing the field's meaning.

Alex and Pat click to the Scenario Manager and request **Add...** to define a new scenario. This time the scenario must consider the effect of changing a whole range of values, the Price values; when the travelers are camping (Yes), the original data is correct, but when they are not camping (No), the entries must show what a bed at the hostel costs.

When the Add Scenario window appears, they enter a name, Hostel Upgrade, and specify the changing cells' names.

The cells include the mpg and buddies as usual, the Price field of the lodging table (J2:J11), and camping. Next, the Scenario Values window appears, and they enter their estimate of $18 per night for the hostels—they didn't take the time to find out the exact cost—and the other values, the last of which is No to camping. Clicking on **Summary** results in the Scenario Summary table shown in Figure 15.12.

Scenario Summary				
	Current Values:	*1 Extra*	*2 Extra*	*Hostel Upgrade*
Changing Cells:				
mpg	22	21	20	20
buddies	2	3	4	4
$J$2	25	25	25	18
$J$3	20	20	20	18
$J$4	20	20	20	18
$J$5	0	0	0	18
$J$6	20	20	20	18
$J$7	20	20	20	18
$J$8	0	0	0	18
$J$9	20	20	20	18
$J$10	20	20	20	18
$J$11	25	25	25	18
camping	Yes	Yes	Yes	No
Result Cells:				
estTotal	$818.66	$577.64	$458.51	$566.01

Notes: Current Values column represents values of changing cells at time Scenario Summary Report was created. Changing cells for each scenario are highlighted in gray.

Figure 15.12 Hostel Upgrade Scenario Summary table for the Arctic Circle road trip.

Notice the form of Figure 15.12. The changing values are shown with gray fill, and are presented for each of the scenarios without regard to whether they are part of the scenario. That is, even though the lodging prices didn't change in the extra travelers scenarios, they are displayed, because they changed in some scenario (Hostel Upgrade).

This model could be used to explore other alternative scenarios.

Analyzing Data Using Filtering

Alex and Pat, joined by friends Ali and Chi, left on their epic road trip to the Arctic Circle. With long hours to pass while driving across the Great Plains of central North America, Pat extends the spreadsheet to a second sheet to record entries for their travels; see Figure 15.13. They called the page the Travel Log.

The Travel Log is an example of a long list of entries that are interesting as a group—that's why they are in the list—and also as subgroups. Filtering is the tool that gives access to subsets of this information. For example, from time to time the friends are interested in seeing only certain entries of their Travel Log record, such as when have they purchased gas.

Auto Filtering Technique

Filtering, as its name implies, selects only certain rows from a list. It applies only to spreadsheet tables that have column headings, as the Travel Log does. Filtering lets users create a customized version of a spreadsheet list that is

Road To Arctic Circle and Back: Stops
Pat, Alex, Chi, Ali

When	Seg. No	Where	Reason	Buy	$	Amt	Mi	Remark
8/4/07 5:45	1	Ali's house IL	Last pick-up			0.00		We're Off!
8/4/07 6:40	1	Toll Booth IL	Alex Fumbles	All tolls	X	2.85		
8/4/07 8:05	1	DriveThru Joe IL	Espresso					Only driver
8/4/07 9:00	1	Beloit WI	Gas & Go	Gas	A	34.50	241	
8/4/07 9:55	1	Madison WI	Snacks					
8/4/07 12:05	1	St. Paul MN	Gas & Go, Eat	Gas	P	28.95	191	Subway
8/4/07 14:45	1	St. Cloud MN	Stretch/Photo					Pretty Here
8/4/07 15:30	1	Sauk Center MN	Snacks					
8/4/07 16:55	1	Fergus Falls MN	Gas & Go	Gas	P	29.22	205	
8/4/07 19:45	1	Fargo ND	Photo in ND					Pat's First
8/4/07 20:25	1	Valley City ND	Supper					Junk Food
8/4/07 22:00	1	Carrington ND	Stay Night	Camp	C	21.45		Great Start
8/5/07 7:25	2	Carrington ND	Gas	Gas	A	37.42	252	
8/5/07 7:55	2	Sykeston ND	Photo					Its flat
8/5/07 10:05	2	Minot ND	Gas & Go,Snx	Gas	X	19.64	135	Ice Cream
8/5/07 11:50	2	Portal ND	Photo in CA					Ali, Pat, 1st
8/5/07 12:25	2	Estevan SK	Lunch					
8/5/07 13:55	2	Weyburn SK	Gas & Go, Eat	Gas	A	*33.82*	151	
8/5/07 15:45	2	Moose Jaw SK	Snacks					I Scream!

Figure 15.13 Start of the Travel Log of the Arctic Circle road trip. Seg. No corresponds to a segment of the original plan (Sheet 1), $ refers to who paid a shared expense, Mi is distance traveled since last fuel.

limited to the rows meeting some criterion. For example, to find out how many times they've stopped for gas so far, the travelers could look through the record in Figure 15.13 to find all those times and places where they filled up. Or they could filter the list, which is much easier.

The easiest form of filtering, called *AutoFilter*, is trivial to apply. Select any cell in the list, then choose *Data* > *Filter* > *AutoFilter*. The result will be a redrawn spreadsheet list with triangle menu buttons by each column heading.

When ⬍	Seg. No ⬍	Where ⬍	Reason ⬍	Buy ⬍	$ ⬍	Amt ⬍	Mi ⬍	Remark ⬍
8/4/07 5:45	1	Ali's house IL	Last pick-up			0.00		We're Off!
8/4/07 6:40	1	Toll Booth IL	Alex Fumbles	All tolls	X	2.85		

The menu buttons give you options for filtering the list based on data in that column. Clicking on a button opens the menu and presents the options, which include sorting rows, displaying rows containing a limited number of values, or displaying only those rows matching a specific value in the column. For example, clicking on the Buy menu button presents the travelers with these options:

Reason ⬍	Buy ⬍	$ ⬍	Amt ⬍
Last pick-up			).00
Alex Fumbles			2.85
Espresso			
Gas & Go			4.50
Snacks			
Gas & Go, Eat			3.95
Stretch/Photo			
Snacks			
Gas & Go			9.22
Photo in ND			

Sort Ascending
Sort Descending
✓ (Show All)
(Show Top 10...)
(Custom Filter...)
All tolls
Camp
Gas
(Show Blanks)
(Show NonBlanks)

Notice that the three values occurring in the column are listed near the bottom. Choosing one of them, such as Gas, causes the list to be filtered, leaving only those rows that match the selected item.

Road To Arctic Circle and Back: Stops
Pat, Alex, Chi, Ali

When	Seg. No	Where	Reason	Buy	$	Amt	Mi	Remark
8/4/07 9:00	1	Beloit WI	Gas & Go	Gas	A	34.50	241	
8/4/07 12:05	1	St. Paul MN	Gas & Go, Eat	Gas	P	28.95	191	Subway
8/4/07 16:55	1	Fergus Falls MN	Gas & Go	Gas	P	29.22	205	
8/5/07 7:25	2	Carrington ND	Gas	Gas	A	37.42	252	
8/5/07 10:05	2	Minot ND	Gas & Go,Snx	Gas	X	19.64	135	Ice Cream
8/5/07 13:55	2	Weyburn SK	Gas & Go, Eat	Gas	A	*33.82*	151	

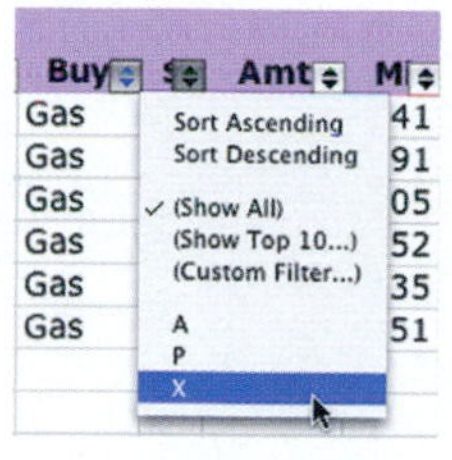

So, at this point in the trip, the friends have purchased fuel six times. These rows can be further filtered. For example, by clicking on the $ menu selector and selecting X, a personalized version of the Travel Log Gas purchases is shown for Alex.

When	Seg. No	Where	Reason	Buy	$	Amt	Mi	Remark
8/5/07 10:05	2	Minot ND	Gas & Go,Snx	Gas	X	19.64	135	Ice Cream

Notice that in Figure 15.13 Alex also paid tolls, but that is not reflected in this version of the table, because the first filter was Buy column matches Gas, and the second was $ column matches X. Of course, the same result would have been found by executing the two filters in the opposite order.

These changes to the list are only logical, that is, the actual list has not been modified. We turn off the AutoFilter simply by selecting it again, that is, it is a toggle, and the original list will be redrawn.

Advanced Filtering Technique

AutoFiltering is easy because the software gives us access to a variety of standard filtering criteria. But most lists contain data that requires more refined analysis. Advanced Filtering is the tool to use to develop precise filtering criteria.

Advanced filtering setup. To apply advanced filtering, we give a column name and a filtering criterion. These are presented to the spreadsheet software in a curious way: by adding a new column. The new column will have the *same heading* as the column containing the data to be filtered. Then, in the cell below the heading, users enter a criterion like >175 to indicate that values in the other column by the same name should be filtered to be greater than 175. Once the setup is complete, we can run the filtering operation.

For example, the travelers decide to analyze their gas purchases. So, they add a new column, which must be labeled exactly like the column to be filtered, that is, Mi. To filter out the smaller gas purchases, they set the criterion to be >175. The result is

When	Seg. No	Where	Reason	Buy	$	Amt	Mi	Mi
8/4/07 5:45	1	Ali's house IL	Last pick-up			0.00		>175
8/4/07 6:40	1	Toll Booth IL	Alex Fumbles	All tolls	X	2.85		

This two-step process completes the setup for the Advanced Search facility.

Executing an advanced filter. To run the actual filtering operation, select a cell in the column to be filtered—not the setup column. This tells the Advanced Filter software which list is to be filtered and which column is considered the source of the filter. Forgetting to select a cell in the filtered column is a common mistake. Next, choose *Data > Filter > Advanced Filter...*, which displays the Advanced Filter window.

The *List range* specification simply gives the dimensions of the list that is going to be filtered; the software generally figures it out on its own and preloads it. The *Criteria range* is where users specify the setup column. Enter the range covering the heading and the criterion. (The *Copy to* option is explained momentarily.) Clicking **OK** produces a filtered table.

When	Seg. No	Where	Reason	Buy	$	Amt	Mi	Mi
8/4/07 9:00	1	Beloit WI	Gas & Go	Gas	A	34.50	241	
8/4/07 12:05	1	St. Paul MN	Gas & Go, Eat	Gas	P	28.95	191	
8/4/07 16:55	1	Fergus Falls MN	Gas & Go	Gas	P	29.22	205	
8/5/07 7:25	2	Carrington ND	Gas	Gas	A	37.42	252	

The table appears on the spreadsheet in the position of the original table. To restore the original table, choose *Data > Filter > Show All*. (Notice that the criterion (>175) is not visible because the first row of the original table isn't in the filtered result.)

The *Copy to* option in the *Advanced Filter* window specifies a new place on the spreadsheet to place the filtered result. It is often handy to have both the original and filtered result to compare. Also, once created, the copy can be treated like any other list and analyzed separately. In the *Advanced Filter* window, specify the range in which to place the filtered result. The specification should be as wide as the original list including the setup, but it can be only one row high, because the size of the result is unknown prior to filtering.

Filtering on Multiple Criteria

The Advanced Filtering facility allows multiple criteria. They are specified during setup by defining multiple columns; then, during execution, the *Criteria range* is enlarged to cover all criteria.

For example, having filtered out the smaller gas purchases, the travelers decide to filter out the large purchases. They define another `Mi` column and enter the criterion `<225`. The result

When	Seg. No	Where	Reason	Buy	$	Amt	Mi	Mi	Mi
8/4/07 5:45	1	Ali's house IL	Last pick-up			0.00		>175	<225

is ready to execute. They select a cell in the original `Mi` column, navigate to the *Advanced Filter* command, enter the *Criteria range* as `$J$1:$K$2` (that is, a 2 × 2 range), and click **OK**. The result is

When	Seg. No	Where	Reason	Buy	$	Amt	Mi	Mi	Mi
8/4/07 12:05	1	St. Paul MN	Gas & Go, Eat	Gas	P	28.95	191		
8/4/07 16:55	1	Fergus Falls MN	Gas & Go	Gas	P	29.22	205		

which has eliminated the larger and smaller gas purchases, revealing the curious fact that Pat pays for the fuel when the purchase is in the midrange.

Filtering is extremely useful. For example, when the trip is over and the friends are settling up their accounts, a list of each traveler's payments can be created, processed, and analyzed. In fact, when the trip is over, Pat and Alex can determine how accurate their original predictions about the trip's cost were.

Summary

This chapter has taught several advanced spreadsheet techniques. You learned that:

- Two basic principles underline the design of effective spreadsheets: (1) focus on form and (2) explain everything.
- Conditional formatting can apply an interpretation to the data in a spreadsheet in a manner that is easy to perceive.
- Conditional formulas using the `IF( )` function allow complex, case-specific data definition and analysis.
- Naming the cells and regions of a spreadsheet allows the parts of a spreadsheet to be referenced in a convenient and less error-prone way.
- "What if" analysis is a particularly powerful application of spreadsheets in which the consequences of alternative information can be assessed.
- Filtering effectively customizes spreadsheet data to particular cases.

There are other handy spreadsheet operations that have not been covered, and for each of the techniques we *have* discussed, there are other applications. When you start using spreadsheets as a daily computing tool, you will undoubtedly migrate toward these more powerful facilities.

Try It Solutions

15.1 The entries are "Cell Value Is", "equal to", and "=min($c2:$c12)".

15.2 The entry is "Formula Is". The conditional formatting rule applies to "=if(c2=min(c2:c7)), TRUE, FALSE)". It applies to Column A.

15.3 The formula is =IF(RIGHT(D2,2)="MN",E2 + 0.1*E2,E2).

Review Questions

Multiple Choice

1. The most useful general-purpose computer application is
   a. email
   b. Windows
   c. a spreadsheet
   d. a browser
2. All of the following are basic spreadsheet principles except
   a. logical form
   b. clean layout
   c. no text
   d. clear and understandable entries
3. "Explain everything" in a spreadsheet means:
   a. you should easily be able to tell what every cell means
   b. each cell and cell range should be labeled
   c. each formula should be explained with a label
   d. all of the above
4. Conditional formatting
   a. allows you to display information in more than one way
   b. allows you to write more than one formula for a cell
   c. automatically finds and flags errors in formulas and formatting
   d. all of the above
5. To get the first characters in a cell you should use the
   a. Begin function
   b. Start function
   c. Left function
   d. Get function

6. Conditional formatting can change the
   a. text color
   b. text format
   c. cell color
   d. more than one of the above
7. Defining names for a spreadsheet allows you to refer to cells
   a. by location
   b. symbolically
   c. conditionally
   d. alphabetically
8. If you found `regHours` in a spreadsheet formula you'd know it's a
   a. mistake
   b. named reference
   c. constant
   d. function
9. Spreadsheets recalculate
   a. whenever a number is changed
   b. only when saved
   c. only when opened
   d. once a minute
10. AutoFiltering can only be used on
    a. named ranges
    b. tables that have column headings
    c. cells containing formulas
    d. rows with unique entries
11. AutoFiltering allows
    a. sorting rows
    b. displaying rows with a limited number of values
    c. displaying rows that match specific criteria
    d. all of the above
12. Conditional formatting allows
    a. customized colors for cells in a spreadsheet
    b. cells to be automatically updated from the Internet
    c. for the interpretation of the data in a spreadsheet
    d. none of the above

Short Answer

1. Spreadsheets are great for playing _______, that is, they are useful for putting together various possible scenarios.
2. _______ are a good way to explain a spreadsheet formula.
3. "Post-it-notes" for a spreadsheet are called _______.
4. _______ allows for the application of interpretation to the data in a spreadsheet.

5. Individual pages in a spreadsheet are called _______.
6. When you _______ for a spreadsheet, you create a symbolic reference for a range of cells.
7. A single cell or a related group of cells is called a(n) _______.
8. A(n) _______ is a named alternative to a spreadsheet based on different inputs.
9. The _______ is the interface for managing scenarios.
10. _______ allows the selection of certain spreadsheet rows based on a specified criteria.

Exercises

1. Create a spreadsheet to plan your own trip.
2. Plan a trip using airlines, car rentals, and hotel stays. Don't forget to budget for sightseeing. Play "What If" with various scenarios for your trip.
3. Create a table to calculate free-throw percentages. Use `IF( )` functions to prevent an error when no free throws are shot. Format the results using bold for percentages greater than or equal to 75 percent.
4. Create a spreadsheet for apartment costs based on the number of bedrooms, the number of roommates, and typical living expenses. Plot various scenarios depending on the price, number of roommates, and monthly expenses.
5. Create a spreadsheet to track your monthly expenses. Create categories for the expenses and filter them. Include columns for the day and date and track expenses by the day of the week.
6. Create a spreadsheet to track your computer usage. Create categories as needed and filter activities such as email, browsing, downloading, entertainment, word processing, spreadsheets, etc.
7. Organize your CD or DVD collection. Create categories as needed and filter by genre, year, stars, producers, directors, etc.
8. Create a spreadsheet to track the stats for your favorite basketball team. Create formulas as needed to calculate shooting percentages. Total the columns as needed.
9. Create a spreadsheet of multiple choice questions. Use a column for the question, a column for each possible answer, a column for the correct answer, and a column for the topic. Set up filtering for it based on topic and correct answer.
10. Create a spreadsheet to track your eating habits. Use columns for food types, calories, time of day, and nutritional value. Set up filtering to see how much junk food is eaten and when it's eaten.

11. Set up a spreadsheet to do stock analysis. Track a stock's open, close, high, low, change, and volume. Track it for 30 days and see how many days are up and how many are down. Use conditional formatting with green for up days and red for down days.
12. Create a monthly budget for yourself. Track the actual expenses to see how close you are. Use green for items that are under budget and red for those that are over budget.
13. Create a spreadsheet for your college classes. List each in its own row. Track whether a class is required or an elective. Include the semester it was (will be) taken. Include the prerequisites, delivery method, instructor, and grade. Filter them as needed to analyze your curriculum.
14. Create a spreadsheet to balance your checkbook. Set up a column for the date, check number, payee, amount, and comment. Create a column to track deposits and another to track the balance. Write formulas as needed to keep the running balance. Set up conditional formatting to let you know when the balance falls below a certain level. Filter it as needed to see your spending habits.
15. Do an analysis of various real estate investments. Compare the price, the mortgage amount, interest rate, and term. Create various scenarios to see which investments are best.
16. Do an analysis of various cars purchases. Compare the price, the loan amount, payments, maintenance, insurance, and driving costs. Create various scenarios to see which is the best buy.

16

chapter

Introduction to Database Concepts

A Table with a View

learning objectives

- Use XML to describe the metadata for a table of information, and classify the uses of the tags as identification, affinity, or collection
- Explain the differences between everyday tables and database tables
- Explain how the concepts of entities and attributes are used to design a database table
- Use the six database operations: **Select**, **Project**, **Union**, **Difference**, **Product**, and **Join**
- Describe the differences between physical and logical databases
- Express a query using Query By Example

Computers are useless. They only give answers.

—PABLO PICASSO

Now that we have all this useful information, it would be nice to do something with it. (Actually, it can be emotionally fulfilling just to get the information. This is usually only true, however, if you have the social life of a kumquat.)

—UNIX PROGRAMMER'S MANUAL

WE HAVE seen the benefits of using spreadsheets to organize lists of information. By arranging similar information into columns and using a separate row for each new list item, we can easily sort data, use formulas to summarize and compute values, get help from the computer to set up series, and so forth. Spreadsheets are very powerful, but with databases it's possible to apply even greater degrees of organization and receive even more help from the computer.

The key idea is to supply metadata describing the properties of the collected information. Recall that metadata is simply information describing (the properties of) other information. We have seen the idea of specifying metadata in Chapter 8, when we saw tags—the metadata—describe the content of the *Oxford English Dictionary*, enabling the computer to help us search for words and definitions. Some databases use tags for metadata, others use different kinds of metadata, but the same principles apply: Knowing the structure and properties of the data, the computer can help us retrieve, organize, and manage it.

In this chapter we distinguish between the everyday concept of a table and a relational database table. Next, we explain how to set up the metadata for collections of information to create a database. The principles are straightforward and intuitive. We will make the metadata tangible by using a notation called XML. After introducing basic table concepts, we present the five fundamental operations on tables and the Join operation. The concepts of physical database and logical database are connected by the concept of queries, and we illustrate how to build a user's logical view from physical tables. Finally, the convenience of Query By Example is illustrated using simple examples.

Differences Between Tables and Databases

When we think of databases, we often think of tables of information. For example, your iTunes or similar application records the title, artist, running time, and so on in addition to the actual MP3 data (the music). Your favorite song is a row in that table. Another example is your state's database of automobile registrations recording the owner's name and address, the vehicle identification number (VIN), the license plate number, and such. Your car is a row in the registration database table. And as a last example, the U.S. Central Intelligence Agency (CIA) keeps an interesting database called the World Factbook; see https://www.cia.gov/library/publications/the-world-factbook/index.html. They have a demographic table that records the country name, population, life expectancy, and so on. The U.S. is a row in the demography table.

Comparing Tables

To see the difference between these database tables and other forms of tables, such as spreadsheets and HTML tables, consider the row for Canada in the CIA's demographic database. This row is displayed as

Canada	32805041	1.61	5	80.1

in a table with column headings such as Country, Population, and Birthrate. In the file it is represented as

```
<demogData>
    <country>Canada</country>
    <population>32805041</population>
    <fertility>1.61</fertility>
    <infant>5</infant>
    <lifeExpct>80.1</lifeExpct>
</demogData>
```

where the tags identify the population, fertility or birthrate, infant mortality (per 1,000 live births), and life expectancy. That is, we are shown a row of data as it appears in any other table, but inside the computer it has a tag identifying each of the data fields.

How does this data appear in other table forms? In a spreadsheet, the following is the row for Canada.

36	Cameroon	16988132	4.47	65	50.89	
37	Canada	32805041	1.61	5	80.1	
38	Cape Verde	418224	3.48	48	70.45	

The entries for Canada are the same, but the software knows the values only by position, not by their meaning. So, if a cell is inserted at the beginning, causing all of the data to shift right one position,

36	Cameroon	16988132	4.47	65	50.89	
37		Canada	32805041	1.61	5	80.1
38	Cape Verde	418224	3.48	48	70.45	

the identity of the information is lost. Spreadsheets rely on position to keep the integrity of their data; the information is not known by its <country> tag, but rather as A37.

HTML tables are possibly even worse. The usual Web page presentation of the data for Canada is represented in HTML as

```
<tr>
    <td>Canada</td>
    <td>32805041</td>
    <td>1.61</td>
    <td>5</td>
    <td>80.1</td>
</tr>
```

where we recall that <tr> is a table row tag and <td> is a table data tag. These tags simply identify Canada's data as table entries with no unique identity at all; that is, the same kind of <td> tags surround all of the different forms of data. HTML is concerned only with how to display the data, not with its meaning.

The Database's Advantage

The metadata is the key advantage of databases over other approaches to recording data as tables. Here's why. Suppose we want to know the life expectancy of Canadians. Database software can search for the <country> tag surrounding Canada. When it's found, the <country> tag will be one of several tags surrounded by <demogData> tags. These constitute the entry for Canada in the database. The software can then look for the <lifeExpct> tag among those tags and report the data that they surround as the data for Canada. The computer knew which data to return based on the availability of the metadata.

The tags for the CIA database just discussed fulfill two of the most important roles in defining metadata.

- **Identify the type of data:** Each different type of value is given a unique tag.
- **Define the affinity of the data:** Tags enclose all data that is logically related.

The <country>, <population>, and similar tags have the role of identification because they label the content. The <demogData> tag has the role of implementing affinity because it keeps an entry's data together. There are other properties of data that metadata must record, as you will see throughout this chapter, but these are perhaps the most fundamental.

XML: A Language for Metadata Tags

To emphasize the importance of metadata and to prepare for our own applications of database technology, let's take a moment to discuss the basics of **XML**. XML stands for the **Extensible Markup Language**, and like the Hypertext Markup Language (HTML), it is basically a tagging scheme, making it rather intuitive. The tagging scheme used for the *Oxford English Dictionary* (*OED*) in Chapter 8 was a precursor to XML, and the demographic data of the last section was written in XML.

What makes XML easy and intuitive is that there are no standard tags to learn. *We think up the tags we need!* Computer scientists call this a *self-describing language*, because whatever we create becomes the language (tags) to structure the data. There are a couple of rules—for example, always match tags—but basically anything goes. Perhaps XML is the world's easiest-to-learn "foreign" language.

The same people who coordinate the Web—the **World Wide Web Consortium** (**W3C**)—developed XML. As a result, it works very well with browsers and other Web-based applications. So, it comes as no surprise that just as XHTML must be written with a text editor rather than a word processor to avoid unintentionally including the word processor's tags, we must also write XML in a simple text editor for the same reason. Use the same editor that you used in Chapter 4 to practice writing Web pages: TextWrangler for Mac users and Notepad++ for Windows users.

Use a Text Editor for XML. Like XHTML, XML should be written using a text editor like Notepad++ or TextWrangler rather than a word processor like Word or Word Perfect. Text editors give you only the text you see, but word processors include their own tags and other information that could confuse XML.

An Example from Tahiti

Let's use XML to define tags to specify the metadata for a small data collection. Given the following size data (area in km^2) for Tahiti and its neighboring islands in the Windward Islands archipelago of the South Pacific,

Tahiti	1048
Moorea	130
Maiao	9.5
Mehetia	2.3
Tetiaroa	12.8

we want to add the metadata, that is, identify which data is an island name and which is the area. As usual, the tag and its companion closing tag surround the data. We choose <iName> and <area> as the tags and write:

```
<iName>Tahiti</iName>          <area>1048</area>
<iName>Moorea</iName>          <area>130</area>
<iName>Maiao</iName>           <area>9.5</area>
<iName>Mehetia</iName>         <area>2.3</area>
<iName>Tetiaroa</iName>        <area>12.8</area>
```

These tags are used in the identification role. Notice that we chose <iName> rather than, say, <island name>. This is because XML tag names cannot contain spaces. But because both uppercase and lowercase are allowed—XML is case sensitive—we capitalize the "N" to make the tag more readable. All XML rules are shown later in this section in Table 16.1.

Though we have labeled each item with a tag describing what it is, we're not done describing the data. We need tags describing what sort of thing the name specifies and the area measures. That's an island, of course. So we enclose each entry with an <island> tag, as in

```
<island><iName>Tahiti</iName>       <area>1048</area></island>
<island><iName>Moorea</iName>       <area>130</area></island>
<island><iName>Maiao</iName>        <area>9.5</area></island>
<island><iName>Mehetia</iName>      <area>2.3</area></island>
<island><iName>Tetiaroa</iName>     <area>12.8</area></island>
```

The <island> tag serves in the affinity role to keep the two facts together; that is, Tahiti is grouped with its area and it is separated from Moorea and its area.

We're nearly done. The islands are not just randomly dispersed around the ocean. They are part of an archipelago, the proper name for a group of islands. So, we naturally invent one more tag, <archipelago>, and surround all of the islands with it. The result is shown in Figure 16.1.

```
<?xml version = "1.0" encoding="ISO-8859-1" ?>
<archipelago>
<island><iName>Tahiti</iName>       <area>1048</area></island>
<island><iName>Moorea</iName>       <area>130</area></island>
<island><iName>Maiao</iName>        <area>9.5</area></island>
<island><iName>Mehetia</iName>      <area>2.3</area></island>
<island><iName>Tetiaroa</iName>     <area>12.8</area></island>
</archipelago>
```

Figure 16.1 XML file encoding data for the Windward Islands database. The first line states that the file contains XML tags.

Notice that in Figure 16.1 an additional line has been added at the beginning of the file. This line, which uses the unusual form of associating question marks (?) within the brackets, identifies the file as containing XML data representations. (It also states that the file's characters are the standard ASCII set used in the U.S.; see Chapter 8.) This first line is required and must be the first line of any XML file. By identifying the file as XML, hundreds of software applications can understand what it contains. In this way the effort to tag all of the information can be repaid by using the data with those applications.

Start Off Right with XML. XML files must be identified as such, and so they are required to begin with the text

```
<?xml version = "1.0" encoding="ISO-8859-1" ?>
```

(or other encoding) as their first line and without leading spaces. The file should be ASCII text, and the file extension should be `.xml`.

16.1 More Islands. Write an XML metadata coding for the following collection of data from the Galápagos archipelago.

Island	Area	Elevation
Isabella	4588	1707
Fernandina	642	1494
Tower	14	76
Santa Cruz	986	846

For the items of the same type as the data from the Windward archipelago, use the same tags; for the elevation, the highest point on the island, think up a new tag.

Expanding the Use of XML

Given the XML encoding of two archipelagos—the Windward Islands and the Galápagos Islands—it seems reasonable to combine the encodings.

To create a database of the two archipelagos, we place them in a file, one after the other. This might seem odd because the Windward Islands have only two data values—name and area—while the Galápagos Islands have three—name, area, and elevation. But this is okay. Both archipelago encodings use the same tags for the common information, which is the key issue to consider when combining them. Extra data is allowed and, in fact, we might want to gather the elevation data for the Windward Islands.

With the two archipelagos combined into one database, we want to include the name of each to tell them apart easily. Of course, this means adding another tag for the name. We could use <name>, which is different from the <iName> tag used before. But in the same way that we added "i" to remind ourselves that it is an island name, it is probably wise to use the same idea to create a more specific tag name. Let's adopt the tag <a_name>. Notice the use of underscore, which is an allowed punctuation symbol for XML. We will place the name inside the <archipelago> tag, since it is data about the archipelago.

Finally, we have two archipelagos and we need to group them together by surrounding them with tags; these tags will serve as the root element of our

XML database. A **root element** is the tag that encloses all of the content of the XML file. In Figure 16.1 the <archipelago> tag was the root element, but now with two archipelagos in the file, we need a new tag to enclose them. They are both geographic features of our planet, so we will use <geo_feature> as the tag that surrounds both archipelagos. The final result of our revisions is shown in Figure 16.2.

Notice that the text in the file has been indented to make it more readable. Like XHTML, XML doesn't care about white space—spaces, tabs, and new lines—when they are between tags. This allows us to format XML files to simplify working with them, but the indenting is only for our use.

Attributes in XML

Recall that XHTML tags can have **attributes** to give additional information, such as src and alt in <img src="photo.jpg"...>. Our invented tags of XML can also have attributes. They have a similar form, and must always be set inside the simple quotation marks—that is, the straight quotes, not the curly "smart" quotes. Tag attribute values can be enclosed either in paired single or

```
<?xml version = "1.0"
  encoding="ISO-8859-1" ?>
<geo_feature>
  <archipelago>
    <a_name>Windward Islands
    </a_name>
    <island>
      <iName>Tahiti</iName>
      <area>1048</area>
    </island>
    <island>
      <iName>Moorea</iName>
      <area>130</area>
    </island>
    <island>
      <iName>Maiao</iName>
      <area>9.5</area>
    </island>
    <island>
      <iName>Mehetia</iName>
      <area>2.3</area>
    </island>
    <island>
      <iName>Tetiaroa</iName>
      <area>12.8</area>
    </island>
  </archipelago>
  <archipelago>
    <a_name>Galapagos Islands
    </a_name>
    <island>
      <iName>Isabella</iName>
      <area>4588</area>
      <elevation>1707</elevation>
    </island>
    <island>
      <iName>Fernandina</iName>
      <area>642</area>
      <elevation>1494</elevation>
    </island>
    <island>
      <iName>Tower</iName>
      <area>14</area>
      <elevation>76</elevation>
    </island>
    <island>
      <iName>Santa Cruz</iName>
      <area>986</area>
      <elevation>846</elevation>
    </island>
  </archipelago>
</geo_feature>
```

Figure 16.2 XML file for the Geographic Features database. XML ignores white space, so the text in the file has been indented for easier reading.

paired double quotes. If the content of the tag attribute requires quotes or an apostrophe (the single quote), then enclose the attribute value in the other form of quotes. So, we might have

```
<entry warnIfNone="Ain't there!">The user entered this data.</entry>
```

for one instance, and

```
<entry warnIfNone='I say, "Please enter"'>The data is from a user.</entry>
```

for another.

Understanding how to write tag attributes is easy enough. Even the rules for using quotes are straightforward. But, we want to use them wisely, which requires some thought.

The best advice about attributes is to use them for additional metadata, not for actual content. So, although we could have written

```
<archipelago name="Galapagos">
```

we chose not to because the name of an archipelago is content. A better use is to give an alternate form of the data, as in

```
<a_name accents="Gal&aacute;pagos">Galapagos</a_name>
```

which records that the second "a" in Galápagos is accented. The name of the islands is still given using a normal tag, but specifying accent marks separately simplifies searching and display options.

Effective Design with XML Tags

XML is a very flexible way to encode metadata. As we have described the archipelagos, we have used a few basic guidelines to decide how to use the tags. To emphasize these rules, let's review our thinking in creating metadata tags for the archipelago data, encapsulating it into three encoding rules.

Identification Rule: Label Data with Tags Consistently. *You can choose whatever tag names you wish to name data, but once you've decided on a tag for a particular kind of data, you must always surround that kind of data with that tag.*

Notice that one of the advantages of enclosing data with tags is that it keeps the data together. For example, the island of Santa Cruz in the Galápagos is a two-word name, but we don't have to treat it any differently than the one-word island names since the tags keep the two words together.

You may think that because we can choose our own tag names, it might be difficult to combine databases written by two different people—without planning ahead, they will probably choose different tags. Luckily, such differences are easily resolved: Because the tags are used consistently, it is possible to edit a file using *Find/Replace* to change the tag names. (There are other, more sophisticated ways to make them consistent, too.) For example, if your friend, who gathered the archipelago data for the Northern Hemisphere, used `<Name>` for the archipelago name rather than `<a_name>`, use *Find* to locate

<Name> and *Replace* to substitute <a_name>. Of course, searching for Name alone and replacing it with a_name does not work since it would match and ruin the <iName> tags. (If such cases do get in the way, use the placeholder technique described in Chapter 2.)

Affinity Rule: Group Related Data. *Enclose in a pair of tags all tagged data referring to the same entity. Grouping it keeps it all together, but the idea is much more fundamental: Grouping makes an association of the tagged data items as being related to each other, properties of the same thing.*

We applied this rule when we grouped the island name and area data inside <island> tags. We did this because both items referred to the same thing, the island. This is an important association, because the area data is not just area data about some random place on the earth; it is the area data for a specific place that is named Tahiti. This is an extremely important result from the simple act of enclosing data in tags.

When we added elevation data as an additional feature of islands, we included it inside the <island> tags for the same reason. As the elevation data shows, it is not necessary for every instance of an object to have data for the same set of characteristics.

Collection Rule: Group Related Instances. *When you have several instances of the same kind of data, enclose them in tags; again, it keeps them together and implies that they are related by being instances of the same type.*

When we had a group of five islands from the same area of the ocean, we grouped them inside an <archipelago> tag, and when we had a group of two archipelagos, we grouped them inside a <geo_feature> tag. We also added the names to the archipelagos using <a_name>, because as a collection they also have this additional property that we want to record.

Notice that the Affinity Rule and Collection Rule are different. The Affinity Rule groups together the data for a single thing—an island. Typically, the tags of the data values will all be different reflecting the different properties of the thing. The Collection Rule groups together the data of several instances of the same thing. Typically, in this case the tags—in our case <islands>—will be the same. The first association is among properties of an object, the second is among the objects themselves, which we also call *entities*. Notice that being grouped by the Collection Rule doesn't preclude being an object; the islands grouped together form a larger object, the archipelago, and so it has properties, too, such as a name.

The XML Tree

The rules for producing XML encodings of information produce hierarchical descriptions that can be thought of as trees. (We interpreted hierarchies as trees in Chapter 5.) See Figure 16.3 for the tree structure of the encoding of Figure 16.2. The hierarchy is a consequence of how the tags enclose one another and the data.

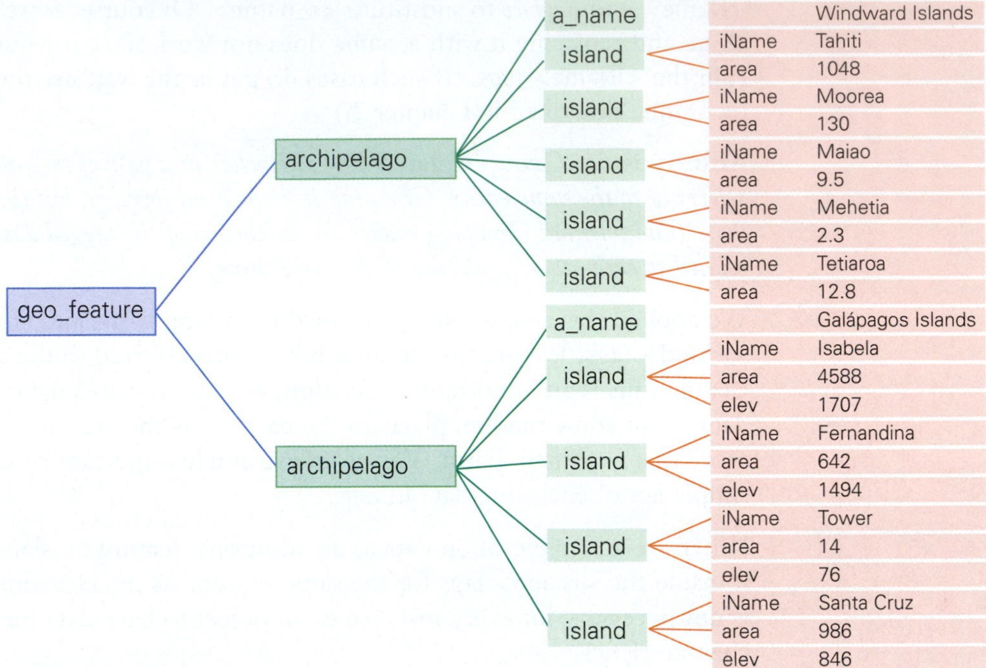

Figure 16.3 The XML displayed as a tree. The encoding from Figure 16.2 is shown with the root element (**geo_feature**) to the left and the leaves (content) shown to the right.

Table 16.1 Rules for writing XML

Required first line	<?xml version="1.0" encoding="ISO-8859-1"?> must appear on the first line, starting in the first position.
First tag	The first tag encountered is the *root* element, and it must enclose all of the file's content; it appears on the second or possibly third line.
Closing tags	All tags must be closed.
Element naming	Observe these rules: • Names can contain letters, numbers, and underscore characters. • Names must not start with a number or punctuation character. • Names must not start with the letters xml (or XML, or Xml, etc.). • Names cannot contain spaces.
Case sensitivity	Tags and attributes are case sensitive.
Proper nesting	All tags must be well-nested.
Attribute quoting	All attribute values must be quoted; paired single quotes (apostrophes) or paired double quotes are okay; use "dumb" quotes only; choose 'opposite' quotes to enclose quoted values.
White space	White space is preserved and converted to a single space.
Comments	XML comments have the form <!-- This is a comment. -->.

Tables and Entities

You have seen how you can record metadata about a collection of data values using XML tags. For the moment, let's set aside the topics of tagging and XML, and focus directly on table database systems generally. I want you to understand the concepts of database organization and the desirable properties embodied in the metadata, not simply the way to encode that structure with tags. We'll return to tagging later in the next chapter, but for now, think of tables pure and simple.

The kind of database approach we will discuss is known as a relational database. **Relational databases** describe the relationships among the different kinds of data—the sort of ideas embodied in Affinity and Collection Rules—allowing the software to answer queries about them. Although every relational database can be described by XML, it is not true that anything described by XML is a relational database. It may seem that relational databases are limited, but their power is enormous.

fluencyBIT

A Bright Idea. Though many people contributed to the creation of relational databases, E. F. Codd of IBM is widely credited with the original concept. He received the Association of Computing Machinery's Turing Award, the field's Nobel Prize, for the idea.

Entities

What *do* we want in database tables? Entities. "Entity" is about as vague as "thing" and "stuff," but the inventors of databases didn't want to limit the kinds of information that can be stored. An **entity** is anything that can be identified by a fixed number of its characteristics, called **attributes**; the attributes have names and values, and the values are the data that is stored in the table. (Unfortunately, *attributes* is an overused word in computing; in relational databases, think of an attribute as a "column of a table," where the "attribute names" are the column headings and the "attribute values" are the entries. We use the term *tag attributes* when we mean the attributes of XML.)

To relate entities and attributes to the metadata discussion earlier in this chapter, think of the attribute's name as the tag used in the Identity role, and the attribute values as the content enclosed in the tags. An entity is a group of attributes collected together by a tag used in the Affinity role. When describing affinity, we noted that the tagged data that we were grouping together all applied to one object, which was why it made sense to enclose it in tags. That object is the entity—the thing that the data applies to. Think of the tag used in affinity as the entity's name, and the tags that we allow within it as its attributes. So, an "island" is an entity, and its attributes include "name," "area," and "elevation"; see Figure 16.4. An "archipelago" is also an entity.

So, an entity defines a table. The name of the entity is the name of the table, and each of its possible attributes is assigned a column with the column

Island		
Name	*Area*	*Elevation*
Isabela	4588	1707
Fernandina	642	1494
Tower	14	76
Santa Cruz	986	846

Figure 16.4 A table instance for the island entity.

heading being the attribute name. The values in the columns are the attributes' values, and the rows are the entity instances. We say **entity instances** for a row because a specific set of values for the attributes of an entity—that is, the content of the row—define one particular object, an instance of the entity. So, "name" and "area" are attributes of "island" generally, but "Tahiti" and "1048" define a specific island; a row with those values is an instance of the "island" entity. Any table containing specific rows is said to be a **table instance**.

In addition to having a name, attributes also have a **data type**, such as number, text, image, and so on. (We haven't been concerned about data types so far.) The data type defines the form of the information that can be stored in a field. By specifying the data type, database software can prevent us from accidentally storing bad information in a table. To connect the data type to the tagging discussed earlier, think of the type as a tag attribute, as in `<name type="text">` or `<area type="number">`, though database software uses other forms of metadata to record the data type.

fluencyBIT

For the Record. Because databases are so important and long-studied, the concepts are known by several terms. The technical term for a row is a **tuple** (short u) from words like quintuple, sextuple, and septuple. Rows are often called **records**, a holdover from computing's punch-card days. Attributes are also known as **fields** and **columns**; an attribute's data type is sometimes referred to as its **format**. Tables are technically known as **relations**.

Properties of Entities

One curious property of a relational database table is that it can be empty. That is, the table has no rows. (Visualize the idea by deleting the last four rows of the table in Figure 16.4.) It seems odd, but it makes sense. Once we agree that an entity is anything defined by a specific set of attributes, then in principle a table exists with a name and column headings. When we specify entity instances, we'll have rows. So, among the instances of any table is the "empty instance."

Instances are unordered. Each distinct table is a different table instance. Two table instances will have a different set of rows. And, tables with the same rows, but reordered—that is, the same rows are listed in different sequence, say one sorted and the other unsorted—are the same table instance. Thus, the order of the rows doesn't matter in databases. We need to list them in some order, of course, but any order will do.

The attributes (columns) are also considered to be unordered, though we must list them in some order. Since the attributes have a name—think of the column heading or the tag—they do not have to be tracked by position.

Notice that the columns are unordered and the rows are unordered, but that doesn't mean that data in the table can go anywhere. Columns stay as columns, because they embody a kind of data being stored, and the items in a row stay as a row, because they are descriptive of an individual entity. The freedom to move the data is limited to exchanging entire rows or exchanging entire columns.

Uniqueness. There are few limits on what an entity can be. Things that can be identified or distinguished from each other based on a fixed set of attributes qualify as entities, which covers almost everything. Amoebas are not entities, because they have no characteristics that allow us to tell them apart. (Perhaps amoebas can tell each other apart, and if we could figure out how, then the characteristics on which they differ could be their attributes, allowing them to become entities.) Of course, one-celled animals *are* entities.

Because entities can be distinguished by their attributes, they are unique. Accordingly, in a database table no two rows can be the same. Unique instances is usually what we intend when we set up a database. For example, the database containing information about registered students at a college intends for each row—corresponding to a student—to be unique since the students are. When we set up the database, we ensure that we store information that uniquely identifies each student—such as name, birth date, parents' names, and permanent address.

In cases where the entities are unique but it is difficult to process the information, we might select an alternate encoding. For example, killer whales can be distinguished by the arrangement of their black-and-white markings. Even though images can be stored in a database, it is difficult to compare two images to determine if they show the same whale. So, we assign names to the killer whales, which are easy to manipulate, letting a human do the recognition and assign the name.

Notice that the two rows can have the same value for some attributes, just not all attributes.

Keys. The fact that no two rows in a database table are identical motivates us to ask which attributes distinguish them. In most cases, there will be several possibilities. Single attributes might be sufficient, like island name, or pairs of attributes like island name and archipelago name may be needed if certain island names, like Santa Maria, are common. Or we may have to consider three or more attributes taken together to ensure uniqueness. Any set of attributes for which all entities are different is called a **candidate key**. Because database tables usually have several candidate keys, we choose one and call it the primary key. The **primary key** is the one that the database system will use to decide uniqueness.

Notice that candidate keys qualify only if they distinguish among all entities forever, not just those that are in the table at the moment, that is, the given instance. For example, all currently registered college students might have different names (first, middle, and last taken together), making the name attribute unique for the current class. But, as we know, there are many people with identical names, and so that triple is not an actual candidate key.

If no combination of attributes qualifies as a candidate key, then a unique ID must be assigned to each entity. That's why your school issues students IDs: Some other student might match you on all of the attributes that the school records in its database, but because the school doesn't want to worry about the possibility of two distinct students matching on its key, it issues an ID number to guarantee that one attribute distinguishes each student.

Atomic data. In addition to requiring a description of each attribute's type of data—for example, number, text, or date—databases also treat the information as **atomic**, that is, not decomposable into any smaller parts. So, for example, an address value

```
1234 Sesame Street
```

is treated in a database table as a single sequence of ASCII characters; the street number and the street name cannot be separated. This is why forms—both paper and Web—have separate fields for street, city, state, and postal code: Most uses of address information must manipulate the city, state, and postal code information independently, which means the data must be assigned to separate fields.

The "only atomic data" rule is usually relaxed for certain types of data, such as dates, time, and currency. Strictly speaking, a date value `01/01/1970` must be treated as a single unity; any use of the date that refers to the month alone has to store the date as three attributes: day, month, and year. But database software usually bends the rules, allowing us to specify the format of the data attribute, say `dd/mm/yyyy`, which allows the program to understand how the field decomposes. This format saves us the trouble of manipulating three attributes.

Database Schemes

Though tags may be a precise way to specify the structure of a table, it is a cumbersome way to define a table. Accordingly, database systems specify a table as a **database scheme** or **database schema**. The scheme is a collection of table definitions that gives the name of the table, lists the attributes and their data types, and identifies the primary key. Each database system has specific requirements for how a scheme is presented, so there are no universal rules. We use an informal approach in which the attributes are given by their name, a data type, and a comment describing the meaning of the field. Figure 16.5 shows a database scheme for the `Island` table.

Island		
iName	text	*Island Name*
area	number	*Area in square kilometers*
elevation	number	*Highest point on the island*
Primary Key: iName		

Figure 16.5 Database table definition for an Island table.

XML Trees and Entities

As mentioned earlier, relational database tables and XML trees are not the same. A full explanation of the differences is for database experts, but basically relational databases are more restrictive than XML trees; the limits make them more powerful and allow them to do more for us, as you'll soon see. For us, the main difference concerns the Collection Rule: When entity instances are grouped, all entities within the tag must have the same structure, because that structure defines the attributes that make up a row.

For example, the Island table for the Galápagos in Figure 16.4, which is a legal relational database table, can be encoded in XML as shown in the answer to *Try It* Exercise 16.1 on page 505. So, the relational formulation and the XML formulation are the same. But, when we added the <a_name> tags inside of the <archipelago> tags, we violated the relational requirement that all entities have the same structure: The <a_name> was not an <island> entity. Including the <a_name> tag made sense for XML, but not for the relational model. So, they are related but not identical.

Database Tables Recap

Summarizing the important points of the last few sections, tables in databases are not simply an arrangement of text, but rather they have a structure that is specified by metadata. The structure of a database table is separate from its content. A table structures a set of entities—things that we can tell apart by their attributes—by naming the attributes and giving their data types. The entities of the table are represented as rows. We understand that rows and columns are unordered in databases, though when they are listed they have to be listed in some order. Tables and fields should have names that describe their contents, the fields must be atomic (i.e., indivisible), and one or more attributes define the primary key (i.e., field(s) with the property of having a different value for every row in any table instance ever).

Operations on Tables

A database is a collection of database tables. The main use of a database is to look up information. Users specify what they want to know and the database software finds it. For example, imagine a database containing Olympic records. There might be a table of participants for each Olympics, including attributes of name, country, and event; there might be a table of the medal winners for each Olympics, including attributes for the medal, the winner's name, the winner's country, and perhaps the score, distance, time, or other measure of the achievement. The database has many tables, but if we want to know how many marathon medalists have come from African countries, there is no table to look in—the table of medalists probably includes all winners in all sports, not just marathon winners from African countries. The data is in the database, but it's not stored in a single table where we, or the computer, can look it up. What we need to do is describe the information we want in such a way that the computer can figure out how to find it for us.

Database operations allow us to ask questions of a database in a way that lets the software find the answer for us. For example, we will ask for the number of African marathon winners by asking:

Put together the medalists for all of the Olympic Games (the operation will be called union*), find the rows of medalists who won in the marathon (the operation will be called* select*), and pick out those who come from African countries (the operation will be called* join*). Count the resulting rows, which is the answer we want.*

This example illustrates two important points. First, we can perform operations on tables to produce tables. It's analogous to familiar operations on numbers: Operations like addition combine two numbers and produce another number; operations like union combine two tables and produce another table. Second, the questions we ask of a database are answered with a whole table. If the question has a single answer—who won the marathon in 2000?—then the table instance answering the question will have only a single row. Generally there will be several answers forming the table. Of course, if there is no answer, the table will be empty.

In this section we illustrate the idea of combining tables to produce new tables. For this example, we imagine a table of the countries of the world as might be used by a travel agency. Its structure and sample entries are shown in Figure 16.6. Using that table, Nations, we'll investigate the five fundamental operations that can be performed on tables: Select, Project, Union, Difference, and Product.

Select Operation

The Select operation takes rows from one table to create a new table. Generally we specify the Select operation by giving the (single) table from which rows are to be selected and the test for selection. We use the syntax:

Select *Test* From *Table*

The *Test* is to be applied to each row of the given table to decide if the row should be included in the new result table. The *Test* is a short formula that tests attribute values. It is written using attribute names, constants like numbers or letter strings, and the relational operators <, ≤, ≠, =, ≥, >. The **relational**

Nations

Name	text	*Common rather than official name*
Domain	text	*Internet top-level domain name*
Capital	text	*Nation's capital*
Latitude	number	*Approx. latitude of capital*
N_S	Boolean	*Latitude is N(orth) or S(outh)*
Longitude	number	*Approx. longitude of capital*
E_W	Boolean	*Longitude is E(ast) or W(est)*
Interest	text	*A short description of the country*

Primary Key: Name

Name	Dom	Capital	Lat	NS	Lon	EW	Interest
Ireland	IE	Dublin	52	N	7	W	History
Israel	IR	Jerusalem	32	N	35	E	History
Italy	IT	Rome	42	N	12	E	Art
Jamaica	JM	Kingston	18	N	77	W	Beach
Japan	JP	Tokyo	35	N	143	E	Kabuki

Figure 16.6 The **Nations** table definition and sample entries.

operators test whether the attribute value has a particular relationship, for example, Interest = 'Beach' or Latitude < 45. If the *Test* is true, the row is included in the new table; otherwise, it is ignored. Notice that the information used to create the new table is a copy, so the original table is not changed by Select (or any of the other table-building operations discussed here).

To use the Nations table to create a table of countries with beaches, we write a Select command to remove all rows for countries that have Beach as their Interest attribute. The operation is

Select Interest = 'Beach' **From** Nations

This gives us a new table, shown in part in Figure 16.7. Notice that the information in the last column is constant because the *Test* required the word "Beach" for that field for all selected rows.

The *Test* can be more than a test of a single value. For example, we can use the logical operations AND and OR in the way they were used to search in

Name	Dom	Capital	Lat	NS	Lon	EW	Interest
Australia	AU	Canberra	37	S	148	E	Beach
Bahamas	BS	Nassau	25	N	78	W	Beach
Barbados	BB	Bridgetown	13	N	59	W	Beach
Belize	BZ	Belmopan	17	N	89	W	Beach
Bermuda	BM	Hamilton	32	N	64	W	Beach

Figure 16.7 Part of the table created by selecting countries with a Test for **Interest** equal to **Beach**.

Chapter 5. So, for example, to find countries whose capitals are at least 60° north latitude, we write

Select Latitude ≥ 60 AND N_S = 'N' **From** Nations

which should produce a four-row table created from the Nations table's rows for Finland, Greenland, Iceland, and Norway.

Project Operation

If we can pick out rows of a table (using Select), we should be able to pick out columns too. Project (pronounced *pro · JECT*) is the operation that builds a new table from the columns of an existing table. We only need to specify the name of a table and the columns (field names) from it to be included in the new table. The syntax is

Project *Field_List* **From** *Table*

For example, to create a new table from the Nations table without the capital and position information—that is, to keep the other three columns—write

Project Name, Domain, Interest **From** Nations

The new table will have as many rows as the Nation table, but just three columns. Figure 16.8 shows part of that table.

Name	Dom	Interest
Nauru	NR	Beach
Nepal	NP	Mountains
Netherlands	NL	Canals
New Caledonia	NC	Beach
New Zealand	NZ	Adventure

Figure 16.8 Sample entries for a **Project** operation on **Nations**.

Project does not *always* result in a table with the same number of rows as the original table. When the new table includes a key from the old table (e.g., Name), the key makes each row distinct, so the new table will include fields from all rows of the original table. But if some of the new table's rows are the same—which can't happen if key columns are included, but can if there is no key among the chosen columns—they will be merged together into a single row. The rows have to be merged because of the rule that the rows of any table must always be distinct. If rows in one table are merged, the two tables will, of course, have different numbers of rows. So, for example, to list the Interest descriptions that travel agents use to summarize countries, we create a new table of only the last column of Nations.

Project Interest **From** Nations

This produces a one-column table with a row for each descriptive word: Beach appears once, Mountains appears once, and so on. Thus, the table has as many rows as unique words, and because of merging, it does not have as many rows as Nations.

We often use Select and Project operations together to "trim" base tables to keep only some of the rows and some of the columns. To illustrate, we define a table of the countries with northern capitals, called Northern, and define it with the command

At60OrAbove = (**Select** Latitude ≥ 60 AND N_S = 'N' **From** Nations)

which is the table we created earlier. To throw away everything except the name, domain, and latitude to produce Northern, we write

Northern = (**Project** Name, Domain, Latitude **From** At60OrAbove)

as shown in Figure 16.9.

Name	Dom	Lat
Finland	FI	61
Greenland	GL	72
Iceland	IS	65
Norway	NO	60

Figure 16.9 Northern, the table of countries with northern capitals.

Another way to achieve the same result is to combine the two operations:

Project Name, Domain, Latitude **From**
(**Select** Latitude ≥ 60 AND N_S = 'N' **From** Nations)

First a temporary table is created with the four countries, just as before. Then the desired columns are selected. It might be a slightly more efficient solution if we don't need the At60OrAbove table for any other purpose, but generally either solution is fine.

Union Operation

Besides picking out rows and columns of a table, another operation on tables is to combine two tables. This only makes sense if they have the same set of attributes, of course. The operation is known as Union, and is written as though it were addition:

Table1 + Table2

The plus sign (+) can be read "combined with." So, if the table of countries with capitals at least 45° south latitude are named At45OrBelow with the command

At45OrBelow = (**Select** Latitude ≥ 45 AND N_S = 'S' **From** Nations)

then we can define places with their capitals closest to the poles using the union operation. Call the result ExtremeGovt and define it by

ExtremeGovt = At60OrAbove + At45OrBelow

The result is shown in Figure 16.10. This table could also have been created with a complex Select command.

Name	Dom	Capital	Lat	NS	Lon	EW	Interest
Falkland Is	FK	Stanley	51	S	58	W	Nature
Finland	FI	Helsinki	61	N	26	E	Nature
Greenland	GL	Nuuk	72	N	40	W	Nature
Iceland	IS	Reykjavik	65	N	18	W	Geysers
Norway	NO	Oslo	60	N	10	E	Vikings

Figure 16.10 The ExtremeGovt table created with Union.

Union can be used to combine separate tables, say, Nations with Canada_Provinces. (Canada_Provinces gives the same data about the provinces as Nations does about countries, except the Domain field is CA for all rows.) For example, had the At60OrAbove table been defined by

```
Select Latitude ≥ 60 AND N_S = 'N'
    From (Nations + Canada_Provinces)
```

then the Yukon would be included because its capital, Whitehorse, is north of 60°.

Difference Operation

The opposite of combining two tables with Union is to remove from one table the rows also listed in a second table. The operation is known as Difference and it is written with the syntax

Table1 – Table2

The operation can be read, "remove from *Table1* any rows also in *Table2*." Like Union, Difference only makes sense when the table's fields are the same. For example,

```
Nations - At60OrAbove
```

produces a table without those countries with northern capitals—that is, without Finland, Greenland, Iceland, and Norway. Interestingly, this command works just as well if At60OrAbove had included Canadian provinces like the Yukon. That is, in a Difference command, the items "subtracted away" do not have to exist in the original table.

Product Operation

Adding and subtracting tables is easy. What is multiplying tables like? The Product operation on tables, which is written as

Table1 × Table2

creates a supertable. The table has the columns from *both* tables. So, if the first table has five attributes and the second table has six attributes, the

Product table has eleven attributes. The rows of the new table are created by *appending* or concatenating each row of the second table to each row of the first table—that is, putting the rows together. The result is the "product" of the rows of each table.

For example, if the first table is Nations with 230 rows, and the second table has 4 rows, there will be 230 × 4 = 920 rows, because each row of the Nations table is appended with each row of the second table to produce a row of the result.

To illustrate, suppose you have a table of your traveling companions, as described in Figure 16.11(a), containing the information shown in Figure 16.11(b).

Travelers

Friend	text	*A Traveling Companion*
Homeland	text	*Friend's Home Country*

Primary Key: Friend

(a)

Friend	Homeland
Isabella	Argentina
Brian	South Africa
Wen	China
Clare	Canada

(b)

Figure 16.11 (a) The definition of the Travelers table, and (b) its values.

Then the Product operation

Super = Nations × Travelers

creates a new table with ten fields—eight fields from Nations and two fields from Travelers—a total of 920 rows. Some of the rows of the new table are shown in Figure 16.12. For each country, there is a row for each of your friends.

The Product operation may seem a little odd at first because its all-combinations approach merges information that may not "belong together." And it's true. But most often, Product is used to create a supertable that contains both useful and useless rows, and then it is "trimmed down" using Select, Project,

Name	Dom	Capital	Lat	NS	Log	EW	Interest	Friend	Homeland
Cyprus	CY	Nicosia	35	N	32	E	History	Clare	Canada
Czech Rep.	CZ	Prague	51	N	15	E	Pilsner	Isabella	Argentina
Czech Rep.	CZ	Prague	51	N	15	E	Pilsner	Brian	South Africa
Czech Rep.	CZ	Prague	51	N	15	E	Pilsner	Wen	China
Czech Rep.	CZ	Prague	51	N	15	E	Pilsner	Clare	Canada
Denmark	DK	Copenhagen	55	N	12	E	History	Isabella	Argentina

Figure 16.12 Some rows from the supertable that is the product of Nations and Travelers. For each row in Nations and each row in Travelers, there is a row in the product table that combines them.

and Difference to contain only the intended information. This is a powerful approach that we will use repeatedly in later sections.

To illustrate, suppose your traveling companions volunteer to tutor students preparing for the National Geographic Society's Geography Bee. Each friend agrees to tutor students "on their part of the world," that is, in the quarter of the planet from which they come. So, Isabella, who comes from Argentina in the southern and western hemispheres, agrees to tutor students on the geography of that part of the world, and so on. Then you can produce a master list of who's responsible for each country. We'll call it the Master table. It is produced by these commands:

```
Super  = Nations × Travelers
Assign =   (Select N_S = 'S' AND E_W = 'W'
           AND Friend = 'Isabella' From Super)
         + (Select N_S = 'S' AND E_W = 'E'
           AND Friend = 'Brian' From Super)
         + (Select N_S = 'N' AND E_W = 'E'
           AND Friend = 'Wen' From Super)
         + (Select N_S = 'N' AND E_W = 'W'
           AND Friend = 'Clare' From Super)
Master = Project Name, Friend From Assign
```

Notice that we have used Product (×), Union (+), Select, and Project.

How do these commands work? The Super table is the product table discussed earlier with a row for each nation paired with each friend (see Figure 16.12). Then the Assign table is created by the Union operation (+) that combines four tables, each created by a Select operation from Super. The first Select keeps only those countries from Super with Isabella's name that are also in the southern and western hemispheres. The second Select keeps only those countries from Super with Brian's name that are in the southern and eastern hemispheres. The same kind of operations are used for Wen and Clare. The resulting Assign table has 230 rows—the same as the original Nations table—with one of your friends' names assigned to each country.

We know that all of the countries are in the Assign table because every country is in one of the four hemisphere pairs, and in Super there is a row for each country for each friend. When the right combination "comes up," the country will be chosen by one of the four Selects. In addition, Assign has the property that each person is given countries in "their" part of the world. (Wen has been assigned the greatest amount of work!) Finally, we throw away all of the location information to create our Master list, keeping only the names of the countries and the friends responsible for tutoring students about that geography. Part of the result is shown in Figure 16.13.

We have introduced five basic operations on tables. They are straightforward and simple. It is surprising, therefore, that these five are the only operations needed to create any table in a relational database. In practice, we will rarely

Name	Friend
Chad	Wen
Chile	Isabella
China	Wen
Christmas Is.	Clare
Cocos Is.	Brian

Figure 16.13 A portion of the **Master** table of your friends' assignments.

use the operations directly, because they are incorporated into database software. When we want to create tables from other tables—an idea that is now quite natural—we will hardly be aware that we're using these operations.

fluencyBIT

Quotient Intelligence. There is a **Divide** operation on tables, but it's complicated and rather bizarre. Because it doesn't give us any new capabilities, we will leave it to the experts.

Join Operation

Another powerful and useful operation for creating database tables is Join. Indeed, it is so useful that although Join can be defined from the five primitive database operations of the last section, it is usually provided as a separate operator.

Join Defined

Join combines two tables, like the Product operation does, but it doesn't necessarily produce all pairings. If the two tables each have fields with a common attribute, the new table produced by Join combines only the rows from the given tables that match on those fields, not all pairings of rows, as does Product. We write the Join operation as follows:

Table1 ⋈ *Table2* **On** *Match*

The unusual "bow tie" symbol suggests a special form of Product in which the two tables "match up." *Match* is a comparison test involving fields from each table, which when true for a row from each table produces a result row that is their concatenation. To refer to attributes in each table, we use the notation *Table.Field*, as in Master.Name.

Join Applied

To show how Join works, recall the Northern table (Figure 16.9) and the Master table of your friends' assignments (Figure 16.13). The Join

Master ⋈ Northern **On** Master.Name = Northern.Name

pairs all rows where the country name matches the home country of a friend. Which rows are those? This is how to find out. Beginning with the first row of the Master table (shown here):

Name	Friend
Afghanistan	Wen
Albania	Wen
. . .	. . .

the Afghanistan row does not have the same Name field as any of the four countries of Northern, so it is not part of the result. Nor does the Name in the second row of Master (Albania) appear as a Name field in Northern. Indeed, only four rows of Master have the same Name field as rows in Northern: Finland, Greenland, Iceland, and Norway. We combine those four rows with their corresponding rows in Northern to produce the four-row result shown in Figure 16.14. As you see, Join associates the information from the rows of two tables in a sensible way. Thus, Join is used to create new associations of information in the database.

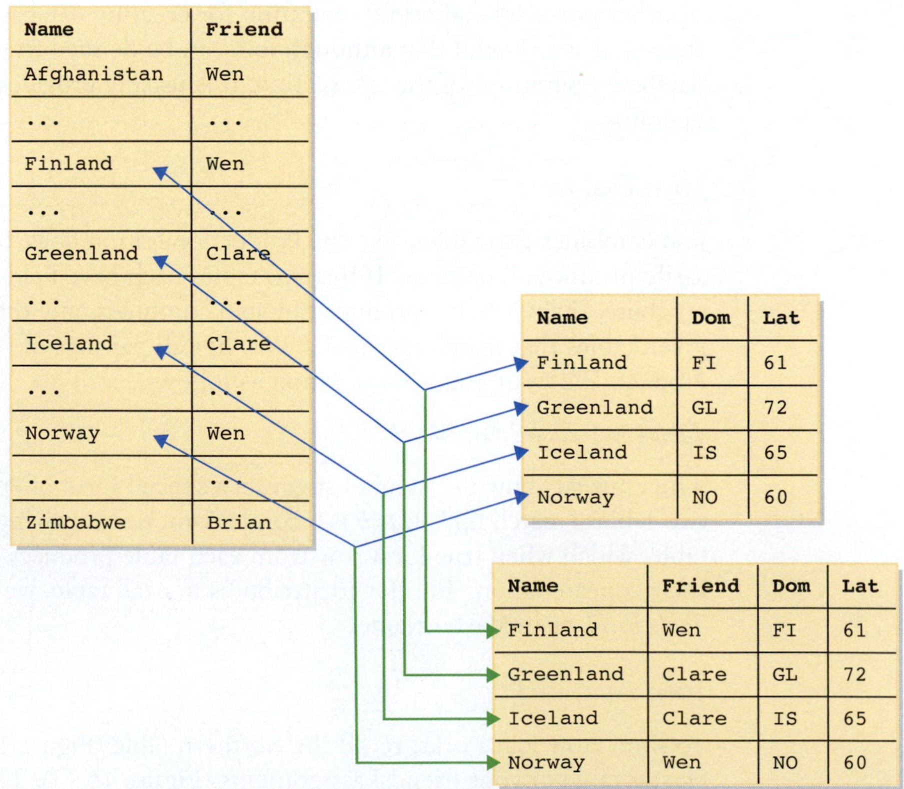

Figure 16.14 The Join operation: Master ⋈ Northern.

There are at least two ways to think about the Join operation. One way is to see it as a "lookup" operation on tables. That is, for each row in one table, locate a row (or rows) in the other table with the same value in the common field; if found, combine the two; if not, look up the next row. That's how we explained it in the last paragraph. Another way is to see it as a Product operation forming all pairs of the two tables, and then eliminating all rows that don't match in the common fields. Both ideas accurately describe the result, and the computer probably uses still another approach to produce the Join table.

Join, as described, is called a *natural* Join *because the natural meaning of "to match" is for the fields to be equal. But as is typical of computing, it is also possible to join using any relational operator* (<, ≤, ≠, =, ≥, >), not just = to compare fields. Unnatural or not, a Join where T1.fieldID < T2.fieldID can be handy.

African Marathon Runners

To complete the task we discussed earlier of finding out how many African men marathon winners there have been in the history of the Olympics, we assume there are tables Medalists1896, Medalists1900, . . ., Medalists2008, and that there is a table, Africa, of African nation names, which includes colonial names like Rhodesia and modern names like Zimbabwe.

Assuming these tables, we write

```
All_Medalists = Medalists1896 + Medalists1900 +
    ... + Medalists2008
```

which is a lot of typing. The All_Medalists table contains the names, medal, event, and country of everyone who won in the Olympics. Next, we pick out the marathon winners with

```
Distance26 = Select medal='gold' AND event='marathon, men'
             From All_Medalists
```

The Distance26 table contains all male runners who received a gold medal in the Olympic marathon event. Next, eliminate everyone but the African winners with

```
Africa_marathon = Distance26 ⋈ Africa
                  On Distance26.country = Africa.name
```

producing a table of African winners. The result is

Kenneth McArthur	South Africa	1912
Abebe Bikila	Ethiopia	1960
Abebe Bikila	Ethiopia	1964
Mamo Wolde	Ethiopia	1968
Josia Thugwane	South Africa	1996
Gezahegne Abera	Ethiopia	2000
Samuel Wanjiru	Kenya	2008

answering the question, except for the count.

Database software provides a function for counting the number of rows in a table, which is applied in the present case as

```
count(Africa_marathon)
```

Using the operators, we specified a set of tables that allowed us to find our solution. We will refine this skill after the next section.

16.2 Joining Tutors. Suppose the **Travelers** relation of Figure 16.11 had the following revised definition:

TravRev

Friend	text	*Companion*
Homeland	text	*Home Country*
NS	text	*Latitude Hemi*
EW	text	*Longitude Hemi*

Primary Key: Friend

Friend	Homeland	NS	EW
Isabella	Argentina	S	W
Brian	South Africa	S	E
Wen	China	N	E
Clare	Canada	N	W

Use **Join** to create the **Assign** table.

Structure of a Database

You have learned that by using the five primitive operations and Join we can create tables from tables to answer questions from a database. But usually these operations are used in a slightly different way. We don't usually ask a single question and quit. Rather, we want to arrange the information of a database in a way that users see a relevant-to-their-needs view of the data that they will use continually. Figure 16.15 shows a schematic of this idea.

In Figure 16.15 you see that there are two forms of tables. The physical database, stored on the disk drives of the computer system, is the permanent repository of the database. The logical database, also known as the *view of the database*, is created for users on-the-fly and is customized for their needs. Why do we use this two-level solution? The answer requires that we look a little closer at the two groups of tables.

Physical and Logical Databases

The point of the two-level system is to separate the management of the data, which is typically done at the physical database level, from the presentation of the data, which typically involves many different versions for many different users.

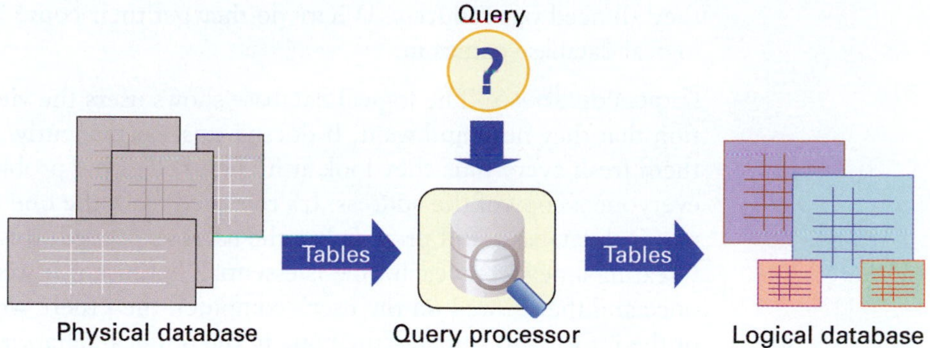

Figure 16.15 Structure of a database system. The physical database is the permanent repository of the data; the logical database, or view of the database, is the form of the database the users see. The transformation is implemented by the query processor, and is based on queries that define the logical database tables from the physical database tables.

Physical database. The physical database is designed by database administrators so that the data is fast to access. More importantly, the physical database is set up to avoid redundancy, that is, duplicating information. It seems obvious that data should not be stored repeatedly because it will waste space, but disk space is *extremely* cheap, implying that that isn't the reason to avoid redundancy. Rather, if data is stored in multiple places in the physical database, there is a chance—possibly, a good chance—that when it's changed in one place, it will not be changed in every other place where it is stored. This causes the data to become *inconsistent*.

For example, if your school stores your home address, and your major department also stores a separate copy of your address, then when you notify the school of your new residence, both addresses should be changed. But, with multiple copies, that might not occur. If the database contains two different addresses for you, then the school has no idea which address is correct; perfectly good information gets turned into garbage because it is inconsistent. For this reason, database administrators make sure that there is only one copy of each piece of data. That is, data is not stored redundantly.

It might seem risky to keep only one copy of the data: What happens if it accidentally gets deleted or the disk crashes? Database administrators worry about this problem all the time, and have a process of making backup copies of the database, which they store in a safe place, *never to be used*. That is, until the data is accidentally deleted or the disk crashes—in other words—when the other copy is gone. There is still only one copy.

Avoiding redundancy is obviously good, but keeping one copy seems to ignore the fact that multiple users need the information. The administration needs to send tuition bills, the dean needs to send notification that you "made the list," and the Sports Center needs to send you the picture of your photo finish;

they all need your address. Where do they get their copy? That's where the logical database comes in.

Logical database. The logical database shows users the view of the information that they need and want. It doesn't exist permanently, but is created for them fresh every time they look at it. This solves the problem of getting everyone a copy of the address. It's retrieved from the one copy stored in the physical database, and provided to the users as needed, fresh every time. Creating a new copy each time is essential, because if it were to be created once and then stored on the user's computer, then there would be two copies of the information again—the copy in the physical database and the one in the logical database—making the data redundantly stored. So, it never stays on the user's computer; it's always recreated. As a result, when you notify the administration that you moved in the morning, the dean can send you a congratulatory letter in the afternoon and have your correct address.

The other advantage of creating specialized versions of the database for each user is that different users want to see different information. For example, the Sports Center needs to record a student's locker number, but no other unit on campus cares. Similarly, the fact that a student is on academic probation is information that most users of the school's database don't need to know, and it should not be included in their view. In principle, each user wants a different view of the database.

Queries. Queries are the key to making this two-level organization work. Each user group, say the dean's office, needs a version of the database created for them. For each user table a query is formulated. A **query** is a specification using the five operations and Join that define a table from other tables. Think of the query as being written as described in the previous sections, but it is actually written in the standard database language **SQL**, short for **Structured Query Language**. Then, when the dean clicks on the table of Spring Term Grades, the database system runs the query that defines that table, creating it and displaying it to the dean. It probably doesn't exist in that form in the physical database, but Select, Project, and the other operations can define how to create it from the data that is physically stored. On the next day, when the dean opens the table of Spring Term Grades again, a new copy will be created, which means that the grade change made the previous afternoon by some physics professor (and stored in the physical database) will be visible to the dean.

It all seems pretty complicated, but it is not. Indeed, in the next section you will see that it is all rather straightforward.

Defining Physical Tables

In this section we define two tables to be used for illustration purposes, focusing on the roles of keys and relationships.

Database schemes. Recall that the metadata specification of a database's tables is given by a database schema, or database scheme. Interactive software can help us define a database schema, but, as we saw earlier, declaring an entity's structure is easy enough to do without software. The database schema is important because it describes the database design. When we want to analyze a database design, we look at its schema.

To illustrate the basics of the two-level approach, imagine a college having a set of tables in its database schema, two of which are Student and Home_Base.

Student

Student_ID	number	*Eight digits*
First_Name	text	*Single name, capitalized*
Middle_Name	text	*All other names, but family*
Last_Name	text	*Family name*
Birthdate	date	
Grade_Point	number	*0 <= GPA <= 4*
Major	text	*None, or degree granting unit*
On_Probation	Boolean	*0 is 'no'; 1 is 'yes'*

Primary Key: Student_ID

Home_Base

Student_ID	number	*Eight digits*
Street	text	*All address info before city*
City	text	*No abbreviations like NYC*
State	text	*Or province, canton, prefecture . . .*
Country	text	*Standard postal abbreviations OK*
Postal_Code	text	*Full postal code*

Primary Key: Student_ID

Figure 16.16 shows the preceding table definitions as they appear in the Microsoft Access database system. Notice that they are different forms of the same thing.

Connecting Database Tables by Relationships

The Student entity records the information basic to the person's identity and associates a student with his or her Student_ID. This is the college's master record of each student. Part of each student's information is where he or she lives. Though we could put addresses in the Student table, we decide not to. This is because other campus units will want to access the address information, but they shouldn't have access to all of the information (especially the sensitive information) about each student. The addresses are stored in a different table, the Home_Base table, which can have a lower security rating. Though these two tables are separate, they are not independent. The Student_ID connects each row in Student with his or her address in Home_Base. We say that there is a relationship between the two entities.

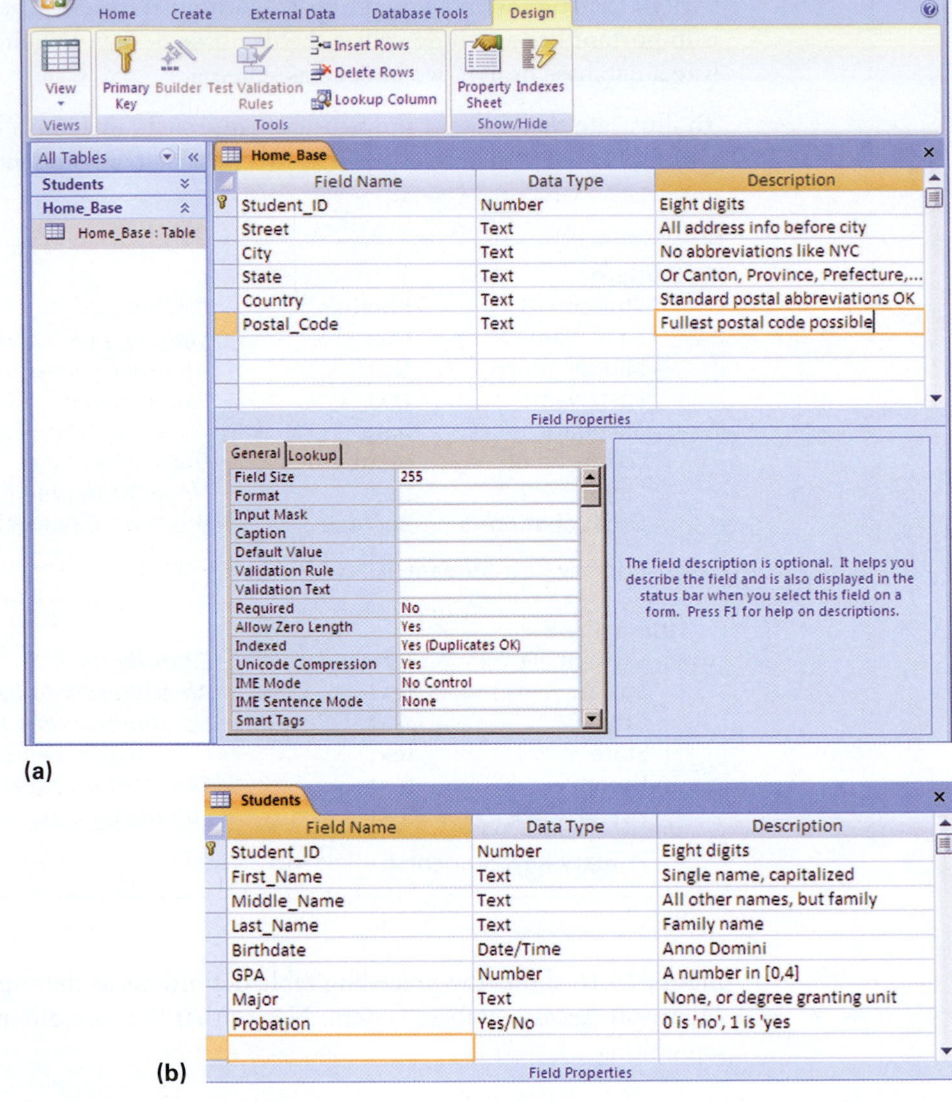

Figure 16.16 Table declarations from Microsoft Access 2007: (a) **Home_Base** table declaration shown in the design view; and (b) students table declaration. Notice that the key is specified by the tiny key next to **Student_ID** in the first column.

The idea of relationships. A **relationship** is a correspondence between rows of one table and the rows of another table. Relationships are part of the metadata of a database, and because they are critical to building the logical database from the physical database, we give them names and characterize their properties.

The relationship between Student and Home_Base—that is, for each row in Student there is a single row in Home_Base (found by the Student_ID)—will be called *Lives_At*. Setting up the tables in this way is largely equivalent to storing the address in Student, but not all relationships are so close. This one is especially close because it is based on the Student_ID, which is the key for both tables. (Recall that keys are unique, meaning no two rows can have the same value.) The *Lives_At* relationship is said to be one-to-one.

Because we used the key Student_ID in both tables, we not only can find the address for each student, but we can also find the student for each address. That is, there is a second relationship in the opposite direction, which we can call *Home_Of*, meaning that the home base entry is the address of the student who has that ID. Like *Lives_At*, *Home_Of* is a one-to-one relationship, because each row in Home_Base corresponds to a single row in Student.

Relationship examples. Familiar relationships that we encounter every day illustrate that their description often ends with a preposition.

- *Father_Of*, the relationship between a man and his child
- *Daughter_Of*, the relationship between a girl and her parent
- *Employed_By*, the relationships between people and companies
- *Stars_In*, the relationships between actors and movies

Names of database relationships should be meaningful to help people working with the database, but like all names in computing, the computer doesn't know whether the name makes sense or not.

Relationships in practice. Database software systems need to know what relationships exist among the tables if they are to help us create the logical databases. The systems allow us to define relationships among tables. The details are specific to each system, of course, but the example of *Lives_At* and *Home_Of* are shown in Figure 16.17 as they would appear in Microsoft Access.

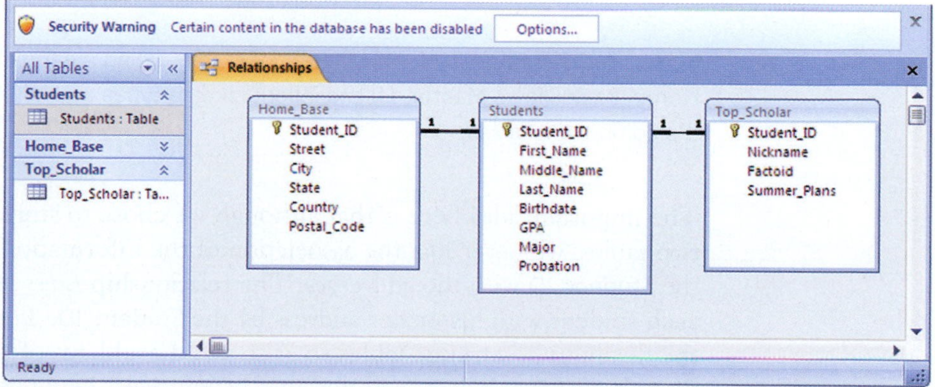

Figure 16.17 The *Relationships* window from the Microsoft Access database system; the 1-to-1 *Lives_At* and *Home_Of* relationships are shown between **Home_Base** and **Students**.

Defining Logical Tables

The school's administration probably thinks there is a single master list recording all of the data for each student. Because that's what they want to see, it's part of the administration's logical view of the database. So, we create it for them from the physical database.

Construction using Join. The relationships between the Student and Home_Base tables allow us to construct a single table, Master_List, which contains the combined information from both tables. How? Using the natural Join operation, described earlier in this chapter. Recall that the natural Join creates a table out of two other tables by joining rows that match—it's an equality test—on specified fields. Thus, we write

```
Master_List = Student ⋈ Home_Base
        On Student.Student_ID = Home_Base.Student_ID
```

where the match is on the common field of Student_ID. Fields of the resulting table are shown in Figure 16.18. We don't lose anything by storing the basic student information in one table and the addresses in another, because with this simple command, we can create a table that recombines the information just as if it were stored in a single table.

Student_ID
First_Name
Middle_Name
Last_Name
Birthdate
On_Probation
Street_Address
City
State
Country
Postal_Code

Figure 16.18 Attributes of the Master_List table. Being created from Student and Home_Base allows Master_List to inherit its data types and key (Student_ID) from the component tables.

The important idea here is that although we chose to store the information in two tables, we never lost the association of the information because we kept the Student_ID with the addresses. The relationship *Lives_At* lets us connect each student with his or her address by the Student_ID. The approach gives us the flexibility to arrange tables so as to avoid problems of redundancy—though we haven't demonstrated that benefit yet—while keeping track of important information, like where a person lives.

Practical construction using QBE. Though it wasn't difficult to write the natural Join query in the last section to create the Master_List table, database systems can make it even easier for us. A technique developed at IBM in the 1970s, called **Query By Example (QBE)**, is available to us in the Microsoft Access system. Basically, the software gives us a template of a table, and we fill in what we want in the fields. That is, we give an example of what we want in the table, referencing fields from other tables that have already been defined. The software then figures out a query that creates the table from the sample table. It couldn't be easier! Figure 16.19 shows the QBE query window that will create Master_List.

The database software automatically creates the query needed for Master_List. What query did it create? We can ask and find out what it generated; see Figure 16.20. The query is expressed in SQL, the standard database query language. If we could read SQL—it's actually not too hard—we'd see that this query is the query we created above for Master_List.

The Dean's View

Because the school administrators probably want to see the entire student record, there isn't much advantage to breaking the files into smaller tables in the physical design, but it does make sense for others who only need to see parts of the database in their view. To illustrate one more logical database, we create a view for the dean.

Storing the dean's data. We imagine that the database administrators have set up a special table with the dean's record of the students in the college. The

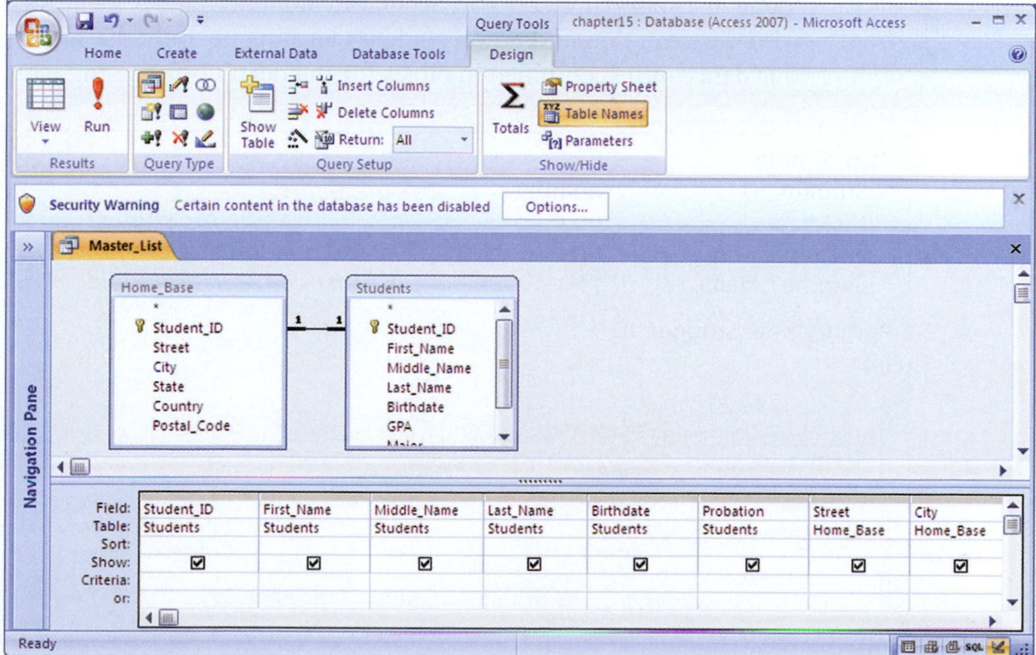

Figure 16.19 The Query By Example definition of the **Master_List** table from MS Access.

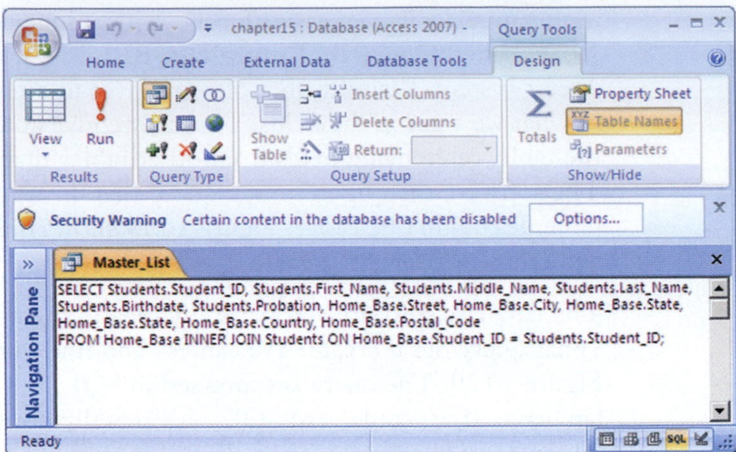

Figure 16.20 SQL query created from the Query By Example data in Figure 16.19.

table definition is shown in Figure 16.21. The Top_Scholar is basically information of interest only to the dean.

The table has a one-to-one relationship with the Home_Base table, based on the Student_ID attribute, just as Student does: For each scholar, there is an address in Home_Base. Therefore, there is a relationship between the Top_Scholar and the Home_Base tables, which we'll call *Resides_At*. The relationship gives the dean access to the student's hometown, which is something the dean wants to be reminded of. Of course, there is a relationship in the opposite direction, too, from Home_Base to Top_Scholar.

Student_ID also connects Top_Scholar to Student. This is lucky, because otherwise the dean doesn't know a student's legal name, only the nickname. All of this data can be combined in tables for the dean's office using natural Join

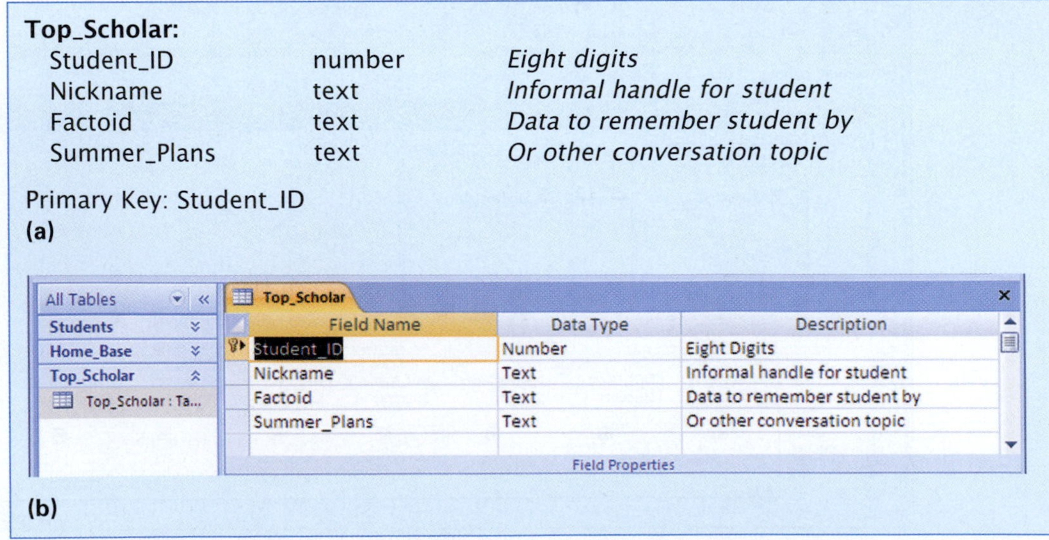

Figure 16.21 The Top_Scholar definition: (a) informal form, (b) in MS Access.

operations like we did in the last section, but the dean doesn't want to see all that information.

Creating a dean's view. Imagine a table, known as the Dean's View, containing information specific to the dean's unique needs. For example, because the dean is not the person who sends letters to top students telling them they made the "Dean's List," the Dean's View doesn't need the students' full home addresses. (Someone else in the dean's office will need them.) The students' hometowns are enough information for the dean to make small talk at parties in honor of the good students. So the Dean's View will include information selected from the physical tables, as shown in Figure 16.22.

Notice that the dean doesn't even want to see the student ID. We use it to create the Dean's View, but it doesn't have to be part of what the dean looks at in the database view.

Join three tables into one. The first step in creating a query for the Dean's View is to note that it contains information from three tables: Top_Scholar, the table actually storing the data the dean wants kept; Student, the college's permanent record of the student; and Home_Base, the college's current address list. The information for each student must be associated to create the Deans_View table, and the Join operation is the key to doing it. The expression

```
Dean_Data_Collect =  (Top_Scholar ⋈ (Student ⋈Home_Base
                     On Student.Student_ID=Home_Base.Student_ID)
                     On Student.Student_ID=Top_Scholar.Student_ID)
```

makes a table that has a row for each student in the dean's Top_Scholar table, but it also has all of the information from all three tables for that student. The association of each student's row in each table is accomplished by matching on the Student_ID attribute.

Deans_View

Name		Source Table
Nickname	Top_Scholar	Used by the dean to seem "chummy"
First_Name	Student	Name information required because
Last_Name	Student	the dean forgets the person's actual name, being so chummy
Birthdate	Student	Is student of "drinking age"?
City	Home_Base	Hometown (given by city, state) is
State	Home_Base	important for small talk, but full address not needed by dean
Major	Student	Indicates what the student's doing in college besides hanging out
Grade_Point	Student	How's student doing grade-wise?
Factoid	Top_Scholar	Data to remember student by
Summer_Plans	Top_Scholar	Or other conversation topic

Figure 16.22 The Dean's View fields showing their source in physical database tables.

Trim the table. The resulting table contains too much information, of course, because it has all the columns from the three tables. The dean doesn't want to see so much information. So, the second step is to retrieve only the columns the dean wants to see.

The Project operation retrieves columns:

```
Deans_View =
    Project Nickname, First_Name, Last_Name, Birthdate,
            City, State, Major, Grade_Point, Factoid, Summer_Plans
    From    Dean_Data_Collect
```

In English, the query says, "Save the Nickname column, First_Name column, and so forth, from the table, Dean_Data_Collect, that is formed by joining—that is, associating on Student_ID—the three tables Top_Scholar, Student, and Home_Base." This is precisely what the dean wants. The query defines the Deans_View table. Although the dean probably thinks the table exists physically, it is created fresh every time it's needed.

The join-then-trim strategy used to create the Dean's View is a standard approach to creating logical tables: a supertable is formed by joining several physical tables. These are then trimmed down to keep only the information of interest to the user. The Deans_View query used Project, but Select and Difference are also frequently used.

Software creates dean's view. If we add Top_Scholar to the Access database schema given in Figure 16.16, and include the one-to-one relationship between it and the other tables based on the Student_ID, as shown in Figure 16.17, then we can use Query By Example again to define the Dean's View, saving ourselves the effort of working out our own query, though writing SQL directly wouldn't be that difficult. Figure 16.23 shows the QBE window from Microsoft Access that defines the Dean's View from the three tables.

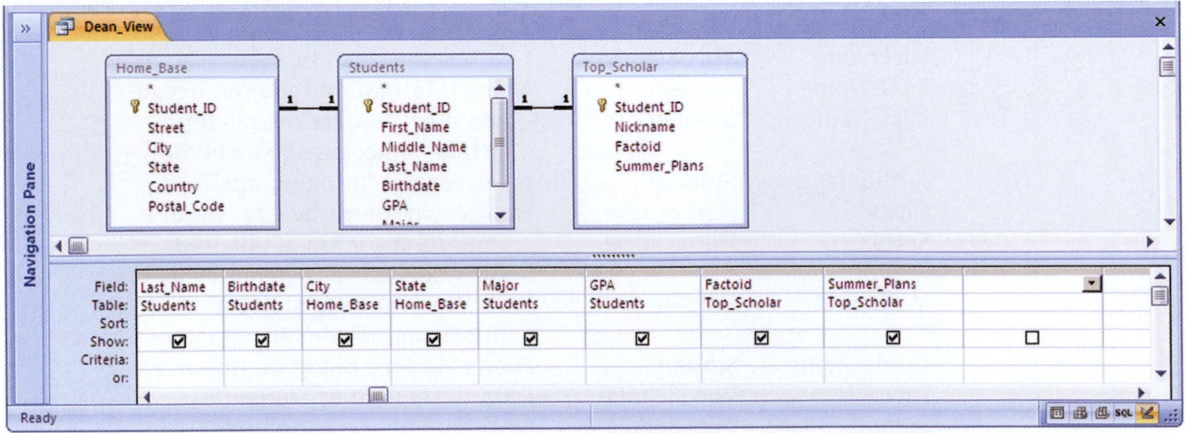

Figure 16.23 The Query By Example definition of the Dean's View table as expressed in Microsoft Access 2007.

For the record, the SQL query that Access produced for us based on our example from Figure 16.23 is shown in Figure 16.24. It is the identical query we developed ourselves, expressed in SQL syntax. (Notice that SQL uses the word "Select" where we used "Project"; the concepts are the same, but the term is different between the theory of relational databases and the SQL language. This naming inconsistency is an annoying feature of the study of databases.)

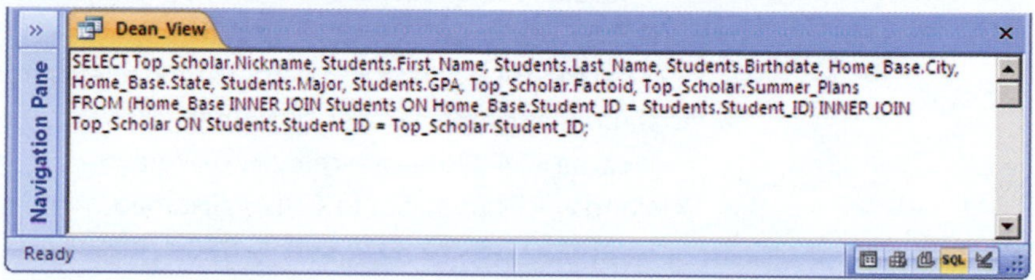

Figure 16.24 SQL query created for the Dean's View by the Query By Example data in Figure 16.22.

Summary

In this chapter we followed a path from XML tagging through to the construction of logical views using QBE. You learned a lot, including:

- XML tags are an effective way to record metadata in a file.
- Metadata is used to identify values, can capture the affinity among values of the same entity, and can collect together a group of entity instances.
- Database tables have names and fields that describe the attributes of the entity contained in the table.
- The data that quantitatively records each property has a specific data type and is atomic.
- There are five fundamental operations on tables: Select, Project, Union, Difference, and Product. These operations are the only ones you need to create new tables from other database tables.
- Join is an especially useful operation that associates information from separate tables in new ways, based on matching fields.
- Relationships are the key to associating fields of the physical database.
- The physical database resides on the disk drive; it avoids storing data redundantly and is optimized for speed.
- The main approach for creating logical views from physical data is the join-and-trim technique.
- There is a direct connection between the theoretical ideas of database tables and the software of database systems.

Try It Solutions

16.1 More Islands Using a tag name different from <elev> for the elevation is possible, but otherwise this is the one solution apart from spacing.

```
<archipelago>
   <island> <iName>Isabella</iName>
      <area>4588</area><elev>1707</elev>  </island>
   <island> <iName>Fernandina</iName>
      <area>642</area> <elev>1494</elev>  </island>
   <island> <iName>Tower</iName>
      <area>14</area>  <elev>76</elev>    </island>
   <island> <iName>Santa Cruz</iName>
      <area>986</area> <elev>846</elev>   </island>
</archipelago>
```

16.2 Joining Tutors

```
Assign = Nations ⋈ TravRev
         On (Nations.EW = TravRev.EW & Nations.NS = TravRev.NS)
```

Review Questions

Multiple Choice

1. If you know the structure and properties of data you can
   a. retrieve it
   b. organize it
   c. manage it
   d. all of the above

2. An important task when defining metadata is to
   a. identify the type of data
   b. normalize the data
   c. define the affinity of the data
   d. more than one of the above

3. Which of the following is an invalid XML tag?
   a. <address>
   b. <stud ID>
   c. <cellPhone>
   d. <SSN>

4. Which of the following is a valid XML tag?
   a. <active?>
   b. <grad-date>
   c. <zip code>
   d. <DOB>

5. The first tag in an XML document is known as a(n)
   a. metatag
   b. tree
   c. root element
   d. entity

6. An XML comment looks like
   a. `<!--Updated 09-26-09-->`
   b. `<! Updated 09-26-09 !>`
   c. `<" Updated 09-26-09 ">`
   d. `</ Updated 09-26-09>`

7. In database terminology, a set of entities refers to
   a. field
   b. column
   c. table
   d. information

8. The kind of information stored in a field in a database is described by the
   a. tuple
   b. field name
   c. data type
   d. record

9. A Project operation will
   a. return a table with as many rows as the original tables
   b. return only unique rows and merge duplicate rows
   c. automatically sort the list in alphabetical order by the first field
   d. all of the above

10. The *Test* in a Select command is used to
    a. add rows to an existing table
    b. remove rows from an existing table
    c. include rows in a new table
    d. describe rows in any table

11. Databases store data just once
    a. in order to avoid data redundancy
    b. because data storage is expensive
    c. because data access is slow
    d. all of the above

Short Answer

1. _______ is information describing other information.
2. A(n) _______ database uses tables to organize information.
3. XML is _______, that is, the tags create the structure of the data.
4. XML should be edited with a _______.
5. XML attribute values must be enclosed in _______.

6. A(n) _______ is a group of related items in an XML document.
7. The rules for XML encodings are a hierarchical description called _______.
8. _______ describe the relationships among the different kinds of data.
9. A(n) _______ is used to ensure that all entities in a database are unique.
10. Data that cannot be decomposed into smaller parts is considered _______.
11. A(n) _______ is a collection of table definitions that give the name of the table, list of the attributes and their data types, and identifies the primary key.
12. A(n) _______ is a specification using the five operations and Join that define a table from other tables.
13. A(n) _______ between two tables means that there is a corresponding row in one table for every row in the other table.

Exercises

1. Use XML to define your class schedule.
2. Create a list of IDs you have that could be considered primary keys in a database.
3. For the following, either indicate that the field is atomic or divide the field to make the result atomic.

Field	Contents
Phone	(212) 555-1212
Name	Maria Murray
Class	CSE100
City	Seattle, WA
DOB	September 26, 1948

4. Take your class schedule from Exercise 1 and define it as a database table.
5. Define the attribute names, data types, and optional comments needed to create a table that could be used as a datebook.
6. Write an operation to display the Name and Interest from the Nations table for those countries with Beach, and store it in a table called Vacation.
7. Create tables that might exist with your student information on campus. Include such areas as Registrar, Bursar, Library, Financial Aid, Food Service, Residence Halls, Parking, and so forth.
8. Take a look at one of your monthly bills, such as the cable bill, phone bill, or utility bill. What fields are used and what is their structure?
9. Using a text editor, create your own XML file containing CD or DVD information. Open the file in a browser.
10. Create a table with information from your driver's license.

A Case Study in Database Organization

The iDiary Database

17

chapter

learning objectives

- Explain the relationship between XML and XSL
- Describe how to express metadata using XML
- Demonstrate the incremental creation of a database
- Explain the relationship between tags and templates
- Show how to use tag attributes to display images
- State how information is hidden in XML databases

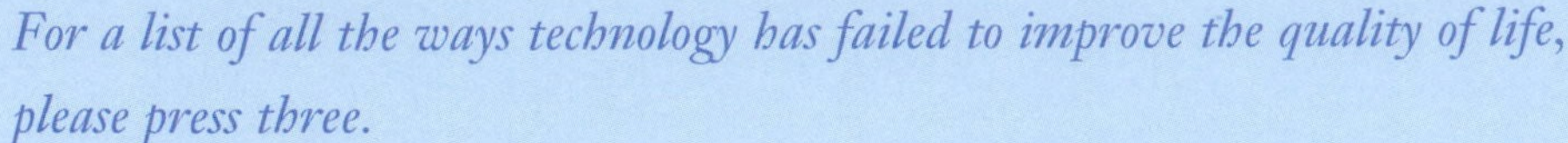
For a list of all the ways technology has failed to improve the quality of life, please press three.

—ALICE KAHN

MANY PEOPLE keep a diary, and in the Information Age it is natural to keep it in digital form. It's not a blog—that's for information to be shared with others. A diary is for one's own personal use, and it is not for public entertainment. Traditionally, diaries have been text only, handwritten, and organized linearly. But in the world of online information, a digital diary can contain a wide variety of electronic information, including links to Web sites, photos, animations, as well as the daily record of one's private thoughts. In this new form, a diary is not a linear chain of text, but a personal database. And that fact makes it an ideal topic for a case study in creating databases, an opportunity to learn database principles in a personally useful way.

In this chapter we build a diary database by applying the XML approach (see Chapter 16) to structure our data. That's our physical database. To display the iDiary, we convert the XML to HTML so it can be viewed with a browser. The conversion uses a language based on XML, called the Extensible Stylesheet Language, or XSL. Since the idea is that each of us will personalize a diary to our own needs, the database of this chapter only illustrates the *principles*. We create a fictional diary built around someone's record of the most interesting thing learned each day.

After illustrating an example of the database we will be creating, we review XML by constructing a small database recording the foreign countries we have visited. We then introduce XSL to display the Travels database. Prepared with the right knowledge, we incrementally build the iDiary database with its companion display information. We include text, titles, captions, images, videos, and poetry to illustrate how irregular data can be organized in a coherent, rational way. Finally, we consider how our database facilities will be used each day.

Thinking About a Personal Database

To start, we analyze the problem of making a personal database that can store any information that catches our interest. Though we will be thinking about how to solve the technical problems of database design, the discussion will guide us in the organization of the chapter as well.

Regular Versus Irregular Data

Relational databases, as discussed in the last chapter, can be expressed in neat tables with regular rows, attributes, keys, relationships, and so on. This regularity and the science of databases enable us to create queries in which computers do all of the difficult work of organizing and displaying the information we want to see. The key is the regularity of the data and the rigid structure imposed on it. Relational databases may be powerful, but very often the information we want to record isn't so regular. We need a more flexible approach. The iDiary database is an example of an irregular data collection.

fluencyALERT

All the Right Attributes. Despite being a chapter about databases, the heavy use of XML and XHTML implies that the word "attribute" will generally mean *tag* attribute in this context.

We record things in the iDiary that we find interesting in our daily lives, which can be almost anything: text, photos, URLs to interesting sites, animations, poems, videos, and so forth. Because we don't want to limit the kinds of information we can store, we will use XML to specify the metadata, implying the database will be an XML tree. In tagging the items stored in the database, we will use the Identity, Affinity, and Collection rules described in Chapter 16. In this way the computer can know what kinds of data it is storing.

Collecting information into a heap, however, is not enough organization. We need to impose some structure on the data. Organizing it helps us keep track of what we have, and it also helps the computer to display it. Since it is natural to think of the iDiary being added to each day, we will organize the database in time sequence, that is, by date. That's not much structure compared to a relational database, but it will be enough to make our irregular data orderly enough to be useful.

Physical Versus Logical

The XML tree will be our physical database. It is the structure into which we store the data. Because our database is mostly an archive rather than a "working database," we do not expect continuous revisions and updates, but only additions. That means we do not worry about the sorts of things that concern database administrators, like redundancy and access speed. All we want is convenience, which will still take some preparation.

The logical database is, of course, our view of the iDiary. If it were a relational database, we could specify queries to show the information of interest to us, merging tables to have just the information of importance. But the XML tree is not a relational database. Instead of using queries, we create a short description using XSL that picks out of the XML tree the data we want and says how to display it. **XSL** stands for **Extensible Stylesheet Language**, and it is a key part of the XML effort to standardize Web databases. The XSL description converts the data into HTML so that it can be displayed on the screen using a browser. As with all database views, the XSL approach gives us flexibility. We can decide to display everything in the XML tree, or we can choose instead only to display part of it—for example, the movie reviews—and leave everything else hidden. Therefore, the XSL description will be like our queries, plucking data from the physical database and showing us exactly what we want to see.

The iDiary

Our strategy will be to build the iDiary database and its stylesheet display together and incrementally. By beginning small and adding as we go, we will not be intimidated by a huge task. Also, if our small database is working and we then add some new feature to it, causing it not to work, we know that the error is in the part that was just added. This is a reliable way to limit the problems of debugging a complicated system. Finally, the step-by-step approach mirrors the way in which databases and other systems are enhanced over time. The plan will ensure success and be a good example for independent database projects.

Figure 17.1 shows a sample from the database we are creating. To familiarize yourself with the database, notice that the image of the database is a long list of daily entries. The entries are quite diverse—science news, poetry, book reviews, and other topics. Not only are these few entries interesting, but we expect that over time this will be a rich archive of factoids that we want to remember.

We build the iDiary after the next section. First, we need to explore the ideas with a practice database.

A Preliminary Exercise

To become familiar with the techniques of creating and displaying XML databases, let's take a moment to construct a separate application, which is a database of countries visited. This database will have a similar organization to the iDiary, but is much simpler, allowing us to focus on how it's done.

Use a Text Editor. Like XHTML, XML and XSL files should be written using a text editor like Notepad++ or TextWrangler rather than a word processor like Word or WordPerfect. Text editors give you only the text you see.

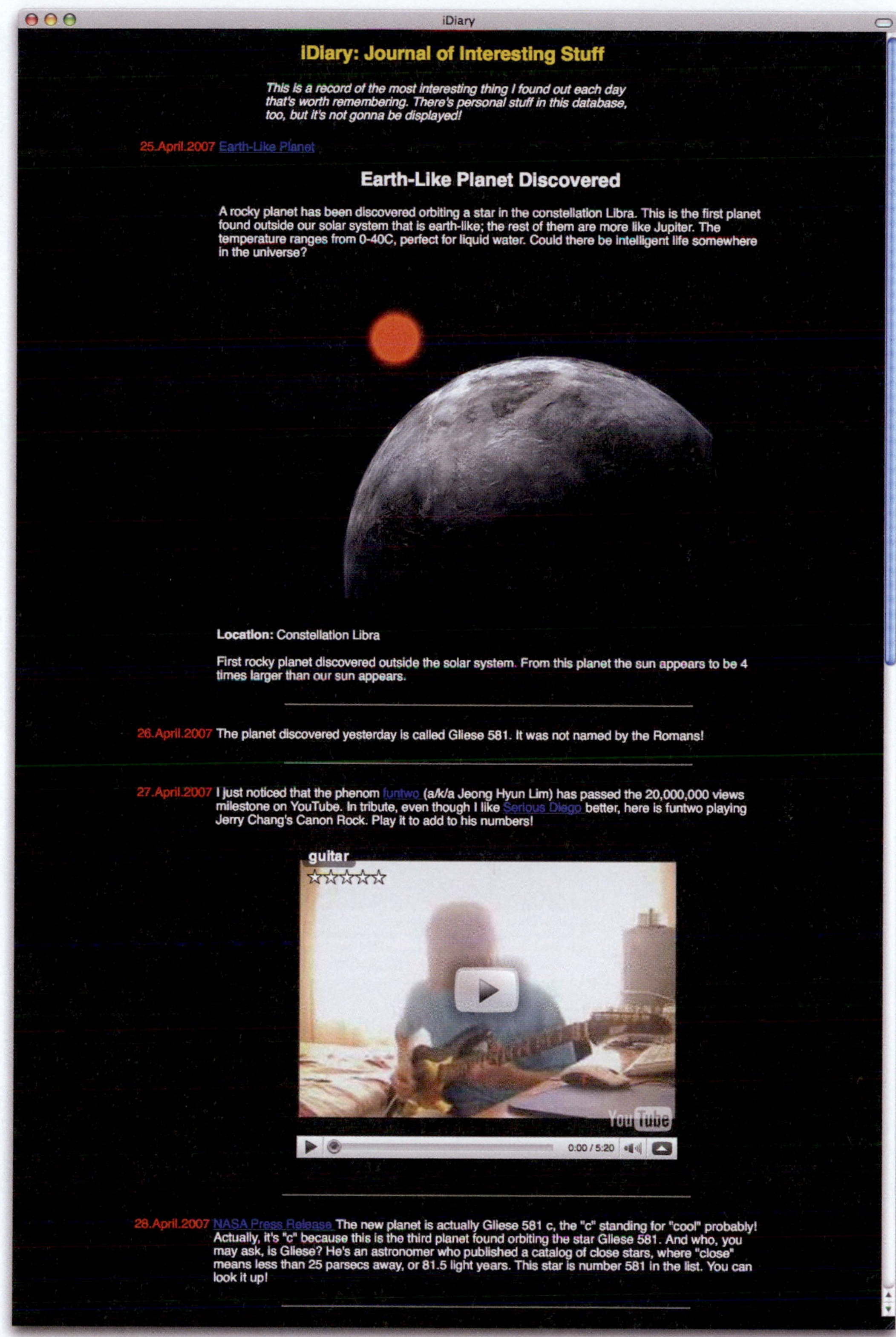

Figure 17.1 Part 1: An example of the planned iDiary.

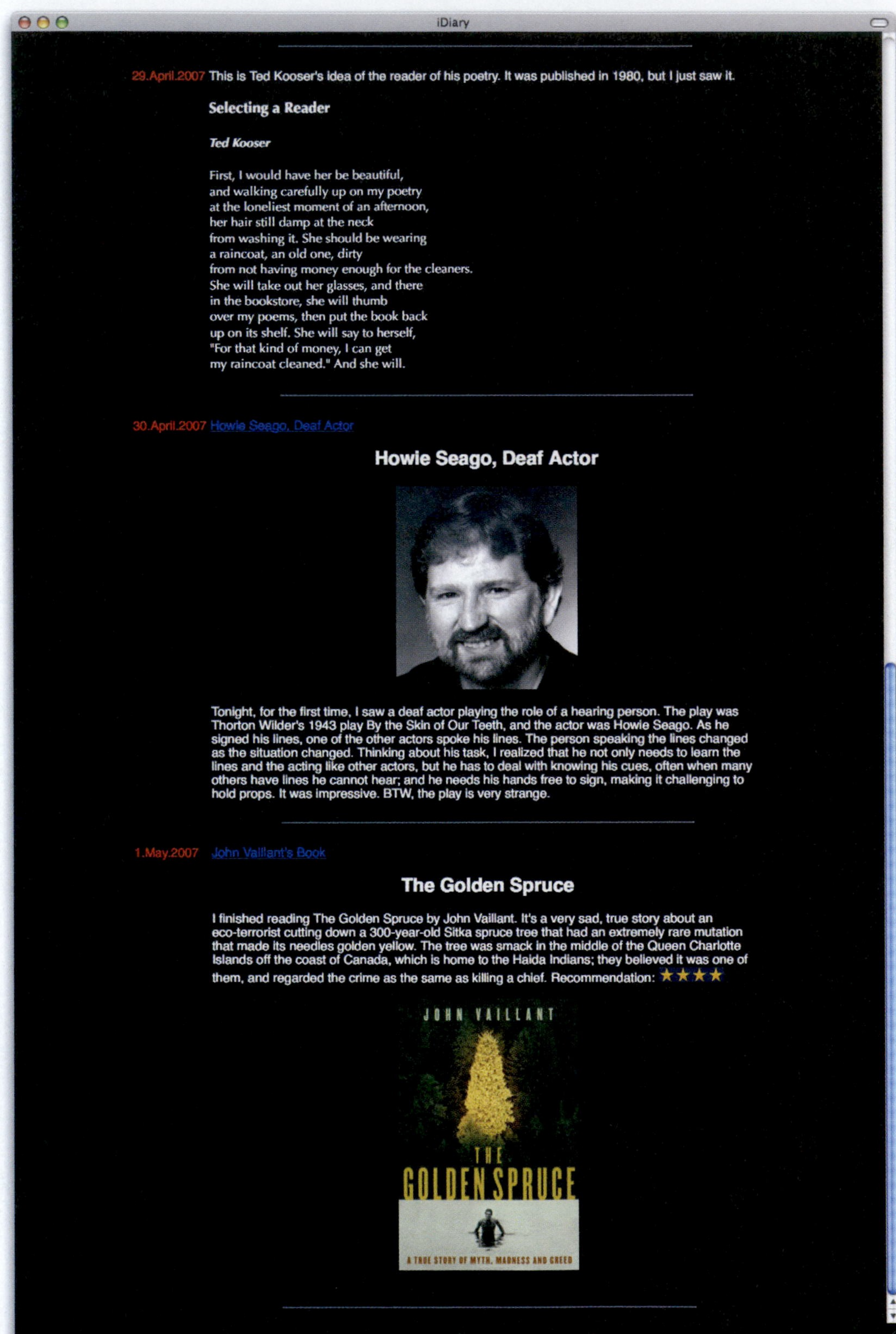

Figure 17.1 Part 2: An example of the planned iDiary.

Travels Database

Imagine that in our travels we have visited Italy, Switzerland, France, and Japan. Our database will list the countries, and for each country list a few places—usually cities—that we visited. We will use nontextual data by displaying the country's flag.

The XML definition. Our entries in the database will be a list of countries, and each will have a name and a tour that contains a list of sights. The name of the file containing the country's flag will be given as a tag attribute for the <name> tag. Therefore, the database will be a sequence of country instances with the structure

```
<country>
    <name flag="file.gif"> Country name </name>
    <tour>
        <sight> Sight name </sight>
        . . .
        <sight> Sight name </sight>
    </tour>
</country>
```

We use a standard text editor to enter the data into a file, tagging as we go. Recall that to identify the file as XML, we must give it the .xml file extension and include as the first line of the file this exact text:

```
<?xml version="1.0" encoding="ISO-8859-1"?>
```

Recalling that the root element is the Collective tag enclosing all items in an XML file, we make <travels> the root element of our tree, and within that we list countries using the structure just shown. Finally, we save the file as travels.xml.

Direct check of XML. We can have a browser display our XML as written by just opening the file with a browser, as shown in Figure 17.2. The browser looks for stylesheet information—we explain that momentarily—and finding none, because we have commented out the second line, it shows the XML tree. The color coding helps us to check that we have the structure right, and we verify that our intended organization is what the file contains. Notice that the display is active in that we can close and open tags used in the Affinity or Collective manner. For example, the inset in Figure 17.2 shows the result of closing the <tour> tags by clicking on the minus (–) signs. Closing parts of the database allows us to see the <country> tags without the clutter of the <tour> tags.

Error Console. Recall that Firefox tells you what it doesn't like about your Web pages on the Error Console (**Tools > Error Console**). Consult it when, for example, it displays your XML completely unformatted.

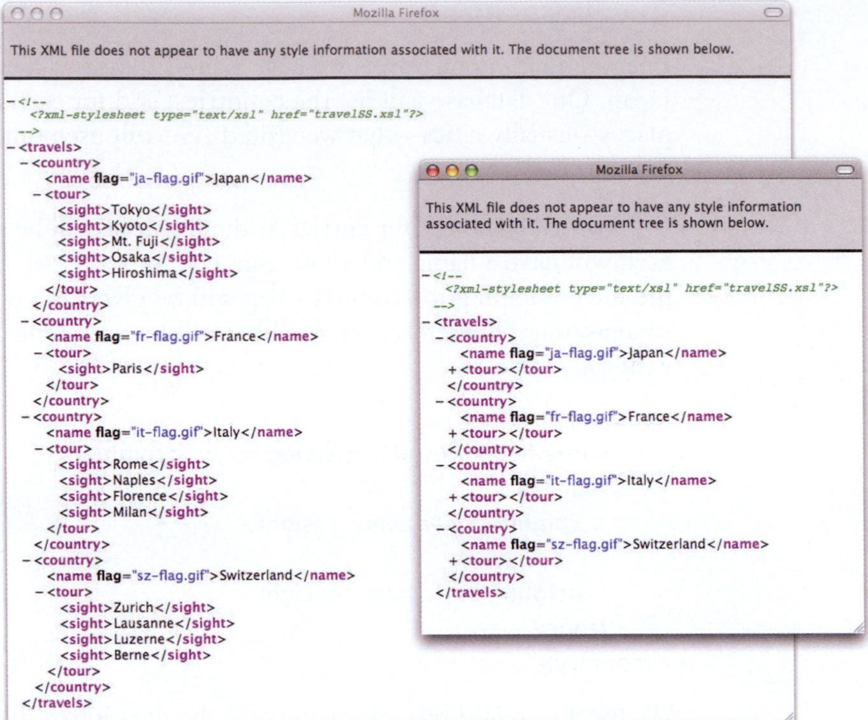

Figure 17.2 The display of the **travels.xml** file using the **Page Source** view of the Firefox browser.

Displaying the Travels with XSL

The message from the browser (in the Error Console) for the file in Figure 17.2 said that no style information was found. Style information tells the browser how to display a markup language like XML. Using the style information, the tags are eliminated and the information is displayed according to the style description. For example, the travels.xml file can be displayed as shown in Figure 17.3 using XSL, which is designed to provide the style information. In this section we discuss how to do this.

Connecting XML with style. Recall from Chapter 4 that the Cascading Style Sheet approach allows an XHTML page to have its style information included in an external file with a .css extension; the browser merges the two. XML uses the same idea, with the style information in an external file with an .xsl extension. So, we will put our style information in a file named travelSS.xsl. These two files get associated because we put in the XML file, as the second line, the text

```
<?xml-stylesheet type="text/xsl" href="travelSS.xsl"?>
```

which tells the browser, when it starts to process the XML file, where to find the style information. This is the line the browser didn't find in Figure 17.2. The line must be exactly as shown, except, of course, for the file name.

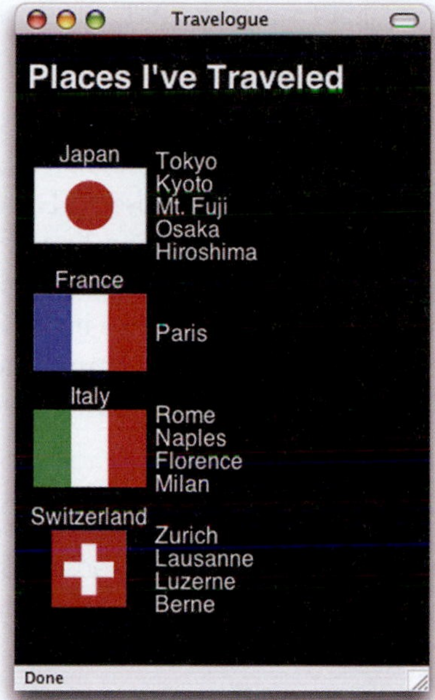

Figure 17.3 The display of the **travels.xml** file using the **travelSS.xsl** style information.

The idea of XSL. Here's how XSL formats XML. The .xsl file contains a series of rules on how to format the information enclosed in XML tags. Expect one rule per tag. The rules are called **templates** in XSL, because they describe how the information is to look without actually having the information. (The information, of course, is in the XML file.) How does the template describe how the information is to be displayed? It uses XHTML. And this is what makes XSL easy to learn: It is basically describing a page with the familiar XHTML.

Figure 17.4 shows this approach schematically. The database (DB) and stylesheet (SS) are input to a *transformer*—a part of the browser software—which "walks" the XML tree, converting all of the tags to HTML according to the template's specification. When an XML tag is found, the transformer looks up the template for that tag in the stylesheet file, and does what the template says, producing HTML, which is accumulated to be displayed at the end. Usually, each template gives a bit of HTML and the transformer "stuffs

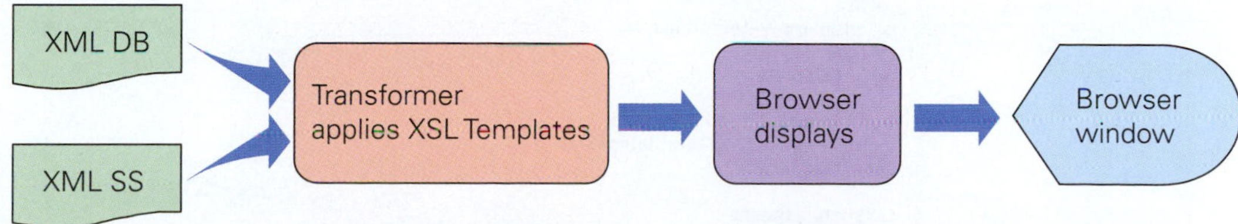

Figure 17.4 Schematic diagram showing how the XML database tree and the XSL style information are merged to produce HTML; the final HTML result is displayed by the browser.

in" the data from the XML file in the right places. Finally, when the "walk" of the XML tree is over, the HTML page is displayed.

XSL templates. It's time to look at some XSL templates. Figure 17.5 shows the XSL file used to display the image in Figure 17.3. Notice that there are tags everywhere. This is because XSL is really just XML! You will recognize the first line as the required first line of any XML file. The second line, also required, is a <xsl:stylesheet . . .> tag with tag attributes specifying the details of the stylesheet; these make it an XSL file. After that come the templates, one for each tag. Notice that because the <xsl:stylesheet . . .> tag is the root element of this XML file, it must be closed with </xsl:stylesheet> at the end.

Plain <html>. Notice that the XSL template in Figure 17.5 uses (in the template for **travels**) an <html> tag with no attributes, unlike Chapter 4. This plain <html> is correct when used in XSL templates.

```
<?xml version="1.0" encoding="utf-8" ?>
<xsl:stylesheet version="1.0"
  xmlns:xsl="http://www.w3.org/1999/XSL/Transform">

<xsl:template match="travels">
  <html>
    <head><title>Travelogue</title>
        <meta http-equiv="Content-Type"
              content="text/html; charset=utf-8"/>
      <style type="text/css">
        body {background-color : black; color : white;
              font-family : helvetica}
      </style>
    </head>
    <body>
      <h2>Places I've Traveled</h2>
        <table>
          <xsl:apply-templates/>
        </table>
    </body>
  </html>
</xsl:template>

<xsl:template match="country">
  <tr>
    <xsl:apply-templates/>
  </tr>
</xsl:template>

<xsl:template match="name">
  <td style="text-align : center">
    <xsl:apply-templates/><br/>
      <img src="{@flag}" alt="Country Flag"/>
  </td>
</xsl:template>

<xsl:template match="tour">
  <td>
    <xsl:apply-templates/>
  </td>
</xsl:template>

<xsl:template match="sight">
  <br/><xsl:apply-templates/>
</xsl:template>

</xsl:stylesheet>
```

Figure 17.5 The contents of the **travelSS.xsl** file that produced Figure 17.3.

There are five different tags used in the XML tree, and five templates in the XSL file, one for each. Notice that the templates have a standard form, which specifies how to display the tags in XHTML.

```
<xsl:template match="tag name">
   . . .
</xsl:template>
```

This match tag attribute tells which XML tag the template is for. Between the start and end tags is the specification in XHTML (and possibly other XSL tags) for how to display the XML.

Use the Right Style for XSL. XSL files must be identified as such, and so they are required to begin with the standard XML tag on the first line

```
<?xml version = "1.0" encoding="ISO-8859-1"?>
```

followed by the required XSL tag

```
<xsl:stylesheet version="1.0"
   xmlns:xsl="http://www.w3.org/1999/XSL/Transform">
```

on the second line. The file should be ASCII text, and the extension should be .xsl.

Because there are tags everywhere, it is important to understand how the computer tells them all apart—it's a good way for us to tell them apart! The tag at the start <?xml . . .?> is the standard XML tag. The tags beginning with <xsl: . . .> are XSL tags. The rest of the tags are XHTML tags. So, when the transformer is using this file to look up how to display the XML, it can keep everything straight.

Next, we explain how each of the templates works.

Creating the travelogue display. Consider the templates of travelSS.xsl. The first template, which matches the <travels> XML tag, has the form

```
<xsl:template match="travels">
  <html>
    <head><title>Travelogue</title>
        <meta http-equiv="Content-Type"
             content="text/html; charset=ISO-8859-1"/>
      <style type="text/css">
        body {background-color : black; color : white;
              font-family : helvetica}
      </style>
    </head>
    <body>
      <h2>Places I've Traveled</h2>
        <table>
          <xsl:apply-templates/>
        </table>
    </body>
  </html>
</xsl:template>
```

Start of the HTML page

End of the HTML page

Notice that between the <xsl:template . . .> tags are XHTML tags, which you might recognize as the start of a Web page and the end of that same Web page. (We explain the <xsl:apply . . .> momentarily.) This template says that whenever the transformer encounters a <travels> tag in the XML file, it should include this XHTML text as a description of how to display the <travels> tag. Of course, there is only one <travels> tag in the XML file, because it is the root element tag of the XML tree. So, the way to display this one tag is to set up the Web page for the display. Then, as the other tags are processed, they will fill in other parts of the page.

You can see that the template includes the necessary heading and body tags to make the image shown in Figure 17.3. At the "deepest point" in these tags are <table> tags, because the content of the travels.xml file is going to be displayed as a table. Each <country> will be a row in this table, with the general structure

Info for <name> tag Flag display here	<sight> entry . . . <sight> entry

This structure calls for two items in the first cell of the table—the name and the flag image—and a list of items in the second cell, depending on how many sights there are in a tour.

We know that a row of the table will correspond to each <country> tag, because the template matching "country" places the <tr> tags for the table rows. Also, the <name> tag and the <tour> tags place the table data tags <td>. The following table summarizes the style roles of the XML tags we have.

XML Tag	XSL Template Task for Displaying the Tag's Data
<travels>	Set up the page, start and finish, including the tags for a table.
<country>	Set up a table row.
<name>	Set up the table data tags for the first cell of a row, place the name, skip to the next line, and place the image of the flag.
<tour>	Set up the table data tags for the second cell.
<sight>	Break to a new line and display the sight.

Each XML tag has a stylistic role to play in the overall creation of the Web page.

How does the data get inside the table data tags? As the transformer is processing the XML file, it is always looking for tags and trying to match them to the templates of the XSL file. Anything it finds that is not a tag—that is, the actual data—it puts directly into the XHTML definition. So, to get the content of the file displayed requires no effort at all.

The apply operation. A curious aspect of the XSL specification in Figure 17.5 is the

```
<xsl:apply-templates/>
```

tag. We know from the /> that this is a stand-alone tag, like <br/>, with no mate. Also, notice that the tag is included once in each of the templates. The <xsl:apply-templates/> tag means, "now process whatever is inside this tag." So, for example, the template matching <tour>:

```
<xsl:template match="tour">
    <td>
        <xsl:apply-templates/>
    </td>
</xsl:template>
```

can be expressed in English as: "When encountering a <tour> tag, place a <td> tag in the accumulating XHTML definition; then process the items found within the <tour> tag, which as we know will be a bunch of <sight> tags; finally, when that processing is over, place the </td> tag to complete the table data specification."

Notice that although the tag is called apply-templates, it really means, "now process whatever is inside this tag," even though it may not have any more tagged items, but only data. As you now know, when actual data is encountered, the transformer simply puts the data into the accumulating XHTML definition, which is what we want.

17.1 Emphasize Paragraphs. Write an XSL template that styles text enclosed in the XML tag <emph> as a paragraph in which all text is both bold and italic.

Tag attributes. Of special interest is the template matching the <name> tag, whose definition is

```
<xsl:template match="name">
    <td style="text-align : center">
        <xsl:apply-templates/><br />
            <img src="{@flag}" alt="Country Flag"/>
    </td>
</xsl:template>
```

The template obviously places <td> tags for the left cell of the table row, but it is also responsible for including in its cell the image of the flag. To display an image requires the <img src . . ./> tag, of course, as can be seen on the fourth line. It has the usual form except for {@flag}. The @flag refers to the value of the tag attribute of the <name> tag, which gives the file name of the *flag*.gif; see the XML in Figure 17.2. By placing a tag attribute reference in braces in the XSL, we cause the tag attribute's value from the XML to be placed inside the quotes specifying the file source name, as shown next.

```
<name flag="fr-flag.gif">
  France        <img src="{@flag}".../> ——> <img src="fr-flag.gif"/>
</name>
```

This is a standard technique for placing information in matched quotes, and we will have several opportunities to use it.

Summary of XSL. When we open our travels.xml file with a browser, it looks to see what style information is provided. It finds that we specifed the travelSS.xsl file. After opening the style file, the browser's transformer begins to process the XML tree. Finding the <travels> tag first, it checks for a template in the .xsl file. Finding one, it does what the template says: Place the starting XHTML commands in the XHTML definition up to a <table> tag, then process the other information within the <travels> tag. When that's done, it appends the remaining XHTML tags to the XHTML definition, and, when finished, displays the resulting Web page.

While processing "the other information within the <travels> tag," the transformer encounters more tags, which it matches with templates and follows their style specifications. Somewhere within each of those templates, there is a <xsl:apply-templates/> tag, which requests processing of the information that the tag encloses. The process continues: match a template, do what needs to be done before processing the enclosed information, process the enclosed information, do what needs to be done after processing the enclosed information, and consider that tag processed. It's a very elegant scheme.

That's all you need to know about XSL, although it is a rich, complex language that gives much more power than we need to manage our iDiary.

The iDiary Database

We are now ready to create the iDiary displayed in Figure 17.1. As explained earlier, we solve the problem incrementally, beginning small and adding more information and greater ability to process it as a Web page. It's a good strategy when creating anything significant.

Computer Tutor. Read the following sections at a computer, and build the database along with the text; this is an extremely effective way to learn these concepts. Moreover, when finished you will have a database into which you can place your own curious information. Find all the necessary files at www.aw.com/snyder/.

The incremental approach will naturally lead us to follow these steps:

1. Getting started
2. Creating a first entry (April 26)

3. Thinking about the nature of things
4. Developing tags and templates
5. Critiquing and evaluating the results

These five steps will be the section headings for the following explanations.

Getting Started

Our first concern is building the XML database that will be the physical repository of our iDiary. Because XML allows us to think up the tags, and therefore lets us have any structure we want, we have a design task: We must figure out our needs and design a structure that meets those needs. In the present case, we need an XML tree in which we can store information about the interesting and curious things that we encounter in our daily lives. This naturally suggests a *sequence* of entries, perhaps one per day, which have a date entry and then the information that we are storing.

Creating the XML database. With only this small amount of thinking, we can make two decisions about our XML database: First, we can decide on <entry> tags as the Affinity tags to enclose the information we add each day, and second, because we need a root element to enclose the <entry> tags, we can choose <idiary> as our Collection tag. So, with these two tags decided upon, we can already create a database that contains no data. We create a file with our text editor called iDiary.xml and enter into it

```
<?xml version = "1.0"
    encoding="ISO-8859-1"?>
<!--<?xml-stylesheet
    type="text/xsl"
    href="iDiarySS.xsl"?> -->

<idiary>
    <entry> This is the first entry </entry>
    <entry> This is the second entry </entry>
</idiary>
```

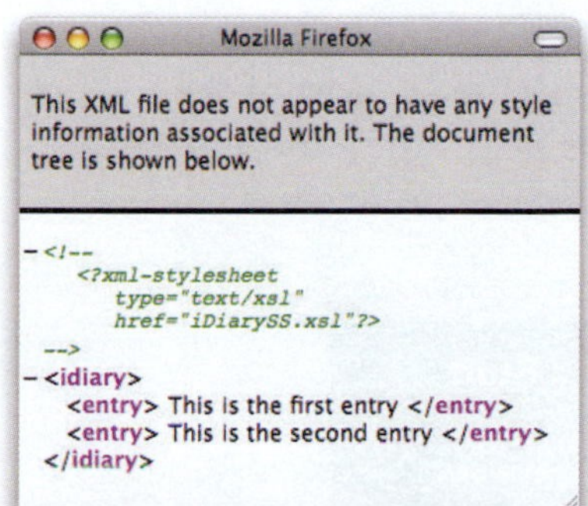

which has the form displayed at left. Notice that the stylesheet specification has been commented out (see the green text in the browser window), because we do not have a style file defined. We know we will need it, and have decided to call it iDiarySS.xsl. We can begin building it, now, too.

Creating the XSL stylesheet. The XSL stylesheet will need to recognize the two kinds of tags. Using our earlier Travels database as a guideline, we decide to set up the page with the root element <idiary>, and have the <entry> tags produce successive rows of a table. (Of course, the table has only one column at the moment.) Using a text editor we enter the following lines in the iDiarySS.xsl file.

```
<?xml version="1.0" encoding="UTF-8"?>
<xsl:stylesheet version="1.0"
    xmlns:xsl="http://www.w3.org/1999/XSL/Transform"
<xsl:template match="idiary">
    <html>
    <head><title>iDiary</title>
        <style type="text/css">
            body {background-color : black; color : white;
                font-family : helvetica}
            h2 {text-align : center }
            table {margin-left : auto; margin-right : auto}
        </style>
    </head>
    <body>
        <h2 style="color:gold">iDiary: Journal of Interesting Stuff</h2>
        <table style="max-width:425px">
            <tr><td>
                <i>This is a record of the most interesting thing I found out
                each day that's worth remembering. There's personal stuff in
                this database, too, but it's not gonna be displayed!</i>
            </td></tr>
        </table><br/>
        <table>
            <xsl:apply-templates/>
        </table>
    </body>
    </html>
</xsl:template>

<xsl:template match="entry">
    <tr><td>
        <xsl:apply-templates/>
    </td></tr>
</xsl:template>

</xsl:stylesheet>
```

This contains the setup for the Web page, with the title, heading, and italicized comment at the start of the page. (A separate table was used for the italicized comment to keep it compact and narrower than the main table of entries.) The table containing the entries is also specified as part of the <idiary> template. The template for <entry> tags places the <tr> and <td> tags, and then processes the entry itself. This stylesheet produces

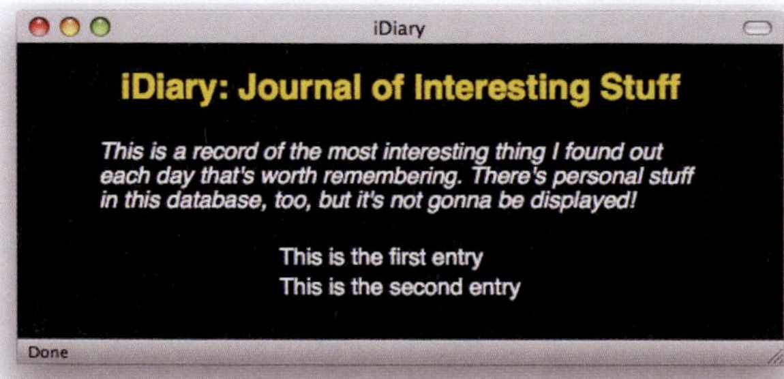

when we uncomment the stylesheet tag (the second line) of the XML file and open the XML file with Firefox.

With the XML and the XSL files started, the iDiary project is well underway.

Creating a First Entry (April 26)

Continuing our design planning, we consider what goes inside of each <entry> tag. We start with the April 26th entry because it is very simple. Since the entry is the entity that we're putting in the database, the items enclosed are the attributes (using the database terminology introduced in the previous chapter). Obviously, the date is one attribute and, of course, there must be some actual content. This motivates two more tags, <date> and <mit>, which is an abbreviation for "most interesting thing." (Tags don't have to make sense to anyone but you, though it is often helpful to put in a comment saying what the tag means since you will almost certainly forget.)

Date tagging. This sounds like a party game, but it refers to the decisions surrounding the metadata for calendar dates. As noted in Chapter 16, data in databases is atomic. If we write

```
<date>April 26, 2007</date>
```

we cannot refer to the day, month, and year separately, though, as we mentioned, some commercial database systems let us cheat. In the XML-XSL approach, if we want to control the formatting specially for dates, we need tags surrounding each of the components.

That might motivate us to put tags around the parts now, even if we don't have immediate plans to do something fancy, because we could add fancy formatting in the future.

On the other hand,

```
<date><month>April</month><day>26</day><year>2007</year></date>
```

is a lot to type just to enter the date, and there are many ways to change the date structure later if we decide we need the whole date tagged. So, being lazy, we decide to let it be atomic, and pick a date format we like and simply surround it with tags.

17.2 It's a date. Assuming the fully tagged form of the date just shown, write the XSL templates to produce *November* 22, 2009, that is, the month is italic, the day is large, and the year is small.

Revising an <entry>. With the two new tags decided upon, we can revise the two temporary <entry> tags used earlier and replace them in the iDiary.xml file with the following single structure:

```
<entry>
    <date>26.April.2007</date>
    <mit> The planet discovered yesterday is called Gliese 581. It was not
        named by the Romans!
    </mit>
</entry>
```

Having added tags, we need to add templates to the iDiary.xsl file. The <entry> tag places the <tr> tags as before, but no longer places <td> tags. Its structure is

```
<xsl:template match="entry">
    <tr>
        <xsl:apply-templates/>
    </tr>
</xsl:template>
```

To handle the two new tags, we make a two-column table. The first column is assigned to the date, and the second column is assigned to the most interesting thing. The appropriate templates are

```
<xsl:template match="date">
    <td>
        <xsl:apply-templates/>
    </td>
</xsl:template>

<xsl:template match="mit"> <!-- Most Interesting Thing -->
    <td>
        <xsl:apply-templates/>
    </td>
</xsl:template>
```

which results in the following page, displaying the data for the April 26th entry in two columns.

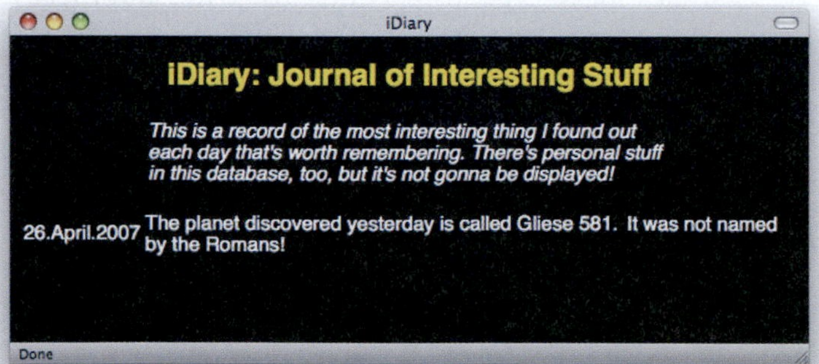

Critiquing the design. In any design, it is wise to critique the result to determine if it meets our needs. The new page has two columns—one for the date and one for the entry—which is a rational way to present the information. The style could use some work, however.

One aspect that could be improved is the position of the date. The table row is two lines wide, causing the date to be centered vertically in its cell. We prefer to have the date at the top of the cell, so we revise its table data styling to include vertical alignment to the top. Another feature we'd like to modify is the color of the date; we prefer red, thinking it might enhance the page. So, we revise the template to

```
<xsl:template match="date">
    <td class="day">
        <xsl:apply-templates/>
    </td>
</xsl:template>
```

and add

```
td.day {vertical-align : top; color : red}
```

to the global style section, which produces the right result.

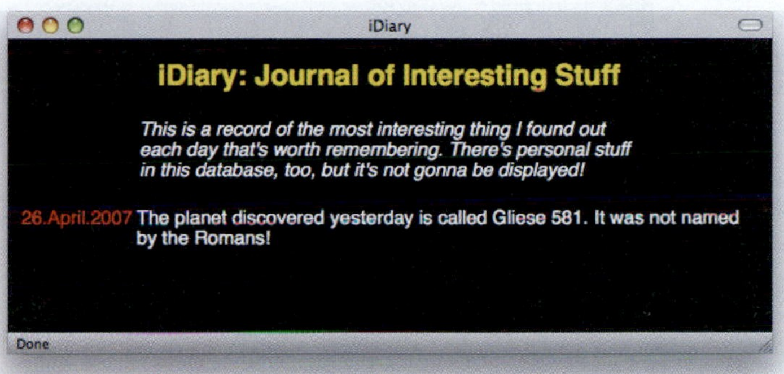

Thinking About the Nature of Things

The second column is for the "most interesting thing" we learn each day, but as Figure 17.1 shows, this entity can take many forms. The different kinds of data—the most interesting thing's attributes—affect both the XML and the XSL definitions.

Recognizing the need for specific tags. When considering the design of the XML, notice that we must specify different data for each type of content that we attribute to an entity. The following list includes some examples.

Type	Specification
Link	URL
Image	Source file, and possibly width and height
Text	Written directly into the file, possibly with a special font
Video	URL, player dimensions, other parameters

Each of these requires that we specify different information. They also require different formatting. Additionally, the text can take several different forms, including:

Type	Style
Titles	Centered with enlarged sized
Captions	Labeled caption, left justified
Poems	Title, author, and line breaks at specific points

We cannot use a single type of tag if we intend to recognize these differences.

Choosing specific tags. Knowing that different kinds of data need different tags—or, stating it in database terms, each attribute requires its own tag—we assign a new tag to each kind of data we store in the iDiary database. Accordingly, we propose to use the following tags for the iDiary.

Tag	Encloses
<fact>	Normal text—the most interesting thing
<title>	Text to be centered; font is enlarged
<link>	Anchor text; the URL is a tag attribute
<pic>	Stand-alone tag with file name, width, and height as tag attributes
<remark>	Text to be left justified; for caption, include the word Caption, etc.
<poem>	Groups <p_title>, <poet>, and <lines> tags
<ytvideo>	URL of video

The <poem> tag is an Affinity tag grouping three other tags that give the title of the poem, the author, and the lines. Notice that in addition to <title> we include a <p-title> for the poems. The difference is that <title> will be centered and larger than the normal text, abstracting the idea of a heading; the <p-title> captures the idea of the title for a literary work, which will be italicized and not centered. Such distinctions are small, but if we recognize differences among the properties of an object or we are fussy about how we want our iDiary to look, we add tags to recognize such differences. And why not? Tags are free, and templates take half a minute to write.

The tags just listed are sufficient to handle the kinds of data displayed in Figure 17.1, but as new kinds of information present themselves, we can introduce more tags. Our database system can evolve to meet our needs.

Notice that because we recognized the need for different tags for different kinds of information that describe the most interesting thing, the role of the <mit> tag changes slightly. Previously it was an Identification tag, and it enclosed the most interesting thing, as if it were just a single thing, such as text. But because we now understand that the most interesting things can have many properties as identified by the foregoing tags, the role of the <mit> tag becomes that of an Affinity tag. It groups together all of the different forms of information that we associate with the most interesting thing for one day.

The change in the way we think of the <mit> tag is only a change in our thinking: The <mit> tag is still a sister to the <date> tag in the XML tree, it still identifies the most interesting thing, and its style role continues to be to place <td> tags.

Developing Tags and Templates

Having worked out that we need several new tags, we take a moment to think about each of them, because some have characteristics that need discussing. With each, we give its companion stylesheet template.

The fact tag. The simplest is the <fact> tag. It encloses text

```
<fact>The planet discovered yesterday is called
   Gliese 581. It was not named by the Romans!
</fact>
```

that is displayed with a line break at the end, as in

```
<xsl:template match="fact">
    <xsl:apply-templates/>
        <br/>
</xsl:template>
```

Keep in mind that the <fact> is enclosed by the <mit> tag.

The title tag. The <title> tag announces the most interesting thing entry, when appropriate.

```
<title>Earth-Like Planet Discovered</title>
```

The text should be centered and can use the XHTML heading tags to enlarge the font.

```
<xsl:template match="title">
    <h2>
        <xsl:apply-templates/>
    </h2>
</xsl:template>
```

The link tag. The <link> tag specifies a Web link. As usual, the Web link has two parts: The tag encloses the anchor text—the highlighted text of the link—and the URL is specified using the tag attribute of that name. For example,

```
<link
   url="http://www.npr.org/templates/story/story.php?storyId=9796321">
   Earth-Like Planet
</link>
```

illustrates the structure. The stylesheet must place an <a href...> tag and enclose the tag attribute value in quotes. A template to do that is

```
<xsl:template match="link">
    <a href="{@url}">
        <xsl:apply-templates/>
    </a>
</xsl:template>
```

As explained earlier in this chapter, the @ symbol is the XSL reference to the tag attribute of the XML tag. By enclosing the reference in curly braces, we can place the tag attribute's value in the XHTML text.

The picture tag. The <pic> tag is a stand-alone tag because all of its information is expressed as tag attributes. The tag encodes the file name of the image and its desired display width and display height, as shown in this next example.

```
<pic file="planet.jpg" width="500" height="360"/>
```

Note that as a stand-alone tag, <pic . . ./> is terminated by the />.

```
<xsl:template match="pic">
    <img src="{@file}" width="{@width}" height="{@height}"
        alt="Picture of Interesting Thing"/>
</xsl:template>
```

Of course, being a stand-alone tag, it does not enclose anything. Accordingly, there is no need for the <xsl:apply-templates/> tag that would normally request continued processing of the enclosed tags or content. This makes the <pic> tag slightly different from those we've seen. To have the pictures centered, we add appropriate styling to the global styling section: img {text-align : center}.

The remark tag. Content such as captions and other small pieces of text that serve in a labeling role will use the <remark> tag. In addition to having a different role than the title, they differ in style: The text is the same size as the <fact> text and it is left justified rather than centered. For example:

```
<remark>Location: Constellation Libra</remark>
```

Because <remark> text may follow facts, pictures, and other items, it is necessary to include a break to ensure that they appear on their own line. Thus, the template is

```
<xsl:template match="remark">
    <br/>
        <xsl:apply-templates/>
    <br/>
</xsl:template>
```

By classifying different types of text, we keep tight control on the format of the page.

The poetry tags. We identify several attributes of poetry—title, author, and lines—and assign tags to each. These will all be enclosed in the Affinity tag <poem>. As noted earlier, we do not use the <title> tag to title a poem. Rather, we invent another, <p_title> tag, which will also allow for different formatting. So, an example is

```
<poem>
    <p_title>Trees, Excerpt</p_title>
    <poet>Joyce Kilmer</poet>
        <line> . . . </line>
        <line>Poems are made by fools like me,</line>
        <line>But only God can make a tree.</line>
</poem>
```

The templates for these new tags are, by now, straightforward. They are

```
<xsl:template match="poem">
    <span style="font-family: optima">
        <xsl:apply-templates/>
    </span>
</xsl:template>
```

which only encloses other tags, and styles them with a more attractive font. These are also:

```
<xsl:template match="p_title">
    <h3>
        <xsl:apply-templates/>
    </h3>
</xsl:template>

<xsl:template match="poet">
    <h4><i>
        <xsl:apply-templates/>
    </i></h4>
</xsl:template>

<xsl:template match="line">
        <xsl:apply-templates/>
    <br/>
</xsl:template>
```

The poetry formatting will not be sufficient for poets like e. e. cummings, but we put that problem off for another day.

The video tag. The best way to include videos in the iDiary is to display a player as an embedded object. The <object> tag is part of XHTML for incorporating multimedia, and the YouTube site, like many others, expecting us to use the <object> tag to run their videos, provides all of the necessary XHTML in a window pane labeled *Embed*, shown just below the URL in Figure 17.6.

Figure 17.6 YouTube display marking the embedding information.

The embedding information, which we can copy and paste, has the following form.

```
<object width="425" height="344">
    <param name="movie"
    value="http://www.youtube.com/v/QjA5faZF1A8&hl=en&fs=1"></param>
    <param name="allowFullScreen" value="true"></param>
    <param name="allowscriptaccess" value="always"></param>
    <embed src="http://www.youtube.com/v/QjA5faZF1A8&hl=en&fs=1"
        type="application/x-shockwave-flash" allowscriptaccess="always"
        allowfullscreen="true" width="425" height="344">
    </embed>
</object>
```

This is obviously XHTML, but mysterious XHTML to us. However, we can avoid learning all of the details of this XHTML by recognizing that the only part that changes from video to video is the URL; all of the rest of it is the same each time we want to embed a YouTube video. So, our new XML video tag needs only to capture the URL in a tag attribute; the rest of the <object> information can go into the template. Using the tag attribute for the URL makes it very similar to the <pic . . ./> tag Thus, our stand-alone video tag has this form:

```
<ytvideo utube="http://www.youtube.com/v/QjA5faZF1A8"/>
```

Notice that we name the tag <ytvideo . . ./> rather than, say, <video . . .>, because we are placing all of the display information in the template, which is special to YouTube. Other video sources might use different embedding tags with different values; if so, we can make a tag for videos from those sources. Also, unlike the <pic . . ./> tag, we do not specify the width and height for each video, because the player is the same dimensions every time.

The <ytvideo . . .> template contains all of the information from the YouTube *Embed* pane, except for the two URLs. We notice that they are the same, so we simply reference them, using the familiar {@ . . .} structure to reference the tag attribute. The template is

```
<xsl:template match="ytvideo">
    <object width="425" height="344">
        <param name="movie" value="{@utube}"></param>
        <param name="allowFullScreen" value="true"></param>
        <param name="allowscriptaccess" value="always"></param>
        <embed src="{@utube}" type="application/x-shockwave-flash"
            allowscriptaccess="always" allowfullscreen="true"
            width="425" height="344">
        </embed>
    </object>
</xsl:template>
```

Notice that because <ytvideo . . .> is a stand-alone tag like <pic . . ./>, we do not need to process any enclosed information, so we do not need an <xsl:apply-templates/> tag.

Finally, we might expect to specify the tag as

```
<ytvideo utube="http://www.youtube.com/v/QjA5faZF1A8&hl=en&fs=1"/>
```

because that is the URL from YouTube's embed information. But, the last 11 characters contain two ampersands. These are parameters (see Chapter 20) specifying that the browser should use English (&hl=en) and it should display with a full screen (&fs=1), which we don't even want. However, the main problem is that we cannot use ampersands literally in XML or XHTML. They have to be escaped: &. So, if we want to include these last 11 characters, we must replace the & with &, but the better thing to do is just to delete them.

A check of the design. We have added a variety of tags and templates. Normally, we check each new tag and each associated template as we create them. To summarize what we have done, we created the small page shown in Figure 17.7, and display it using a browser as shown in Figure 17.8.

Critiquing and Evaluating the Results

As always, once a design is finished, it must be evaluated to see that it meets our needs. In Figure 17.8, we see several features worth reconsidering.

Form of entries. The two sample entries seem to run together. Because this is a digital diary, we are not wasting paper if we space out the entries. So, we decide to add some breaks and a horizontal line at the end of the <mit>

```
<?xml version = "1.0" encoding="ISO-8859-1" ?>
<?xml-stylesheet type="text/xsl" href="iDiarySS.xsl"?>
<idiary>
 <entry>
  <date>25.April.2007</date>
  <mit>
   <link url="http://www.npr.org/ ">Earth-like Planet</link>
   <title>Earth-like Planet Discovered</title>
   <fact>A rocky planet has been discovered orbiting a star in the
       constellation Libra. This is the first planet found outside our
       solar system that is earth-like; the rest of them are more like
       Jupiter. Is there intelligent life somewhere in the universe?
   </fact>
   <pic file="planet.jpg" width="125" height="90"/>
   <remark>Location: Constellation Libra</remark>
  </mit>
 </entry>
 <entry>
  <date>27.April.2007</date>
  <mit>
   <fact>These are Kilmer's most famous lines. </fact>
   <poem>
    <p_title>Trees, Excerpt</p_title>
    <poet>Joyce Kilmer</poet>
     <line> . . . </line>
     <line>Poems are made by fools like me,</line>
     <line>But only God can make a tree.</line>
    </poem>
    <ytvideo utube="http://www.youtube.com/v/QjA5faZF1A8"/>
  </mit>
 </entry>
</idiary>
```

Figure 17.7 Sample database entries for checking the iDiary tags and templates.

template to separate it from the entry that follows. This change is straightforward.

Also, we notice that the entry tends to spread out horizontally, as the browser expands the table to fill the available screen real estate. (The image has been purposely shown tiny to emphasize this point.) It might be more attractive if the entries are more compact, so that the text and pictures are more in scale. How do we make the entry compact? We limit the size of the table by adding a width specification to the template. Adopt a size of, say, 700 pixels, as in `<table style="max-width:700px">`.

Our `<pic . . ./>` tag gives the ability to control the size of the images using the width and height tag attributes. Having adopted 700 pixels as the width of our `<mit>` entry, we should scale our images so their width is no more than 700.

Scaling Images. Recall that images have a width and height given in pixels. This can be adjusted using graphics software, but it is not necessary. Simply scale (divide) both sizes by the same amount (rounding down to give a whole number), and use those values as the **width** and **height**.

Remarks on <remark>. The <remark> tag—the tag used for the Location information in Figure 17.8—should have the word Location emphasized in bold. This change has nothing to do with the type of data; we just prefer a

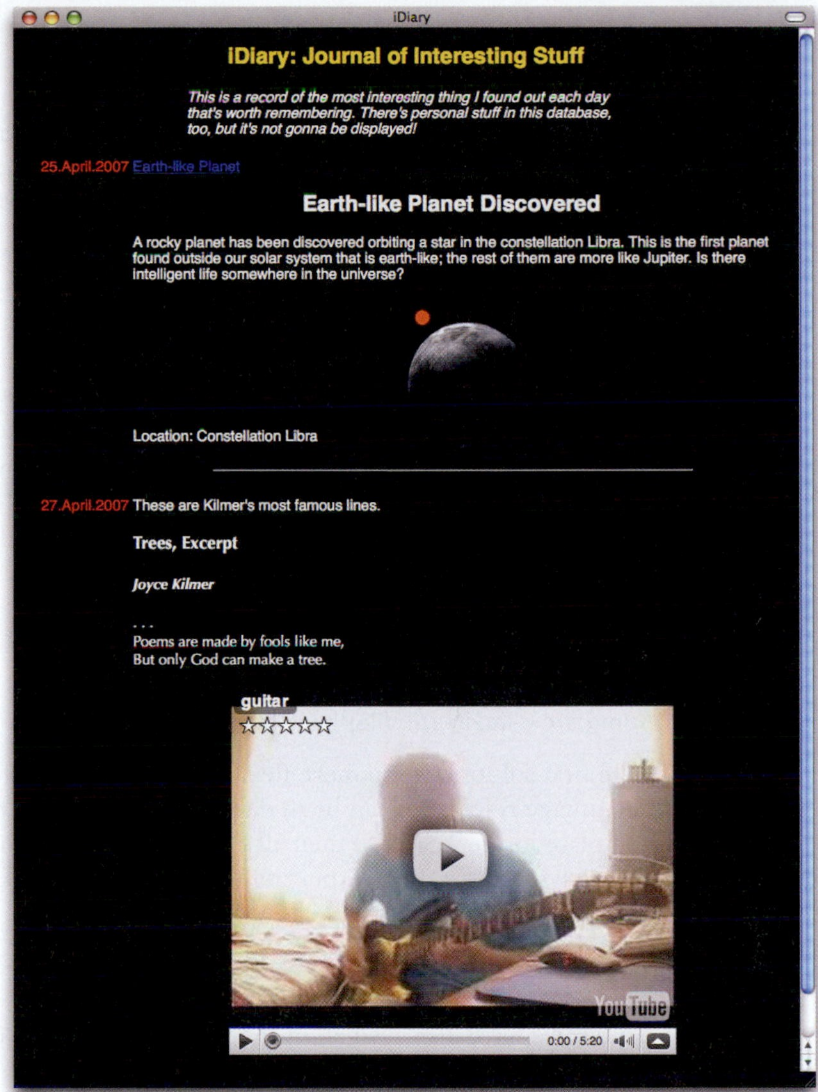

Figure 17.8 Firefox display of the sample diary in Figure 17.7.

different style. If we place <b> and </b> tags in the XML entry, they are treated as (meaningless) XML tags. Rather, we need to add a new tag, say, <label>, that labels the kind of remark we have in the database. For example, we could write

```
<remark><label>Location :</label>Constellation Libra</remark>
```

The <label> tag will have a template that simply places <b> and </b> tags around the information that it encloses.

Those are the only changes that we want now. The XML and XSL files are "living documents" in that we will be adding to the XML file daily, and if we add a new kind of content that we've never included before—say audio—then we will make changes to the XSL templates.

Using the iDiary Daily

The database we created has the flexibility to record any digital data and to display it in an attractive way. We do not have to be constrained when we consider what was the most interesting thing that we learned. So we assume that adding to the iDiary is an activity that we will perform frequently.

Archiving Photos

As we've built the page, the iDiary.xml and iDiarySS.xsl files and the photos have all been on the desktop. They need to be placed in a permanent location. Because the page will likely include many photos, we should store them in a separate folder within the folder containing the two database files. Call the folder imFiles, and notice that we seem to have two choices for specifying the path to these pictures. We can put the path in the XML file as part of the <pic . . ./> tag, as in

```
<pic file="imFiles/planet.jpg" . . . />
```

or maybe we could put it in the XSL file as part of the <pic . . . /> tag template, as in

```
<img src="imFiles/{@file}" . . . >
```

The first solution is the more flexible. By placing the full path in the XML file, image references can be in different places; if the path is specified by the template in the XSL file, then all files referenced by the <pic.../> tag must be in the same place. In fact, putting the path in the XML file allows us to make references to images stored elsewhere on the Internet.

Hiding Information

So far, we have displayed all of the information in the database, but we don't have to. We *do* have to tag everything, and we *must* provide a template to process each tag. But, we don't have to display it.

Suppose we have a tag, <personal>, that encloses our personal thoughts. Though the information can go anywhere in the database, we should consider where we want it placed when we do display it. Assume the <personal> tag is included inside of the <mit> tag, as part of the most interesting thing. Then, the template to display the <personal> content is

```
<xsl:template match="personal">
    <xsl:apply-templates/> <!-- Display personal information-->
</xsl:template>
```

as we expect; it's wise to include a comment to remind ourselves that we're displaying personal information.

Because the <xsl:apply-templates/> tag tells the transformer to "process the information enclosed in the matched tag," all we need to do is leave that tag out of the template. That is, we write

```
<xsl:template match="personal">
  <!--Don't display personal information-->
</xsl:template>
```

When the transformer gets to a <personal> tag, it will check to see what to do, and with no instructions to apply templates to the enclosed information, it will just skip the information inside the tags, as if it were not there. The result is that our personal content is not displayed, though it is part of the database.

Note that including personal information in the file without enclosing it in tags, or tagging it but not providing a template for the tag, both result in the information being displayed. In both cases the transformer doesn't know what to do with the information, so the transformer just adds the information to the XHTML file, causing it to display on the page. Hiding information requires that we treat it properly, including saying how to display it. Not.

Entering Data into the Database

Because we have built our own database system without using commercial database software, we will be adding in new data using our trusty text editor, and we'll be tagging everything ourselves. But we can simplify the task so that it is not an annoyance by setting up our own template in the comments.

In the XML database we include a comment in the form

```
<!--The following tags are available for adding a new entry.
    Change the places containing x's

<entry>
    <date>xx.xxmonthxx.20xx</date>
    <mit>
        <link url="http://www.xxx/xxx"> xx anchor of link xx
        </link>
        <title>xx title of entryxx</title>
        <fact>xx facts are entered here xx </fact>
        <pic file="xxx.jpg" width="xx" height="xx"/>
        <remark><label>xxLabelxx</label> xx remark text xx
        </remark>
        <poem>
            <p_title>xx Poem title xx</p_title>
            <poet>xx author xx</poet>
            <line>xx line of poem xx</line>
        </poem>
        <ytvideo utube="xx YouTube URL xx"/>
    </mit>
</entry>

Edit all places with xx -->
```

Then, by copying and pasting the interior portion of the comment—the <entry> tags and the lines they contain—we have all of the tags we need. We delete tags we don't need and edit those we do. This ensures that we match tags and don't make typing errors in the tags.

Summary

In this chapter we have applied the database ideas from Chapter 16 to a personally relevant task of making a digital diary capable of recording and displaying the many types of media we encounter online. From this case study you now understand:

- XML databases can record irregular data that relational databases cannot.
- An XML database can be directly displayed by opening it in a browser.
- Adding a stylesheet line to XML and building templates in XSL allows the XML file to be displayed formatted using a browser.
- A complex database can be set up incrementally, adding tags and templates one at a time, and checking that they work as planned.
- An XML database can optionally hide some of its information, allowing for the selective display of its contents.

Try It Solutions

17.1

```
<xsl:template match="emph">
<b><i>
    <xsl:apply-templates/>
</i></b>
</xsl:template>
```

Enclosing bold tags with italic tags is also correct.

17.2

```
<xsl:template match="date">
    <xsl:apply-templates/>
</xsl:template>
<xsl:template match="month">
    <i><xsl:apply-templates/></i>
</xsl:template>
<xsl:template match="day">
    <big><xsl:apply-templates/></big>,
</xsl:template>
<xsl:template match="year">
    <small><xsl:apply-templates/></small>
</xsl:template>
```

Did you remember to include the comma?

Review Questions

Multiple Choice

1. The <idiary> tag is a
   a. Collection tag
   b. Affinity tag
   c. Identification tag
   d. none of the above
2. The <country> tag is a
   a. Collection tag
   b. Affinity tag
   c. Identification tag
   d. none of the above
3. The root element <xsl:stylesheet . . .> tag is a
   a. Collection tag
   b. Affinity tag
   c. Identification tag
   d. none of the above
4. XML files are styled for a browser using:
   a. HTML
   b. XSL
   c. SQL
   d. none of the above
5. An incremental approach to development has the advantage of
   a. shortening development time
   b. making the final product smaller
   c. limiting errors to recently developed materials
   d. all of the above
6. When you open an XML file without a stylesheet in a browser, it
   a. won't display and returns an error
   b. displays the text of the file
   c. displays a tree showing the structure of your file
   d. brings up a dialog box to find the stylesheet
7. XSL tag rules are called
   a. licenses
   b. structures
   c. policies
   d. templates
8. The second line of an XML file that uses an XSL template begins with
   a. <xml:stylesheet
   b. <html>
   c. <!--xsl
   d. <xsl:stylesheet

9. iDiary is ordered by
   a. event
   b. date
   c. friend
   d. class
10. Each attribute in an XSL file requires its own
   a. file
   b. tag
   c. table
   d. link
11. To add entries to iDiary you would
   a. modify the XML file
   b. modify the XSL file
   c. make changes to both files
   d. once created the file cannot be changed

Short Answer

1. XSL stands for ______.
2. XSL templates describe how the information should be displayed by using ______.
3. XML and XSL files are combined in a(n) ______, where they're converted to HTML for display in a browser.
4. A(n) ______ tag is the top-most tag in an XSL stylesheet.
5. The root element tag of a stylesheet is a ______ tag.
6. A(n) ______ tag is used to produce successive entries on a page.
7. Items enclosed in an entity are called ______.
8. Each attribute in an XSL file requires its own ______.
9. A description of how a page should be displayed is called a(n) ______.
10. Use the ______ tag to embed multimedia in a page.

Exercises

1. Use XML to define your class schedule.
2. Create a list of other content that could be added to the iDiary database.
3. Design a database similar to iDiary with details for a vacation.
4. Create an online resume using XML and XSL.
5. Create a family history using XML and XSL.
6. Create an iStore database to display items you have for sale.
7. Use XML and XSL to create a testbank of true/false, multiple choice, and short answer questions. Build into it the ability to display pictures.
8. A used car dealer wants you to develop a Web site to display their vehicles. Their inventory changes daily. Explain what you would include on the site and how you would update on a daily basis.

INTERVIEW

with

Alan Kay

Alan Kay is one of the earliest pioneers of personal computing: In the late 1960s he designed one of the first desktop computers (the FLEX Machine) and laptop computers (the Dynabook), and in the early 1970s he invented an early object-oriented programming language, development, and operating system (Smalltalk). Alan also developed the now ubiquitous overlapping window interface. More recently, he helped found the Viewpoints Research Institute, a non-profit organization dedicated to improving education through new computing technologies for the benefit of the world's children. Alan has been a Xerox Fellow, Chief Scientist of Atari, an Apple Fellow, a Disney Fellow, and a Senior Fellow at Hewlett-Packard.

Alan got his B.A. in Mathematics and Molecular Biology with minor concentrations in English and Anthropology from the University of Colorado in 1966, and his M.S. and Ph.D. degrees in Computer Science from the University of Utah in 1968 and 1969. He is the recipient of numerous awards, including the NAE's Charles Stark Draper Prize, the Inamori Foundation Kyoto Prize, and the Turing Award, widely recognized as the highest distinction in Computer Science, for his work on object-oriented programming.

You started out in show business. What led you to become a computer scientist?

I was a professional jazz musician of modest abilities for about 10 years and did some teaching of guitar in that period. My general background included an artistic and musical mother, a scientific and mathematical father, and a grandfather who wrote and illustrated many books. So I grew up interested in many things and didn't make much distinction between what are called the Arts and the Sciences. I came across a number of books about computers and how to build them as a teenager in the 1950s, and when taking a computer aptitude test in the Air Force was an option, I took it, got a good score on it, and starting programming in the early 1960s.

In college I carried full majors in mathematics and biology and supported this by being a programmer at the National Center for Atmospheric Research in Boulder. I was also still playing jazz in clubs at this time.

I wound up at the University of Utah ARPA (Advanced Research Projects Agency) project for grad school in 1966 as a complete fluke without any planning or knowledge about ARPA. From the moment I got there and met (Professor) Dave Evans (later, my advisor) I "got" what ARPA was trying to do and it was a huge stroke of "romance" that I responded to.

How does the musician in you continue to influence the computer scientist?

Analogies can often be misleading, but there are some interesting ones to be made between music and computing (and mathematics and biology). The big ones for me have been the large aesthetic content of music and math and a wish for computing to always be that beautiful, the textures of different kinds of things interacting over time, the incredible ratio of parsimony to effect, etc.

You often talk about education and the art of teaching. Did someone in particular inspire your concept of the ideal teacher?

The initial ideas about "teaching people to think better—even qualitatively better" came from a number of science fiction novels, one of which led me to the General Semantics movement started by Alfred Korzybski. I also had one truly fantastic teacher in the fourth grade. She knew how to reach and realize the potential in the many different kinds of children in her classroom "without teaching," and she has been one of the main models for me for how to go about helping people learn.

You have said that "literacy is not just about being able to read street signs or medicine labels. It means being able to deal in the world of ideas." What does it mean to you for someone to be computer literate?

I like Frank Smith's general definition of literacy as something that starts with important ideas, finds ways to write them down in some kind of language, and helps develop more "readers and writers." The computer has ways of "writing" down representation systems of all kinds—it is a simulator and a metamedium. By metamedium, I mean that it is a holder of all the media you can think of, as well as ones you haven't thought of yet. Computer literacy is all about important ideas written and read as simulations. And the writing and reading are actually some kind of programming, where the programs—like mathematics or a musical score or an essay—are a means for expressing a powerful idea.

What many consider to be the prototype for the laptop computer is a machine you designed about 35 years ago, the Dynabook, yet, you often contend that the Dynabook is still a dream...

It is indeed now possible to not just make a physical Dynabook, but one with many more capabilities than my original conception. However, the physical part of the Dynabook is about 5 percent of the dream. In musical terms, we can now make the body of the violin but we are still struggling with the strings, fingerboard, and bow (the user interface that includes authoring) and we still only have a few instances of what the musical expression will be like (the content of the Dynabook). The other difficult part of the design is that we somehow want the early parts of the Dynabook experience to be a lot more value-laden and fun than learning to play the violin usually is. More importantly, we want users to keep experimenting, move on, and not get complacent as many do, for example, after learning to play three chords on the guitar.

What is Squeak?

Squeak is free and open source software, orignally created by my research team, for getting to better places in all the areas we've been discussing. It is derived from one of the last Xerox PARC Smalltalks and has been brought forward to twenty-first-century graphics, etc. It contains models of itself, which make it easy to port, and now exists on more than 25 platforms running "bit-identically" (exactly the same). From the computer science standpoint it is a little more interesting than most of the other stuff that is around, but pretty much all of its ideas date from the 1970s, so its interesting features are more of a commentary on what didn't happen in computer science in the last 20 years.

We have now done and tested a child's environment that is working out pretty well, and contains a number of new language and structuring ideas. This has been used to implement a much more comprehensive adult/media authoring environment (a kind of super-duper Hypercard) that contains the child's environment as a subset. This is essentially what we think the Dynabook should be like, plus, you can now download it and use it for free.

You have said, "The best way to predict the future is to invent it." What advice do you have for students who are planning a career in the field of technology?

Gain wide perspective by majoring in something else while an undergraduate. Try to find partial answers to Jerome Bruner's questions: What makes humans human? How did we get that way? How can we become more so? In other words, try to understand human beings and the role that representation systems for ideas have played in this journey called "civilization."

4 PART

Problem Solving

chapter

4 PART

Introduction

OUR STUDY of information technology has already covered problem solving in several different forms. We have solved problems related to writing XHTML; finding accurate information sources; answering research questions about Buckminster Fuller; debugging and designing an XML database; and more. In all cases our main tool was logical reasoning applied to a specific situation. In Part 4 we'll become even more effective problem solvers.

Problem solving requires a problem and some medium or mechanism in which to produce a solution. For us, Web pages and familiar applications provide the problems, and JavaScript is our solution medium. The important part of our study—the part that transfers to other aspects of our lives—is neither the problems nor the solutions, but the process by which we find them.

Though problem solving is the "high-order bit" (i.e., most significant information), JavaScript is a programming language. Once you see how programs are written, you will have an understanding of computing which will make you more operationally attuned—and thus a better user. And, the practical bonus from learning JavaScript is that it allows you to create much fancier Web pages.

Fundamental Concepts Expressed in JavaScript

18
chapter

Get with the Program

learning objectives

- Tell the difference between name, value, and variable
- List three basic data types and the rules for specifying them in a program
- Explain the way in which the assignment statement changes a variable's value
- Write expressions using arithmetic, relational, and logical operators
- Write conditional and compound statements

Everything is vague to a degree you do not realize till you have tried to make it precise.

—BERTRAND RUSSELL

PROGRAMMING is a profession, yet we all need to know something about it to be effective computer users. This is analogous to medicine. Doctors and nurses are professionals, but we need to know something about their specialties—our bodies, disease symptoms, nutrition, first aid, and so forth—to care for ourselves and benefit fully from their care. In neither case do we need an expert's knowledge, and in both cases we could probably survive with near total ignorance. But knowing some of what the professionals know is unquestionably beneficial and worth learning, despite its technical nature. What do we need to know?

What we need to know about programming is a fuller elaboration of the concepts already discussed in Chapter 10 on algorithms. These concepts are deep and subtle. We cannot expect to understand them fully the first time we meet them. Indeed, our goal is to change our thinking habits to be more "abstract." Just as we need experience writing, reading, and speaking a foreign language in order to acquire it, so too do we need experience writing, reading, and executing algorithms and programs to acquire the thought processes of computation.

After preliminary remarks, we present a sample program. Though it might look like gibberish at the start, the plan is to introduce all of the concepts used in the program. We begin by explaining about names, variables, and declarations, giving ourselves the ability to refer to the program's data. Then we cover the types of data values: numbers, character strings, and Booleans. Next, we introduce assignment statements and expressions, so we can compute new values. The last concepts are compound statements for grouping and conditional statements for testing. With this list of concepts, we return to the program and work through its execution. By the end of the chapter, we'll be programming!

Overview: Programming Concepts

Programming is the act of formulating an algorithm or program. It entails developing a systematic means of solving a problem so that an agent—someone other than the programmer and usually a computer—can follow the instructions and produce the intended result for every input, every time. The agent must also be able to perform or execute the program without any intervention from the programmer. This means that all of the steps must be spelled out precisely and effectively, and that all contingencies must be planned for.

This summary of programming—that everything must be explained clearly and all contingencies planned for—is perhaps best expressed by Adele Mildred Koss, one of the first programmers of UNIVAC I in 1950. She described her view of this challenge for the *Annals of the History of Computing*.

[Computers] couldn't think in the way a human thinks, but had to be given a set of step-by-step machine instructions to be executed before they could provide answers to a specific problem. Before the computer could solve a problem, a human would have to solve it first, using mathematics, physics, or a business process. The human would have to segment the solution into little building blocks that the machine could handle, and use the machine code to write a program that would execute that process correctly, at high speed and for many iterations without human intervention. Problems could be solved in many different ways, but to devise a correct and elegant solution—and I stress elegant—was the challenge.

Programming has become much easier in the years since Ms. Koss programmed, but the principles are the same. Programming actually requires thinking. But relying on thinking alone makes programming too difficult. Instead, in this and following chapters, we introduce basic programming concepts developed over the years. These are the tools you will need to formulate any computation. And, trying to program an algorithm precisely using English is hopeless. Natural languages are too ambiguous for directing anything as clueless as a computer. So, programming languages have been developed to help programmers in two ways: they are precise, and they are specialized in using the concepts mentioned in the previous paragraphs. Using a programming language is actually easier than writing in English. We will use **JavaScript**, a modern programming language that is especially effective for Web applications. You won't become a JavaScript expert from reading this chapter, but you might learn enough to make a glitzy personal Web page.

This chapter introduces the following programming concepts:

- Names, values, and variables
- Declarations
- Data types, numbers, string literals, and Booleans
- Assignment
- Expressions
- Conditionals

With just these few concepts, you will be able to write actual programs. The program in Figure 18.1 is an example. It probably looks like gibberish to you at this moment, but by the end of this chapter you'll be able to read and understand it. (We present it now to make it clear where we are headed, but skip it if it appears intimidating.)

Finally, in introducing the deep ideas of the chapter, we must set down the practical details of programming. These rules can be as burdensome as a chapter-long list of dos and don'ts. So, we skip the more obvious rules here—the ones you would guess intuitively—you can reference them in Appendix C.

At the Espresso Stand

Espresso is concentrated liquid coffee. Some people enjoy drinking espresso straight, but others prefer a café latte, espresso in steamed milk; a cappuccino, espresso in equal parts of steamed milk and milk foam; or an Americano, espresso in near-boiling water. Espresso drinks are sold in three sizes: short (8 oz.), tall (12 oz.), and grande (16 oz.). These drinks are made with a standard amount of espresso, but coffee addicts often order additional shots of espresso. The price of the additional shots is added to the base price of the drink, and tax is figured in to produce the charge for the drink. The program to compute the price of an espresso drink is:

Input:

drink, a character string with one of the values: "espresso", "latte", "cappuccino", "Americano"

ounce, an integer, giving the size of the drink in ounces

shots, an integer, giving the number of shots

Output:

price in dollars of an order, including 8.8% sales tax

Program:

```
var price;
var taxRate = 0.088;
if (drink == "espresso")
   price = 1.40;
if (drink == "latte" || drink == "cappuccino") {
   if (ounce == 8)
      price = 1.95;
   if (ounce == 12)
      price = 2.35;
   if (ounce == 16)
      price = 2.75;
}
if (drink == "Americano")
   price = 1.20 + .30 * (ounce/8);
price = price + (shots - 1) * .50;
price = price + price * taxRate;
```

Figure 18.1 Sample JavaScript computation to figure the cost of espresso drinks.

This allows us to emphasize the few rules that you cannot guess on your own. When in doubt, refer to Appendix C. All of the rules are listed there.

Names, Values, and Variables

Though we are familiar with the concepts of a name (the letter sequence used to refer to something), and a value (the thing itself), in normal conversation we tend not to distinguish carefully between the two. Thus, when we use the letter sequences "Kate Winslet" or "Harrison Ford," we mean those specific movie stars. There are many people with those names, of course, and if your friend from geology class is also named Harrison Ford, that name has one value for you in the context of that class and another in the context of the movies. People understand this distinction in everyday conversation. In everyday life we treat names as "bound to" their values.

Names Have Changing Values

Names and values are separable in programming. The best way to think of names and values in programming is to think of names as if they were offices or titles, or other designations purposely selected to have changing values. There are plenty of examples:

Name	Current Value (7/1/2009)	Previous Values
U.S. President	Barack Obama	Bill Clinton, George Washington
Chief Justice U.S. Supreme Court	John Roberts	Warren Burger, Earl Warren
James Bond	Daniel Craig	Sean Connery, Roger Moore
Queen of England	Elizabeth II	Victoria I, Elizabeth I
U.N. Secretary General	Ban Ki-moon	Boutros Boutros-Ghali, Kofi Annan

The names used in the middle and right columns are, of course, the informal usage of names from everyday conversation.

The reason we focus on the case where the values associated with a name can change is because they change in programs. A program is a fixed specification of a process. As the process evolves and the program transforms data to produce new values, the old names must refer to these new values, that is, the names have changed values. This is a natural result of the fixed specification of the process. So, for example, the U.S. Constitution contains this specification of a process: "The President-elect will be sworn into office by the Chief Justice on the January 20 following the election." The intent of this command is to describe a process that applies no matter who wins the presidential election, that is, the value of "President-elect," and who is the senior justice of the Supreme Court on that date, that is, the value of "Chief Justice." We naturally interpret the U.S. Constitution this way. The names "President-elect" and "Chief Justice" have changing values.

Names used in this way—a single letter sequence with a varying value—are an already familiar concept to you from your previous computing experience. The file named `EnglishPaper` changes its value every time you save a version of your composition. In computing, the name is always separable from the value, and the value can be changed. It's a basic idea worth thinking about.

18.1 What's in a Name? Explain the difference between the names "Best Picture" and the name "Slumdog Millionaire."

Names in a Program Are Called Variables

In programming terminology, the names just discussed are called **variables**, a term that reminds us that their values *vary*. For example, in the *Alphabetize CDs* program in Chapter 10, two variables, *Alpha* and *Beta*, were used. Nearly every step in that program changed the value of one or the other of those variables. That's typical. The most commonly used programming language operation is the command to change the value of a variable. That command is called **assignment**, and it will be discussed shortly.

Names and Values. We've seen one other example of names having multiple values over time. Memory locations—their names are called *addresses*—have different values at different times. This is not a coincidence. Variables *are* memory locations in the computer. Variables are simply a more readable and convenient way to reference computer memory than are the actual numerical addresses. The value of the address is the current contents of the memory location, and it is the value of the corresponding variable.

Identifiers and Their Rules

The letter sequence that makes up a variable's name is called the **identifier**. In every programming language, identifiers must have a particular form, although the form is somewhat different from language to language. Generally, identifiers must begin with a letter, followed by any sequence of letters, numerals (the digits 0 through 9), or the underscore symbol (_). (JavaScript permits slightly more general identifiers than suggested here, but throughout this book, tiny limitations are implied to make it easier to learn and to help avoid errors. There is no loss of expressiveness in programming.)

Identifiers are not allowed to contain spaces. The following are eight identifiers:

```
X
x
ru4it
```

```
nineteen_eighty_four
Time_O_Day
Identifiers_can_B_long_but_if_so_typing_them_can_be_a_pain
oO000Oo
elizaBETH
```

Notice two features of identifiers: The underscore symbol can be used as a word separator to make identifiers more readable, and identifiers in most programming languages, including JavaScript, are case sensitive, meaning that uppercase and lowercase letters are different.

fluencyBIT

Form Rules. User IDs, logins, and email names follow similar rules, but with a few important differences. For example, login and email names often allow a dash (-), but variable names do not, because a dash could be confused with a minus sign between variables.

A Variable Declaration Statement

Programs are usually written "starting from scratch." That is, when you begin to program, you can think of the computer as if it were newly manufactured; it knows nothing except how to understand the programming language. So the first thing to do when writing any program is to state what variables will be used. This is called **declaring variables**, and we do it using a command called a declaration. In JavaScript, the **declaration command** is the word var, short for *variable*, followed by a list of the identifiers for the variables to be declared, separated by commas. For example, to write a computation that computes the area of a circle given its radius, we need variables area and radius. So we declare,

```
var area, radius;
```

This command *declares* that in the program we will use these two identifiers as variables. Notice that the first command in the espresso computation in Figure 18.1

```
var price;
```

is a variable declaration of this type. (The program uses other variables that will be explained momentarily.)

The declaration was just called a *command*, because it is commanding the computer to record which identifiers will be used as variables. But everything we tell a computer to do is a command, so we should call the declaration by its proper term, declaration **statement**.

The Statement Terminator

A program is simply a list of statements. Because we can't always write one statement per line as in a normal list, the statements are often run together, which means that each statement must be terminated by some punctuation symbol. The **statement terminator** in JavaScript is the semicolon (;). It's the same idea as terminating sentences in English with periods, question marks, or exclamation points. The main difference is this If I forget to terminate an English sentence, like I just did, you still understand—both from the meaning and from the capital letter beginning the next sentence—that the sentence is over, that is, terminated. The computer isn't that clever. It needs the semicolon. So, the rule is: Terminate every statement with a semicolon.

First Mistake. Everyone makes mistakes when programming. Everyone. One of the most common mistakes for beginners is to forget the semicolon. When the semicolon is missing the computer becomes confused and debugging is necessary. Remembering semicolons makes programming easier.

Rules for Declaring Variables

Every variable used in a program must be declared. JavaScript allows declaration statements anywhere in the list of program statements. But because variable declarations announce what variables *will* be used in the program, programmers like to place them first in the program. It's like saying, "Here's the list of variables I'll be using in the program that follows." We will declare variables first.

Undefined values. The declaration states that the identifier is the name of a variable. But what is the name's value? It has no value at first! The value of a declared variable is not defined. It's a name that doesn't yet name anything. Similarly, when a group of people forms an intramural basketball team, say, Crunch, the intramural sports office can refer to the Crunch captain, even if the person who will be captain hasn't been chosen. The name is declared—it will be meaningful when the season is under way—but there is no value assigned yet. The value is **undefined**.

Initializing a declaration. Often we know an *initial value* for the identifiers we declare. So JavaScript allows us to set the initial value as part of the declaration, that is, to **initialize** the variable. To declare that `taxRate` and `balanceDue` will be variables in the program, and that their initial values are .088 and 0, respectively, we write

```
var taxRate = .088;
var balanceDue = 0;
```

We don't have to declare and initialize just one variable at a time in the `var` statement. We can declare and initialize any number of variables by separating them with commas:

```
var taxRate = .088, balanceDue = 0;
```

The computer doesn't care which style is used. They're equivalent. Typically, programmers include several variables in a single declaration statement when the variables are logically related. This serves as a reminder that the variables are related. For example, variables describing a person's features might be declared

```
var height, weight, hairColor, eyeColor, astrological_sign;
```

If the variables are not related, they are usually specified in separate statements. All approaches are equivalent; there is no "proper" way.

18.2 **Make a Declaration.** The *Alphabetize CDs* program used two variables, *Alpha* and *Beta*. Write a JavaScript declaration statement to declare them.

Three Basic Data Types of JavaScript

We will use three types of data in our JavaScript programs: numbers, strings, and Booleans.

Rules for Writing Numbers

The values assigned to the variables taxRate and balanceDue are **numbers**. Like everything in programming, there are rules for writing numbers, but basically numbers are written in the "usual way." (Details are provided in Appendix C.)

One "unusual" aspect of numbers in programming is that there are no "units." We can't write 33% or $10.89; we must write 0.33 and 10.89. This explains why there are no dollar signs in the program in Figure 18.1 even though it is a computation to figure the price of a coffee drink in dollars. Standard computer numbers can have about ten significant digits and range from as small as 10^{-324} to as large as 10^{308}. (Numbers and computer arithmetic are unexpectedly subtle. Our uses of numbers will be trivial to avoid any difficulties. As a general rule, the "safe zone" is the range from 2 billionths to 2 billion plus or minus. Outside that range, we must learn more about computer arithmetic.)

Though computers frequently compute on numbers, they compute on other kinds of data as well.

Strings

For us, strings will be the most common kind of data. **Strings** are sequences of keyboard characters. For example, here are nine strings:

```
"abcdefghijklmnopqrstuvwxyz"   "May"   '!@#$%^&*( )_+|}{ : ]['
"strings are surrounded by quotes"   " "   "M&M's"
'strings can contain blanks'   ""   '"No," she said.'
```

Notice that a string is always surrounded by single (') or double (") quotes.

Strings can initialize a declaration. Like numbers, strings can be used to initialize variables in a declaration. For example,

```
var hairColor = "black", eyeColor = "brown", astrological_sign = "Leo";
```

We need strings when manipulating text, as when we're building Web pages, for example. The program in Figure 18.1 uses several string constants: "espresso", "latte", "cappuccino", and "Americano".

Rules for writing strings in JavaScript. The rules for writing strings in JavaScript, most of which can be seen in the preceding examples, are as follows:

1. Strings must be surrounded by quotes, either single (') or double ("), *which are not curly*.
2. Most characters are allowed within quotes except the return character (Enter), backspace character, tab character, \, and two others (little used).
3. Double quoted strings can contain single quotes, and vice versa.
4. The apostrophe (') is the same as the single quote.
5. Any number of characters is allowed in a string.
6. The minimum number of characters in a string is zero (""), which is called the **empty string**.

Rule (3) lets us include quotes in a string. To use double quotes in a string, for example, we enclose the string in single quotes, as in 'He said, "No!"'. If our string contains single quotes, we enclose it in double quotes, as in "Guide to B&B's". Because the apostrophe is commonly used in English's possessives and contractions, it's a good idea to use double quotes as the default. This allows the free use of apostrophes. We change to single quotes only when the string contains double quotes. Both methods work, and the computer doesn't care which one we use.

Notice that by rule (6) the empty string is a legitimate value. That is, writing

```
var exValDef = "";
var exValUndef;
```

results in two quite different situations. After these two statements, if we ask the computer what kind of value exValDef has, the answer would be "a string," but the answer for exValUndef would be "an undefined value."

Literals. The numbers and strings discussed are known as either **string constants** or **string literals**. The term *literal* conveys the idea that the characters are typed literally in the program. So there are rules about how to write these values explicitly in a computation. However, when literals become the values of variables and are stored in the computer, the representation changes slightly, especially for strings.

String literals stored in the computer. First, because the surrounding quotes or double quotes are used only to delimit the string literal, they are removed when the literal is stored in the computer. That's why the empty string "" has a length of 0, rather than 2.

Second, any character can be stored in the computer's memory. Specifically, although a prohibited character such as a tab character cannot be *typed* in a literal, it can be the value of a string in the computer. To do this we use the "escape" mechanism, which we discussed in Chapter 4.

For JavaScript, the escape symbol is the backslash (\) and the escape sequences are shown in Table 18.1. Thus we can write declarations such as

```
var fourTabs = "\t\t\t\t", backUp = "\b",
    bothQuotesInOne = " '\" ";
```

which give values to the variables that cannot be typed literally. The escape sequences are converted to the single characters they represent when they are stored in the computer's memory. So, the lengths of the values of these three string variables are 4, 1, and 2, respectively.

Table 18.1 Escape sequences for characters prohibited from string literals

Sequence	Character	Sequence	Character
\b	Backspace	\f	Form feed
\n	New line	\r	Carriage return
\t	Tab	\'	Apostrophe or single quote
\"	Double quote	\\	Backslash

Boolean Values

Another kind of value is the **Boolean value** (**Booleans**). Unlike numbers and strings, there are only two Boolean values: true and false. Boolean values have their obvious logical meaning. We should emphasize that although true and false are written as letter sequences, they are *values*, like 1 is a value, not identifiers or strings. Although Booleans are used implicitly throughout the programming process, as you'll see, they are used only occasionally for initializing variables. Examples might be

```
var foreignLanguageReq = false, mathReq = true, totalCredits = 0;
```

This last declaration illustrates that variables appearing in the same declaration can be initialized with different kinds of values.

fluencyBIT

> **It's True.** Boolean values get their name from George Boole. True. Boole was an English mathematician who invented true and false. False. True and false have been around since humans began to reason. Boole invented an algebra based on these two values that is basic to computer engineering and other fields.

The different kinds of values of a programming language are called its **data types** or its **value types** or simply its types. We have introduced three types for JavaScript: numbers, strings, and Booleans. There are several other types, but these are sufficient for most of what we will do in JavaScript. JavaScript is very kind to programmers with respect to types, as you will see later in the chapter.

18.3 Literary Work. Declare variables (of your choosing) to describe literary personalities, and initialize them to values appropriate for Mark Twain: his real name, the century in which he wrote *Tom Sawyer*, whether he was a humorist, and a famous quotation in quotation marks: *Nothing so needs reforming as other people's habits.*

Meta-Brackets. In discussing programming languages, we often need to describe syntactic structures, such as declaration statements. To separate the language being defined from the language doing the defining, we enclose terms of the defining language in "angle brackets," (< >), known as **meta-brackets**. Thus, the general form of the earlier initializing variable declaration would be var <*variable name*> = <*initial value*>, where the symbols not in meta-brackets are written literally, and symbols or words in the meta-brackets represent things of the sort indicated, as a kind of placeholder. Notice that these are not tags.

The Assignment Statement

If variables are to change values in an algorithm or program, there should be a command to do so. The **assignment statement** changes a variable's value; it is the workhorse of programming.

An assignment statement has three parts that always occur in this order:

<*variable*> <*assignment symbol*> <*expression*>;

Here <*variable*> is any declared variable in the program, <*assignment symbol*> is the language's notation for the assignment operation (discussed next), and <*expression*> is a kind of formula telling the computer how to compute the new value. Like any other statement, an assignment statement is terminated by a semicolon. JavaScript's <*assignment symbol*> is the equal sign (=), and you've already seen the assignment operation as the initializer for variable declarations.

Assignment Symbol

Different programming languages use different symbols for indicating assignment. The three most widely used symbols are the equal sign (=); the colon, equal sign pair (:=); and the left pointing arrow (←). There are others, but these are the most common. The := is considered a single symbol even though it is formed from two keyboard characters. Like JavaScript, most languages use =. Pascal uses := and more mathematical languages like APL use ←. Regardless of which symbol the language uses, assignment is a standard and commonly used operation in every programming language.

An example of an assignment statement is

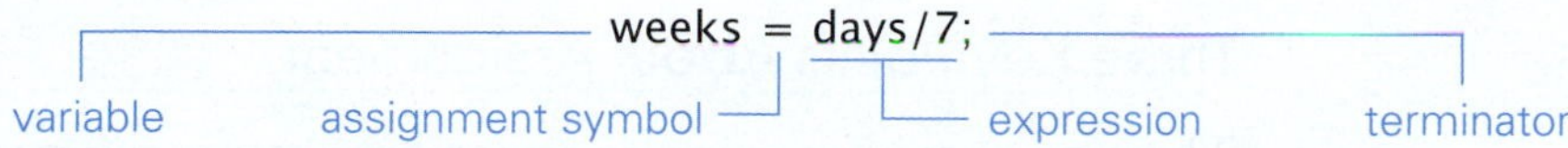

where weeks is the variable whose value is being changed, = is the assignment symbol, and days/7 is the expression. Therefore, this assignment statement illustrates the standard form.

Interpreting an Assignment Statement

To understand how assignment works, you *must* think of a value flowing from the right side (expression side) of the assignment symbol to the left side (variable side). (This view makes the left arrow, ←, perhaps the most intuitive assignment symbol.) The *assignment symbol* should be read as "*is assigned*" or "*becomes*" or "*gets*." Therefore, our example can be read

- "the variable weeks *is assigned* the value resulting from dividing the value of the variable days by 7"
- "the value of weeks *becomes* the value resulting from dividing the value of the variable days by 7"
- "the variable weeks *gets* the value resulting from dividing the value of the variable days by 7"

fluencyBIT

Get with the Program. Most programmers prefer *gets* when reading assignments. It conveys the idea of filling a container, as in a "mailbox *gets* a letter" or a "flour tin *gets* refilled." The variable is the container.

Terms like *is assigned*, *becomes*, and *gets* emphasize the role that the assignment symbol plays, namely, to change the value of the variable named on the left side.

In an assignment statement, the expression (that is, everything to the right of the assignment symbol) is computed or evaluated first. If there are any variables used in the expression, their current values are used. This evaluation produces a value that then becomes the new value of the variable named on the left side. So, the effect of executing the sample assignment statement

```
weeks = days/7;
```

is that the current value of the variable days is determined by looking in the memory (suppose it is 77), and that value is divided by 7, producing a new value, 11. This new value then becomes the new value of the variable weeks, that is, weeks is assigned 11.

fluencyBIT

Assignment to Memory. In the computer, an assignment statement causes the value in the memory location(s) corresponding to the variable to be replaced by the new value resulting from the expression.

Three Key Points About Assignment

There are three key points to remember about assignment statements. First, all three of the components must be given; if anything is missing, the statement is meaningless. Second, the flow of the value to the name is always right to left. Thus the two variable names in the assignment statement

```
variable_receiving_new_value = newly_computed_value;
```

correctly show the motion of information. Notice that the expression can simply be some other variable; it doesn't have to be a complicated formula. Third, the values of any variables used in the expression are their values before the start of execution of the assignment. This point is extremely important, because the variable being changed in the assignment statement might also be used in the expression.

For example, a program simulating a basketball game would probably use the assignment statement

```
totalScore = totalScore + 3;
```

for a basket from outside the three-point circle. When the expression on the right side of the assignment statement, totalScore + 3, is evaluated, the value of totalScore used in the computation is its value before starting this statement, that is, the score before the shot. When the assignment statement is completed, totalScore is the updated value reflecting the three-point shot.

Similarly, the program might contain the code

```
shotClock = shotClock - 1;
```

to implement the "tick" of the shot clock. Again, when evaluating the right side expression, the values used for variables are those *before* the statement is executed.

Repeating, because this is the most important of all of the ideas in this chapter: The role of = is to *assign* the value computed on the right side to be the new value of the variable named on the left side.

fluencyBIT

Programming Is Not Algebra. Like algebra, many programming languages use an equal sign in assignments. In programming "=" is read "becomes," which suggests the dynamic meaning of the right-to-left value flow. In algebra "=" is read "equals," which emphasizes the static meaning that both sides are identical. In programming, the statement "$x = x + 1$" means the value of x becomes 1 larger; in algebra, the equation "$x = x + 1$" is meaningless because there is no number that is identical to itself plus 1. The unknowns in algebra are names whose values do not change.

18.4 An Assignment. Declare a variable **bestPicture** and then write an assignment statement to give it the value *Slumdog Millionaire*.

An Expression and Its Syntax

Although programming is not mathematics, it has its roots in higher math. So, it is not surprising that one of the concepts in programming is an algebra-like formula called an **expression**. Expressions describe the means of performing the actual computation. As you've already seen in earlier spreadsheet chapters and in the expression days/7, expressions are built out of variables and **operators**, which are standard arithmetic operations, such as addition or subtraction, found on the keys of a calculator.

The symbols of basic arithmetic are called the **arithmetic operators**. The actual symbols used for some operators may be different, depending on the programming language, so we limit ourselves here to JavaScript operators. Examples of expressions include

```
a * (b + c)
height * width / 2
pi * diameter
(((days * 24) + hours) * 60 + minutes) * 60 + seconds
```

Arithmetic Operators

Expressions usually follow rules similar to algebraic formulas, but not quite. Multiplication must be given explicitly with the asterisk (*) multiply operator, so we write a * b rather than ab or a · b or a × b. As with algebra, multiplication and division are performed before addition and subtraction—multiplication and division have *higher precedence* than addition and subtraction—unless parentheses group the operations differently. Therefore, a*b + a*c is equivalent to (a*b) + (a*c) because multiplication is automatically performed before addition. Also, because expressions must be typed on a single line, superscripts, as in x^2, are prohibited. Some languages have an operator for exponents or powers, but JavaScript does not. If we want to compute the area of a circle, we must multiply R times itself because we can't square it. So

```
pi * R * R
```

is the expression for computing the area of a circle (πr^2), assuming that the variable pi has the value 3.1415962.

Operators like + and * are called **binary operators** because they operate on two values. The values they operate on are called **operands**. There are also **unary operators**, like negate (–), which have only one operand. (Language parsers—the part of a compiler that "diagrams" programs so a computer can understand them—can easily figure out whether the minus means negate or subtract.)

One very useful operator in future chapters will be mod. The **modulus** (mod) **operation** (%) divides two integers and returns the remainder. So, the result of a%b for integers a and b is the remainder of the division a/b. In particular, the result of 4%2 is 0 because 2 evenly divides 4, whereas 5%2 is 1 because 2 into 5 leaves a remainder of 1.

Relational Operators

Expressions involving addition, subtraction, and so on are similar to algebra, but programmers use other kinds of expressions. **Relational operators** are used to make comparisons between numerical values—that is, to test the relationship between two numbers. The outcome of the comparison is a Boolean value, either true or false. The operators are illustrated here with sample operands a and b that should be replaced with variables or expressions:

a < b	Is a less than b?
a <= b	Is a less than or equal to b?
a == b	Is a equal to b?
a != b	Is a not equal to b?
a >= b	Is a greater than or equal to b?
a > b	Is a greater than b?

Notice that the "equal to" relational operator (==) is a double equal sign, making it different from assignment.

Examples of relational expressions include

```
bondRate > certificateDeposit
temperature <= 212
drink == "espresso"
```

Notice that relational tests can apply to string variables, as in the last example, which is taken from the program in Figure 18.1. Both equal (==) and not equal (!=) can be applied to string variables.

fluencyBIT

> **One Character or Two?** Several operators, such as <=, >=, and !=, are composed of two keyboard characters. They cannot contain a space and are considered a single character. They were invented years ago to make up for the limited number of characters on a standard keyboard. If programming language research started today, compounds would not be necessary because it's now easy to introduce new symbols that are not on the keyboard, such as ≤, ≥, and ≠.

Logical Operators

The relational test results in a true or false outcome; that is, either the two operands are related to each other as the relational operator asks, making the test outcome true, or they are not, making the test outcome false. It is common to test two or more relationships together, requiring that relational expression results be combined. For example, teenagers are older than 12 and younger than 20. In programming, "teenagerness" is determined by establishing that the relational tests age > 12 and age < 20 are both true. In JavaScript the "teenage" expression is

```
age > 12 && age < 20
```

Logical and. The && is the **logical and** operator, playing the same role AND plays in query expressions (Chapters 5 and 16). The outcome of *a* && *b* is true if both *a* and *b* are true; otherwise, it is false. (The operands *a* and *b* can be variables, in which case they have Boolean values, or expressions, or a mixture.)

Thus, in the teenager expression, the current value of age is compared to 12, which yields a true or a false outcome. Then the current value of age is compared to 20, yielding another true or false outcome. Finally, these two outcomes, the operands of &&, are tested, and if they are both true, the entire expression has a true outcome; otherwise, it is false. For example,

Value of age	age > 12	age < 20	age > 12 && age < 20
4	false	true	false
16	true	true	true
50	true	false	false

Notice that the operands for relational expressions must be numeric, but the operands for logical expressions must be Boolean (that is, true or false).

fluencyBIT

Programming Is Still Not Algebra. In algebra, the notation *12 < age < 20* would be used to assert "teenagerness," the static condition of an age within the indicated limits. In programming, both tests must be specified and the two results "anded" (combined using &&) to produce the final answer. The difference, again, is that in algebra we are just stating a fact, whereas in programming we are *commanding* the computer to perform the operation of testing the two conditions.

Logical or. Not surprisingly, there is also a **logical or** operator, ||. The outcome of *a* || *b* is true if either *a* is true or *b* is true, and it is also true if they are both true; it is false only if both are false. A "preteen" test expression

```
age == 11 || age == 12
```

illustrates the use of the logical operator ||. Because && and || have lower precedence than the relational operators, the relationals are always tested first. To include 10-year-olds as preteens, we write an expression that states that either the person is age 10 or their age satisfies the previous preteen definition:

```
age == 10 || (age == 11 || age == 12)
```

Notice that the subexpression in parentheses produces a true or false value when evaluated, just like a relational test does. It doesn't matter how the operands of || are produced; it only matters that they are true or false values. Another way to achieve the same result is

```
(age == 10 || age == 11) || age == 12
```

Of course, it is also possible to test this definition of preteen with the expression

```
age >= 10 && age <= 12
```

which takes a bit less typing, and is like the teenager test. All of these expressions seem equally clear to a person, and the computer doesn't care which is used.

Logical Not. The **logical not** (!) is a unary operator—it takes only a single operand—and its outcome is the opposite of the value of its operand. To command the computer to check if the age is not that of a teenager, write

```
! (age > 12 && age < 20)
```

It works as follows. The subexpression in parentheses tests whether the age qualifies as a teenager, that is, more than 12 and less than 20. The outcome of the test is either true, the age qualifies as a teenager, or false, it does not. By placing the logical not operator in front of the parenthesized expression, we have a new expression, which has the opposite outcome: The whole expression is false if the age is that of a teenager, and it is true if the age is not that of a teenager.

18.5 In the Tropics. The Tropic of Cancer is 23.5° North latitude and the Tropic of Capricorn is 23.5° South latitude; the Arctic Circle is 66.5° North latitude and the Antarctic Circle is 66.5° South latitude. Assume lat is a variable giving the latitude of a location on the globe. Write a relational expression that is true if the location is hot or cold; that is, either tropical or polar.

Operator overload. Finally, we've reached **operator overload.** That might sound like the description of someone trying to learn too many new operators at a time—a state you have no doubt achieved!—but it is a technical term meaning the "use of an operator with different data types." The case of interest is +. Operators usually apply to a single data type, like numbers. So, we expect 4 + 5 to produce the numerical result of 9. And it does when the operands are numbers. But if the operands are the strings "four" + "five" the result is the string "fourfive".

Concatenation. When we use + with strings, it joins the strings together by the operation of **concatenation.** In everyday writing, we simply place two strings together if we want them joined, but in programming, we command the computer to do the work, so we need the operator concatenation to tell the computer to put two strings together. We have "overloaded" the meaning of + to mean addition when operands are numeric and concatenation when the operands are strings. Though overloading is common in some programming languages, + is the only example you'll see here with our use of JavaScript.

fluencyTIP

> **Quote Note.** When manipulating strings, as in the statement
>
> `fullName = firstName + " " + middleName + " " + lastName;`
>
> which creates a name from its parts using blanks as separators, it's easy to understand + as concatenation. But for a statement like
>
> `colt = "4" + "5";`
>
> the variable **colt** will be assigned the string **"45"**, not **9**, because the operands are (length 1) strings. Thus, you must be alert for quotes that tell you the operand is a string rather than a numerical value.

A Conditional Statement

The *Alphabetize CDs* program in Chapter 10 required many tests. For example, there was a test to determine if the titles of two CDs were in alphabetical order. A specific statement type, called a **conditional statement** or a **conditional**, has been invented to make testing simpler. The conditional statement of JavaScript, which differs from the IF( ) function of spreadsheets, has the form

```
if (<Boolean expression>)
    <then-statement>;
```

Here the *<Boolean expression>* is any expression evaluating to a Boolean true or false outcome, such as relational expressions, and the *<then-statement>* is any JavaScript statement, such as an assignment statement.

if Statements and Their Flow of Control

For example, an if statement that checks waterTemp in Fahrenheit

```
if (waterTemp < 32)
    waterState = "Frozen";
```

is a typical conditional statement. In a conditional the *<Boolean expression>*, called a **predicate**, is evaluated, producing a true or false outcome. If the outcome is true, the *<then-statement>* is performed. If the outcome is false, the *<then-statement>* is skipped. Therefore, in the example the value of the variable waterTemp is determined and compared to 32. If it is less than 32, the value of the variable waterState is changed to "Frozen". Otherwise, the statement is passed over, and waterState remains unchanged. The following conditional

```
if (waterTemp >= 32 && waterTemp <= 212)
    waterState = "Liquid";
```

tests a range of values using relational operators and the and operator.

Some programming languages use the word *then* to separate the predicate from the <*then-statement*>, but JavaScript does not, because it is unnecessary. Writing the <*then-statement*> indented on the following line is actually only common practice, not a rule; the <*then-statement*> could be on the same line as the predicate,

```
if (waterTempC >= 0 && waterTempC <= 100) waterState = "Liquid";
```

It has the same meaning because white space is ignored in JavaScript. But programmers write the <*then-statement*> indented on the following line to set it off and emphasize its conditional nature for anyone reading the program. By the way, when you read a conditional statement you *say* "then" after the predicate.

Sometimes we need to perform more than one statement on a true outcome of the predicate test. We could just repeat the test for each statement, as in

```
if (waterTemp < 32) waterState = "Frozen";
if (waterTemp < 32) description = "Ice";
```

Repeating statements can become tedious, however.

Compound Statements

Programming languages allow for a sequence of statements in the <*then-statement*>. The problem is that if there are several statements, how will we know how many to skip in case the predicate has a false outcome? The solution is easy: We group the statements by surrounding them with "curly braces," {}, which collects them to become a single statement known as a **compound statement**. Then they fulfill the requirements of the earlier definition because now the <*then-statement*> refers to the single (compound) statement; it is skipped when the predicate outcome is false. For example,

```
if (waterTempC < 0) {
    waterState = "Frozen";
    description = "Ice";
}
```

Notice the location of the curly braces. One immediately follows the predicate to signal that a compound statement is next, and the other is placed conspicuously on its own line below the *i* of if. Programmers do this so that compound statement grouping symbols are easy to see, because they are easily overlooked if they are in an unexpected place in a program. As always, the computer doesn't care where the curly braces are placed.

The "exception proving the rule" that every statement must be terminated by a semicolon is the compound statement. The closing curly brace, }, should not be followed by a semicolon.

Show Your Braces. Since compound statement braces have a huge impact on program behavior, always put them in the standard place, where they will be noticed.

Another example of the use of the compound statement is from the espresso computation of Figure 18.1:

```
if (drink == "latte" || drink == "cappuccino") {
    if (ounce == 8)
        price = 1.95;
    if (ounce == 12)
        price = 2.35;
    if (ounce == 16)
        price = 2.75;
}
```

This code illustrates an if with a compound statement containing three simple if statements. If drink is neither a "latte" nor a "cappuccino", the three statements will be skipped. Otherwise, if drink equals "latte" or drink equals "cappuccino", the three statements will be performed. Notice that at most one predicate of the three statements of the compound statement can be true, because ounce can have only one value at a time: 8, 12, 16, or something else. So, price will be changed at most once.

if/else Statements

Of course, performing statements when a condition is true is handy, but how can statements be executed when the condition's outcome is false? There is another form of the if statement known as the **if/else statement**. It has the form

```
if  (<Boolean expression>)
    <then-statement>;
else
    <else-statement>;
```

The <*Boolean expression*> is evaluated first. If the outcome is true, the <*then-statement*> is executed and the <*else-statement*> is skipped. If the <*Boolean expression*>'s outcome is false, the <*then-statement*> is skipped and the <*else-statement*> is executed. For example,

```
if (day == 'Friday' || day == 'Saturday')
    calendarEntry = "Party!";
else
    calendarEntry = "Study";
```

The <*then-statement*> and <*else-statement*> are single statements, but several statements can be grouped into a compound statement with curly braces when necessary. For example,

```
if ((year % 4) == 0) {
    leapYear = true;
    febDays = febDays + 1;
}
else
    leapYear = false;
```

This example uses the mod operator %, so the outcome of (year%4) is the remainder of year / 4; that is, the result is 0, 1, 2, or 3.

A typical example sets the same variables in both parts of the conditional. Consider a coin toss at the start of a soccer game, which can be expressed as

```
if (sideUp == sideCalled) {
    coinTossWinner = visitorTeam;
    firstHalfOffensive = visitorTeam;
    secondHalfOffensive = hostTeam;
}
else {
    coinTossWinner = hostTeam;
    firstHalfOffensive = hostTeam;
    secondHalfOffensive = visitorTeam;
}
```

Notice that the opening curly brace for the <*else-statement*> is placed right after the else, and the closing curly brace is placed conspicuously on its own line directly below the *e* of else.

18.6 Even or Odd? After executing the conditional statement

```
if (monthDays < 31 && monthNumber < 8)
    evenOrOdd = "even";
else
    evenOrOdd = "odd";
```

what is the value of **evenOrOdd** for May, the fifth month, which has 31 days?

Nested **if/else** Statements

The <*then-statement*> and the <*else-statement*> can contain an if/else, but you have to be careful, because it can be ambiguous which if an else goes with. The rule in JavaScript and most other programming languages is that the else associates with the (immediately) preceding if. For example, the code

Caution: This code is deceptive!

```
if (Pooh == "bear")
    if (Eeyore == "bear")
        report = "Pooh and Eeyore are the same kind of animal";
else
    report = "Pooh is not a bear";
```

has been *deceptively* indented so that it *appears* that the else associates with the first if. But white space is ignored. The JavaScript rule means that the else associates with the "inner" if, so that the following indentation matches the actual meaning:

```
if (Pooh == "bear")
    if (Eeyore == "bear")
        report = "Pooh and Eeyore are the same kind of animal";
    else
        report = "Pooh is not a bear";        Caution: This conclusion is wrong!
```

In fact, assuming Pooh is a bear and Eeyore is a donkey or any animal other than a bear, report gives the wrong answer. The best policy—the one successful programmers follow—is to enclose the *<then-statement>* or *<else-statement>* in compound curly braces whenever they contain an if/else. Thus the right way to express the statement is

```
if (Pooh == "bear") {
    if (Eeyore == "bear")
        report = "Pooh and Eeyore are the same kind of animal";
}
else
    report = "Pooh is not a bear";
```

The braces ensure that the else matches with its if. This policy saves a lot of grief.

As one final example of **nested conditionals**, consider the four outcomes from flipping two coins expressed by nested conditionals:

```
if (flip1 == guess1) {
    if (flip2 == guess2)
        score = "win win";
    else
        score = "win lose";
}
else {
    if (flip2 == guess2)
        score = "lose win";
    else
        score = "lose lose";
}
```


This example shows clearly the logic of the true and false outcomes of the predicates.

The Espresso Program

We now return to the program shown in Figure 18.1. The program (shown on the next page) computes the price of four kinds of espresso drinks based on the type of drink, the size of drink, and the number of additional shots, plus tax. The input variables are listed at the start of the program, as is the output.

The input variables are assumed to be given; see Chapter 19 for details on how this is done with a GUI. Because the program will create the output, we declare the output to be a variable in the first statement of the program.

Statements 3 through 5 determine the kind of drink and establish the base price. These statements have been written to show different programming techniques:

- **Line 3:** If the order is straight espresso, the first shot is priced at $1.40. This is an example of a basic conditional statement.
- **Lines 4–4c:** These statements establish the base prices for lattes and cappuccinos using an if statement with conditionals in the *<then-statement>* compound statement.
- **Line 5:** This line uses a basic if statement to compute the base price for Americanos.
- **Lines 6, 7:** Finally, the total price is computed in lines 6 and 7. In Line 6 the cost of additional shots is added to the base price. In line 7 the tax is added in. This is accomplished by multiplying the total price by the taxRate, then adding the result to the total price.

Notice that the if statements on lines 3, 4, and 5 will always be executed, but because they apply to different drinks, the statement(s) of their *<then-statement>* will be executed in at most one of the cases.

Input:

drink—a character string with one of the values: "espresso", "latte", "cappuccino", "Americano"
ounce— an integer, giving the size of the drink in ounces
shots—an integer, giving the number of shots

Output:

price in dollars of an order, including 8.8% sales tax

Program:

```
1.    var price;
2.    var taxRate = 0.088;
3.    if (drink == "espresso")
          price = 1.40;
4.    if (drink == "latte" || drink == "cappuccino") {
4a.       if (ounce == 8)
              price = 1.95;
4b.       if (ounce == 12)
              price = 2.35;
4c.       if (ounce == 16)
              price = 2.75;
      }
5.    if (drink == "Americano")
          price = 1.20 + .30 * (ounce/8);
6.    price = price + (shots - 1) * .50;
7.    price = price + price * taxRate;
```

Execution for a Double Tall Latte

To see the espresso program in action, compute the price of a double tall latte, the second most common phrase used in Seattle after "it's still raining." A "double" means a total of two shots in the drink, that is, one extra shot. Thus the input variables to the program are

drink ⟺ "latte"
ounce ⟺ 12
shots ⟺ 2

where ⟺ means "has the value of" or "contains." This notation allows us to give the value of a variable without using the equal sign, which would look like an assignment statement.

The first statements are declarations, which are like definitions. In particular, we should treat price as not yet having any value. The following lines are executed:

- **Line 3** is executed first. The test drink == "espresso" fails, because the variable drink has the value "latte". As a result its then statement is skipped.
- **Line 4** is executed next. The test drink == "latte" || drink == "cappuccino" has a true outcome because the subexpression drink == "latte" is true; the relational test drink == "cappuccino" is false, of course, but because one of the operands of the || is true, the whole expression is true. This means that the then statement containing the conditionals 4a–4c will be executed.
- **Line 4a** is executed next. The test ounce == 8 has a false outcome, so its then statement is skipped.
- **Line 4b** is nexecuted. (I made up *nexecuted* for "next executed." Isn't it a great word?) The ounce == 12 test is true, so the then statement is executed, giving price its initial value, price ⟺ 2.35.
- **Line 4c** is nexecuted. The ounce == 16 test fails, so its then statement is skipped.
- **Line 5** is nexecuted. The drink == "Americano" test fails, so its then statement is skipped.
- **Line 6** is nexecuted. This causes the value of shots minus 1 to be multiplied by .50, resulting in the value .50, which is added to price, yielding price ⟺ 2.85.
- **Line 7** is nexecuted. The current value of price is multiplied by taxRate, whose value was initialized on line 2 (taxRate ⟺ 0.088), resulting in 0.25, which is added to price to compute the final value of 3.10, which is assigned to price.

Thus, price ⟺ 3.10, so a "double tall latte" costs $3.10.

Summary

In this chapter, we introduced enough programming concepts—and their JavaScript syntax—for you to read and understand basic programs. The chapter began by introducing the idea that a name can be separated from its value. Captain is a name for a team leader, but its value, that is, the person who is the captain, can change. In fact, the name exists, though with an undefined value, as soon as a team is formed. Names-with-changing-values is a familiar idea. File names work this way as we progressively update a file with, say, a word processor. Variables in programming languages have changing values, too. The reason is simple. A program is a fixed, finite specification for a computation written out in a few pages of code. Yet, when the computation is executed, many values may be created to produce the final answer. In the espresso computation, for example, the variable `price`, which is initially undefined, has three different values: the base price, the total price before tax, and the final price. At any point, the value of `price` is the price as computed so far, but the process of computing `price` continues until the program is finished.

In basic programming, you now understand that:

- Name–value separation is an important concept. It's one of the ways that programming differs from algebra.
- Letter sequences that make up a variable's name (identifiers) must be declared. Variables can be initialized when they are declared. Changing the value of a variable is possible by using assignment.
- An assignment statement has a variable on the left side of the symbol and an expression on the right side. The operation is to compute the value of the expression and make the result the new value of the variable. This makes information flow from right to left in an assignment statement. Statements like `x = x + 1;` make sense in programming, but not in algebra. This statement is a command to the computer to find the current value of the variable `x`, add 1 to it, and make the result of the addition the new value of `x`.
- There are three JavaScript data types—numbers, strings, and Booleans—and we can build expressions to compute values of these types.
- Standard arithmetic operators and relationals compute on numbers, and logical operations on Booleans. (See Appendix C for a full listing.) In defining concatenation, you learned about "operator overload." Expressions "do the computing" in programs and are generally a familiar idea.
- As a rule, all programming statements are executed one after another, starting at the beginning. The conditional statements are the exception. JavaScript's two conditional forms are `if` and `if/else`.

These allow statements to be executed depending on the outcome of a Boolean expression called a predicate. Using conditionals, we can organize our computations so that operations are performed when "the conditions are right."

- We must be careful to group statements within a compound statement to make it clear which statements are skipped or executed. We also must be careful when using `if/else` in a conditional so that the `if` and `else` associate correctly.
- The espresso program in Figure 18.1 illustrates most of the ideas in this chapter. The program uses both numeric and string data types, as well as the declaration, assignment, and conditional statement forms.
- All that keeps us from running the program and demonstrating our knowledge is setting up the input to acquire the values for `drink`, `ounce`, and `shots`, and outputting the `price`. This requires a GUI written in HTML (the topic of Chapter 19).

Try It Solutions

18.1 "Slumdog Millionaire" is a name bound to a specific movie that will always be the movie's name; "Best _Picture" is a variable that changes value each year.

18.2
```
var Alpha, Beta;
```

18.3
```
var real_first_name = 'Samuel', real_last_name = "Clemens";
var humorist = true;
var century = 19;
var famous_quote = '"Nothing so needs reforming as other
   people\'s habits." '
```

Notice the use of escape apostrophe (\') in `famous_quote`. It is required because the entire quotation is enclosed in single quotes to allow the text to include double quotes. In the computer's memory the value of `famous_quote` is the 54-character string:

```
"Nothing so needs reforming as other people's habits."
```

That is, the enclosing single quotes and the backslash are gone.

18.4
```
var bestPicture;
bestPicture = "Slumdog Millionaire";
```

Did you remember the semicolon terminators?

18.5 lat <= 23.5 | | lat >= 66.5

18.6 `evenOrOdd` has the value `odd`.

Review Questions

Multiple Choice

1. JavaScript is mainly used for
   a. mainframe applications
   b. Web applications
   c. operating systems
   d. all of the above
2. On the computer, variables are
   a. memory locations
   b. programs
   c. files
   d. all of the above
3. Which of the following can be used as part of a variable name?
   a. - hyphen
   b. ƀ (space)
   c. _ underscore
   d. ( ) parentheses
4. The symbol to terminate a statement in JavaScript is
   a. : colon
   b. Enter
   c. ! exclamation
   d. ; semicolon
5. When declared, JavaScript variables are
   a. automatically assigned a 0
   b. automatically assigned a blank
   c. undefined
   d. assigned a random number
6. Which of the following is not a term used to change the value of a variable?
   a. assign
   b. gets
   c. sets
   d. becomes
7. The right side of an assignment statement
   a. must contain a formula
   b. must contain more than just a variable
   c. uses the values in the variables before the start of the execution of the statement
   d. all of the above
8. `grade = num_right * 2.5` is a(n)
   a. variable
   b. operator
   c. assignment statement
   d. relational operator

A JavaScript Program

The Bean Counter

19
chapter

learning objectives

- Use the Bean Counter application as a model to
  - Write input elements
  - Create a button table
  - Write an event handler in JavaScript
  - Produce a GUI similar to that of the Bean Counter
- Trace the execution of the Bean Counter, saying what output is produced by a given input
- Explain event-based programming in JavaScript and the use of event handlers

Programming today is a race between software engineers striving to build bigger and better idiot-proof programs, and the Universe trying to produce bigger and better idiots. So far the Universe is winning.

—RICH COOK

MUCH OF MODERN programming requires two activities. The first is creating the algorithm that directs the computer to solve a problem. The second is creating a user interface to assist with the human/computer interaction; specifically, a way to enter the input and a way to display the computed output. JavaScript (JS) is designed for Web applications, which means that JavaScript code is included in Web page source code written in XHTML. The Web page is the graphical user interface; the JavaScript does the computing.

In Chapter 18, we wrote a program in JavaScript to charge for espresso drinks. That program is the computational part of our solution. In this chapter, we focus on creating a user interface and connecting it to the espresso program. So, our main goal is to produce a user-friendly GUI for the program.

We will create the Bean Counter application. The first step is to make sure that the computation from Chapter 18 is correct. Then, after covering two preliminaries, we will follow these steps.

1. Review Web page programming, recalling some XHTML basics, and introduce the idea of HTML input elements.
2. Build the GUI for the Bean Counter program, so that the graphic looks right. Only the picture will be complete; the buttons will not work yet.
3. Introduce the idea of event programming and connect the buttons to the program logic.
4. Test the Web page, evaluating it for its usefulness.
5. Revise the Web page and the logic to improve the solution to the problem.

When the Web page is complete, we will have created our first complete JavaScript program.

Preliminaries

Recall from Chapter 4 that XHTML files are simple ASCII text. The fancy formatting of word processors like WordPerfect and Microsoft Word confuses Web browsers and must be avoided. Instead we'll use the basic text editor such as Notepad++ or TextWrangler discussed in Lab Practice I of Chapter 4. The file format must be `text` or `txt`, and the file name's extension (the characters following the last dot) must be `html`. So, `bean.html` is an appropriate file name. The operating system knows that the file will be processed by a Web browser, and the browser will be able to understand everything in the file without becoming confused.

fluencyTIP

> **Build as You Go.** The best way to learn the ideas and the practical skills in this chapter is to build the program yourself as you read along.

To create your program, start by opening your `starterPage.html` in your text editor, and rename the file, `bean.html`. To include JavaScript in an XHTML file, enclose the JavaScript text in `<script type="text/javascript"> </script>` tags. The information that you include between these tags is the subject of this chapter. When it's time to test your program, Save it. Then find the file on your computer and open the file with Firefox. Your JavaScript will run with your XHTML. It's that simple.

To work through the mechanics of running a JavaScript program, we will ignore the user interface for the moment and simply run the computational part of the program from Chapter 18. This is mostly an exercise, because we will not be able to interact with the result, and all that we will see is one number printed out. We begin this way to make sure the Bean Counter code is working. We'll use this code later in the chapter, so typing it in now is a good way to become familiar with the code. The program structure needed to run just the computation part is shown in Figure 19.1. You should *accurately* type it into a file, save it as `beanV0.html`, and run it.

Because we have not yet built the user interface, we have no way to give inputs. So we fake the input. We declare and initialize three new variables—`drink`, `shots`, and `ounce`—as the first three statements of the JavaScript code. We'll take these out later, when we add the buttons. These initializers are for a "double tall latte," that is, a 12-ounce latte made with two shots of espresso. After you type in and run the program with Firefox, you should see the result shown in Figure 19.2.

The `alert(price)` command prints out the amount that the program computed for the `price`. We verify that the program did produce the same price for a "double tall latte" that we computed in Chapter 18. (The answer isn't rounded to a whole penny, but we'll solve that problem later.) Our next step is to construct the graphical user interface.

```
<!DOCTYPE html PUBLIC "-//W3C//DTD XHTML 1.0 Strict//EN"
"http://www.w3.org/TR/xhtml1/DTD/xhtml1-strict.dtd">

<html xmlns="http://www.w3.org/1999/xhtml">
  <head>
    <meta http-equiv="Content-Type" content="text/html; charset=utf-8"/>
    <title>Version 0</title></head>
  <body>
    <h1>Here's Version 0 of the Bean Counter</h1>
    <script language = "JavaScript">
      var drink = "latte";  //Temporary Decl. for Version 0; to be removed
      var shots = 2;        //Temporary Decl. for Version 0; to be removed
      var ounce = 12;       //Temporary Decl. for Version 0; to be removed
      var price;
      var taxRate = 0.088;
      if (drink == "espresso")
        price = 1.40;
      if (drink == "latte" || drink == "cappuccino") {
        if (ounce == 8)
          price = 1.95;
        if (ounce == 12)
          price = 2.35;
        if (ounce == 16)
          price = 2.75;
      }
      if (drink == "Americano")
        price = 1.20 + .30 * (ounce/8);
      price = price + (shots - 1) * .50;
      price = price + price * taxRate;
      alert(price);   //Temporary statement to print result; to be changed
    </script>
  </body>
</html>
```

Figure 19.1 Version 0 of the Bean Counter program without the user interface, and with fixed inputs:

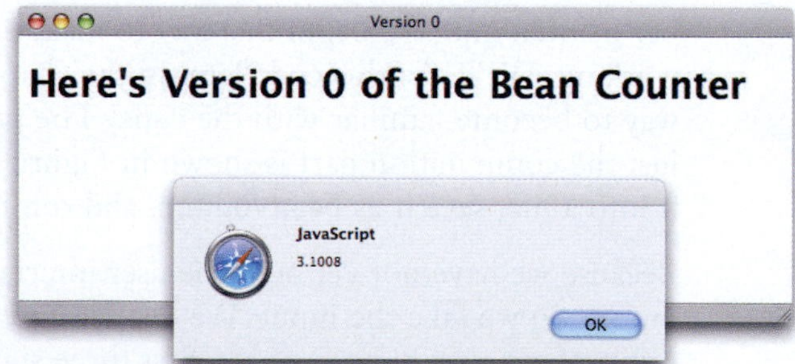

Figure 19.2 Web page displayed by Version 0 of the Bean Counter program of Figure 19.1.

Background for the GUI

This section covers two introductory topics that you need to understand to create the JavaScript graphical user interface. First we present a quick review of XHTML. If you need more information, consult Chapter 4. Next we explain a new XHTML tag, the <input.../> tag. This allows us to create buttons and print output.

The Bean Counter GUI (see Figure 19.3) offers the user rows and columns of buttons, and a window in the lower right corner to display the total price of the espresso drink. The first column of buttons specifies the number of shots. The second column specifies the size of the drink, where S, T, and G stand for short, tall, and grande. The next column specifies the type of espresso drink. The meanings of the last two buttons in the rightmost column are obvious.

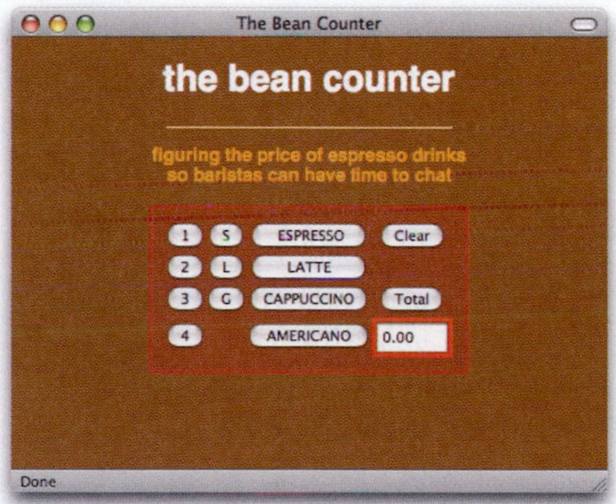

Figure 19.3 Web interface for the Bean Counter program displayed with Firefox.

Review XHTML Basics

Our review of XHTML—covered thoroughly in Chapter 4—entails a quick development of the starting XHTML for the bean.html page.

Beginning with the starterPage.html, change the title to <title>The Bean Counter</title>. We will need a global <style> section in the head, so this is a good time to place those tags. And in the body, we replace "Hello, World" with an <h1> heading that reads "the bean counter," an <hr/> for a horizontal line, and a paragraph with the text "figuring the price of espresso drinks so baristas can have time to chat." A <br/> is needed to display the short slogan on two lines. Now all that remains is to format the text.

Though we will follow the color and font choices of Figure 19.3, if we were "starting from scratch" on this page we would probably experiment at this point with various background colors, font colors, and font faces. A convenient way to do this is to open three windows: one for the text editor, to modify the page; another for the browser, to display the page; and a third one to display a list of color names, probably at www.w3schools.com/css/css_colornames.asp, to show the color choices with their names. Having the three windows open makes it easy to switch from one window to the next, choosing a color, updating the style information with the editor, and then checking out the result. Design couldn't be easier.

We will choose saddlebrown as the background color, darkorange for the font color, and Helvetica for the font family. The heading, however, will be white, and the horizontal line must be styled, too, to be shorter than the full window. So, the styling components for the start of the page are

```
<style type="text/css">
    body {background-color : saddlebrown; color : darkorange;
          font-family : helvetica; text-align : center}
</style>
. . .
<h1 style="color : white"> the bean counter</h1>
<hr style="width : 50%; color : darkorange"/>
<p><b>figuring the price of espresso drinks<br/>
        so baristas can have time to chat</b></p>
```

Notice that we chose a color for the line, changing it from its default gray.

If this discussion reminds you what you've forgotten about XHTML, review Chapter 4 or check Appendix A for more information.

Interacting with a GUI

Curiously, the input facilities like **buttons** and **checkboxes** are known as elements of **forms**. They were introduced into HTML to assist with activities like ordering products or answering survey questions. As you know, users fill out the form by clicking on buttons or entering data in text windows. When the form is complete, it is sent to the computer for processing. Although our application doesn't involve questionnaires, we use the input elements, and so must use the form tags.

Forms. The form tags <form> and </form> must surround all of the input elements. Though <form> has several attributes, only one is required, the action attribute. Normally, this explains to the browser how to process the form, but because we will not be using this feature, we simply make the action the empty string, action="". Thus, to allow us to use input buttons, the next item in our XHTML program is the pair

```
<form action="">
</form>
```

The rest of our GUI programming will be placed between these two tags. Figure 19.4 shows the code for the page as it looks so far.

Events and event handlers. When the GUI inputs are used, such as clicking a button, they cause an event to occur. In the case of a button, the event is called a "click event." An **event** is an indication from the computer (operating system) that something just happened (mouse click).

We want our JavaScript program to respond to that click—that is, perform the operation corresponding to the button command. When JavaScript finds out about the event, it runs a piece of program called the event handler for that event. An **event handler** is the program that performs the task to respond to an event. We will explain this concept further in a moment.

```
<!DOCTYPE html PUBLIC "-//W3C//DTD XHTML 1.0 Strict//EN"
"http://www.w3.org/TR/xhtml1/DTD/xhtml1-strict.dtd">

<html xmlns="http://www.w3.org/1999/xhtml">
  <head>
    <meta http-equiv="Content-Type" content="text/html; charset=utf-8"/>
     <title>The Bean Counter</title>
     <style type="text/css">
          body {background-color : saddlebrown; color : darkorange;
                   font-family : helvetica; text-align : center}
     </style>
  </head>
  <body>
    <h1 style="color : white"> the bean counter</h1>
    <hr style="width : 50%; color : darkorange "/>
    <p><b>figuring the price of espresso drinks<br />
           so baristas can have time to chat</b></p>
     <form action="">
     </form>
</body>
</html>
```

The Bean Counter

the bean counter

figuring the price of espresso drinks
so baristas can have time to chat

Done

Figure 19.4 The Bean Counter interface to this point, and the HTML that produced it.

Three Input Elements

The <input ... /> tag, a singleton tag ending in />, specifies all of the input types—buttons, text boxes, check boxes, and so on. The easiest way to learn the types is simply to study an example of each. The three input elements used in this book are the button, text box, and radio buttons.

- **Button.** The form of the button input is

  <input type="button" value="*label*" onclick="*event_handler*" />

  where value gives the text to be printed on the button, and onclick gives the event handler's JavaScript instructions. When the user clicks on the button, the JavaScript code of the event handler is executed. (Event handling will be discussed momentarily.) The image for the button is placed in the next position in the text of the XHTML program.

- **Text Box.** The text box can be used to input or output numbers or words. Its general form is

  <input type="text" name="*identifier*" size="6"
      onchange="*event_handler*" />

  where *identifier* is the name of the element and onchange gives the event handler's JavaScript instructions. After the user has changed the contents in the text window, the JavaScript program instructions are performed. The image for the text input is placed in the next position in the text of the HTML program.

- **Radio Button.** Radio buttons give a selection of preprogrammed settings. Their general form is

  <input type="radio" name="*identifier*"
      onclick="*event_handler*" />*label text*

where *identifier* is the name of the element, *label text* is shown beside the button, and onclick gives the event handler. When the user clicks on a radio button, the center darkens to indicate that it is set, and the event handler's JavaScript instructions are performed. If there are other radio buttons with the same name, they are also cleared. The image is placed in the next position in the text of the HTML program.

For the Bean Counter application, we need only the text and button inputs. We will use radio buttons later.

Creating the Graphical User Interface

We are well on our way to creating the Bean Counter interface, as shown in Figure 19.3. The XHTML in Figure 19.4 has the heading information, the horizontal line, and the slogan. "All" we have to do is create a table and fill in the entries. We should place the table between the form tags to ensure that the browser understands the inputs.

Focus Point. When faced with a task, it's a good idea to "think it through" before starting. List the required steps in the order you will do them. Then you can focus your attention on one step at a time. This process, which is a main topic of Chapter 22, is illustrated here by writing down our plan before starting.

Notice that the table in Figure 19.3 is a four-row, four-column table with two empty cells. (The columns are not all the same size, but the browser will take care of making them the right size.) Buttons appear in all of the occupied cells but one, so our table is mostly a table of buttons. This suggests the following algorithm for building the table.

1. **Create a button table.** Program the XHTML for a four-row, four-column table with a generic button in each cell. This is a good strategy because we can build such a table quickly using *Copy/Paste*.
2. **Delete two buttons.** Two of the cells in the table should be empty. Delete the buttons, but not the cells.
3. **Insert text box.** Replace the button for the last cell and make it a text control.
4. **Label the buttons.** Pass through the table and set the value attribute of each button so that the label on the button is correct.
5. **Primp the interface.** Check the interface and adjust the specification where it is necessary.

Once these five steps are complete, the image of the Bean Counter interface will be finished. Consider each step in detail.

Table Trick. A fast way to build a table in HTML is to create a skeleton first, then fill it in. This is easy because the skeleton can be constructed inside out using copy and paste. Begin with a generic cell such as `<td>` and `</td>` tags; copy and paste these as many times as needed to build a row, and enclose the result in `<tr>` and `</tr>` tags; copy and paste that for as many rows as needed, and surround the result with `<table>` and `</table>` tags. Finally, fill in the entries.

1. Create a Button Table

We use the "inside out" scheme to build the table. Given the information about the button input, we decide that the generic cell can have the form

```
<td>
    <input type="button" value="b" onclick = ''/>
</td>
```

Here "b" is a placeholder for the button label that we'll fix in Step 4, and '' is a placeholder for the JavaScript text of the event handler that we'll write later.

We make four copies of the cell in the file from Figure 19.4 and surround them by row tags. We make four copies of the row and surround them with table tags. We save the page and review it, and immediately notice that the table is left justified. We want it centered. This is more complicated than it ought to be using CSS, but the proper solution is to add a global styling definition for the table element, specifying that the left and right margins should be automatically positioned—this will balance and center the table:

```
table {margin-left : auto; margin-right : auto}
```

(Because Internet Explorer does not follow widely accepted Web standards, `text-align : center` must also be included if we want IE users to see the table centered, which we do.) The result is shown in Figure 19.5(a).

2. Delete Two Buttons

In row 2, cell 4, and row 4, cell 2, we remove the `<input.../>` because these cells must be empty. Of course, we can leave a cell empty, but we still need to surround it with the `<td>` and `</td>` tags for it to be a cell.

3. Insert Text Box

From the last section, we know we need a text box in the lower right corner, so the next step is to modify the button input to be a text input. Begin by changing the type to text. Next, we decide to name the text box "price" because that's the information that we compute with our program code and want displayed. The window can be five characters wide because no combination of drink inputs will result in a price of more than four digits plus the decimal point. Finally, we change the onclick event handler to onchange. So the button in row 4, cell 4 should be replaced by

```
<input type="text" name="price" value="0.00" size="5"
    onchange=' '/>
```

which produces the result shown in Figure 19.5(b). This looks a little lopsided, but we haven't labeled the buttons yet.

4. Label the Buttons

The next task is to pass through the table cells and change the value attribute of each button from "b" to its proper button label. The first column is the number of shots (1, 2, 3, 4), the second column is the sizes (S, T, G), and the third column is the drinks (espresso, latte, cappuccino, Americano), which will be given in all uppercase letters. The two items in the last column are the controls (Clear, Total).

Because of the row formulation of HTML tables, it is easiest to work row-wise through the table rather than column-wise. The result of our work is shown in Figure 19.5(c). We're close to achieving what we want, but we still need to fix the buttons a bit.

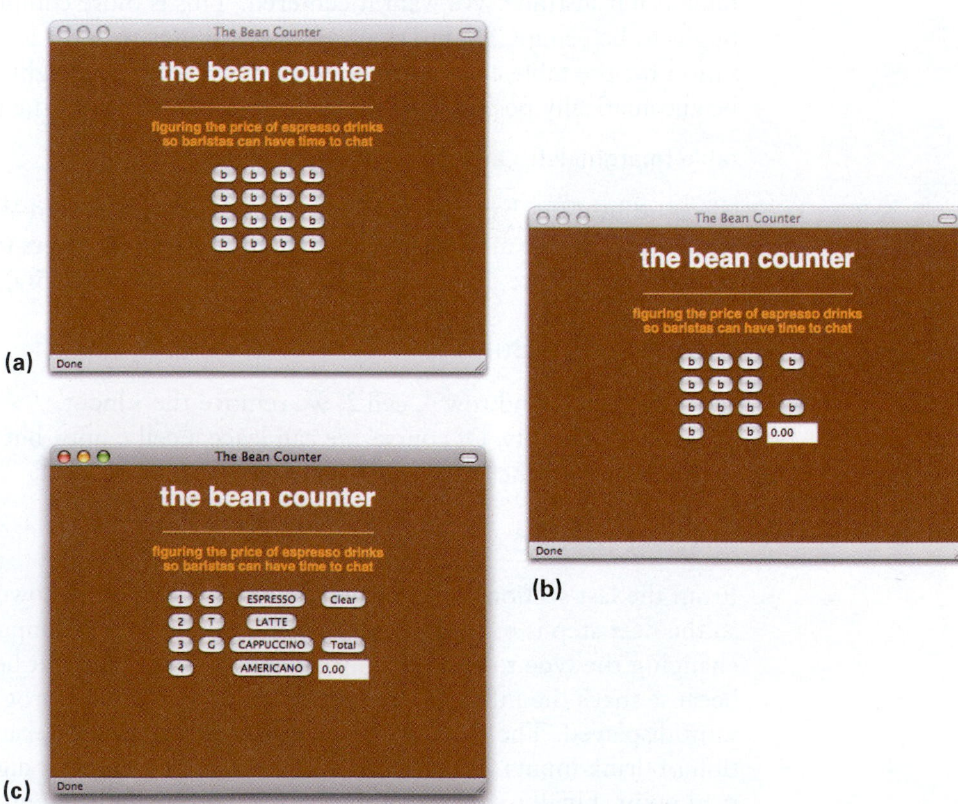

Figure 19.5 Intermediate stages in the construction of the Bean Counter interface: (a) after Step 1, (b) after Step 3, (c) after Step 4.

5. Primp the Interface

Our guess that the form of the form wouldn't be quite right was right. Looking at the design in Figure 19.5(c), we notice that the buttons, though centered, look ragged; the appearance would look more polished if they were all about the same width. Because the button is as wide as its value text, we simply add spaces before and after the drink name to make the button wider and to balance the position of the text.

The only remaining difference is that the table in Figure 19.3 has borders and colors. Giving the table a background color requires that we add to the table's global style specification. As we recall from Chapter 11, colors can be numeric; a good choice for this table might be background-color : #993300. In addition, we add a border to the table styling, making it a medium solid line colored firebrick. Also, because the buttons seem crowded in the table, we add 8 pixels of padding.

Finally, we add a medium red border to the price text box; because it applies only to the cell, we use a style attribute on its <td> tag. Now our interface matches Figure 19.3 exactly.

Event-Based Programming

How should the Bean Counter program work? Like a calculator, something should happen as each button is clicked, that is, in response to user-caused events. The rest of the time nothing should happen. Programming the Bean Counter application amounts to defining in JavaScript the actions that should be performed when each button is clicked. This is called **event-based programming**. In this section we'll write the event-handling code.

The **onclick** Event Handler

The greatest part of the programming task is already done, because the action for the Total button is to compute the final price, and that computation, shown between the <script> and </script> tags in Figure 19.1, is already programmed. Because this code defines the action we want the computer to perform when the Total button is clicked, we make it the onclick event handler for the Total button. Our XHTML input element for the Total button is presently

```
<td>
    <input type = "button" value = "Total" onclick =' '/>
</td>
```

where onclick is the **event-handling attribute** for the Total button. To use JavaScript to calculate the price, we insert the price computation code *inside the quotes* for the onclick attribute, as shown in Figure 19.6, and it becomes the onclick event handler. Notice that we do not need <script> tags because the browser assumes that the event handler is written in JavaScript.

```
<td>
  <input type="button" value="Total" onclick=
    'var price;
     var taxRate = 0.088;
     if (drink == "espresso")
        price = 1.40;
     if (drink == "latte" || drink == "cappuccino") {
     if (ounce == 8)
        price = 1.95;
     if (ounce == 12)
        price = 2.35;
     if (ounce == 16)
        price = 2.75;
     }
     if (drink == "Americano")
        price = 1.20 + .30 * (ounce/8);
     price = price + (shots - 1) * .50;
     price = price + price * taxRate;
     document.forms[0].price.value = price;
     //one more assignment is required here
  '/>
</td>
```

Figure 19.6 The Total text box input element with the price computation inserted as the event handler. (Notice that the three temporary declarations of Figure 19.1 have been removed, as has the temporary "alert" command.)

Click Event

Here's what happens. When the barista clicks on the Total button, it causes a **click event** in the browser. The browser, designed to perform an action in response to the click event, looks for the onclick event handler in the Total button input tag. The browser should find the JavaScript instructions to perform the action associated with the button. The browser runs those instructions, which implement the action, and then waits for the next event. That's why we move the price computation instructions—the JavaScript text of Figure 19.1 with the temporary assignments removed—to between the quotes of the onclick attribute. Doing so specifies what action the browser is to perform on the click event and how it is to be performed. The browser can now *handle* this click event. (One more instruction is required, as explained at the end of this section.)

Shots Button

Handling the click events for the other buttons is even easier. In each case, we ask what action should be performed when a particular button is clicked. For the first column of buttons—the shots buttons—the answer is to specify the number of shots the customer requests. For example, clicking on the 1 button should cause the shots variable to get the value 1. (Recall that "get" is how we pronounce the assignment operator =, suggesting how we will write the program.) To handle the click event for the 1 button input, we need to assign shots as follows:

```
<td>
    <input type = "button" value = "1" onclick = 'shots = 1' />
</td>
```

Notice that the 2 button assigns shots the value 2, and so on. Thus the event handlers for the shots buttons require only one JavaScript command each: an assignment of the right number to shots.

Size and Drink Buttons

The buttons in the size and drink columns are similar. The action to be performed on a click event for the size buttons is to assign the ounce variable the appropriate value, 8, 12, or 16, as in

```
<td>
    <input type = "button" value = " S " onclick = 'ounce = 8' />
</td>
```

For the drink column, the drink variable gets the name of the drink quoted:

```
<td align="center">
    <input type = "button" value = " ESPRESSO "
        onclick = 'drink = "espresso"' />
</td>
```

Notice that single quotes surround the assignment statement, which uses double quotes. To plan for the use of double-quoted string literals, we chose single quotes for the event handler placeholder in the generic button of the last section.

Also, notice that drink was assigned the string "espresso", not "ESPRESSO", as written on the button. The reason is that when the JavaScript code computes the price, the if statement compares the value of the drink with the string literal "espresso", and since the comparison is case sensitive, the two strings have to be the same case to match.

19.1 Second Row. The second row of the table has the form

```
<tr>
   <td>
      <input type="button" value="2" onclick=' '/>
   </td>
   <td>
      <input type="button" value="T" onclick=' '/>
   </td>
   <td>
      <input type="button" value="LATTE" onclick=' '/>
   </td>
   <td>
   </td>
</tr>
```

Give the **onclick** event handler code for each of the three input elements.

Match Point. You need to be careful when typing string literals like "**espresso**", because when the computer compares this value with the string literal in the **Total** button's event handler (Figure 19.6, line 5), they must match exactly. Misspellings ("**expresso**"), case differences ("**Espresso**"), or even unintentional blanks (" **espresso**") will fail to match.

Clear Button and Initializations

Clicking on the Clear button should reset all of the variables (drink, ounce, and shots) to their initial values. When we think about what those initial values are, we realize that we haven't initialized them yet. In fact, we haven't even declared the variables yet. As is common in programming, working on the solution to one task—setting up the Clear event handler—reminds us that we have another task to do—declare the variables. So, we first handle the declaration with initialization, and then return to the Clear event handler.

The declarations should be placed at the beginning of the program, but we don't really have a single program. Rather, we have many little program pieces in the form of event handlers. So, referring to Figure 19.1, we place the declarations for the three variables at the start of the body just after the <body> tag. As usual, the declarations must be enclosed in <script> tags. (Recall that <script> tags are not needed for the event handlers, because they *expect* JavaScript.) The declarations are

```
<script type = 'text/javascript'>
    var shots = 1;
    var drink = "none";
    var ounce = 0;
</script>
```

The initial value for shots is 1 because every espresso drink will have at least one shot. The initial values for drink and ounce are chosen to be illegal values, so that if the barista forgets to specify either one, he or she will receive an error message, indicating that an input has been forgotten. Finally, the Clear button should make these same assignments, resulting in its onclick event handler being

```
<td>
    <input type = "button" value = "Clear" onclick = 'shots = 1;
        drink = "none";
        ounce = 0;
        document.forms[0].price.value = "0.00"' />
</td>
```

completing both the initialization and Clear event handler specifications.

The last assignment statement of the Clear event handler

```
document.forms[0].price.value = "0.00"
```

is important. It places 0.00 in the price window, reinitializing it. The next section explains how the assignment statement works.

Referencing Data Across Controls

The browser records all of the information about a Web page in a data structure called the **Document Object Model**, or **DOM**. When we use JavaScript we will often refer to information in the DOM, so it is important that we know just a bit about it. The main thing is that the DOM has areas where it records information about the forms used in the page, the images used on the page, and so on. Entries are created for forms, images, and the other elements in the order in which the information is encountered in the XHTML description. So, for example, our one form is recorded as forms[0], because computer counting always starts at 0. We'll have just a bit more to say about the DOM later.

For each form, the input controls are recorded. Our form has an input named price. Input controls can have several attributes, and these are recorded, too. The price input control has a value attribute, which was initially assigned "0.00". (See *3. Insert text box* on page 584.) The value attribute of the price element of the forms[0] form of the document is displayed by the window.

When we program in JavaScript and want a statement in one element (e.g., the Clear button) to change a value in another element (e.g., the value attribute of the price text window), we must tell the browser how to navigate among the elements. For that we need the **dot operator**.

Dot operator. The dot operator provides a means of navigation to the proper object. So, the reference

object.property

selects the **property of the object**. We usually read this reference *right to left*, saying the dot as "of," as in "*property of object*." So, the assignment in the Clear button event handler reinitializing the window

```
document.forms[0].price.value = "0.00"
```

can be read "the value attribute *of* the price input *of* the forms[0] form *of* the document is assigned 0.00." Said another way, when the Clear button wants to change the window of the price element, it tells the browser to find the 0th form in the document, and then within it, find the price input, and then within it, find the value attribute, and change it.

Changing the window. Because the value attribute is the content displayed in the price window, when the assignment changes the value back to 0.00, the browser displays the assigned value. In this way, the event handler of one element can refer to an attribute of another input element.

Notice that when the value is reassigned, the window displays the 0.00 and thus acts as an output. The idea that something called an *input* is used to output information may seem strange. But the window can be seen from both the user's and the computer's point of view. If one side gets information (input) from it, the other must have put (output) the information. And vice versa. Input elements are for both input and output.

Displaying the total. There is one other case where the event handler of one element must refer to the value attribute of price. The Total event handler, the one we built first, must output the price. It does this the same way the Clear button event handler clears the price window—by assigning to the value attribute of price. Thus the final line of the Total event handler—the one that is a comment in Figure 19.6 promising one more assignment statement—should be replaced by

```
document.forms[0].price.value = price;
```

in order to display the final price. That change completes the Total event handler, which means we've finished the Bean Counter application. Run it!

19.2 Double-Click. Using the fact that the value of the price window can be tested using an expression such as document.forms[0].price.value == "0.00", change the Clear button event handler using an if/else statement so that if clicked and the price window already contains "0.00", then it is filled with "No Sale".

Critiquing the Bean Counter

Every design must be critiqued to ensure that it meets the requirements of solving the problem and to determine if it can be improved. Therefore, the next task is to experiment with the Bean Counter application, trying a dozen or more sample values to see how well it works.

Be a Reviewer. This critique is most valuable if you have taken a moment to try the application. If you didn't program it, you can find it at: www.aw.com/snyder/.

Does our design fulfill the barista's needs? We'll organize our analysis by topic.

Numbers Versus Money

The most obvious and annoying problem with the Bean Counter application is that the final price is shown as a decimal number with several digits of precision rather than as currency with only two digits to the right of the decimal point. This problem can be almost completely fixed by changing the last line of the Total button event handler to

```
document.forms[0].price.value = Math.round(price*100)/100;
```

The computation works as follows: The price is first multiplied by 100. This changes the price from a "dollars amount" to a "cents amount," that is, the price is expressed as the total number of pennies. That result is then rounded by using the built-in JavaScript function Math.round() to eliminate any digits to the right of the decimal point that now represent less than a penny. Finally, that result is divided by 100 again to convert back to a "dollars amount." The computation is a standard way to remove unwanted digits.

The solution doesn't quite solve the problem, because trailing zeros are dropped; that is, the price of $3.10 for a double tall latte would print as 3.1. But this is a small problem that doesn't come up much, so we'll ignore it. The full solution requires some advanced concepts, resulting in the assignment statement:

```
document.forms[0].price.value =
    (Math.round(price*100)/100).toString().match(/ \.\d]{4}/);
```

Organization

The organization of the buttons is generally consistent with how the application will be used. Because espresso drinks are typically named with syntax of the form

<shots> *<size>* *<kind>*

as in "double tall latte," the buttons are in a good order for the left-to-right cursor flow. It might make sense to put the Clear button on the left side to start the process, but because there is no obvious place for it and because the cursor will generally be positioned on the Total button at the end of the previous purchase—that is, on the right side of the table below the Clear button—the design is not inconvenient. We will leave the page organized as it is.

Feedback

One problem with the design is that it doesn't give the barista any feedback about the current settings of the variables. One principle of user interfaces from Chapter 2 is that there should always be feedback for every operation. For some browsers there is *a bit of* feedback because buttons are automatically highlighted when they are clicked. But once another button is clicked, the automatic highlighting moves to that button. Adding feedback—for example, a window above each column of buttons that gives the current setting—might be better; see Figure 19.7.

Recap of the Bean Counter Application

The sample program of Chapter 18 is now a "useful" application. In the process, we learned the basics of event-based programming using JavaScript. Because this chapter focused on building the application, we didn't spend much time discussing the ideas generally. So, let's review the major ideas now.

We created a graphical user interface for the Bean Counter application by first creating the XHTML text to produce the image of the interface, and

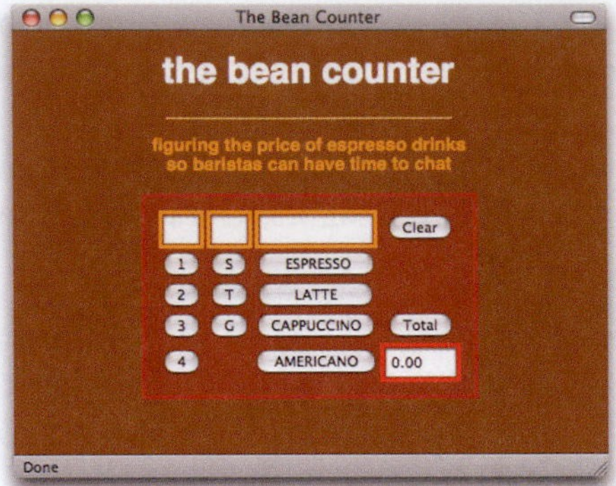

Figure 19.7 The Bean Counter application improved to give the barista feedback.

then adding JavaScript—mostly in event handlers for inputs—to make the application work. Though we discussed programs in Chapter 18 as if they were single, monolithic sequences of statements, the Bean Counter application is actually many tiny code segments that are mostly one or two statements long. This is typical of event-based programming. Other, less interactive forms of computing are more monolithic.

Referencing Variables

The only problem that the many-tiny-code-segments property caused is that we didn't immediately know where to place the declarations for the variables, `shots`, `ounce`, and `drink`. Declarations are usually placed at the start of a program. With many event handlers, however, it's as though we have many program "starts." We placed the declarations right after the `<body>` tag, which is not the start of a JavaScript program, just the start of the body of the XHTML program. That's why the declarations had to go inside the `<script>` and `</script>` tags.

Though any event handler can reference the globally declared variables, the same is not true for the values of the input elements, such as the `price`. The `value` property of this window is local to the element. So, if an event handler of one element needs to place a value in the window of another element, it must describe how to navigate to the item it wants to change. That was the purpose of this code:

```
document.forms[0].price.value = "0.00";
```

It uses the dot operator to navigate from the enclosing document to the target element value, by naming the appropriate item at each step along the path. The dot operator is best read right to left and can then be pronounced "of." So the statement reads, "assign `0.00` to the `value` attribute *of* the `price` window *of* the `0th` form *of* the `document`."

The Bean Counter application illustrates three different ways to reference data values in an event-handling program: as variables local to a handler (taxRate), as variables global to all the handlers (drink), and as a variable in another element (document.forms[0].price.value). In the first two cases the reference simply requires the variable name because they are defined in the handler (in the case of locals) or in an "enclosing" program (in the case of globals). Only cross-element references require the dot operator.

Program and Test

The programming process for the Bean Counter application was incremental. We began by producing a minimal 14-line XHTML program (see Figure 19.4), and then we tested it. We added a skeleton table and tested it. We improved the table one feature at a time, testing as we went. We wrote JavaScript to solve one event handler at a time. And, recognizing similarities among the various events, we developed their event handlers together. Finally, we critiqued the result.

The result is a 107-line program of more than 3,000 characters. Compared to other first programs, it's huge! This strategy—the result of breaking the task into tiny pieces and testing the program after each small milestone—had two advantages: At no point did we have to solve a complex task that taxed our brains, and the continual testing meant that we immediately knew where any errors were located, namely, in the part we just added. Though the program in Appendix D looks impressive, it is not hard to produce by the program-and-test method. Obviously the approach works generally, as you'll see again in Chapter 22.

Assess the Program Design

When the initial design was completed, we critiqued the result. We were not critiquing the programming. Rather, we were critiquing how well our solution fulfilled the barista's needs. This is an important part of any design effort, but it is especially critical for software. Since software can do anything, it should perfectly match the solution requirements. We found that our design did not give the barista feedback, and so violated one of the principles listed in Chapter 2. This shortcoming could be remedied by adding feedback windows.

Summary

We created the Bean Counter application using the price computation of Chapter 18 and a GUI developed in this chapter. The result is a substantial program that performs a useful computation, at least if you are a barista. The application is analogous to the calculator applications provided by operating systems: the user uses the application by clicking or typing. The requested computation is performed immediately in response to the input events. In the process of creating this application we:

- Used XHTML to set up a context in which event handlers perform the actual work. The setup involved placing buttons and other input elements on a Web page, so a user could enter data and receive results. This is the input/output part of the application and it is principally written in XHTML.

- Wrote JavaScript code for the event handlers. This is the processing part of the application. We used the event-based programming style and the basic instructions discussed in Chapter 18. The style, which is ideal for interactive applications, will be used throughout the rest of the book. Though XHTML and JavaScript are separate languages, that won't matter much. Generally, XHTML will simply be the input/output part of a program written in JavaScript.

Try It Solutions

19.1 Column 2 contents:

```
onclick = 'shots = 2' onclick = 'ounce = 12' onclick = 'drink = "latte"'
```

19.2 Replace the assignment to the price window (last line) of the Clear button event handler to

```
if (document.forms[0].price.value == "0.00")
    document.forms[0].price.value = "No Sale";
else
    document.forms[0].price.value = "0.00";
```

Review Questions

Multiple Choice

1. HTML pages are made from
   a. JavaScript
   b. ASCII text
   c. word processing files
   d. any of the above

2. The first tag of a Web page is
   a. <script>
   b. <head>
   c. <top>
   d. <html>

3. Most of the content of a Web page goes inside the
   a. <head> tag
   b. <body> tag
   c. <content> tag
   d. <page> tag

4. The `color` property sets the
   a. text color
   b. background color
   c. border color
   d. none of the above
5. The `<p>` tag is used to
   a. insert a picture
   b. print a page
   c. insert a paragraph
   d. load a page
6. All of the following are input elements except
   a. print
   b. radio button
   c. text box
   d. checkbox
7. In JavaScript, `onclick` is a(n)
   a. variable
   b. event
   c. event handler
   d. button
8. The operating system signals that a mouse click has occurred. This is called a(n)
   a. handler
   b. event
   c. trigger
   d. action
9. When a button is clicked, the browser
   a. looks for an `onclick` event handler
   b. looks for the JavaScript program to download
   c. creates the button for the program
   d. none of the above
10. The GUI for a Web-based application is built with
    a. XHTML
    b. JavaScript
    c. both of the above
    d. none of the above

Short Answer

1. The interface for a JavaScript program is a(n) _______.
2. The extension for an XHTML page must be _______
3. The _______ tag is used to place a line horizontally across a Web page.
4. The _______ tag is used to place text in italic.

5. A(n) _______ is an indication from the computer that something just happened.
6. A(n) _______ is programming code that responds to an event.
7. A(n) _______ is used to change a value in another element.
8. In the line, `document.forms[0].price.value = "0.00"` the input element is _______, the attribute is _______, and _______ is the form.
9. _______ elements are used for both input and output.
10. _______ is a function used in JavaScript to round numbers.
11. The _______ principle of user interfaces states that a computer should indicate when it has completed the action.
12. JavaScript is used mainly for _______.
13. In XHTML, _______ are used to place and display content.
14. A(n) _______ approach to programming breaks a task into small pieces and tests each piece along the way.

Exercises

1. How many inputs are needed for the Bean Counter program (Figure 19.1) to run correctly?
2. How many outputs does the Bean Counter program have?
3. Explain how variables are initialized. Why do variables need to be initialized?
4. Could radio buttons be used for this application? What would they be like?
5. What would the variable for storing a person's age be called? Create an input element that asks for a person's age.
6. The tax rate for the Bean Counter program is 8.8 percent. What needs to be changed if the tax rate drops to 7 percent?
7. What events are coded into the Bean Counter program?
8. Why won't you know how much your coffee costs until you click on the `Total` button?
9. Explain why none of these strings match:

   `Espresso', 'espresso', 'ESPRESSO', 'Expresso', ' espresso'`
10. In layman's terms, explain what happens when the user clicks on the `Tall` button.
11. Why is a dot operator needed when referencing some variables and not others?
12. Can the user make this program crash?

Programming Functions

20
chapter

Thinking Big

learning objectives

- Apply JavaScript rules for functions, declarations, return values, function calls, scope of reference, and local/global variable reference
- Write JavaScript functions with the proper structure
- Build a GUI that contains functions, analogous to the Memory Bank Web page
- Explain how computers generate random numbers

Civilization advances by extending the number of important operations which we can perform without thinking about them.

—ALFRED NORTH WHITEHEAD, 1911

AS YOU KNOW, an algorithm is a precise and systematic method for producing a specific outcome. If we want an algorithm that we can "carry around" and use in different settings—say while we're programming JavaScript—we put it into a function. A function is simply the standard package into which we place algorithms so they are useful in practice.

We have two motives for packaging algorithms into functions. The first benefit of functions is *reuse*; once we work out the details of how an algorithm produces its outcome, we'd rather not think about it again. Functions allow us to reuse our thinking over and over without repeating the actual thinking. That's a great advantage. The second benefit is to *reduce complexity*, that is, to simplify our thinking. Many times—you'll see a specific case in Chapter 22—problems get so complicated that we experience "brain fry" trying to figure out how to solve them. Functions allow us to encapsulate parts of the solution so that we can set them aside where they no longer confuse us. That's a great advantage, too.

In this chapter you learn how to create functions in JavaScript. While discussing the syntax and operation of functions, we will show many simple examples. The task of learning about functions is not too difficult, so there is time at the end of the chapter to create the *interactive* Memory Bank Web page, a personal page where you can file away your functions as well as all those facts you need to know, but would rather not spend time remembering.

Anatomy of a Function

Functions are packages for algorithms, which implies they have three parts:

- Name
- Parameters
- Definition

Together these parts form the **function declaration**; they are present in functions of all sorts, including JavaScript and other programming languages, spreadsheets, databases, mathematics, and so forth. As we consider each, we'll use the process of converting from the Celsius to Fahrenheit temperature scales as a running example, since it's a computation many Americans struggle with. (We'll do the Fahrenheit to Celsius conversion, the one the rest of the world struggles with, later.) Recall that the relationship between Celsius and Fahrenheit is

$$Fahrenheit = \frac{9}{5} Celsius + 32$$

This is an equation, not an assignment statement. It is this simple computation that we want to package up into a function.

Alternate Function. Functions are also known as *procedures* in both informal and computing languages. *Subroutine* is an antiquated computing term for the same idea. Another technical term is *method.*

Pick a Name

Obviously, the *name* is the identifier for the function, and it is common to use it to describe what the function does. Although computers would be happy with any unique name, it's best to try to pick a name that will be meaningful to humans. We will want a suggestive name to remind ourselves what computation the function performs when we encounter it weeks or years later.

Names in JavaScript follow the usual rules for identifiers, that is, they begin with a letter, use any mix of letters, numbers, and underscores (_), avoid reserved words (see Appendix C), and are case sensitive. Let's pick `convertC2F` for our conversion function.

Naturally, programming languages have a standard form for writing function declarations, and JavaScript's form is quite typical

```
function <name> ( <parameter list> ) {
    <statement list>
}
```

We have just picked the name; the other two parts will be described momentarily. Look at the punctuation. Parentheses always follow a function name, even if there is no *<parameter list>*. And the curly braces, although they can be positioned anywhere to enclose the *<statement list>*, should always be placed where they are obvious. Like the curly braces used with if statements, they are easy to miss. So programmers adopt the convention of placing them where shown so that everyone knows where to look for them.

Parameters

The **parameters** are the values that the function will compute on, the input to the function. For our example, the input is the Celsius temperature. In order for the statements of the algorithm to refer to the input values, they are given names. The *<parameter list>* is simply the list of names for the input values separated by commas. Parameter names follow the usual rules for identifiers in all programming languages. If we pick tempInC as the name for our one parameter in our conversion function, that is, the Celsius temperature we want to convert to Fahrenheit, then our definition so far is

```
function convertC2F ( tempInC ) {
    <statement list>
}
```

When writing our algorithm statements, the parameters are like normal variables; the only differences are that they begin with a value—the function's input—and they don't have to be declared. Because they're parameters, JavaScript automatically declares them for us.

Definition

The **function definition** is the algorithm written in a programming language. A function definition follows the language's general rules for program statements, so for JavaScript, the rules that apply are those covered in Chapters 18–21 and Appendix C.

Because the function definition is computing an algorithm—a precise and systematic method for producing a specified result—there must be some way to say what the result is, that is, some way to give the answer. Different languages do this differently, but JavaScript uses the statement

```
return <expression>
```

where the answer is whatever value the *<expression>* produces. We call the answer the function's *value* or *result*. For example, the function

```
function cheshireCat ( ) {
    return "Smile!";
}
```

is a function that returns the letter string Smile!. It is also a function with no parameters.

Converting from Celsius to Fahrenheit is so easy—the answer we want to produce is simply $\frac{9}{5}$ *Celsius* + 32—that our entire function definition is a single line

```
function convertC2F ( tempInC ) {
    return 9/5*tempInC + 32;
}
```

First, notice that we use our parameter tempInC, which is the input to the function, as the variable in the conversion computation, and second, that we must write the multiplication operation (*) explicitly, as is normal in programming.

That's it. We never have to think about how to convert Celsius to Fahrenheit again. This function will do it for us, saving our brainpower for more important stuff, like movies.

20.1 Fahrenheit to Celsius: Write a JavaScript function to convert from Fahrenheit to Celsius. The equation for the relationship just described implies that *Celsius* = $\frac{5}{9}$(*Fahrenheit* – 32).

The convertC2F( ) function defines the algorithm for converting from Celsius to Fahrenheit, but how exactly will we get the answers? We must *call* the function.

Calling a function is asking the computer to run or execute the statements of the function to produce the answers. We simply write the function's name and put the input values, known as **arguments**, in parentheses after it, as in convertC2F(38). The computer follows the definition of the function and returns the answer, 100.4. Now, that's hot! Getting answers couldn't be easier.

Since we wrote our function in JavaScript, we will have to illustrate the function call by setting up a little Web page to host the JavaScript and to provide a situation in which to call the function. Figure 20.1 shows the page. It begins with the standard XHTML; it gives the definition of the function—we say the function is *declared*—and it computes the result using an alert( ) call, as was

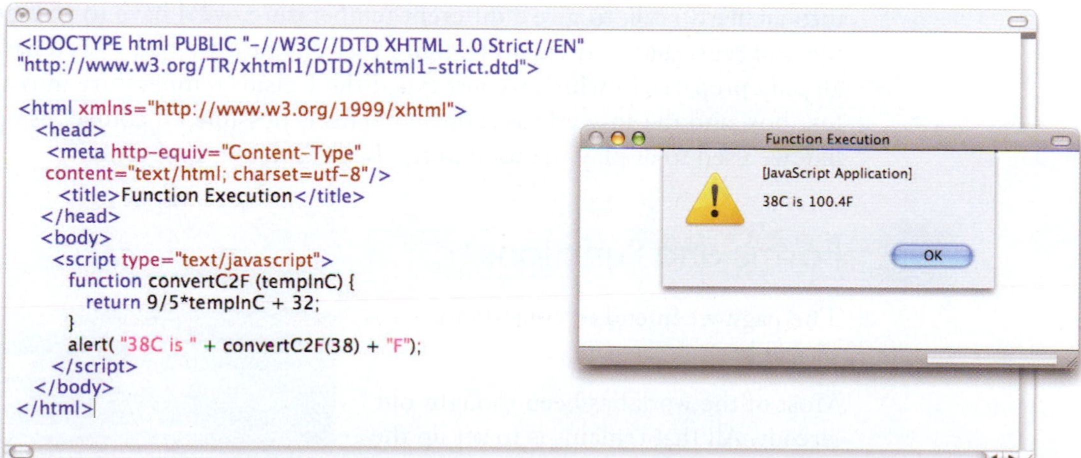

Figure 20.1 The convertC2F( ) function in JavaScript called from an alert( ).

used for version 0 of the Bean Counter computation in Chapter 19. (Of course, alert( ) is itself a built-in JavaScript function.)

Arguments Versus Parameters. Notice that parameters and arguments are two different ways to refer to the same thing. In the function *declaration* we write **function convertC2F(tempInC)** and use the term *parameter* for **tempInC**. In the function *call* we write **convertC2F(38)** and use the term *argument* for 38. It's a parameter when the function's input is viewed from the "inside" of the function; it's an argument when the function's input is viewed from "outside" of the function. They are opposite sides of the same thing.

Declaration Versus Call

Figure 20.1 illustrates an important point about functions: A function's declaration (specification) is different from its call (use). To emphasize the distinction, let's review what we just did.

We *declared* the function right after the <script ...> tag by writing down its three parts in the form required by JavaScript. Functions are only declared once, because it's unnecessary to tell the computer more than once how the function works. Notice that for built-in functions like alert( ), we don't even have to do that much: Some other programmer declared alert( ) while writing the JavaScript interpreter; all we have to do is call it.

We *called* the function convertC2F( ) in an alert( ) call as part of the composition of a string of characters for displaying the answer. Functions are typically called many times because the answers they give are needed many times. For example, we expect to call convertC2F( ) every time someone mentions a Celsius temperature we don't understand. *One declaration, many calls.*

The main problem with convertC2F( ) is that it is inconvenient to write a Web page to find out the answer, even a little one like Figure 20.1. The problem is that in Figure 20.1 the solution to the argument, 38, had to be typed directly into an alert( ) call; to give a different temperature, we'd have to change the file and reexecute it. It would be more convenient if we had a Web page already prepared in which we just typed the Celsius temperature into an input text box, and the answer was returned. This is possible, of course, using forms like we used to display the total in the Bean Counter application.

Forms and Functions

The page we intend to construct is shown here.

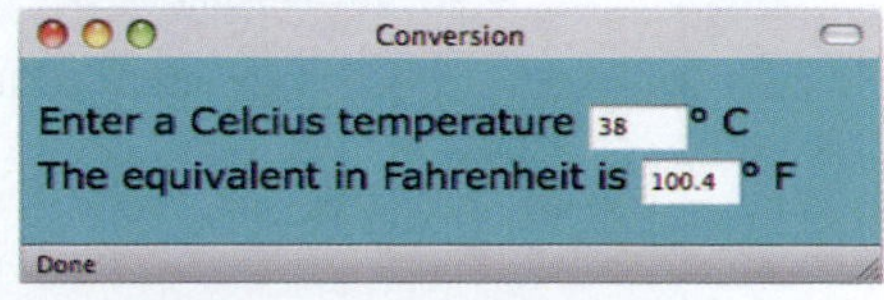

Most of the work has been thought out already. All that remains is to set up the forms.

Recall from Chapter 19 that

- forms must be enclosed in <form> tags
- text boxes are specified by an <input type="text" ... /> tag
- text boxes have a name, size, and other attributes
- to refer to the value or contents of a text box named tb in the first form of a page, we write document.form[0].tb.value
- the main event handler of interest is onchange

The onchange event handler recognizes when a value is entered into the Celsius window (by the cursor moving out of the window) and handles it as we direct. Of course, the operation is pretty easy—we call the convertC2F( ) function with the number typed into the window as the argument. More specifically, let's set up the forms as follows.

```
<form action="">
    <input type="text" name="tempIn" size="4"
        onchange=""/>                              For Celsius input
    <input type="text" name="tempOut" size="4"/>   For Fahrenheit output
</form>
```

The tempIn window will be where we type the Celsius temperature, and the tempOut window will show the result. (Recall that even though we use it as an output in this case, JavaScript uses the <input .../> tag for both input and output text boxes.) So, with these names, we handle the onchange event with the function call

```
onchange = "document.forms[0].tempOut.value =
    convertC2F(document.forms[0].tempIn.value)"
```

In English, this line says when the input window (tempIn) is changed, use the value in that window document.forms[0].tempIn.value as an argument to convertC2F( ) and assign the result to display as the value document.forms[0].tempOut.value of the output window. Putting some text around the text boxes and styling it yields the page we want, as shown in Figure 20.2.

Calling to Customize a Page

In JavaScript there are three ways to get the result of a function call to print on the monitor, and you've just seen two: before the page is created, as you saw with the alert( ) call, and interactively after the page is displayed, as you saw with the Conversion page. The third case applies *while* the page is being created. Calling functions while the browser is creating the page is handy because we can customize pages on-the-fly.

First, let's discuss how a browser builds a page. It begins by reading through the XHTML file, figuring out all of the tags and preparing to build the page. As it's reading the file, it finds our JavaScript tags. The browser removes those tags and all of the text between them, that is, our JavaScript. Then it does whatever the JavaScript tells it to do. One thing that the JavaScript could tell

```
<!DOCTYPE html PUBLIC "-//W3C//DTD XHTML 1.0 Strict//EN"
"http://www.w3.org/TR/xhtml1/DTD/xhtml1-strict.dtd">

<html xmlns="http://www.w3.org/1999/xhtml">
  <head>
   <meta http-equiv="Content-Type" content="text/html; charset=utf-8"/>
    <title>Conversion</title>
    <style type="text/css">
      body {background-color : lightseagreen; font-family : verdana;
              font-size : large;
              }
    </style>
  </head>
  <body>
    <script type="text/javascript">
      function convertC2F (tempInC) {
        return 9/5*tempInC + 32;
      }
    </script>
    <form action="">
      <p>Enter a Celcius temperature
        <input type="text" name="tempIn" size="4" onchange=
        "document.forms[0].tempOut.value =
              convertC2F(document.forms[0].tempIn.value)"/>&#176; C <br/>
       The equivalent in Fahrenheit is
        <input type="text" name="tempOut" size="4"/>&#176;  F
      </p>
    </form>
  </body>
</html>
```


Figure 20.2 The HTML/JavaScript source for the Conversion application.

the browser to do is to put some text back into the file, where the JavaScript just came from. There is a built-in function, document.write( ), that does just that: It inserts the text of its argument into the Web page at the point of the JavaScript tags, as shown in Figure 20.3.

We can use this idea to build a page on-the-fly. Suppose we want a table of temperature conversions for a Web page with a column for Celsius and a column for Fahrenheit (see Figure 20.4). It is easy to set up the page and specify the table tags using normal XHTML. Place <script> tags where the table

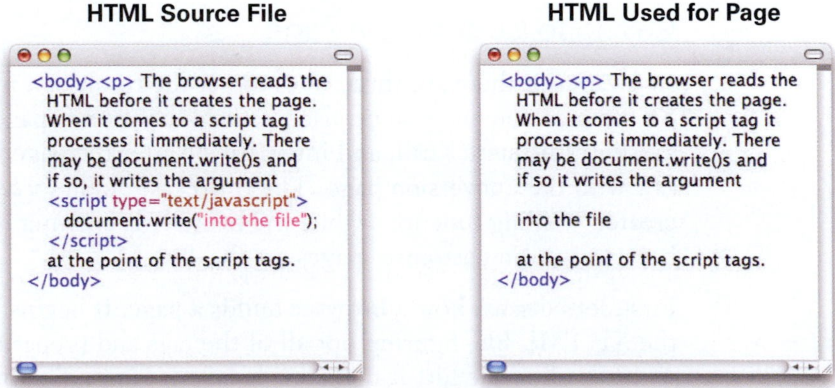

Figure 20.3 An HTML source file containing a JavaScript document.write( ), and the HTML text used by the browser to create the page.

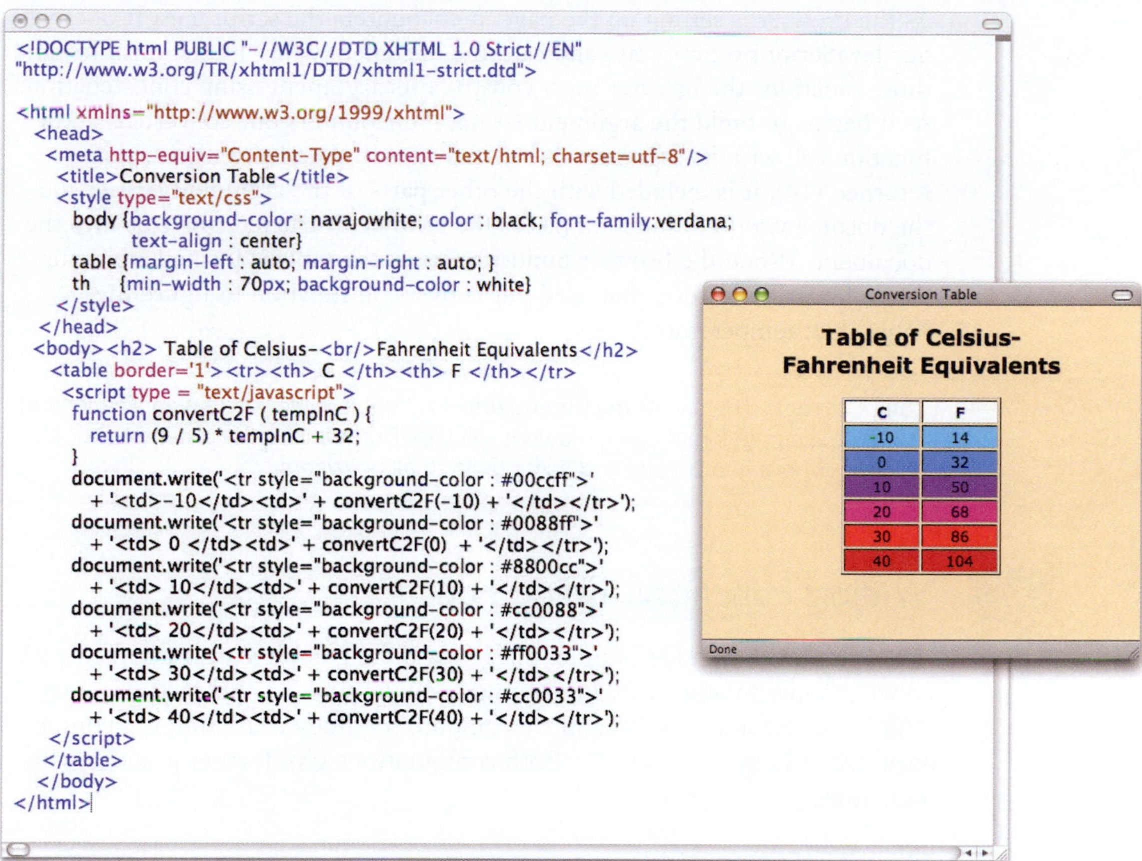

```
<!DOCTYPE html PUBLIC "-//W3C//DTD XHTML 1.0 Strict//EN"
"http://www.w3.org/TR/xhtml1/DTD/xhtml1-strict.dtd">

<html xmlns="http://www.w3.org/1999/xhtml">
  <head>
   <meta http-equiv="Content-Type" content="text/html; charset=utf-8"/>
    <title>Conversion Table</title>
    <style type="text/css">
      body {background-color : navajowhite; color : black; font-family:verdana;
              text-align : center}
      table {margin-left : auto; margin-right : auto; }
      th     {min-width : 70px; background-color : white}
    </style>
  </head>
 <body><h2> Table of Celsius-<br/>Fahrenheit Equivalents</h2>
   <table border='1'><tr><th> C </th><th> F </th></tr>
    <script type = "text/javascript">
      function convertC2F ( tempInC ) {
         return (9 / 5) * tempInC + 32;
      }
      document.write('<tr style="background-color : #00ccff">'
         + '<td>-10</td><td>' + convertC2F(-10) + '</td></tr>');
      document.write('<tr style="background-color : #0088ff">'
         + '<td> 0 </td><td>' + convertC2F(0)  + '</td></tr>');
      document.write('<tr style="background-color : #8800cc">'
         + '<td> 10</td><td>' + convertC2F(10) + '</td></tr>');
      document.write('<tr style="background-color : #cc0088">'
         + '<td> 20</td><td>' + convertC2F(20) + '</td></tr>');
      document.write('<tr style="background-color : #ff0033">'
         + '<td> 30</td><td>' + convertC2F(30) + '</td></tr>');
      document.write('<tr style="background-color : #cc0033">'
         + '<td> 40</td><td>' + convertC2F(40) + '</td></tr>');
   </script>
  </table>
  </body>
</html>
```


Figure 20.4 Source text and image for the Conversion Table computation. (Because of document.write( ) this program does not validate.)

rows will go. Then, using document.write( ) within the JavaScript tags, create the rows of the table. A row will be composed of several components joined (concatenated) together. For example, the first row is built from

<tr style="background-color : #00ccff">	*Table row tag and attribute*
<td>-10</td>	*Table data tags for first entry*
<td>	*Table data tag for second entry*
convertC2F(-10)	*Call to conversion function*
</td></tr>	*Closing tags for data and row*

Notice that the first table entry (–10) is also the value converted by the function call that creates the second table entry; that is, –10 is the argument to convertC2F( ).

When the components are combined into a document.write( ) call with the proper quotes and concatenations, it has the form

```
document.write('<tr style="background-color : #00ccff">'
                  + '<td>–10</td><td>' + convertC2F(–10) + '</td></tr>');
```

All of the rows have a similar structure.

As the browser is setting up the page, it encounters the script tags. It does what our JavaScript program says and calls the `document.write( )` functions. To call those functions the browser must construct its argument using concatenation. As it begins to build the argument string, it encounters our `convertC2F(-10)` function call with its argument (`-10`), and runs it. The Fahrenheit value is returned (`14`); it is included with the other parts of the argument string, and the `document.write( )` function places the newly constructed row tags into the document. When the browser builds the page, the table is formed from our created-on-the-fly rows that used our conversion function to figure the Fahrenheit temperature.

fluency ALERT

> **Still Correct.** The use of **document.write( )** is not legal for certain applications of XHTML, so pages that use it may not validate. But, we use **document.write( )** for HTML, where it is correct and acceptable to all browsers.

Writing Functions, Using Functions

Though our knowledge of functions is not quite complete, it is good enough to write some functions for interesting computations. In this section we try flipping electronic "coins," and we compute the Body Mass Index, a combined measure of height and weight. Both computations give further practice with functions.

Flipping Electronic Coins

How can a computer flip a coin? It seems impossible, except for robots, because computers have no moving parts. The answer is not to focus on the act of flipping, but on the fact that a coin flip is an unpredictable event whose two outcomes are "equally probable." We might guess that a computer could generate a random number between 0 and 1, and round to the nearest whole number; 0 could represent tails and 1 could represent heads. About half the time the outcome would be tails (the random number was less than 0.5) and the rest of the time it would be heads. The only problem is that computers are completely deterministic, as we learned in Chapter 9: Given a program and its input, the outcome is perfectly predictable. It's not random in any way. It would be possible to create truly random numbers based on an unpredictable physical process such as counting the particle emissions from a radioactive material like U_{238}, but computers don't have to be radioactive to generate random numbers. They can generate pseudo-random numbers.

> **Flipping Out.** The mathematician John von Neumann, one of the computing pioneers, once said, "Anyone who attempts to generate random numbers by deterministic means is, of course, living in a state of sin."

Pseudo-random numbers are an invention of computer science in which an algorithm produces a sequence of numbers that passes the statistical tests for randomness. For example, a sequence of pseudo-random numbers between 0 and 1 has the property that about half are closer to 0 and the others are closer to 1; that is, the sequence of items, when rounded to the nearest whole number, behave like a coin flip. (It's still deterministic: If you know the algorithm and the starting point, you can perfectly predict the sequence; but you don't!) Because pseudo-random numbers are so good, we'll drop the "pseudo" part from here on.

Random numbers are important in many applications, so programming languages come with a built-in function for generating them. In JavaScript the random number generator is called Math.random( ). It's part of a library of handy mathematical functions, which includes Math.round( ). Each time Math.random( ) is called, it generates a random number between 0 (inclusive) and 1 (exclusive); that is, it could be 0, but never 1. So, a function to flip electronic coins—that is, to generate a 0 or a 1 with roughly equal probability—would have the form

```
function coinFlip( ) {
    return Math.round(Math.random( ));
}
```

When coinFlip( ) is called, it returns with equal probability a 0 or a 1, which can represent tails and heads.

The obvious improvement to the coinFlip( ) function is to return the text Heads and Tails rather than numbers. So, we create a new function

```
function flipText( ) {
    if (coinFlip( )==0)
        return 'Tails';
    else
        return 'Heads';
}
```

Notice that we have called the previous coinFlip( ) function in the if statement test of the flipText( ) function. Calling functions from inside other functions is the most common way to use functions because it allows us to build more complex programs progressively.

Our flipping function would be even more useful if it gave the outcome in response to clicking a button on a Web page. As you learned in Chapter 19, buttons are inputs just like text boxes, so creating such a Web page is not too difficult. We will need a form, which we call eCoin, and the functions we've just finished programming. Figure 20.5 shows the image and source for this program.

```
<!DOCTYPE html PUBLIC "-//W3C//DTD XHTML 1.0 Strict//EN"
"http://www.w3.org/TR/xhtml1/DTD/xhtml1-strict.dtd">
<html xmlns="http://www.w3.org/1999/xhtml">
  <head>
   <meta http-equiv="Content-Type"
          content="text/html; charset=utf-8"/>
    <title>eCoin Flipping</title>
    <style type="text/css">
      body {background-color : #ccffcc; color : green;
            font-family : verdana; text-align : center}
    </style>
  </head>
  <body>
    <script type="text/javascript">
      function coinFlip() {
        return Math.round(Math.random());
      }
      function flipText() {
        if (coinFlip()==0)
            return 'Tails';
        else
            return 'Heads';
      }
    </script>
    <form action="">
      <h2>Heads or Tails? <br/>
      <input type="button" value="Flip"
        onclick='document.forms[0].ans.value=flipText()'/>
        <input type="text" name="ans" size="5"/></h2>
    </form>
  </body>
</html>
```

eCoin Flipping

Heads or Tails?

Flip

Done

Figure 20.5 The JavaScript and image for the eCoin Flipping page.

Bug Report. When you cannot figure out why a JavaScript program is not working, you can often find helpful information from Firefox's Error Console, where the browser informs us what it doesn't like about a JavaScript program:

Tools > Error Console.

The Body Mass Index Computation

The Body Mass Index (BMI) is a standard measure of a person's weight in proportion to his or her height. (An "acceptable" BMI is generally in the range of 18.5 to 25, but as usual, experts disagree.) What is your BMI? The formula for determining BMI, using metric units, that is, height in meters and weight in kilos, is

$Index = weight/height^2$

In the same way that it was easy to translate the Celsius conversion into a function, it is easy to translate the metric BMI into a function, though this time we need two parameters, one for weight and one for height. Also, let's take the height in centimeters and convert:

```
function bmiM ( weightKg, heightCm ) {          //Compute BMI in metric
    var heightM = heightCm / 100;               //Change cm to meters
    return weightKg / (heightM * heightM);
}
```

We have used var to declare an extra variable (heightM) for use in converting from centimeters to meters. In fact, the conversion is part of the initialization for the variable. Also, there's no "square" in JavaScript, so we must multiply heightM times itself.

For weight and height in English units, the formula is

$$Index = 703\ weight / height^2$$

where weight is given in pounds and height is given in inches. (The constant 703 corrects for our use of English units in a quantity defined in metric units.) Of course, Americans give their height in feet and inches—that is, a person says, "I'm 5 feet, 6 inches" rather than "I'm 66 inches"—but working with feet and inches is a little messy. So, we use inches. The solution parallels the function for metric units

```
function bmiE ( weightLbs, heightIn ) {         //Compute BMI in English
    return 703 * weightLbs / (heightIn * heightIn);
}
```

The two functions are quite similar.

It would be more universal if the function could compute the BMI in whatever units the user specified. That would require a new function with three inputs, one for the kind of units and the other two for weight and height. Such a function could use our previous functions—another example of calling a function within a function. The declaration for the universal BMI is

```
function BMI ( units, weight, height ) {
   if (units == 'E')
      return bmiE(weight, height);              //Answer for English
   else
      return bmiM(weight, height);              //Answer for Metric
}
```

Notice first that we check the units parameter to call the correct function. Second, we have simply passed the weight and height parameters as arguments to our previously programmed BMI functions.

Counting Arguments. A function must be given as many arguments as it has parameters, because they correspond one-to-one. For this reason, for multiparameter functions, it is also important that the arguments are given in the right order.

How should the BMI function be used? Perhaps the most convenient way would be to have a Web page similar to the Conversion Table and Coin

Flipping pages. For that, we need to define the functions, set up the forms, and define the event handlers, as we've done before. The final result is shown in Figure 20.6.

Code Breaking. Notice the structure of the Figure BMI page in Figure 20.6. Besides the HTML tags at the beginning and end, the program has two main parts: A section enclosed in script tags, where functions and other JavaScript computations are given, and a section enclosed in form tags, where input, output, and other text of the page are given. Most programs in this chapter (and this book) have that structure; recognizing it helps with understanding long sequences of text.

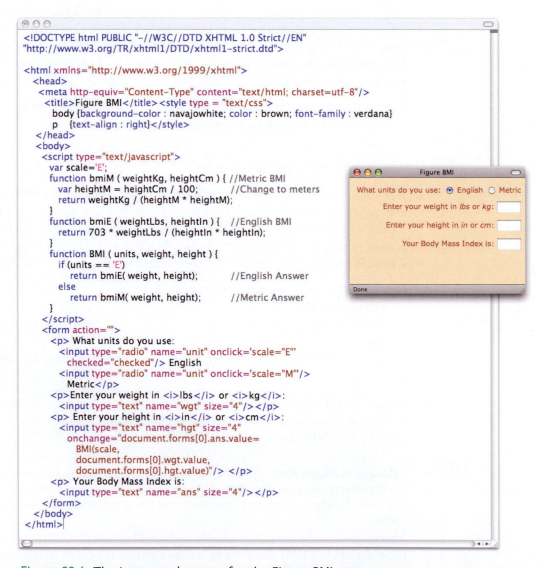

```
<!DOCTYPE html PUBLIC "-//W3C//DTD XHTML 1.0 Strict//EN"
"http://www.w3.org/TR/xhtml1/DTD/xhtml1-strict.dtd">

<html xmlns="http://www.w3.org/1999/xhtml">
  <head>
   <meta http-equiv="Content-Type" content="text/html; charset=utf-8"/>
    <title>Figure BMI</title><style type = "text/css">
     body {background-color : navajowhite; color : brown; font-family : verdana}
     p    {text-align : right}</style>
   </head>
   <body>
     <script type="text/javascript">
       var scale='E';
       function bmiM ( weightKg, heightCm ) { //Metric BMI
         var heightM = heightCm / 100;         //Change to meters
         return weightKg / (heightM * heightM);
       }
       function bmiE ( weightLbs, heightIn ) {  //English BMI
         return 703 * weightLbs / (heightIn * heightIn);
       }
       function BMI ( units, weight, height ) {
         if (units == 'E')
            return bmiE( weight, height);          //English Answer
         else
            return bmiM( weight, height);          //Metric Answer
       }
     </script>
     <form action="">
       <p> What units do you use:
         <input type="radio" name="unit" onclick='scale="E"'
           checked="checked"/> English
         <input type="radio" name="unit" onclick='scale="M"'/>
           Metric</p>
       <p>Enter your weight in <i>lbs</i> or <i>kg</i>:
         <input type="text" name="wgt" size="4"/></p>
       <p> Enter your height in <i>in</i> or <i>cm</i>:
         <input type="text" name="hgt" size="4"
           onchange="document.forms[0].ans.value=
              BMI(scale,
              document.forms[0].wgt.value,
              document.forms[0].hgt.value)"/> </p>
       <p> Your Body Mass Index is:
         <input type="text" name="ans" size="4"/></p>
     </form>
   </body>
</html>
```

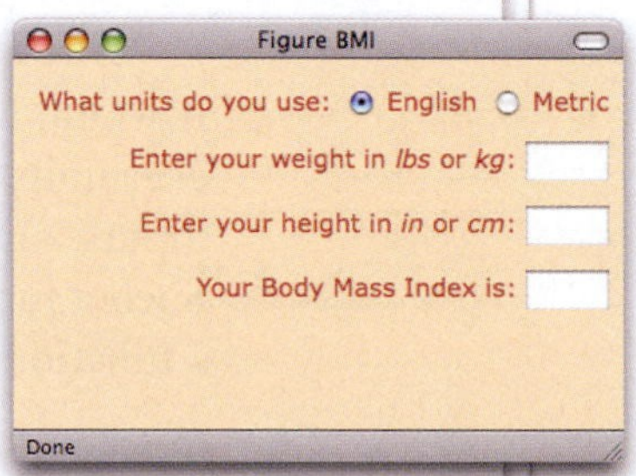

Figure BMI
What units do you use: English Metric
Enter your weight in *lbs* or *kg*:
Enter your height in *in* or *cm*:
Your Body Mass Index is:
Done

Figure 20.6 The image and source for the Figure BMI page.

We have used radio buttons to select the units as English or metric. Recall from Chapter 19 that radio buttons, like command buttons, are specified with <input .../> tags, and so must be placed within <form> tags. The two new features of radio buttons are

- all related radio buttons share the same name; that is, if when clicking on one the other should click off, then they must have the same name
- radio buttons can be preset by writing checked='checked'

The button has been preset to English units, but can easily be preset to metric.

In addition to presetting a radio button we must also write the onclick event handlers for them. What should happen when the user clicks on the radio button? Obviously, we need to remember the type of units chosen. But we are not quite ready to call the BMI( ) function—the other inputs are not yet available—so we need to store the values in a variable that we will pass to BMI( ). At the start of the JavaScript code we declare and initialize

```
var scale = "E";
```

Thus, scale starts out with the value that was preset in the radio button. When the Metric button is clicked, we want

```
scale = "M";
```

as the response to the click-event. So, that becomes the onclick event handler for Metric. Similarly, when the English button is clicked we should assign scale the value "E" again.

Finally, notice that we call the BMI( ) function from the onchange event handler for the height (hgt) input. Since we assume the values will be filled in sequentially, all of the inputs will be available after the height has been entered. So the computation can be performed. The arguments to the call

```
onchange = "document.forms[0].ans.value=
    BMI(scale,
        document.forms[0].wgt.value,
        document.forms[0].hgt.value)"
```

require some explanation. As you learned in Chapter 19, the “dot notation” allows the browser to navigate among the different forms to locate the values in the other input boxes. The scale variable, having been declared outside of any function or form, is a global variable. No navigation is required, because it is known to all functions and forms.

Global variables, like scale, are considered in greater detail in the next section. It is the last topic we need to mention about functions.

Scoping: When to Use Names

There is one thing left to learn about functions: name scoping. Once you've learned about it, all that remains is practice.

The scope of a name—any name in a program—defines how "far" from its declaration it can be used. Every programming language has its own scoping constraints, but the general rules for scoping are fairly simple.

- Variable names declared in a function can be used only within that function. They are said to be *local to the function* and are called **local variables** or simply **locals**. Parameters, for example, are considered local variables.
- Variable names declared outside any function can be used throughout the program. They are said to be *global to the function* and are called **global variables** or simply **globals**. For example, variables defined outside of a function are global variables.

The consequences of this distinction are global variables can be used inside of functions, but local variables cannot be used outside of the functions they are declared in. Examples will make this clear.

An annotated example. Consider the JavaScript program shown in Figure 20.7, which illustrates different cases of the preceding rules. The functions in the program are a variation on the BMI computation of Figure 20.6. However, rather than choosing between English and metric each time, the page is customized to one kind of unit when it is created. (This is another way—besides presetting the radio button—to specialize the solution to the default settings of the common case when most users want the same units.) Since the page will have different text for each case, the forms are created

```
<script type="text/javascript">
  var scale='E';                                    //Declare global variable
  var reportErr=true;                               //Declare global variable
  function bmiM ( weightKg, heightCm ) {            //Parameters are locals
    var heightM = heightCm / 100;                   //Declare local, set w/local
    return weightKg / (heightM*heightM);            //Reference local variables
  }
  function bmiE ( weightLbs, heightIn ) {           //Parameters are local
    var heightFt = heightIn / 12;                   //Declare local; set with local
    return 4.89*weightLbs/(heightFt*heightFt);      //Reference locals
  }
  function BMI ( units, weight, height ) {          //Parameters are locals
    if (height==0) {                                //Reference local variable
      if (reportErr)                                //Reference global variable
        alert("Height is 0!");
      return 'Huh?';
    }
    if (units == 'E')                               //Reference local variable
      return bmiE(weight, height);                  //Use locals as arguments
    else
      return bmiM(weight, height);                  //Use locals as arguments
    if (scale=='E')                                 //Reference global variable
      document.write('<h1>BMI in English</h1>');
    else
      document.write('<h1>BMI in Metric</h1>');
  }
</script>
```

Figure 20.7 Annotated functions showing the scope of each variable reference.

with document.write( ) calls, which haven't been filled in because they are not important to our example. In addition, there is a test to see if the height is zero, so as to avoid a divide-by-zero error. If it is zero, the reportErr variable is checked to see if errors are supposed to be reported, and in that case "Huh?" is returned as the function's value.

Figure 20.7 classifies all of the variable uses in the program as to whether they are local or global. The classification is simply an application of the scoping rules: The variables declared within a function—both the user-defined variables like heightM and the parameters like heightCm—are locals. The two global variables, scale and reportErr, are declared at the start of the JavaScript, outside of any function. scale and reportErr are referenced inside BMI( ), illustrating that globals can be referenced from inside functions.

The only way to figure out the scoping information shown in Figure 20.7 is to notice where the variables are declared and where they are used, and then apply the rules.

So, why is scoping so important? Local and global variables behave differently. *Locals come into existence when a function begins, and when it ends, they vanish. Global variables are around all the time.* So, if information must be saved from one function call to the next, it must be a global variable.

Global/local scope interaction. There is one tricky case to consider: where a global variable and a local variable have the same name. For example:

```
var y=0;
. . .
function tricky (x) {
    var y;
        y = x;
    . . .
}
```

In the example, y is globally declared and can be referenced anywhere. The same name is declared as a local in the tricky( ) function. They are two different variables. Which y is being assigned the parameter x? It's the local y because it is declared in the function's scope, making it the "closest" declaration and hiding the global y.

Because programmers tend to reuse names, the tricky( ) case *does* arise. Luckily, programmers almost always intend for the reference to be to the local variable, so the program usually works right. When they don't, it's usually a tough bug to find!

Perhaps scoping is analogous to using pronouns—he, she, them—in natural language: When speaking it is always necessary for the speaker and the listener to know who a pronoun refers to, and it's the speaker's responsibility to make it clear. In the same way, the programmer and computer have to agree on what a variable name refers to, and it's the programmer's responsibility to get it right.

The Memory Bank Web Page

Remembering useless trivia is easy, probably because it's fun to know. For example:

Q: *Who was the fifth Beatle?*

A: *Stuart Sutcliffe was a founding member of The Beatles with Lennon, McCartney, and Harrison.*

Remembering useful stuff seems to be more difficult for some reason. So, in this section we create the Memory Bank Web page for remembering useful computations. It will be a place for us to store information in an interactive form. The Web page will also give us a chance to practice programming with functions.

Plan the Memory Bank Web Page

Figure 20.8 shows the HTML image for the initial Memory Bank Web page. Here is how it is supposed to work. Each row of the table will present a computation. Each text box in the row except the last will be an input to the computation; the last text box will be the output. The user types inputs into the text box(es), and when they are all filled, gets the answer back in the output text box by clicking.

We have started the page with a row for the BMI computation. It's a form of the Figure BMI program of Figure 20.6, except for one improvement: We now allow users to specify their weight and height in either order. (Recall that previously, weight had to be specified before height because we called the `BMI( )` function from the `hgt onchange` event handler.) Now, we call it from both the `wgt` and `hgt onchange` event handlers if the other text box already contains a value; otherwise we do nothing, and wait for the other value. This is a more convenient way to present the computation to users.

Our plan is to add more rows to the table using the computations we've programmed, plus others. We will add embellishments to the page to make it more useful to us personally. The idea is to create a page to keep in our Web space that we can add to from time to time as we progress through college. After all, if functions save us some thinking, we might as well present them on a respectable Web page for convenience.

Random Additions

We begin by adding our coin-flipping computation to the Memory Bank page, so we can decide with a friend who buys coffee. (If we're going to use electronic money, we'll need electronic coins!) However, anyone who loses will be skeptical about the fairness of our electronic coin flip. (It's fair—computer theorists can prove it!) So, we will improve the computation by adding a

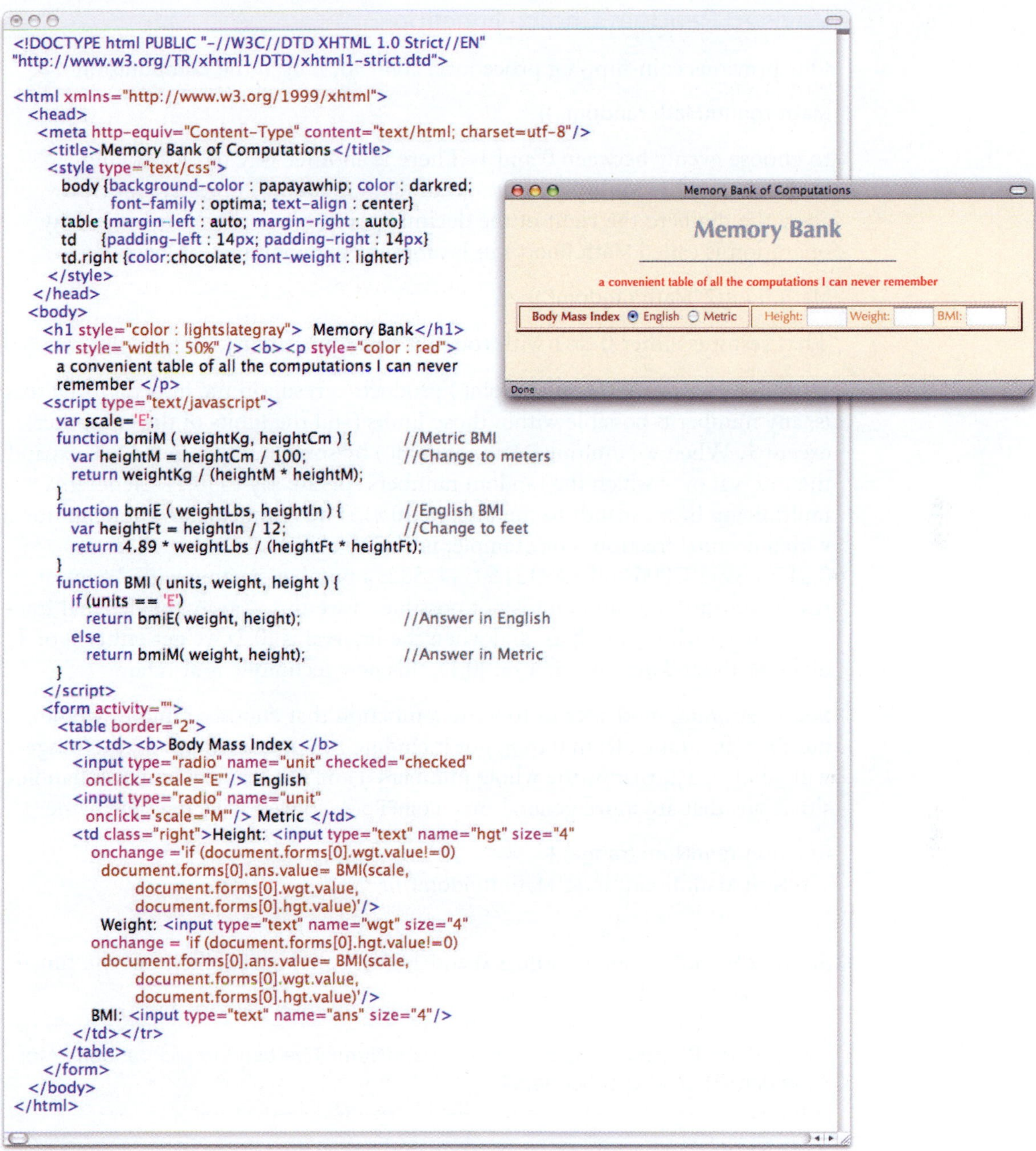

```
<!DOCTYPE html PUBLIC "-//W3C//DTD XHTML 1.0 Strict//EN"
"http://www.w3.org/TR/xhtml1/DTD/xhtml1-strict.dtd">

<html xmlns="http://www.w3.org/1999/xhtml">
  <head>
    <meta http-equiv="Content-Type" content="text/html; charset=utf-8"/>
     <title>Memory Bank of Computations</title>
     <style type="text/css">
       body {background-color : papayawhip; color : darkred;
             font-family : optima; text-align : center}
       table {margin-left : auto; margin-right : auto}
       td    {padding-left : 14px; padding-right : 14px}
       td.right {color:chocolate; font-weight : lighter}
     </style>
   </head>
  <body>
    <h1 style="color : lightslategray"> Memory Bank</h1>
    <hr style="width : 50%" /> <b><p style="color : red">
      a convenient table of all the computations I can never
      remember </p>
    <script type="text/javascript">
      var scale='E';
      function bmiM ( weightKg, heightCm ) {        //Metric BMI
        var heightM = heightCm / 100;               //Change to meters
        return weightKg / (heightM * heightM);
      }
      function bmiE ( weightLbs, heightIn ) {       //English BMI
        var heightFt = heightIn / 12;               //Change to feet
        return 4.89 * weightLbs / (heightFt * heightFt);
      }
      function BMI ( units, weight, height ) {
        if (units == 'E')
          return bmiE( weight, height);             //Answer in English
        else
          return bmiM( weight, height);             //Answer in Metric
      }
    </script>
    <form activity="">
      <table border="2">
      <tr><td> <b>Body Mass Index </b>
        <input type="radio" name="unit" checked="checked"
          onclick='scale="E"'/> English
        <input type="radio" name="unit"
          onclick='scale="M"'/> Metric </td>
        <td class="right">Height: <input type="text" name="hgt" size="4"
          onchange ='if (document.forms[0].wgt.value!=0)
            document.forms[0].ans.value= BMI(scale,
                document.forms[0].wgt.value,
                document.forms[0].hgt.value)'/>
            Weight: <input type="text" name="wgt" size="4"
          onchange = 'if (document.forms[0].hgt.value!=0)
            document.forms[0].ans.value= BMI(scale,
                document.forms[0].wgt.value,
                document.forms[0].hgt.value)'/>
          BMI: <input type="text" name="ans" size="4"/>
        </td></tr>
      </table>
    </form>
  </body>
</html>
```


Figure 20.8 The initial Memory Bank interface and its source. This program can be downloaded from **www.aw.com/snyder/**.

count of the number of heads and tails that have been flipped. That way, a skeptic can click the Flip button several times and verify that the outcomes are roughly split between heads and tails.

Revised Random Choice Function

Our previous coin-flipping procedure, coinFlip( ), used the computation

```
Math.round(Math.random( ))
```

to choose evenly between 0 and 1. There is another way to pick evenly between 0 and 1: Multiply the result of Math.random( ) times 2, and throw away the digits to the right of the decimal point. Since the "throwing away" operation is called Math.floor( ) in JavaScript, the computation becomes

```
Math.floor(2*Math.random( ))
```

That result is either 0 or 1 with roughly equal probability.

How does this work? Math.random( ) produces a result in the interval [0,1); that is, any number is possible within those limits (and the limits of the computer) except 1. When we multiply Math.random( ) by some number, say 2, we expand the interval over which the random numbers spread, say to [0,2). Generally, multiplying by *n* expands to the interval [0,*n*). The numbers are whole numbers with a decimal fraction. For example, in [0,2) we'll have numbers like 0.21598895302006 and 1.84151605441332; a number starting with 2 cannot result, because the end point is not possible. If we throw away the decimal fraction, we get whole numbers, and when the interval is [0,2) we get either 0 or 1. Since Math.random( ) was fair on [0,1), this new technique is also fair.

Such reasoning motivates us to write a function that chooses random whole numbers in a range from 0 to *n*, not including *n*. For coin-flipping, the range will be of size 2, that is, the whole numbers 0 and 1. Our new function handles situations that are more general than coinFlip( ), so we'll give it a new name:

```
function randNum (range) {
  return Math.floor(range*Math.random( ));
}
```

So, randNum(2) produces values 0 and 1 with equal probability, but the function picks from larger intervals, too.

> **20.2 Rock-Paper-Scissors.** How can **randNum( )** be used to pick randomly for the game Rock-Paper-Scissors?

The Coin-Flipping Row

The coin-flipping row of the table

is defined by text and text boxes of the form:

```
<tr><td><b> Electronic Coin Flip </b></td>
    <td class="right"> <input type="button" value="Flip"
        onclick='flipCoin( )'/>
            Outcome: <input type="text" name="oc" size="4"/>
            Heads: <input type="text" name="nH" size="3" value="0"/>
            Tails: <input type="text" name="nT" size="3" value="0"/>
    </td>
</tr>
```

The components are by now self-explanatory. All that remains is to program the event handler, flipCoin( ).

To keep track of the numbers of heads and tails flipped, we will need global variables—numHeads, numTails—that can be incremented from the flipCoin( ) function each time the user clicks Flip. We choose global variables rather than defining local variables in flipCoin( )because local variables come into existence when a function is called and they vanish after the function returns; they will not keep their values "across function calls." Accordingly, we add declarations

```
var numHeads=0, numTails=0;
```

just after the <script . . .> tag.

With the global counters defined, all that remains is to flip the coin, check the outcome, and update two of the three windows depending on the results of the flip. The following logic implements the function.

```
function flipCoin ( ) {
    if (randNum(2)==0) {
        document.forms[0].oc.value="Heads";
        numHeads=numHeads+1;
        document.forms[0].nH.value=numHeads;
    }
    else {
        document.forms[0].oc.value="Tails";
        numTails=numTails+1;
        document.forms[0].nT.value=numTails;
    }
}
```

Notice that the random number is generated in the test of the if statement. Also, the <then-*statement*> list and the <else-*statement*> list must have curly braces around them because they involve multiple statements. By also adding the definition of randNum( ) to our accumulating XHTML file, the newly added row is complete.

The "I'm Thinking of a Number" Row

The Rock-Paper-Scissors example in Try It Exercise 20.2 is a reminder that not all guessing games involve making a binary choice. We could choose a number from 1 to *n*. Since we have already programmed the new randNum( ) function that chooses a random integer from a range—although it is a range from 0 to *n*–1 — it is a simple matter to shift the range by one: The computation

```
randNum(n)+1
```

does the job.

The row in the Memory Bank page is quite similar to the coin-flipping row, though it has a text box to set the upper end of the range.

```
<tr><td><b> I'm thinking of a number from 1 to </b>
    <input type="text" name="limit" size="2" value="10"
       onchange='if (document.forms[0].limit.value > 0)
                    topEnd=document.forms[0].limit.value;
                 else
                    document.forms[0].limit.value="?"'/></td>
    <td class="right"><input type="button" value="Pick"
       onclick='document.forms[0].res.value=randNum(topEnd)+1'/>
       a number from the range:
       <input type="text" name="res" size="4"/>
    </td></tr>
```

As before, we need to declare a global variable, topEnd, that says what the limit of the range is. This value is initialized to 10, which is the default value shown in the limit text box. Changing the text box produces a new topEnd value if that value is greater than 0; otherwise, a question mark is displayed.

When the user clicks Pick, the randNum( ) function is called with the topEnd argument and the result is incremented to shift its range. That value is displayed.

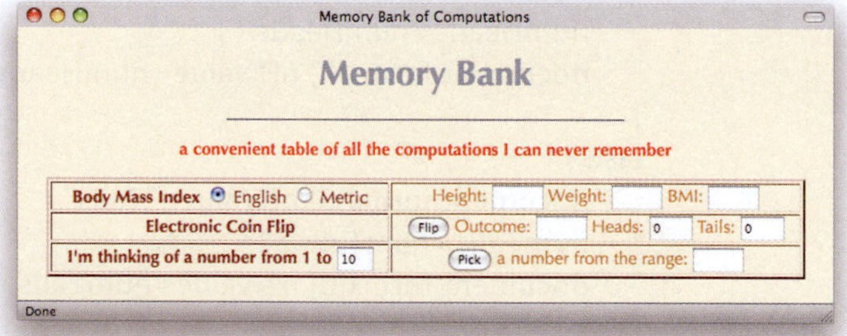

Improving the Memory Bank Web Page

The Memory Bank Web page is useful, but it needs to be fancier and include some other cool features. In this section we program the Memory Bank page to splash new pages onto the screen. Opening a new window differs from linking to a new page, because a link replaces the page being displayed, while the new window allows both to be displayed. It's very easy to open a new window, and it's handy if we want a page to remain on the screen even when the Memory Bank page is closed.

Splashing a New Page

Figure 20.9 shows a revised Memory Bank page with two new rows. These differ from the rows above. They have a title on the left side, as usual, but they have a single button on the right. When the user clicks on the button a new page is displayed. The result of clicking on the Convert button is shown. The page is a variation of our Celsius and Fahrenheit conversions, but it is slightly improved. Specifically, rather than giving users a single solution—converting from Celsius to Fahrenheit or converting from Fahrenheit to Celsius—the new page simply gives two temperature text boxes. When the user fills one in, the other is filled in with the converted temperature. The program is shown in Figure 20.10.

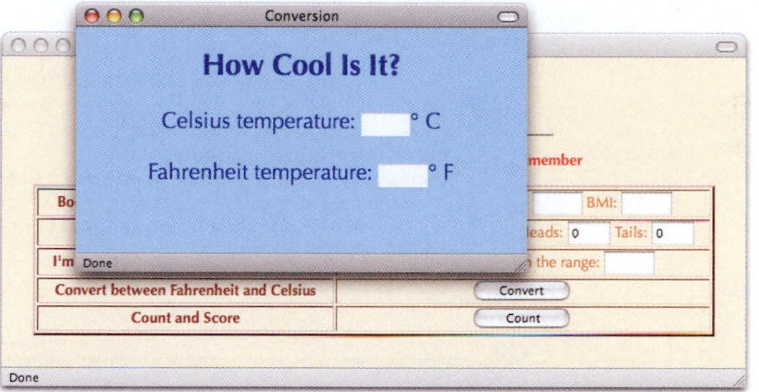

Figure 20.9 The revised Memory Bank page and the Conversion page that displays when Convert is clicked.

It's easy to get a new page to display. All we need to do is open it. In order to open a page we must give the location of the page just as if we were using a <a href= . . .> or <img src= . . ./>, as described in Chapter 4. If the HTML file for the page is in the same directory as the page from which it is being opened, then giving the name is enough. Otherwise, navigation to lower or higher (../) directories is necessary. And, it is possible to give a full URL.

For the Memory Bank page, the Conversion page from Figure 20.10 is saved in a file named temperature.html, which is in the same directory as memoryBank.html. So, the Convert line for the Memory Bank table is

```
<tr><td><b>Convert between Fahrenheit and Celsius</b></td>
    <td class="right"><input type="button" value="    Convert    "
        onclick="window.open('temperature.html','jack','resizable=yes')"/>
    </td>
</tr>
```

The window.open( ) function loads the page whose location is given as its first argument. The second argument is the window's name, and because we won't need the name for other purposes, we give it any unique name. The third

```
<html xmlns="http://www.w3.org/1999/xhtml">
  <head>
    <meta http-equiv="Content-Type" content="text/html; charset=utf-8"/>
     <title>Conversion</title>
     <style type="text/css">
       body {background-color : dodgerblue; font-family : optima;
             color: midnightblue; text-align : center}
       p     {font-size : x-large}
     </style>
   </head>

  <body>
    <h1>How Cool Is It? </h1>
    <script type="text/javascript">
      function convertC2F (tempInC) {
        return 9/5*tempInC + 32;
      }
      function convertF2C (tempInF) {
        return 5/9*(tempInF - 32);
      }
    </script>
    <form activity="">
      <p> Celsius temperature:
        <input type="text" name="textTempC" size="4"
          onchange="document.forms[0].textTempF.value
          =convertC2F(document.forms[0].textTempC.value)"/>&#176;  C</p>
      <p> Fahrenheit temperature:
        <input type="text" name="textTempF" size="4"
          onchange="document.forms[0].textTempC.value
          =convertF2C(document.forms[0].textTempF.value)"/>&#176;  F</p>
    </form>
  </body>
</html>
```

Figure 20.10 The file **temperature.html** for the new Conversion page in Figure 20.9.

argument allows the page to be resized; there is a fourth argument, which we ignore. We always follow this form.

The last row of the Memory Bank page will reference a new page, which we will write momentarily. The new page will be stored in a file named counter.html. So, the XHTML for the last row of the Memory Bank page is

```
<tr><td><b> Count and Score </b></td>
    <td class="right"><input type="button" value=" Count "
        onclick="window.open('counter.html','jill', 'resizable=yes')"/>
    </td>
</tr>
```

If there are other pages we wish to display in new windows, we follow this same process.

A Counting Page

It is common when searching for things or watching sports to keep track of counts. It's easy enough to get a scrap of paper and tally the number, but it is equally easy to click a mouse. So, we write the Counter Assistant application; see Figure 20.11.

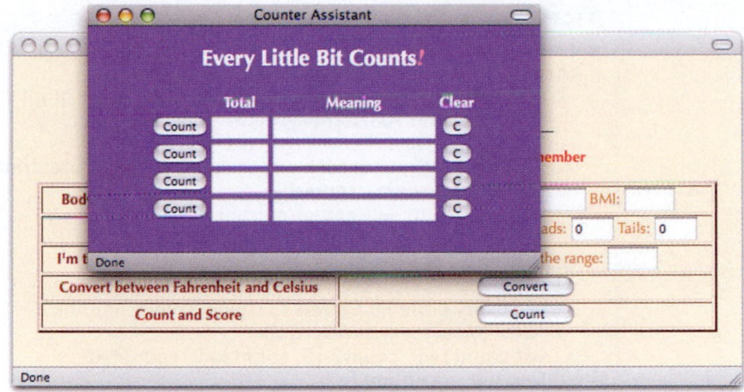

Figure 20.11 The revised Memory Bank page and the Counter Assistant page that displays when **Count** is clicked.

Its operation is pretty obvious: Clicking on the Count button increments the Total field; the Meaning field can be filled with any text to remind us which counter is which among several; the C button clears the fields.

The Counter Assistant page uses an interesting approach: We write a function to create a row of the table, placing the entire XHTML text in the function. The strategy requires us to use a sequence of document.write( ) functions. The program is shown in Figure 20.12.

Checking the code, we see that it relies on four global variables to keep track of the counts, count1 through count4. After declaring these variables, the row( ) procedure is declared. It has a single parameter, which is the number of the row being specified. Then comes a series of document.write( ) calls in which the value of the parameter is concatenated with other text to produce the required code. The XHTML is familiar, by now. The onclick event handlers for the two buttons perform the obvious operations. The Count button increments the correct counter; the C button overwrites the two text boxes with a space and reinitializes the proper counter to 0. The table is easily constructed by writing four calls to row( ). A Counter Assistant with more rows could be constructed by editing the counter.html file so that more counter variables are declared, and more calls to row( ) are placed.

Recap: Two Reasons to Write Functions

Most of our functions—convertC2F( ), BMI( ), randNum( ), and so on—are general. We wrote them for our application, but we hope that we will have a chance to use them again. Think of them as building blocks for programs that we may write in the future. But flipCoin( ) and row( ) are not building blocks.

Because flipCoin( ) and row( ) contain explicit references like document.forms[0].oc.value, they must run within a document with a form, and that form must have within it input controls *with specific names*. We do not expect this situation ever to happen again. Instead, we wrote these two functions to encapsulate the complexity of handling the Flip click-event and

```
<html xmlns="http://www.w3.org/1999/xhtml">
  <head>
   <meta http-equiv="Content-Type" content="text/html; charset=utf-8"/>
    <title>Counter Assistant</title>
    <style type="text/css">
      body {background-color : blueviolet; color : white; font-family : optima;
             text-align : center}
      table {margin-left : auto; margin-right : auto}
    </style>
  </head>
  <body>
   <h2>Every Little Bit Counts<i style="color : hotpink">!</i></h2>
   <script type="text/javascript">
     var count1=0, count2=0, count3=0, count4=0;
     function row(num) {
       document.write('<tr><td><input type="button" value="Count"' );
       document.write(' onclick="count'+num+'=count'+num+'+1;' );
       document.write(' document.forms[0].arch'+num+'.value=count'+num+'"/></td>' );
       document.write('<td><input type="text" size="5" name="arch'+num+'"/></td>' );
       document.write('<td><input type="text" size="20" name="what'+num+'"/></td>' );
       document.write('<td><input type="button" value="C" ' );
       document.write( ' onclick="document.forms[0].arch'+num+'.value='+"' ';" );
       document.write("document.forms[0].what"+num+".value=' ';" );
       document.write('count'+num+'=0"/></td></tr>' );
     }
   </script>
   <form activity="">
     <table>
       <tr><th> </th><th> Total </th><th> Meaning </th><th>Clear</th></tr>
       <script type="text/javascript">
         row(1); row(2); row(3); row(4);
       </script>
     </table>
   </form>
  </body>
</html>
```

Figure 20.12 The Counter Assistant application, saved in a file **counter.html**.

generating a table row. Packaging the event-handling operation and the row construction processes allowed us to get them out of the way.

So, we have had an opportunity to write functions that reflect the two reasons for packaging algorithms into functions: reuse and complexity management. The former are the building blocks of future programming; the latter help us to keep our sanity while we're solving problems.

Add Final Touches to Memory Bank

To wrap up our discussion of functions and the Memory Bank page development, we add two finishing touches: a date and Web links. Both features are simple, but they make the page more useful. Also, we add one bonus feature.

Add a Date

The date can be added at the top after the red motto text, centered. JavaScript gives us many ways to manipulate dates, but here we use only the `Date( )` function. We could write a function to insert the date into the XHTML document, but it is only a single line, so we write the code

```
<script type = 'text/javascript'>
    document.write('<p>' + (Date( ).toString( )) + '</p>');
</script>
```

placing it just after the motto line. Because the document.write( ) operation is a JavaScript statement, <script> tags must surround it, as usual.

The expression in the center of the string, (Date( ).toString( )), references the date object, which contains the current date and time in numeric form. The numeric form can be converted to a printable form using toString( ). So the expression says, "Get the current date and time converted to a printable string."

Add Web Links

Our Memory Bank page has concentrated on programming computations, but it's a Web page, so we can include useful links, too. These links are probably bookmarked in your browser, but by placing them on the Memory Bank page, they are available even when you're using a different computer or browser. What should those links be? Anything that is useful—an online dictionary and thesaurus for writing term papers, a link to the Fluency class's home page, a periodic table for chemistry class, and maybe the CIA's factbook of country information for geography class.

Where should the links be located? We could add another column to the table, placing one link per row. Because the links are highlighted with a different color, they would appear to be in their own column. But, why should the number of links match the number of rows of the table? And furthermore, it's cumbersome to add columns to HTML tables.

An alternative is to add another row at the bottom of the table that spans both columns, and fill it with the links. We choose this solution for two reasons. First, it gives us a free-form region in which to list the links and organize them by topic. Second, we can set it up so that adding more links is easy, encouraging us to include new ones. The XHTML is shown in Figure 20.13.

Assess the Web Page Design

First, notice that to get the table data to span two columns, XHTML's colspan = 2 attribute is included with the <td> tag. Second, the links are grouped by topic, which uses the standard text color to stand out from the differently colored links. Third, a red bullet—a .gif image—is used to separate the entries because some of them are two or three words. (Of course, a file named bullet.gif must be in the same directory as this page, as explained in Chapter 4.) Finally, and most important, the link area has a very neat structure that makes adding new links almost trivial. The headings and entries all have a standard structure, and a schema has been developed and placed in a comment, so setting up for a new link is a simple *Copy/Paste* operation. This should encourage us to keep the content current.

```
<tr>
  <!-- The standard form for the links is...
  <br /><b>topic name . . . </b>
  <a href='http:// URL GOES HERE'>ANCHOR TERM(S) HERE</a> |
So, just copy/paste/edit it.-->
  <td colspan = "2" style="text-align:left"><h4>IMPORTANT LINKS</h4>
    <b> Resource Links ...</b>
    <a href='http://dictionary.cambridge.org'>Cambridge Dictionary</a> |
    <a href='http://www.wordsmyth.net'>Thesaurus</a> |
    <a href="http://www.etymonline.com/">Etymology Dictionary</a>
<br /><b>Classes...</b>
    <a href='http://www.cs.washington.edu/100/'>Fluency Home Page</a> |
    <a href='http://www.chemsoc.org/viselements/pages/pertable_j.htm'> Periodic Table</a> |
    <a href='https://www.cia.gov/library/publications/the-world-factbook/'> CIA Fact Book</a>
<br /><b>XHTML References ...</b>
    <a href="http://www.w3schools.com/css/css_reference.asp">CSS Ref</a> |
    <a href="http://www.w3schools.com/css/css_colornames.asp">Color Names </a> |
    <a href="http://www.w3schools.com/tags/default.asp">XHTML Tags</a> |
     <a href="http://http://www.w3schools.com/tags/ref_symbols.asp"> Odd Symbols</a>
</td></tr>
```

Figure 20.13 HTML for the link area of the Memory Bank Web page.

We'll add one more feature to our Web page. See the Fluency Byte *Time of Your Life* below.

With these additions, the Memory Bank page is complete for the moment. (An XHTML and JavaScript listing is given in Appendix E.) More functions can be added in the future.

Time of Your Life. Computers can easily work with dates because they usually keep track of dates and time with "UNIX dates." The UNIX operating system began recording dates as the number of milliseconds since 1 January 1970 at 00:00:00 Universal Time, that is, New Year's Day 1970 in Greenwich, England. Thus the number of milliseconds between any two dates after New Year's Day 1970 can be found by subtracting the two UNIX dates, making it much easier to compute than if time were recorded in years, days, and hours.

JavaScript uses UNIX dates. It also provides functions to refer to time as if it were recorded in days and hours, when that is convenient for us. We use these features to compute your age in seconds. (Of course, your age in milliseconds is just 1,000 times more.) See Figure 20.14.

The JavaScript code, to be placed just after the </table> tag at the end of the Memory Bank program inside of script tags, is:

```
<script type="text/javascript">
   var today = new Date( );            // Get today's date
   var myBdate = new Date( );          // Get a date object to modify
   var difference;                     // Declare a temporary variable
   myBdate.setFullYear(1990);          // Set my birth year to 1990
   myBdate.setMonth(6);                // Set my birth mo to July (mos start at 0)
   myBdate.setDate(4);                 // Set my birth day to 4th
   myBdate.setHours(12);               // Set my hour of birth to noon
   myBdate.setMinutes(0);              // Set my minute of birth to o'clock
```

```
    myBdate.setSeconds(0);          // Set my second of birth on the hour
    difference = today.getTime( ) - myBdate.getTime( );
    difference = Math.floor(difference/1000);
    document.write("<p> I'm " + difference +
        " seconds old. What <i>am</i> I doing with my life?</p>");
</script>
```

The code creates two date objects, one for today and one for your birthday. (Objects are a complex subject and will not be covered here.) In the six statements after the declarations, we set your birthday as if it were exactly noon, July 4, 1990. To do this, we use JavaScript functions that allow us to refer to the time using months and hours. Once your birthday has been set, we compute **difference**, the difference between the present time and that date. This computation uses UNIX dates. Then we divide the result by 1,000 to convert it to seconds and print it out at the bottom of the Memory Bank page.

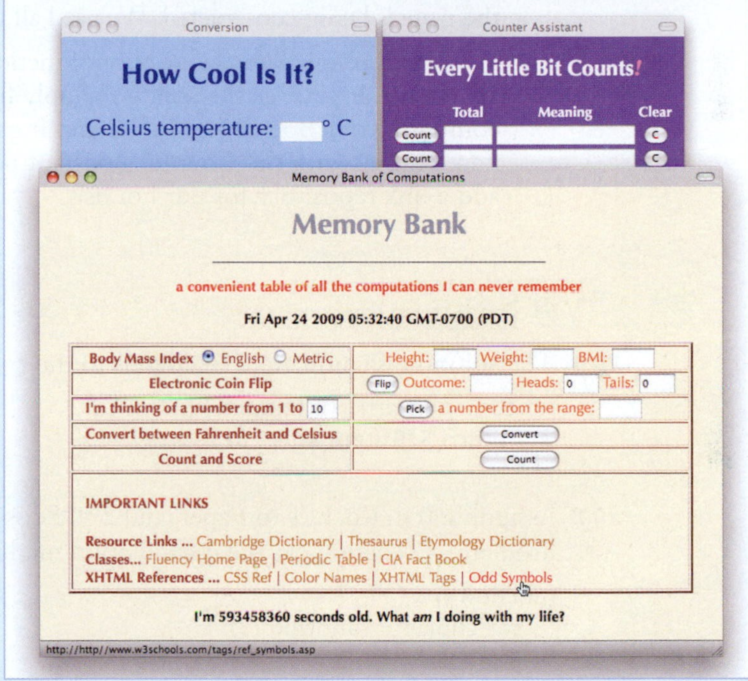

Figure 20.14 Final version of the Memory Bank, Conversion, and Counter Assistant pages.

Summary

This chapter began by introducing the concept of a function as a package for an algorithm. Two motivations led us to study functions: They are a means of reusing our thinking and a tool for managing complexity. Both benefits were demonstrated in the chapter, specifically:

- The three parts of a function—name, parameter list, and definition—are specified in a function declaration using a standard form.

We illustrated their use in defining convertC2F( ), bmiE( ), randNum( ), and many others.

- The function declaration specifies to the computer how the function works, so we give it only once. To use the function—something we will likely do many times—requires that we give the function name and its input values, known as arguments. The arguments correspond one-to-one with the parameters of the function.
- Writing functions packages algorithms, but to get their benefit in JavaScript and XHTML requires that we develop Web pages with which we give the inputs to the functions and get their answers displayed.
- We showed three different ways to display the results of a function in XHTML: using alert( ), interacting with a page that has text boxes, and using document.write( ) to include the results of a function while the page is being constructed. We used all three techniques repeatedly.
- We put all of our knowledge about functions into the Memory Bank Web page. It gave us the ability to apply functions directly, as for computing our Body Mass Index, and it gave us the ability to open a new page, as with the Counter Assistant page. We also decided to add a link repository for our hot list.

Try It Solutions

20.1 The solution is completely analogous to the convertC2F( ) function:

```
function convertF2C (tempInF) {
   return 5/9*(tempInF – 32);
}
```

20.2 Assigning 0 to Rock, 1 to Paper, and 2 to Scissors, randNum(3) solves the problem. A function for the computation might have the form

```
function rps ( ) {
   var choice = randNum(3);
   if (choice==0)
      return "Rock";
   if (choice==1)
      return "Paper";
   if (choice==2)
      return "Scissors";
}
```

Review Questions

Multiple Choice

1. The building blocks of programming are
   a. programming languages

   b. functions
   c. HTML and JavaScript
   d. variables and events

2. A curly brace, }, in a piece of JavaScript code
   a. must be placed on its own line to work
   b. indicates the end of the code
   c. should be on its own line for clarity
   d. all of the above

3. In JavaScript, a line beginning with `//` is a(n)
   a. assignment
   b. comparison
   c. comment
   d. function

4. In a function
   a. each argument must be supplied with a parameter
   b. each parameter must have an argument
   c. parameters are input values
   d. parameters are output values

5. The event associated with the input control is
   a. `onclick`
   b. `textchange`
   c. `onchange`
   d. `sparechange`

6. Radio buttons will work together when
   a. the `checked` attribute is set to `checked`
   b. they are on the same form
   c. when all of them are selected
   d. when all of them have the same name

7. Random numbers in JavaScript are generated by using
   a. `Math.random( )`
   b. `Rnd`
   c. `Math.rnd`
   d. `Random.Math( )`

8. The JavaScript `Date( )` function
   a. returns the date as a string
   b. returns the current date and time as a number
   c. is displayed as a decimal
   d. none of the above

9. In HTML, `href`
   a. creates an image
   b. displays the answer to a JavaScript function
   c. creates a Web link
   d. is the extension for a Web page

10. UNIX is
    a. an international date standard
    b. a program
    c. an operating system
    d. a cookie

Short Answer

1. _______ is a process where simple steps are grouped together and given a name that describes the process.
2. _______ statement specifies what value results from a function.
3. A(n) _______ is all the code needed to define a function.
4. _______ are variables in a function that do not need to be declared with a var statement.
5. The _______ of a variable describes where and when it can be referenced.
6. Input values for a function are called _______.
7. When you divide by zero in JavaScript, _______ is returned as the answer.
8. Computer-generated numbers for a coin toss are technically called _______.
9. A random number generated in JavaScript is always between _______ and _______.
10. In JavaScript, time is tracked in _______, each of which is one one-thousandth of a second.
11. JavaScript keeps track of dates using _______ dates, which are expressed as the number of milliseconds since January 1, 1970, at 00:00:00 Universal Time.
12. What is the difference between a declaration and a call?
13. Describe how you would write a function for randomly picking "rock, paper, scissors."

Exercises

1. Describe how random numbers could be used to simulate the roll of a die. How could two dice be simulated using this function?
2. Identify the three parts of a function.
3. Describe how dates are tracked in JavaScript.
4. Calculate your age as a UNIX date.
5. How would the banking industry make use of the computer's ability to calculate the difference between two dates?
6. What are five words that cannot be used to name a function or a variable? What are five more?
7. Describe a function in terms of input, processing, and output.
8. Write a function to calculate your wages for a part-time job. (Don't worry about calculating overtime.)

21
chapter

Iteration Principles

Once Is Not Enough

learning objectives

- Trace the execution of a given **for** loop
- Write a World-Famous Iteration **for** loop
- Discuss the structure of nested loops
- Explain the use of indexes
- List the rules for arrays; describe the syntax of an array reference
- Explain the main programming tasks for online animations

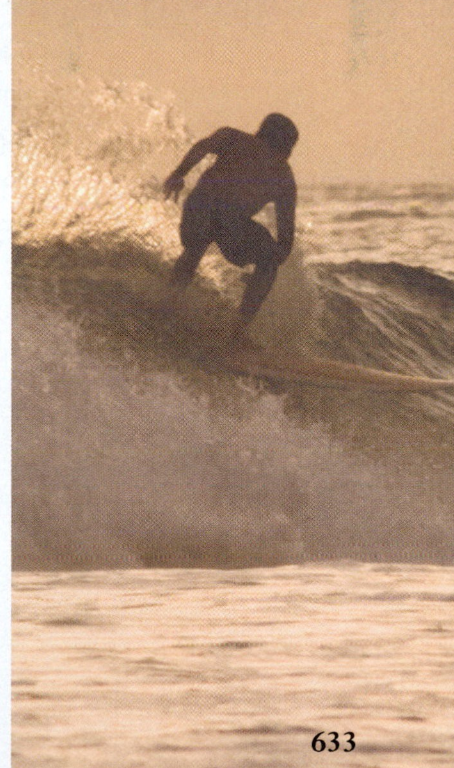

There are three kinds of programmers: those who make off-by-one errors, and those who don't.

—ANONYMOUS

THE TOPIC of this chapter is iteration—the process of repetition. You are familiar with the English word *reiterate*, which means to repeat something, as in "The attorney reiterated her client's position." Because *iterate* means to repeat, *reiterate* sounds redundant. But repetition is redundant; that's what it's about. So, English has both words, and maybe it needs a third, *rereiterate*, meaning, perhaps, "repeated endlessly," as in "Beer commercials are rereiterated." Repetition is usually tiresome, but learning about it is not. And, iteration is the source of considerable computational power, making it a very important topic. By learning how to use iteration, you can make the computer perform the tiresome parts of programming.

In this chapter, you complete your study of programming concepts by learning about iteration and applying it to computational problems. We begin by explaining the `for` statement, one of JavaScript's iteration statements and the key to iterative computation. Then we explore iteration more deeply by discussing how its components can vary. The key to understanding iteration is to focus on how the iteration variable changes values. We mention the Fundamental Principle of Iteration and then we return to the topic of random numbers. After that, we consider the companion topics of indexing and arrays. Together, indexing and arrays can be used with iteration to perform almost unlimited amounts of computation, making them a major source of computing power. Finally, to bring all of these topics together, we study online animation, which allows us to add action to our Web pages. We work through the animation of a familiar icon to prepare us for more interesting animations.

Iteration: *Play It Again, Sam*

There is a slight difference between the meanings of *iterate* and *repeat*. When your mother said, "I've repeated myself four times," she meant, strictly speaking, she'd said the same thing five times. Usually, the first time isn't considered a "repeat." Only the second through the last are "repeats." If she'd actually said the sentence exactly four times, she should have used *iterate*. (Pointing this out to her would *not* have been smart.) We often ignore this difference in terminology in common speech. For example, "reps" (for *repetitions*) in weight training count the total number. In this book, we follow common usage and use *repeat* and *iterate* interchangeably, except where precision is essential, in which case we use *iterate*. When something is iterated five times, there are five instances; you can't be off by one.

The **for** Loop Basic Syntax

Iteration—probably the fourth most important programming idea after assignment, conditionals, and functions—means looping through a series of statements to repeat them. In JavaScript, the main **iteration statement** is the **for loop**, which has the following syntax:

```
for ( <initialization>; <continuation>; <next iteration> ) {
    <statement list>
}
```

Here the text that is not in meta-brackets must be given literally. (Notice the prominent position of the closed curly brace.) The statement sequence to be repeated is in the *<statement list>*, and the constructs in parentheses—which we'll explain in a moment—control how many times the *<statement list>* is iterated. The whole statement sequence is performed for each iteration. So, if the for loop

```
for ( <initialization>; <continuation>; <next iteration> ) {
    document.write('First');
    document.write('Second');
    document.write('Third');
    document.write('Home');
}
```

iterates three times, it will produce the sequence →

```
First
Second
Third
Home
First
Second
Third
Home
First
Second
Third
Home
```

That is, the computer completes the whole statement sequence of the *<statement list>* *before* beginning the next iteration.

The iteration variable. The three operations in the parentheses of the for loop, <*initialization*>, <*continuation*>, and <*next iteration*>, control the number of times the loop iterates. They are called the *control specification*. They control the loop by using an **iteration variable**. Iteration variables are normal variables, so they must be declared. They are called iteration variables only while they are serving to control the loop. Here's a typical example in which the iteration variable is j:

```
for ( j = 1 ; j <= 3 ; j = j + 1 ) {
    <statement list>
}
```

To see how these statements work, imagine that the for loop has been replaced with the schematic form

General Form	**Specific Example with j**
<initialization>;	j = 1;
→ if (<continuation>) {	→ if (j <= 3) {
<statement list>;	<statement list>;
<next iteration>;	j = j + 1;
}	}

The arrow means to go back to do the if statement again.

Here's what happens. The first operation of a for loop is the <*initialization*>. The **initialization** sets the iteration variable's value for the first (if any) iteration of the loop. Next, the **continuation** has the same form as the predicate in a conditional statement. If the <*continuation*> test has a false outcome, the loop terminates, the <*statement list*> is skipped, and it is as if nothing happened except that the iteration variable got assigned its initial value.

However, if the <*continuation*> test has a true outcome, the <*statement list*> is performed. The statement list can be any sequence of statements, including other for statements. When the statements are completed, the <*next iteration*> operation is performed. The next iteration expression changes the iteration variable. That completes the first iteration. The next iteration starts with the <*continuation*> test, performing the same sequence of operations. All following iterations proceed as the first one until the <*continuation*> test has a false outcome, terminating the loop. In this way, the statement sequence can be performed many times without having to write each of the statements to be performed.

Terminator, Too. The second item among the control operations is called the <*continuation*> test here, because if its outcome is **true**, the iteration continues, and if its outcome is **false**, it ends. But the proper programming term for this test is **termination test** because it checks to see if the loop should terminate. However, as a termination test, the outcomes are backward: **true** means continue, **false** means terminate! Both terms are useful. To remember the meanings of the outcomes, think of the test as asking "Continue?"

Following the iteration variable. In the for loop with iteration variable j—and in all for loops—we can understand what's happening by following the iteration variable. Consider the sequence of operations on j shown in Table 21.1.

Table 21.1 The sequence of operations on j from the **for** loop with control specification (j=1; j<=3; j=j+1)

Operation	Operation Result	Role
j = 1	j's value is 1	Initialize iteration variable
j <= 3	true, j is *less than* 3	First <*continuation*> test, continue
j = j + 1	j's value is 2	First <*next iteration*> operation
j <= 3	true, j *is less than* 3	Second <*continuation*> test, continue
j = j + 1	j's value is 3	Second <*next iteration*> operation
j <= 3	true, j *is equal to* 3	Third <*continuation*> test, continue
j = j + 1	j's value is 4	Third <*next iteration*> operation
j <= 3	false, j *is greater than* 3	Fourth <*continuation*> test, terminate

The loop iterates three times by beginning at 1 and, after assigning a new value to j, testing to see if it should continue. The statements of the <*statement list*> are executed between the <*continuation*> test and the <*next iteration*> operation. Notice that j counts from 1 to 4, but at 4, the test determines that j has counted too far, so it quits before performing the <*statement list*> again. Thus the <*statement list*> is performed the right number of times.

fluencyBIT

No Planning. The for loop *might have been* designed to figure the number of iterations to perform before starting out, and then doing them. But iteration doesn't work that way. Instead, the computer just plods along, testing to see if it should continue before starting an iteration, doing the statement sequence, changing the iteration variable, and repeating. Plodding is more powerful, because it's not always possible to predict the number of iterations.

How a **for** Loop Works

To get a little experience programming with for loops, consider this computation on declared variables j and text,

```
text = "She said ";                    //Set text to a string
for (j = 1; j <= 3; j = j + 1) {       //Define a 3 cycle loop
  text = text + "Never! ";             //Concatenate on a string
}                                      //... end of loop
alert(text);                           //Show result
```

which produces the following alert box.

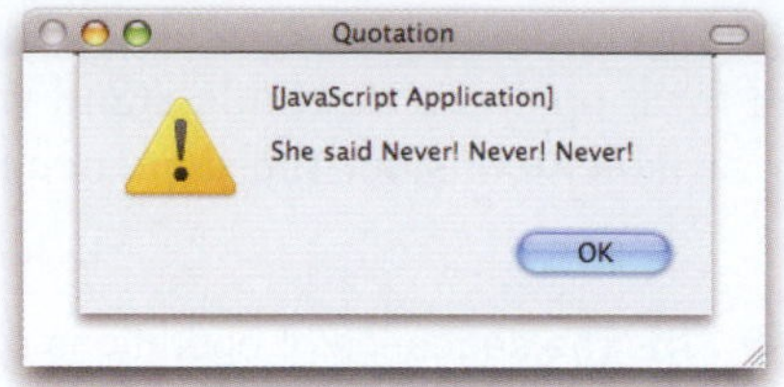

This for loop, which iterates three times, was used with two assignment statements to produce the value of text by appending three copies of the string "Never! ". To check the code's operation, notice that through the four continuation tests, text has the following values:

"She said "	*Before the loop is entered*
"She said Never! "	*After one iteration*
"She said Never! Never! "	*After two iterations*
"She said Never! Never! Never! "	*After three iterations*

So the for loop allowed us to build the phrase one word at a time. Of course, this phrase could have been typed out, "She said Never! Never! Never! ". But the more emphatic phrase in which she says "Never! " 1,000 times would be much harder to type. Using a for loop, we can simply change the 3 to 1,000. It's easy to be emphatic with for loops.

JavaScript Rules for **for** Loops

A programmer would say that our "emphatic" for loop "iterates from 1 to 3 by 1." This is different from saying the for loop iterates three times. The programmer's description focuses on the most relevant feature of a for loop—its control. The key parts of the control are the starting point (1, in the "emphatic" loop), the ending point (3), and the step size (1).

In this section, we consider some of the possibilities:

- The iteration variable
- A starting point
- Continuation/termination test
- Step size
- Reference to the iteration variable
- A World-Famous Iteration
- Avoiding infinite loops

The Iteration Variable

Iteration variables are normal variables that are used in an iteration. They must be declared, and they follow the usual rules for identifiers. Programmers tend to choose short or even single-letter identifiers for iteration variables because they are usually typed frequently, as you'll see. By far, i, j, and k are the most common.

A Starting Point

An iteration can begin anywhere, including with negative numbers. So, for example, in

```
for (j = -10; j <= 10; j = j + 1) { . . .}
```

the iteration variable j assumes each of the 21 values from –10 to 10, that is, including 0. And, similarly, in

```
for (j = 990; j <= 1010; j = j + 1) { . . .}
```

j assumes each of the 21 values around 1,000. Finally, it's possible to start at a fractional number. So, in the loop

```
for (j = 2.5; j <= 6; j = j + 1) { . . .}
```

j assumes the values 2.5, 3.5, 4.5, and 5.5 because the continuation test will finally fail at 6.5.

Continuation/Termination Test

If it's possible to begin an iteration anywhere, it must be possible to end it anywhere. The *<continuation>* test follows the rules for predicates—the tests in if statements. That is, the test is any expression resulting in a Boolean value.

The key point to remember about the continuation test is that to avoid an infinite loop (explained later in the section Avoiding Infinite Loops), it must involve the iteration variable. Other variables can be used as well as the logical operations and (&&), or (||), and not (!). For example, a loop that is supposed to stop at j <= 6 could also be terminated by either ((j < 6) || (j == 6)) or j < 7.

Step Size

The *<next iteration>* also allows considerable freedom. It allows us to specify an amount of change, known as the **step** or **step size**. For example, it's possible to step by units of 2, say, to iterate through the even numbers from 0 to 20:

```
for (j = 0; j < 20; j = j + 2) { . . .}
```

In this case j takes the values of ten numbers because 20 is not included. The *<next iteration>* computation is often called the **increment** by programmers because, as you've seen, it almost always *increases* the value of the iteration variable. But it doesn't have to. The step can be negative, resulting in a **decrement**, and so we call it the *<next iteration>* computation to cover both the increasing and decreasing cases. For example, to count the 21 integers around 0, from *positive* to *negative* this time, we use the following:

```
for (j = 10; j >= -10; j = j - 1) { . . .}
```

The successive values of j are 10, 9, 8, . . . , –9, –10. Notice that reversing the direction of the enumeration of the values means the *<continuation>* test has to be adjusted, too.

Pluses and Minuses. Because incrementing and decrementing by 1 are so common, JavaScript has a special "post increment/decrement" notation. Thus, i++ means i = i + 1, and i-- means i = i – 1. (The variable can be anything, of course.) This notation is handy for the <*next iteration*> component of a **for** loop.

Reference to the Iteration Variable

As you will soon see, the iteration variable is often used in the computations of the <*statement list*>, which is why we focus on the values of the iteration variable during the looping. We care what these values are because we compute with them. So, for example, the iteration variable j is used in the statement that computes 5 factorial (5!):

```
fact = 1;
for (j = 1; j <= 5; j = j + 1) {
    fact = fact * j;
}
```

That is, it computes ((((1 * 1) * 2) * 3) * 4) * 5 ⟺ 120. Using the iteration variable in the computation is necessary and useful.

The World-Famous Iteration

Because JavaScript has the same for loop statement structure as the most popular programming languages (e.g., C, C++, and Java), thousands of for loops with the form just described are written every day—millions have been written in the past decade. With so many loops, programmers have gotten in the habit of using one standard form most of the time:

```
for (j=0; j<n; j++) { . . .}
```

Without a doubt this is the most frequently written for loop of all time, so we will call it the **World-Famous Iteration** (**WFI**). Of course, j and n can be replaced with other declared variables. It is worth taking a moment to study this form because you will see it again and again.

Notice first that the iteration variable starts at 0. You will soon see why starting at 0 is better than starting at 1. The iteration counts up from 0 in steps of 1 because the post-increment j++ is used. And the iteration ends when the iteration variable is no longer strictly less than n—that is, the loop's last iteration is when j ⟺ n–1. Thus the for loop <*statement list*> is performed n times: 0, 1, 2, . . . , n–1. When used in this stylized form, the variable or expression following the < symbol—the n in this case—is *exactly the number of times through the loop*. Thus, we can determine the number of times around the loop in an instant without thinking hard about it. And this form saves on typing, which is important if you consider how difficult it is to type programming symbols. When you see JavaScript in the *Source* listing of the Web pages you download (by choosing *View* > *Page Source*), chances are you will see this World-Famous Iteration. Nearly every iteration in the rest of this book has this WFI form.

Off Again. An extremely common error in computing—you've probably made it several times in *this* section—is to miscount by one. It's so common it has a name, *Off by One Error*. "Exam week is from the 3rd to the 10th," so how many days is it? We tend to subtract to get seven, but it's eight because it includes the end points. Figuring the number of iterations is similarly error prone. Happily, the World-Famous Iteration helps. The **n** following < in the WFI form is the *exact* iteration count.

21.1 Emphatically WFI. Rewrite the first line of the **for** loop in the "She said..." example from the How a **for** Loop Works section using the World-Famous Iteration.

Avoiding Infinite Loops

For loops are relatively error free, especially if we follow the world-famous form, but it's still possible to create infinite loops. To avoid this, think about what could go wrong. It's a fact that every loop in a program must have a continuation test or it will never terminate. As you learned in Chapter 10, the fifth property of algorithms is that they must be finite, that is, stop and report an answer, or stop and report that no answer is possible. For loops have a <*continuation*> test, so they meet the requirement of testing in each iteration. But just because there is a test doesn't mean that it will stop the loop. It must test a condition based on a value that is changing during the loop, such as the value changed by the <*next iteration*> operation. If the test is based on values that don't change in the loop, the outcome of the test will never change, and the loop will never complete. Again, if we follow the rules, things will work out.

Nevertheless, it's not too difficult to make a mistake and create an infinite loop. For example,

```
for ( j = 1 ; j <= 3; i = i + 1) { ... }
```

looks almost like our earlier "emphatic" for loop, but it is broken and will loop forever. (Very emphatic, indeed!) The problem is that the variable being compared in the <*continuation*> test (j) is not the one incremented in the <*next iteration*> operation (i). Unless the iteration variable is changed in the loop—iteration variables should never be changed by statements in the <*statement list*>—the iteration will loop forever. Anyone carefully analyzing this for statement will spot the problem, but it's easy to miss. It's also easy enough to create, say, by making incomplete edits. (Imagine that the statement had previously used i as an iteration variable and was incompletely revised.)

fluencyBIT

Infinite Loops. Infinite loops happen. It's a fact of programming. Luckily, JavaScript is kind to programmers who make this mistake. Firefox and Internet Explorer warn you that the script is running slowly and ask if you want to terminate it; other browsers can simply be forced to close. In the past, you had to turn off the computer to stop an infinite loop.

Experiments with Flipping Coins

To practice for loops, we experiment with flipping electronic coins. Recall that in Chapter 20 we wrote a function randNum(); its parameter is the range of integers from which the random choice is made. So, randNum(2), which returns either 0 (tails) or 1 (heads), can be used for our experiments.

The first experiment is to find out how many heads and tails we get in 100 flips. We expect the numbers to be roughly equal. To run the experiment, we must set up an iteration in which our randNum() function is performed 100 times and statistics are gathered along the way. The code is

```
<body><script type='text/javascript'>
var heads=0, tails=0;                              //Counters
var i;                                             //Iteration variable
for (i=0; i<100; i++ ){                            //WFI
    if (randNum(2) == 1)                           //Is random pick 1?
        heads++;                                   //Yes, count heads
    else
        tails++;                                   //No, count tails
}
alert("Heads: " + heads + " and Tails: " + tails);
function randNum(range) {
    return Math.floor(range*Math.random( ));
}
</script></body>
```

Note that because the output will be reported using alert(), the page doesn't matter, so we can compress the XHTML.

The for loop, which uses the WFI form, loops 100 times—i ranges from 0 through 99—and uses a conditional statement to check and record the outcomes of the random number generation. The post-increment (++) notation has been used three times, allowing us to replace statements like heads = heads + 1 with the briefer heads++. Running the program gave me the results shown in the following alert the first time I tried it on my computer. But you should experiment on your computer; expect to get different results.

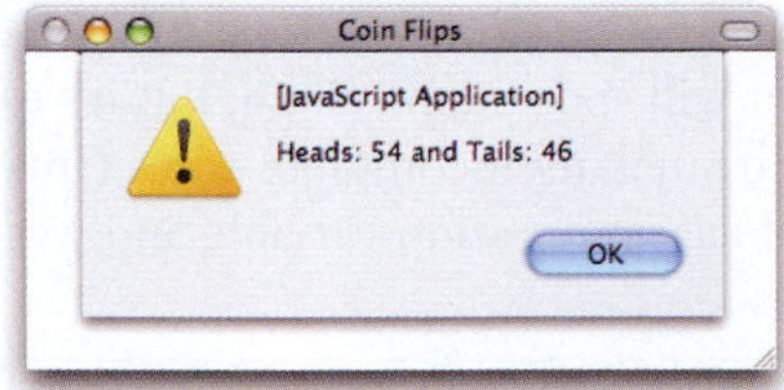

Running the program several times gives us different answers. My five runs ranged from a 50–50 outcome to a 57–43 outcome. This motivates us to run several trials.

Our trial will be the 100-sample iteration just described. To run several trials, we want to iterate them. That is, we will iterate an iteration. Think of the earlier iteration

```
for (i=0; i<100; i++ ){                                   //Trial line 1
    if (randNum(2) == 1)                                  //Trial line 2
        heads++;                                          //Trial line 3
    else                                                  //Trial line 4
        tails++;                                          //Trial line 5
}                                                         //Trial line 6
    alert("Heads: " + heads + " and Tails: " + tails);    //Trial line 7
```

as a unit called a Trial. (Notice that thinking of the loop as a unit is an *abstraction*, as discussed in Chapter 10.)

A Nested Loop

To iterate these statements, we create another for loop with the *<statement list>* containing this Trial unit and a couple of additional statements needed to make the whole process work out. The additional statements must reinitialize the counters, because they should begin at 0 for each new trial. The result is

```
var heads = 0, tails = 0;
var i, j;                                         //Iteration vars
for (j = 0; j < 5; j++){                          //Outer loop start
    for (i=0; i<100; i++){                        //Trial line 1
        if (randNum(2) == 1)                      //Trial line 2
            heads++;                              //Trial line 3
        else                                      //Trial line 4
            tails++;                              //Trial line 5
    }                                             //Trial line 6
    alert("Heads: "+heads+" and Tails: "+tails);  //Trial line 7
    heads = 0; tails = 0;                         //Additional
}                                                 //Outer loop end
```

This structure—a loop within a loop—is called a **nested loop**. Notice that another iteration variable, j, had to be declared because the outer loop cannot use the same iteration variable as the inner loop, because they would interfere.

The behavior of the nested loop should be clear: The outer loop on j, which also uses the WFI form, iterates five times; that is, j assumes the values 0 to 4. *For each of these* j *values*, the whole *<statement list>* is executed; that is, the inner loop on i iterates 100 times, the alert is printed out, and the counters are reinitialized. That is a total of five trials of 100 flips each, or 500 total flips. Run the program and see the range of results.

21.2 Rock On. Rewrite this Coin Flips example to count the three possible outcomes of Rock-Paper-Scissors and have it iterate 300 times. (The simple test logic is shown in Chapter 20.)

A Diagram of Results

Suppose we are interested in how far off from a perfect 50–50 score a trial is. Such information is easily displayed with a diagram. We compute the difference of the coin flip from 50–50 and show that number using asterisks. For example, the first trial, 49–51, is represented by a single asterisk because it differs from perfect by one coin flip. Either of the quantities `heads-50` or `tails-50` gives us the right number of asterisks, but one expression is positive and the other one is negative. JavaScript has the function `Math.abs()` for the absolute value; that is, it makes all numbers—positive or negative—positive, implying that `Math.abs(heads-50)` is the number of asterisks to display.

As with the raw data, the line of asterisks is added to `text` at the end of the inner loop. (Declare `text` and initialize it to `''`, the empty string.) But how do we include a variable number of asterisks? With another iteration, of course. We replace the previous `alert` statement with the statement sequence

```
text = text + 'Trial ' + j + ': ';
for (i = 0; i < (Math.abs(heads-50)); i++) {
    text = text + '*';
}
text = text + '\n';
```

The line for the *j*th trial result begins with the text "Trial *j*: ". Then, an iteration is performed in which asterisks are added one at a time, up to a total of `Math.abs(heads-50)`. We can reuse the iteration variable `i` because its previous use as an iteration variable is complete. It is also fine to put the math function in the <*continuation*> test. (Notice that the WFI form tells us immediately that we have the right number of iterations.) Finally, after the iteration, the new line character is added, so each experiment starts on a new line. Add `alert(text)` as the last line. My program generated the output shown here.

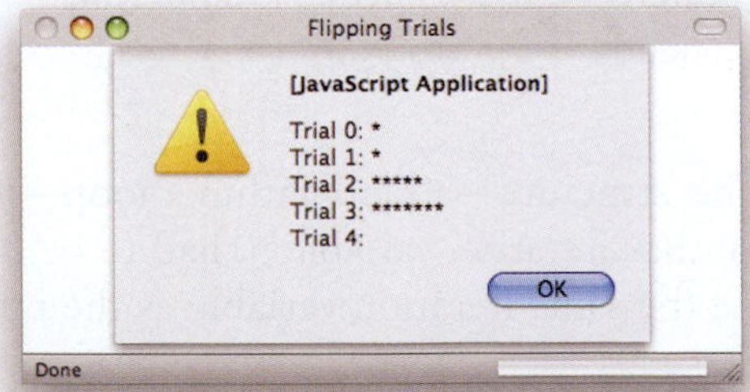

In the sample output, notice that the successive values of `j` do indeed start at 0, that Trial 4 evidently resulted in a 50–50 outcome, and that Trial 3 had the widest variation, being 7 away from perfect, that is, either 43–57 or 57–43.

We can revise the program to print the trials starting at 1 by changing the `text` assignment to

```
text = text + 'Trial ' + (j + 1) + ': ';
```

This is a very unusual statement because the + has two different meanings. The third + is addition, while the other three are concatenation. How does the computer know which one we mean? It looks to see if we are combining numbers (in which case it adds) or strings (in which case it concatenates). The special rule is that if there is one number and one string, it concatenates. So, we need the parentheses around `j + 1` to cause the addition.

The final version of the coin-flipping program, as shown in Figure 21.1, uses three iterations, all in the WFI form.

```
var heads = 0, tails = 0;         //Counters
var i, j;                         //Iteration variables
var text = '';                    //Output accumulator
for (j=0; j<5; j++){              //"Trials" iteration
  for (i=0; i<100; i++){          //"Flips" iteration
    if (randNum(2))
      heads++;
    else
      tails++;
  }
  text = text + 'Trial ' + (j + 1) + ': ';
  for (i = 0; i < (Math.abs(heads-50)); i++) { //"Stars"
    text = text + '*';
  }
  text = text + '\n';
  heads = 0; tails = 0;
}
alert(text);
function randNum(range) {
  return Math.floor(range*Math.random());
}
```

Figure 21.1 The final version of the coin-flipping program.

Though it is only 21 lines long, the program performs hundreds of statements' worth of computation. We could easily change to 1,000 sample trials with no additional programming. And that's the importance of iteration: it allows us to command the computer to do a lot of work with very few program lines.

Indexing

If you're familiar with Elizabeth II, Super Bowl XXV, *Rocky 3*, and Apollo 13, you are acquainted with indexing. **Indexing** is the process of creating a sequence of names by associating a base name ("Apollo") with a number ("13"). When a new name is needed, the next number in sequence is used ("Apollo 14"). Each indexed item is called an **element** of the base-named sequence.

Index Syntax

Naturally, in programming, indexing has a special syntax. An index is enclosed in square brackets in JavaScript, for example, `Apollo[13]`. The index can be a constant, variable, or expression. It must evaluate to a non-negative integer, the index value. (See the section Array Reference Syntax for more information.) Indexing is important in computing because of its close link to iteration: Iterations can be used to refer to all elements of a name; that is, a notation like A[j] can, on successive iterations over j, refer to different elements of A.

fluencyBIT

Index Terms. The terms *indexes* and *indices* are both commonly used to refer to more than one index.

Index Origin

When indexing queens, Super Bowls, popes, and so on, we usually start counting at 1, though often the first item doesn't initially get an index; for example, Queen Elizabeth I was just called Queen Elizabeth until Elizabeth II came along. Yard lines in football begin indexing with 0 (goal = 0). Movie sequels start at 2 because there can't be a *sequel* to nothing. The point at which indexing begins, that is, the least index, is known as the **index origin**.

Arrays

In programming, an indexed base name is called an **array**. Arrays must be declared; in JavaScript, arrays are declared with the syntax

var <*variable*> = new Array(<*number of elements*>)

Notice that Array starts with a capital letter A. Also unlike queens, variables either are or are not arrays; they don't change. In the sample declaration

```
var week = new Array(7);
```

week is the identifier being declared, and new Array(7) specifies that the identifier will be an array variable. The number in parentheses gives the number of **array elements**. *JavaScript uses index origin 0*, meaning that the least index of any array is always 0, and the greatest index is the number of elements minus 1. Thus, the array just declared has elements week[0], week[1], ... , week[6], that is, seven elements. The **array length** refers to the number of elements in an array. To refer to an array's length, we use <*variable*>.length. For example, week.length ⟺ 7.

Rules for Arrays

To summarize, here are the rules for arrays in JavaScript.

- Arrays are normal variables initialized by new Array(<*number of elements*>).
- <*number of elements*> in the declaration is just that—the number of array elements.
- Array indexing begins at 0.

- The number of elements in an array is its *length*.
- The greatest index of an array is *<number of elements>* – 1 because of the 0 origin.

Array Reference Syntax

An **array reference** consists of the array name together with an index—a constant, variable, or expression—enclosed in brackets and evaluating to a non-negative integer, the **index value**. The value to which the index evaluates must be less than the array's length. Thus, the statements

```
var dwarf = new Array(7);           //Declarations use parentheses
var deux = 2;                       //Create value for examples
dwarf[0] = "Happy";                 //References use brackets
dwarf[1] = "Sleepy";                //Index by a constant
dwarf[deux] = "Dopey";              //Index by a variable
dwarf[deux+1] = "Sneezy";           //Index by an expression
dwarf[2*deux] = "Bashful";
dwarf[3*deux–1] = "Grumpy";
dwarf[10–(2*deux)] = "Doc";
```

assign values to the array elements using a variety of index alternatives.

fluencyBIT

> Sub Standard. The index is also known as a *subscript*. In mathematics, indexes, written below the line as in x_1 and y_1, are called subscripts. Programming inherits the same term but writes them in brackets.

When introducing the World-Famous Iteration, we said that the reason for indexing from 0 to n–1 would soon be evident. Now you can see that 0-origin iteration is perfect for 0-origin indexing. Study the following version of the WFI:

```
for (j = 0; j < week.length ; j++) {
    week[j] = dwarf[j] + " & " + dwarf[(j+1)%7] + " do dishes";
}
```

The variable j ranges over all of the elements of the array week, that is, 0 through 6. By using *<array name>*.length in the *<continuation>* clause of the control, we set up to enumerate all of the array's elements. This iteration creates the values

```
week[0] ⟺ "Happy & Sleepy do dishes"
week[1] ⟺ "Sleepy & Dopey do dishes"
week[2] ⟺ "Dopey & Sneezy do dishes"
week[3] ⟺ "Sneezy & Bashful do dishes"
week[4] ⟺ "Bashful & Grumpy do dishes"
week[5] ⟺ "Grumpy & Doc do dishes"
week[6] ⟺ "Doc & Happy do dishes"
```

for the array week by referring to a consecutive pair of elements from dwarf.

The final pair—Doc & Happy—which must "wraparound," uses (*j* +1) *mod* 7 to index the dwarf array in the second reference. That is, (j+1)%7 results in an index value of 0 because (6+1) divided by 7 has a 0 remainder, which is Happy.

Why So Famous? Our focus on computing the index with an expression explains why the WFI is so popular. Because it's common to have to program *some* expression for the index values, it doesn't matter much whether the iteration variable counts starting at 0 or at 1 or at 14. The index expression can adjust the value as long as the *total* number of values is correct. The WFI does this, and does it better than other iterations.

21.3 Indexes Simplify. Revise your Rock-Paper-Scissors code from Try It Exercise 21.2 to save the counts in a three-element array. By using indexing you should be able to solve the problem without an **if** statement.

The Busy Animation

As you know, movies, cartoons, and flipbooks animate by the rapid display of many still pictures known as **frames**. Human visual perception is relatively slow—presumably because of the amazingly complicated tasks it performs—so it is fooled into observing smooth motion when the **display rate** is about 30 frames per second, that is, 30 Hz. In this section, we discuss the principles of online animation and practice using iteration, arrays, and indexing.

The animation we plan to construct is a familiar "busy" indicator. In Figure 21.2 the 12 frames contributing to the animation are shown with their names. The rapid display of the frames makes the black bar appear to revolve. Creating this Busy Animation is the goal of this section.

Fast Forward. The quickest way to learn both the ideas and the practical skills of animation is to build the animation program yourself as you read along.

Before you can successfully program an animation in JavaScript, you must understand three concepts:

- Using a timer to initiate animation events
- Prefetching the frames of the animation
- Redrawing a Web page image

As the ideas are introduced, we program the Busy Animation.

Using a Timer to Initiate Animation

The animation we produce will be displayed by a Web browser. As you know, Web browsers are *event driven*. That is, they are told to perform a task, they

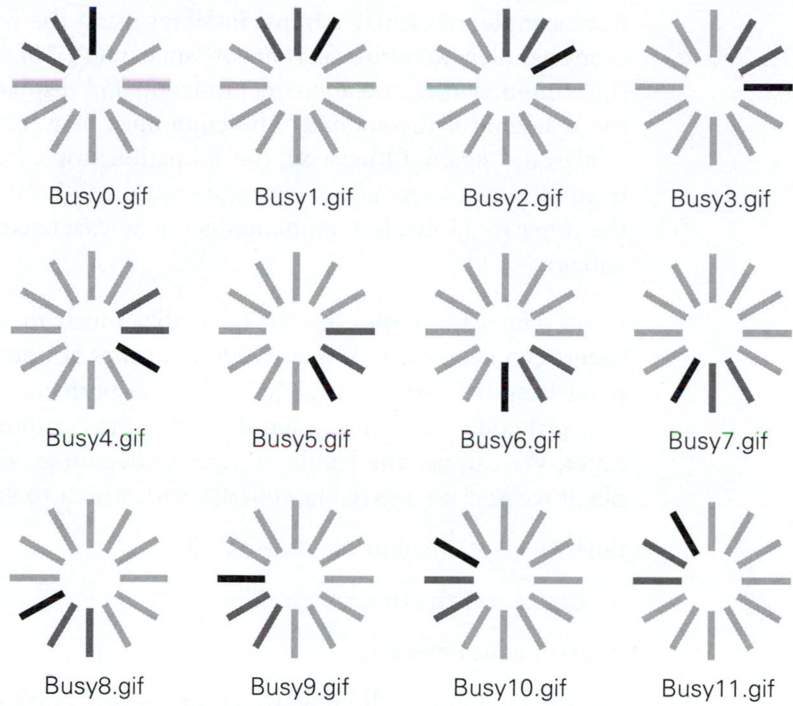

Figure 21.2 The **.gif** images for the Busy Animation. These files are available at www.aw.com/snyder/.

do it, and then they sit idle waiting for an event, which will cause them to do the next task. If browsers are idle when they are not working on a task, how can they animate anything? Animations require action every 30 milliseconds (ms). The obvious solution is to turn the activity of drawing the next frame into an event. The event will be the regular "ticking" of a clock. We'll use a timer analogy.

We set a timer to wake up the browser to tell it to display the next frame, and then set it again for 30 ms into the future. In 30 ms, we repeat the process. In this way, we draw the frames at regular intervals and create an animation. We use such a scheme for *online animations*. (Animations like *WALL•E* apply these ideas differently.) Not surprisingly, JavaScript comes equipped with all of the features, for example, timers needed to implement online animation.

Setting a timer. Computers have extremely fast internal clocks, which are too fast for most programming purposes. Instead, programmers' timers typically "tick" once per millisecond. Timers are pretty intuitive. In JavaScript, the command to set a timer is

setTimeout("<*event handler*>", <*duration*>)

where <*event handler*> is a string giving the JavaScript computation that will run when the timer goes off, and <*duration*> is any positive number of milliseconds, saying how far into the future the timer should go off.

For example, to display a frame in 30 ms using the function animate() as an event handler, we write setTimeout("animate( )", 30). Thirty milliseconds later, the computer runs the animate( ) function and displays the frame. Of course, the last step for the animate( ) function must be to set the timer so that it "wakes up" again. Otherwise, the animation stops. ("Every 30 ms" is different from 30 times a second, of course, because 1,000/30 = 33.333 ms. We can set the timer to 33 ms, but animation is not an exact science and 30 is close enough.)

Using a handle to refer to a timer. Unlike mechanical timers, computer timers can keep track of many different times at once. How does the computer keep the settings straight? When we perform setTimeout( ), we get back a special code—it's called a **handle**—that the computer uses to identify our timer. We can use the handle to refer to our timer, say, to cancel it. For example, if we declare a variable, timerID, with which to save the handle, and write

```
timerID = setTimeout("animate( )", 30);
```

we can cancel the timer by writing

```
clearTimeout(timerID);
```

and the computer will know which of the timers it's tracking should be canceled.

Using buttons to start/stop the animation. Because timers can be set and canceled, we will include two buttons to start and stop our animation. Their definitions are

```
<input type="button" value="Start"
   onclick='setTimeout("animate( )",30)'/>
<input type="button" value="Stop"
   onclick='clearTimeout(timerID)'/>
```

The **Start** button sets the timer for the first time. The animation keeps going on its own thereafter. Each time animate() sets the timer, the handle is stored in timerID. Then, when the **Stop** button is clicked, its event handler clears the timer and stops the animation.

Prefetching Images

Next, we'll consider displaying images. Recall from Chapter 4 that to keep our Web pages tidy, we keep the .gif and .jpg images in a separate directory or folder. So, assume that the graphics files shown in Figure 21.2 are in a folder gifpix. The first of the images would be displayed on a Web page with the HTML

```
<img src="gifpix/Busy0.gif" alt="spinner"/>
```

We begin with this skeleton XHTML page that includes the <form> tags and the two buttons.

```
<body style="text-align:center"><p>
    <img src="gifpix/Busy0.gif" alt="spinner"/>   <!--Initial Frame -->
    <form>
        <input type="button" value="Start"
            onclick='setTimeout("animate( )",30);'/>
        <input type="button" value="Stop"
            onclick='clearTimeout(timerID);'/>
    </form>
</p></body>
```

We would like to overwrite that single image with all of the other .gif files in gifpix in sequence, one every 30 ms. But we can't do so directly. The problem is that loading the images is generally too slow to allow us to show a new image so quickly. Web images must be transferred from the Web server across the Internet, where they encounter all sorts of delays. (We don't notice this while we're developing a Web application on our computers because all of the files are already stored locally.) Consequently, the strategy is to get the images first, store them locally so they are available in the computer's memory, and then display them. The process of loading the images ahead of time is called **prefetching**.

Where will the 12 images (Busy0.gif through Busy11.gif) of the gifpix folder be put? Because they are indexed already, it's logical to use an array. We'll name the array pics and declare it

```
var pics = new Array (12);
```

indicating that it will have 12 elements.

Initializing to an image object. In order for the elements of the array to store an image, they must be initialized to an **image object**. An image object is a blank instance of an image (Chapter 2). Think of an image object as a skeleton that provides places for all the information needed to store an image, such as its name, size of its two dimensions, and its actual pixels. To initialize the 12 array elements to image objects requires an iteration and the new Image() operation:

```
for (i = 0; i < pics.length; i++) {
    pics[i] = new Image( );
}
```

Notice that Image( ) begins with a capital I.

Using the src component. Among the places in the image object is a field called src where the image's source is stored—that is, the file name of the file containing the image. This is the string that we give in the <img src="..."/> tag. When we assign to the src field using dot notation, the browser saves the name and gets the file, storing it in memory, just as we require. Thus,

```
pics[0].src = "gifpix/Busy0.gif"
```

parallels our earlier explicit fetch of the initial frame. Because there are 12 images in total, we use a loop,

```
for (i = 0; i < pics.length; i++) {
    pics[i].src = "gifpix/Busy" + i + ".gif";
}
```

which constructs the file names on-the-fly. That is, we build up file name gifpix/Busy*i*.gif using the iteration variable and concatenation.

There is an important difference between the prefetching by assigning to the .src field of an image variable, and using <img src=". . ."/> in XHTML. The former is not visible on the screen, whereas the latter is. This works to our advantage both ways. The image variable, which is just a part of our JavaScript program, is not visible because it hasn't been placed on the page. But that's fine, because we don't want the user to see the prefetch happening anyway. The <img src=". . ."/> tag places an image on the page, and so is visible. We need both.

Redrawing an Image

To animate the initial frame that we placed earlier with <img src=". . ."/>, we need to overwrite it with the images that we just prefetched at a rate of one every 30 ms. How do we refer to the initial frame in order to overwrite it? As with forms (recall Chapter 19), Web browsers keep an array of the images used on the page in the DOM; it is just like our pics array. As the <img src=". . ."/> commands are encountered, the browser fills its images array just like we filled pics. So, document.images[0] is the name of the first image—that is, our initial frame Busy0.gif. Any additional <img src=". . ."/> images are indexed with higher numbers in sequence. The browser's images array elements each have the src property too, and assigning to it overwrites the image. Thus, to change the initial frame, we write the assignment

```
document.images[0].src = pics[i].src;
```

which replaces the initial frame with the *i*th element of the pics array, causing it to be displayed. All that needs to happen to animate the Busy icon is to sweep through all of the i values, cyclically, one every 30 ms.

Defining the animate( ) event handler. The animate( ) event handler overwrites the image, sets up for the next frame, and sets the timer to call itself again:

```
function animate () {
    document.images[0].src = pics[frame].src;
    frame = (frame + 1)%12;
    timerID = setTimeout ("animate( )", 100);
}
```

We set the timer for 100 ms rather than 30 ms because it makes the bar appear to revolve at a nice pace.

```
<body style="text-align : center">
    <img src="gifpix/Busy0.gif" alt="spinner"/>
    <script type="text/javascript">
        var i, frame = 0;                              //Iteration vars
        var timerID;                                   //Timer handle
        var pics = new Array (12);                     //Array to prefetch into
        for (i=0;i<pics.length ; i++) {                //Init. array for images
            pics[i] = new Image();
        }
        for (i=0;i<pics.length; i++) {                 //Prefetch images
            pics[i].src = "gifpix/Busy" + i + ".gif";
        }
        function animate () {                          //Draw pic, call self
            document.images[0].src = pics[frame].src;  //Change pic
            frame = (frame+1)%12;                      //Move to next frame
            timerID = setTimeout("animate()", 100);    //Schedule next tick
        }
    </script>
    <form activity="">
    <input type="button" value="Start" onclick='timerID=setTimeout("animate()",30)'/>
    <input type="button" value="Stop" onclick='clearTimeout(timerID)'/>
    </form>
</body>
```

Figure 21.3 The Busy Animation program, assuming that the 12 .gif files are stored in a folder gifpix.

The whole Busy Animation program, including the familiar Start and Stop buttons, is shown in Figure 21.3, with the concepts explained. As a postscript to the Busy Animation, try clicking Start several times, followed by an equal number of Stop clicks. Can you explain what happens?

Summary

We studied the fundamentals of programming to understand the sources of power in computation. The concepts of this chapter—iteration, indexing, and arrays—account for much of it. There is much more to say about programming, but we'll leave the rest of it to the experts. In this chapter we discussed:

- The basics of for loop iteration. The control part of a for statement is written in parentheses and the <*statement list*> is enclosed in curly braces. With each iteration, the entire statement list is performed. The number of iterations is determined by assignments to, and tests of, the iteration variable as specified in the control part.
- In the JavaScript for statement, the <*initialization*> component is executed first. Then, prior to each iteration, including the first, the <*continuation*> predicate is tested. If it is true, the <*statement list*> is performed; otherwise, it is skipped, and the for statement terminates. After each iteration, the <*next iteration*> operation is performed.
- The principles of iteration ensure that every iteration contains a test and that the test is dependent on variables that change in the loop.

- The for statement is very flexible. The <*initialization*> can begin with any number, the <*continuation*> test can stop the loop at any number, and the <*next iteration*> operation can increment by various amounts and count upward or downward.
- Programmers routinely use the World-Famous Iteration (WFI)—a stylized iteration that begins at 0, tests that the iteration variable is strictly less than some limit, and increments by 1. There is no obligation to use the WFI, but it allows us to quickly determine the number of times around the loop—it's the limit to the right of <. Because it is common to make errors figuring out the number of iterations, programmers use the WFI to recognize the number of iterations quickly.
- In indexing, we create a series of names by associating a number with a base name. If we need more names, we count out more numbers. Indexed variables are known as arrays in programming. Like ordinary variables, arrays must be declared, but they use the new Array(<*length*>) syntax, in which <*length*> is the number of elements of the array.
- Array elements—referenced by giving the name and a non-negative index in brackets—can be used like ordinary variables. Arrays and iterations can be effectively used together.
- Basic concepts of online animation. All animations achieve the appearance of motion by rapidly displaying a series of still frames.
- When animating information displayed by a Web browser, we should prefetch the images so that they are readily accessible for rapid display. The key idea is to use a timer to create events, and then use the timer-event handler to redraw an image that has been placed on the Web page by the <img src="..."/> tag. These are referenced as the elements of the document's images array.

Try It Solutions

21.1
```
for (j = 0; j < 3; j++)
```

21.2
```
var rock=0, paper=0, scissors=0;          //Counters
var i, pick;                              //Loop variable
for (i=0; i<300; i++ ){                   //WFI
   pick = randNum(3);                     //Make random choice
   if (pick == 0)                         //Is it rock?
      rock++;                             //Yes, count rock
   else {
      if (pick == 1)                      //OK, is it paper?
         paper++;                         //Yes, count paper
      else
```

```
            scissors++;                              //No, count scissors
    }
}
alert("Rock: " + rock + ", Paper: " + paper + " and Scissors: " + scissors);
```

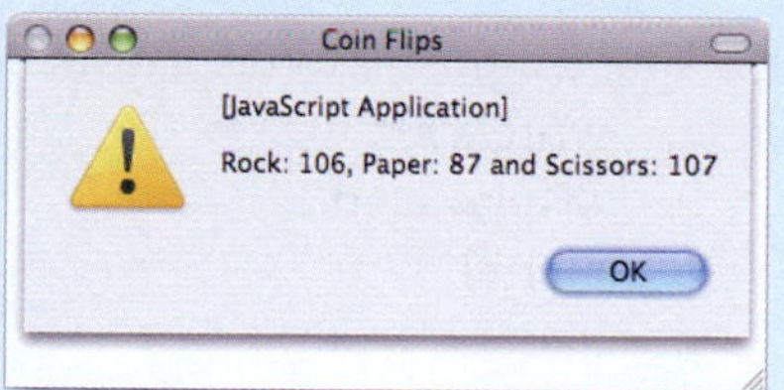

21.3

```
var rps = new Array(3);                          //Counters
var i, pick;                                     //Loop variable
rps[0] = 0; rps[1] = 0; rps[2] = 0               //Initialize counters
for (i=0; i<300; i++ ){                          //WFI
   pick = randNum(3);                            //Make random choice
   rps[pick]++;                                  //Index array by pick
}                                                //   and add 1
alert("Rock: " + rps[0] + ", Paper: " + rps[1]
               + " and Scissors: " + rps[2]);
```

Notice that the array has three elements, numbered 0, 1, and 2; by indexing with the number, we don't have to handle the separate cases. The right element is incremented.

Review Questions

Multiple Choice

1. In JavaScript the for statement is used for
   a. assignment
   b. increment
   c. iteration
   d. selection
2. If your mother told you four times to clean up your room (or in the computer age, to clean up your Desktop), there were
   a. four repetitions
   b. four iterations
   c. three iterations
   d. five iterations
3. In a for loop, the iteration value is changed by
   a. the <*continuation*> test
   b. the <*next iteration*>
   c. a false <*continuation*> test
   d. the end of the statement sequence

4. A false outcome for a termination test means
   a. terminate the loop
   b. terminate the program
   c. continue the loop
   d. do not enter the loop
5. The command to display an alert box in JavaScript is
   a. write.alert
   b. display.alert
   c. alert()
   d. alert = "text"
6. The maximum number of times a loop can iterate is
   a. 1,024
   b. 65,536
   c. 1,048,576
   d. infinite
7. i++ means
   a. add the value of i to itself and store the result in i
   b. add 1 to i
   c. multiply i by itself
   d. check to see if i is positive
8. For the statement below, which of the following is true?
   `for (j = 0; j < n; j++) {...}`
   a. the loop starts at 0
   b. the loop increments by 1
   c. the loop stops after n iterations
   d. all of the above
9. Array elements cannot be numbered with
   a. negative numbers
   b. decimals
   c. numbers greater or equal to their number of elements
   d. all of the above
10. The timer in JavaScript is called
    a. setTimeout
    b. Math.Timer
    c. Timer
    d. setTick
11. Given the line below, which of the following is a valid array reference?
    `var cols = New Array(9)`
    a. cols[0]
    b. cols[4.5]
    c. cols[9]
    d. cols[10]

12. Loading an image ahead of time is known as
    a. buffering
    b. prefetching
    c. caching
    d. backlogging

Short Answer

1. _______ means to loop through a series of statements to repeat them.
2. The _______ statement is used to start a loop in JavaScript.
3. A `for` loop is controlled by a _______.
4. _______ is the first operation of a `for` loop.
5. The first step of the second iteration of a loop is the _______ test.
6. The shortcut to subtract 1 from `i` is _______.
7. A loop that never ends is known as a(n) _______.
8. A loop inside a loop is called a(n) _______.
9. In JavaScript, the command to force a new line is _______.
10. `Math.abs()` is used in JavaScript to find _______.
11. _______ is the creation of a sequence of names by associating a base name with a number.
12. An indexed item is called a(n) _______.
13. The number of elements in an array is its _______.
14. A(n) _______ is an array name with its index.
15. The _______ is the number of frames per second that is displayed in an animation.

Exercises

1. You're making cookies (the real ones) and the directions say to stir until thoroughly mixed. Explain how a loop like this works.
2. What property of a loop ensures it will terminate?
3. Write the code for a loop that starts at 0 and iterates seven times.
4. Write the code for a loop that starts at your birth year and iterates for each year of your age.
5. Young lovers often use a daisy to determine the true feelings of the other. With each petal they count, they alternate "She loves me" and "She loves me, not." Generate a random number up to 25 and then use that to determine if your girlfriend (or boyfriend) loves you. Even numbers mean love. Other numbers mean not. Display the process.

6. Use nested loops to "count" from 1 to 100. Use the inner loop for the ones digit and the outer loop for the tens digit. Concatenate them to display the "number."
7. What would it take to "count" to 1,000 in Exercise 6?
8. Create a loop to display a set of asterisks to create a set of "stairs."

```
      *
     **
    ***
   ****
  *****
 ******
*******
```

9. Create a loop to display a set of "stairs" that go down instead of up.
10. Compile a list of everyday items that make up an array.
11. Explain why loops can use negative numbers and decimals but an array cannot.
12. Explain how an animation uses still images and loops to create the illusion of motion.

A Case Study in Algorithmic Problem Solving

22

chapter

The Smooth Motion Application

learning objectives

- State and apply the Decomposition Principle
- Explain the problem-solving strategy used in creating the Smooth Motion application
- Explain the use of the JavaScript operations for iteration, indexing, arrays, functions, animation controls, and event handlers in Smooth Motion
- Explain how mouse events are handled in Smooth Motion

You think of yourself as writing for a human being, explaining to a human being what a computer should do, instead of thinking of yourself as talking to the computer telling it what to do.

—DONALD KNUTH

THE PROGRAMMING that you've learned indicates how computers solve problems and demonstrates the source of their speed and versatility. You've learned enough programming to be able to embellish Web pages, making them more adaptive and dynamic. But the great value of the knowledge you've learned is neither insight nor embellishment. Rather, you can apply the programming ideas to general problem-solving situations. Processes, procedures, instructions and directions, decision-making, and so forth are phenomena we meet in daily life beyond the sphere of computers. Your knowledge applies in all of those cases, making you more effective at learning, performing, and planning tasks. In this chapter we apply this knowledge by solving a more substantial task.

Though the ideas have broad application, our interest and preparation are still Web related. Accordingly, the task at hand is a Web application, Smooth Motion, that tests a user's coordination at manipulating a mouse. How smooth are you? The application will use event programming, including "mouse events," animation, controls, somewhat more sophisticated XHTML, functions, iteration, indexing, and arrays. Smooth Motion is a generic application that allows us to focus on the problem-solving activity. By patiently following this fully explained case study, there will be opportunities to discuss when and how to apply the ideas you have learned.

The Smooth Motion Application

Step 0 in solving any problem is to understand what must be accomplished. (Almost everything in this chapter is 0-origin!) The Smooth Motion application is a coordination test. (Try Smooth Motion at www.aw.com/snyder/.) The graphical user interface is shown in Figure 22.1. Naming the components from top to bottom we have these parts:

- **Heading:** The text "Smooth Motion"
- **Grid:** The 7 × 20 grid of squares
- **Keys:** The row of seven brown/orange boxes
- **Controls:** The buttons and radio settings
- **Instructions:** The text at the bottom

Further, the components are enclosed in a one-column, five-row table with a border and a colored background.

How the Smooth Motion Application Should Work

Smooth Motion works as follows. The application starts up automatically five seconds after it is loaded. It begins filling the grid from the right with stacks of blocks of random height. The blocks move steadily to the left at a rate determined by the controls. Examples of the random stacks of blocks are shown in the left side of the grid in Figure 22.1.

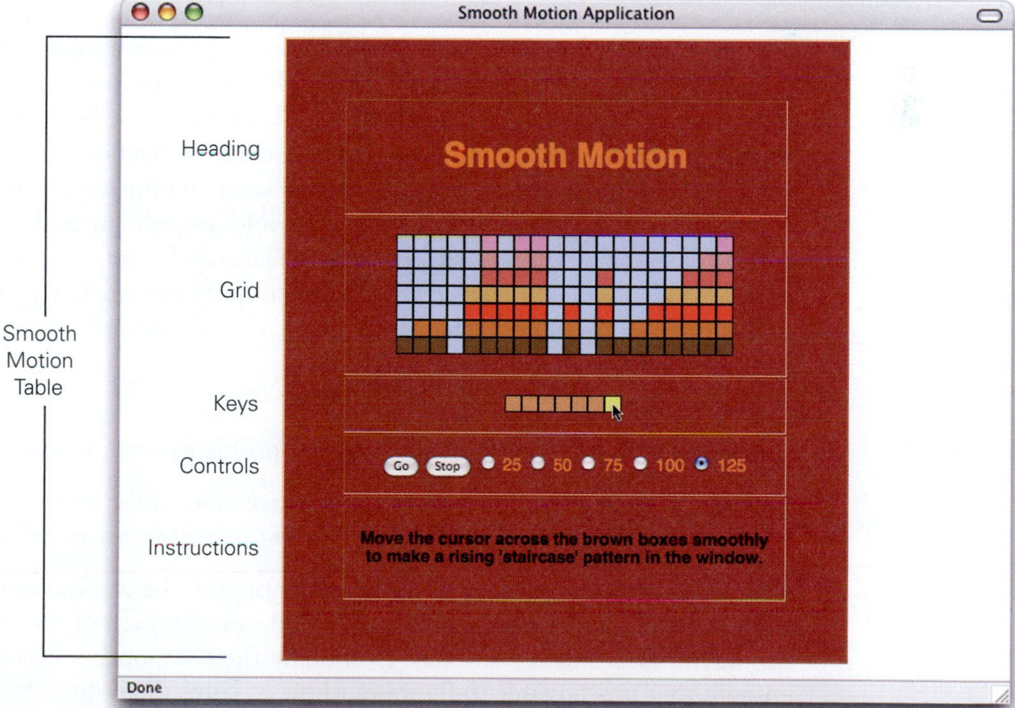

Figure 22.1 The Smooth Motion application user interface. Try it at www.aw.com/snyder/.

The random stack generation continues until the user places the mouse cursor over one of the brown keys. At that point, the user is in control of the stacks of blocks displayed in the grid. If we call the leftmost key, key 1, and the rightmost key, key 7, then when the mouse hovers over key *n*, a stack of *n* blocks appears in the grid. Figure 22.1 shows the mouse hovering over key 7.

The user's goal is to move the mouse across the brown keys as smoothly as possible. When the user has moved the mouse smoothly enough to create a perfect staircase rising to the right in the grid, the action stops. The process can be started or stopped at any point using the Go and Stop buttons. The speed selections are given in milliseconds and describe the rate at which the blocks move left. The test requires a smooth mouse motion across the keys from left to right at a rate corresponding to the frame rate of the grid animation.

Programming the Smooth Motion application is a substantial project, but surprisingly it requires only a modest amount of XHTML and JavaScript.

Smooth Move. How would you program Smooth Motion? Before reading about problem solving in this chapter, spend two minutes thinking about how you would create the Smooth Motion application. Truly, thinking about your own solution first will help you to understand the chapter more readily.

Planning Smooth Motion

The goal is to design and construct the Smooth Motion application. Achieving such a goal entails a substantial design with several functions and some intricate logic. A complicating factor is that we have both timer events for the animation and mouse events for the controls happening simultaneously. Most of us would never succeed with such an effort by trying to "brain it out." The complications of the project would overwhelm us. Instead, we will succeed by approaching it in a methodical step-by-step way, applying a standard divide-and-conquer technique to simplify our work. By breaking the project into convenient, manageable pieces, we will succeed.

Apply the Decomposition Principle

A fundamental strategy for solving complex problems is the following principle.

Decomposition Principle: *Divide a large task into smaller subtasks that can be solved separately and then combine their solutions to produce the overall solution.*

Of course, the subtasks may not be small enough to be worked out easily, so the Decomposition Principle can be applied again to each of the subtasks, producing even smaller subtasks. Eventually the components become small enough that it is possible to figure out how to solve them directly. When the subtasks are all solved, we begin the assembly process, combining the most primitive components to produce the more complex components, and so on until the overall problem is solved. The Decomposition Principle is little more than common sense, but when applied judiciously, it is a powerful technique for achieving significant results.

List the Tasks

The Smooth Motion application has several parts that provide an obvious beginning point for applying the Decomposition Principle.

Task	Description
Build GUI	Create a Web page with the table and its five parts: heading, grid, keys, controls, and instructions
Animate Grid	Move the block stacks to the left
Sense Keys	Handle the mouse events and transfer the control information to the grid animator
Detect Staircase	Recognize when, among a stream of events, the user has "met the test"
Build Controls	Implement the actions to control the application
Assemble Overall Design	Build the automatic random start-up, handle the starting and stopping, set the speeds, and interconnect the other components
Primp the Design	Make the page attractive and functional

Only the Build GUI task is simple enough to be solved directly, and even it is fancier than the other Web pages we've constructed so far. All of the other tasks will require further decomposition when we start to solve them.

Decide on a Problem-Solving Strategy

Decomposing the problem into tasks is step number one in solving it. Step number two is to strategize how to solve each of the parts. The strategy is concerned mostly with the order in which we'll solve the parts.

Build a basic Web page first. First, because JavaScript programming usually needs a Web page to host the computation, it makes sense to begin with the Build GUI task rather than any of the others. Such an approach gives us a place to test and save the solutions to the other tasks. The page becomes an organizing structure, a location where we record our progress by adding our JavaScript code to it.

fluency ALERT

Total Waste. One pitfall to avoid in any JavaScript design is spending hours constructing a splashy Web page only to discover that it doesn't fit well with the solutions to the other tasks. Such a mistake won't happen here—this is a "textbook example," after all—but it is an error to avoid on your other projects.

So, we begin by building the host page, but to avoid wasting time on a splashy-but-inappropriate page, we will build only the basic primitive page, and wait to embellish the design until after the parts are all working. Thus, we're splitting the GUI construction into two parts.

Though our problem is too small to illustrate it, there is a problem-solving strategy that creates a working prototype first before completing the whole design. This strategy is smart because it is easier to add to an already-working primitive design. Our plan to focus on the basic Web page and leave the cosmetic features to the end is in the spirit of this approach.

Solve independent tasks before dependent tasks. Deciding the order in which to solve the other tasks requires us to consider the **task dependencies**. That is, some tasks—for example, Detect Staircase—*rely on* or *depend on* the solution of other tasks, such as Sense Keys. Tasks that do not rely on the solution of any other tasks are *independent*, and should be done first. Tasks that depend on the independent tasks are done next, tasks that depend on them follow, and so on. Plan to schedule the tasks based on the rule: *Perform any task when all of the tasks it depends on are solved.* All of the tasks could be mutually dependent, though this is rare. In that case the dependent tasks are started, pushed as far as possible until they absolutely need the results of another task, and then are interrupted to work on the other task. For us, Build GUI is the independent task, and the Animate Grid task is dependent only on it. So, we'll schedule it second. Sense Keys is also dependent only on the GUI, but it is easier to test when the Animate Grid task is completed. It will be our third task.

PERT chart. Keeping track of many dependencies can be confusing, so systems engineers and managers draw a **task dependency graph**, or **PERT chart**. Standing for Program Evaluation and Review Technique, PERT charts were developed by the U.S. Navy in the 1950s.

There are several ways to draw them; we place tasks in circles and use arrows to show dependencies. In Figure 22.2 we have placed an arrow between two

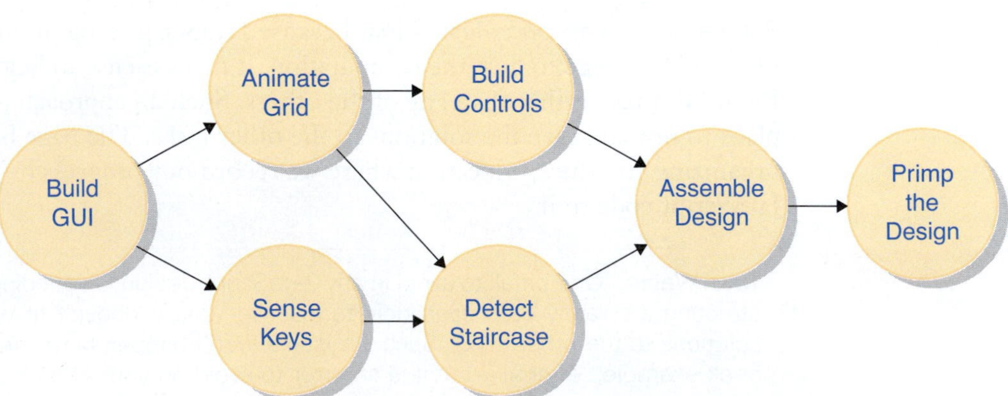

Figure 22.2 A task dependency diagram, also known as a PERT chart. Tasks are in circles and arrows are read as "task at head of arrow depends on task at tail of arrow."

circles so that the task at the head of the arrow depends on the task at the tail of the arrow. In this (very common) form of a PERT chart, we begin with circles that have no incoming arrows. From any circle, the arrows show which tasks can be done next when the task in the circle is completed.

✓checkLIST

Our strategy is to solve the tasks in this order:

- *Build GUI, to give us the basic Web page.*
- *Animate Grid, which is dependent only on the Build GUI task.*
- *Sense Keys, which is dependent only on the Build GUI task.*
- *Detect Staircase, which is dependent on Animate Grid and Sense Keys.*
- *Build Controls, which is dependent on Animate Grid.*
- *Assemble Overall Design, wrapping up those parts not yet complete.*
- *Primp the Design, embellishing the Web page.*

Usually each of these tasks would be further simplified using the Decomposition Principle until all of its subtasks were simple enough to solve directly. Doing so ensures that the decomposition has produced a practical solution. For our purposes, we will use a slightly different strategy, choosing instead to assign a section of this chapter to each task and to apply the Decomposition Principle at the start of the section.

Build the Basic Web Page GUI

The full graphical user interface for Smooth Motion will have a table with constituent parts: heading, grid, keys, controls, and instructions. For now, we'll create the basic structure. We'll call this the *structural page*. The "basic" features include the table, heading, and instructions as well as the background color, font style and color, and the centering of the application on the page. We'll improve it later when the application is completely working.

The Structural Page

The structural page contains a five-row, one-column table; the text for the Smooth Motion heading and instructions are placed in the first and last rows. As you learned from making the Bean Counter Web application page in Chapter 19, it is easiest to build tables "inside out" using *Copy/Paste*. That is, we construct a generic table cell with `<td>` tags, replicate that to make a row which we enclose in `<tr>` tags, and then replicate the row to make the whole table which we enclose in `<table>` tags. Then we fill it in. Because the present table has only one column, it's not necessary to replicate the cells to make a row for this situation. For us, the "generic" table cell is centered and contains a single blank character, that is, `<td> </td>`. The "basic" table has a border.

The Structural Page Heading

For the heading text, we use an <h1> heading, and for the instructions, we use a paragraph tag. Because the instructions text has a different text color than the other text on the page, we must set its font color.

The graphic and the XHTML for the structural page definition are shown in Figure 22.3. Notice that the middle three rows of Figure 22.1 are empty in Figure 22.3 because they are white space. However, they are defined in the XHTML, providing a site for our next programming step, the Animate Grid task.

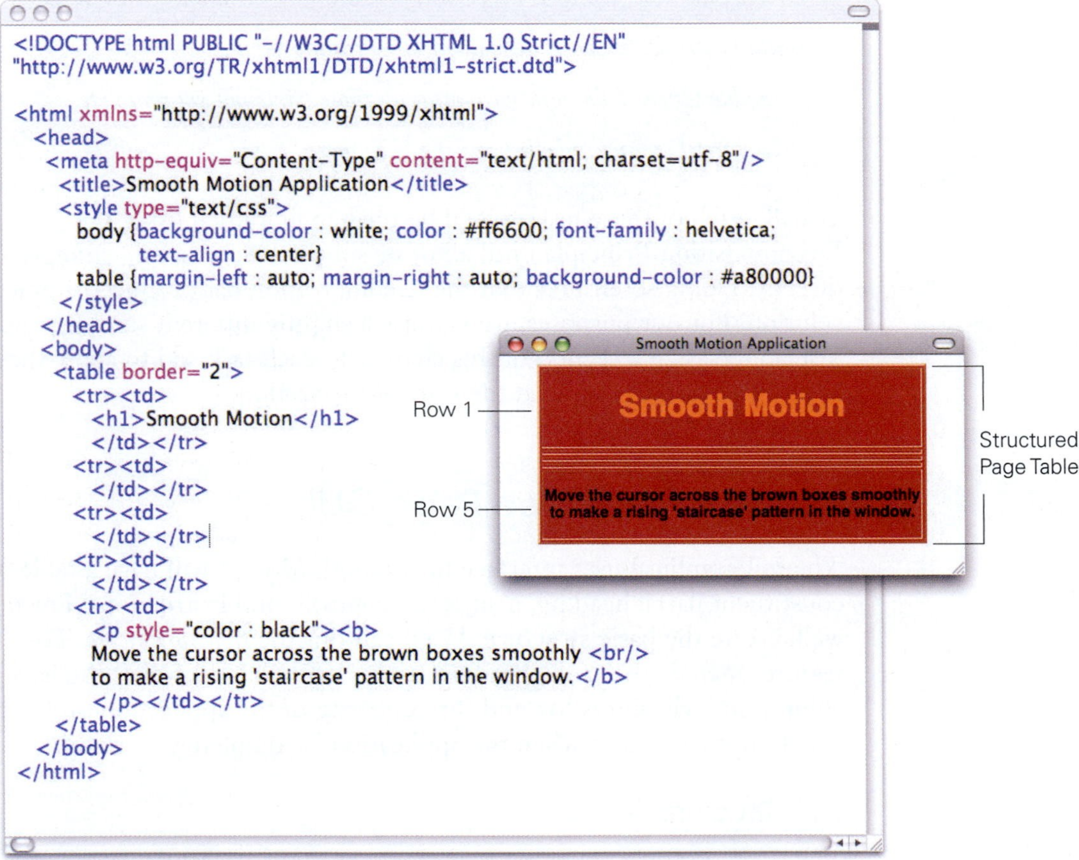

Figure 22.3 Image and HTML for the structural page. The table appears compressed because rows 2–4 contain nothing. Remember, your browser image may be slightly different.

Animate the Grid

The Animate Grid task must animate the 7 × 20 = 140 grid of blocks moving from right to left. This task is much too complicated to solve directly, so we apply the Decomposition Principle again.

First Analysis

The Busy Animation of Chapter 21 illustrated the basic steps of animation:

- Define and place the initial image.
- Prefetch the frames for updating the image.
- Set a timer and build a timer event handler, which updates the image.

These are the starting decomposition steps for the Animate Grid task. But these three steps don't fully solve the problem. We need to think and strategize further.

Frames for the columns of blocks. How will we organize the rapid redrawing of 140 images, keeping track of each block's trajectory? Reviewing how the application is supposed to work, we first notice that it only discusses "stacks" of blocks. This implies that there is no "motion" of images vertically, only horizontally. (This is obvious by the color scheme, too.) And, the horizontal motion is limited only to moving from right to left. From these observations we can conclude that we don't have to animate individual squares at all. The images can be whole columns. That simplification reduces the total number of images in the grid to 20, that is, the number of columns. Of course, we will need a frame image for each stack of blocks: a 0-stack, a 1-stack, … , and a 7-stack, resulting in a total of eight frames. So, a new subtask to add to our list of three is to define and organize the column frames.

Indexing columns left to right. Next we consider the "motion of an image." On each time step, a given column is replaced by the column to its right. If the 20 columns are indexed left to right, then the image in column *i* of the grid at a time step is replaced on the next time step by the image in column *i*+1 (see Figure 22.4). (The columns will be indexed from 0, left to right, because, as was mentioned in Chapter 21, when browsers place images on a page, they record them in the array `document.images` in the order encountered; that order is the construction sequence of an XHTML page, left to right, top to

Figure 22.4 With column 0 at the left, the image in column *i* should be replaced by the image in column *i* + 1 to implement the left-moving motion for the Grid Animation event handler.

bottom. So, the leftmost column of the grid is `document.images[0]`.) The action replaces the contents of `document.images[i]` with the contents of `document.images[i+1]`. Shifting each column to the left is quite easy, and it leaves only the last column to be handled differently.

Handling column 19 (last) is also easy because we only need to assign a new image—that is, one of the eight frames. Which frame do we assign? If we are in the random start-up phase, it should be a random frame. If we are in the user-controlled phase, it should be whichever frame the user has specified by the mouse position, if any. We will leave this choice of the frame open for the time being, because the Assemble Overall Design task will set the frame selection properly.

Second Analysis

From our first analysis it seems that we should add subtasks for defining an image-shifting process and for defining a column-19 fill process, but it's not necessary. Both activities will be part of the timer event handler, which is already on our list. So, our subtask list for the Animate Grid task has increased by only one new item:

1. Define and organize the eight columnar frames.
2. Define and place the initial images, 0 through 19.
3. Prefetch the eight frames for updating the image.
4. Set a timer with an event handler that shifts the images in columns 1 through 19 to columns 0 through 18, respectively, and introduce a new frame into column 19.

We'll assign a subsection to each subtask.

Subtask: Define and Organize the Frames

The eight frames for the Smooth Motion application are shown in Figure 22.5. The files are available online (www.aw.com/snyder/) so we don't need to create them here. Notice that they have names indexed in accordance with the block height. Also, the images have the necessary colors and lines that will be placed densely side-by-side to construct the grid.

If the `gif` frames had not been available, we would have had to create them. Numerous tools are available for this purpose, from simple paint programs to

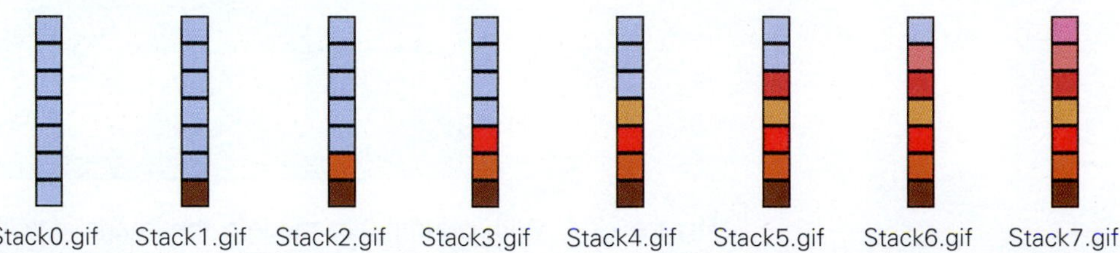

Figure 22.5 The eight frames required for the Smooth Motion application.

sophisticated image editing facilities. Though the tools vary in capabilities, convenience, and sophistication, there are only two guidelines to follow when creating frame images for JavaScript animations.

- Ensure that all images overwriting one another have the same dimensions in pixels. An easy way to meet this constraint is to create an initial "blank" frame instance, save it, and use it as the base for creating all of the other frame instances.
- Ensure that all files are saved using either the .gif or .jpg formats, and that they are used consistently; that is, only overwrite .gifs with .gifs.

To use images in HTML, it is recommended that they be placed in a separate folder, simply as an organizing technique (Chapter 3). Following that advice, the stack gifs in Figure 22.5 are saved in a folder called gifpix, meaning that their names relative to the HTML file are gifpix/Stack0.gif, gifpix/Stack1.gif, and so on.

Subtask: Define and Place Initial Images

This subtask constructs the grid in the second row of the structural page (see Figure 22.3). The initial state of the grid is created from 20 copies of Stack0.gif. As usual, to place an image on a page, we use the <img src="..."/> tag. But the 20 images will require 20 such tags. This calls for a loop. To use JavaScript's for statement, we place the <script> tags inside of the second row's <td> tags, and within them we write the necessary JavaScript. To have the images appear on the structural page, we must place them using the document.write() function.

The iteration can use the World-Famous Iteration form and must declare an iteration variable. The necessary code to implement these objectives is

```
<script type='text/javascript'>
    var j;                              //Declare iteration var
    for (j = 0; j < 20; j++) {          //Initialize grid images
        document.write('<img src="gifpix/Stack0.gif" alt=" "/>');
    }
</script>
```

which completes the image initialization. (Notice that the alt tag is left blank because these images will be overwritten.)

Subtask: Prefetch the Frame Images

As explained in Chapter 21, animating with images fetched from across the Internet is not likely to work because of delays that the .gif files might encounter during transfer. So, prefetching is necessary, and it is the goal of this subtask. (Review prefetching from the Busy Animation of Chapter 21, if necessary.)

Relative to the creation of the Web page, the prefetching activity can be performed at any time prior to the start of the animation. Because the prefetching also requires JavaScript code, we decide to place it with the code from the initialization subtask just completed, say, after the declaration. This is a good location because to prefetch the frames, we need an eight-element image array to prefetch into, and so we need another declaration for that array.

The three steps of prefetching are:

1. Declare the array into which the images will be fetched.
2. Initialize the array elements to be image objects; that is, define the image structure for each array element using the new Image() specification.
3. Assign the names of the files to the src fields of the image objects, causing the browser to record the names and get the files, thus implementing the prefetch.

The file names are those given in Figure 22.5. We call the array pics, and use a separate iteration for the second and third tasks, though combining the two operations into a single iteration is equivalent. The resulting code

```
var pics = new Array(8);                    //Declare array for gifs
for (j = 0; j < 8; j++) {                   //Make the elements images
    pics[j] = new Image( );
}
for (j = 0; j < 8; j++) {                   //Name source file, prefetch
    pics[j].src = "gifpix/Stack" + j + ".gif";
}
```

is inserted within the previous <script> tags, after the declaration. Notice that the file names are constructed on-the-fly to save us from typing separate statements.

22.1 **Pharaoh's Pyramid.** Using the idea of "building the name" for a file using concatenation, write two **for** loops that together would display the files of Figure 22.5 as a pyramid, as shown.

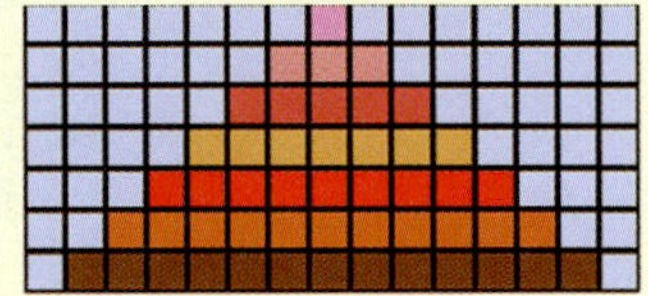

Subtask: Set Timer and Build Timer Event Handler

This subtask is mostly concerned with writing the event handler to move each of the grid's images one position left, obliterating the 0 image and assigning a new image to position 19. So we begin by constructing that event handler, called animate( ). As we work on it, several additional details arise that require our attention.

The timer event handler animate( ) has three operations:

1. To move all images but the first, one position left
2. To assign a new frame to image 19
3. To schedule itself for some time in the future

The mechanism for choosing the new frame is not yet worked out, but the Assemble Overall Design task will resolve it. For the moment, we simply assign a random frame as an easy way to have something different happening on each tick. And, assigning random frames is the way the application is to begin anyway.

Recall that browsers store the details of the images they display in an array called images in the DOM, that the array is referenced as document.images, and that the source field, src, is the relevant one to change if we want to display a new image. We use document.images and we program the three steps of the animate( ) function as

```
function animate( ) {
    for (j = 0; j < 19; j++) {                                //Shift left 1
        document.images[j].src = document.images[j+1].src;
    }
    document.images[19].src = pics[randNum(8)].src;           //New image
    timerId = setTimeout("animate( )", duration);             //Set timer
}
```

We have used the randNum() function developed in Chapter 20

```
function randNum (range) {
    return Math.floor(range * Math.random( ));
}
```

so we must include its declaration in order to reuse it. Also, we added a variable duration to the accumulating list of declarations:

```
var duration = 125;
```

To get the process started automatically after five seconds, we include the additional statement before the function definitions

```
timerId = setTimeout("animate( )", 5000);
```

which sets the animate( ) function to be run 5,000 ms after the browser starts. As with the Busy Animation, we save the handle received from the setTimeout function in a variable timerId (it must be declared!) so that the animation can be stopped. And, with that code, the Set Timer subtask is finished, completing the Animate Grid task. Figure 22.6 shows the state of the structural page at this point.

The Best Laid Plans . . .

The next step in our task decomposition strategy is to solve key sensing. However, now that we have the grid animation worked out, we find it very cumbersome not to be able to start and stop the animation on demand. It would be very helpful to have the controls available to stop the animation so that we don't have to kill the browser window each time to do so. But the

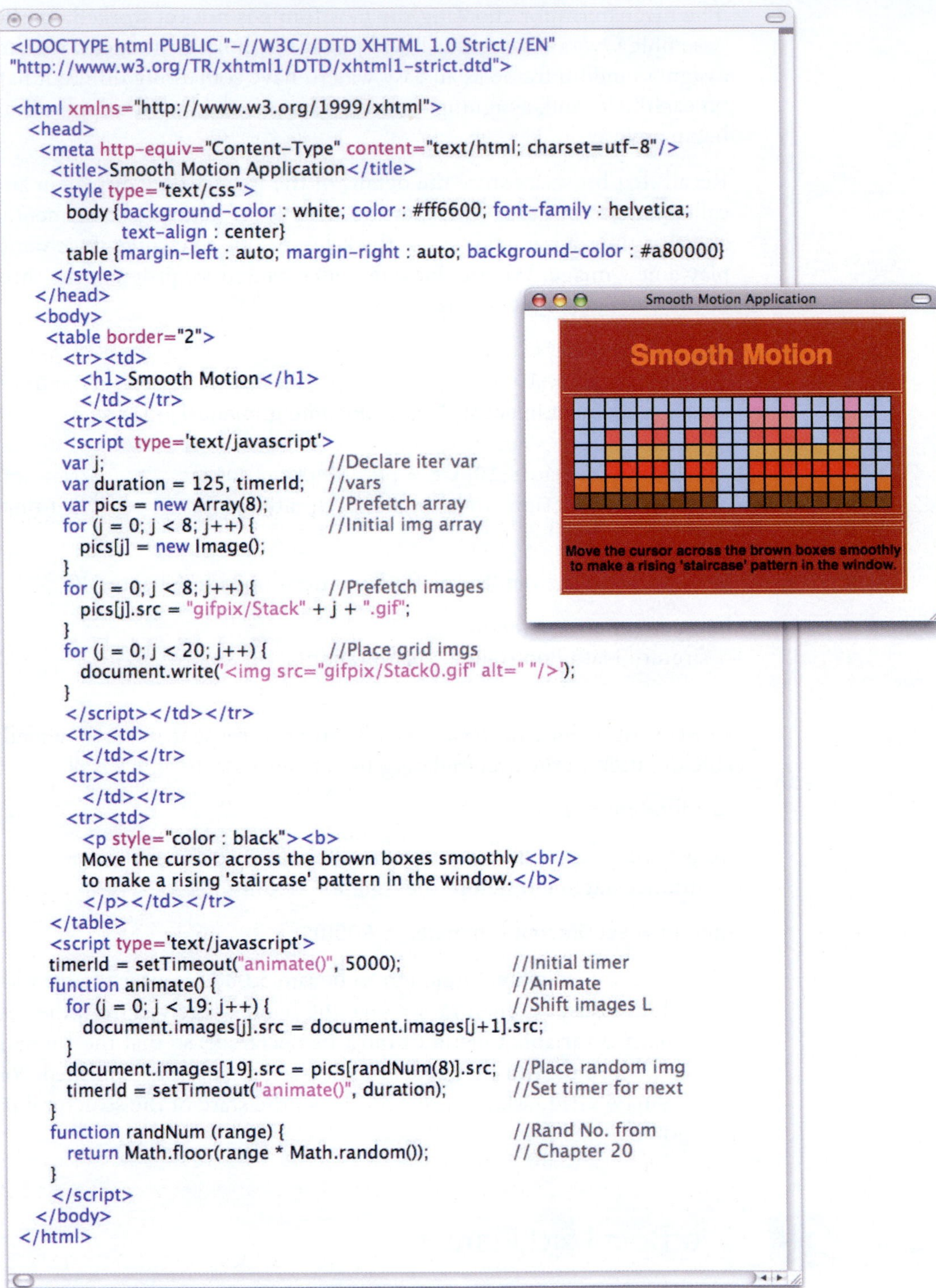

```
<!DOCTYPE html PUBLIC "-//W3C//DTD XHTML 1.0 Strict//EN"
"http://www.w3.org/TR/xhtml1/DTD/xhtml1-strict.dtd">

<html xmlns="http://www.w3.org/1999/xhtml">
  <head>
   <meta http-equiv="Content-Type" content="text/html; charset=utf-8"/>
    <title>Smooth Motion Application</title>
    <style type="text/css">
      body {background-color : white; color : #ff6600; font-family : helvetica;
            text-align : center}
      table {margin-left : auto; margin-right : auto; background-color : #a80000}
    </style>
  </head>
  <body>
   <table border="2">
     <tr><td>
       <h1>Smooth Motion</h1>
       </td></tr>
     <tr><td>
     <script type='text/javascript'>
     var j;                        //Declare iter var
     var duration = 125, timerId;  //vars
     var pics = new Array(8);      //Prefetch array
     for (j = 0; j < 8; j++) {     //Initial img array
       pics[j] = new Image();
     }
     for (j = 0; j < 8; j++) {     //Prefetch images
       pics[j].src = "gifpix/Stack" + j + ".gif";
     }
     for (j = 0; j < 20; j++) {    //Place grid imgs
       document.write('<img src="gifpix/Stack0.gif" alt=" "/>');
     }
     </script></td></tr>
     <tr><td>
       </td></tr>
     <tr><td>
       </td></tr>
     <tr><td>
       <p style="color : black"><b>
       Move the cursor across the brown boxes smoothly <br/>
       to make a rising 'staircase' pattern in the window.</b>
       </p></td></tr>
   </table>
   <script type='text/javascript'>
   timerId = setTimeout("animate()", 5000);                //Initial timer
   function animate() {                                    //Animate
     for (j = 0; j < 19; j++) {                            //Shift images L
       document.images[j].src = document.images[j+1].src;
     }
     document.images[19].src = pics[randNum(8)].src;       //Place random img
     timerId = setTimeout("animate()", duration);          //Set timer for next
   }
   function randNum (range) {                              //Rand No. from
     return Math.floor(range * Math.random());             // Chapter 20
   }
   </script>
  </body>
</html>
```


Figure 22.6 XHTML, JavaScript, and image for the table of the Smooth Motion implementation after the completion of the Animate Grid task.

Build Controls task is planned for later. Perhaps it makes more sense to solve it now to simplify our work. As Robert Burns noted, plans don't always work out, no matter how hard we try. (Burns put it more poetically: *The best laid schemes o' mice and men gang aft agley.*) Adjusting the order of tasks is very typical of large projects because it isn't always possible to figure out ahead of time all of the relevant interactions. So, we proceed to the Build Controls task.

Build Controls

Inspecting the GUI in Figure 22.1, we see that the controls entry of the table contains seven input controls. Thus, the fourth row of the table must contain <form> tags so that we can specify the controls. (Chapters 20 and 21 covered <form> tags.) The only challenge is how to handle the click-events. As always, we ask, "What should happen when the control is clicked?" There are three scenarios:

- **Go button click-event.** Start the animation with setTimeout( ), keeping track of the handle.
- **Stop button click-event.** End the animation by clearing the timer using the handle.
- **Radio button click-event.** Set the timer interval by assigning to duration.

None of these activities is more than a single statement, so rather than creating functions for the event handlers, we simply place the code in an input control.

```
<form activity=" ">
    <input type="button" value="Go" onclick='animate( )'/>
    <input type="button" value="Stop" onclick="clearTimeout(timerId)"/>
    <input type="radio" name="speed" onclick="duration=25"/> 25
    <input type="radio" name="speed" onclick="duration=50"/> 50
    <input type="radio" name="speed" onclick="duration=75"/> 75
    <input type="radio" name="speed" onclick="duration=100"/> 100
    <input type="radio" name="speed"
       onclick="duration=125" checked="checked"/> 125
</form>
```

Notice that the last button is checked to indicate that duration ⟺ 125 is the default. We place the code in the fourth row of the structural page table.

fluencyTIP

Easily Repeated. We could have used a **for** loop to place the radio buttons, though only the first four have the consistent structure suitable for a loop. Looping would require <script> tags, **document.write**, and so on. With so few repetitions, it's simpler to use *Copy/Paste/Edit* rather than a loop.

Having completed the Build Controls task, we can start and stop the animation. "We now return to our originally scheduled program."

Sense the Keys

The Sense Keys task implements the ability to recognize when the mouse hovers over a given key. The task requires us to understand how mouse motions are sensed, a topic that has not yet been introduced. But, it's typical when solving a large problem not to know the details of the constituent parts and to have to learn a new concept, system, or operation to solve the task. That's our situation with respect to sensing mouse motions. So, before attempting the task decomposition, we find out about mouse motions.

Actually, sensing mouse motions is very easy. Browsers recognize events on the objects of a Web page, such as images, just as they recognize events caused by controls. For example, if we click on an image, we cause a click-event, which we can process with an event handler. We specify the event handler by using the `onclick` attribute of the image tag, as in `<img src=". . ." onclick= "doSomething( )"/>`. This enables a mouse click on an image of a Web page to be recognized.

The browser, with the help of the operating system, keeps track of where the mouse pointer is at any moment. (After all, it's the operating system that is drawing the mouse pointer in the first place.) When the mouse pointer moves over an image or other Web page object, a *mouseover* event is recognized. When the mouse pointer moves off of the object, a *mouseout* event is recognized. We need these two events to follow the mouse cursor across the Smooth Motion keys. The keys are images, so we write an event handler for each of the two mouse events. We specify them to the browser with the `onmouseover` and `onmouseout` event handler specifications in the `<img src=". . ."/>` tag defining the key's image.

With that information, we can decompose the Sense Keys task by asking, "How should key sensing work?" First, we notice that there are no keys yet (see Figure 22.6), so we have to define them. Second, after thinking about their operation—they change their color from brown to orange on *mouseover* and then change back to brown on *mouseout*—it's clear that the keys are effectively another animation. The difference between other animations we've written and the keys' animation is that the former are updated by a timer, whereas the latter are updated by mouse motions. This observation is a tremendous help in our planning, because we have solved animation problems before. So, we begin our problem decomposition with the standard animation decomposition used for the Animate Grid task:

1. Define and organize the necessary frames.
2. Place the initial images and create the keys.
3. Prefetch the frames.
4. Build the event handlers.

This is a sufficient strategy to solve the problem.

Subtask: Define and Organize the Frames

The first subtask involves only two images, ■ and ■. They are named `BrownBox.gif` and `OrangeBox.gif` and are stored in the `gifpix` directory with the `Stack` images. Moving the files to that directory completes the first subtask.

Subtask: Place the Initial Images

Placing the images creates the keys. Seven images will be placed in the center of the third row of the structural page's table. They are all `BrownBox.gif`. As before, we write a JavaScript loop to iterate the `document.write` of the `<img src=". . ."/>` tags. The resulting code, which is still incomplete—but will be fixed momentarily—is

```
for (j = 0; j < 7; j++) {                          //Incomplete
    document.write('<img src="gifpix/BrownBox.gif" alt=" "/>');
}
```

This completes the placement subtask for the time being.

Subtask: Prefetch the Frames

Prefetching the frames is also completely analogous to our earlier animations, and by now its three-subtask sequence is becoming familiar. There are only two frames to prefetch, leading to the declaration of a small array:

```
var keypix = new Array(2);
```

We add simple code for image initialization,

```
keypix[0] = new Image( );
keypix[1] = new Image( );
```

and prefetching,

```
keypix[0].src = "gifpix/BrownBox.gif";
keypix[1].src = "gifpix/OrangeBox.gif";
```

because it isn't worth writing loops. These lines complete the prefetch subtask.

Subtask: Build the Event Handlers

Finally, we build the two event handlers, `here( )` for `mouseover` and `gone()` for `mouseout`. They're not difficult to build.

As with any event handler, we ask, "What should happen when the mouse moves over a key?" First, the key must change color to give feedback to the user that the mouse is on or off the key. This involves simply updating the key's image with the `OrangeBox.gif` or the `BrownBox.gif` image. But how do we refer to the key's image? We know that it is listed in the `images` array that the browser keeps of the images on the page. Because the keys come *after* the grid, the key images are obviously stored in the array *after* the grid images. The grid images are images[0], . . . , images[19], so by the preceding loop, the keys must be images[20], . . . , images[26]. Of course, if we know the position of the key, say, pos, we can refer to the image as images[20+pos]. We conclude that we need to record the position of each key in the sequence.

Next, the mouse-sensing event handlers must tell the Grid Animation event handler which new Stack image to draw in the last position of the grid. All that event handler needs is the key's position, so if we assign it to a global variable, say, frame, we've done the job. These observations lead us to declare a variable frame and to define the two mouse event handlers.

```
function here (pos) {
    document.images[20+pos].src = "gifpix/OrangeBox.gif";
    frame = pos + 1;
}
function gone (pos) {
    document.images[20+pos].src = "gifpix/BrownBox.gif";
    frame = 0;
}
```

We have made the key's position a parameter.

Notice how here( ) solves a problem of mismatched indices. The keys are 0-origin indexed (i.e., 0, 1, . . . , 6); pos will have one of these values. The stacks of blocks are 1-origin indexed (i.e., Stack1.gif, Stack2.gif, . . . , Stack7.gif); frame should have one of these values. That is, the mouse over key[0] means draw Stack1.gif. The here( ) function makes up for this mismatch with the assignment

```
frame = pos + 1;
```

Also, notice that for gone( ), we don't know where the mouse is moving to. It could be moving to another key, or it could be moving off the keys entirely, which should draw the Stack0.gif. The safe thing is to set frame = 0. If the mouse moves to another key, its mouseover event handler will be called immediately, setting frame to the right number.

22.2 **Quick Mouse.** When the mouse moves over the rightmost sense key image, the function here( ) will be called; what is the value of pos for that call? What is the index of the element in the document.images array that is changed? What is the name of the image that should be displayed in document.images[19] as a result of the call?

Combine the Subtasks

With the two mouse event handlers defined, we return to the image initialization subtask to add the event handler specifications to the <img src="..."/> tags. The revised and final form of the initialization is

```
for (j = 0; j < 7; j++) {
    document.write('<img src="gifpix/BrownBox.gif" ' +
      'onmouseover = "here(' + j + ')" ' +
      'onmouseout = "gone(' + j + ')" alt=" "/>');
}
```

The two mouse event handler functions have their position parameters specified by the for loop's iteration variable j. To test the Sense Keys task solution, we make one tiny change in the Grid Animation event handler, animate( ), namely, to change the frame assigned to the last column from the random choice to the frame variable. The new line has the form

```
document.images[19].src = pics[frame].src;
```

allowing us to test the code.

Having completed the Sense Keys task, Figure 22.7 shows the code entered into the structural page in the third row. (The two declarations—keypix and frame—are included with the earlier declarations, and the event handling functions are included with the previously defined functions.)

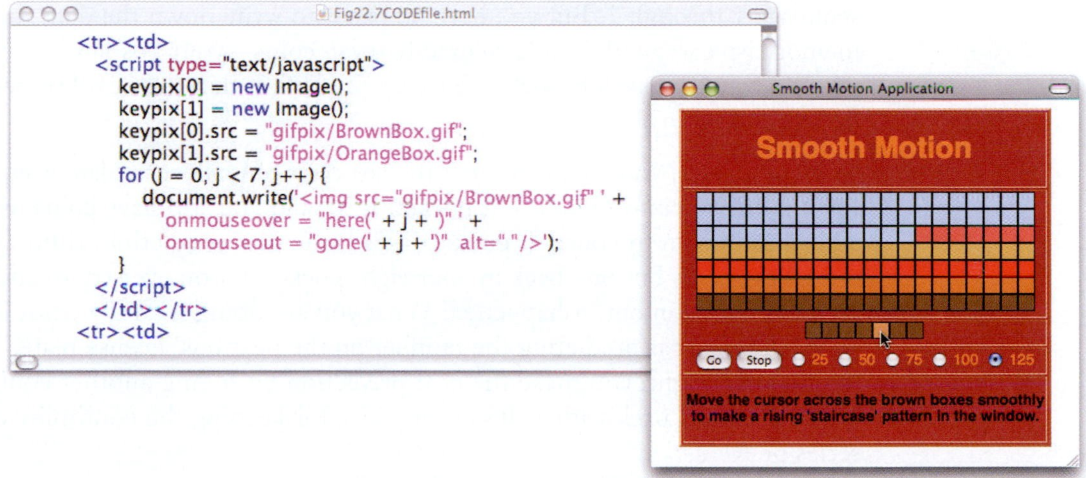

Figure 22.7 JavaScript for the Sense Keys task (the two declarations and the two event handlers are not shown).

Staircase Detection

When the user has manipulated the mouse in such a way as to create a rising "staircase" of blocks in the grid, the animation should stop. How do we recognize the "staircase"? It's not possible to look at the grid, of course, so we must identify it by other characteristics. Observe that the user will have created a staircase when the frame values for seven consecutive animate( ) calls are 1, 2, 3, 4, 5, 6, 7.

This is true because the value of frame tells the animate( ) event handler which Stack frame to display, and if it is directed to display the seven frames in order on seven consecutive ticks, there will be a staircase in the grid.

Subtask: Recognizing the Staircase

How do we recognize the seven consecutive frame values? There are many techniques. Some involve keeping an array of the seven most recent frame values and checking each time to see if the desired sequence occurs. Another involves looking at the src fields in the last seven images of the grid—it's almost like looking at the picture—to see if they have the right sequence of file names. But the technique we will employ requires slightly less programming and seems cleverer. The idea is to keep predicting the next frame value.

Subtask: Recognizing Continuity

Notice that we are trying to recognize continuity across a sequence of events, that is, seven events in which the value for frame is 1, 2, 3, 4, 5, 6, 7. By analogy, imagine you are sitting at a bus stop trying to determine if seven consecutive buses ever pass by with the last digit of their license numbers making the sequence 1 through 7. But you have no paper to write down the data and your memory isn't so good. You have exactly seven coins—your bus fare—so you put one coin in your left pocket. That's a prediction that the next bus has a license ending in 1.

As a bus arrives, you check to see if the last digit of its license plate is equal to the number of coins in your left pocket. If so, and you still have coins, you add another coin to your left pocket. This is the next prediction. If not, you put all the coins but one back in your right pocket. If you ever try to add a coin but have run out, it happened! What you are doing with the coins in your left pocket is predicting the number on the next bus' license plate. If the prediction is right, you make the next prediction by adding another coin; but if not, you start back with 1. It's an easy idea for keeping the continuity of a series of events.

Implementing the bus analogy, we modify the animate( ) function at the point where it is about to set the timer for the next tick, because if the staircase is found, there should be no next tick. Additionally, we'll declare another variable, next1, that corresponds to the coins in your left pocket, that is, as if predicting an event. The following code implements the steps of this process.

```
if (frame == next1)                                //Is the prediction correct?
    next1 = next1 + 1;                             //Yes, make next prediction
else                                               //No
    next1 = 1;                                     //Go back to the start
if (next1 != 8)                                    //Are we still looking?
    timerId = setTimeout("animate()",duration);    //Yes, set timer
```

Notice that the test in the last if statement compares to 8 rather than 7 because next1 was already incremented previously, and so the condition of "no more coins left" is equivalent to next1 ⟺ 8. With that addition to animate( ) we have completed the Detect Staircase task.

Assemble Overall Design

With the Build Controls task performed out of order and parts of the Assemble Overall Design task performed ahead of time, there is not much left to do to complete the programming of the Smooth Motion application. Nevertheless, this is the point at which we make sure that the whole application works as planned.

Reviewing the description at the start of the chapter, we notice that the display of randomly selected stacks of blocks isn't presently working. Originally we generated random stacks when we solved the Animate Grid task. But we took that feature out to test the keys. Now we want to put it back in.

Basically we should set image 19 to frame or randNum(8), depending on whether or not the user has ever passed the mouse over a key. How will we know? The mouseover event handlers will recognize the situation, but at the moment they are programmed only to return a frame value from 1 through 7. So, if we started out with frame initialized to some erroneous number, say, –1, and test it in the animate( ) event handler before using the frame value, we could recognize the two situations: –1 means the mouse has not yet passed over the keys for the first time; anything else means the mouse has passed over the keys the first time. Thus, we must change the initialization of frame in its declaration to

```
var frame = -1;                //Set for initial random generation
```

and rewrite the assignment to the last column of the grid one more time:

```
if (frame == -1)
    document.images[19].src = pics[randNum(8)].src;
else
    document.images[19].src = pics[frame].src;
```

This last change to animate( ) makes it quite cluttered with if statements, as shown in Figure 22.8. The clutter obscures the simple two-part logic of shifting the grid and checking for the staircase. So, we relegate both operations to functions. The resulting solution is no shorter—in fact, it is longer by four lines—but it makes the important animate( ) event handler clearer, making the exercise worthwhile.

After checking the operation of the Smooth Motion application, it seems that we've taken care of all of the design elements, except the fancy GUI, which is the last remaining task.

```
function animate() {
  for (j = 0; j < 19; j++) {
    document.images[j].src = document.images[j+1].src;
  }
  if (frame == -1)
    document.images[19].src = pics[randNum(8)].src;
  else
    document.images[19].src = pics[frame].src;
  if (frame == next1)
    next1 = next1 + 1;
  else
    next1 = 1;
  if (next1 != 8)
    timerId = setTimeout("animate()",duration);
}
```

becomes...

```
function animate() {
  shiftGrid ();
  checkStairAndContinue ();
}
function shiftGrid() {
  for (j = 0; j < 19; j++) {
    document.images[j].src = document.images[j+1].src;
  }
  if (frame == -1)
    document.images[19].src = pics[randNum(8)].src;
  else
    document.images[19].src = pics[frame].src;
}
function checkStairAndContinue() {
  if (frame == next1)
    next1 = next1 + 1;
  else
    next1 = 1;
  if (next1 != 8)
    timerId = setTimeout("animate()",duration);
}
```

Figure 22.8 Revision of the function **animate( )** to encapsulate portions of the computation into functions.

Primp the Design

The structural page we've built our application around can be made more attractive. In fact, the task of improving the aesthetics of Web pages is probably an unending task. We recognize the following improvements that will produce the page shown in Figure 22.1:

- Cell padding
- Sense key color upgrade

Cell padding is a somewhat complicated topic that will not be covered here. For the record, the two enhancements can be programmed using properties of the table element:

```
padding : 5%
```

which adds space around the table, and the td element

```
padding : 15px
```

which adds space around the contents of the cells. An explanation of this topic is found at www.w3.org/TR/CSS2/box.html and nearby pages. It's left to the interested reader to explore alternative styles.

The sense keys seem a little dull. So, we create a new YellowBox.gif as the color for mouse over, and use OrangeBox.gif for the base case. This brightens up the display, and can be implemented by two Find and commands.

Assessment and Retrospective

When we are asked to design a solution to someone else's problem, we are usually finished when we verify that we've done what we've been asked to do. If the design is to achieve a goal of our own choice, however, an assessment step remains. When we pick a goal, we usually do not have a fixed target like Figure 22.1 to work toward. Rather, we design a solution to our original "best guess"; then we consider whether the result is the best possible solution. (We have used such assessments in Chapters 17 and 19.) Generally, having a working solution suggests many worthwhile improvements.

In this chapter, the first case applies, and so we are finished. Instead of an assessment, consider the ideas from earlier chapters applied in this chapter. There are three primary topics:

- Loops
- Parameterizing functions for reuse
- Managing complexity with functions

Applying these ideas has produced a better program. Consider how.

Loops. The Smooth Motion application used several for loops. These saved us from tedious activities like writing 20 <img src=". . ."/> statements in a row. Such loops simplified the programming. But at times, when we might have used loops, we chose not to. For example, we explicitly wrote the instructions for defining the radio buttons and for prefetching the key images. We used *Copy*, *Paste*, and *Edit* commands rather than a loop, because it was easier to program. Had there been more iterations, or had the specification been slightly simpler, we might have used a loop. The computer does the same work either way; we decide which method is more convenient.

Parameterizing functions for reuse. The here( ) and gone( ) functions each use a single parameter that is the position of the key in sequence. The actual value is passed to the functions in the event handler specifications. For example, the third key from the left was defined by a document.write that produces

```
<img src="gifpix/BrownBox.gif"
    onmouseover = "here(2)" onmouseout = "gone(2)" alt=" "/>
```

where the "2" indicates the key's 0-origin number. The parameter customizes the event handler for each key. We could have written separate functions in which the key's position is used explicitly everywhere pos occurs, but this would create a proliferation of almost-identical functions. The parameter says where and how the event handlers differ from each other, and their use produces a more abstract—and easier to understand—solution.

Managing complexity with functions. The functions shiftGrid() and checkStairAndContinue() shown in Figure 22.8 are examples of creating functions to manage complexity. Both functions "package" program logic allowing us to *name them* and *move them* out of the way, revealing the simple two-part logic of the animate( ) function.

```
function animate( ) {
    shiftGrid ( );
    checkStairAndContinue ( );
}
```

As with loops and parameters, functions clarify to humans how the animation function works; it's all the same to the computer. Humans will see our choice of function names—for example, shiftGrid( )—and correctly interpret them as describing what the function does. If people need to know how the program shifts the grid, they can check the function; otherwise, it's out of the way, replaced by a succinct statement of what it does (its name). This role of shifting the grid might have been expressed as a comment at the start of the code sequence, but comments are often overlooked. The abstraction—naming the function and giving its definition—creates a new concept in our minds, raising our level of understanding of Smooth Motion's animation process. Though these two functions will never be used again, the goal of simplifying the program justifies our effort to define them. See Appendix F for a complete listing of the Smooth Motion application.

Thus, we see that programming is as much about teaching viewers of our program how we solved the problem as it is about instructing the computer. Even for programs that are not textbook examples, helping humans understand programs is essential. It helps with debugging—an important concern for us—and by organizing the solution in an understandable way, and instills confidence in others about the correctness of our solution.

Summary

We have programmed a substantial application that would have been too complicated to achieve directly. To succeed, we applied the Decomposition Principle, first to create the high-level tasks that guided our overall solution, and then again, when it came time to solve the tasks that were still too complicated. Though it is mostly common sense, the Decomposition Principle provides a strategy that works to solve all difficult problems. To solve the problem at hand we:

- Defined the tasks and strategized about the order in which to solve them. Because there were dependencies among the tasks, we defined a feasible plan to solve them.
- Used a dependency diagram to show which tasks depended on others and to assist us in strategizing. We planned an order consistent with the diagram—that is, no task was scheduled ahead of the tasks it depended on—and produced a workable plan.
- Considered other features, such as ease of testing, and adjusted the schedule to address these aspects.
- Developed the actual solution of the Smooth Motion program directly. We decomposed each task into several subtasks. There was similarity among these subtasks. For example, the timer-driven animation and the key-driven animation used a similar set of subtasks.
- Decided to solve the tasks out of order from our original schedule, to give ourselves the ability to start and stop the animation. Convenience motivated us to depart from our original schedule, but originally it was not possible to predict the benefits of the alternative plan.
- Learned about mouse events, a topic we had not previously encountered. This was not a difficult concept to grasp, but it illustrated a common feature of any large task—that it is often necessary to learn new information to solve a complex problem.
- Used the programming facilities covered in earlier chapters—loops, functions, parameters, and so on—as tools to instruct both the computer and humans looking at the program. Those facilities clarified the program, making it plain how the problem was solved.
- Developed an IT application with techniques that have wide application. You can expect to use decomposition in other problem solving, to abstract the components of a solution by giving them names and precise definitions, and to reduce the complexity of a solution to an understandable level.
- Learned powerful problem-solving techniques.

Try It Solutions

22.1
```
<script type="text/javascript">
    var i;
    for (i=0; i < 8; i++) {
        document.write('<img src="gifpix/Stack' + i + '.gif"/>');
    }
```

```
for (i=0; i < 7; i++) {
    document.write('<img src="gifpix/Stack' + (6-i) + '.gif"/>');
}
</script>
```

22.2 The value of pos for that call is 6, because the seven sense keys are indexed 0 to 6, and the rightmost key is the last one. The element in `document.images` that is changed is 26, because 20 + 6 = 26. The image displayed, the `frame`, is `Stack7.gif`, because the images containing more than 0 blocks are indexed 1 through 7.

Review Questions

Multiple Choice

1. The first step in problem solving is
   a. develop an algorithm
   b. understand the problem
   c. create the interface
   d. determine the functions needed
2. The second step in problem solving is
   a. break the problem into smaller tasks
   b. plan how to solve the problems
   c. design the interface
   d. build the functions
3. The Build Controls task is dependent on
   a. Assemble Overall Design
   b. Detect Staircase
   c. Sense Keys
   d. Animate Grid
4. Before the Animate Grid task can be completed, the
   a. Build Controls task must be completed
   b. Detect Staircase task must be completed
   c. Build GUI task must be completed
   d. Sense Keys task must be completed
5. The Detect Staircase task is not dependent on
   a. Build Controls
   b. Sense Keys
   c. Animate Grid
   d. Build GUI
6. Which of the following is an example of the World-Famous Iteration form?
   a. `for (j = 0; j < 10; j++)`
   b. `for (i = 1; i <=5; i = i +1)`
   c. `for (k = 10; k > 1; k--)`
   d. `for (j = 1; j++; j<=5)`

7. To use a graphic that has been prefetched
   a. the `href` command must be used
   b. the `src` command must be used
   c. a specific image must be placed in a specific location
   d. none of the above
8. To get the browser to delay 5 seconds, you need to set the `setTimeout` function to
   a. 5
   b. 500
   c. 5000
   d. .5
9. It is worthwhile to write a loop to do a repetitive task when there are
   a. 2 or more tasks
   b. more than 3–5 tasks
   c. more than 8–10 tasks
   d. 20 or more tasks
10. A meaningful name for a function
    a. makes the code easier to read
    b. raises the level of understanding for those who read the code
    c. means as much to the computer as a meaningless name
    d. all of the above

Short Answer

1. The _______ is used to break a task into smaller, easy-to-solve tasks.
2. _______ is the second step in problem solving.
3. _______ are the relationships between tasks that determines the order in which the tasks in a program are solved.
4. When solving a problem, the _______ should be solved first.
5. PERT stands for _______.
6. A(n) _______ can be used to visually keep track of which tasks depend on another.
7. The _______ task must be completed before the Sense Keys task can be completed.
8. The Animate Grid task and the Sense Keys task both must be completed before the _______ task can be completed.
9. An array called _______ is where a browser stores information about the images on a page.
10. Clicking on a button on a Web page will trigger a(n) _______.
11. _______ are objects that, when placed in a group, work together to allow the user to select one item from the group.
12. The unit used for timing JavaScript events on the computer is called a _______.

Exercises

1. Describe the Decomposition Principle.
2. Apply the Decomposition Principle to cooking a meal.
3. Create a PERT chart for the preceding exercise.
4. List the dependent tasks and the independent tasks for cooking a meal.
5. On the Smooth Motion Web page, what objects are used for user input?
6. Explain why it's a good idea to create the GUI early in the process, but not finalize it until the end of the process.
7. What is the advantage of prefetching images for an animation?
8. How would you modify the Smooth Motion code to keep track of how long the user can keep the animation running and display it at the end?
9. Explain how the `onmouseover` and `onmouseout` events work.

Limits to Computation

Computers Can Do Almost {❑ Everything, ❑ Nothing}

23
chapter

learning objectives

- Explain what the Turing test was designed to show
- Discuss the issue of a computer being intelligent and able to think; refer to Deep Blue
- Discuss the issue of computer creativity; refer to computer-generated music and art
- State the meaning of the Universality Principle
- State the way in which the amount of work in a program is related to the speed of the program

The real danger is not that computers will begin to think like men, but that men will begin to think like computers.

—SYDNEY J HARRIS

Artificial Intelligence is no match for natural stupidity.

—ANONYMOUS

Rules have no existence outside of individuals.

—HENRI MATISSE

COMPUTERS have achieved sustained speeds of well over 1,000 trillion additions per second. On a pocket calculator, at one operation per second, it takes 1,000 lifetimes (assuming 60 years of daily calculating for 14 hours each day) to perform 1 trillion operations. But so what? Everyone knows computers are amazingly fast at arithmetic. Shouldn't we be more impressed if a computer ever had an original thought, no matter how trivial? Absolutely! But it probably won't happen. As you have learned, for a computer to do anything, it must be programmed to do it, and so far "thought" in the sense we usually mean the term has eluded researchers. So, we have a curious situation. Computers can be truly awesome at some tasks and completely hopeless at others. Because they're so different from humans, it's reasonable to wonder what computers can and cannot do.

This chapter addresses philosophical issues. First we ask whether a computer can think. Thinking about thinking leads us to the famous Turing test. Chess—a game requiring smarts—became a *de facto* goal of artificial intelligence research. We explore how computers play chess, summarize the advancements, and report the victory of Deep Blue. We also speculate on how creative computers can be. Next, we consider the easy-to-understand but significant idea—the Universality Principle—that asks how different computers can be. Any "new and improved" computer will be faster or larger, but not more capable. How important is more speed? We explore how fast computers can solve various problems by revisiting the *Alphabetize CDs* algorithm from Chapter 10. Finally, there are problems that cannot be solved by a computer even in principle, not because they are too nebulous to specify for a computer, but because to do so would be a contradiction.

Can Computers Think?

The inventors of electronic computers thought that they were discovering how to "think with electricity." And to the extent that operations like addition and multiplication require humans to think, it's easy to see their point. Previously, electricity had been used directly as an energy source for driving motors and powering light bulbs. With the digital computer, electricity switched complex circuits, implementing logical operations. The power was applied to manipulate information. The phenomenon was truly new.

Today, electronic devices that manipulate information are so common, we are less impressed by them. It is difficult to regard a calculator as "thinking." But our view of what constitutes thinking has changed over time, too. In the Middle Ages, when very few people could read or reckon, as performing arithmetic was called, anyone who could add and multiply was thought to have special powers, divinely or perhaps mystically conferred. Reckoning was a uniquely human activity. It took centuries for addition and multiplication to be codified into the algorithms that we all learn in elementary school. Is a capability, once classified as thinking and believed to be a divine gift, no longer thinking when it turns out to be algorithmic? It required thinking when we learned it. Maybe all thought is algorithmic. Maybe it's thinking only as long as no one understands how it's accomplished.

fluencyBIT

Sub Text. Computer scientist Edsger Dijkstra is quoted as saying, "The question of whether a computer can think is no more interesting than the question of whether a submarine can swim." But he seems to be in the minority.

The Turing Test

The problem of defining thinking for the purposes of deciding whether a computer thinks concerned Alan M. Turing, one of the pioneers of computation. Turing was aware of definitions like "thinking is what people do," and the tendency for people to call an activity "thinking" until it turns out to be algorithmic. So, he decided to forget trying to define what thinking is and proposed a simple experiment that would demonstrate intelligence. Turing designed the following experimental setting, which has since become known as the **Turing test**.

Turing test: *Two identical rooms labeled A and B are connected electronically to a judge who can type questions directed to the occupant of either room. A human being occupies one room, and the other contains a computer. The judge's goal is to decide, based on the questions asked and the answers received, which room contains the computer. If after a reasonable period of time the judge cannot decide for certain, the computer can be said to be intelligent.*

Thus, the computer is intelligent if it acts enough like a human to deceive the judge.

Passing the Test

Turing's experiment not only sidestepped the problem of defining thinking or intelligence, but it also got away from focusing on any specific ability such as performing arithmetic. The judge can ask any questions, so as to explore the entire range of thought processes. Apparent stumpers for the computer like

In Hamlet's famous soliloquy, what metaphors does Shakespeare use for "death"?

might not be so hard if the computer has access to online sources of Shakespearean criticism. Apparent "gimmes" for the computer like

What are the prime factors of 72,914,426?

might be answered in more human-like ways such as being slow or refusing to answer such questions at all. When Turing proposed the test in 1950, there was little prospect that a computer could deceive the judge. Nevertheless, it emphasized the important point that thinking is a process; how it is accomplished—with synapses or transistors—shouldn't matter.

Advances in the past 60 years have definitely improved the computer's chances of "passing" the Turing test, though perhaps they are still not very good. Researchers reading Turing's paper in 1950 might have conceded that computers could be better than people at arithmetic, but probably all of them would have believed that "natural language"—a true human invention—was beyond the abilities of computers. For example, when Turing conceived the test, no algorithmic process was known for parsing (analyzing) English into its grammatical structure, as word processors' grammar checkers do today. Nor was "machine translation"—converting text from one language into its semantic equivalent in another language—anything more than science fiction. Nor was recognizing semantically meaningful information something a computer could perform, as Google does today.

Admittedly, computers are still a long way from being perfect at any of these tasks, but they are pretty good at all three—at least good enough to be the basis for useful applications. More important, they are good enough at these language tasks that we can imagine a day when computers are better than most humans. And then, like reckoning, the tasks of parsing, translation, and semantic searching in natural language will have been reduced to algorithmic

fluency FLASHBACK

Grand Turing. Englishman Alan Mathison Turing (1912–1954) was probably the most brilliant of all of the computer pioneers. In addition to the Turing test, he invented the first theoretical computer, now known as the Turing Machine, and discovered the Universality Principle (explained later in this chapter). During World War II he worked at the British Government's Code and Cipher School at Bletchley Park breaking Germany's Enigma Code. The Cambridge-educated mathematician and marathon runner was awarded the Order of the British Empire (OBE) and was a member of the Royal Society. He died in 1954 of potassium cyanide poisoning under suspicious circumstances.

fluencyBIT

Motto. IBM, the dominant computer manufacturer of the 1950s–1970s, used "Think" as its corporate motto. It was common to see the command in computer rooms and on programmers' desks. Perhaps one of the best signs employed "negative space" to get the reader's brain working.

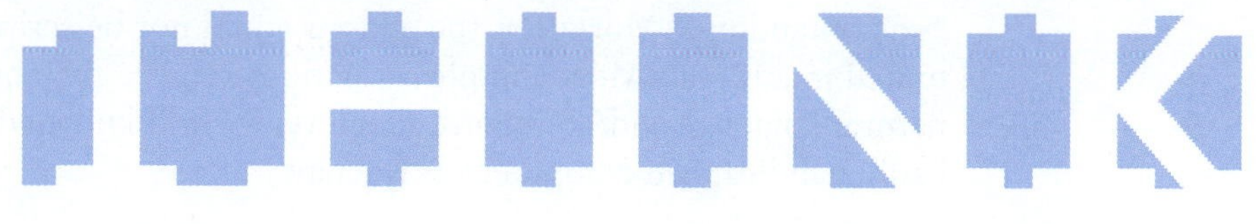

form. Does it add to our admiration of computers that they are closer to passing the Turing test? Or does it detract from our opinion of ourselves, suggesting that instead of computers being more like people, perhaps people are just computers? The questions are truly profound.

Acting Intelligently?

Anyone with even passing experience with grammar or spell checkers knows that these programs don't "understand" the sentences. They know the parts of speech such as prepositions and verbs, concepts like subject/object agreement, passive voice, and so on, but they don't understand complete sentences. Such concepts are not trivialities. It takes tremendously complex software and substantial dictionary resources to implement grammar and spell checking, and they're occasionally good enough to be helpful. But they definitely do not "understand" English.

The distinction between being intelligent and being programmed to seem intelligent concerned researchers in the 1950s and 1960s. The Doctor program (also known as Eliza) developed by MIT researcher Joseph Weizenbaum demonstrated this difference clearly. Doctor was programmed to ask questions in a dialog like a psychotherapist and a patient:

User: I'm depressed.

Doctor: Why are you depressed?

User: My mother is not speaking to me.

Doctor: Tell me about your mother.

User: She doesn't want me to major in engineering.

Doctor: No?

User: No, she wants me to go into medicine.

Doctor was programmed to keep the dialog going by asking questions and requesting more information. It would take cues from words like *mother*, including a reference to them in its next response. It would also notice uses of negative sentences, but the dialog was essentially preplanned. It may have appeared to be intelligent, but it definitely was not. What would a computer have to do to be intelligent or to demonstrate that it "understands" something?

As the research field of artificial intelligence (AI) came into existence, a consensus grew that to exhibit intelligence, a computer would have to "understand" a complex situation and reason well enough to act on its "understanding." Moreover, the actions could not be scripted or predetermined in any way. Most complex situations require the ability to understand natural language and/or require much real-world knowledge. Both properties badly handicapped computers of the day.

fluencyBIT

It's Therapeutic. There are Web-based programs that conduct Doctor-type dialogs. Search for "eliza" to find one.

Playing Chess

Playing chess, however, was much cleaner. It offered a challenging task that humans were both good at and interested in. The rules were clear, and success could be easily defined: beat a grand master in a tournament. Indeed, in the initial exuberance over computing, it was predicted as early as 1952 that a computer would beat a grand master "sometime in the next decade." Though it took more than a decade before computers could do much more than know the legal chess moves, the problem was well established as a litmus test for AI.

fluencyBIT

A Modest Proposal. Claude Shannon, a pioneer in information theory, was the first to propose how a computer might play chess in 1949.

The board configuration. How does a computer play chess? First, like all computational problems, the information must be represented in bits. The chess "world" is especially easy to represent because it is completely defined by an 8 × 8 checkered board, 32 pieces of two colors and six different types, and a single bit indicating whose turn it is to move. Because details are unimportant, think of the graphic of a chessboard as printed in game books or newspapers; see Figure 23.1. Call it a board configuration, or simply a board.

The game tree. Next the computer must decide on a move. It does this in roughly the same way we do, by exploring moves to determine,

"Will a move of this piece to that position make me better off or worse off?"

"Better off or worse off" are determined with respect to winning, of course, but it is very difficult to "compute" such information. Humans use intuition and experience. A computer uses an **evaluation function**, a procedure that assigns a numerical value to each piece and, taking into account things like captures and board position, computes a score for the move. If the score is positive, it's better; if it's negative, it's worse. Then, starting from the current board configuration, the computer checks the evaluation function on the

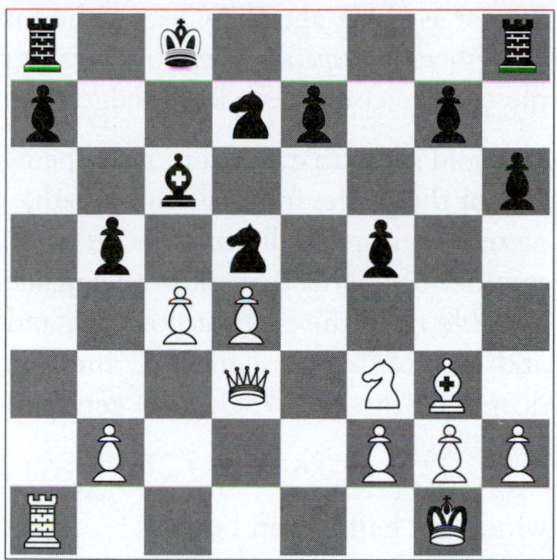

Figure 23.1 A chessboard configuration.

result of every possible single legal move, as shown in the **game tree** in Figure 23.2. One of these moves—suppose there are 28 legal moves—will give the highest score, which might be the one that the computer should pick.

Using the game tree tactically. Before picking a move, the computer should consider what the opponent might do. So for each of these "1-move" board configurations considered so far, the computer considers every possible next move from each and evaluates them. These boards are two moves away from the current board configuration. Furthermore, because the opponent makes the second move, the interpretation of the evaluation function is reversed. That is, the best move for the opponent is presumably the worst move for the computer, so the computer assumes the opponent will choose the move with the most negative score in the computer's evaluation function. This process is

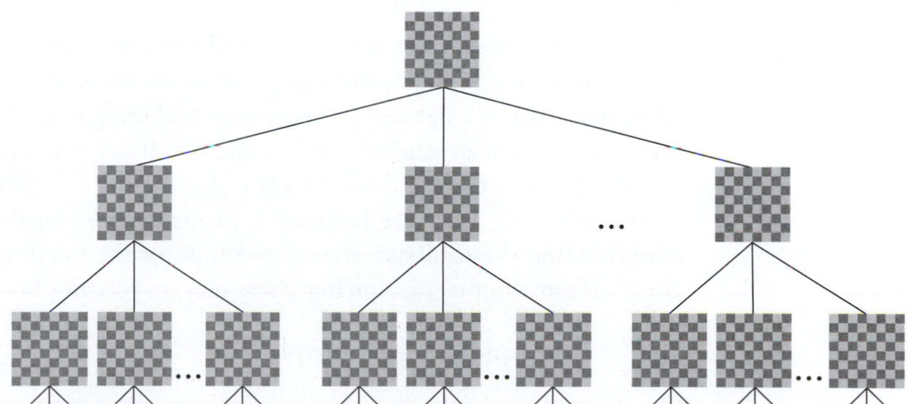

Figure 23.2 A schematic diagram of a game tree for chess. The current board position is at the top (root). The boards produced in a single move are on the layer below, those reachable in two moves are on the layer below that, and so forth.

known as "look ahead." Clearly, the further ahead the computer looks—it's described as *deeper* in chess because of the tree formulation—the more complete is the computer's knowledge about possible outcomes of the game.

It would seem that the computer, being very fast, could look all the way to the end of the game, find a winning path, and follow that. But checking the whole game tree is generally impossible because of the geometric increase in the number of boards that must be considered. For example, if there are 28 moves possible from the current position, and an average of 28 from each of those, and each of their descendants, and so on, then considering only six moves deep (i.e., three for each side) generates

$$28 + 28^2 + 28^3 + 28^4 + 28^5 + 28^6 = 499{,}738{,}092$$

which is a half billion boards. It's infeasible for a computer to look 50 moves into the future.

23.1 Look Forward. Compute the size of the 3-move tic-tac-toe (naughts and crosses) game tree beginning from an empty board. The size is the number of game boards required to draw the 3-move tree; the boards at the bottom of the tree will have three marks—two X's and one O.

Which move should the computer select? Picking the best move at the first level is not the best strategy, because the evaluation function is generally a static assessment of the board configuration. If in that one move the computer could reach a checkmate, the evaluation function would be very positive and the computer should pick it. But if not, the situation needs more strategy, because the most positive evaluation might come from a capture that would give the computer a piece advantage, whereas another choice, though less desirable at the moment, might lead in a few moves to a win. To play an intelligent game—that is, to strategize, to sacrifice pieces, to force the opponent into specific behaviors—requires the computer to analyze the game tree much more carefully.

Using a database of knowledge. Finally, in addition to representing the game and making moves, the computer needs some knowledge. In chess, this takes the form of a database of openings and endgames. Because chess is interesting and has been studied for so long, much is known about how to start and finish chess games. Providing this database is like giving the computer chess experience. Because learning is probably even harder than being intelligent, loading the database saves the computer the need to "learn from experience." It's analogous to aspiring chess players reading books by grand masters.

Using Parallel Computation

Slowly, as the basic logic just discussed got worked out, chess programs got better and better. Eventually they were beating duffers, then serious players, and then masters. Progress came as a combination of faster computers, more complete databases, and better evaluation and "strategizing" functions. In time, **parallel computation**—the application of several computers to one task—and custom hardware allowed computer researchers to entertain the possibility of beating a grand master in tournament conditions.

The Deep Blue matches. In 1996, reigning grand master Garry Kasparov trounced an IBM computer dubbed Deep Blue. Deep Blue was a parallel computer composed of 32 general-purpose computers (IBM RS/6000 SP) and 256 custom chess processors, enabling it to consider on average 200 million board positions per second. In one of the six games of the match, the computer played very well and won. Kasparov saw himself as victorious in defending the human race, but AI researchers were also ecstatic. At last a computer had played world-class chess in tournament conditions. A rematch was inevitable. On May 11, 1997, Kasparov lost 3.5–2.5 to an improved Deep Blue, achieving the "in the next decade" goal of the 1950s in a mere 45 years.

Interpreting the Outcome of the Matches

Did Deep Blue settle the question of whether computers can be intelligent? Not to everyone's satisfaction. To its credit, it answered one of the greatest technical challenges of the century. To do so required a large database of prior knowledge on openings and endgames, but that's analogous to reading books and playing chess. It also required special-purpose hardware that allowed rapid evaluation of board positions, but that's probably analogous to synaptic development in the brains of chess experts, giving them the ability over time to encapsulate whole board configurations as single mental units. But disappointingly—at least to some observers, and probably the AI pioneers who made the predictions in the first place—the problem was basically solved by speed. Deep Blue simply looked deeper. It did so *intelligently*, of course, because the geometric explosion of boards prevents success based simply on raw power. And that may be the strongest message from the Deep Blue/Kasparov matches. Intelligence may be the ability to consider many alternatives in an informed and directed way. Deep Blue surely demonstrated that.

The Deep Blue experience may have demonstrated that computers can be intelligent, or it may have demonstrated that IBM's team of chess experts and computer programmers is very intelligent. In the final analysis, the hardware was simply following the instructions that the programmers and engineers gave it. Such an objection has been raised in the "intelligence" debate since the beginning. It is a weak criticism because we can imagine intelligence, or creativity, or any other intellectual process being encoded in a general form, so that once started on a body of information, the program operates autonomously, responding to new inputs and realizing states not planned by its designers. Deep Blue operates autonomously in this sense and thus transcends its designers.

The main cautionary note regarding Deep Blue is that it is completely specialized to chess. That is, the 256 chess processors only evaluate board positions and are not useful for any other purpose. The 32 general-purpose processors can run other programs, of course, but none of Deep Blue's "intelligence" is transferable to another computation unless a programmer abstracts the ideas from Deep Blue and incorporates them into that computation. The "intelligence" isn't formulated in any general-purpose way. Thus Deep Blue speaks only indirectly to the subject of general-purpose intelligence.

Acting Creatively?

An alternative approach to understanding the limitation and potential of computers is to consider whether they can be "creative." For example, can a computer create art? It's not a question of whether a computer can be the art medium—artists have manipulated computers to produce art for decades. Rather the question is whether a computer can prevail in, perhaps, a "graphic version" of the Turing test: A judge visits an art gallery and decides whether a person or a computer produced the art. Could a computer be successful at fooling the judge? The task may be more daunting even than the original Turing test because creativity is by definition a process of breaking the rules, and computers only follow rules. How could they ever succeed at being creative? Perhaps there are rules—**metarules**—that describe how to break the rules or, perhaps, transcend existing rules. A computer could follow those. To see how this might be, let's first look at a program to create fine art.

There are several clever Web applications to create graphic designs after artists such as the famed cubist Piet Mondrian (1872–1944) and Jackson Pollack (1912–1956), whose paintings are exhibited in the great art collections of the world (see Figure 23.3).

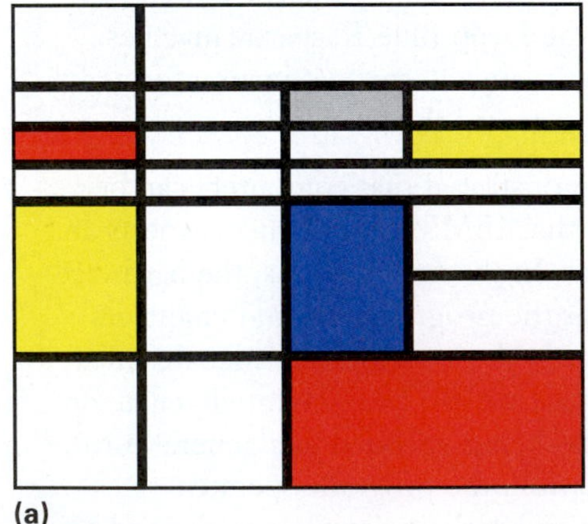

(a)

(b)

Figure 23.3 Examples of artist-free art. (a) Graphic design suggestive of the style of Piet Mondrian (find programs on the Web by searching *mondrian AND java*.) (b) Graphic design suggestive of the style of Jackson Pollock (go to **www.jacksonpollock.org**, and move and click the mouse).

The first program displays a new Mondrian-like picture with each mouse click. Inspecting the code, we find that the programs use random numbers to steer a deterministic process for placing lines and filling regions with color. That is, the program encodes a set of rules for creating graphics in the style of Mondrian, using what looks to the casual observer like the same design elements, same colors, and so on. The graphics are new in the sense that they have never before existed, but as art critics love to say, "The work is derivative."

In the Pollack case we provide the randomization by the timing and motions of the mouse. As with Mondrian the program translates this random data into form and color suggestive of Pollack's work.

Mondrian and Pollack are famous not because they created pleasing pictures with distinctive elements, but because they had something to say about their experiences that they expressed through art. That is, they're famous for a body of work from which the program's rules have been (reasonably faithfully) abstracted. The program only produces variations on the application of the rules using random numbers. But to many, creativity means inventing the rules in the first place.

Creativity as a Spectrum

Computer scientist Bruce Jacob distinguishes between the form of creativity that comes from inspiration—"a flash out of the blue"—and the form that comes from hard work—"incremental revision." Inspiration remains a mystery; in Jacob's view the hard work is algorithmic. (This is reminiscent of Thomas Edison's famous description of genius: 1 percent inspiration, 99 percent perspiration.)

To organize our discussion, think of creativity as a spectrum ranging from "flash out of the blue" to "Mondrian in a click." To be creative in fine art at the "flash out of the blue" end, the computer would have to step outside of the "established order," inventing its own rules, whereas at the Mondrian-in-a-click end of the spectrum, the computer just randomly assembles parts by the rules some programmer gave it, never extending or modifying them. Between those two extremes, there are many alternatives.

The hard work forms. Jacob illustrates the hard work form of creativity using canons (musical compositions that have the incremental-variation-on-a-theme property).

Jacob has developed a music composition system, Variations, which attempts to create canons by extending a repertoire of base themes by (randomly) generating new themes, assessing them as "good" or "bad," and discarding the "bad" ones. Interestingly, Jacob points out that because the program must work within the underlying characteristics of the base themes, getting a random variation to "fit" within those constraints "sometimes requires creativity!" That is, forcing a random variation on the constraints imposed by a set of rules produces new techniques.

Calling Jacob's work *computer creativity* may seem difficult, because the program appears to embody much of the designer—the test for "bad," for instance—and there is a certain "stumbling onto a solution" quality from the randomness. Nevertheless, this and similar efforts, which span creative pursuits from inventing typefaces to making analogies, focus on the rule-making aspect of creativity and demonstrate that incremental revision is algorithmic. So, the conclusion seems to be that creativity does represent a huge range of different kinds of invention.

fluencyBIT

Classical Question. In an interesting demonstration at the University of Oregon, three pianists played three different pieces of music in the style of Bach, one composed by Bach, one composed by Steven Larson (a UO professor), and one composed by EMI, a computer program. The audience voted on who they thought wrote which piece.

	Audience Guess	**True Composer**
Composition 1	EMI	Larson
Composition 2	Larson	Bach
Composition 3	Bach	EMI

What Part of Creativity Is Algorithmic?

When the Turing test was invented, "Draw a picture in the style of Mondrian" would have been a request that a computer would have utterly failed at. Today it is a three-page Java program.

AI researchers have demonstrated in various contexts that the "hard work" form of creativity is algorithmic. If the matter of whether a computer can be creative is not taken to be a yes/no question, but rather is seen as an expedition into the process of creativity, we find our answer. The more deeply we understand creativity, the more we find ways in which it is algorithmic. Will it be found to be entirely algorithmic at some point in the future? Will there be rules for breaking the rules? Will it become like reckoning? Or will there necessarily be a nonalgorithmic part at the inspirational end? No matter how it turns out, aspects of creativity are algorithmic. To the extent that creativity is algorithmic, a computer can be creative. But who needs a computer? If creativity is algorithmic, we can all be creative by following the rules. Progress in understanding creativity can benefit us, too. And how it is accomplished—with synapses or transistors—shouldn't matter.

fluencyBIT

Fill in the Blank. In an essay on creativity published in *Science*, Jacob Goldenberg, David Mazursky, and Sorin Solomon report that, in one study, 89 percent of award-winning advertisements contain a use of one of six "creativity templates," that is, follow-the-rules techniques, and that one simple template, *Replacement*, accounted for 25 percent of all award-winning ads.

The Universality Principle

Another problem that concerned Turing and other computer pioneers was to determine what makes one computer more powerful than another. Their amazing discovery was that any computer using only very simple instructions could simulate any other computer. This fact—known as the **Universality Principle**—means, for example, that all computers have the same power!

fluencyBIT

All Computers Are Created Equal. Though computer scientists have found different fundamental instruction sets, the six instructions **Add** (as described in Chapter 9), **Subtract**, **Set_To_One**, **Load**, **Store**, and **Branch_On_Zero** are sufficient to program any computation.

It goes without saying that every computer has these primitive instructions and much more. From the commercial point of view, the Universality Principle means that Intel and IBM cannot compete with each other to build a computer that can compute more computations. Every computer the two companies have ever made is equivalent to all other computers in terms of what they can compute. The Universality Principle says that all computers compute the same set of computations. It's surprising.

The Universality Principle has deep theoretical implications, but there are important practical consequences, too.

fluencyBIT

Getting Down to Basics. Another startling consequence of the Universality Principle is that programs, in effect, reduce *all* computation—playing chess or checking grammar or figuring income tax—to the point where it is expressible with only a half dozen different operations.

Universal Information Processor

Perhaps the most important aspect of universality is that if we want to do some new information-processing task, we don't need to buy a new computer. The computer we have is sufficient if we can write or buy the software for the task.

This is quite different, say, from wanting to perform a new task in the kitchen or the shop, where we would have to buy a new gadget. Machines that transform material must be specialized to each activity, requiring us—or enabling us, if you like to get new gadgets!—to buy a specialized device. By contrast, there is only one information-processing machine, the computer.

Because computers are general purpose, people play a greater role in setting them up and configuring them for a specific task—installing software, for example—than they do for single-purpose machines like food processors or table saws. This greater role in customizing the general-purpose device to our needs is one reason why it is important to become fluent with computing.

Competing Machines and the Universality Principle. To understand why all computers are equivalent, imagine two computers, the ZAP^2 and the BXLE, and suppose they have the same hardwired instructions, except that ZAP^2 has one additional instruction. Its manufacturer claims, contrary to the Universality Principle, that the new instruction enables new computations on the ZAP^2 that are not possible on the BXLE. "Baloney," says BXLE's CEO. "Using the instructions already in BXLE, we will program a function that performs the operation of ZAP^2's special hardwired instruction. Then, in any program, we will replace every use of their special instruction with a call to our function. Anything ZAP^2 can do, BXLE can do, too." For a schematic diagram, see Figure 23.4.

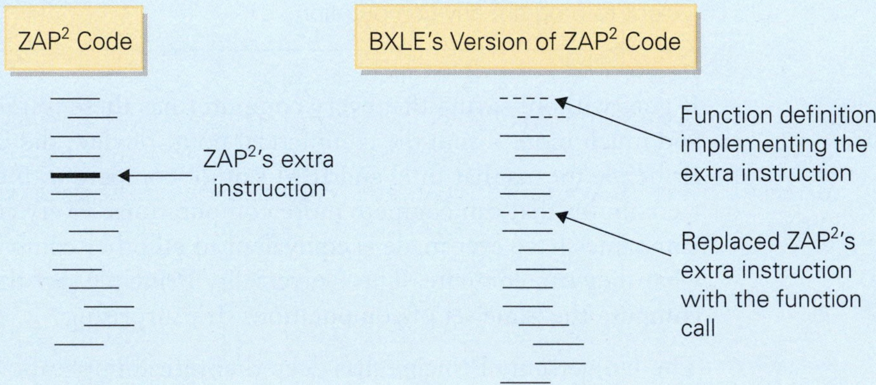

Figure 23.4 Schematic diagram showing a revision of ZAP^2's program to run on the BXLE, in which the special instruction has been replaced by a function call.

In effect, ZAP^2 performs the instruction in hardware while the BXLE performs the instruction in software, that is, by using a function. The argument holds up as long as the special instruction can be programmed with the basic instructions of the BXLE, which we can be confident, will be possible. But the skeptic needn't accept that on faith. Rather, it's possible to write a program for the BXLE to simulate circuits and to simulate the entire circuitry of ZAP^2. Simulating ZAP^2 by the BXLE is possible because ZAP^2 is built from (zillions of) two-input logic gates. There are only 16 different gates, and they can be trivially simulated with the six basic instructions, which the BXLE surely has. Because BXLE can exactly duplicate the ZAP^2 operation in the simulator, it is possible to do all of the same computations, too. Notice that this solution also solves the problem in software.

Because all computers do the same computations, the main basis for technical competition among manufacturers is speed.

Practical Consequences of the Universality Principle

The Universality Principle says that all computers compute the same way, and their speed is the only difference. Unfortunately, the Universality Principle's claim that any computer can simulate any other computer has the disadvantage that simulation does the work much more slowly.

In the first solution of the ZAP²/BXLE example, BXLE was only slower on the special instruction, which presumably takes several basic instructions to implement. The second case was much slower because each instruction of the ZAP² might take thousands of logical operations, and the BXLE must simulate each of these. So, although both computers can realize the same computations, they perform them at different rates. For that reason, manufacturers *do* include special instructions for tasks such as digital signal processing, graphics, and encryption, hoping that their frequent use will speed up their computer.

The Universality Principle seems to conflict with our everyday experience, however. Three obvious difficulties arise:

- Macintosh software didn't run on the PC in the past; if Macs and PCs are the same, why not?
- People say old machines become outmoded; how so, if they're all the same?
- Is it really true that the computer in my laptop is the same as the one in my microwave oven?

Despite these apparent problems, the Universality Principle is a practical fact. Consider each objection in turn.

Macintosh versus PC. Until recently, the PC and Mac used different processors—Intel's Pentium and Motorola's PowerPC. The Mac now uses an Intel chip, but because the problem still remains in other less familiar settings, let's assume they still run different processors; we handle the new chips in a moment. Obviously, the Pentium and PowerPC each have a different *combination* of instructions, though they include the six most basic ones mentioned earlier. These instruction sets are encoded differently, they operate slightly differently, each has instructions the other doesn't have, and so on. None of these differences is fundamental. It is possible to write a program for each machine to perform the instructions of the other machine, just as was argued earlier. It is not only possible in principle, computer scientists write such programs frequently.

But consumer software relies heavily on operating system facilities, too. OS software extends the basic instruction set of the computer—as you learned in Chapter 9—so it can perform useful operations like booting itself up and locating files on the hard disk. And this is the real difference between the Mac and PC: These operating systems do things very differently. None of the differences is fundamental, and it's possible in principle to simulate each OS on the other platform. Business considerations keep the two separate.

The alternative solution, which software companies like Adobe, Microsoft, and Oracle use, is to translate their programs to each computer family, as explained in Chapter 9. That's how Apple got the Macintosh software running on the new Intel chip. The software is written in a programming language like Basic, C, or Java, and then it is compiled—that is, translated—into the machine language of whatever processor type, Pentium, PowerPC, or other processor that will run the code. Special care is taken to ensure that operating system incompatibilities are removed. The result is that rather than simulating the software of one computer on another computer, there is a separate custom version of the software for each vendor's computer. So, the Universality Principle is applied daily, but not along the lines of our original discussion.

Outmoded computers. As noted, speed is the main difference among computers. Often, the reason why someone buys a new computer is that they own new software, doubtless loaded with slick new features, that runs slowly on their old machine. With the new software doing more, it is not surprising that a faster computer would help. But, for those who are patient, there is no need to upgrade.

People usually give two reasons in support of their claim that older computers become "outmoded." The first reason is that hardware and/or software products are often incompatible with older machines. For example, input/output devices, such as printers, are often incompatible with older computers because of other internal parts, such as the system bus. (See the computer components diagram, Figure 9.2, in Chapter 9.) As a result, it is not possible to connect the new devices. However, these parts are not closely connected with instruction execution.

The second reason is that software vendors simply don't support old machines. As explained, software vendors compile their programs to each platform—usually a processor/OS combination—to sell to customers. But, if there are too few customers running an old processor/OS combination, the vendor may decide that it isn't profitable to sell and maintain a version for that machine. Thus new software is often not available for old computers. This is a business decision; there is no technical impediment.

The laptop and the microwave. The computers embedded in consumer products like microwave ovens, brakes, and other devices are there not because the task of running a microwave is so complex that it needs a computer. Rather, it's cheaper to implement the system with a computer and a read-only memory (ROM) chip containing a fixed program than it is to implement it with custom electronics. It's a matter of economics, not a technical requirement.

Embedded computers have a rich enough instruction set to run any other computer application. Their main handicap as computers is usually neither their instruction repertoire nor their speed. Rather, embedded computers are, well, embedded. The program is fixed—giving only options like popping popcorn or defrosting dinner—and it is connected to a very limited set of input/output devices, usually only the sensors and actuators of the system they control. If the embedded computer were connected to a keyboard and a monitor, as is the personal computer we're accustomed to, it could run the software just fine.

So, the Universality Principle is not only a theoretical fact, it is a practical fact, too.

More Work, Slower Speed

When we use computers, they are simply idling most of the time, waiting for us to give them something to do. For tasks like word processing, even including continuous grammar and spell checking doesn't keep them busy. So we listen to MP3 tunes too, which still doesn't stress them. Eventually, perhaps when we are manipulating digital images, we notice that certain activities, like making the image brighter, are computed very fast, but others, like rotating the image, are noticeably slower. This is curious when we think about it, because the image has the same number of pixels in both cases. What causes some tasks to take longer to compute?

Comparing *Alphabetize CDs* with *Face Forward*

The obvious and correct answer is that it takes more time to do more work. Recall the *Alphabetize CDs* example from Chapter 10. If the CD rack were smaller, the algorithm would complete sooner because fewer CDs would have to be considered. But it is not just the number of inputs that determines the amount of work; the operation of the algorithm does, too. Consider a task like making sure the CDs all face forward.

The *Face Forward* algorithm requires only that we start at the beginning of the rack, inspect each CD to see which way it faces, and if it is not facing forward, reorient it and return it; in either case, we then move on to the next CD. If the rack holds 24 CDs, the algorithm takes 24 iterations of the inspect-and-reorient operations because just one pass through the rack is sufficient. If the rack contains 48 CDs, 48 iterations will be required. The amount of work is proportional to the amount of data.

Cases of this type, where the amount of work is directly proportional to the amount of data, are said to be **work-proportional-to-*n* algorithms**. That is, the running time is at most the number of basic steps devoted to each item times the number *n* of data items. We say "at most" because all of the steps may not be necessary on each data item. If some CDs are already facing forward, there will be no need for a reorient step. In the worst case, all CDs are facing backward, and it takes the maximum predicted time.

Orienting the CDs to face forward is an easier task than alphabetizing them. Recall that the *Alphabetize CDs* algorithm did not solve the problem in "one pass" through the rack. In fact, for each CD referenced by *Alpha*, all of the CDs after it had to be considered; we called this a *Beta* sweep. So, if there are 24 CDs in the rack, 23 CDs must be considered to get the first CD into position in the front because *Alpha*'s reference doesn't change, but *Beta* references the other 23 CDs. Thus the "In Order?" test must be made 23 times to locate the alphabetically first CD. Then *Alpha* moves to the second position, referencing the next slot, and *Beta* must visit the 22 CDs after it. This continues until the last step, when *Alpha* references the next-to-last CD and *Beta* references only the last slot—that is, only one interchange of CDs is considered at the very end. Adding these numbers yields

$$23 + 22 + \ldots + 1 = 276$$

That is, we test 276 times to put the CDs in order in a 24-slot rack. In the same way, if the CD rack contains 48 CDs, locating the alphabetically first CD would require 47 CD references in the first *Beta* sweep, finding the second would require 46, and so on. Adding these numbers we get

$$47 + 46 + \ldots + 1 = 1{,}128$$

which is surprising because the rack is only twice as large, but the number of tests is more than four times larger. Clearly the repeated *Beta* sweeps of *Alphabetize CDs* require more work than the single sweep of the *Face Forward* algorithm.

Brainy Kid. At age seven, Johann Karl Friedrich Gauss (1777–1855), the mathematician whose face once graced the Ten Deutsche Mark note, was asked by his teacher to add the numbers 1 to 100. He found the answer 5,050 immediately by noting that adding the first plus last numbers (1 + 100) equals 101, adding the next-to-first and next-to-last numbers (2 + 99) also equals 101, and so on, and that there are 50 pairs summing to 101. Young Gauss's idea always works, so adding numbers from 1 to n is $(n + 1)n/2$.

Work Proportional to n^2

Thus, although the *Face Forward* computation took only one pass through the rack, *Alphabetize CDs* took many passes. In the former case, the number of repetitions is proportional to n for an n-slot rack, and in the latter case, the number of repetitions is proportional to $(n + 1)n/2 = (n^2 + n)/2$. Whereas *Face Forward* is said to be a work-proportional-to-n algorithm, *Alphabetize CDs* is said to be a **work-proportional-to-n^2 algorithm**. (Computer people don't worry about the other terms of the equation, only the most significant term, the n^2 here.)

Thus, if there are $n = 1{,}000$ pieces of data, and a problem can be solved by a work-proportional-to-n algorithm, it will take about a thousand times the amount of work needed to do the task on one data item. But, if the problem is solved by a work-proportional-to-n^2 algorithm, the amount of work will be about a *million* = $1{,}000 \times 1{,}000$ times the amount of work needed to solve the problem on one data item. So, when we observe that one computation is taking more time than another despite requiring the same amount of data, it is generally because the algorithm does more work to solve the problem.

Notice that the explanation is that "the algorithm does more work to solve the problem," not that the problem *requires* more work to be solved. That is, the algorithm the programmer chose to solve the problem may not be the fastest. The fastest known algorithm is rarely the solution of choice. For example, there are faster ways to alphabetize CDs than the solution presented, though none of them works in time proportional to n. And the alternatives are somewhat more complicated. Complexity and other factors contribute to a programmer's decision, and besides the computer is idle most of the time anyway.

23.2 Working Harder. How much more work would *Alphabetize CDs* require if you owned the 64-slot "Aye, Tunes" CD rack?

How Hard Can a Problem Be?

With algorithms requiring work proportional to n and proportional to n^2, it is a good guess that there are algorithms requiring work proportional to n^3, n^4, and so on. There are, and they are all considered practical for computers to solve, though as the example in the last section made clear, the exponent does matter a lot to the user sitting and waiting for the answer.

NP-Complete Problems

There are much more difficult computations, many of which are important to business, science, and engineering. In fact, one of the most significant discoveries of the 1970s was that many problems of interest—for example, finding the cheapest set of plane tickets for touring n cities—don't have any known "practical" algorithmic solutions. Such problems are known by the rather curious name of **NP-complete problems**. In essence, the best-known algorithms do little more than try all possible solutions, and then pick the best. It seems that there should be cleverer algorithms than that. If there are, the person who discovers one will enjoy tremendous fame. In the meantime, such problems are said to be **intractable**—the best way to solve them is so difficult that large data sets cannot be solved with a realistic amount of computer time on any computer. Computers can solve them in principle, but not in practice.

fluencyBIT

Hard Problems. Steve Cook of the University of Toronto and Dick Karp of UC Berkeley discovered NP-completeness. They also discovered the amazing fact that if anyone finds a better algorithm for just one NP-complete problem, their algorithm will improve *every* NP-complete problem.

Unsolvable Problems

Perhaps more surprisingly, there are problems computers cannot solve at all. It's not that the algorithms take too long, but that there are no algorithms, period! These are not problems like being intelligent or creative, but precisely definable problems with a clear quantifiable objective. For example, it's impossible for an algorithm to determine if a program has a bug in it, like looping forever. Such an algorithm would have been quite handy in Chapter 21 in our study of looping, when we messed up the *<next iteration>* step, causing infinite loops. We'd simply give our program to this imagined Loop-Checker algorithm, and it would tell us whether or not our program loops forever. Notice that the Loop-Checker would be especially useful for computations having, say, work proportional to n^4 because we have to wait a long time for the results. While we're waiting, we'd like to be sure we're going to get a result eventually, rather than have the program caught in an infinite loop, forcing us to wait forever.

The nonexistent loop checker. But the Loop-Checker can't exist. Suppose it did. That is, suppose there is a program LC(P, x) that takes as its input any program P and input data x, analyzes P, and answers back "Yes" or "No" as to whether P will loop forever on input x. This actually seems plausible, because LC could look through P, checking every loop to see if the *<next iteration>* and *<continuation>* tests are set right. And then it could follow the execution of P on x, looking to see if anything could go wrong. It seems plausible, but it's not. Here's why.

Create another program, CD(P), that also takes as input a program P. CD is an abbreviation for "contradiction." The program works according to the flowchart shown in Figure 23.5. What does CD(CD) compute? We're not sure what the assumed LC(CD,CD) will answer back, but suppose it says "No," CD does not loop forever when the CD program is its input. In that case, the left arrow out of the diamond is taken and CD loops forever. So, LC would have been wrong. Perhaps LC answers "Yes," that CD will loop forever when CD is its input. In that case, the right arrow out of the diamond is taken and the program doesn't loop forever, but just stops. Wrong again. The Loop-Checker cannot answer correctly—neither "Yes" nor "No" is the right answer. This problem cannot be algorithmically solved.

The halting problem. The Loop-Checker is trying to solve a famous computation known as the **Halting Problem**. Alan M. Turing was the first to recog-

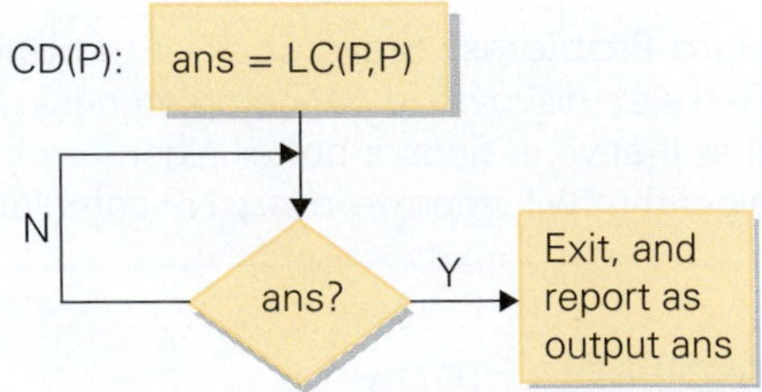

Figure 23.5 The logic of the CD program, given the assumed program LC.

nize the impossibility of creating the perfect debugger, like the theoretical Loop-Checker. It's too bad one can't be created, because having such a debugger would be handy. Interestingly, debugging—the topic of Chapter 7—is something that humans can do, admittedly with great difficulty sometimes. In fact, it requires considerable intelligence to figure out what has gone wrong when a computing task doesn't work. It's something that computers won't ever be able to do in any general way. So, maybe we were looking in the wrong place for capabilities that are uniquely human. Making computers solve our problems *properly* is something only humans can do!

Summary

We have explored the limits of computation. We began by asking a question that has puzzled people since computers were invented—can computers think? The question challenged us to define what thinking is. In this chapter we:

- Identified a tendency for people to decide that an intellectual activity isn't considered thinking if it is algorithmic. Thinking is probably best defined as what humans do, and therefore something computers can't do.
- Discussed the Turing test, an experimental setting in which we can compare the capabilities of humans with those of computers.
- Studied the question of computer chess and learned that computers use a game tree formulation, an evaluation function to assess board positions, and a database of openings and endgames. Deep Blue became the chess champion of the world in 1997, a monumental achievement, but not one that closed the book on the algorithmic nature of intelligence.
- Studied creativity, deciding it occurs on a spectrum: from algorithmic variation (Mondrian and Pollock graphics-in-a-click) through incremental revision to a flash of inspiration. The degree to which the activities along the spectrum are algorithmic has advanced over the years.
- Presumed that there will be further advancement, but we do not know where the "algorithmic frontier" will be drawn. It's too early to tell if creativity, like reckoning, is entirely algorithmic. Computers will be creative insofar as creativity is algorithmic. And so will we all.
- Considered the Universality Principle, which implies that computers are equal in terms of what they can compute. This is not only a theoretical statement. We benefit from its practical consequences daily.
- Discussed that software companies can write a single application program and translate it into the machine language of any computer, making it available to everyone regardless of the kind of computer

they own. This implied that computer vendors could only compete on speed, which led us to consider how fast computers can solve problems.

- Discussed that the many proportional-to-n computations require less work than the proportional-to-n^2 computations even though both require n data values. Such computations are practical and form the large part of computing.
- Learned that important problems—the so-called NP-complete problems—require much more computational work. Many of the problems we would like to solve are NP-complete problems, but unfortunately the NP-complete problems are intractable—large instances are solvable by computer only in principle, not in practice.
- Learned the amazing fact that some computations—for example, general-purpose debugging—cannot be solved by computers, even in principle. If it were possible, we could solve the Halting Problem, and that's not logically possible. We should remember this when it seems computers can do anything!

Try It Solutions

23.1 By level, $1 + 9 + (9 \times 8) + (9 \times 8 \times 7) = 586$

23.2 $63 + 62 + . . . + 1 = (63 + 1) \times 63/2 = 2016 - 1128 = 888$ more operations for only 24 more slots.

Review Questions

Multiple Choice

1. Computers can
   a. think
   b. manipulate information
   c. be creative
   d. all of the above

2. For the computer, chess is a series of
   a. algorithms
   b. computations
   c. possible moves reduced to an evaluation of the "best" move
   d. all of the above

3. Creativity can be
   a. "a flash out of the blue"
   b. incremental revision of existing work
   c. hard work
   d. perhaps some of each, depending on the definition

4. The ability of any computer to imitate another computer is known as
   a. mimicry
   b. the Imitation Principle
   c. the Universality Principle
   d. the Turing Test

5. The fastest computers can calculate up to
   a. ten billion instructions per second
   b. a trillion instructions per second
   c. a million instructions per minute
   d. a thousand trillion instructions per second

6. Work-proportional-to-*n* algorithms
   a. increase processing time proportionally to the data
   b. process data in roughly the same amount of time regardless of the amount of data
   c. work so fast that modern computers spend most of their time idling
   d. geometrically increase in processing time as the amount of data increases

7. The *Alphabetize CDs* algorithm is a(n)
   a. work-proportional-to-*n* algorithm
   b. work-proportional-to-n^2 algorithm
   c. either A or B, depending on the initial order of the CDs
   d. A XOR B

8. NP-complete problems
   a. have no known solution
   b. have too many possibilities to solve
   c. must consider every possible solution to find the best one
   d. can be solved with a work-proportional-to-*n* algorithm

9. The one thing humans can do that computers can't is
   a. play games of chance
   b. perform sort algorithms
   c. make computers work properly
   d. solve the Halting Problem

10. Putting together a puzzle by trying every possible combination and selecting the best result is an example of a(n)
    a. work-proportional-to-*n* algorithm
    b. work-proportional-to-n^2 algorithm
    c. NP-complete problem
    d. intractable problem

11. To play checkers with a computer
    a. would be too complicated for Deep Blue to compute
    b. the algorithm for Deep Blue would work
    c. the possible "deep" moves would be much simpler than in chess
    d. all of the above

12. Calculating every possible move in a chess game is known as a
    a. game tree
    b. Turing Test
    c. work-proportional-to-n algorithm
    d. none of the above
13. In a game, looking ahead for potential moves is called
    a. deeper
    b. drill down
    c. variations
    d. none of the above
14. Putting several computers to work on the same problem is called
    a. algorithmic thinking
    b. parallel computation
    c. Universality
    d. none of the above
15. All computer computations can be completed with just
    a. 4 instructions
    b. 6 instructions
    c. 9 instructions
    d. 11 instructions
16. The simplest of the listed algorithmic solutions is the
    a. work-proportional-to-n algorithm
    b. work-proportional-to-n^2 algorithm
    c. NP-complete problem
    d. intractable problem
17. A program debugger
    a. works only on syntax errors
    b. works on logic errors
    c. works on both types of errors
    d. doesn't exist

Short Answer

1. _______ is the name of the IBM computer designed for chess.
2. The _______ is a test of computer intelligence.
3. AI is short for _______.
4. For computer chess, a(n) _______ shows the result of every possible legal move for the computer along with a numeric evaluation of each move.
5. Deep Blue is a good example of computer intelligence that is ______, not general purpose.
6. _______ are rules about rules.
7. The _______ maintains that any computer can be made to imitate any other computer.

8. All computer programming can be done with only _______ basic instructions.
9. The _______ is the only information-processing machine.
10. Any hardwired computer instructions can be simulated in _______.
11. _______ considerations rather than technical considerations explain why some applications run only on Microsoft Windows or the Apple's MacOS.
12. _______ is the process of translating a computer program into the machine language of the computer.
13. Lack of _______ and _______ are the two major claims put forth for computers becoming outdated.
14. _______ computers are computers built into other devices to implement them with custom electronics.
15. _______ are problems with no practical algorithmic solutions.

Exercises

1. How many 0's in a trillion?
2. How long would it take a human to do a billion calculations?
3. Explain how computer art is derivative and not creative.
4. Where on the list does a chess algorithm fall for solving computer problems?
5. What type of algorithm is needed to solve a problem of finding the best route to take for a cross-country trip?
6. Explain how a game tree could be used for card games.
7. Describe why the argument on whether computers can think has little impact on our daily lives. Use your word processor to answer this.
8. What does a computer have to do to pass the Turing test?

24
chapter

A Fluency Summary

Click to Close

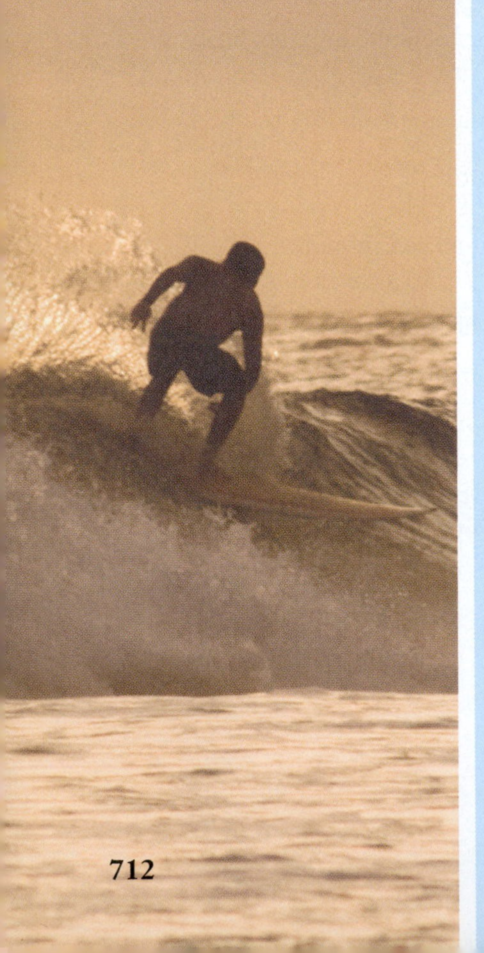

learning objectives

- Discuss the differences in remembering IT details and ideas when you are Fluent
- Discuss lifelong IT learning through finding new uses, asking for help, and noticing new technology
- Discuss the benefits of achieving Fluency now and in the future

Whatever a man prays for, he prays for a miracle ... "Great God, let not two times two make four."

—IVAN TURGENEV 1862

WE HAVE COME to the final chapter. There has been no miracle—two times two still makes four—and the parts of computing we've discussed make sense. It has been a substantive and, at times, challenging tour. But your ability to apply computing ideas has dramatically improved. You have acquired basic information about a broad spectrum of topics. Though you may not be an expert, you know enough to know when you need to learn more. As your study proceeded, you integrated the basic information into a powerful intuitive computing model. As you acquire new knowledge, this model gives it a place to "fit into."

In this chapter we wrap up our Fluency study by summarizing two of several repeating ideas. Then we consider the two most pressing matters: How much of the information in this book do you have to remember, and how do you learn the technology that hasn't yet been invented? Both topics have unexpected outcomes. Finally, we reflect on the fact that in the world of IT, we can shift for ourselves.

Two Big IT Ideas

Thinking back over the chapter summaries, several ideas have recurred in our study. Two examples are information structuring and strategies for nonalgorithmic tasks. We consider each in turn.

Information Structuring

In Chapter 5 we learned that collections of information are structured hierarchically—that is, organized by descriptive metadata into groups and subgroups—in order to assist us in locating specific items. In Chapter 8 we found that the *Oxford English Dictionary*'s digitization includes metadata structural tags that enclose the constituents of each definition. Knowing the purpose of each part of the *OED's* content (headword, citation, etc.) allows the computer to perform complex searches and analysis. In Chapters 14–17, specifying the structure of the information gave the same powerful advantage when we built spreadsheets and databases. Specifying the characteristics of the data stored in a table—its type, whether it is a key, and so on—allowed for sophisticated queries and prevented erroneous uses that would have produced garbage.

The idea is that *specifying structure is as essential as specifying content.* This idea comes up again and again because the value of information depends on how effectively we can use it, and all of the powerful applications rely on the computer's knowing the structure. The truth of this observation is clear from our studies. But we can learn more from it!

As we become increasingly more effective users, we will acquire a growing collection of personally important digital information. Years of old email correspondence, digital photos, collections of MP3 tunes, and other items will fill our hard disks. As our collections grow, we may eventually decide to move certain information into databases or other structured archives in order to manipulate them efficiently. But as we accumulate the information as independent files, it's smart to keep it structured—simply by the way we arrange it in folders and subfolders. We should assign our MP3s and JPEGs to their own folders—substructured perhaps into folders based on content—so that we can find files when we want them; the details of the organization could be a private part of our iDiary. This simple directory hierarchy organization is not as effective as the examples cited earlier because the computer does not know the structure. But *we* know it and it will assist us in a manual navigation of our collections.

Strategies for Nonalgorithmic Tasks

Algorithms have been an important topic in our Fluency study. We learned the placeholder technique for reformatting text (Chapter 2), an exchange sort for alphabetizing CDs (Chapter 10), an effective query construction (Chapter 16)—build a supertable with joins and then trim it down using `Select` and `Project`—and many other algorithms.

But perhaps the most significant content of our study concerned capabilities that are not algorithmic. Finding accurate information (Chapter 5), satisfying our curiosity through research (Chapter 6), debugging (Chapter 7), formulating a password (Chapter 12), designing a database (Chapter 17), testing and assessing a user interface (Chapter 19), and programming a complex Web application (Chapter 22) are all examples in which there are no deterministic, guaranteed-to-yield-a-solution rules. In each case we could only give guidelines. For example, debugging is facilitated by these guidelines:

✓checkLIST

Debugging Guidelines

- *Make sure that you can reproduce the error.*
- *Determine exactly what the problem is.*
- *Eliminate the "obvious" causes.*
- *Divide the process, separating the parts that work from the parts that don't.*
- *When you reach a dead end, reassess your information, ask where you may be making wrong assumptions or conclusions, and then step through the process again.*
- *As you work through the process from start to finish, make predictions about what should happen and verify that the predictions are fulfilled.*

The steps prescribe a rational approach to the task, but they don't form an algorithm.

The nonalgorithmic capabilities have been presented as though they form a separate knowledge base, and they do, in the sense that they each entail a separate list of guidelines. But generally the capabilities are all applications of logical reasoning in service of achieving some higher goal—true information, correct program, convenient application, and so on. Reasoning is the key. It is applied in small ways on nearly every page of the book. Indeed, an overarching theme of this text is that *precision and the directed application of logical reasoning can solve problems great and small, algorithmic and nonalgorithmic.* The more we apply such thinking, the better we become at it!

Fluency: Less Is More

In reviewing the material discussed in this book, it is sobering to realize the enormous amount of detailed information covered. You've learned about anchor tags in XHTML, the `if/else` statement in JavaScript, the Vacation Message, the Nyquist rule, `Select` operations, and on and on. How can anyone ever remember it all?

Recall that the Fluency knowledge is compartmentalized into three components:

- **Skills**—competency with contemporary IT applications like word processing.
- **Concepts**—understanding the foundations on which computing is built, like the Fetch/Execute Cycle.
- **Capabilities**—facility with higher-level thinking processes like reasoning.

These three kinds of knowledge are co-equal and interdependent. But when we analyze the three types of knowledge from the point of view of how much we have to remember, we realize that they are very much *unequal.*

- The skills all require much detailed knowledge. For example, is the length of the line in the `<hr/>` tag of XHTML, `size` or `length`? It is impossible to have short lines in XHTML without knowing which is correct. Furthermore, an annoying property of this detail is that the computer demands that we are *exactly right;* it is unforgiving. We can't use computers without knowing such facts, or, more likely, looking them up.
- The concepts might be quite detailed, but the "basic ideas" are not. We know a computer's Fetch/Execute Cycle is an infinite process for interpreting instructions, but now that we understand the core idea, we don't really need to remember that the third of the five steps is called Data Fetch. It's the concept of an instruction execution engine that is important. Computing concepts are like other scientific information: Ideas must be explained in full detail to be understood; but after they're learned, only the ideas themselves, not the particulars, are important for the nonspecialist.
- The capabilities are the least detailed of all. Capabilities are mainly approaches to thinking. For example, problem decomposition, in which a complex task is broken into smaller tasks that are either solved directly or are themselves broken into smaller pieces still, is simply a rational way to tackle complex problems. Debugging—thinking objectively about a faulty IT application—is mostly a matter of being a good detective. Yes, there are guidelines on how to proceed, but debugging mainly comes down to forcing yourself to look at a situation the way it is rather than the way it seems so far. The capabilities require you to remember almost no detail whatsoever.

So there is a spectrum of detail from skills through concepts to capabilities.

Curiously, our Fluency study allows us to remember less, rather than requiring us to remember more. How can this be? We remember less *detail* because we remember the *basic ideas* instead.

The clearest example—much of our Fluency study works this way—was our discussion of what the digerati know (Chapter 2). The chapter seemed to cover necessary skill-level information about how to use a GUI, what's behind the *File* and *Edit* menus, how to use shift-select, and so on. But the chapter is really about the capability of *thinking abstractly about technology*, and how we learn to think abstractly. We asked sweeping questions like:

- How do we learn technology?
- How do software designers, indeed any tool designers, expect users to learn to use their new creations?
- When we're confronted with a task that requires technology, how do we figure out what to do?

The answers to these questions were not "Memorize thick, boring manuals." Rather, we pointed out that thinking abstractly about technology implies an adaptive approach to learning. Tool creators exploit consistent interfaces—every music player uses the same icons—so we should look for the consistency. Look for metaphors. When presented with a tool, explore it by "clicking around" to see what the inventor provided. Wonder what you're expected to do. And finally, simply "blaze away," trying things out and watching what happens, knowing that the garbage created when mistakes are made must be thrown away (at no cost) before starting over. In other words, don't memorize the tool's details. Rather, learn the details as you need them. If you use software frequently, you will become adept at the specifics, memorizing the details through use. If you use software rarely, you will forget the specifics. But even that's fine, because you will know abstractly what to do and how to figure out the details again.

Thus the higher-level capabilities make us rational people, approaching IT tasks thoughtfully, enabling us to proceed in a directed and disciplined way toward the goal, solving problems as they arise, figuring out what to do as required, logically figuring out what's wrong when a bug has us blocked. You've learned how to learn IT. Fluency doesn't require that you use your head to memorize details. It only requires that you use your head.

24.1 Remembering. Capabilities require little recall—the debugging guidelines list has only six items in it. Similarly, the problem decomposition idea used to design the Web page in Chapter 22 had only one rule for building a plan from the task dependency graph. Do you remember it?

Lifelong IT Learning

Information technology learning is a process of lifelong learning, but that doesn't mean you have to read 20 pages of *C++ GUI Programmer's Guide* every night before bed. In fact, it doesn't mean that you have to do much at all. To learn computing throughout life requires only that you engage in three activities:

- Pursue new IT uses that fulfill your personal needs.
- Be rational about asking for help.
- Notice new ideas and technology as they arise.

There's no course of study to attend.

Pursuing New Uses

While studying Fluency, you have had to learn many new and unfamiliar applications. Though learning new skills may initially have been daunting, the process should have become steadily easier as your experience broadened and your facility with "clicking around" and "blazing away" developed. This success, and the fact that learning becomes easier the more you know, should give you confidence that you can learn IT on your own. And that's the best way to advance your knowledge. When you are engaged in information processing tasks—addressing envelopes, paying bills, or looking up Manila's time zone—determine whether you should use information technology to help you. If so, be confident that you can learn the new application, and take the time to do so. Expanding your IT use is the best way to continue to learn.

If you think objectively when you ask the question, "Can IT help in this situation?" the answer will not always be "yes." Your grandparents like to chat with you on the phone; should you encourage them to get a camera and Skype? You could help them set it up, but would they adopt this new-for-them technology? Perhaps not. Should you Skype with your lab partner, who lives in the next building? Probably not. In the first case the technology presents a barrier that might be difficult for your grandparents to adjust to; in the second case, the technology's advantage—face-to-face interaction over distance—is no real benefit; it's more fun to get together. Should you Skype with close friends in other cities? Of course. In summary, apply IT only if it can help, and if it can help, don't hesitate to apply it.

Asking for Help

One goal of our study is to convert you into a self-reliant computer and information user. Does that mean that you should solve all of your problems yourself? Of course not. In fact, it is certain that there are problems that are beyond your knowledge now, and there always will be. We always need experts. So, eventually we need to get assistance from someone more knowledgeable than we are.

But acknowledging that we need help doesn't mean that the moment things go awry we throw up our hands in desperation. Fluency has taught you how to troubleshoot your problems, and this experience has given you some perspective. We should assess whether the problem is probably due to our own stupidity—and eagerly fix it on our own to save the embarrassment of revealing that stupidity to someone else—or something more fundamental that requires greater expertise. Only after we've applied reasonable efforts to solving the problem ourselves will we need to ask for help. But when we do need assistance, we should ask. Of course, one reason to limit our asking professionals for help is that it usually takes longer to solve the problem than we are willing to wait.

As a contributor to lifelong learning, trying to solve our own problems and asking for help when we're truly stuck can contribute to greater understanding. If we figure it out ourselves, we're at least more experienced at troubleshooting. If someone else helps us, we may learn some facts we didn't know. Either way, we win.

Noticing New Technology

If the technological changes of the last half-century are any guide to the changes to come, IT will be quite different at the end of the next half-century. To learn about and apply the upcoming advances requires attention. Is the "advance" being touted in the press a fundamental leap forward that's potentially beneficial to you, or is it just hype about an old product in a different package? The latter is far more common than the former. You must be attentive and skeptical.

When there is a fundamental advancement—it happens more like once a decade than once a month—we need to be willing to learn about it. The media often covers the "science" of new technologies; following these technologies should be easy now that you've learned the concepts taught in this book. Using the technology might require taking a class, but more likely it won't. After all, thinking about technology abstractly, we know that those eager to deploy a new technology will prepare a "migration path" for those of us who are competent, daily users of the current technology. Innovations will likely be harder to use than the mature technologies with which we are familiar, of course. But if, as Fluent users, we don't have the background and experience to overcome those difficulties—that is, if we can't succeed with a new technology—then it isn't ready.

It often happens that technologies—small advances as well as large ones—are rushed to market before they're ready, so there is considerable risk in being an early adopter. But waiting involves risks too. One of technology's defining characteristics is that it steadily improves. Inventing technology is a difficult creative activity, and engineering it to perfection the first time never happens. So, there are steady improvements—automobiles improved throughout the entire twentieth century. There will always be a next-generation technology that is more convenient, more functional, and more versatile with better price performance, and so on. But waiting for perfection might require a hundred-year wait, and during that time you won't benefit from the technology. The lesson: Adopt a technology as soon as there's a high probability that it will assist you, but expect it to continue to improve.

Shifting for Yourself

Ted Nelson, the inventor of hypertext, tells a story of his first meeting with a software development team for a project he was to direct. He was depressed to find that everyone on the team drove a car with a standard transmission (a car requiring the driver to shift gears manually). Nelson's point in telling the story is that software should be as easy for people to use as automatic transmissions are, and that programmers who enjoy shifting their own gears may not produce such software. Whether his point is correct or not, his story gives us a valuable—if different—perspective.

Fluency enables *us*, the users, to shift gears. It doesn't give us the ability to build a car, to repair it, or to modify it. But, we can control computing devices to extract their full power, to be in command, and to reach our destination. Nelson may be right regarding builders, but for users, the ability to manipulate the levers of IT is not an ability to deplore.

Whatever the IT equivalent of the automatic transmission is, it is still on the drawing board. It took 60 years for cars to come equipped with automatic transmissions. With personal computing's 60th birthday still years away, we can't wait. We'll shift for ourselves.

Try It Solutions

24.1 Perform any task when all of the tasks it depends on are solved.

Review Questions

Multiple Choice

1. Specifying structure is
   a. more important than specifying content
   b. less important than specifying content
   c. just as important as specifying content
   d. the same as specifying content
2. Examples of nonalgorithmic tasks include all of the following except
   a. finding information
   b. using placeholders to reformat text
   c. database design
   d. creating a password
3. The first step in debugging is to
   a. determine what the problem is
   b. reproduce the error
   c. eliminate obvious causes
   d. divide the problem into smaller parts

4. Debugging is
   a. algorithmic
   b. procedural
   c. ordinal
   d. none of the above
5. Problems can be solved by approaching them
   a. through the use of algorithms
   b. by applying more and faster computers to the problem
   c. by using logical reasoning
   d. through trial and error
6. Which of the following is not a component of Fluency knowledge?
   a. Skills
   b. Capabilities
   c. Content
   d. Concepts
7. Put the three Fluency components in order from the least detailed to the most detailed.
   a. Capabilities, Concepts, Skills
   b. Concepts, Capabilities, Skills
   c. Skills, Concepts, Capabilities
   d. Skills, Capabilities, Concepts
8. Thinking Fluently involves the use of
   a. memorization
   b. repetition and practice
   c. abstract thinking
   d. attention to detail
9. You should adopt technology
   a. when the price/performance ratio is in your favor
   b. as soon as you can get your hands on it
   c. only after most of the rest of the public has adopted it
   d. when there is a high probability that it will prove beneficial to you
10. Fundamental advances in IT come along
    a. daily
    b. monthly
    c. yearly
    d. less often than yearly

Short Answer

1. _______ is involved when there is no deterministic, unfailing method to solve a problem.
2. _______ is a series of steps that, when taken, guarantees the successful completion of a task.
3. Debugging is not algorithmic, but, rather, it is _______.

4. Of the three Fluency components, the ability to use email is considered a _______.
5. Of the three Fluency components, the understanding of networking principles is considered a _______.
6. Of the three Fluency components, the understanding of algorithmic thinking is considered a _______.
7. _______ is the process of asking questions, pursuing ideas and interests, and being curious.
8. A list of files provides _______ for storing them, but it gives no indication of their _______.
9. Examples of _______ include the Smooth Motion program, the insertion sort, and query construction.
10. With Fluency, _______ are to details what _______ are to the "big picture."

Exercises

1. Explain how knowledge of program debugging can be used to solve other problems.
2. Describe the debugging process as a loop. What condition allows you to end the loop?
3. Describe how the development of the GUI is like the shift (pardon the pun) from manual to automatic transmissions.
4. Why are computers very good at structure but very poor on content?
5. Why is the best technology often the most overlooked?
6. Why is structure as important as content?
7. At what point should you be satisfied with your knowledge of IT?
8. How are skills tied to details while capabilities are tied to the "big picture?"

INTERVIEW

with

Tim Berners-Lee

Sir Timothy Berners-Lee is called the "father of the World Wide Web." He invented an Internet-based hypermedia initiative for global information sharing, which became known as the World Wide Web, in 1989 while working at the European Particle Physics Laboratory CERN. A year later, he wrote the first Web client and server.

Tim is the 3COM Founders Professor of Engineering in the School of Engineering and the Computer Science and Artificial Intelligence Laboratory at MIT, and Professor of Computer Science at the University of Southampton's School of Electronics and Computer Science in England. He is the also the director of the World Wide Web Consortium (W3C), co-director of the Web Science Research Initiative (WSRI), and director of the Word Wide Web Foundation. Tim advocates for Net neutrality—limiting proprietary systems while advancing open standards to encourage innovation.

Tim received his degree in physics from Oxford University in 1976. He has been awarded numerous honors, including the NAE's Charles Stark Draper Prize and the Japan Prize. In 2004 he was knighted by H. M. Queen Elizabeth II, and in 2007 he received Britain's Order of Merit.

You earned your first degree in physics. Why did you later pursue your Ph.D. in Computer Science?

After my physics degree, the telecommunications research companies seemed to be the most interesting places to be. The microprocessor had just come out, and telecommunications was switching very fast from hardwired logic to microprocessor-based systems. It was very exciting.

How did your foundation in physics influence your design of the Web?

When you study physics, you imagine what rules of behavior on the very small scale could possibly give rise to the large-scale world as we see it. When you design a global system like the Web, you try to invent rules of behavior of Web pages and links and things that could create a large-scale world as we would like it. One is analysis and the other synthesis, but they are very similar.

You've often said that the Web is simply "not done yet." What do you envision it to be like when it is done?

As I say in my book, *Weaving the Web*, I have a dream for the Web … and it has two parts.

In the first part, the Web becomes a much more powerful means for collaboration between people. I have always imagined the information space as something to which everyone has immediate and intuitive access, and not just to browse, but to create. Furthermore, the dream of people-to-people communication through shared knowledge must be possible for groups of all sizes, interacting electronically with as much ease as they do now in person.

In the second part of the dream, collaborations extend to computers. Machines become capable of analyzing all the data on the Web—the content, links, and transactions between people and computers. A "Semantic Web," which should make this possible, has yet to emerge, but when it does, the day-to-day mechanisms of trade, bureaucracy, and our daily lives will be handled by machines talking to machines, leaving humans to provide inspiration and intuition ... This machine-understandable Web will come about through the implementation of a series of technical advances and social agreements that are now beginning.

Once the two-part dream is reached, the Web will be a place where the whim of a human being and the reasoning of a machine coexist in an ideal, powerful mixture.

And what does that mixture look like?

There is just one Web, whatever your browser, it's always available, and anyone can access it no matter what hardware device, software vendor, geographical position, disability, language, or culture.

What do you find most challenging about your work?

When two groups disagree strongly about something, but want in the end to achieve a common goal, finding exactly what they each mean and where the misunderstandings are can be very demanding. The chair of any working group knows that. However, this is what it takes to make progress toward consensus on a large scale.

What challenges are you facing in trying to achieve the Semantic Web?

Technically, there are many standards to make in the area of rules of query languages and Web services, and at the same time there is the job of working out how these will all fit together as logical systems.

Commercially, it is difficult to find a short-term business model for anything Web-like, because its value depends on the extent to which others are also using it.

Legally, the threat of patents hangs over any standards area until everyone involved has agreed to make the common infrastructure royalty-free.

These are three of the larger challenges we are facing, but overcoming them is the excitement, creativity, and business wisdom of many people who are working together in different ways.

What do you think students should be aware of as Web technology advances?

Be aware that what you can make with communications and computing technology is limited only by your imagination. Be aware also that while technology gives us more choices as to what we do, it does not change the essential nature, limitations, and strengths of a human being.

XHTML Reference

THE FOLLOWING brief descriptions form an alphabetical list of the XHTML tags used in this book. Check Chapter 4 for further explanation or consult

www.w3.org/hypertext/WWW/MarkUp/MarkUp.html.

Other useful links from W3C are:

Tags	www.w3schools.com/tags/default.asp
Special characters like Ö	www.w3schools.com/tags/ref_entities.asp
XHTML validation	validator.w3.org/#validate_by_upload
Attributes	www.w3.org/TR/html4/index/attributes.html
Color names	www.w3schools.com/css/css_colornames.asp
Properties	www.w3.org/TR/CSS2/propidx.html

Every XHTML source file must contain the following tags in the given order:

```
<html xmlns="http://www.w3.org/1999/xhtml">
    <head>
    <title> Title goes here </title>
        All other header content goes here
    </head>
    <body>
        All body content goes here
    </body>
</html>
```

XHTML Document Structure for Validation

To validate the XHTML, the following two lines

```
<!DOCTYPE html PUBLIC "-//W3C//DTD XHTML 1.0 Strict//EN"
    "http://www.w3.org/TR/xhtml1/DTD/xhtml1-strict.dtd">
```

must be the first two lines of the file. In addition, the line

```
<meta http-equiv="Content-Type" content="text/html; charset=utf-8"/>
```

must be included between <head> and <title> in the head section.

XHTML Tags

Anchor (<a> </a>): Defines a hyperlink using the href="*fn*" attribute, where *fn* is a file name. The text between the two tags is known as the link and is highlighted.

```
<a href="nextPage.html">Click here for next page</a>
```

fluency ALERT

> **Text Only!** Remember, XHTML source files must contain standard keyboard text (ASCII) only. Word processors include fancy formatting that confuses browsers. Use simple text editors only, such as Notepad++ or TextWrangler. Also, the file name extension—the characters after the last dot in the file name—must be **html**

Body (<body> </body>): Specifies the extent of the body of the XHTML document (see the XHTML Document Structure section at the beginning of this appendix for an example). Useful style attributes include:

- "background-color : *color*" paints the background the specified *color*
- "color : *color*" displays text in the specified *color*
- "font-family : *face*" displays the text in the specified font *face*

Bold (<b> </b>): Specifies that the style of the enclosed text is to be a bold font.

```
<b>This text prints as bold</b>
```

Caption (<caption> </caption>): Specifies a table caption, and must be enclosed by table tags (see the entry for "Table" for an example).

Comment (<!-- *comment goes here* -->): The comment text is enclosed within angle brackets; avoid using angle brackets in the comments.

```
<!-- This text will not be displayed -->
```

Definitional List (<dl> </dl>): Defines a definitional list, which is composed of two-part entries, called the definitional-list term (<dt> </dt>) and the definitional-list definition (<dd> </dd>). Terms are on separate lines and the definitions are on the following lines.

```
<dl>
    <dt>First term</dt>
    <dd>First definition goes here</dd>
    <dt>Second term</dt>
    <dd>Second definition goes here</dd>
</dl>
```

Header (<head> </head>): Defines the extent of the header of the XHTML document, which must include a title (see the XHTML Document Structure section at the beginning of this appendix for an example).

Headings (<h1> </h1> . . . <h8> </h8>): Specifies that the enclosed text is to be one of eight heading levels. The smaller the number, the larger and more prominent the text.

```
<h1> Heading level 1 </h1>        Most prominent
<h2> Heading level 2 </h2>
. . .
<h7> Heading level 7 </h7>
<h8> Heading level 8 </h8>        Least prominent
```

Horizontal Rule (<hr/>): Defines a line that spans the window, though it can be reduced in size using the width="*p*%" attribute. The attribute size="*n*" specifies the (point) thickness of the line.

```
<hr width="75%"/>
```

HTML (<html> </html>): Defines the beginning and end of the document (see the XHTML Document Structure section at the beginning of this appendix for detailed information).

Image (<img . . . />): Causes an image—specified by the src="*fn*" attribute—to be placed in the document at the current position. In addition to the src attribute, the alt="*text*" attribute is required to give the image a text interpretation. Position styling information uses the float property. Also, height and width attributes specify the displayed image's size in pixels.

```
<img src="prettyPic.jpg" style='float:left' alt='Sunset' width='140'/>
```

Italics (<i> </i>): Specifies that the style of the enclosed text is to be italic.

```
<i>This text is emphasized by italics</i>
```

Line Break (<br/>): Ends the current line and continues the text on the next line.

```
This text is on one line.<br/> This text is on the next line.
```

List Item (<li> </li>): Specifies an entry in either an ordered or an unordered list (see the entries for "Ordered List" and "Unordered List" for examples).

Ordered List (<ol> </ol>): Specifies the extent of an ordered list, whose entries are list items. The list items are prefixed with a number.

```
<ol>
    <li>First list item</li>
    <li>Second list item</li>
</ol>
```

Paragraph (<p> </p>): Specifies the extent of a paragraph. Paragraphs begin on a new line.

```
<p> This text forms a one-line paragraph.</p>
```

Table (<table> </table>): Defines a table of table rows; the rows contain table data. Optionally, the first row of the definition can be formed with table heading tags. A useful attribute is border, giving the table a border.

```
<table border="1">
    <caption>Description</caption>
    <tr>
        <th>Head Col 1</th>
        <th>Head Col 2</th>
        <th>Head Col 3</th>
    </tr>
    <tr>
        <td>Row 1, Cell 1</td>
        <td>Row 1, Cell 2</td>
        <td>Row 1, Cell 3</td>
    </tr>
    <tr>
        <td>Row 2, Cell 1</td>
        <td>Row 2, Cell 2</td>
        <td>Row 2, Cell 3</td>
    </tr>
    <tr>
        <td>Row 3, Cell 1</td>
        <td>Row 3, Cell 2</td>
        <td>Row 3, Cell 3</td>
    </tr>
</table>
```

Table Data (<td> </td>): Specifies a cell in a table, and must be enclosed by table row tags. A useful styling property is "background-color=*color*".

Table Heading (<th> </th>): Specifies a cell in the heading row of a table, and must be enclosed by table row tags. A useful styling property is "background-color=*color*".

Table Row (<tr> </tr>): Specifies a row in a table, and must be enclosed by table tags. See the entry for "Table" for an example.

Title (<title> </title>): Defines the page title; it must be given in the header section of the XHTML source.

```
<title> Title displays at the top of the browser window</title>
```

Unordered List (<ul> </ul>): Specifies the extent of an unordered list, whose entries are list items. The list items are preceded by a bullet. A list item can enclose another list.

```
<ul>
    <li>First list item</li>
    <li>Second list item</li>
</ul>
```

RGB Colors

Table A.1 shows the hexadecimal coding for commonly used colors that are consistently displayed by all browsers; the decimal equivalents. The six digit hex numbers abcdef, when used in attribute specifications, should have the form "#abcdef".

Table A.1 Web-safe colors for Web page design

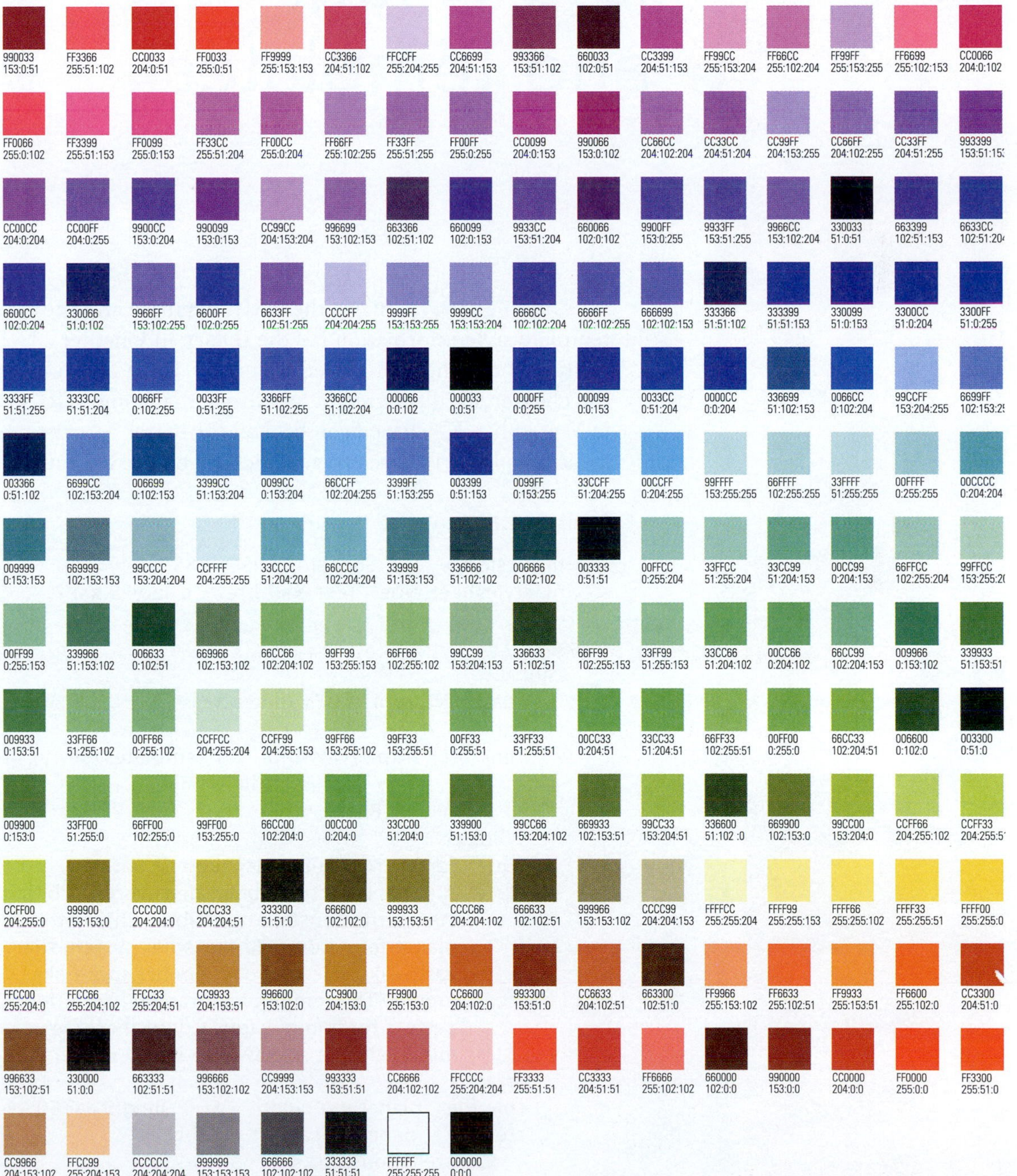

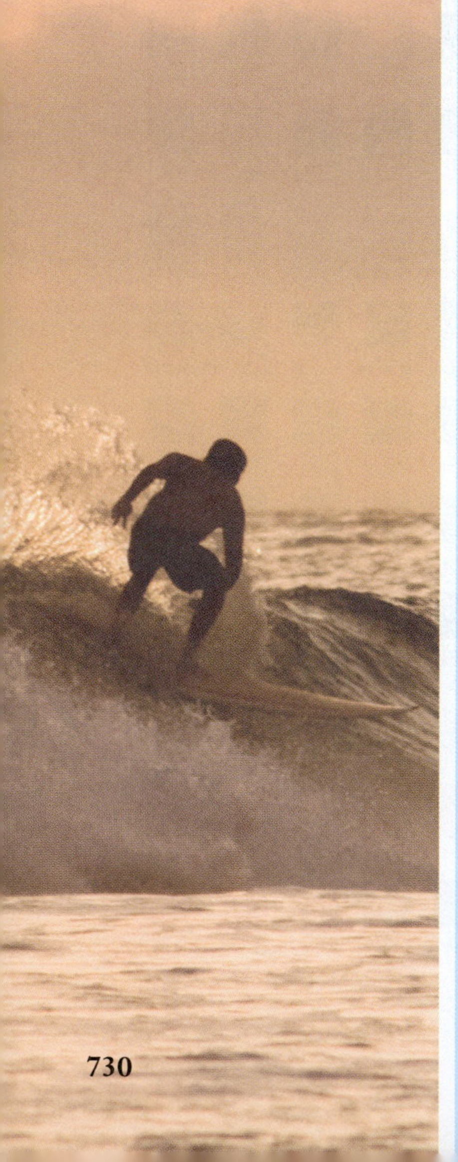

B

appendix

iDiary: Tags and Templates

THIS APPENDIX contains the XML database and the XSL template style information for the iDiary in Chapter 17. The content shown here produced Figure 17.1. All tags used in the chapter are illustrated here. Notice that some URLs, indicated by ⤵, have been broken for better formatting; these should be restored to a single line before executing.

XML Database File iDiary.xml

```
<?xml version = "1.0" encoding="ISO-8859-1" ?>
<?xml-stylesheet type="text/xsl" href="iDiarySS.xsl"?>

<idiary>
    <entry>
        <date>25.April.2007</date>
        <mit>
        <link url="http://www.npr.org/templates/story/⤵
                story.php?storyId=9796321">
            Earth-Like Planet
        </link>
        <title>Earth-Like Planet Discovered</title>
        <fact> A rocky planet has been discovered orbiting a
               star in the constellation Libra. This is the first
               planet found outside our solar system that is
               earth-like; the rest of them are more like
               Jupiter. The temperature ranges from 0-40C,
               perfect for liquid water. Could there be
               intelligent life somewhere in the universe?
        </fact>
        <pic file="planet.jpg" width="500" height="360"/>
        <remark><label>Location: </label>
            Constellation Libra</remark>
```

```
        <remark>First rocky planet discovered outside the
          solar system. From this planet the sun appears to be 4 times larger
          than our sun appears.</remark>
        </mit>
    </entry>

    <entry>
        <date>26.April.2007</date>
        <mit>
            <fact>The planet discovered yesterday is called Gliese 581. It was
                not named by the Romans!
            </fact>
        </mit>
    </entry>

    <entry>
        <date>27.April.2007</date>
        <mit>
            <fact>I just noticed that the phenom
            <link url="http://en.wikipedia.org/wiki/Jeong-Hyun_Lim">funtwo
            </link>
                (a/k/a Jeong Hyun Lim) has passed the 20,000,000 views
                milestone on YouTube. In tribute, even though I like
            <link url="http://www.youtube.com/watch?v=xn9yVLabCN8">
                Serious Diego </link>
                better, here is funtwo playing Jerry Chang's Canon Rock. Play it
                to add to his numbers! </fact>
            <ytvideo utube="http://www.youtube.com/v/QjA5faZF1A8"/>
        </mit>
    </entry>

    <entry>
        <date>28.April.2007</date>
        <mit>
            <link url="http://www.eso.org/public/outreach/press-rel/➥
                    pr-2007/pr-22-07.html">
                NASA Press Release
            </link>
            <fact>The new planet is actually Gliese 581 c, the "c" standing for
                "cool" probably! Actually, it's "c" because this is the third planet
                found orbiting the star Gliese 581. And who, you may ask, is
                Gliese? He's an astronomer who published a catalog of close
                stars, where "close" means less than 25 parsecs away, or 81.5
                light years. This star is number 581 in the list. You can look it
                up!
            </fact>
        </mit>
    </entry>

    <entry>
        <date>29.April.2007</date>
        <mit>
```

```
            <fact> This is Ted Kooser's idea of the reader of his poetry. It was
                published in 1980, but I just saw it.
            </fact>
            <poem>
                <p_title>Selecting a Reader</p_title>
                <poet>Ted Kooser</poet>
                <line>First, I would have her be beautiful,</line>
                <line>and walking carefully up on my poetry</line>
                <line>at the loneliest moment of an afternoon,</line>
                <line>her hair still damp at the neck</line>
                <line>from washing it. She should be wearing</line>
                <line>a raincoat, an old one, dirty</line>
                <line>from not having money enough for the cleaners.</line>
                <line>She will take out her glasses, and there</line>
                <line>in the bookstore, she will thumb</line>
                <line>over my poems, then put the book back</line>
                <line>up on its shelf. She will say to herself,</line>
                <line>"For that kind of money, I can get</line>
                <line>my raincoat cleaned." And she will.</line>
            </poem>
        </mit>
    </entry>

    <entry>
        <date>30.April.2007</date>
        <mit>
            <link url="http://www.imdb.com/name/nm0780462/bio">
                Howie Seago, Deaf Actor
            </link>
            <title>Howie Seago, Deaf Actor</title>
            <pic file="howie-seago.jpg" width="202" height="224"/>
            <fact> Tonight, for the first time, I saw a deaf actor playing the
                role of a hearing person. The play was Thornton Wilder's 1943
                play By the Skin of Our Teeth, and the actor was Howie Seago.
                As he signed his lines, one of the other actors spoke his lines.
                The person speaking the lines changed as the situation
                changed. Thinking about his task, I realized that he not only
                needs to learn the lines and the acting like other actors, but he
                has to deal with knowing his cues, often when many others
                have lines he cannot hear; and he needs his hands free to sign,
                making it challenging to hold props. It was impressive. BTW, the
                play is very strange.
            </fact>
        </mit>
    </entry>

    <entry>
        <date>1.May.2007</date>
        <mit>
            <link url="http://www.npr.org/templates/story/
                    story.php?storyId=4679760">
                John Vaillant's Book
```

```
                </link>
                <title>The Golden Spruce</title>
                <fact>I finished reading The Golden Spruce by John Vaillant. It's a
                    very sad, true story about an eco-terrorist cutting down a 300-
                    year-old Sitka spruce tree that had an extremely rare mutation
                    that made its needles golden yellow. The tree was smack in the
                    middle of the Queen Charlotte Islands off the coast of Canada,
                    which is home to the Haida Indians; they believed it was one of
                    them, and regarded the crime as the same as killing a chief.
                    Recommendation:
                    <rate uri="1star.gif"/><rate uri="1star.gif"/>
                    <rate uri="1star.gif"/><rate uri="1star.gif"/>
                </fact>
                <pic file="sitkaSpruce.jpg" width="200" height="300"/>
            </mit>
        </entry>
</idiary>
```

XSL Database File iDiarySS.xsl

```
<?xml version="1.0" encoding="UTF-8"?>
<xsl:stylesheet version="1.0"
    xmlns:xsl="http://www.w3.org/1999/XSL/Transform">

<xsl:template match="idiary">
    <html><head><title>iDiary</title>
        <style type="text/css">
            body    {background-color : black; color : white;
                    font-family : helvetica}
            h2      {text-align : center}
            table   {margin-left : auto; margin-right : auto}
            td.day  {vertical-align : top; color : red}
            p       {text-align : center}
        </style>
    </head>
    <body>
        <h2 style="color : gold">iDiary: Journal of Interesting Stuff</h2>
            <table style="max-width:425px">
                <tr><td>
                    <i>This is a record of the most interesting thing I found
                    out each day that's worth remembering. There's personal
                    stuff in this database, too, but it's not gonna be displayed!
                    </i>
                </td></tr>
            </table><br/>
            <table style="max-width:700px">
                <xsl:apply-templates/>
            </table>
        </body>
    </html>
</xsl:template>
```

```
<xsl:template match="entry">
    <tr>
        <xsl:apply-templates/>
    </tr>
</xsl:template>

<xsl:template match="date">
    <td class="day">
        <xsl:apply-templates/>
    </td>
</xsl:template>

<xsl:template match="mit"> <!-- Most Interesting Thing -->
    <td>
        <xsl:apply-templates/>
        <br/><hr style="width:75%"/><br/>
    </td>
</xsl:template>

<xsl:template match="fact">
    <xsl:apply-templates/>
    <br/>
</xsl:template>

<xsl:template match="title">
    <h2>
        <xsl:apply-templates/>
    </h2>
</xsl:template>

<xsl:template match="link">
    <a href="{@url}">
        <xsl:apply-templates/>
    </a>
</xsl:template>

<xsl:template match="pic">
    <p>
        <img src="{@file}" width="{@width}" height="{@height}"
            alt="Picture of Interesting Thing"/>
    </p>
</xsl:template>

<xsl:template match="rate">
    <img src="{@uri}" alt="Star"/>
</xsl:template>

<xsl:template match="remark">
    <br/>
        <xsl:apply-templates/>
    <br/>
</xsl:template>
```

```
<xsl:template match="ytvideo">
    <p><object width="425" height="344">
        <param name="movie" value="{@utube}"></param>
        <param name="wmode" value="transparent"></param>
        <embed src="{@utube}"
            type="application/x-shockwave-flash"
            wmode="transparent" width="425" height="350">
        </embed>
    </object></p>
</xsl:template>

<xsl:template match="poem">
    <span style="font-family : optima">
        <xsl:apply-templates/>
    </span>
</xsl:template>

<xsl:template match="p_title">
    <xsl:apply-templates/>
    </h3>
</xsl:template>

<xsl:template match="poet">
    <h4><i>
        <xsl:apply-templates/>
    </i></h4>
</xsl:template>

<xsl:template match="line">
    <xsl:apply-templates/>
    <br/>
</xsl:template>

<xsl:template match="label">
    <b>
        <xsl:apply-templates/>
    </b>
</xsl:template>

<xsl:template match="personal">
    <xsl:apply-templates/> <!-- Display personal information-->
</xsl:template>

</xsl:stylesheet>
```

appendix

JavaScript Programming Rules

THIS APPENDIX summarizes in brief statements the "rules" for writing JavaScript and the rules that JavaScript follows when executing programs. The chapter in which each rule was introduced is given in brackets. Notice Tables C.1, escape sequences; C.2, reserved words; and C.3, JavaScript operators.

Program Structure

White space is ignored [18]. Any number of spaces, tabs, or new line characters can generally separate the components of a program. Avoid breaking up identifiers and literals such as numbers and strings.

Place declarations first [18]. Declarations should appear before other statements. If there are multiple blocks of JavaScript code, place global declarations at the beginning of the first block.

First-to-last execution [18]. Program statements are all executed from first to last, unless specifically commanded to skip using conditional `if` statements or told to repeat using `for` statements.

Terminate statements with semicolons [18]. Every statement, including those on their own line, must be terminated with a semicolon (;), except the compound statement (i.e., the curly brace (}) is *not* followed by a semicolon).

Slash slash comment [18]. Text from // to the end of the line is treated as a comment. For example,

```
x = 3.1; //Set rate
```

Slash star–star slash comment [18]. All text enclosed by the symbols /* and */ is treated as a comment, and so can span several lines. For example,

```
/* The text in a Slash Star-Star Slash comment can spill across lines of a pro-
gram, but the Slash Slash comment is limited to the end of one line. */
```

Data Types

Four rules for numbers [18]. Numerical constants:

1. Keep the digits together without spaces, so 3.141 596 is wrong, whereas 3.141596 is right.
2. Don't use digit grouping symbols of any type, so 1,000,000 is wrong, whereas 1000000 is right.
3. Use a period as the decimal point, so 0,221 is wrong, whereas 0.221 is right.
4. Use no units, so 33% and $10.89 are wrong, whereas 0.33 and 10.89 are right.

Six rules for strings [18]. When typing string literals:

1. The characters must be surrounded by quotes, either single (') or double (").
2. Most characters are allowed within quotes except new line, backspace, tab, \, form feed, and return.
3. Double-quoted strings can contain single quotes and vice versa.
4. The apostrophe (') is the same as the single quote.
5. Any number of characters is allowed in a string.
6. The minimum number of characters in a string is zero (""), which is called the empty string.

String literal escape characters [18]. Table C.1 gives the escape sequences for the special characters of string literals that cannot be typed directly. For example, "\b\b" is a string of two backspaces.

Boolean data type [18]. There are two Boolean values: true and false.

Table C.1 Escape sequences for characters prohibited from string literals

Sequence	Character	Sequence	Character
\b	Backspace	\f	Form feed
\n	New line	\r	Carriage return
\t	Tab	\'	Apostrophe or single quote
\"	Double quote	\\	Backslash

Variables and Declarations

Identifier structure [18]. Identifiers must begin with a letter and may contain any combination of letters, numerals, or underscores (_). Identifiers cannot contain white space. For example, green, eGGs, ham_and_2_eggs are three identifiers.

Case sensitivity [18]. JavaScript identifiers are case sensitive, so y and Y are different.

Reserved words [18]. Some words, such as var and true, are reserved by JavaScript and cannot be identifiers. Table C.2 lists these words. To use a word in the list as an identifier, prefix it with an underscore (for example, _true), but it's safer (and smarter) to think up a different identifier.

Table C.2 Reserved words and property terms in JavaScript. These words cannot or should not be used as identifiers.

abstract	eval	moveBy	scrollbars
alert	export	moveTo	scrollBy
arguments	extends	name	scrollTo
Array	false	NaN	self
blur	final	native	setInterval
boolean	finally	netscape	setTimeout
Boolean	find	new	short
break	float	null	static
byte	for	number	status
callee	focus	Object	statusbar
caller	frames	open	stop
captureEvents	function	opener	String
case	Function	outerHeight	super
catch	goto	outerWidth	switch
char	history	package	synchronized
class	home	Packages	this
clearInterval	if	pageXOffset	throw
clearTimeout	implements	pageYOffset	throws
close	import	parent	toolbar
closed	in	parseFloat	top
confirm	infinity	parseInt	toString
const	innerHeight	personalbar	transient
constructor	innerWidth	print	true
continue	instanceof	private	try
Date	int	prompt	typeof
debugger	interface	protected	unescape
default	isFinite	prototype	unwatch
defaultStatus	isNaN	public	valueOf
delete	java	RegExp	var
do	length	releaseEvents	void
document	location	resizeBy	watch
double	locationbar	resizeTo	while
else	long	return	window
enum	Math	routeEvent	with
escape	menubar	scroll	

Declare variables [18]. All variables must be declared using var. Do not declare any variable more than once.

Variable declaration list separated by commas [18]. For example,

```
var prices, hemlines, interestRates;
```

Variable declaration initializers can be expressions [18]. For example,

```
var minutesInDay = 60 * 24;
```

Expressions

Operators [18]. A selection of JavaScript operators is given in Table C.3.

Table C.3 JavaScript operators used in this book

Name	Symbol	# of Operands and Data Type	Example	Comment	Result of Example
Addition	+	2 Numeric	4 + 5		9
Concatenation	+	2 String	"four"+"five" 6 + "pack"	1 numeric operand implies concatenate	"fourfive" "6 pack"
Subtraction	-	2 Numeric	9 - 5		4
Multiplication	*	2 Numeric	-2 * 4		-8
Division	/	2 Numeric	10/3		0.33333...
Modulus	%	2 Numeric	10%3	Remainder	1
Increment	++	1 Numeric	3++	See Chapter 20	4
Decrement	--	1 Numeric	3--	See Chapter 20	2
Less Than	<	2 Numeric	4 < 4		false
Less Than or Equal	<=	2 Numeric	4 <= 4		true
Equal	==	2 Numeric 2 String	4 == 4 "a" == "A"		true false
Not Equal	!=	2 Numeric 2 String	4 != 4 "a" != " a"		false true
Greater Than or Equal	>=	2 Numeric	4 >= 4		true
Greater Than	>	2 Numeric	4 > 4		false
Negation	-	1 Numeric	- 4		-4
Logical Not	!	1 Boolean	! true		false
Logical And	&&	2 Boolean	true && true		true
Logical Or	||	2 Boolean	false || true		true

Note: The examples use literal data (actual numbers) to show the operation; in practice the operands are variables.

Use parentheses [18]. Though JavaScript uses precedence to determine the order in which to perform operators when no parentheses are given, that feature is for professionals. To be safe, parenthesize all complex expressions.

Operator overloading [18]. Plus (+) means addition for numerical operands; it means concatenation for string operands. If + has an operand of each type (e.g., `4 + "5"`), the number converts to a string and returns a string (e.g., `"45"`).

Arrays and Indexes

Array declarations [21]. Arrays are declared using the `var` statement and the `new Array (`<*elements*>`)` designation, where <*elements*> is the number of array elements. For example,

```
var zodiacSigns = new Array (12);
```

Arrays are 0-origin, meaning the least index value is 0, and the largest index is <*elements*> `- 1`.

Array references [21]. Array elements can be referenced by the syntax

<*array_name*>[<*index*>]

where <*array_name*> is a declared array and <*index*> is any integer value from 0 to <*elements*> `- 1`. An array reference, for example, `A[i]`, is a variable and can be used wherever variables can be used.

Index values [21]. An index value can be any expression, including a constant (e.g., 3), a variable (e.g., `i`), or an expression involving operators (e.g., `(i + 12)%5`) that evaluates to an integer in the range from 0 to the highest index of the array, <*elements*> `- 1`.

Statements

Assignment statement [18]. The assignment statement (e.g., `lap = lap + 1`) updates the value of a variable on the left side of the = (e.g., `lap`) by computing the value of the expression on the right side of = (e.g., `lap + 1`) and making it the new value of the variable. The value flow is from the right side to the left side.

Compound statements [18]. A sequence of statements enclosed by { } is a compound statement and is treated as one statement, say, for purposes of the <*statement*> in `if`, `if/else`, iteration statements, and function declarations. The compound statement is not terminated by a semicolon, though statements it contains must be.

if statement [18]. The `if` statement, or conditional statement, has the form

```
if(<Boolean expression>)
    <then-statement>;
```

If the value of the Boolean expression is `true`, the <*then-statement*> is performed; if the Boolean expression is `false`, the <*then-statement*> is skipped.

if/else statement [18]. The if/else statement, or conditional statement, has the form

```
if( <Boolean expression> )
    <then-statement>;
else
    <else-statement>;
```

If the result of the Boolean expression is true, the *<then-statement>* is performed and the *<else-statement>* is skipped. If the Boolean expression is false, the *<then-statement>* is skipped and the *<else-statement>* is performed.

Conditional within a conditional [18]. If a conditional's *<then-statement>* or *<else-statement>* contains another conditional, make it a compound statement (enclose it in { }) to avoid ambiguity as to which if statement the else associates with.

for loops [21]. The for statement has the syntax

```
for( <initialization>; <continuation>; <next iteration> ) {
    <statement list>
}
```

The *<initialization>* is an assignment to the iteration variable, the *<continuation>* is a Boolean expression like those used in if statements, and the *<next iteration>* is an assignment to the iteration variable.

for loop operation [21]. A for loop works as follows: The initialization assignment is performed first, followed by the continuation test. If the test result is false, the *<statement list>* is skipped and the for loop ends. If the test result is true, the *<statement list>* is performed followed by the next iteration assignment. That completes one iteration. At the completion of an iteration, the process repeats with the continuation test.

World-Famous Iteration [21]. The World-Famous Iteration (WFI) is a for statement that has the following standard form:

```
for( <iteration var> = 0; <iteration var> < <limit> ; <iteration var>++ ) {
    <statement list>
}
```

The *<iteration var>* is any declared variable, and the *<limit>* is any expression or variable. An example is

```
for( j = 0; j < n ; j++ ) {
    <statement list>
}
```

The number of iterations—the number of times the loop loops—is n.

Functions

Function declaration [20]. Functions are declared using the following syntax:

```
function <name> ( <parameter list> ) {
    <statement list>
}
```

Notice the conspicuous position of the closed brace on its own line, below the *f* in function. The brace is not followed by a semicolon. An example is

```
function prefixTitle ( familyName, mORf ) {
    if (mORf = "M")
        return "Mr. " + familyName;
    else
        return "Ms " + familyName;
}
```

Function names are identifiers [20]. Function names, for example, prefixTitle, follow the rules for identifiers. It is best if the chosen name says what the function does.

Parameters are identifiers [20]. Function parameters, for example, familyName, follow the rules for identifiers.

Parameters are not declared [20]. Function parameters should not be declared because the JavaScript interpreter automatically declares them.

Return statement [20]. A function completes when it reaches a return statement:

return <*expression*>

The result of the function is the result of <*expression*>, which could simply be a variable.

Guidelines

Programmer's rules: Professional programmers have a set of good programming practices, including:

- Choose meaningful identifiers for variables. For example, interestRate is better than, say, p.
- Insert white space liberally to improve code readability. For example,

  ```
  if(input!="")name=first+last;
  ```

  is poor, while

  ```
  if( input != "" )
    name = first + last;
  ```

  is preferred.
- Comment programs liberally, saying what the variables mean and what the logic is doing.
- Align code—especially when the statements are logically related—and be consistent; it helps to locate errors.

Wrong:	Right:
`  able="a;`	`able    = "a";`
`baker = 'b';`	`baker   = "b";`
`    charlie = "c";`	`charlie = "c";`

D

appendix

Bean Counter Program

THE FINAL XHTML and JavaScript code for the Bean Counter application in Chapter 19 appears on the following pages. Note that variations in Web browsers will affect how closely it matches the sample output in the figure.

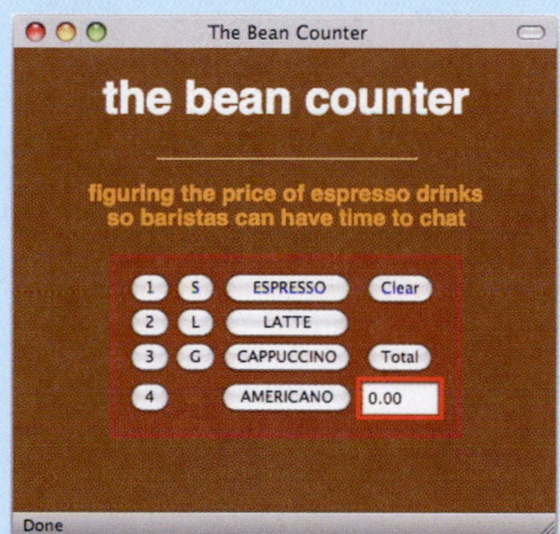

```
<!DOCTYPE html PUBLIC "-//W3C//DTD XHTML 1.0 Strict//EN"
    "http://www.w3.org/TR/xhtml1/DTD/xhtml1-strict.dtd">
<html xmlns="http://www.w3.org/1999/xhtml">
    <head>
        <meta http-equiv="Content-Type" content="text/html;
            charset=utf-8"/>
        <title>The Bean Counter</title>
        <style type="text/css">
            body {background-color : saddlebrown;
                color : darkorange;
```

```
            font-family : helvetica; text-align : center}
            table {margin-left : auto; margin-right : auto; text-align : center;
                  background-color : #993300; border-style : solid;
                  border-color : firebrick; border-width : medium; padding :
                  8px }
        </style>
    </head>
    <body>
        <script type = "text/javascript">
            var shots = 1;
            var drink = "none";
            var ounce = 0;
        </script>
        <h1 style="color : white"> the bean counter</h1>
        <hr style="width : 50%; color : darkorange  "/>
        <p><b>figuring the price of espresso drinks<br />
            so baristas can have time to chat</b></p>
        <form action="" >
        <table>
            <tr>
                <td>
                    <input type="button" value="1" onclick='shots = 1'/>
                </td>
                <td>
                    <input type="button" value="S" onclick='ounce = 8'/>
                </td>
                <td>
                    <input type="button" value="    ESPRESSO    "
                        onclick='drink = "espresso"'/>
                </td>
                <td>
                    <input type="button" value="Clear" onclick=
                        'shots = 1;
                        drink = "none";
                        ounce = 0;
                        document.forms[0].price.value = "0.00"
                    '/>
                </td>
            </tr>
            <tr>
                <td>
                    <input type="button" value="2" onclick='shots = 2'/>
                </td>
                <td>
                    <input type="button" value="L" onclick='ounce = 12'/>
                </td>
                <td>
                    <input type="button" value="      LATTE      "
                        onclick='drink = "latte"'/>
                </td>
                <td>
                </td>
            </tr>
```

```
        <tr>
            <td>
                <input type="button" value="3" onclick='shots = 3'/>
            </td>
            <td>
                <input type="button" value="G" onclick='ounce = 16'/>
            </td>
            <td>
                <input type="button" value="CAPPUCCINO"
                    onclick='drink = "cappuccino"'/>
            </td>
            <td>
                <input type="button" value="Total" onclick=
                    ' var price;
                    var taxRate = 0.088;
                    if (drink == "espresso")
                        price = 1.40;
                    if (drink == "latte" || drink == "cappuccino") {
                    if (ounce == 8)
                        price = 1.95;
                    if (ounce == 12)
                        price = 2.35;
                    if (ounce == 16)
                        price = 2.75;
                    }
                    if (drink == "Americano")
                        price = 1.20 + .30 * (ounce/8);
                    price = price + (shots - 1) * .50;
                    price = price + price * taxRate;
                    document.forms[0].price.value = price;
                '/>
            </td>
        </tr>
        <tr>
            <td>
                <input type="button" value="4" onclick='shots = 4'/>
            </td>
            <td>
            </td>
            <td>
                <input type="button" value="  AMERICANO  "
                    onclick='drink = "Americano"'/>
            </td>
            <td style="border-style : solid; border-width : medium;
                border-color : red">
                <input type="text" name="price" value="0.00" size="5"
                    onchange=' '/>
            </td>
        </tr>
    </table>
    </form>
  </body>
</html>
```

Memory Bank Code

THE FOLLOWING XHTML and JavaScript code produces the Memory Bank page in Chapter 20 (Figure 20.14). Notice that some URLs, indicated by ↩, have been broken for better formatting; these should be restored to a single line before executing.

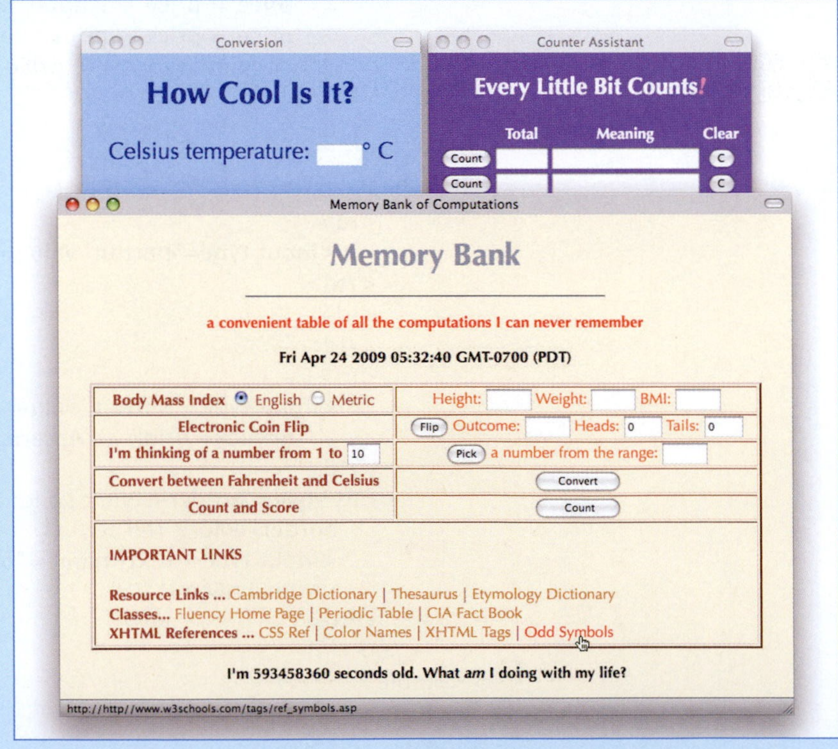

```
<!DOCTYPE html PUBLIC "-//W3C//DTD XHTML 1.0 Strict//EN"
   "http://www.w3.org/TR/xhtml1/DTD/xhtml1-strict.dtd">
<html xmlns="http://www.w3.org/1999/xhtml">
   <head>
      <meta http-equiv="Content-Type" content="text/html; charset=utf-8"/>
      <title>Memory Bank of Computations</title>
      <style type="text/css">
         body       {background-color : papayawhip; color : brown;
                        font-family : optima; text-align : center}
         table      {margin-left : auto; margin-right : auto}
         td         {padding-left : 14px; padding-right : 14px}
         td.right   {color:orangered; font-weight : lighter}
         p          {color : black}
         a:link     {color : chocolate; text-decoration : none}
         a:hover    {color : red; text-decoration : none}
         a:visited  {color : chocolate; text-decoration : none}
      </style>
   </head>
   <body>
      <h1 style="color : lightslategray">  Memory Bank</h1>
      <hr style="width : 50%" /> <b><p style="color : red">
         a convenient table of all the computations I can never remember </p>
      <script type="text/javascript">
         var scale='E'; var numHeads = 0, numTails = 0; var topEnd = 10;
         document.write('<p>' +  (Date().toString()) + '</p>');
         function bmiM ( weightKg, heightCm ) {            //Metric BMI
            var heightM = heightCm / 100;                  //Change to meters
            return weightKg / (heightM * heightM);
         }
         function bmiE ( weightLbs, heightIn ) {           //English BMI
            var heightFt = heightIn / 12;                  //Change to feet
            return 4.89 * weightLbs / (heightFt * heightFt);
         }
         function BMI ( units, weight, height ) {
            if (units == 'E')
               return bmiE( weight, height);               //Answer in English
            else
               return bmiM( weight, height);               //Answer in Metric
         }
         function randNum (range) {
            return Math.floor(range*Math.random());
         }
         function flipCoin () {
            if (randNum(2)==0) {
               document.forms[0].oc.value="Heads";
               numHeads=numHeads+1;
               document.forms[0].nH.value=numHeads;
            }
            else {
               document.forms[0].oc.value="Tails";
               numTails=numTails+1;
               document.forms[0].nT.value=numTails;
```

```
            }
        }
    </script>
    <form activity="">
        <table border="2">
            <tr><td><b>Body Mass Index </b>
                <input type="radio" name="unit" checked="checked"
                    onclick='scale="E"'/> English
                <input type="radio" name="unit"
                    onclick='scale="M"'/> Metric </td>
                <td class="right">Height: <input type="text" name="hgt"
                        size="4"
                    onchange ='if (document.forms[0].wgt.value!=0)
                        document.forms[0].ans.value= BMI(scale,
                            document.forms[0].wgt.value,
                            document.forms[0].hgt.value)'/>
                        Weight: <input type="text" name="wgt" size="4"
                    onchange = 'if (document.forms[0].hgt.value!=0)
                        document.forms[0].ans.value= BMI(scale,
                            document.forms[0].wgt.value,
                            document.forms[0].hgt.value)'/>
                        BMI: <input type="text" name="ans" size="4"/>
                </td></tr>
            <tr><td><b> Electronic Coin Flip </b></td>
                <td class="right">
                    <input type="button" value="Flip" onclick='flipCoin()'/>
                    Outcome: <input type="text" name="oc" size="4"/>
                    Heads: <input type="text" name="nH" size="3" value="0"/>
                    Tails: <input type="text" name="nT" size="3" value="0"/>
                </td></tr>
            <tr><td><b> I'm thinking of a number from 1 to </b>
                <input type="text" name='limit' size="2" value="10"
                    onchange='if (document.forms[0].limit.value > 0)
                        topEnd=document.forms[0].limit.value;
                    else
                        document.forms[0].limit.value="?"'/></td>
                <td class="right"><input type="button" value="Pick"
                    onclick='document.forms[0].res.value=randNum(topEnd)+1'/>
                    a number from the range:
                    <input type="text" name="res" size="4"/>
            <tr><td><b>Convert between Fahrenheit and Celsius</b></td>
                <td class="right"><input type="button" value="     Convert     "
                    onclick="window.open('temperature.html', 'jack',
                        'resizable=yes')"/>
                </td></tr>
            <tr><td><b> Count and Score </b></td>
                <td class="right"><input type="button" value="       Count       "
                    onclick="window.open('counter.html', 'jill',
                        'resizable=yes')"/>
                </td></tr>
```

```
            <tr>
                <!--- The standard form for the links is . . .
                    <br /><b>topic name . . . </b>
                    <a href='http:// url goes here'>anchor term(s) here</a> |
                So, just copy/paste/edit it.-->
                <td colspan = "2" style="text-align:left"><h4>IMPORTANT
                    LINKS</h4>
                    <b> Resource Links ...</b>
                    <a href='http://dictionary.cambridge.org'>Cambridge
                        Dictionary</a> |
                     <a href='http://www.wordsmyth.net'>Thesaurus</a> |
                     <a href="http://www.etymonline.com/">Etymology
                        Dictionary</a>
                <br /><b>Classes . . . </b>
                    <a href='http://www.cs.washington.edu/100/'>Fluency
                        Home Page</a> |
                    <a href='http://www.chemsoc.org/viselements/pages/
                        pertable_j.htm'>Periodic Table</a> |
                    <a href='https://www.cia.gov/library/publications/
                        the-world-factbook/'> CIA Fact Book</a>
                <br /><b>XHTML References . . . </b>
                    <a href="http://www.w3schools.com/css/
                        css_reference.asp">CSS Ref</a> |
                    <a href="http://www.w3schools.com/css/
                        css_colornames.asp">Color Names</a> |
                    <a href="http://www.w3schools.com/tags/
                        default.asp">XHTML Tags</a> |
                    <a href="http://http://www.w3schools.com/tags/
                        ref_symbols.asp">Odd Symbols</a>
                </td>
            </tr>
        </table>
        </form>
    <script type="text/javascript">
        var today = new Date();       // Get today's date
        var myBdate = new Date();     // Get a date object to modify
        var difference;               // Declare a temporary variable
        myBdate.setFullYear(1990);    // Set my birth year to 1990
        myBdate.setMonth(6);          // Set my birth mo to July (mos start at 0)
        myBdate.setDate(4);           // Set my birth day to 4th
        myBdate.setHours(12);         // Set my hour of birth to noon
        myBdate.setMinutes(0);        // Set my minute of birth to o'clock
        myBdate.setSeconds(0);        // Set my second of birth on the hour
        difference = today.getTime() - myBdate.getTime();
        difference = Math.floor(difference/1000);
        document.write("<p> I'm " + difference + " seconds old. What
            <i>am</i> I doing with my life?</p>");
    </script>
  </body>
</html>
```

How Cool Page of temperature.html

```
<!DOCTYPE html PUBLIC "-//W3C//DTD XHTML 1.0 Strict//EN"
"http://www.w3.org/TR/xhtml1/DTD/xhtml1-strict.dtd">
<html xmlns="http://www.w3.org/1999/xhtml">
    <head>
        <meta http-equiv="Content-Type" content="text/html; charset=utf-8"/>
        <title>Conversion</title>
        <style type="text/css">
            body   {background-color : dodgerblue; font-family : optima;
                        color: midnightblue; text-align : center}
            p      {font-size : x-large}
        </style>
    </head>
  <body>
    <h1>How Cool Is It? </h1>
    <script type="text/javascript">
      function convertC2F (tempInC) {
        return 9/5*tempInC + 32;
      }
      function convertF2C (tempInF) {
        return 5/9*(tempInF - 32);
      }
    </script>
    <form activity="">
      <p> Celsius temperature:
        <input type="text" name="textTempC" size="4"
          onchange="document.forms[0].textTempF.value
          =convertC2F(document.forms[0].textTempC.value)"/>&#176; C</p>
      <p> Fahrenheit temperature:
        <input type="text" name="textTempF" size="4"
          onchange="document.forms[0].textTempC.value
          =convertF2C(document.forms[0].textTempF.value)"/>&#176; F</p>
    </form>
  </body>
</html>
```

Every Little Bit Page of counter.html

```
<!DOCTYPE html PUBLIC "-//W3C//DTD XHTML 1.0 Strict//EN"
"http://www.w3.org/TR/xhtml1/DTD/xhtml1-strict.dtd">
<html xmlns="http://www.w3.org/1999/xhtml">
    <head>
    <meta http-equiv="Content-Type" content="text/html; charset=utf-8"/>
        <title>Counter Assistant</title>
        <style type="text/css">
            body {background-color : blueviolet; color : white; font-family : optima;
                text-align : center}
            table {margin-left : auto; margin-right : auto}
        </style>
    </head>
```

```
    <body>
        <h2>Every Little Bit Counts<i style="color : hotpink">!</i></h2>
        <script type="text/javascript">
            var count1=0, count2=0, count3=0, count4=0;
            function row(num) {
                document.write('<tr><td> <input type="button" value="Count"' );
                document.write(' onclick="count'+num+'=count'+num+'+1;' );
                document.write(' document.forms[0].arch'+num+'.value
                    =count'+num+'"/></td>' );
                document.write('<td><input type="text" size="5" name
                    ="arch'+num+'"/></td>' );
                document.write('<td><input type="text" size="20" name
                    ="what'+num+'"/></td>' );
                document.write('<td><input type="button" value="C" ' );
                document.write( ' onclick="document.forms[0].arch'+num+'.value
                    ='+"' ';" );
                document.write("document.forms[0].what"+num+".value=' ';" );
                document.write('count'+num+'=0"/></td></tr>' );
            }
        </script>
        <form activity="">
            <table>
                <tr><th> </th><th> Total </th><th> Meaning </th>
                    <th>Clear</th></tr>
                <script type="text/javascript">
                    row(1); row(2); row(3); row(4);
                </script>
            </table>
        </form>
    </body>
</html>
```

appendix

Smooth Motion Program

THE FOLLOWING XHTML and JavaScript code produces the Smooth Motion program in Chapter 22 (Figure 22.1).

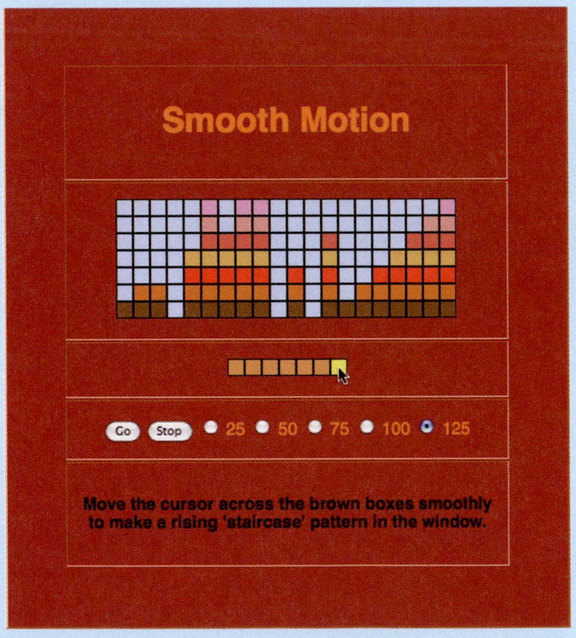


```
<!DOCTYPE html PUBLIC "-//W3C//DTD XHTML 1.0 Strict//EN"
    "http://www.w3.org/TR/xhtml1/DTD/xhtml1-strict.dtd">
<html xmlns="http://www.w3.org/1999/xhtml">
    <head>
        <meta http-equiv="Content-Type" content="text/html;
                charset=utf-8"/>
```

```
    <title>Smooth Motion Application</title>
    <style type="text/css">
        body  {background-color : white; color : #ff6600;
                  font-family : helvetica; text-align : center}
        table {margin-left : auto; margin-right : auto;
                  background-color : #a80000; padding : 5%}
        td    {padding : 15px}
    </style>
</head>
<body>
    <table border="2">
        <tr><td>
            <h1>Smooth Motion</h1>
        </td></tr>
        <tr><td>
            <script type="text/javascript">
                var j;                                  //Declare iter var
                var duration = 125, timerId;            // vars
                var pics = new Array(8);                // array
                var keypix = new Array(2);
                var next1 = 0, frame = -1;
                for (j = 0; j < 8; j++) {               //Initial img array
                    pics[j] = new Image();
                }
                for (j = 0; j < 8; j++) {               //Prefetch images
                    pics[j].src = "gifpix/Stack" + j + ".gif";
                }
                for (j = 0; j < 20; j++) {              //Place grid imgs
                    document.write('<img src="gifpix/Stack0.gif" alt=" "/>');
                }
            </script>
        </td></tr>
        <tr><td>
            <script type="text/javascript">
                keypix[0] = new Image();
                keypix[1] = new Image();
                keypix[0].src = "gifpix/OrangeBox.gif";
                keypix[1].src = "gifpix/YellowBox.gif";
                for (j = 0; j < 7; j++) {
                    document.write('<img src="gifpix/OrangeBox.gif" ' +
                    'onmouseover = "here(' + j + ')" ' +
                    'onmouseout = "gone(' + j + ')"  alt=" "/>');
                }
            </script>
        </td></tr>
        <tr><td>
            <form action="">
                <input type="button" value="Go"
                    onclick='timerId=setTimeout("animate()",duration)'/>
                <input type="button" value="Stop"
                    onclick="clearTimeout(timerId)"/>
```

```
                <input type="radio" name="speed" onclick="duration=25"/> 25
                <input type="radio" name="speed" onclick="duration=50"/> 50
                <input type="radio" name="speed" onclick="duration=75"/> 75
                <input type="radio" name="speed" onclick="duration=100"/> 100
                <input type="radio" name="speed" onclick="duration=125"
                    checked="checked"/> 125
            </form>
        </td></tr>
        <tr><td>
            <p style="color : black"><b>
                Move the cursor across the brown boxes smoothly <br/>
                to make a rising 'staircase' pattern in the
                window.</b></p>
        </td></tr>
    </table>
    <script type="text/javascript">
        timerId = setTimeout("animate()", 5000);                //Initial timer
        function animate() {
            shiftGrid()
            checkStairAndContinue();
        }
        function shiftGrid() {
            for (j = 0; j < 19; j++) {
                document.images[j].src = document.images[j+1].src;
            }
            if (frame == -1)
                document.images[19].src = pics[randNum(8)].src;
            else
                document.images[19].src = pics[frame].src;
        }
        function checkStairAndContinue() {
            if (frame == next1)
                next1 = next1 + 1;
            else
                next1 = 1;
            if (next1 != 8)
                timerId = setTimeout("animate()",duration);
        }
        function here (pos) {
            document.images[20+pos].src = "gifpix/YellowBox.gif";
            frame = pos + 1;
        }
        function gone (pos) {
            document.images[20+pos].src = "gifpix/OrangeBox.gif";
            frame = 0;
        }
        function randNum (range) {                              //Rand No. fcn from
            return Math.floor(range * Math.random());           // Chapter 20
        }
    </script>
  </body>
</html>
```

Glossary

1-way cipher, *see* one-way cipher

419 fraud, the name for advance-fee fraud derived from the applicable section number of the Nigerian Criminal Code

802.11 (eight-oh-two eleven), wireless communications protocol

A

absolute cell reference, an address or pointer that does not change; in a spreadsheet, a cell with an absolute reference does not change even if copied

absolute pathname, navigation information for locating files in HTML using complete URLs

abstract, to remove an idea, concept, or process from a specific situation

abstraction, the central idea or concept removed from a situation

ADC, *see* analog-to-digital converter

administrative authority, having the ability to access all functions of a computer or software system, including overriding passwords; also called *superuser*

administrator, one who has complete access to a computer system; also called *superuser*

advance-fee fraud, an online scam often called the *Nigerian Widow scam* or the *419 fraud*

algorithm, a precise and systematic method for producing a specified result

algorithmic thinking, devising algorithms that achieve specific goals and solve problems effectively

alphanumeric, describing characters or text as being composed solely of letters, numbers, and possibly a few special characters like spaces and tabs, but not punctuation

ALU, *see* arithmetic/logic unit

American Standard Code for Information Interchange (ASCII), a standard for assigning numerical values to the letters in the Roman alphabet and to typographical characters; pronounced *AS·key*

analog signal, a continuously varying representation of a phenomenon, e.g., a sound wave

analog-to-digital converter (ADC), in digitizing sound, takes the continuous sound wave and samples it at regular intervals, outputting binary numbers that are written to memory for each sample

anchor tag, the HTML tag that specifies a link, or the text associated with the reference that is highlighted in the document

anchor text, the highlighted (often blue) text indicating the presence of a hyperlink

AND-query, a search request for items in which all keywords must apply

append, to add to the end of an existing structure

applet, a small application program, often written in Java, which is executed on a client

arguments, the values given for the function's parameters in a function call

arithmetic/logic unit (ALU), a subsystem of a computer that performs the operations of an instruction

arithmetic operators, the symbols of basic arithmetic

array, a multi-element variable in a programming language, formed from a base name indexed by one or more integers

array element, an indexed item; also called an *element*

array length, the number of elements of an array; also the array size

array reference, the specification of an element of an array by giving the array name and index or index expression

ASCII, *see* American Standard Code for Information Interchange

assembly language, a symbolic form of a binary machine language

assignment statement, a programming command expressed with a variable on the left and a variable or expression on the right of an assignment symbol, usually =

asynchronous communication, indicates that the actions of senders and receivers occur at separate times, as in the exchange of email

atomic, in database theory, treating data as primitive or undecomposable

attribute, in HTML, a parameter used within the tags to specify additional information; in a database, a property of an entity; also called a *field*

authoritative name server, a computer of the Domain Name System that knows for its domain the identity of all computers and domains in it

automated reply, a function of mail servers that allows a user to set up a message saying that he or she is temporarily away and unable to reply to emails; also called a *vacation message*

B

b, abbreviation for bit, e.g., Kb is kilobits

B, abbreviation for byte, e.g., KB is kilobytes

backdoor access, a program that enters a computer and configures it so that it can be controlled remotely without the user's awareness

bandwidth, the bit-transmission capacity of a channel, usually measured in bits per second

base, the number that is raised to various powers to generate the counting units of a number system; e.g., the base of the decimal system is 10 and the base of the binary system is 2; also called *radix*

binary, having two related components

binary number, a quantity expressed in radix 2 number representation

binary object file, a program form directly executable by a computer, often shortened to *binary*

binary operator, an operator such as addition (+) having two operands

binary system, any information encoding using symbols formed from two patterns; also called *PandA representation* in this book

bit, basic unit of information representation having two states, usually denoted as 0 and 1

bit-mapped, as in bit-mapped display, indicates that the display's video image is stored pixel-by-pixel in the computer's memory

blazing away, assertively trying unfamiliar software by exploring its features

Boolean, having the property of being either true or false

boot, to start a computer and load its operating system

broadcast communication, a type of transmission of information from one sender to all receivers

browsing information, on a Web page, used for casual perusing; contrast with *navigational information*

bug, an error in a computer, program, or process

byte, a sequence of eight bits treated as a unit

C

cable, a bundle of wires carrying power and/or signals between computer components; also called *cord* or *wires*

candidate key, a relational database field that could potentially be chosen as the table's key

card, a small printed circuit board plugged into a motherboard to provide additional functionality; also called a *daughter board*

Cascading Style Sheets (CSS), a system for globally styling Web pages written in HTML

cathode ray tube (CRT), a video display technology

cell, in a spreadsheet, the intersection of a row and a column

cell range, in a spreadsheet, a naming scheme that allows the user to refer to a group of cells by naming the first cell and the last cell and placing a colon (:) in between

CGI, *see* Common Gateway Interface

channel, the physical medium, e.g., wires, over which signals are sent; in silicon technology, the area under the gate of a transistor

character, an uppercase or lowercase Latin letter, Arabic numeral, or English punctuation; can be used generally to include the alphabet and punctuation for other natural languages

cipher text, in a cryptosystem, an encrypted form of the cleartext

class, a family of styling specifications in CSS given a common name

classifier, a component of an optical character recognition system that ranks characters by the probability that they match a given set of features

cleartext, information before encryption or after decryption

click event, the result caused by a user clicking a command button

clicking around, exploring a user interface

click-with-shift, a GUI command in which the Shift key is pressed while the mouse selects an item to avoid deselecting the items already selected; also called *shift-select*

client, a computer that receives the services in a client/server structure

client/server structure, a relationship between two computers in which the client computer requests services from the server computer

clock, in computing, determines the rate of the Fetch/Execute Cycle

CMOS (Complementary Metal Oxide Semiconductor), the most widely used integrated circuit technology; pronounced *SEE·moss*

collating sequence, an ordering for a set of symbols used to sort them; for example, alphabetical ordering

command button, an image in a GUI that looks like a physical button used to cause an operation to be performed; the HTML button input control

Common Gateway Interface (CGI), an extension to HTML allowing browsers to cause a Web server to run programs on their behalf with specific data

compile, to translate programming language into language a computer can interpret (machine language)

compliance/enforcement, how organizations meet their obligations regarding privacy issues

compound statement, in programming, a group of statements surrounded by curly braces to become a single statement

compression, encoding information with fewer bits than a given representation by exploiting properties of regularity or unimportance

compression ratio, the factor by which compression reduces an encoding from its uncompressed size

computable, a task that can be performed by a computer; algorithmic

computer, a device that deterministically follows instructions to process information

concatenation, in programming, to join strings

conditional or **conditional statement**, a programming statement, usually identified by `if`, that optionally executes statements depending on the outcome of a Boolean test

conditional formatting, controlling the display of text in spreadsheet cells based on the values stored in the cell

conditional formulas, spreadsheet formulas that use the `IF()` function

continuation test, a Boolean expression to determine whether an iteration statement will execute its statement sequence again; also called a *termination test*

control unit, a subsystem of a computer that is the hardware implementation of the Fetch/Execute Cycle

cookie, information stored on a Web client computer by an HTTP server computer

copyright, the legal protection of many forms of intellectual property

cracker, a person who attempts to break a code

crawler, a program that navigates the Internet, cataloging and indexing Web pages by the words they contain for use by a query processor

CRT, *see* cathode ray tube

cryptography, the study of encryption and decryption methods

cryptosystem, collective term for operations to encrypt and decrypt information

CSS, see *Cascading Style Sheets*

cycle power, to turn a computer off, wait a moment, and then turn it back on

D

DAC, *see* digital-to-analog converter

daemon, a program that periodically "wakes up" to perform a system management task

data controller, in Fair Information Practices, the person who sets policies, responds to individuals regarding information, and is accountable for those policies and actions

Data Fetch (DF), the third step in the Fetch/Execute Cycle; the action of retrieving the instruction's operands from memory

data types, the different kinds of values of a programming language; also called *value types*

database operations, select, project, union, difference, and product; often includes join
database query, an operation that creates a database view
database scheme or **schema**, the declaration of entities and relationships of a database
database view, a restructured version of the data designed for a specific user
daughter board, a small printed circuit board plugged into a motherboard to provide additional functionality; also called a *card*
debugging, the act of discovering why a system does not work properly
declaration command, in programming, the command used to declare variables
declaring variables, stating what variables will be used in a program
decrement, an amount by which a variable is decreased; a negative increment
decrypt, to recover the original information from a digitally encrypted representation; also called *digitally decrypt*
definiteness, a property of algorithms requiring that a specific sequence of steps is defined
definitional list, in HTML, a list form usually comprising a sequence of terms and their definitions
delimited or **delimited by**, ends with
device driver, software that enables a computer to communicate with a peripheral device
DF, *see* Data Fetch
DHCP, *see* Dynamic Host Configuration Protocol
digital signal, a discrete or step levels representation of a phenomenon, varying instantaneously
digital subscriber line (DSL), a dedicated connection to an Internet service provider
digital-to-analog converter (DAC), in playing sound, creates an electrical wave by interpolation between the digital values; the signal is input to a speaker, which converts it to a sound wave
digitally decrypt, to recover the original information from a digitally encrypted representation; also called *decrypt*
digitally encrypt, to transform a digital representation so that the information cannot be readily discerned; also called *encrypt*
digitize, originally to encode with decimal numerals, now to encode in bits
directory, a named collection of files, other directories, or both; also called a *folder*
directory hierarchy, the complete file structure of a computer
discrete, distinct or separable; not able to be changed by continuous variation
disk, a magnetic medium (floppy or hard)
display rate, in animation, the frequency with which images are changed
DNS, *see* Domain Name System
Document Object Model (DOM), the browser's representation (data structure) for the components of a Web page
DOM, *see* Document Object Model
domain, in networking, a related set of networked computers, e.g., `.edu` is the set of education-related computers
Domain Name System (DNS), the collection of Internet-connected computers that translate domain addresses into IP addresses
dot operator, in JavaScript, provides a means of navigation to the proper object
download, to transfer information from a server to a client
drop-down, menu type in a GUI; when selected, a menu drops down and is displayed; also called a *pull-down menu*
DSL, *see* digital subscriber line
dual booting, loading two operating systems at once
Dynamic Host Configuration Protocol (DHCP), a networking protocol in which an IP address is assigned to a computer at startup and returned at shutdown.

E

eCommerce, electronic commerce; the use of electronic data communication to conduct business
effectiveness, a property of algorithms requiring that all instructions are performed mechanically within the capabilities of the executing agent
element, an indexed item; also called an *array element*
email attachment, a file that is sent with an email message
emoticon, a character sequence that is common in email and that expresses an emotion by its physical form, e.g., the "smiley face" :) or ☺ to express happiness or humor
empty string, a character sequence of zero length
empty table, in a database, a table with name and column headings, but no rows
encrypt, to transform a digital representation so that the information cannot be readily discerned; also called *digitally encrypt*
end tag, the second of a pair of tags, such as `</i>`
entity, something that can be identified by a fixed number of its characteristics
entity instance, a specific data value for an entity
entity-relationship diagram (ER diagram), a visual illustration of some or all of a database

schema in which relationships are drawn as arrows between boxes that represent entities

ER diagram, *see* entity-relationship diagram

escape symbol, a character, often & or \, that is a prefix to another character or word used to enlarge a character's encoding, e.g., &infinity to encode ∞

evaluation function, in computer games, e.g., in chess, a procedure that assigns a numerical value to each piece, accounts for captures and board position, and computes a score for the move

even parity, a property of binary numbers in which the number of 1-bits is even

event, an indication from the operating system that a mouse click or other action has occurred

event-based programming, a programming style that responds to events, such as mouse clicks

event handler, the program that performs the task that responds to an event

event-handling attribute, in JavaScript, tells the browser how to respond to an event like onClick

EX, *see* Instruction Execution

Exchange Sort, a standard algorithm that compares pairs of items chosen in a particular way

execute, to perform the instructions of a program, usually by a computer; to run a program

exploit, in computer security, a program that takes advantage of a security vulnerability in software

expression, in programming, a formula-like description of how to compute a value

Extended ASCII, improved standard character representation with 256 symbols, enough to encode English and Western European languages

Extensible Hypertext Markup Language (XHTML), a W3C standard dialect of HTML compatible with XML.

Extensible Markup Language (XML), a W3C standard for structured information encoding

Extensible Stylesheet Language (XSL), a Web standard language for specifying formatting information for XML

F

factor, in arithmetic, any number that divides a given number evenly, i.e., without a remainder

factor of improvement, the amount by which a first measurement must be multiplied to be equivalent to the second measurement when computing scale of change

fail-safe, in software, a program that stops operating to avoid harm

fail-soft, in software, a program that continues to operate but with possibly degraded functionality

fair use, a concept in copyright law in which copyright limitations are waived for explicitly listed, socially valuable purposes

feature, a component of a character in an optical character recognition system

feedback, in a GUI, an indication that the computer is working or has completed a request

Fetch/Execute Cycle, the basic instruction execution process of a computer

field, in a database, a property of an entity; also called an *attribute*

field effect transistor, in semiconductors, a device used to control conductivity

field inputs, character input, such as telephone numbers, with a specific structure

file extension, the letters after the last dot in a file name giving the file's type, e.g., .pdf

file structure, directories and files of a computer

file type, the kind of information in a file describing how it is to be processed

fill handle or **tab**, in a spreadsheet, used to drag a selection to extend a series or fill a selection

filling, in a spreadsheet, automated copying and pasting; allows the user to replicate the contents of a cell

filtering, a process (especially in spreadsheets) for selecting items based on one or more criteria

finiteness, a property of algorithms requiring that they terminate with the intended result or an indication that no solution is possible

firewall, a barrier between two computers on a network, or between the Internet and a personal computer

flame-a-thon, email battle; also called a *flame war*

flame war, nasty email exchanges in which many uninvolved users are copied

floppy disk (drive), a storage device that provides persistent memory using (removable) diskettes

focus words, search terms chosen to identify more authoritative sites

folder, a named collection of files, other directories, or both; also called a *directory*

for loop, a common programming structure for iterating a sequence of instructions over a regular range of index values

foreign data, data from another application that one wants to import into a spreadsheet

foreign key, in a database, a field in a record that points to a key field of another database record in another table

form, in HTML, used to collect user input, e.g., when ordering a product on the Web

formal language, a synthetic notation designed for expressing algorithms and programs

formula, in a spreadsheet, an expression that indicates how data in a specific number of cells should be calculated
frame, in animation, one of many images rapidly redrawn to create the illusion of motion
frame grabber, in OCR, an electronic device that recognizes when to snap an image and send it to a computer for processing
freeware, software available on the Web at no cost
frequency, in sound, the number of waves per second
full backup, a complete copy of a body of information usually performed at a specific point in time
function, a programming structure with a name, optional parameter list, and a definition that encapsulates an algorithm
function body, the definition of a function's computation
function declaration, the specification of a function, including its name, parameters, and body
function definition, a function body, the program implementing the function; one of three parts of a function declaration
functional composition, the ability to create software by combining other software
functions, in a spreadsheet, for computing common summary operations such as totals, maximums, averages, etc.

G

game tree, a conceptualization of the possible future configurations of a multiperson game
garbage, in a database, inconsistent data
gate, a part of a transistor that controls the flow of charge
GB, *see* gigabyte
generalization, statement of a rule deduced by generalizing
generalize, to formulate an idea, concept, or process so that it abstracts multiple situations
GIF (Graphics Interchange Format), file extension, e.g., `picture.gif`, that specifies a graphic image format; pronounced with either a soft or hard *g*
giga-, prefix for billion; pronounced with a hard *g*
gigabyte, 1 billion (exactly 1,073,741,824) bytes
gigahertz, one billion cycles per second
global variable, a variable declared outside the scope of a function, usually at the start of a program
graphical user interface (GUI), the synthesized visual medium of interaction between a user and a computer; pronounced *GOO·ey*
GUI, *see* graphical user interface

H

Halting Problem, determining if a computation halts for a given input; a problem that cannot be solved by a computer
handle, in programming, a binary value returned by a function or server and used for subsequent references
haptic device, an input/output technology that interfaces with the sense of touch
hard disk, a high-capacity, persistent peripheral storage device; also called a *disk* or *hard drive*
hard drive, *see* hard disk
hardware, the physical implementation of a computer, usually electronic, which includes the processor, memory, and typically its peripheral devices
hard-wired, in a computer, operations done directly with wires and transistors
heuristic, a guideline used to solve a problem that usually results in a solution; for example, "when looking for a lost item check the last place you had it"
hex digit, one of the sixteen numerals of hexadecimal, 0, 1, 2, 3, 4, 5, 6, 7, 8, 9, A, B, C, D, E, F
hexadecimal, radix 16 number representation
hierarchical index, a structure for organizing information using descriptive terms that partition the information
hierarchy, an organizing structure composed of a sequence of levels that partition all items so that those of one level are partitioned into smaller groups at the next level
high-level programming languages, used in all software programming today; programs are compiled into assembly languages, which are then assembled into binary
hit, in a Web search, a match to a query; for a Web site, a visit
hop, in networking, the transfer of a packet or message to an adjacent router
HTML, *see* Hypertext Markup Language
HTTP, *see* Hypertext Transfer Protocol
hyperlink, a mechanism that allows the linear sequence of text to be interrupted to visit another location, and return to the point of interruption
hyperlink reference, the destination Web address of a hyperlink
Hypertext Markup Language (HTML), a notation for specifying the form of a Web page to a browser
Hypertext Transfer Protocol (HTTP), the rules governing the interaction between client and server on the Web
Hz (Hertz), cycles, or repetitions per second

I

IC, *see* integrated circuit
icon, a graphic that pictorially describes a thing or action
ID, *see* Instruction Decode
identifier, a legal sequence of letters, numerals, or punctuation marks forming the name of variable, file, directory, etc.
identity theft, the crime of posing as someone else for fraudulent purposes
`if/else` statement, a programming structure that allows the conditional execution of statements based on the outcome of a Boolean test
IF, *see* Instruction Fetch
image object, a blank instance of an image
image tag, a singleton HTML tag used to place an image in a document, e.g., `<img ... />`
inconsistency, in a database, the same information stored differently in rows or tables
increment, in JavaScript, the next iteration computation; it almost always increases the value of the iteration variable
index, in information structures, an organizing mechanism used to find information in a large collection; in programming, the number that together with an identifier forms an array reference
index origin, the number at which indexing begins; the least index
index value, the result of evaluating an index expression; the number of an array element
indexing, in programming, the mechanism of associating a number and an identifier to locate an element
infix operator, a binary operator, e.g., +, whose syntax requires that it is written between its operands, as in 4 + 3
initialization, in JavaScript, the first operation of a `for` loop
initialize, in JavaScript, setting the initial value of a variable as part of the declaration
input, data put into a communication system for transmission or into a computer system for processing
Input Unit, a subsystem of a computer transferring information from the physical world via an input device to the computer's memory
input/output (I/O), in a computer, transferring data between the memory and a peripheral device
instance, one of whatever type of information the application processes; the current values of an entity, table, or database
Instruction Decode (ID), the second step in the Fetch/Execute Cycle; the action of determining which operation is to be performed and computing the addresses of the operands
Instruction Execution (EX), the fourth step in the Fetch/Execute Cycle; the action of performing a machine instruction
Instruction Fetch (IF), the first step in the Fetch/Execute Cycle; the action of retrieving a machine instruction from the memory address given by the program counter
instruction interpretation, the process of executing a program
integer, a whole number; in programming, a data type for a whole number, either positive or negative
integrated circuit (IC), a complex set of electronic components and their interconnections that are etched or imprinted on a computer chip
integration, in silicon technology, the ability to fabricate both active and connective parts of a circuit using a family of compatible materials in a single complexity-independent process
intellectual property, creations of the human mind that have value to others
Internet, the total of all wires, fibers, switches, routers, satellite links, and other hardware used to transport information between named computers
Internet Protocol address (IP address), a unique address given to each computer connected to the Internet composed of four numbers in the range 0–255
Internet service provider (ISP), a utility that connects private and business computers to the Internet
interpolation, filling in intermediate values between two points
interpret, to follow a computer program's instruction
intersect, to determine if two data objects have members in common
intractable, a description for computations solvable by computer in principle, but not in practice
intranet, local network that supports communication within an organization and connects to the Internet by a gateway
invoke (a function or operation), to call a function or cause an operation to perform
IP, acronym for Internet Protocol
IP address, *see* Internet Protocol address
IP packet, a fixed quantum of information packaged together with an IP address and other data for sending information over the Internet
ISO, acronym for the International Standards Organization

ISO-8859-1, an international standard for encoding into binary alphabets used in North American and Western European languages
ISP, *see* Internet service provider
iteration, in programming, looping through a series of statements to repeat them
iteration statement, in programming, a loop that repeatedly executes a statement
iteration variable, any variable controlling an iteration statement, e.g., a `for` statement

J

JavaScript, a programming language
JPEG, acronym for Joint Photographic Experts Group, a committee of the ISO; pronounced *JAY·peg*
JPG, file extension, e.g., `picture.jpg`, for JPEG encoding

K

Kb, kilobits
KB, kilobytes
key, in a database, field(s) that make the rows of an entity (table) unique; in cryptography, selectable code used to encrypt and subsequently decrypt information
key escrow, in encryption software, registering a secret key with a trusted third party
kilo-, prefix for thousand; if prefixing a quantity counted in binary, e.g., memory, prefix for 1,024

L

LAN, *see* local area network
latency, the time required to deliver or generate information
LCD, *see* liquid crystal display
length (of an array), the number of elements in an array
lexical structure, a specification of the form of character input; e.g., telephone numbers in North America are formed of ten Arabic numerals with a space following the third and a hyphen following the sixth
liquid crystal display (LCD), a video display technology
list-server, a mailing list application
local area network (LAN), a network connecting computers within a small physical space such as a building; acronym usually pronounced
local variable, a variable declared within a function
logical and, in programming, the operator && that represents "and"
logical not, in programming, the operator ! that changes its operand to the opposite logical value
logical operator, a connective (*and*, *or*, or *not)*
logical or, in programming, the operator || that represents "or"
lossless compression, the process of reducing the number of bits required to represent information in which the original form can be exactly reconstructed
lossy compression, the process of reducing the number of bits required to represent information in which the original cannot be exactly reconstructed

M

machine language, computer instructions expressed in binary, respecting the form required for a specific machine
malware, collective term for software intended to compromise or do harm to a computer
many-to-one, in a database, a relation where many rows of one table refer to one row of a second table
mask, in fabrication technology, a material similar to a photographic negative containing the pattern to be transferred to the silicon surface in the process of constructing a chip
MB, *see* megabyte
mega-, prefix for million; if prefixing a quantity in binary, e.g., memory, prefix for 1,048,576
megabyte (MB), 1 million (exactly 1,048,576) bytes
megahertz (MHz), 1 million cycles per second
memory, a device capable of storing information, usually in fixed-size, addressable units; a subsystem of a computer used to store programs and their data while they execute
memory address, a whole number that designates a specific location in a computer's memory
menu, a list of available operations from which a user can select by clicking on one item
meta-brackets, angle brackets, < and >, used to enclose syntactically defined terms
metadata, information describing the properties of other information
metaphor, an object or an idea used as an analogy in computing, e.g., a desktop
metarules, in programming, rules that describe how to operate on other rules
MHz, *see* megahertz
microprocessor, component of a computer that computes or performs instructions; also called a *processor*
mnemonic, an aid for remembering something
moderator, a person responsible for deciding what is to be sent to a mailing list

modulus operation, in JavaScript, divides two integers and returns the remainder
monitor, a computer's video output device or display; also called a *screen*
monolithic, a computer having all its devices bundled together, e.g., an Apple iMac or a laptop
MOS (Metal Oxide Semiconductor), a transistor made of metal, oxide, and semiconductors (cross sections, top to bottom)
motherboard, contains the processor chip, memory, and other computer electronics; also called a *printed circuit*
MPEG (Motion Picture Experts Group), a committee of the ISO; pronounced *EM·peg*
MPG, file extension, e.g., `flick.mpg`, for MPEG encoding
multicast, a type of transmission of information from one sender to many receivers

N

name conflict, the attempt to give a different definition, e.g., variable declaration, to an identifier with an existing meaning
navigation, in searching, following a series of links to locate specific information often in a hierarchy
nested conditionals, in JavaScript, an `if` statement as the `then` or `else` statement of another conditional
nested loop, the condition of a loop (inner loop) appearing in the statement sequence of another loop (outer loop)
netiquette, Internet etiquette
new line, in word processing, represented by ↲ or ¶
NOT-queries, a search request for items in which no keywords are to apply
NP-complete problems, a measure of difficulty of problems believed to be intractable for computers
Nyquist rule, a digitization guideline stating that the sampling frequency should exceed the signal frequency by at least two times

O

OCR, *see* optical character recognition
one-way cipher, a form of encryption that cannot easily be reversed, i.e., decrypted, often used for passwords
operand, the data used in computer instructions; the value(s) that operators operate on
operating system (OS), software that performs tasks for the computer; it controls input and output, keeps track of files and directories, and controls peripheral devices such as disk drives and printers
operationally attuned, applying what one knows about how a device or system works to simplify its use
operator, in programming, a symbol used to perform an operation on some value
operator overloading, a property of some programming languages in which operators like + have different meanings depending on their operand data types, e.g., + used for both addition and concatenation in JavaScript
optical character recognition (OCR), a computer application in which printed text is converted to the ASCII letters that represent it
Opt-in/Opt-out, the choice of approving or objecting to a use of information
OR-queries, a search request for items in which one or more of the keywords apply
OS, *see* operating system
output, the information produced by a program or process from a specific input
Output Unit, a subsystem of a computer that transfers information from the computer's memory to the physical world via an output device
overflow exception, an error condition for operations such as addition, in which a result is too large to be represented in the available number of bits

P

p2p, acronym for peer-to-peer
PageRank, in Google, computing the importance of a Web page based on its relevancy, determined by links to that page
PandA, in this book, a mnemonic for "present and absent encoding," the fundamental physical representation of information; also called *binary encoding*
paragraph symbol (¶), represents a new line in some word processing programs
parallel computation, the use of multiple computers to solve a single problem
parameter, an input to a function
parity, refers to whether a number is even or odd
partial backup, new information copied to another medium that has been added to a system since the last full or partial backup
partitionings, in hierarchies, a classification where leaves appear only once
password, a sequence of characters that one must input to gain access to a file, application, or computer system
pathname, the sequence following the IP address; tells the server which file (page) is requested and where to find it

PC, acronym for program counter, printed circuit (board), and personal computer

peer-to-peer, a communication protocol in which processors are equals; contrast with *client/server structure*

peripherals, devices connected to a computer, usually for I/O purposes

PERT (Program Evaluation and Review Technique) chart, a task-dependency graph used by systems engineers and managers in project management; acronym pronounced

phishing, a social engineering technique to trick people into voluntarily giving up personal (security) information; short for password harvesting fishing

photolithography, a process of transferring a pattern by means of light shown through a mask or negative

photoresist, a material used in a silicon chip fabrication process that is chemically changed by light, allowing it to be patterned by a mask

physical database, in a database, the tables stored on the disk drive

picture element or **pixel**, the smallest displayable unit of a video monitor

pins, stiff wires in a cable's plug that insert into sockets to make the connection

pixel, contraction for picture element

place value, in decimal numbers, positions representing the next higher power of 10, starting from the right

placeholder technique, a searching algorithm in which strings are temporarily replaced with a special character to protect them from change by other substitution commands

plaintext, synonym for *cleartext*

point-to-point communication, a type of transmission of information from one sender to one receiver

pop-up, a menu type in a GUI that is displayed at the cursor position when the mouse is clicked

power cable, connects a computer system to a power supply

power switch, in a monolithic computer system, turns the system on and off

precedence, the relationship among operators describing which is to be performed first

predicate, the Boolean expression in a conditional statement that is evaluated to produce a true or false outcome

prefetching, in online animation, the process of loading the images prior to beginning an animation

preformatted, in HTML, text that is enclosed between `<pre>` and `</pre>` tags

primary key, the column in a database table that always has a unique value for every row

primary source, a person who provides information based on direct knowledge or experience

prime number, a number that can only be divided evenly by itself and one

print queue, an operating system's list of in-process or waiting printing jobs

printed circuit, a stiff composite board containing the processor chip, memory, and other computer electronics; also called a *motherboard*

privacy, the right to choose freely the circumstances under which and the extent to which people will reveal themselves, their attitudes, and their behaviors

process, a synonym for *algorithm*

processor, the component of a computer that computes, i.e., performs the instructions; also called a *microprocessor*

processor box, in a component system, houses the computer and most of its parts (hard disk, floppy disk drive, and CD drive

processor core, one of multiple processors fabricated together on a chip

program, an algorithm encoded for a specific situation

program counter, a register in a computer that stores the address of the next instruction to be executed

programming, the act of encoding an algorithm that is to be executed by a computer

properties, stylistic characteristics of a Web page that can be set using the `style` attribute

protocol, a standard procedure for regulating data transmission between computers

public domain, the status of a work in which the copyright owner has explicitly given up rights

public key, a key published by the receiver and used by the sender to encrypt messages

public key cryptosystem, software that uses a public key

pull-down, menu type in a GUI; when selected, a menu drops down and is displayed; also called a *drop-down menu*

Q

QBE, *see* Query By Example

query, database command defining a table expressed using the five database operators

Query By Example (QBE), a method for defining queries in a database

query processor, the part of a search engine that uses the crawler's index to report Web pages associated with keywords provided by a user

quotient-remainder form of division, a means of expressing the division of *a/b* as the solution to the equation $a = b \cdot c + d$, where *c* is the quotient and *d* is the remainder

R

radix, the number that is raised to various powers to generate the counting units of a number system; e.g., the radix of the decimal system is 10 and the radix of the binary system is 2; also called *base*

RAM, *see* random access memory

random access, referencing an item directly; contrast with *sequential access*

random access memory (RAM), a subsystem of a computer used for storing programs and data while they execute; acronym pronounced

reachable configurations, in software, the possible configurations that a program can define

read-only memory (ROM), permanently set memory; acronym pronounced

reboot, to restart a computer by clearing its memory and reloading its operating system

redirection, on the Web, the substitution of one URL for another

redundancy, used to resolve hardware failures by having computers perform computations of a safety critical system and make decisions based on majority vote; in databases, duplicated information

reference, in HTML, the displayed and highlighted portion of an anchor tag

refresh rate, the frequency with which a video display is redisplayed

relational database, a table-based organization for a database in which queries can be specified using relational operators

relational operator, one of six operators ($< \; \leq \; = \; \neq \; \geq \; >$) that compare two values; in JavaScript, one of the six operators (< <= == != >= >)

relationship, a correspondence between two tables of a database

relative cell reference, an address or pointer that changes when the target item is moved or the relationship to it has changed; in a spreadsheet, a cell with a relative reference changes its formula when copied

relative pathname, navigation information for locating an HTML file on the local site

remainder, the whole number less than the devisor that is left after completing a division

replacement string, in editing, the letter sequence that substitutes for the search string

Result Return (RR), the fifth and final step of the Fetch/Execute Cycle, the action of storing in memory the value produced by executing a machine instruction

RGB, red, green, blue; name for a color encoding method

ROM, *see* read-only memory

root element, in XML, the tag that encloses all content in a file

root name server, one of several Internet DNS servers that contain the IP addresses of the top-level domain registry organizations that maintain global domains (.com, .net, .org, .gov, .edu, etc.)

rootkit, malware that directly manipulates operating system tables to hide its presence

router, a computer in a network with several wired connections or a wireless connection to other computers in the network, which forwards arriving traffic to destination computers

row, a set of values for the fields of a table; also called a *tuple*

RR, *see* Result Return

RSA public key cryptosystem, an encryption method invented by Rivest, Shamir, and Adelman

run, what a computer does to a program when one asks it to perform a task

run-length encoding, a representation in which numbers are used to give the lengths of consecutive sequences of 0's or 1's

S

safe software, the goal of software programs to be reliable in safety-critical situations, such as life support

sample, to take measurements at regular intervals, as in sound digitization

sampling rate, the number of samples per second

schema, the abstract structure of an entity or entities; the metadata of a database's tables

scope, in programming, the range of statements over which a variable or other defined object is known

screen, a computer's video output device or display; also called a *monitor*

scroll bar, a slider control appearing at the side and/or bottom of a window when the information cannot be fully displayed

SCSI (Small Computer System Interface), acronym pronounced *scuzzy*

search engine, a software system composed of a crawler and a query processor that helps users locate specific information on the Web or on a specific Web site

search string, the series of characters sought in a text search

search text, in searches, a sequence formed by tokens

seat, to firmly insert a plug into a socket after an initial alignment

secondary source, a person providing information without direct knowledge of or experience with the topic

semiconductor, matter such as silicon capable of conducting, or not conducting, electrons

sequential access, a memory reference pattern in which no item can be referenced without passing (skipping or referencing) the items that precede it; contrast with *random access*

series, in a spreadsheet, results from the automatic incrementing of data by adding one to days, dates, times, etc.

series fill, in a spreadsheet, allows the user to enter a series of numbers or dates into a range of cells

server, a computer providing the services in a client/server structure

shareware, software available on the Web, paid for on the honor system

shift-select, a GUI command in which the Shift key is pressed while the mouse selects an item, to avoid deselecting the items already selected; also called *click-with-shift*

shortcut, a keystroke combination available as an alternative to selecting a menu item in a GUI

signal, an electrical or light pulse or frequency in a wire, fiber, or wireless transmission; refers to anything that is generated and transmitted (power, data, control systems)

singleton tag, a tag such as the image tag <img ... /> that has no end tag

site search, a search restricted to a single domain

slider control, a synthesized slot in which a bar can be moved to select a position within a continuous range

social engineering, a technique such as phishing designed to trick people into revealing information by faking a normal social situation

software, a collective term for programs

software license, generally allows use of the software; the ownership remains with the party who markets the program

source, on the Web, the HTML or other text description of how a Web page should be displayed

spam, unsolicited commercial email

specification, in programming, a precise definition of the input; how the system should behave and how the output should be produced

spyware, malware that snoops private information

SQL, *see* Structured Query Language

standard functionality, the basic operations that all PC applications should be able to perform

start tag, the first of a pair of tags, such as <i>

statement, in JavaScript, a program instruction

statement terminator, in JavaScript, the semicolon (;) used to end each statement

step or **step size**, the amount an iteration variable is changed after each cycle of a loop

string, in searching, a sequence of characters; in programming, a data type for a sequence of characters

string constants, in JavaScript, numbers or strings; characters typed literally in a program; also called *string literals*

string literals, in JavaScript, numbers or strings; characters typed literally in a program; also called *string constants*

strong encryption, a public key encryption technique; a communicating party can use the technology to protect communications so that no one else can read it

structure, something made up of a number of parts that are held or put together in a particular way, e.g., a hierarchy

Structured Query Language (SQL), a standard notation for defining tables from tables in a database; sometimes pronounced *SEE·quel*

subscript, an index

substitution, in searching, the result of replacing a substring of a character sequence with another string

superuser, having the capability to access all functions of a computer or software system, including overriding passwords; also called *administrative authority*

symbol, an information code formed from a specific sequence of base patterns; for example, 01000001 is the ASCII symbol for *A* formed from patterns of 0's and 1's

synchronous communication, requires that both the sender and the receiver are simultaneously active, e.g., a telephone conversation

T

tab, in word processing, a formatting character often represented by →

tab-delimited text, in a spreadsheet, how foreign data is imported; each cell's entry ends with a tab and each row ends with a return

table, an organizing mechanism for database entities

table instance, a relational database table containing specific data values

tag, a word or abbreviation enclosed in angle brackets, usually paired with a companion starting with a slash, which describes a property of data or expresses a command to be performed; e.g., `<italic>You're it!</italic>`

task dependencies, when solving tasks, the fact that some tasks rely or depend on the resolution of other tasks

task-dependency graph, used by systems engineers and managers in project management; also called a *PERT chart*

TCP/IP, acronym for Transmission Control Protocol/Internet Protocol

template, the structural information of a document with placeholders for content that is later filled in to produce a complete document

tera-, prefix for trillion; in prefixing, a quantity counted in binary, e.g., memory, prefix for 1,099,511,627,776

termination test, a Boolean expression to determine whether an iteration statement will execute its statement sequence again; also called a *continuation test*

test, in algorithmic thinking, included in a loop to determine if the instructions should be repeated

text, a sequence of characters; in searching, the material being searched

text editor, basic software to create and modify text files; contrast with *word processor*

third-party cookie, in a browser, a cookie from a site the user didn't explicitly request

tiling, in graphics, copying a small image repeatedly to create a background pattern

TLD, *see* top-level domain

toggling, reversing the state of an item, e.g., toggling between selected and deselected

token, a symbol sequence treated as a single unit in searching or in languages

top-level domain (TLD), is a domain, such as `.com` or `.edu`, that is not a member of any higher level domain (except root)

transceiver, a device capable of sending and receiving signals; used in wireless communication

transducer, a device that converts waves of one form into waves of another, usually electrical

transistor, a connection between two wires that can be controlled by a third wire to allow or disallow a charge to flow

translate, in graphics, to move an image to a new position unchanged; in programming, to compile a programming language into a language that the computer can interpret (machine language)

trapdoor, in encryption software, incorporated by the programmer as a way to gain access to particular cleartext; works like a telephone wiretap

tree, a graphic representation of a hierarchical directory

triangle pointers, small triangular icon used as a button in a GUI to indicate presence of hidden information

Trojan program, a seemingly innocuous program that takes its name from the Trojan Horse of Greek mythology; it contains hidden code that allows the unauthorized collection, exploitation, or destruction of data

troubleshoot, in computing, determining why something does not work due to malfunctioning hardware or buggy or outdated software

tuple, a set of values for the attributes of an entity; also called a *row*

Turing test, an experimental setting to determine if a computer and a person can be distinguished by their answers to a judge's questions

type, a kind of information, such as number, text, or image

U

unary operator, an operator, such as negation (–), with a single operand

undefined, in JavaScript, the value of declared variables before they are assigned

Universal Resource Locator (URL), a two-part name for a Web page composed of an IP address followed by the file name, which can default to `index.html`

universality principle, a property of computation that all computers with a minimal set of instructions can compute the same set of computations

unsubscribe, a process of being removed from an email list

upload, to transfer information from a client to a server

URL, *see* Universal Resource Locator

UTF-8, Unicode Translation Format for bytes

V

vacation message, a function of mail servers that allows a user to set up a message saying that he or she is temporarily away and unable to reply to email; also called an *automated reply*

value types, the different kinds of values of a programming language; also called *data types*

variable, a named quantity in a programming language

vector of attack, the method by which malware gets into your computer
virtual, a modifier meaning not actually, but as if
virtual reality, a digital representation of the world
virus, a program that infects another program by embedding a (possibly evolved) copy of itself
virus-checking software, programs that check for known viruses, worms, etc.

W

W3C, *see* World Wide Web Consortium
WAN, *see* wide area network
Web, short form of World Wide Web
Web browser, a software application that locates and reads HTML pages. Modern browsers can display sound and video as well as text and graphics (although plug-ins may be required for multimedia)
Web client, a computer requesting services from a Web server; a computer running a Web browser
Web server, a computer providing pages to Web clients; a computer hosting a Web page
WFI, *see* World-Famous Iteration
"what if" analysis, a spreadsheet tool that temporarily recomputes entries based on alternative cell values
white space, in HTML, space inserted for readability
wide area network (WAN), a network connecting computers over a wider area than a few kilometers
window, an area of a computer screen that displays its own file or message independent of the rest of the screen
wired equivalent privacy (WEP2), an encryption standard for wireless networks
wireless network, a network connecting computers using radio frequency (RF) signals; a network using the 802.11 standard
word processor, software to create and modify text files that include formatting; contrast with *text editor*
work-proportional-to-*n* algorithm, a description of the time required to solve a problem with input of size *n*
workaround, the process of achieving a goal by avoiding buggy or failing parts of a system
World-Famous Iteration (WFI), in JavaScript, the most frequently written `for` loop used by programmers
World Wide Web (WWW), the collection of all HTML servers connected by the Internet and their information resources
World Wide Web Consortium (W3C), a standards body composed mainly of companies that produce Web software
worm, an independent program that replicates itself from machine to machine across network connections
wrap, in HTML, when there is insufficient window space for the full sequence of text, the browser continues the text on the next line
WYSIWYG (what you see is what you get), pronounced *WHIZ·ee·wig*

X

XHTML, *see* Extensible Hypertext Markup Language
XML, *see* Extensible Markup Language
XSL, *see* Extensible Stylesheet Language

Answers to Selected Questions

Chapter 1

Multiple Choice

1. A. Monitors use bit-mapped technology generated by the computer whereas TVs display recorded images.
3. C. A laptop has an LCD display and uses RGB color.
5. D. Follow the acronym, PILPOF, plug in last, pull out first.
7. C. Red and green light combine to make yellow.
9. B. The grid is 19×16 or 304 pixels.

Short Answer

1. processor or microprocessor
3. screen saver
5. 786,432 or 1024×768
7. tip of the arrow
9. Execute or run (or interpret, though this is introduced in Chapter 9)
11. abstraction
13. word processor
15. generalization

Chapter 2

Multiple Choice

1. A. Those with computer skills are sometimes called digerati.
3. D. Both A and B are correct. Ease of use is one of the driving forces behind software development and one of the reasons for the popularity of some software.
5. B. You'll find all except door handles in a typical GUI. (Who knows maybe one day . . .)
7. B. When a menu option cannot be used, it is shown in gray and it cannot be selected.
9. C. Leave the replacement window blank.

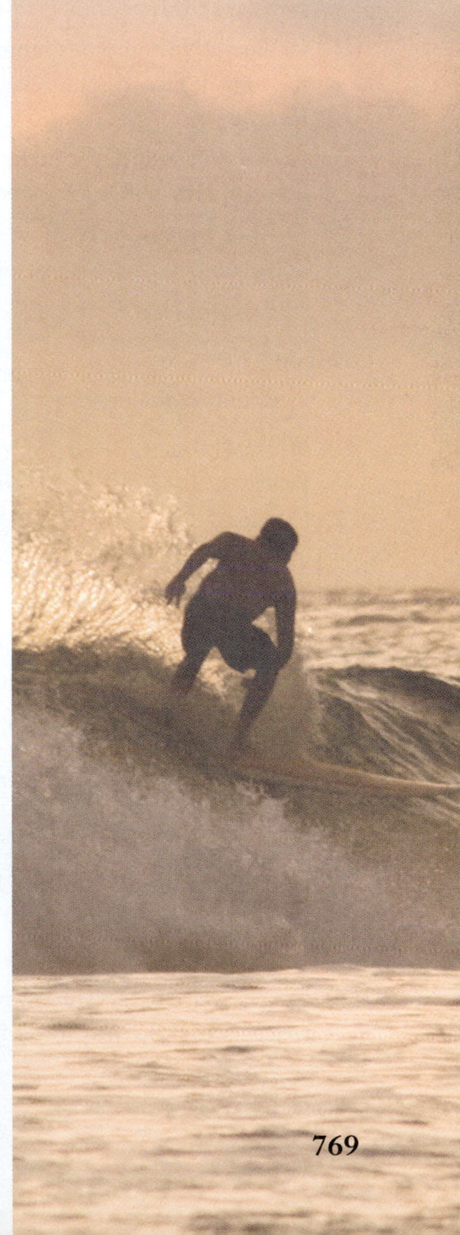

Short Answer

1. Digerati
3. analogies
5. Triangle pointers
7. menus
9. Help
11. gray

Chapter 3

Multiple Choice

1. C. There are 256 * 256 * 256 * 256 potential connections. Some are reserved for testing and some are restricted.
3. C. The DNS translates human IP addresses into the four-number IP addresses needed for the Internet.
5. C. Tuvalu uses TV for its top-level country domain. How's that for a hook?
7. C. Root name servers allow surfers to use symbolic computer names instead of arcane IP addresses.

Short Answer

1. electronic commerce
3. multicast
5. peers
7. channel
9. gateways
11. Web servers
13. FTP
15. Hypertext Markup Language
17. blog

Chapter 4

Multiple Choice

1. C. The commands used in HTML are called tags. They are enclosed in < >.
3. A. The first one has the tags properly paired.
5. C. These are paragraph tags and put a double space around the text to set it off from the rest of the page.
7. C.
9. A. `img src = "filename.ext"` will get the image. Then use `align =` and enclose the proper alignment in quotes.

Short Answer

1. Web authoring software
3. `<br/>` or `<pre>`
5. attributes
7. relative
9. Graphics Interchange Format
11. ordered list

Chapter 5

Multiple Choice

1. A. Some use the Web for their own gains and slant their content accordingly.
3. D. Libraries have large online collections and services for Internet users. Resources are free and open to everyone.
5. B. The query processor looks at the search information and performs the search.
7. C. Use the minus sign (–) in front of the word to exclude pages that have that word.
9. WWW Consortium approval

Short Answer

1. library
3. Single links
5. Google
7. logical (or Boolean) operators
9. hierarchy
11. hits
13. AND
15. InterNIC

Chapter 6

True/False and Multiple Choice

1. F. A tertiary source is removed from the source by time or space. A tertiary source reports what happened but isn't an eyewitness.
3. D. In addition, mistakes in print tend to stay mistakes.

5. B. An eyewitness and a participant are examples of primary sources.
7. C. We obtain online information from primary and secondary sources. It is important to check the credentials of online authors, especially those who are secondary sources of information.
9. D. Page rank on a search engine is usually based on popularity, that is, the number of hits it gets.
11. B. Biography.com would probably have the most-accurate information. All of them might have accurate information, but Biography.com would probably have better references and would be maintained by experts.

Short Answer

1. Curiosity-driven research
3. primary source
5. secondary source

Chapter 7

Multiple Choice

1. B. The computer doesn't understand the information it was given. This usually means the user didn't understand what the computer wanted or the user simply entered the wrong information.
3. B. See if the error repeats itself. If it doesn't, then you're in the clear. If it does, then you need to work through the debugging process.
5. A. Look again for the error.

Short Answer

1. Field inputs
3. ~~b~~
5. bug
7. workaround
9. fail-soft

Chapter 8

Multiple Choice

1. C. You learned the alphabet in a particular order that everyone agrees on.
3. D. None of these need to be quantified. While all are usually thought of as numbers, none of them are treated as numbers.
5. A. A clock with hands is analog. If the clock displays digits, it is digital.
7. D. It's called a syllogism. From the two statements, I can deduce the third statement.
9. A. The coating on floppies and hard disks is an iron compound that can store a magnetic charge.

Short Answer

1. molecules
3. Present and Absent
5. collating sequence
7. nibble
9. Bit
11. Hex
13. ASCII code

Chapter 9

Multiple Choice

1. A. The computer executes its instructions literally. There is no allowance for free will, creativity, or intuition.
3. D. The fastest personal computers can sustain speeds even higher than that, and each generation of computers is faster.
5. B. The ALU performs instructions.
7. B. Branch and jump make the computer switch tasks so it doesn't always grab the next instruction.
9. B. The correct order is thousands, millions, billions, trillions.
11. C. Assembly language is the most primitive software level that humans work with, and rarely used.

Short Answer

1. Computers
3. RAM
5. deterministically
7. information processing
9. keyboard
11. Programming
13. Instruction interpretation

15. gate
17. high-level

Chapter 10

Multiple Choice

1. C. There are five basic requirements: inputs specified, outputs specified, definiteness, effectiveness, and finiteness.
3. A. A natural language lacks the rigorous structure and precise meaning of the others.
5. C. These steps must be repeated in order to put the whole set of CDs in order.
7. A. You took a specific example and generated an idea from it.
9. D. After the Alpha sweep, the algorithm is complete.
11. D. Both A and C. Output is the intended result and it must include its type, amount, and form.

Short Answer

1. algorithm
3. algorithm, program
5. Beta sweep
7. nonredundant
9. loop

Chapter 11

Multiple Choice

1. B. Each intensity has a range from 0–255. That gives you 256 possible settings for each color or 16,777,216 possible colors.
3. B. Analog information is not discrete. It can always be divided into a smaller sampling.
5. D.
7. A. MP3 is the audio layer of MPEG movies.
9. C. A supermarket uses UPC codes, the little sets of numbers and black and white lines on packages.

Short Answer

1. black
3. Interpolation
5. ADC
7. ISO
9. optical character recognition (OCR)
11. virtual reality
13. Haptic devices
15. Bias-free Universal Medium Principle

Chapter 12

Multiple Choice

1. B. Although it can happen, messages for a listserve are seldom edited or censored.
3. C. The first was accidentally released in 1988.
5. D. Under the "fair use" policy, educational and scholarly use of small parts of a copyrighted piece is allowed.

Short Answer

1. Netiquette
3. moderator
5. virus
7. Intellectual property
9. public domain

Chapter 13

Multiple Choice

1. D. There are few limits on how businesses can use the information.
3. D. Each is an instance of using another's identity for personal profit or gain.
5. B. According to the Quality principle, your personal information should be accurate.
7. B. The EU requires others to follow its guidelines when information on EU citizens is used outside their countries.
9. C.
11. C. XOR means you can have x or y, but not both.
13. D. All of the above are attributes of social networking.

Short Answer

1. Privacy
3. Cash

5. due diligence test
7. European Data Protection Directive
9. cryptosystem
11. one-way cipher
13. Identity theft
15. partial backup
17. Social networking

Chapter 14

True/False

1. F. It will spill over into the cell to the right if that cell is empty. If text is in the cell, it will display as much as possible. If a number is in the cell, it will display crosshatches (#).
3. T.
5. F. It is used to fill other cells with the contents of the selected cell.
7. F. You should use the dollar sign ($).
9. T.

Multiple Choice

1. C. It is sometimes called a range as well.
3. D. All of the above are valid ranges.
5. C. There are six rows and three columns for a total of 18 cells.
7. C. The results are displayed in the cell. Look at the formula line at the top of the spreadsheet to see the formula.
9. A. When the dollar sign is used in a cell reference it makes that part of the reference absolute.
11. A. The dollar sign in front of the G makes it absolute. Without the dollar sign, the 5 is relative.
13. C. The Return and Enter keys will both create a carriage return.

Short Answer

1. atomic or monolithic
3. row
5. fill handle
7. absolute
9. max or maximum
11. series
13. Pmt or payment
15. Concatenate

Chapter 15

Multiple Choice

1. C. Spreadsheets are flexible and powerful.
3. A. To avoid confusion, comments and labels should be used to clarify a spreadsheet.
5. C. The Left function looks at a specified number of characters at the beginning of a cell.
7. B. By defining names, you can refer to a cell or range of cells by name instead of cell reference.
9. A. A spreadsheet recalculates automatically whenever a number in a cell is changed.
11. D. All of the above can be done with auto-filtering

Short Answer

1. "what if"
3. comments
5. worksheets
7. range
9. Scenario manager

Chapter 16

Multiple Choice

1. D. Relational database are used for this.
3. B. XML tags cannot have a space in them.
5. C. The first tag encountered is the root element and must enclose all of the file content.
7. C. When entities are grouped, they become a table.
9. B. Duplicate records are combined.
11. A. Data redundancy is a major concern for databases.

Short Answer

1. Metadata
3. self-describing
5. quotes
7. trees
9. primary key

11. database
13. one-to-one relationship

Chapter 17

Multiple Choice

1. A. Collection tag
3. A. Collection tag
5. C. Debugging is easier because the errors are usually limited to newly developed materials.
7. D. The rules are called templates in XSL.
9. B. iDiary is organized by date. Each new date brings a new entry to it.
11. A. To add entries, simply add the changes to the XML file.

Short Answer

1. Extensible Stylesheet Language
3. Transformer
5. Collective
7. attributes
9. stylesheet

Chapter 18

Multiple Choice

1. B. JavaScript is used mainly for the Web.
3. C. An underscore can be used to separate words in a variable name. That makes the variable name easier to read.
5. C. When declared, the value of a variable is undefined. Be sure to assign a value to it before you use it.
7. C. The values of the variables before the start of the statement are used in a calculation.
9. C. Multiplication and division are done before addition and subtraction.
11. B. Both must be true for the operator to work.

Short Answer

1. program
3. declaration
5. initialize
7. operators
9. unary
11. !
13. conditional statement
15. {} or curly braces

Chapter 19

Multiple Choice

1. B. HTML pages are saved as ASCII text.
3. B. The `<body>` tag holds the body of the page, what the viewer will see.
5. C. The `<p>` tag starts a new paragraph.
7. C. When there is a click event, it is handled by this event handler.
9. A. A click triggers an `onClick` event handler.

Short Answer

1. Web page
3. `<hr/>`
5. event
7. dot operator
9. Input
11. feedback
13. tags

Chapter 20

Multiple Choice

1. B. Functions are used to solve simple tasks. When put together, they solve complicated tasks.
3. C. Two slashes are used to start a comment.
5. C. `onchange` is used. When the input is changed, the event is triggered.
7. A. `Math.random()` returns a number greater than 0 and less than 1.
9. C. Links are created using `href`, short for hypertext reference.

Short Answer

1. Abstraction
3. declaration
5. scope
7. infinity

9. 0, 1
11. Unix
13. Assigning 0 to rock, 1 to paper, and 2 to scissors, `randNum(3)` solves the problem.

Chapter 21

Multiple Choice

1. C. The `for` statement is used for iteration.
3. B. The *<next iteration>* changes the value of the iteration value.
5. C. The `alert()` command is used.
7. B. It means to add 1 to `i`.
9. D. All of the above are elements with invalid numbers.
11. A. The array starts at 0, ends at 8, has nine elements, and does not have any with decimals.

Short Answer

1. Iteration
3. variable
5. continuation or termination
7. infinite loop
9. `"\n"`
11. Indexing
13. length
15. display rate

Chapter 22

Multiple Choice

1. B. You must understand the problem before you can do anything else.
3. D. The Animate Grid task must be completed before the Build Controls task can be completed.
5. A. Build Controls is not dependent on the Detect Staircase task.
7. B. Graphics are placed using the `src` command.
9. B. Usually, when there are 3 to 5 tasks or more, it becomes useful to use a loop.

Short Answer

1. Decomposition Principle
3. Task dependencies
5. Program Evaluation and Review Technique
7. Build GUI
9. `document.images`
11. Radio buttons

Chapter 23

Multiple Choice

1. B. Computers are great at manipulating information, but that's about it.
3. D. Creativity is hard to define and hard to explain.
5. D.
7. B. Regardless of the order the CDs are in, the computer must make a pass to check it.
9. C. Getting computers to work properly is one thing humans can do better than computers.
11. C. Checkers is a much simpler game than chess so the algorithm is much simpler.
13. A. The process is called deeper.
15. B. Six basic instructions are sufficient.
17. A. A program debugger can detect syntax errors, but it cannot find logical errors.

Short Answer

1. Deep Blue
3. artificial intelligence
5. specialized
7. Universality Principle
9. computer
11. business
13. compatibility and support
15. NP-complete problems

Chapter 24

Multiple Choice

1. C. The value of information depends on how we use it.

3. B. The first step is to make sure the error happens again. If you cannot duplicate the error, then there probably isn't a bug.
5. C. Logical reasoning can be applied to most problems with successful results.
7. A. The Capabilities component has the broadest range. Skills has the most detail.
9. D. There are risks to being too early or too late with new developments.

Short Answer

1. Heuristic thinking
3. heuristic
5. Concept
7. Lifelong learning
9. algorithms

Index

Credits

Chapter 2

Page 49: Excerpt from United Nations Universal Declaration of Human Rights. From http://www.un.org/en/documents/udhr/. Copyright © United Nations 2009. Reprinted with permission.

Chapter 3

Fig. 3.9: Robert Metcalf

Chapter 4

Fig. 4.4: W3C screenshot courtesy of W3C. Copyright © 2009 W3C.

Chapter 5

Fig. 5.1: Reprinted with permission of the University of Washington Libraries.

Figs. 5.3, 5.4: NPR screenshot courtesy of National Public Radio. Copyright © 2009 NPR.

Page 147: Screenshot © 2009 Columbia College Chicago. All Rights Reserved.

Chapter 6

Fig. 6.2: (http://en.wikipedia.org/wiki/Buckminster_Fuller) Wikipedia® is a registered trademark of the Wikimedia Foundation, Inc. (http://www.wikimediafoundation.org/), a non-profit organization. See the full terms of the GNU Free Documentation License on the following page.

Fig. 6.6: © 2009 About.com, a part of The New York Times Company. All Rights Reserved.

Fig. 6.7: © 2009 WNET.ORG Properties, LLC. All Rights Reserved.

Page 165: Video Shot © 2009 WNET.ORG Properties, LLC. All Rights Reserved.

Fig. 6.8: As posted on Thirteen/WNET New York. www.thirteen.org. © Allegra Fuller Snyder. All Rights Reserved.

Fig. 6.9: Used with permission from the Buckminster Fuller Institute. http://bfi.org. All Rights Reserved.

Fig. 6.10: As posted on Thirteen/WNET New York. www.thirteen.org. © Sarah Feldman. All Rights Reserved.

Fig. 6.11: © 2009 WNET.ORG Properties, LLC. All Rights Reserved.

Fig. 6.12: Used with permission from the Buckminster Fuller Institute. http://bfi.org. All Rights Reserved.

Fig. 6.13: Screenshot courtesy of Stanford University. © 2009 Stanford University. All Rights Reserved. Photo used with permission from the Buckminster Fuller Institute. http://bfi.org. All Rights Reserved.

Pages 172–173: Excerpt used with permission from the Buckminster Fuller Institute. http://bfi.org. All Rights Reserved.

Fig. 6.14: Courtesy Chris Rywalt.

Fig. 6.18: Source: Nobelprize.org, the official Web site of the Nobel Foundation Copyright © Nobel Web AB 2009 Nobelprize.org®, Nobel Prize® and the Nobel Medal® design mark are registered trademarks of the Nobel Foundation.

Fig. 6.19: Used with permission from the Buckminster Fuller Institute. http://bfi.org. All Rights Reserved.

Chapter 7

Fig. 7.2: Copyright © 2009 Regents of the University of California. All Rights Reserved.

Chapter 10:

Page 285: Map © 2009 Google. Map data © 2009 Google.

Chapter 14

Fig. 14.6: Courtesy of the King County Department of Transportation.

Chapter 15

Fig. 15.1: Map © 2009 Google. Map data © 2009 LeadDog Consulting, Google, Tele Atlas, INEGI.

Chapter 17

Fig. 17.1 Part 1: Image courtesy of the Eastern Southern Observatory, Germany. Copyright © 2007 ESO. Video Shot Copyright © Lim Jeong Hyun. All Rights Reserved.

Fig. 17.1 Part 2: Poem Copyright © Ted Kooser. All Rights Reserved. Photo Courtesy of the John F. Kennedy Center for the Performing Arts. All Rights Reserved. Book cover © 2005 by John Vaillant. All Rights Reserved.

The following license agreement applies only to the following Wikipedia material:
"Buckminster Fuller" on page 160: http://en.wikipedia.org/wiki/Buckminster_Fuller.

Wikipedia: Text of the GNU Free Documentation License From Wikipedia, the free encyclopedia, Version 1.3 3 November 2008.

0. PREAMBLE

The purpose of this License is to make a manual, textbook, or other functional and useful document "free" in the sense of freedom: to assure everyone the effective freedom to copy and redistribute it, with or without modifying it, either commercially or noncommercially. Secondarily, this License preserves for the author and publisher a way to get credit for their work, while not being considered responsible for modifications made by others.

This License is a kind of "copyleft", which means that derivative works of the document must themselves be free in the same sense. It complements the GNU General Public License, which is a copyleft license designed for free software.

We have designed this License in order to use it for manuals for free software, because free software needs free documentation: a free program should come with manuals providing the same freedoms that the software does. But this License is not limited to software manuals; it can be used for any textual work, regardless of subject matter or whether it is published as a printed book. We recommend this License principally for works whose purpose is instruction or reference.

1. APPLICABILITY AND DEFINITIONS

This License applies to any manual or other work, in any medium, that contains a notice placed by the copyright holder saying it can be distributed under the terms of this License. Such a notice grants a world-wide, royalty-free license, unlimited in duration, to use that work under the conditions stated herein. The "Document", below, refers to any such manual or work. Any member of the public is a licensee, and is addressed as "you". You accept the license if you copy, modify or distribute the work in a way requiring permission under copyright law.

A "Modified Version" of the Document means any work containing the Document or a portion of it, either copied verbatim, or with modifications and/or translated into another language.

A "Secondary Section" is a named appendix or a front-matter section of the Document that deals exclusively with the relationship of the publishers or authors of the Document to the Document's overall subject (or to related matters) and contains nothing that could fall directly within that overall subject. (Thus, if the Document is in part a textbook of mathematics, a Secondary Section may not explain any mathematics.) The relationship could be a matter of historical connection with the subject or with related matters, or of legal, commercial, philosophical, ethical or political position regarding them.

The "Invariant Sections" are certain Secondary Sections whose titles are designated, as being those of Invariant Sections, in the notice that says that the Document is released under this License. If a section does not fit the above definition of Secondary then it is not allowed to be designated as Invariant. The Document may contain zero Invariant Sections. If the Document does not identify any Invariant Sections then there are none.

The "Cover Texts" are certain short passages of text that are listed, as Front-Cover Texts or Back-Cover Texts, in the notice that says that the Document is released under this License. A Front-Cover Text may be at most 5 words, and a Back-Cover Text may be at most 25 words.

A "Transparent" copy of the Document means a machine-readable copy, represented in a format whose specification is available to the general public, that is suitable for revising the document straightforwardly with generic text editors or (for images composed of pixels) generic paint programs or (for drawings) some widely available drawing editor, and that is suitable for input to text formatters or for automatic translation to a variety of formats suitable for input to text formatters. A copy made in an otherwise Transparent file format whose markup, or absence of markup, has been arranged to thwart or discourage subsequent modification by readers is not Transparent. An image format is not Transparent if used for any substantial amount of text. A copy that is not "Transparent" is called "Opaque".

Examples of suitable formats for Transparent copies include plain ASCII without markup, Texinfo input format, LaTeX input format, SGML or XML using a publicly available DTD, and standard-conforming simple HTML, PostScript or PDF designed for human modification. Examples of transparent image formats include PNG, XCF and JPG. Opaque formats include proprietary formats that can be read and edited only by proprietary word processors, SGML or XML for which the DTD and/or processing tools are not generally available, and the machine-generated HTML, PostScript or PDF produced by some word processors for output purposes only.

The "Title Page" means, for a printed book, the title page itself, plus such following pages as are needed to hold, legibly, the material this License requires to appear in the title page. For works in formats which do not have any title page as such, "Title Page" means the text near the most prominent appearance of the work's title, preceding the beginning of the body of the text.

The "publisher" means any person or entity that distributes copies of the Document to the public.

A section "Entitled XYZ" means a named subunit of the Document whose title either is precisely XYZ or contains XYZ in parentheses following text that translates XYZ in another language. (Here XYZ stands for a specific section name mentioned below, such as "Acknowledgements", "Dedications", "Endorsements", or "History".) To "Preserve the Title" of such a section when you modify the Document means that it remains a section "Entitled XYZ" according to this definition.

The Document may include Warranty Disclaimers next to the notice which states that this License applies to the Document. These Warranty Disclaimers are considered to be included by reference in this License, but only as regards disclaiming warranties: any other implication that these Warranty Disclaimers may have is void and has no effect on the meaning of this License.

2. VERBATIM COPYING

You may copy and distribute the Document in any medium, either commercially or noncommercially, provided that this License, the copyright notices, and the license notice saying this License applies to the Document are reproduced in all copies, and that you add no other conditions whatsoever to those of this License. You may not use technical measures to obstruct or control the reading or further copying of the copies you make or distribute. However, you may accept compensation in exchange for copies. If you distribute a large enough number of copies you must also follow the conditions in section 3.

You may also lend copies, under the same conditions stated above, and you may publicly display copies.

3. COPYING IN QUANTITY

If you publish printed copies (or copies in media that commonly have printed covers) of the Document, numbering more than 100, and the Document's license notice requires Cover Texts, you must enclose the copies in covers that carry, clearly and legibly, all these Cover Texts: Front-Cover Texts on the front cover, and Back-Cover Texts on the back cover. Both covers must also clearly and legibly identify you as the publisher of these copies. The front cover must present the full title with all words of the title equally prominent and visible. You may add other material on the covers in addition. Copying with changes limited to the covers, as long as they preserve the title of the Document and satisfy these conditions, can be treated as verbatim copying in other respects.

If the required texts for either cover are too voluminous to fit legibly, you should put the first ones listed (as many as fit reasonably) on the actual cover, and continue the rest onto adjacent pages.

If you publish or distribute Opaque copies of the Document numbering more than 100, you must either include a machine-readable Transparent copy along with each Opaque copy, or state in or with each Opaque copy a computer-network location from which the general network-using public has access to download using public-standard network protocols a complete Transparent copy of the Document, free of added material. If you use the latter option, you must take reasonably prudent steps, when you begin distribution of Opaque copies in quantity, to ensure that this Transparent copy will remain thus accessible at the stated location until at least one year after the last time you distribute an Opaque copy (directly or through your agents or retailers) of that edition to the public.

It is requested, but not required, that you contact the authors of the Document well before redistributing any large number of copies, to give them a chance to provide you with an updated version of the Document.

4. MODIFICATIONS

You may copy and distribute a Modified Version of the Document under the conditions of sections 2 and 3 above, provided that you release the Modified Version under precisely this License, with the Modified Version filling the role of the Document, thus licensing distribution and modification of the Modified Version to whoever possesses a copy of it. In addition, you must do these things in the Modified Version:

A. versions (which should, if there were any, be listed in the History section of the Document). You may use the same title as a previous version if the original publisher of that version gives permission.

B. List on the Title Page, as authors, one or more persons or entities responsible for authorship of the modifications in the Modified Version, together with at least five of the principal authors of the Document (all of its principal authors, if it has fewer than five), unless they release you from this requirement.

C. State on the Title page the name of the publisher of the Modified Version, as the publisher.

D. Preserve all the copyright notices of the Document.

E. Add an appropriate copyright notice for your modifications adjacent to the other copyright notices.

F. Include, immediately after the copyright notices, a license notice giving the public permission to use the Modified Version under the terms of this License, in the form shown in the Addendum below.

G. Preserve in that license notice the full lists of Invariant Sections and required Cover Texts given in the Document's license notice.

H. Include an unaltered copy of this License.

I. Preserve the section Entitled "History", Preserve its Title, and add to it an item stating at least the title, year, new authors, and publisher of the Modified Version as given on the Title Page. If there is no section Entitled "History" in the Document, create one stating the title, year, authors, and publisher of the Document as given on its Title Page, then add an item describing the Modified Version as stated in the previous sentence.

J. Preserve the network location, if any, given in the Document for public access to a Transparent copy of the Document, and likewise the network locations given in the Document for previous versions it was based on. These may be placed in the "History" section. You may omit a network location for a work that was published at least four years before the Document itself, or if the original publisher of the version it refers to gives permission.

K. For any section Entitled "Acknowledgements" or "Dedications", Preserve the Title of the section, and preserve in the section all the substance and tone of each of the contributor acknowledgements and/or dedications given therein.

L. Preserve all the Invariant Sections of the Document, unaltered in their text and in their titles. Section numbers or the equivalent are not considered part of the section titles.

M. Delete any section Entitled "Endorsements". Such a section may not be included in the Modified version.

N. Do not retitle any existing section to be Entitled "Endorsements" or to conflict in title with any Invariant Section.

O. Preserve any Warranty Disclaimers.

If the Modified Version includes new front-matter sections or appendices that qualify as Secondary Sections and contain no material copied from the Document, you may at your option designate some or all of these sections as invariant. To do this, add their titles to the list of Invariant Sections in the Modified Version's license notice. These titles must be distinct from any other section titles.

You may add a section Entitled "Endorsements", provided it contains nothing but endorsements of your Modified Version by various parties—for example, statements of peer review or that the text has been approved by an organization as the authoritative definition of a standard.

You may add a passage of up to five words as a Front-Cover Text, and a passage of up to 25 words as a Back-Cover Text, to the end of the list of Cover Texts in the Modified Version. Only one passage of Front-Cover Text and one of Back-Cover Text may be added by (or through arrangements made by) any one entity. If the Document already includes a cover text for the same cover, previously added by you or by arrangement made by the same entity you are acting on behalf of, you may not add another; but you may replace the old one, on explicit permission from the previous publisher that added the old one.

The author(s) and publisher(s) of the Document do not by this License give permission to use their names for publicity for or to assert or imply endorsement of any Modified Version.

5. COMBINING DOCUMENTS

You may combine the Document with other documents released under this License, under the terms defined in section 4 above for modified versions, provided that you include in the combination all of the Invariant Sections of all of the original documents, unmodified, and list them all as Invariant Sections of your combined work in its license notice, and that you preserve all their Warranty Disclaimers.

The combined work need only contain one copy of this License, and multiple identical Invariant Sections may be replaced with a single copy. If there are multiple Invariant Sections with the same name but different contents, make the title of each such section unique by adding at the end of it, in parentheses, the name of the original author or publisher of that section if known, or else a unique number. Make the same adjustment to the section titles in the list of Invariant Sections in the license notice of the combined work.

In the combination, you must combine any sections Entitled "History" in the various original documents, forming one section Entitled "History"; likewise combine any sections Entitled "Acknowledgements", and any sections Entitled "Dedications". You must delete all sections Entitled "Endorsements".

6. COLLECTIONS OF DOCUMENTS

You may make a collection consisting of the Document and other documents released under this License, and replace the individual copies of this License in the various documents with a single copy that is included in the collection, provided that you follow the rules of this License for verbatim copying of each of the documents in all other respects.

You may extract a single document from such a collection, and distribute it individually under this License, provided you insert a copy of this License into the extracted document, and follow this License in all other respects regarding verbatim copying of that document.

7. AGGREGATION WITH INDEPENDENT WORKS

A compilation of the Document or its derivatives with other separate and independent documents or works, in or on a volume of a storage or distribution medium, is called an "aggregate" if the copyright resulting from the compilation is not used to limit the legal rights of the compilation's users beyond what the individual works permit. When the Document is included in an aggregate, this License does not apply to the other works in the aggregate which are not themselves derivative works of the Document.

If the Cover Text requirement of section 3 is applicable to these copies of the Document, then if the Document is less than one half of the entire aggregate, the Document's Cover Texts may be placed on covers that bracket the Document within the aggregate, or the electronic equivalent of covers if the Document is in electronic form. Otherwise they must appear on printed covers that bracket the whole aggregate.

8. TRANSLATION

Translation is considered a kind of modification, so you may distribute translations of the Document under the terms of section 4. Replacing Invariant Sections with translations requires special permission from their copyright holders, but you may include translations of some or all Invariant Sections in addition to the original versions of these Invariant Sections. You may include a translation of this License, and all the license notices in the Document, and any Warranty Disclaimers, provided that you also include the original English version of this License and the original versions of those notices and disclaimers. In case of a disagreement between the translation and the original version of this License or a notice or disclaimer, the original version will prevail.

If a section in the Document is Entitled "Acknowledgements", "Dedications", or "History", the requirement (section 4) to Preserve its Title (section 1) will typically require changing the actual title.

9. TERMINATION

You may not copy, modify, sublicense, or distribute the Document except as expressly provided under this License. Any attempt otherwise to copy, modify, sublicense, or distribute it is void, and will automatically terminate your rights under this License.

However, if you cease all violation of this License, then your license from a particular copyright holder is reinstated (a) provisionally, unless and until the copyright holder explicitly and finally terminates your license, and (b) permanently, if the copyright holder fails to notify you of the violation by some reasonable means prior to 60 days after the cessation.

Moreover, your license from a particular copyright holder is reinstated permanently if the copyright holder notifies you of the violation by some reasonable means, this is the first time you have received notice of violation of this License (for any work) from that copyright holder, and you cure the violation prior to 30 days after your receipt of the notice.

Termination of your rights under this section does not terminate the licenses of parties who have received copies or rights from you under this License. If your rights have been terminated and not permanently reinstated, receipt of a copy of some or all of the same material does not give you any rights to use it.

10. FUTURE REVISIONS OF THIS LICENSE

The Free Software Foundation may publish new, revised versions of the GNU Free Documentation License from time to time. Such new versions will be similar in spirit to the present version, but may differ in detail to address new problems or concerns. See http://www.gnu.org/copyleft/.

Each version of the License is given a distinguishing version number. If the Document specifies that a particular numbered version of this License "or any later version" applies to it, you have the option of following the terms and conditions either of that specified version or of any later version that has been published (not as a draft) by the Free Software Foundation. If the Document does not specify a version number of this License, you may choose any version ever published (not as a draft) by the Free Software Foundation. If the Document specifies that a proxy can decide which future versions of this License can be used, that proxy's public statement of acceptance of a version permanently authorizes you to choose that version for the Document.

11. RELICENSING

"Massive Multiauthor Collaboration Site" (or "MMC Site") means any World Wide Web server that publishes copyrightable works and also provides prominent facilities for anybody to edit those works. A public wiki that anybody can edit is an example of such a server. A "Massive Multiauthor Collaboration" (or "MMC") contained in the site means any set of copyrightable works thus published on the MMC site.

"CC-BY-SA" means the Creative Commons Attribution-Share Alike 3.0 license published by Creative Commons Corporation, a not-for-profit corporation with a principal place of business in San Francisco, California, as well as future copyleft versions of that license published by that same organization.

"Incorporate" means to publish or republish a Document, in whole or in part, as part of another Document.

An MMC is "eligible for relicensing" if it is licensed under this License, and if all works that were first published under this License somewhere other than this MMC, and subsequently incorporated in whole or in part into the MMC, (1) had no cover texts or invariant sections, and (2) were thus incorporated prior to November 1, 2008.

The operator of an MMC Site may republish an MMC contained in the site under CC-BY-SA on the same site at any time before August 1, 2009, provided the MMC is eligible for relicensing.